Fundamentals of C++
Understanding Programming
and Problem Solving

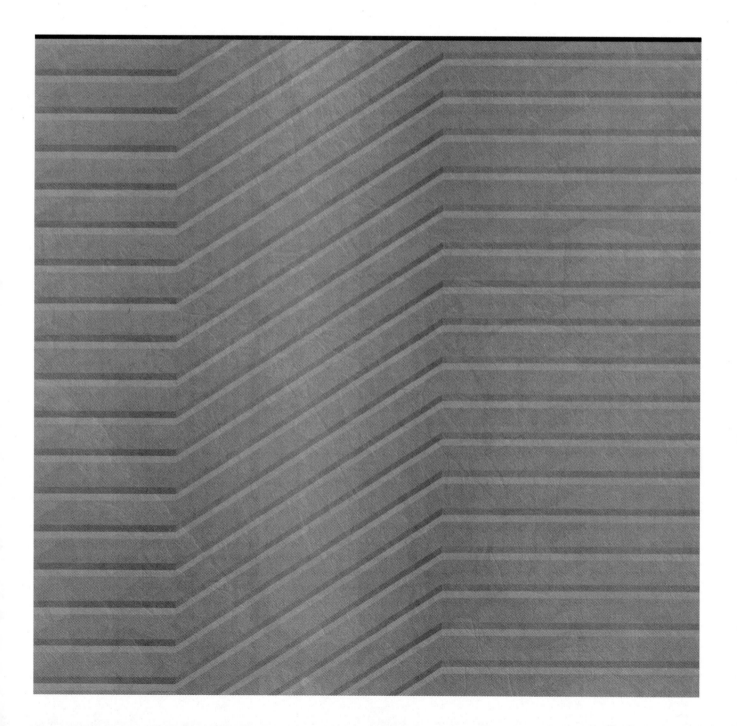

Fundamentals of C++
Understanding Programming and Problem Solving

Kenneth A. Lambert
Washington & Lee University

Douglas W. Nance
Central Michigan University

JOIN US ON THE INTERNET
WWW: http://www.thomson.com
EMAIL: findit@kiosk.thomson.com   A service of I(T)P®

South-Western Educational Publishing
an International Thomson Publishing company I(T)P®

Cincinnati • Albany, NY • Belmont, CA • Bonn • Boston • Detroit • Johannesburg • London • Madrid
Melbourne • Mexico City • New York • Paris • Singapore • Tokyo • Toronto • Washington

To Savannah.

To our children and their families. We are thankful they are also our friends.

Copyeditor: Lorretta Palagi
Composition: Carlisle Communications, Ltd.
Cover image: Pamela J. Vermeer
Photo credits follow the Index.

ISBN 0-314-20493-8

8 9 10 QWT 02

Printed in the United States of America

I(T)P

International Thomson Publishing

South-Western Educational Publishing is a division of International Thomson Publishing, Inc. The ITP trademark is used under license.

Contents

CHAPTER 3

Arithmetic, Variables, Input, Constants, and Library Functions

63

CHAPTER 4   Subprograms: Functions for Problem Solving   **127**

CHAPTER 6   Repetition Statements   293

CHAPTER 7

Files

373

CHAPTER 8

Arrays

415

CHAPTER 9   Building Structured Data: Structs and Classes   495

CHAPTER 12

Advanced Topics: Recursion and Efficient Searching and Sorting   667

Glossary   G.1

Appendixes   A.1

Answers to Selected Exercises   AN.1

Index   I.1

Preface

Those who teach entry-level courses in computer science are familiar with the problems encountered by beginning students. Initially, students can get so involved in learning the syntax and features of a programming language that they may fail to grasp the significance of using the language to solve problems. On the other hand, the solutions to really interesting problems require a student to learn a great many features of a programming language. The intent of this text is to provide a happy medium between these two extremes. Besides providing a complete, introductory course in the essential features of C++, the broader goals are for students to understand programming techniques and subsequently be able to use them to solve interesting problems.

Overview and Organization

The material in Chapters 1 through 6 covers the basics of problem solving and algorithm development, using the standard control structures of expression evaluation, sequencing, selection, iteration, and procedural abstraction. This material is presented at a deliberate pace. If students in the class have already had some programming experience, these chapters may be covered rapidly. However, students must be able to solve problems with top-down design and stepwise refinement. If these skills are overlooked, students will have difficulty designing solutions to more complex problems later.

In addition to the character and numeric data types, a string data type is introduced in Chapter 3 and used throughout the text. Thus, students can quickly start solving problems that require the use of strings as well as numbers.

Beginning with Chapter 2, a section on graphics applications appears at the end of the chapters. Using a small library of graphics operations, students can learn many of the fundamentals of graphics programming.

Beginning with a discussion of the ACM Code of Ethics in Chapter 2, we have made an effort to highlight the ethical and social dimensions of computer science. Exercises dealing with ethical issues are included at the end of several early chapters.

Subprograms are presented fairly early in the text. User-defined functions with input and output parameters are presented in Chapter 4 before either selection statements (Chapter 5) or iteration statements (Chapter 6). This facilitates good problem-solving habits in that a completely modular approach can be emphasized early in the course.

Chapter 7 introduces file stream processing. The focus of this chapter is the use of file stream operations, primarily in conjunction with numeric, character, and string data. Because of its simple approach, this chapter could be used earlier or later in the course if desired.

Chapter 8 discusses array operations in detail. Students learn the appropriate applications of one-dimensional and two-dimensional arrays. The potential pitfalls of using C++ arrays are examined to prepare students to remedy these problems by developing safer data structures in Chapter 10.

We have made a tremendous effort to acknowledge the increasing importance of object-oriented methods in the computer science community. In the first eight chapters, this effort takes the form of the use of objects, such as strings and file streams, and of allusions to object-oriented design when appropriate. However, we have deliberately avoided presenting the object-oriented features of C++ in the first eight chapters. We believe that students can best learn the fundamentals of algorithm development if they are provided with a simple model of computation and a small subset of C++ syntax. The object-oriented model of computation and the object-oriented features of C++ are neither simple nor small; they are best introduced only when needed, primarily to develop data structures in the second half of an introductory course in computer science.

Chapter 9 provides a transition from a procedural approach to an object-oriented approach. The chapter begins with a discussion of the C++ struct, which is similar to the record type of other languages. We then explore the use of classes and objects as an alternative method to the use of structs for developing data structures. Examples are taken from data processing (a bank account management system) and mathematics (rational numbers). Careful attention is paid to the specification and implementation of all data structures as abstract data types. We introduce a standard method of discussing user requirements, specifying attributes and behavior, and declaring and implementing a class, and then we use this method in the remaining chapters. Appropriate features of object-oriented design, such as operator overloading, inheritance, and software reuse, are discussed and developed in these examples.

Chapter 10 develops several important classes using arrays—a vector class with range checking, a string class, an ordered collection class, a sorted collection class, and a matrix class. The use of dynamic arrays to implement these classes is treated in detail. Issues of data security and data abstraction alluded to in earlier chapters come into detailed focus. This chapter also provides an opportunity to discuss other important concepts in object-oriented design, such as the difference between container classes and derived classes.

Chapter 11 examines pointers and dynamic memory as means of developing linked lists. We first discuss the logical requirements of a linked list class, making extensive use of box and pointer diagrams. We then examine the use of pointers in manipulating areas of dynamic memory within the implementation of the linked list class. The chapter closes with a discussion of the representation of arrays and linked structures in computer memory and the efficiency trade-offs of the two different data structures.

Chapter 12 gives a preview of topics normally presented in a second course in computer science—recursion and analysis of algorithms. We illustrate the use of recursion as a divide-and-conquer method of problem solving in implementing the quick sort and binary search algorithms. A brief comparison of the behavior of these algorithms with that of selection sort and linear search is provided.

Throughout the text we have attempted to explain and develop concepts carefully. These are illustrated by frequent examples and diagrams. New concepts are then used in complete programs to show how they aid in solving problems. We place an early and consistent emphasis on good writing habits and neat, readable documentation. We frequently offer communication and style tips where appropriate.

Features

This text has a number of noteworthy pedagogical features.

◆ *Chapter outlines:* Lists of the important topics covered are given at the beginning of each chapter.

◆ *Objectives:* Each section starts with a concise list of topics and learning objectives in each section.

◆ *Communication and Style Tips:* These are suggestions for programming style that are intended to enhance readability. The ACM has recently encouraged the development of communication skills to enhance the portability of programs.

◆ *Exercises:* Short-answer questions that are intended to build analytical skills appear at the end of each section.

◆ *Chapter Review Exercises:* Lengthy lists of exercises designed to prepare students to answer questions on quizzes or exams are given at the end of each chapter.

◆ *Programming Problems and Activities:* Starting with Chapter 2, lengthy lists of suggestions for complete programs and projects are given at the end of each chapter. These cover different problem areas in computer science, such as data processing and mathematics. Some problems and projects run from chapter to chapter, providing students with a sense of problem solving as a cumulative enterprise that often requires programming in the large. Several assignments focus explicitly on improving students' communication skills in refining designs and writing documentation.

◆ *Module specifications:* Specifications are given for many program modules.

◆ *Structure charts:* We provide charts that reflect modular development and include the use of data flow arrows to emphasize transmission of data to and/or from each module. These charts set the stage for understanding the use of value and reference parameters when functions are introduced.

◆ *Notes of Interest:* These are tidbits of information intended to create awareness of and interest in various aspects of computer science, including its historical context. Special attention is paid to issues of computer ethics and security.

◆ *Suggestions for test programs:* Ideas included in the exercises are intended to encourage students to use the computer to determine answers to questions and to see how to implement concepts in short programs.

◆ *Case Studies:* With the exception of Chapters 1, 2, and 11, a complete program is presented at the end of the chapter that illustrates utilization of the concepts developed within the chapter. This section includes the complete development of a project, from user requirements to specifications to pseudocode design to implementation and testing.

◆ *AP classes:* The AP classes for strings, vectors, and matrices are used, discussed, and developed in several chapters of the text, particularly Chapter 10.

◆ *Running, Debugging, and Testing Hints:* These hints will be useful to students as they work on the programming problems at the end of each chapter.

◆ *Graphics programming:* With the exception of Chapters 1 and 11, the final section of each chapter covers an aspect of graphics applications related to the material covered in that chapter. Primitive graphics operations are introduced, example algorithms are developed, and complete program examples are provided to give students a start in programming and problem solving with graphics.

◆ *Reading References:* When appropriate, suggestions are given for excellent sources for further reading on topics introduced in the text.

◆ New terms are highlighted when introduced and definitions are supplied in the margins.

In the back of the book there is a complete glossary, as well as appendixes on reserved words, useful library functions, syntax diagrams, a character set, graphics functions, and the AP class libraries. The final section of the book provides answers to selected exercises.

This book covers only that portion of C++ necessary for a first course in computer science. Students wanting to learn more about the language are referred to the excellent source mentioned in Appendix 1.

Ancillaries

It is our belief that a broad-based teaching support package is essential for an introductory course using C++. Thus, the following ancillary materials are available from South-Western Educational Publishing.

1. *Teacher's manual and test bank:* This manual, written by Marjorie L. Parker, contains the following for each chapter:
   a. Outline
   b. Suggestions for presenting the material
   c. Answers to Section exercises and to selected Programming Problems and Activities
   d. Chapter test questions
   e. Answers to test questions.
2. *Program disk:* To give students direct access to programs from the text, a disk containing most of these programs is bundled with the Teacher's Manual. The disk is in DOS format, but the programs are written in platform-independent C++, which can be run immediately on most implementations.
3. *Transparency masters:* More than 75 transparency masters are available to adopters of the text. The set of masters includes figures, tables, and other selected material from the text.
4. *Laboratory Manual:* In keeping with our intent to provide a modern approach and to meet the growing need for laboratory experience as put forth by the new ACM curriculum guidelines, a laboratory manual is available that is closely tied to the text's pedagogy. The manual provides

two kinds of exercises. Each lab experience begins with a few exercises relating to a small set of new concepts, such as the use of reference parameters with functions. The lab experience then uses these new concepts to extend several cumulative, semester-long programming projects. Students thus use the lab experience to build their competence incrementally, and to get a sense of how various concepts play a role in programming in the large. The example programs in the lab experiences are written in platform-independent C++.

5. *Computerized test bank:* Adopters of this edition will receive a computerized test-generation system. This provides a test bank system that allows adopters to edit, add, or delete test questions.

Each program segment in the text and in the lab manual has been compiled and run. Hence, original versions were all working. Unfortunately, the publication process does allow errors in code to occur after a program has been run. Every effort has been made to produce an error-free text, although this cannot be guaranteed with certainty. We assume full responsibility for all errors and omissions. If you detect any, please be tolerant and notify us or South-Western Educational Publishing so they can be corrected in subsequent printings and editions.

Acknowledgments

We would like to take this opportunity to thank those who in some way contributed to the completion of this text. Several reviewers contributed significant constructive comments during various phases of this project. They are all high school teachers, and we appreciate the time they took from their busy schedules to assess our work. They include:

Ms. Constance Byrnes
Abraham Lincoln High School
Council Bluffs, Iowa

Mr. Steve Carr
Lincoln Northeast High School
Lincoln, Nebraska

Mr. John Adrian Hood
Merkel High School
Merkel, Texas

Ms. Judith Hromcik
Arlington High School
Arlington, Texas

Ms. Peggy Mica
Round Rock High School
Round Rock, Texas

Ms. Karen North
Elsik High School
Houston, Texas

Mr. Don Parsons
Sunray Independent School District
Sunray, Texas

Mr. Steve Peerman
Las Cruces High School
Las Cruces, New Mexico

Ms. Charlotte Shepperd
Seguin High School
Seguin, Texas

Mr. Ronald Smith
Holmes High School
San Antonio, Texas

Mr. Chris Van Dyke
Channelview High School
Houston, Texas

Pam Vermeer, of Washington and Lee University, has classroom tested the college-level version of this text for several terms and contributed much to the design and content of the laboratory manual. Tom Whaley, also of Washington and Lee University, offered many helpful suggestions on making the minefield of C++ safer for beginning students.

Eight other people deserve special mention because, without their expertise, this book would not exist:

Lorretta Palagi, copyeditor. This is our fourth book with Lorretta. She has a wonderful sense of where to apply Occam's razor to a sentence or paragraph, and made many useful suggestions for improving not only style, but content as well.

Elliot Simon, technical proofreader. Elliot provided careful eyes and judgment during the layout and proofing stages of the book.

Regan Stilo and Deanna Quinn, production editors. Regan and Deanna monitored the production process and kept things running smoothly.

Cindy Trickel, editorial manager at Carlisle Publishers Services, our typesetter. Cindy handled all the details of turning a copyedited manuscript into a printed text.

Phyllis Jelinek, project manager. Phyllis lined up great reviewers and provided them with all of the relevant questions. She then digested the reviews into analyses that focused our attention immediately on the improvements that needed to be made at each phase of the development process.

Denis Ralling, editor. Denis plotted the strategy for the approach and focus we took in the book, and kept the entire process on schedule.

Jerry Westby, executive editor. Jerry initiated our collaboration on this project. His insight into what makes a book useful is uncanny. It is a privilege to work with an editor who is right at the top of his field.

Computer Science, Computer Architecture, and Computer Languages

A jet airplane crash-lands near a large American city. Though the plane catches fire on impact, all of the passengers and crew members miraculously survive. Investigators find no clues from the crew or the flight recorders that point to the cause of the crash. However, using reports of observers on the ground about the behavior of the plane, they construct a computer simulation of the plane's behavior in the air. From this simulation, they hypothesize that a flaw in the plane's rudder might have caused it to go into a tailspin. They examine the parts of the rudder found at the crash site and confirm their hypothesis. The results of their investigation will be used to correct the flaw in the rudders of several hundred airplanes.

The investigators who constructed this simulation solved a problem by designing a program and running it on a computer. They may not have been trained as computer scientists, but they used techniques that have come to be associated with the exciting field of computing.

This chapter provides a quick introduction to computer science, computer architecture, and computer languages. Section 1.1 provides a preview of the study of computer science. Section 1.2 examines the structure and parts of a computer and introduces the idea of computer software. Section 1.3 analyzes how computer languages are used to make a computer run.

As you read this chapter, do not be overly concerned about the introduction and early use of technical terminology. All terms will be subsequently developed. A good approach to an introductory chapter like this is to reread it periodically. This will help you maintain a good perspective on how new concepts and techniques fit into the broader picture of using computers. Finally, remember that learning a language that will make a computer work can be exciting; being able to control such a machine can lead to quite a sense of accomplishment.

1.1 Computer Science: A Preview

Objectives

♦ to understand that computer science is

    computer literacy

    mathematics and logic

    science

    engineering

    communication

    interdisciplinary

algorithm: A finite sequence of effective statements that, when applied to a problem, will solve it.

programming language: A formal language that computer scientists use to give instructions to a computer.

Computer science is a very young discipline. Electronic computers were initially developed in the 1940s. Those who worked with computers in the 1940s and 1950s often did so by teaching themselves about computers because at that time most schools did not offer any instruction in computer science. However, as these early pioneers in computers learned more about their machines, a collection of principles began to evolve into the discipline we now call computer science. Because it emerged from the efforts of people using computers in a variety of disciplines, the influence of these disciplines can often be seen in computer science. With that in mind, in the next sections we briefly describe what computer science is.

Computer Science as Computer Literacy

In the 1990s, computer-literate people know how to use a variety of computer software to make their professional and domestic lives more productive and easier. This software includes, for instance, word processors for writing and data management systems for storing every conceivable form of information (from address lists to recipes).

The computer-literate person who wants to acquire an understanding of computer science is in much the same position as the driver of a car who wants to learn how to change its spark plugs. For the driver, this curiosity can lead to a study of how automobile engines function generally. For the literate user of computer software, this curiosity can lead from the software's instruction manual to designing and writing a program with that software, and then to a deep understanding of a computer as a general-purpose problem-solving tool. The computer-literate person will come to understand that the collection of problems encompassed by computer science and the techniques used to solve those problems are the real substance of this rapidly expanding discipline.

Computer Science as Mathematics and Logic

The problem-solving emphasis of computer science borrows heavily from the areas of mathematics and logic. Faced with a problem, computer scientists must first formulate a solution. This method of solution, or **algorithm** as it is often called in computer science, must be thoroughly understood before the computer scientists make any attempt to implement the solution on the computer. Thus, at the early stages of problem solution, computer scientists work solely with their minds and do not rely on the machine (except, perhaps, as a word processor for making notes).

Once the solution is understood, computer scientists must then state the solution to this problem in a formal language called a **programming language.** This parallels the fashion in which mathematicians or logicians must develop a proof or argument in the formal language of mathematics. This formal solution as stated in a programming language must then be evaluated in terms of its correctness, style, and efficiency. Part of this evaluation process involves inputting the formally stated algorithm as a programmed series of steps for the computer to follow.

Another part of the evaluation process is distinctly separate from a consideration of whether or not the computer produces the "right answer" when the program is executed. Indeed, one of the main areas of emphasis throughout this book is in developing well-designed solutions to problems and in recognizing the difference between such solutions and ones that work but are not elegant. True computer scientists seek not just solutions to problems, but the best possible solutions.

Computer Science as Science

Perhaps nothing is as intrinsic to the scientific method as the formulation of hypotheses to explain phenomena and the careful testing of these hypotheses to prove them right or wrong. This same process plays an integral role in the way computer scientists work.

When confronted with a problem, such as a long list of names that needs to be arranged in alphabetical order, computer scientists formulate a hypothesis in the form of an algorithm that they believe will effectively solve the problem. Using mathematical techniques, they can make predictions about how such a proposed algorithm will solve the problem. But because the problems facing computer scientists arise from the world of real applications, predictive techniques relying solely on mathematical theory are not sufficient to prove an algorithm correct. Ultimately, computer scientists must implement their solutions on computers and test them in the complex situations that originally gave rise to the problems. Only after such thorough testing can the hypothetical solutions be declared right or wrong.

Moreover, just as many scientific principles are not 100% right or wrong, the hypothetical solutions posed by computer scientists are often subject to limitations. An understanding of those limitations—of when the method is appropriate and when it is not—is a crucial part of the knowledge that computer scientists must have. This is analogous to the way in which any scientist must be aware of the particular limitations of a scientific theory in explaining a given set of phenomena.

Do not forget the experimental nature of computer science as you study this book. You must participate in computer science to truly learn it. Although a good book can help, *you* must solve the problems, implement those solutions on the computer, and then test the results. View each of the problems you are assigned as an experiment for which you are to propose a solution and then verify the correctness of your solution by testing it on the computer. If the solution does not work exactly as you hypothesized, do not become discouraged. Instead, ask yourself why it did not work; by doing so you will acquire a deeper understanding of the problem and your solution. In this sense, the computer represents the experimental tool of the computer scientist. Do not be afraid to use it for exploration.

Computer Science as Engineering

Whatever the area of specialization, an engineer must neatly combine a firm grasp of scientific principles with implementation techniques. Without knowledge of the principles, the engineer's ability to design creative models for a problem's solution is severely limited. Such model building is crucial to the engineering design process. The ultimate design of a bridge, for instance, is the result of an engineer considering many possible models of the bridge and then selecting the best one. The transformation of abstract ideas into models of a problem's solution is thus central to the engineering design process. The ability to generate a variety of models that can be explored is the hallmark of creative engineering.

Similarly, the computer scientist is a model builder. Faced with a problem, the computer scientist must construct models for its solution. Such models take the form of an information structure that holds the data pertinent to the problem and the algorithmic method to manipulate that information structure to solve the problem. Just as an engineer must have an in-depth understanding of scientific principles to build a model, so must a computer scientist. With these principles, the computer scientist can conceive of models that are elegant, efficient, and appropriate to the problem at hand.

An understanding of principles alone is not sufficient for either the engineer or the computer scientist. Experience with the actual implementation of hypothetical models is also necessary. Without such experience, you can have only very limited intuition about what is feasible and how a large-scale project should be organized to reach a successful conclusion. Ultimately, computers are used to solve problems in the real world. In the real world, you will need to design programs that come in on time, that are within (if not under) the budget, and that solve all aspects of the original problem. The experience you acquire in designing problem solutions and then implementing them is vital to your being a complete computer scientist. Hence, remember that you cannot actually study computer science without actively doing it. To merely read about computer science techniques will leave you with an unrealistic perspective of what is possible.

Computer Science as Communication

As the discipline of computer science continues to evolve, communication is assuming a more significant role in the curriculum. The Association for Computing Machinery, Inc., guidelines for 1991 state, ". . . undergraduate programs should prepare students to . . . define a problem clearly; . . . document that solution; . . . and to communicate that solution to colleagues, professionals in other fields, and the general public" (p. 7).

It is no longer sufficient to be content with a program that runs correctly. Extra attention should be devoted to the communication aspects associated with such a program. For instance, you might be asked to submit a written proposal prior to designing a solution, or to document a program carefully and completely as it is being designed, or to write a follow-up report after a program has been completed.

These are some ways in which communication can be emphasized as an integral part of computer science. Several opportunities are provided in the exercise and problem lists of this text for you to focus on the communication aspects associated with computer science.

Ethics and Computer Science

Ethical issues in computer science are rapidly gaining public attention. As evidence, consider the following article from the Washington Post, October 14, 1990.

Should law-enforcement agencies be allowed to use computers to help them determine whether a person ought to be jailed or allowed out on bond? Should the military let computers decide when and on whom nuclear weapons should be used?

While theft and computer viruses have not gone away as industry problems, a group of 30 computer engineers and ethicists who gathered in Washington recently agreed that questions about the proper use of computers is taking center stage. At issue is to what degree computers should be allowed to make significant decisions that human beings normally make.

Already, judges are consulting computers, which have been programmed to predict how certain personality types will behave. Judges are basing their decisions more on what the computer tells them than on their own analysis of the arrested person's history. Computers are helping doctors decide treatments for patients. They played a major role in the July 1988 shooting of the Iranian jetliner by the USS Vincennes, and they are the backbone of this country's Strategic Defense Initiative ("Star Wars").

Representatives from universities, IBM Corp., the Brookings Institution, and several Washington theological seminaries [recently discussed] what they could do to build a conscience in the computer field.

The computer industry has been marked by "cre-ativity and drive for improvement and advancement," not by ethical concerns, said Robert Melford, chairman of the computing-ethics subcommittee of the Institute of Electrical and Electronics Engineers.

Computer professionals, Melford said, often spend much of their time in solitude, separated from the people affected by their programs who could provide valuable feedback.

Unlike hospitals, computer companies and most organized computer users have no staff ethicists or ethics committees to ponder the consequences of what they do. Few businesses have written policies about the proper way to govern computers. But there is evidence that technical schools, at least, are beginning to work an ethical component into their curricula. [For example, in recent years,] all computer engineering majors at Polytechnic University in Brooklyn [have been required to take a course in ethics.] The Massachusetts Institute of Technology is considering mandating five years of study instead of the current four to include work in ethics.

Affirmation that such questions should be addressed by computer scientists is contained in the 1991 curriculum guidelines of the Association for Computing Machinery, Inc. These guidelines state that "Undergraduates should also develop an understanding of the historical, social, and ethical context of the discipline and the profession."

You will see further **Notes of Interest** on this area of critical concern later in this book.

Computer Science as an Interdisciplinary Field

The problems solved by computer scientists come from a variety of disciplines—mathematics, physics, chemistry, biology, geology, economics, business, engineering, linguistics, and psychology, to name but a few. As a computer scientist working on a problem in one of these areas, you must be a quasi-expert in that discipline as well as in computer science. For instance, you cannot write a program to manage the checking account system of a bank unless you thoroughly understand how banks work and how that bank runs its checking accounts. As a minimum, you must be literate enough in other disciplines to converse with the

Development of computers

Era	Early Computing Devices		Mechanical Computers	Electro-mechanical Computers
Year	1000 B.C. A.D. 1614	1650	1900	1945
Development	Abacus Napier's bones		Adding machine	Cogged wheels
				Instruction register
			Slide rule	Operation code
				Address
			Difference engine	Plug board
				Harvard Mark I
			Analytic engine	Tabulating machine

<table>
<tr><td>

1.2 Computer Architecture

Objectives

◆ to understand the historical development of computers

◆ to know what constitutes computer hardware

◆ to know what constitutes computer software

</td><td>

people for whom you are writing programs and to learn precisely what it is they want the computer to do for them. Because such people may be naive about the computer and its capabilities, you will have to possess considerable communication skills as well as a knowledge of that other discipline.

Are you beginning to think that a computer scientist must be knowledgeable about much more than just the computer? If so, you are correct. Too often, computer scientists are viewed as technicians, tucked away in their own little worlds and not thinking or caring about anything other than computers. Nothing could be further from the truth. The successful computer scientist must be able to communicate, to learn new ideas quickly, and to adapt to ever-changing conditions. Computer science is emerging from its early dark ages into a mature field, one that we hope you will find rewarding and exciting. In studying computer science, you will develop many talents; this text can get you started on the road to that development process.

This section is intended to provide you with a brief overview of what computers are and how they are used. Although various sizes, makes, and models of computers are available, you will see that they all operate in basically the same straightforward manner. Whether you work on a personal computer that costs a few hundred dollars or on a mainframe that costs millions of dollars, the principles of making the machine work are essentially the same.

</td></tr>
</table>

◆ Figure 1.1

Development of computers (continued)

Noncommercial Electronic Computers	Batch Processing	Time-Sharing Systems	Personal Computers
1945 1950	1965	1975	Present
First-generation computers	Second-generation computers	Third-generation computers	Fourth-generation computers
Vacuum tubes	Transistors	Integrated circuit technology	Fifth-generation computers (supercomputers)
	Magnetic core memory		
Machine language programming	Assemblers	Operating system software	Microprocessors
	Compilers		
		Teleprocessing	Workstations
ENIAC	UNIVAC I		
	IBM 704		

Modern Computers

The search for aids to perform calculations is almost as old as number systems. Early devices included the abacus, Napier's bones, the slide rule, and mechanical adding machines. More recently, calculators have changed the nature of personal computing as a result of their availability, low cost, and high speed. The development of computers over time is highlighted in Figure 1.1. For more complete information, see People and Computers, Partners in Problem Solving by John F. Vinsonhaler, Christian C. Wagner, and Castelle G. Gentry, West Publishing Company, 1989.

The last three decades have seen the most significant changes in computing machines. As recently as the 1960s, a computer required several rooms because of its size. However, the advent of silicon chips has reduced the size and increased the availability of computers so that parents are able to purchase personal computers as presents for their children. These smaller computers are also more powerful than the early behemoths.

What is a computer? According to Webster's New World Dictionary of the American Language (2nd College Edition), a computer is "an electronic machine which, by means of stored instructions and information, performs rapid, often complex calculations or compiles, correlates, and selects data." Basically, a computer can be thought of as a machine that manipulates information in the form of numbers and characters. This information is referred to as **data.** What

data: The particular characters that are used to represent information in a form suitable for storage, processing, and communication.

mainframe: A large computer typically used by major companies and universities.

minicomputer: A small version of a mainframe computer. It is usually used by several people at once.

microcomputer: A computer capable of fitting on a laptop or desktop, generally used by one person at a time.

workstation: A powerful desktop computer that uses microprocessor technology.

network: A group of computers that are linked to share resources.

client/server relationship: A means of describing the organization of computing resources in which one resource provides a service to another resource.

hardware: The physical computing machine and its support devices.

makes computers remarkable is the extreme speed and precision with which they can store, retrieve, and manipulate data.

Several types of computers currently are available. An oversimplification is to categorize computers as mainframes, minicomputers, microcomputers, or workstations. In this grouping, **mainframe** computers are the large machines used by major companies, government agencies, and universities. They can be used by as many as 100 or more people at the same time and can cost millions of dollars. **Minicomputers,** in a sense, are smaller versions of large computers. They can be used by several people at once but have less storage capacity and cost far less than mainframes. **Microcomputers** are frequently referred to as personal computers. They have limited storage capacity (in a relative sense), are generally used by one person at a time, and can be purchased for as little as a few hundred dollars. **Workstations** have a larger storage capacity and faster processing speeds than microcomputers, but can still sit on a desktop and rely on similar microprocessing technology.

Most modern computers in organizations such as companies and universities are linked in a network. A **network** allows users of different computers to communicate and share resources. For example, the user of a microcomputer might receive electronic mail from a colleague in another office, send a file to a departmental laser printer, or connect to a cluster of workstations to perform tasks that require intensive processing.

Networked computers make use of a **client/server relationship.** One can think of clients as users requiring services, and servers as agents that perform services. For example, a single workstation might be an electronic mail server for 100 personal computers (the clients) in an organization.

As you begin your work with computers, you will hear people talking about **hardware** and **software.** Hardware refers to the physical machine and its support devices. Software refers to programs that make the machine do something. Many software packages exist for today's computers. They include word processing, database programs, spreadsheets, games, operating systems, and compilers. You can (and will!) learn to create your own software. In fact, that is what this book is all about.

A **program** can be thought of as a set of instructions that tells the machine what to do. When you have written a program, the computer will behave exactly as you have instructed it. It will do no more or no less than what is contained in your specific instructions. For example, the following listing is a C++ program that allows a student's last name and three scores to be entered from a keyboard. The program computes the average of the scores and then displays the student's name and average:

```
// Program file: average.cpp
// This program reads a student's name and
// three scores and displays their average.

#include <iostream.h>
#include <iomanip.h>
#include "apstring.h"
```

```
int main ()
{
        int score1, score2, score3;
        double average;
        apstring last_name;

        cout << "Enter the student's last name and press <Enter>: ";
        cin >> last_name;
        cout << "Enter the first score and press <Enter>: " ;
        cin >> score1;
        cout << "Enter the second score and press <Enter>: " ;
        cin >> score2;
        cout << "Enter the third score and press <Enter>: " ;
        cin >> score3;
        average = (score1 + score2 + score3) / 3.0;
        cout << setiosflags (ios::fixed | ios::showpoint) << setprecision(2);
        cout << "The average score for " << last_name;
        cout << " is " << average << endl;
        return 0;
}
```

software: Programs that make the machine (the hardware) do something, such as word processing, database management, or games.

program: A set of instructions that tells the machine (the hardware) what to do.

main unit: A computer's main unit contains the central processing unit (CPU) and the main (primary) memory; it is hooked to an input device and an output device.

central processing unit (CPU): A major hardware component that consists of the arithmetic/logic unit and the control unit.

Do not be concerned about specific parts of this program. It is intended only to illustrate the idea of a set of instructions. Very soon, you will be able to write significantly more sophisticated programs.

Learning to write programs requires two skills.

1. You need to be able to use specific terminology and punctuation that can be understood by the machine; that is, you need to learn a programming language.

2. You need to be able to develop a plan for solving a particular problem. This plan—or algorithm—is a sequence of steps that, when followed, will lead to a solution of the problem.

Initially, you may think that learning a language is the more difficult task because your problems will have relatively easy solutions. Nothing could be further from the truth! **The single most important thing you can do as a student of computer science is to develop the skill to solve problems in an organized fashion.** Once you have this skill, you can learn to write programs in several different languages.

Computer Hardware

Let's take another look at the question "What is a computer?" Our previous answer indicated it is a machine. Although there are several forms, names, and brands of computers, each consists of a **main unit** that is subsequently connected to peripheral devices. The main unit of a computer consists of a **central processing unit (CPU)** and **main (primary) memory.** The CPU is the "brain" of the computer. It contains an **arithmetic/logic unit,** which is capable of performing arithmetic operations and evaluating expressions to see if they are true or false, and the **control unit,** which controls the action of remaining components so your program can be followed step by step, or **executed.**

main (primary) memory (synonym: **random access memory**): Memory contained in the computer.

arithmetic/logic unit (ALU): The part of the central processing unit (CPU) that performs arithmetic operations and evaluates expressions.

control unit: The part of the central processing unit that controls the operation of the rest of the computer.

execute: To carry out the instructions of a program.

Main memory can be thought of as mailboxes in a post office. It is a sequence of locations where information representing instructions, numbers, characters, and so on can be stored. Main memory, also called *random access memory* (RAM), is usable only while the computer is turned on. It is where the program being executed is stored along with data it is manipulating.

As you develop a greater appreciation of how the computer works, you might wonder "How are data stored in memory?" Each memory location has an address and is capable of holding a sequence of **binary digits** (0 or 1), which are commonly referred to as *bits*. Instructions, symbols, letters, numbers, and so on are translated into an appropriate pattern of binary digits and then stored in various memory locations. These are retrieved, used, and changed according to instructions in your program. In fact, the program itself is similarly translated and stored in part of main memory. Main memory can be envisioned as in Figure 1.2, and the main unit can be envisioned as in Figure 1.3.

Peripherals can be divided into three categories: **input devices, output devices,** and **secondary (auxiliary) memory devices.** Input devices are necessary to give information to a computer. Programs are entered through an input device and then program statements are translated and stored as previously indicated. One input device (a typical keyboard) is shown in Figure 1.4.

Output devices are necessary to show the results of a program. These devices include a screen, line printer, impact printer, or laser printer (Figure 1.5). Input and output devices are frequently referred to as **I/O devices.**

Secondary (auxiliary) memory devices are used if additional memory is needed. On small computers, these secondary memory devices could be floppy disks or hard disks (Figure 1.6), CD-ROM disks, or magnetic tapes. Programs and data to be executed and processed are kept "waiting in the wings" in secondary memory.

◆ Figure 1.2

Main memory

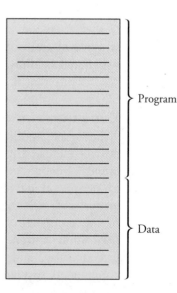

◆ Figure 1.3

Main unit

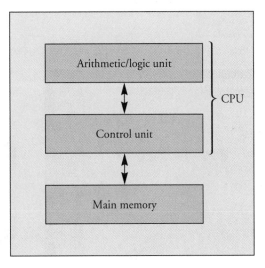

◆ Figure 1.4

Keyboard

binary digit (synonym: **bit**): A digit, either 0 or 1, in the binary number system. Program instructions are stored in memory using a sequence of binary digits. Binary digits are called bits.

input device: A device that provides information to the computer. Typical devices are keyboards, disk drives, card readers, and tape drives.

Communication between components of a computer is frequently organized around a group of wires called a **bus.** The relationship between a bus and various computer components can be envisioned as in Figure 1.7.

A photograph of a bus is shown in Figure 1.8. What appear to be lines between the slots are actually wires imprinted on the underlying board. Boards with wires connected to peripheral devices can be inserted into the slots.

Communication among different computers on a network is usually handled in two ways. A personal computer in the home might use a device called a **modem** to connect to a phone line. The user then connects to a remote computer by dialing a phone number. Computers in organizations are usually connected by cables that run between offices or buildings. These connections allow much faster transmission of information than modems and phone lines.

◆ Figure 1.5

(a) Screen, (b) line printer (mainframe), (c) impact printer (microcomputer), and (d) laser printer

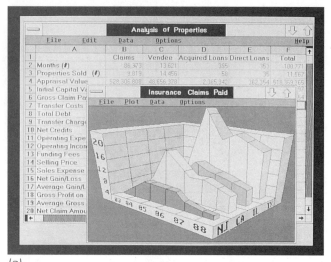

(a)

(b)

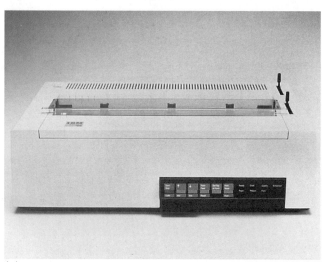

(c)

(d)

output device: A device that allows you to see the results of a program. Typically it is a monitor or printer.

secondary memory device: An auxiliary device for memory, usually a disk or magnetic tape.

Computer Software

As previously stated, software refers to programs that make the machine do something. Software consists of two kinds of programs: **system software** and **application software.**

System software includes what is often called the **operating system.** (For instance, the ubiquitous DOS stands for Disk Operating System.) The operating system for a computer is a large program and is usually supplied with the computer. This program allows the user to communicate with the hardware. More specifically, an operating system might control computer access (via passwords), allocate peripheral resources (perhaps with a printer queue), schedule shared

◆ Figure 1.6

(a) Disk drive and (b) microcomputer with hard disk

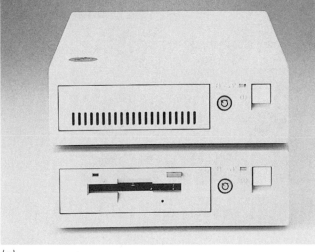

(a)

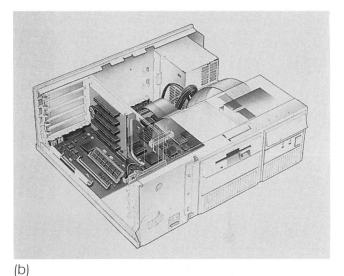

(b)

◆ Figure 1.7

An illustration of a bus

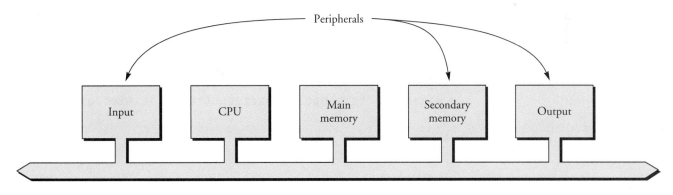

I/O devices: Any devices used for input or output.

bus: A group of wires imprinted on a circuit board to facilitate communication between components of a computer.

resources (for CPU use), connect to other computers (via networks), or control execution of other programs.

Applications software consists of programs designed for a specific use. Examples of applications software include programs for word processing, text editing, simulating spreadsheets, playing games, designing machinery, and figuring payrolls. Most computer users work with applications software and have little need to learn a computer language; the programs they require have already been written to accomplish their tasks.

◆ Figure 1.8

Bus

1.3 Computer Languages

Objectives

◆ to understand what a computer language is

◆ to understand the difference between a low-level language and a high-level language

◆ to understand the difference between a source program and an object program

modem: A device that connects a computer to a telephone system to transmit data.

system software: The programs that allow users to write and execute other programs, including operating systems such as DOS.

What is a computer language? All data transmission, manipulation, storage, and retrieval are actually done by the machine using electrical pulses representing sequences of binary digits. If eight-digit binary codes are used, there are 256 numbered instructions from 00000000 to 11111111. Instructions for adding two numbers would consist of a sequence of these eight-digit codes. Instructions written in this form are referred to as **machine language.** It is possible to write an entire program in machine language. However, this is very time consuming and difficult to read and understand.

Therefore, the next level of computer language allows words and symbols to be used in an unsophisticated manner to accomplish simple tasks. For example, the machine code for adding two integers might be

```
0100001100111010001111010100001001010101101000010
```

This is replaced by

```
LOAD A

ADD B

STORE C
```

This causes the number in **A** to be added to the number in **B** and the result to be stored for later use in **C**. This computer language is an **assembly language,** which is generally referred to as a *low-level language.* What actually happens is that words and symbols are translated into appropriate binary digits and the machine uses the translated form.

Although assembly language is an improvement over machine language for readability and program development, it is still a bit cumbersome. Consequently,

application software: Programs designed for a specific use.

operating system: A large program that allows the user to communicate with the hardware and performs various management tasks.

machine language: The language used directly by the computer in all its calculations and processing.

assembly language (synonym: **low-level language**): A computer language that allows words and symbols to be used in an unsophisticated manner to accomplish simple tasks.

high-level language: Any programming language that uses words and symbols to make it relatively easy to read and write a program.

compiler: A computer program that automatically converts instructions in a high-level language to machine language.

source program: A program written by a programmer.

object program (synonym: **object code**): The machine code version of the source program.

many **high-level languages** have been developed; these include Pascal, PL/I, FORTRAN, BASIC, COBOL, C, Ada, Modula-2, Logo, and others. These languages simplify even further the terminology and symbolism necessary for directing the machine to perform various manipulations of data. For example, in these languages, the task of adding two integers would be written as

```
C := A + B;          (Pascal, Modula-2, Ada)
C = A + B;           (PL/I, C++)
C = A + B            FORTRAN, BASIC
ADD A, B GIVING C    (COBOL)
MAKE "C :A + :B      (Logo)
```

A high-level language makes it easier to read, write, and understand a program. This book develops the concepts, symbolism, and terminology necessary for using C++ as a programming language for solving problems. After you have become proficient with C++, you should find it relatively easy to learn the nuances of other high-level languages.

For a moment, let's consider how an instruction such as

```
C = A + B;
```

gets translated into machine code. The actual bit pattern for this code varies according to the machine and software version, but it could be as previously indicated. In order for the translation to happen, a special program called a **compiler** "reads" the high-level instructions and translates them into machine code. This compiled version is then run using some appropriate data, and the results are presented through some form of output device. The special programs that activate the compiler, run the machine-code version, and cause output to be printed are examples of system programs (software). The written program is a **source program,** and the machine-code version generated by the compiler is an **object program** (also referred to as *object code*).

As you will soon see, the compiler does more than just translate instructions into machine code. It also detects certain errors in your source program and prints appropriate messages. For example, if you write the instruction

```
C = (A + B;
```

in which a parenthesis is missing, when the compiler attempts to translate this line into machine code, it will detect that "**)**" is needed to close the parenthetical expression. It will then give you an error message such as

```
Error: ')' expected
```

You should correct the error (and any others) and recompile your source program before running it with the data.

A Note of Interest

Why Learn C++?

C++ is a superset of C. C is a programming language developed at AT&T Bell Laboratories by Dennis Ritchie in 1972. Ritchie originally intended C to be used to write the UNIX operating system and to write tools to be used with that system. Over the years, however, C has achieved widespread popularity for writing various programs in industry, and it is now the language of choice in most graduate schools of computer science. According to Richard P. Gabriel ("The end of history and the last programming language," Journal of Object-Oriented Programming, July–August 1993), C and C++ are among the few programming languages that are not either dead or moribund. There are several reasons for this. C is available on a wide range of computers and requires few computer resources to design, implement, and run programs. C represents a simple machine model, one that closely corresponds to the structure of actual computers. This property supports the development of very efficient programs. C is also similar to several different popular programming languages, like Pascal, FORTRAN, and assembly language. Finally, C requires almost no mathematical sophistication to learn.

Critics claim that C is a dangerous language in two respects. First, C encourages programmers to write programs that lack structure and are difficult to read and maintain. Second, C lacks many of the fail-safe features of modern programming languages, such as thorough compile-time type checking.

Responding to this challenge, Bjarne Stroustrup, also of AT&T Bell Laboratories, developed C++ in the 1980s. C++ incorporates all of the desirable and undesirable features of C enumerated above. However, some additional features, if used properly, make C++ a safer language and support the design and implementation of well-structured, easily maintained programs for both beginners and professionals. For example, C++ has strong support for data types and type checking, and also has features that support the discipline of **object-oriented programming** (OOP). Object-oriented programming is a method of developing and maintaining large software systems. OOP is introduced and discussed in later chapters in this text.

Critics claim that C++ introduces its own costs: The language is enormous, the machine model that it represents is more complex than that of C, and programmers must have more mathematical sophistication to make use of its improved features. However, if Gabriel is right, students will do well to learn this language, because it will be used in industry for many years to come.

Our approach in this text will be to focus on those features of C++ that support the design and implementation of well-structured programs that are easy to read and maintain. C++ is a powerful tool that should be wielded carefully.

You are now ready to begin a detailed study of C++. You will undoubtedly spend much time and encounter some frustration during the course of your work. We hope your efforts result in an exciting and rewarding learning experience. Good luck!

Summary

Key Terms

algorithm	binary digit (bit)	control unit
application software	bus	data
arithmetic/logic unit (ALU)	central processing unit (CPU)	execute
assembly language (low-level language)	client/server relationship	hardware
	compiler	high-level language
		input device

I/O devices   modem   programming language
machine language   network   secondary (auxiliary)
main (primary) memory   object program (object   memory device
main unit   code)   software
mainframe   operating system   source program
microcomputer   output device   system software
minicomputer   program   workstation

Chapter Review Exercises

1. State and discuss the characteristics of each of the four classifications of computers.
2. Discuss the skills needed by students of computer science.
3. What are the three major components of any computer?
4. What are the two parts of the central processing unit?
5. Name three input devices.
6. Name two output devices.
7. Name five high-level languages.
8. Give three reasons for studying C++.

Answer each of the following fill-in-the-blank exercises with a single word or phrase.

9. The advent of _____ has reduced the size and increased the availability of computers.
10. The information (in the form of characters and numbers) manipulated by computers is known as _____.
11. The actual machine and its support devices are known as _____.
12. The programs run by a machine are called _____.
13. A set of instructions telling a computer what to do is called a(n) _____.
14. A sequence of steps used to solve a problem is called a(n) _____.
15. CPU stands for _____.
16. The two parts of a CPU are the _____ and the _____.
17. Auxiliary memory exists on _____, _____, or _____.
18. I/O devices are also known as _____.
19. All work inside the computer is done by sequences of _____. This lowest level language is referred to as _____.
20. The next lowest level of language is _____.
21. The program you write in a high-level language is called _____; its compiled version is called _____.

Chapter

Writing Your First Programs

Chapter Outline

2.1 Program Development: Top-Down Design

A Note of Interest: Software Verification

2.2 Writing Programs

A Note of Interest: Program Libraries

2.3 Data Types and Output

A Note of Interest: The ACM Code of Ethics

2.4 Graphics

C hapter 1 presented an overview of computers and computer languages. We are now ready to examine problems that computers can solve. First we need to know how to solve a problem and then we need to learn how to use a programming language to implement our solution on the computer. Section 2.1 lays the foundation for what many consider to be the most important aspect of entry-level courses in computer science—program development. The problem-solving theme in this section is continued throughout the text.

Before looking at problem solving and writing programs for the computer, we should consider some psychological aspects of working in computer science. Studying computer science can cause a significant amount of frustration for these reasons:

1. *Planning is a critical issue.* First, you must plan to develop instructions to solve your problem and then you should plan to translate those instructions into code before you sit down at the keyboard. You should not attempt to type in code "off the top of your head."

2. *Time is a major problem.* You cannot expect to complete a programming assignment by staying up late the night before it is due. You must begin early and expect to make several revisions before your final version is ready.

3. *Successful problem solving and programming require extreme precision.* Generally, concepts in computer science are not difficult; however, implementation of these concepts allows no room for error. For example, one misplaced word in a 1000-line program could prevent the program from working.

In other words, you must be prepared to plan well, start early, be patient, handle frustration, and work hard to succeed in software development. If you cannot do this, you may not enjoy software development or be successful at it.

19

Objectives

- to understand what an algorithm is
- to understand what top-down design is
- to understand what stepwise refinement is
- to understand what modularity is
- to be able to develop algorithms

effective statement:
A clear, unambiguous instruction that can be carried out.

The key to writing a successful program is planning. Good programs do not just happen; they are the result of careful design and patience. Just as an artist commissioned to paint a portrait would not start out by shading in the lips and eyes, a good computer programmer would not attack a problem by immediately trying to write code for a program to solve the problem. Writing a program is like writing an essay: An overall theme is envisioned, an outline of major ideas is developed, each major idea is subdivided into several parts, and each part is developed using individual sentences.

Six Steps to Good Programming Habits

In developing a program to solve a problem, six steps should be followed: analyze the problem, develop an algorithm, document the program, write code for the program, run the program, and test the results. These steps will help develop good problem-solving habits and, in turn, solve programming problems correctly. A brief discussion of each of these steps follows:

Step 1:   Analyze the Problem. This is not a trivial task. Before you can do anything, you must know exactly what it is you are to do. You must be able to formulate a clear and precise statement of what is to be done. You should understand completely what data are available and what may be assumed. You should also know exactly what output is desired and the form it should take. When analyzing a complex problem, it helps to divide the problem into subproblems whose solutions can be developed and tested independently before they are combined into a complete solution.

Step 2:   Develop an Algorithm. An algorithm is a finite sequence of effective statements that, when applied to the problem, will solve it. An **effective statement** is a clear, unambiguous instruction that can be carried out. Each algorithm you develop should have a specific beginning and an ending that is reached in a reasonable amount of time. When each step is completed, the next step should be uniquely determined.

Step 3:   Document the Program. It is very important to completely document a program. The writer knows how the program works, but if others are to modify it, they must know the logic used. Moreover, users will need to know how to use the program effectively. Documentation can come directly out of steps 1 and 2 before you write any code.

Step 4:   Write Code for the Program. When the algorithm correctly solves the problem, you can start to translate your algorithm into a high-level language. An effective algorithm will significantly reduce the time you need to complete this step.

Step 5:   Run the Program. After writing the code, you are ready to run the program. This means that, using an editor, you type the program code into the computer, compile the program, and run the program. At compile time, you may discover syntax errors, which are mistakes in the way you have formed sentences in the program. Once these errors have been corrected, you may discover other errors at run time. Some of these mistakes may be as simple as an attempt to divide by zero. Other errors, called logic errors, may be more subtle and cause the program to produce mysterious results. They may require a reevaluation of all or parts of your algorithm. The probability of having to make some corrections or changes is quite high.

Step 6: **Test the Results.** After your program has run, you need to be sure that the results are correct, that they are in a form you like, and that your program produces the correct solution in all cases. To be sure the results are correct, you must look at them and compare them with what you expect. In the case of a program that uses arithmetic operations, this means checking some results with pencil and paper. With complex programs, you will need to test the program thoroughly by running it many times using data that you have carefully selected. Often you will need to make revisions by returning to one of the previous steps.

You should bear in mind that programs of any significant size (more than 100 lines of code) are never constructed all at once. The six steps just described are used to build programs incrementally. That is, a program is created out of small pieces that are designed, coded, tested, and documented to solve small problems. These pieces are then glued together to solve the problem set for the overall program.

Developing Algorithms

Algorithms for solving a problem can be developed by stating the problem and then subdividing the problem into major subtasks. Each subtask can then be subdivided into smaller tasks. This process is repeated until each remaining task is one that is easily solved. This process is known as **top-down design,** and each successive subdivision is referred to as a **stepwise refinement.** Tasks identified at each stage of this process are called **modules.** The relationship between modules can be shown graphically in a **structure chart** (see Figure 2.1).

To illustrate how to develop an algorithm, we will use the problem of updating a checkbook after a transaction has been made. A first-level refinement is shown in Figure 2.2. An arrow pointing into a module means information is needed before the task can be performed. An arrow pointing out of a module means the module task has been completed and information required for subsequent work is available. Each of these modules could be further refined as shown in Figure 2.3. Finally, one of the last modules could be refined as shown in Figure 2.4. The complete top-down design could then be envisioned as illustrated in Figure 2.5. Notice that each remaining task can be accomplished in a very direct manner.

As a further aid to understanding how data are transmitted, we will list **module specifications** for each main (first-level) module. Each module specification includes a description of inputs or data received, outputs or information returned, and the task performed by the module. In cases for which there are no inputs or outputs, none are specified.

For the checkbook-balancing problem, complete module specifications are as follows:

Module: Get information
Task: Have the user enter information from the keyboard.
Output: Starting balance, transaction type, transaction amount

---

top-down design: A methodology for solving a problem whereby you first state the problem and then repeatedly subdivide the main task into subtasks until each remaining subtask is easily solved.

stepwise refinement: The process of repeatedly subdividing tasks into subtasks until each subtask is easily accomplished.

module: An independent unit that is part of a larger development. Can be a function or a class (set of functions and related data).

structure chart: A graphic method of indicating the relationship between modules when designing the solution to a problem.

module specifications: A description of data received, information returned, and task performed by a function.

◆ **Figure 2.1**

◆ **Figure 2.1**

Structure chart illustrating
top-down design

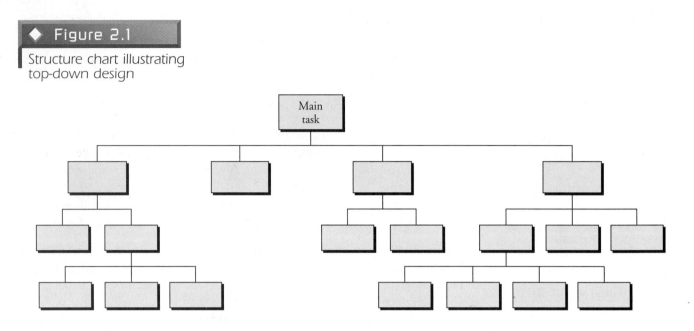

Module: Perform computations
Task: If transaction is a deposit, add it to the starting balance; otherwise, subtract it.
Input: Starting balance, transaction type, transaction amount
Output: Ending balance

Module: Display results
Task: Display results in a readable form.
Input: Starting balance, transaction type, transaction amount, ending balance

At least two comments should be made about top-down design. First, different people can (and probably will) have different designs for the solution of a problem. However, each good design will have well-defined modules with functional subtasks. Second, the graphic method just used helps to formulate general logic for solving a problem but is somewhat awkward for translating to code. Thus, we will use a stylized, half-English, half-code method called

◆ **Figure 2.2**

First-level refinement

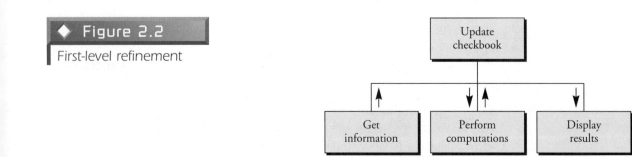

◆ Figure 2.3

Second-level refinement

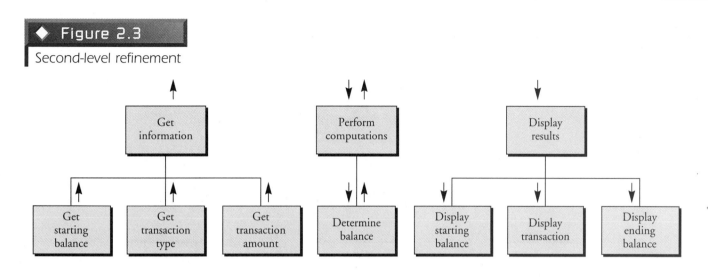

pseudocode: A stylized half-English, half-code language written in English but suggesting C++ code.

pseudocode to illustrate stepwise refinement in such a design. Pseudocode is written in English, but the sentence structure and indentations suggest C++ code. Major tasks are numbered with whole numbers and subtasks with decimal numbers. After you become used to the pseudocode notation, the numbering of lines will be omitted. First-level pseudocode for the checkbook-balancing problem is

1.   Get information
2.   Perform computations
3.   Display results

A second-level pseudocode development produces

1.   Get information
     1.1 Get starting balance
     1.2 Get transaction type
     1.3 Get transaction amount

◆ Figure 2.4

Third-level refinement

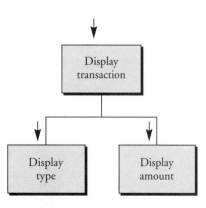

◆ **Figure 2.5**

Structure chart for top-down design

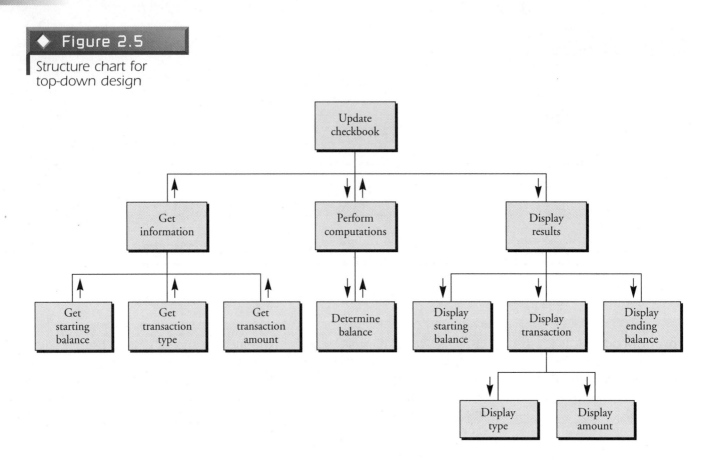

2. Perform computations
   2.1 If deposit then
        add to balance
   Else
        Subtract from balance
3. Display results
   3.1 Display starting balance
   3.2 Display transaction
   3.3 Display ending balance

Finally, step 3.2 of the pseudocode is subdivided as previously indicated into

   3.2 Display transaction
        3.2.1 Display transaction type
        3.2.2 Display transaction amount

Two final comments are in order. First, each module developed should be tested with data for that module. Once you are sure each module does what you want, the whole program should work when the modules are used together. Second, the process of dividing a task into subtasks is especially suitable for writing programs in C++. As you will see, the language supports development of subprograms for specific subtasks.

A C++ program for the checkbook-balancing problem follows:

```cpp
// Program file: chbook.cpp
// This program updates a checkbook.

#include <iostream.h>
#include <iomanip.h>

int main ()
{
        double starting_balance, ending_balance, trans_amount;
        char trans_type;
```

```cpp
// Module for getting the data.
        cout << "Enter the starting balance and press <Enter>: " ;
        cin >> starting_balance;
        cout << "Enter the transaction type (D) deposit or (W) withdrawal " ;
        cout << "and press <Enter>: " ;
        cin >> trans_type;
        cout << "Enter the transaction amount and press <Enter>: " ;
        cin >> trans_amount;
```

1

```cpp
// Module for performing computations.

        if (trans_type == 'D')
                ending_balance = starting_balance + trans_amount;
        else
                ending_balance = starting_balance - trans_amount;
```

2

```cpp
// Module for displaying results.

        cout << setiosflags (ios::fixed | ios::showpoint | ios::right)
             << setprecision(2);
        cout << endl;
        cout << "Starting balance      $" << setw(8)
             << starting_balance << endl;
        cout << "Transaction           $" << setw(8)
             << trans_amount << setw(2) << trans_type << endl;
        cout << setw(30) << "-------" << endl;
        cout << "Ending  balance       $" << setw(8)
             << ending_balance << endl ;
```

3

```cpp
        return 0;
}
```

Notice how sections of the program correspond to module specifications. Sample runs of the program produce this output:

```
Enter the starting balance and press <Enter>: 235.16
Enter the transaction type (D) deposit or (W) withdrawal and press <Enter>: D
Enter the transaction amount and press <Enter>: 75.00

Starting Balance              $   235.16

Transaction                   $    75.00 D
                                  -------

Ending Balance                $   310.16

Enter the starting balance and press <Enter>: 310.16
Enter the transaction type (D) deposit or (W) withdrawal and press <Enter>: W
Enter the transaction amount and press <Enter>: 65.75

Starting Balance              $   310.16

Transaction                   $    65.75 W
                                  -------

Ending Balance                $   244.41
```

You probably would not use the power of a computer for something as simple as this program. You could just press a few calculator keys instead. However, as you will see, the language supports development of subprograms for specific subtasks. You will, for example, soon be able to enhance this program to check for overdrafts, save the new balance for later use, and repeat the process for several transactions. Learning to think in terms of modular development now will aid you not just in creating algorithms to solve problems, but in writing programs to solve problems.

Software Engineering

software engineering:
The process of developing and maintaining large software systems.

The term **software engineering** is used roughly to refer to the process of developing and maintaining very large software systems. Before becoming engrossed in the specifics of solving problems and writing relatively small programs, it is instructive to consider the broader picture faced by those who develop software for "real-world" use.

It is not unusual for software systems to be programs that, if written in this size type, would require between 100 and 150 pages of text. These systems must be reliable, economical, and subject to use by a diverse audience. Because of these requirements, software developers must be aware of and practice certain techniques.

As you might imagine, such large programs are not the work of a single individual but are developed by teams of programmers. Issues such as communication, writing style, and technique become as important as the development of

A Note of Interest

Software Verification

Sitting 70 kilometers east of Toronto on the shore of Lake Ontario, the Darlington Nuclear Generating Station looks much like any other large nuclear power plant of the Canadian variety. But behind its ordinary exterior lies an unusual design feature.

Darlington is the first Canadian nuclear station to use computers to operate the two emergency shutdown systems that safeguard each of its four reactors. In both shutdown systems, a computer program replaces an array of electrically operated mechanical devices—switches and relays—designed to respond to sensors that are monitoring conditions critical to a reactor's safe operation, such as water levels in boilers.

Darlington's four reactors supply enough electricity to serve a city of two million people. Its Toronto-based builder, Ontario Hydro, opted for sophisticated software rather than old-fashioned hardware in the belief that a computer-operated shutdown system would be more economical, flexible, reliable, and safe than one under mechanical control.

But this new approach turned out to have unanticipated costs. To satisfy regulators that the shutdown software would function as advertised, Ontario Hydro engineers had to go through a frustrating but essential checking process that required nearly three years of extra effort. "There are lots of examples where software has gone wrong with serious consequences," says engineer Glenn H. Archinoff of Ontario Hydro. "If you want a shutdown system to work when you need it, you have to have a high level of assurance."

The Darlington experience demonstrates the tremendous effort involved in establishing the correctness of even relatively short and straightforward computer programs. The 10,000 "lines" of instructions, or code, required for each shutdown system pale in comparison with the 100,000 lines that constitute a typical word processing program or the millions of lines needed to operate a long-distance telephone network or a space shuttle.

algorithms to solve particular parts of the problem. Management, coordination, and design are major considerations that need resolution very early in the process. Although you will not face these larger organizational issues in this course, you will see how some of what you learn has implications for larger design issues.

Software engineering has been so titled because techniques and principles from the more established engineering disciplines are used to guide the large-scale development required in major software. To illustrate, consider the problems faced by an engineer who is to design and supervise construction of a bridge. This analysis was presented by Alfred Spector and David Gifford in an article entitled "A computer science perspective on bridge design," published in Communications of the ACM (April 1986).

> Engineers designing a bridge view it first as a hierarchy of substructures. This decomposition process continues on the substructures themselves until a level of very fundamental objects (such as beams and plates) ultimately is reached. This decomposition technique is similar to the stepwise refinement technique used by software designers, who break a complex problem down into a hierarchy of subproblems each of which ultimately can be solved by a relatively simple algorithm.
>
> Engineers build conceptual models before actually constructing a bridge. This model-building allows them to evaluate various design alternatives in a way which eventually leads to the best possible design for the application

being considered. This process is analogous to the way in which a skilled software designer builds models of a software system using structure charts and first-level pseudocode descriptions of modules. The designer then studies these conceptual models and eventually chooses the most elegant and efficient model for the application.

By the fashion in which engineers initially break down the bridge design, they insure that different aspects of the design can be addressed by different subordinate groups of design engineers working in a relatively independent fashion. This is similar to the goal of a software designer who oversees a program development team. The design of the software system must insure that individual components may be developed simultaneously by separate groups whose work will not have harmful side effects when the components are finally pulled together.

This overview is presented to give you a better perspective on how developments in this text are part of a greater whole. As you progress through your study of C++, you will see specific illustrations of how concepts and techniques can be viewed as part of the software engineering process.

Software System Life Cycle

Software engineering is the process by which large software systems are produced. As you might imagine, these systems need to be maintained and modified, and ultimately they are replaced with other systems. This entire process parallels that of an organism. That is, there is a development, maintenance, and subsequent demise. This process is referred to as the **software system life cycle.** Specifically, a system life cycle can be viewed in the following phases:

software system life cycle: The process of development, maintenance, and demise of a software system.

1. Analysis
2. Design
3. Coding
4. Testing/verification
5. Maintenance
6. Obsolescence

It may come as a surprise that the design phase is not the first phase. It is extremely critical that a problem be completely understood before any attempt is made to design a solution; that is why the analysis phase comes first. The analysis phase is complicated by the fact that potential users may not supply enough information when describing their intended use of a system. Analysis requires careful attention to items such as exact form of input, exact form of output, how data entry errors (there will be some) should be handled, how large the databases will become, how much training in the use of the system will be provided, and what possible modifications might be required as the intended audience increases/decreases. Clearly, the analysis phase requires an experienced communicator.

The design phase is what much of this book is about. This is where the solution is developed using a modular approach. Attention must be paid to techniques that include communication, algorithm development, writing style, teamwork, and so on. The key product of this phase is a detailed specification of the intended software product.

Coding closely follows design. Unfortunately, many beginning students want to write code too quickly. This can be a painful lesson if you have to scrap several days' worth of work because your original design was not sufficient. You are encouraged to make sure your designs are complete before writing any code. In the real world, teams of designers work long hours before programmers ever get a chance to start writing code.

The testing phase of a large system is a significant undertaking. Early testing is done on individual modules to get them running properly. Larger data sets must then be run on the entire program to make sure the modules interact properly with the main program. When the system appears ready to the designers, it is usually field tested by selected users. Each of these testing levels is likely to require changes in the design and coding of the system.

Finally, the system is released to the public and the maintenance phase begins. This phase lasts throughout the remainder of the program's useful life. During this phase, we are concerned with repairing problems that arise after the system has been put into use. These problems are not necessarily bugs introduced during the coding phases. More often they are the result of user needs that change over time. For instance, annual changes in the tax laws necessitate changes in even the best payroll programs. Or problems may arise as a result of misinterpretation of user needs during the early analysis phase. Whatever the reason, we must expect that a program will have to undergo numerous changes during its lifetime. During the maintenance phase, the time spent documenting the original program will be repaid many times over. One of the worst tasks imaginable in software development is to be asked to maintain an undocumented program. Undocumented code can quickly become virtually unintelligible, even to the program's original author. Indeed, one of the measures of a good program is how well it stands up to the maintenance phase.

Of course, no matter how good a program is, it will eventually become obsolete. At that time, the system life cycle starts all over again with the development of a new system to replace the obsolete one. Hence, the system life cycle is never ending, being itself part of a larger repetitive pattern that continues to evolve with changing user needs and more powerful technology.

Object-Oriented Design

During the last few years, a methodology has emerged that promises to make the task of maintaining large software systems easier. According to this method, large software systems should be constructed from smaller software components called *objects*. Software objects are a bit like building blocks, in that they can be pulled out of a box and put together in different ways to construct different applications. Objects can also be customized, that is, they can be adapted if they do not quite fit the task at hand. It is claimed that the use of software objects results in several benefits:

1. Because software objects can represent the behavior of the "real" objects that a software system is created to model, the differences between the analysis, design, and coding phases of the software life cycle tend to collapse.
2. Instead of changing existing code or writing new code, software maintenance involves plugging objects into a system or unplugging them from a system.

3. Systems can be more easily developed in increments, starting with a rough prototype whose detailed functions are eventually filled in until they are complete.

object-oriented design: A methodology that uses small, reusable components to construct large software systems.

Although **object-oriented design** holds much promise for the development of solutions to complex problems, it is not necessarily the easiest and most straightforward way to learn to solve problems with a computer. In particular, the need for objects will not become apparent until we begin to define and use our own data structures for solving problems in Chapters 8 and 9. After we have explored some other typical problem-solving techniques, we will introduce object-oriented problem solving and programming with C++ in Chapters 9 through 11.

■ Exercises 2.1

1. Which of the following can be considered effective statements; that is, considered to be clear, unambiguous instructions that can be carried out? For each statement, explain why it is effective or why it is not.
   a. Pay the cashier $9.15.
   b. Water the plants a day before they die.
   c. Determine all positive prime numbers less than 1,000,000.
   d. Choose x to be the smallest positive fraction.
   e. Invest your money in a stock that will increase in value.

2. What additional information must be obtained in order to understand each of the following problems?
   a. Find the largest number of a set of numbers.
   b. Alphabetize a list of names.
   c. Compute charges for a telephone bill.

3. Outline the main tasks for solving each of the following problems:
   a. Write a good term paper.
   b. Take a vacation.
   c. Choose a college.
   d. Get a summer job.
   e. Compute the semester average for a student in a computer science course and print all pertinent data.

4. Refine the main tasks in each part of Exercise 3 into a sufficient number of levels so that each problem can be solved in a well-defined manner.

5. Use pseudocode to write a solution for each of the following problems. Indicate each stage of your development.
   a. Compute the wages for two employees of a company. The input information will consist of the hourly wage and the number of hours worked in one week. The output should contain a list of all deductions, gross pay, and net pay. For this problem, assume deductions are made for federal withholding taxes, state withholding taxes, social security, and union dues.
   b. Compute the average test score for five students in a class. Input for this problem will consist of five scores. Output should include each score and the average of these scores.

6. Develop an algorithm to find the total, average, and largest number in a given list of 25 numbers.

7. Develop an algorithm to find the greatest common divisor (GCD) of two positive integers.

8. Develop an algorithm for solving the following system of equations:

$$ax + by = c$$
$$dx + ey = f$$

9. Draw a structure chart and write module specifications for each of the following exercises.
   a. Exercise 5-a
   b. Exercise 5-b
   c. Exercise 6
10. Discuss how the top-down design principles of software engineering are similar to the design problems faced by a construction engineer for a building. Be sure to include anticipated work with all subcontractors.
11. Using the construction analogy of Exercise 10, give an example of some specific communication required between electricians and the masons who finish the interior walls. Discuss why this information flow should be coordinated by a construction engineer.
12. State the phases of the software system life cycle.
13. Contact some company or major user of a software system to see what kinds of modifications might be required in a system after it has been released to the public. (Your own computer center might be sufficient.)

2.2 Writing Programs

Objectives

- to be able to recognize reserved words and standard library identifiers
- to be able to recognize and declare valid identifiers
- to know the basic components of a program
- to understand the basic structure of a C++ program

The Vocabulary of C++

Consider the following complete C++ program:

```cpp
// Program file: reswords.cpp
// This program illustrates the use of reserved words.

#include <iostream.h>
#include <iomanip.h>

const int LOOP_LIMIT = 10;

int main ()
{
    int j, number, sum;
    double average;

    sum = 0;
    for (j = 1; j <= LOOP_LIMIT; ++j)
    {
        cout << "Enter a number and press <Enter>: ";
        cin >> number;
        sum = sum + number;
    }
    average = double(sum) / LOOP_LIMIT;
    cout << setiosflags (ios::fixed | ios::showpoint
        | ios::right)
        << setprecision(2);
```

```
          cout << endl;
          cout << setw(10) << "The average is"
               << setw(8) << average << endl;
          cout << endl;
          cout << setw(10) << "The number of scores is"
               << setw(3) << LOOP_LIMIT << endl;
          return 0;
     }
```

reserved words: *Words that have predefined meanings that cannot be changed.*

library identifiers: *Words defined in standard C++ libraries.*

programmer-supplied identifiers: *Words defined by the programmer.*

The vocabulary of C++ consists of several kinds of words. Words that have a predefined meaning that cannot be changed are called **reserved words.** Some other predefined words **(library identifiers)** can have their meanings changed if the programmer has strong reasons for doing so. Other words **(programmer-supplied identifiers)** must be created according to a well-defined set of rules, but can have any meaning, subject to those rules.

Case Sensitivity

C++ is case sensitive. This means that the word **while** will have a different meaning to the compiler than the word **While**, even though the two words might appear to mean the same thing to a human being. All reserved words and many library identifiers in C++ must be typed in lowercase letters only. Constant identifiers in C++ are typed in uppercase by convention. Identifiers that you create for your own purposes may be typed in any case you like, as long as you remember that the same words written in different cases will mean different things.

Reserved Words

In C++, reserved words are predefined and cannot be used in a program for anything other than the purpose for which they are reserved. Some examples are **for**, **if**, **while**, **do**, **switch**, and **int**. As you continue with your study of C++, you will learn where and how these words are used. The C++ reserved words are listed in Table 2.1.

▼ **Table 2.1**

Reserved words

asm	continue	float	new	signed	try
auto	default	for	operator	sizeof	typedef
break	delete	friend	private	static	union
case	do	goto	protected	struct	unsigned
catch	double	if	public	switch	virtual
char	else	inline	register	template	void
class	enum	int	return	this	volatile
const	extern	long	short	throw	while

Library Identifiers

A second set of predefined words, library identifiers, can have their meanings changed by the programmer. For example, if you could develop a better algorithm for the trigonometric function **sin**, you could then substitute it in the program. However, these words should not be used for anything other than their intended use. This list will vary somewhat from compiler to compiler, so you should obtain a list of library identifiers used in your local implementation of C++. Some library identifiers are listed in Table 2.2 and in Appendix 2. The term **keywords** is used to refer to both reserved words and library identifiers in subsequent discussions.

keywords: Either reserved words or library identifiers.

▼ Table 2.2

Some library identifiers

```
cin
cout
pow
setprecision
setw
sin
sqrt
apstring
```

Syntax

syntax: The formal rules governing construction of valid statements.

Syntax refers to the rules governing construction of valid statements. This includes the order in which words and statements occur, together with appropriate punctuation. We use two methods of expressing syntax rules in this book. In the body of the text, the form of most new expressions in the language will be written using an angle bracket notation. In this notation, words that appear directly in the expression, such as **if** and **==**, will be written as is. Other components of the expression requiring further definition, such as type names or parameter lists, will be described by enclosing a term, such as **type name** or **parameter list**, within angle brackets (**<** and **>**). Thus, the rule for function call expressions looks like this:

<function name> (<actual parameter list>)

This rule means that a function call expression is a function name, followed by a left parenthesis, followed by a list of actual parameters if the function expects any, followed by a right parenthesis.

Another method of expressing a syntax rule uses a diagram. A list of syntax diagrams covering the portion of C++ used in this text appears in Appendix 3.

A Note of Interest

Program Libraries

When the computer scientist John Backus developed the programming language FORTRAN in 1954, he decided to place the code for frequently used mathematical functions in compiled libraries. Programmers writing applications in FORTRAN had merely to link their own programs with the libraries to use these functions. Soon they began to construct and share libraries of their own functions. The practice of borrowing software tools "off the shelf" from libraries became a standard way of constructing large software systems quickly and safely. A library enhanced program safety, in that its tools were already debugged or shown to work correctly. A library

enhanced system maintenance, in that changes to the importing application or to the exporting library could be made independently. Finally, a library enhanced the portability of a software system from one hardware installation to another, in that low-level, machine-dependent tasks could be packaged in the library and thereby insulated from the rest of the system.

One of the reasons C++ is so popular is that there are so many program libraries that enhance the safety, maintenance, and portability of systems written in the language.

Identifiers

Reserved words and library identifiers are restricted in their use. Most C++ programs require programmer-supplied identifiers; the more complicated the program, the more identifiers are needed. **A valid identifier must start with a letter of the alphabet or an underscore (_) and must consist of only letters, digits, and underscores.**

Table 2.3 gives some valid and invalid identifiers along with reasons for those that are invalid. A valid identifier can be of any length. However, some versions of C++ recognize only the first part of a long identifier, for example, the first 8 or the first 10 characters. Therefore, identifiers such as **MathTestScore1** and **MathTestScore2** might be the same identifier to a computer and could not be used as different identifiers in a program. Thus, you should learn what restrictions are imposed by your compiler.

The most common use of identifiers is to name the variables to be used in a program. Other uses for identifiers include symbolic constants, new data types,

▼ Table 2.3	Identifier	Valid	If Invalid, Reason
Valid and invalid identifiers	`Sum`	Yes	
	`X+Y`	No	'+' is not allowed
	`Average`	Yes	
	`Text1`	Yes	
	`1stNum`	No	Must start with a letter or '_'
	`X30`	Yes	
	`K mart`	No	Spaces are not allowed
	`this_is_a_long_one`	Yes	

and subprogram names, all of which are discussed later. Even though single-letter identifiers are permitted, you should always use descriptive names for identifiers because, as you will see, descriptive names are easier to follow in a program.

Basic Program Components

A large, well-structured C++ program normally consists of many small modules whose text appears in different files. A small, simple program like many of those used in this text appears in a single file. For now, a simple program in C++ consists of five components: an optional set of *preprocessor directives,* an optional *constant and type definition section,* a *main program heading,* an optional *declaration section,* and a *statement section.* These five components are illustrated in the program shown in Figure 2.6. Figure 2.7 illustrates the program components of the sample program that started this section; appropriate program parts are indicated.

The **preprocessor directives** are usually the first part of any C++ program. Preprocessor directives are preceded by the symbol **#**. One of them, **#include**, should be used if you wish to use certain library identifiers in your program. **#include** directs the preprocessor to include the contents of the designated library file with your source program for compilation. **#include** should be followed by the name of a library header file. For now, the name of the library header file should be enclosed in angle brackets. In later chapters of this text, we will see some library header file names enclosed in double quotes.

The **constant and type definition section** contains the definitions of symbolic constants and names of data types used in the rest of the program.

Constants name values that cannot change in a program. The form for defining a constant is

preprocessor directives: *Statements that tell the C++ preprocessor to perform such tasks as combining source program files prior to compilation.*

constant and type definition section: *An area of a C++ program where constant and type definitions are placed, usually near the beginning of the text.*

const   \<type identifier> \<identifier> **=** \<value>**;**

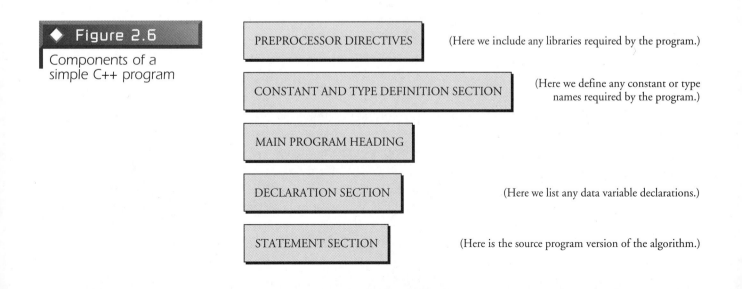

◆ Figure 2.6

Components of a simple C++ program

PREPROCESSOR DIRECTIVES   (Here we include any libraries required by the program.)

CONSTANT AND TYPE DEFINITION SECTION   (Here we define any constant or type names required by the program.)

MAIN PROGRAM HEADING

DECLARATION SECTION   (Here we list any data variable declarations.)

STATEMENT SECTION   (Here is the source program version of the algorithm.)

◆ Figure 2.7

Components of example
program

```cpp
// Program file: reswords.cpp
// This program illustrates the use of reserved words.

#include <iostream.h>
#include <iomanip.h>

const int LOOP_LIMIT = 10;

int main ()
{
    int j, number, sum;
    double average;

    sum = 0;
    for (j = 1; j <= LOOP_LIMIT; ++j)
    {
        cout << "Enter a number and press <Enter>:";
        cin >> number;
        sum = sum + number;
    }
    average = double (sum) / LOOP_LIMIT;
    cout << setiosflags(ios::fixed | ios::showpoint | ios::right)
        << setprecision(2);
    cout << andl;
    cout << setw(10) << "The average is"
        << setw(8)
        << average << endl;
    cout << endl;
    cout << setw(10) << "The number of scores is"
        << setw(3)
        << LOOP_LIMIT << endl;
    return 0;
}
```

Preprocessor
directives →

Constant
definition section →

Main program
heading →

Declaration
section →

Statement
section →

An example of a constant definition is

```cpp
const int LOOP_LIMIT = 10;
```

If a constant is used that has not been declared, an error will occur when the program is compiled. Values of constant identifiers cannot be changed during program execution.

If a value is of type **char**, it must be enclosed in single quotation marks (apostrophes).

Any number of constants can be defined in this section. A typical constant definition portion of the declaration section could be

```
const int CLASS_SIZE = 35;
const int SPEED_LIMIT = 65;
const double CM_TO_INCHES = 0.3937;
```

We will discuss the mechanisms for defining new data types in Chapters 5, 8, and 9.

main program heading: *A syntactic form that marks the beginning of the main part of a C++ program.*

The **main program heading** is required in any C++ program. It consists of the word **int**, followed by the word **main**, followed by a set of parentheses. The program heading indicates the starting point of execution at run time.

The remainder of the program is sometimes referred to as the **main block.** A main block must begin with a left curly brace (**{**) and end with a right curly brace (**}**). The major parts of a main block are a declaration section and a statement section. The **declaration section** is used to declare (name) variables that are necessary to the program. If a variable is used that has not been declared, an error will occur when the program is compiled. For now, we assume all data used in a C++ program must be one of three *simple types:* **int**, **double**, or **char**. Types **int**, **double**, and **char** are discussed in Section 2.3.

main block: *The main part of a program.*

declaration section: *The section used to declare (name) variables that are necessary to the program.*

Variables name values that can change in a program. The form required for declaring variables is somewhat different from that used for defining constants. One form simply omits the reserved word **const**:

```
<type identifier> <identifier> = <value>;
```

```
int sum = 0;
char ch = 'a';
```

When you need to declare more than one variable of the same type, it is convenient to list the variable names after the type on one line:

```
int length = 0, width = 0, area = 0;
```

Alternatively, one might declare some variables without giving them initial values:

```
int length, width, area;
```

In general, it is considered good, defensive programming practice to provide variables with initial values when they are declared. Failure to do so can be the cause of mysterious program errors at execution time.

statement section: *An area of a C++ program where the executable statements are placed.*

The fifth basic component of a simple C++ program is the **statement section.** This section contains the statements that cause the computer to do something.

Writing Code in C++

We are now ready to examine the use of the statement section of a program. In C++, a basic unit of grammar is an **executable statement,** which consists of library identifiers, programmer-defined identifiers, reserved words, numbers, and/or characters together with appropriate punctuation.

executable statement:
The basic unit of grammar in C++ consisting of valid identifiers, standard identifiers, reserved words, numbers, and/or characters, together with appropriate punctuation.

One of the main rules for writing code in C++ is that a semicolon almost always terminates executable statements. For example, if the expression

```
cout << setw(20) << "The results are" << setw(8) << sum
        << "and" << setw(6) << aver
```

is to be used in a program, it will not be treated as a statement unless it is followed by a semicolon. Thus, it should be

```
cout << setw(20) << "The results are" << setw(8) << sum
        << "and" << setw(6) << aver;
```

There is one typical instance in which a semicolon is not needed. Occasionally, you will wish to enclose a series of statements within curly braces, so that they can be treated as a statement unit (the main program block is a good example). In this case, a semicolon is not needed after the right curly brace. You can visualize the statement section as shown in Figure 2.8.

◆ **Figure 2.8**

Executable section

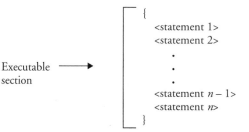

C++ does not require each statement to be on a separate line. Actually, you could write a program as one long line (which may wrap around to fit the screen) if you wish; however, it would be difficult to read. Compare, for example, the readability of the following two programs.

```
// Program file: format.cpp // This program illustrates the use of formatting.
#include <iostream.h> #include <iomanip.h> const int AGE = 26; int main () { int j,
sum; sum = 0; for (j = 1; j <= 10; ++j) {sum = sum + j;} cout <<
setiosflags(ios::right); cout << setw(28) << "My name is George" << endl; cout <<
setw(27) << "My age is " << AGE << endl; cout << endl; cout << setw(28) << "The sum is
" << sum << endl; return 0;}


// Program file: format.cpp
// This program illustrates the use of formatting.
```

```
#include <iostream.h>
#include <iomanip.h>

const int AGE = 26;

int main ()
{
        int j, sum;

        sum = 0;
        for (j = 1; j <= 10; ++j)
        {
                sum = sum + j;
        }
        cout << setiosflags(ios::right);
        cout << setw(28) << "My name is George" << endl;
        cout << setw(27) << "My age is " << AGE << endl;
        cout << endl;
        cout << setw(28) << "The sum is " << sum << endl;
        return 0;
}
```

You are not expected to know exactly what the statements mean at this point, but it should be obvious that the second program is much more readable than the first. In addition, it is easier to change if corrections are necessary. Note, however, that these programs would be executed similarly because C++ ignores extra spaces and line boundaries.

We discuss many kinds of statements in the following chapters. In every program in this text, you will see the statement

```
    return 0;
```

at the end. When it occurs in the main program, this statement tells the computer that the program is finished running.

Formatting Conventions for Identifiers

You will have noticed by now that in our examples, constant identifiers have been written in uppercase letters, and all other identifiers, including variable and function names, have been written in lowercase letters. We believe that this convention helps the reader to pick out the constant names from the other names, when no other cues are available from the context. In addition, underscores are used to make multiword identifiers, such as **monthly_pay**, more readable.

Program Comments

comment: *A non-executable statement used to make a program more readable.*

Programming languages typically include some provision for putting **comments** in a program. These comments are nonexecutable and are used to document and explain various parts of the program. In C++, programmers commonly use an *end-of-line comment*. An end-of-line comment begins with two slash characters (**//**)

and runs for just one line. For multiline comments, we merely place the slash characters at the beginning of each line.

1. List the rules for forming valid identifiers.
2. Which of the following are valid identifiers? Give an explanation for those that are invalid.
   a. **7Up**
   b. **Payroll**
   c. **Room222**
   d. **Name List**
   e. **A**
   f. **A1**
   g. **1A**
   h. **Time&Place**
   i. **const**
   j. **X*Y**
   k. **ListOfEmployees**
   l. **Lima,Ohio**
3. Which of the following are valid program headings? Give an explanation for those that are invalid.
   a. **int main()**
   b. **PROGRAM GettingBetter (output);**
   c. **main(input, output)**
   d. **MAIN();**
4. Name the five main sections of a simple C++ program.
5. Write constant definition statements for the following:
   a. your gender
   b. your age
   c. pi
6. Find all errors in the following definitions and declarations:
   a. **const char ch 'a';**   c. **int 32;**
      double salary;   d. **area int;**
   b. **int const;**   e. **char int;**
7. Discuss the significance of a semicolon in writing C++ statements. Include an explanation of when semicolons are not required in a program.

2.3 Data Types and Output

Objectives

◆ to understand and be able to use the data types **int**, **double**, and **char**

◆ to understand the difference between the floating-point form and the fixed-point form of decimal numbers

◆ to understand the syntax for and use of output statements

◆ to be able to format output

Type **int**

C++ requires that all variables used in a program be given a **data type.** Since numbers in some form will be used in computer programs, we will first look at numbers of type **int**. Values of this type are used to represent integers or whole numbers.

Some rules that must be observed when using integers follow:

1. Plus (+) signs do not have to be written before a positive integer, though they can be.

data type: *A formal description of the set of values that a variable can have.*

2. Minus (−) signs must be written when using a negative number.
3. Decimal points cannot be used when writing integers. Although 14 and 14.0 have the same value, 14.0 is not of type **int**.
4. Commas cannot be used when writing integers; hence, 271,362 is not allowed; it must be written as 271362.
5. Leading zeros should be avoided. If you use leading zeros, the compiler will interpret the number as an octal (base 8) number.

There is a limit on the largest and the smallest integer constants. How you determine this limit is discussed in Chapter 3. Different machines have different values for these constants; you should check your C++ implementation to see what they are. Operations with integers and integer variables are examined in Chapter 3.

C++ also supports the data types **short int** and **long int**, which represent, respectively, a smaller and a larger range of integer values than **int**. Adding the prefix **unsigned** to any of these types means that you wish to represent nonnegative integers only. For example, the declaration

```
unsigned short int x, y;
```

reserves memory for representing two relatively small nonnegative integers.

Type double

Values of type **double** are used to represent real numbers. Plus (+) and minus (−) signs for data of type **double** are treated exactly as with integers. When working with real numbers, however, trailing zeros are ignored. As with integers, leading zeros should be avoided. Thus, +23.45, 23.45, and 23.450 have the same value, but 023.45 may be interpreted by some C++ compilers as an octal number followed by a decimal point, which is a syntax error.

fixed-point form: *A method of writing decimal numbers in which the decimal is placed where it belongs in the number.*

floating-point form: *A method for writing numbers in scientific notation to accommodate numbers that may have very large or very small values.*

All real numbers seen thus far have been in **fixed-point form.** The computer will also accept real numbers in floating-point or exponential form. **Floating-point form** is an equivalent method for writing numbers in scientific notation to accommodate numbers that may have very large or very small values. The difference is that, instead of writing the base decimal times some power of 10, the base decimal is followed by E and the appropriate power of 10. For example, 231.6 in scientific notation would be 2.316×10^2; in floating-point form it would be 2.316E2. Table 2.4 sets forth several fixed-point decimal numbers with the equivalent scientific notation and floating-point form. Floating-point form for real numbers does not require exactly one digit on the left of the decimal point. In fact, it can be used with no decimal points written. To illustrate, 4.16E1, 41.6, 416.0E−1, and 416E−1 have the same value and all are permissible. However, it is not a good habit to use floating-point form for decimal numbers unless exactly one nonzero digit appears on the left of the decimal. In most other cases, fixed-point form is preferable.

In addition to **double**, C++ supports the types **float** and **long double**. **float** supports a less precise representation of real numbers but uses less memory than **double**. **long double** supports a more precise representation of

▼ Table 2.4	Fixed-Point Form	Scientific Notation	Floating-Point Form
Forms for equivalent numbers	46.345	4.6345×10^1	4.6345E1
	59214.3	5.92143×10^4	5.92143E4
	0.00042	4.2×10^{-4}	4.2E−4
	36000000000.0	3.6×10^{10}	3.6E10
	0.000000005	5.0×10^{-9}	5.0E−9
	−341000.0	-3.41×10^5	−3.41E5

real numbers, at the cost of more computer memory. However, to avoid confusion, we will use the term "real number" or **double** to characterize fixed-point numeric literals in this text.

When using real numbers in a program, you may use either fixed-point or floating-point form. But the computer prints out real numbers in floating-point form unless you specify otherwise. Formatting of output is discussed later in this section.

Type **char**

Another data type available in C++ is **char**, which is used to represent character data. In standard C++, data of type **char** can be only a single character (which could be a blank space). These characters come from an available character set that differs somewhat from computer to computer, but always includes the letters of the alphabet (uppercase and lowercase); the digits 0, 1 , 2, 3, 4, 5, 6, 7, 8, and 9; and special symbols such as #, &, !, +, −, *, /, and so on. A common character set is given in Appendix 4.

Character constants of type **char** must be enclosed in single quotation marks when used in a program. Otherwise, they are treated as variables and subsequent use may cause a compilation error. Thus, to use the letter **A** as a constant, you would type **'A'**. The use of digits and standard operation symbols as characters is also permitted; for example, **'7'** would be considered a character, but **7** is an integer.

Several nonprintable characters, such as the backspace, the horizontal tab, the newline, and the bell, are represented by using the backslash (**'\'**) in an escape sequence. For example, to use the backspace character, one would type **'\b'** in a C++ program. Some commonly used escape sequences are listed in Table 2.5.

▼ Table 2.5	Escape Sequence	Character Value
Some escape sequences for special characters	**'\b'**	Blank space
	'\n'	Newline
	'\t'	Tab
	'\\'	Backslash
	'\''	Apostrophe
	'\"'	Double quote

Strings

string: A data type used to represent a word or a line of text.

string constant: A word or a line of text enclosed in double quotes.

Strings are used in programs to represent textual information, such as the names of people and companies. In C++, a **string constant** must be enclosed in double quotation marks. The following are examples of strings:

1. `"Hello world!"`
2. `"125"`
3. `""`
4. `"\n"`
5. `"\t"`
6. `"the word \"hello\""`

Note the difference between the second string, `"125"`, and the integer value 125. They are different data types in C++. The third string, `""`, is the empty string, because it contains no characters.

The fourth string contains a backslash (\) or escape character. This character tells the compiler to treat the following character, **n**, not as a literal character, but as a special code that represents a special character, in this case, a newline character. Thus, the string `"\n"` really contains just one character, the newline character. The fifth string represents a horizontal tab character. The last string uses two backslash characters to wrap double quotes around the word `"hello"`. Note that when you wish the double quotes to appear literally in a string, they must be escaped with the backslash character. In general, to mention any special character in a string, including the backslash character itself, you prefix it with a backslash character. Consult your local implementation for a list of these special characters.

String variables can be declared and manipulated with several functions. Programs that use these must include the C++ library header file **apstring.h**:

```
#include "apstring.h"
```

The use of string variables and string operations is discussed in detail in Chapter 3.

Output

The goal of most programs is to output something. What gets printed (either on paper, on a screen, or in a file) is referred to as output. The simplest way to produce screen output in C++ is to direct a value to the **standard output stream.** This stream is made available to a program by including the C++ library header file **iostream.h**:

standard output stream: An object to which a program sends data for output to a device, normally the terminal screen.

```
#include <iostream.h>
```

The name of this stream is **cout**, and the operator used to direct output to this stream is **<<**. Output values are usually character strings, numbers, numerical expressions, or variable names. The general form of an output statement is

```
cout << <expression 1> << <expression 2> << . . . << <expression n>;
```

You can think of **cout** as the name of an intelligent agent. This agent receives a message from you that you wish to display a value on the terminal screen and it then performs the desired action. The agent also understands messages to format the output in a special way. We discuss the methods for creating our own intelligent agents when we introduce object-oriented programming in Chapters 9 and 10.

Normally, the output statement causes subsequent output to be on the same line. If you wish subsequent output to begin on the next line, you must direct an end-of-line character to the standard output stream. When output is to a monitor, the following two lines each cause the cursor to move to the next line for the next I/O operation:

```
cout << '\n';

cout << endl;
```

The following are examples of single-line and multiline output:

```
cout << "This is a test. ";

cout << "How many lines are printed?" << endl;
```

causes the output

```
This is a test. How many lines are printed?
```

whereas

```
cout << "This is a test." << endl;

cout << "How many lines are printed?" << endl;
```

causes the output

```
This is a test.
How many lines are printed?
```

Character strings can be printed by enclosing the string in double quotation marks. Numerical data can be printed by typing the desired number or numbers. Thus,

```
cout << 100;
```

produces

```
100
```

| Example 2.1 | Let's write a complete C++ program to print the following address: |

1403 South Drive
Apartment 3B
Pittsburgh, PA 15238

A complete program to print this is

```cpp
// Program file: printaddr.cpp
// This program prints an address

#include <iostream.h>

int main()
{
    cout << "1403 South Drive" << endl;

    cout <<  "Apartment 3B" << '\n';

    cout << "Pittsburgh, PA  15238" << "\n";

    return 0;
}
```

Note the different ways of instructing the computer to output a newline to the terminal screen.

Formatting Integers

Output of integers can be controlled with **format manipulators.** First, you must include the library header file **iomanip.h** (short for "input/output manipulators") to gain access to the format manipulators:

> **format manipulator:** A symbol that instructs the computer to display output in a specified format, such as right justified.

```cpp
#include <iomanip.h>
```

Second, you instruct the computer to right justify the output by running the statement

```cpp
cout << setiosflags(ios::right);
```

Third, you specify the field width for the next output operation by using the **setw** manipulator with the size of the number of columns to be filled. Then, on the next output operation, the value of an integer, identifier, or integer expression will be printed on the right side of the specified field. Thus,

```cpp
cout << setw(10) << 100 << setw(10) << 50 << setw(10) << 25;
```

produces

```
*******100********50********25
```

where each * indicates a blank.

Some illustrations for formatting integer output are given in Table 2.6.

▼ Table 2.6	Program Statement	Output
Samples of formatted output	`cout << setw(6) << 123;`	`***123`
	`cout << 15 << setw(5) << 10;`	`15***10`
	`cout << setw(7) << −263 << setw(3)`	
	`    << 21;`	`***−263*21`
	`cout << setw(6) << +5062;`	`**5062`
	`cout << setw(3) << 65221;`	`65221`

End-of-line output at the beginning and end of the executable section will separate desired output from other messages or directions. Thus, the previous program for printing an address could have been written as follows:

```
int main()
{
    cout << endl << endl;

    cout << "1403 South Drive" << endl;

    cout <<  "Apartment 3B" << endl;

    cout << "Pittsburgh, PA, 15238" << endl;

    return 0;
}
```

Formatting Real Numbers

Output of real numbers can also be controlled by formatting. First, you must include the **iomanip** library to gain access to the format manipulators. As with integers, you use **setw** to specify the total field width of each real number. However, if you wish real numbers to be displayed in decimal form, you must specify a fixed-point format with the number of positions to the right of the decimal. The following output statement does this for a desired precision of two places to the right of the decimal:

```
cout << setiosflags (ios::fixed | ios::showpoint | ios::right) << setprecision(2);
```

Then,

```
cout << setw(8) << 736.23;
```

produces

```
**736.23
```

The expression `setiosflags(ios::fixed | ios::showpoint | ios::right)` instructs the output stream to display real numbers in fixed-point format using a decimal point. The general form for using `setiosflags` is

---

`setiosflags(<flag₁> | <flag₂> | . . . | <flag_n>)`

Some useful flags are listed in Table 2.7.

▼ Table 2.7	Flag Name	Meaning
Useful format flags	`ios::showpoint`	Display decimal point with trailing zeros
	`ios::fixed`	Display real numbers in fixed-point notation
	`ios::scientific`	Display real numbers in floating-point notation
	`ios::right`	Display values right justified

The function `setprecision` specifies the number of digits to the right of the decimal point to be displayed. In the previous example, precision of 2 will remain in effect for all subsequent outputs of real numbers, until the programmer specifies a change with another `setprecision` function.

Formatting real numbers causes the following to happen:

1. The decimal point uses one position in the specified field width.
2. Trailing zeros are printed to the specified number of positions to the right of the decimal.
3. Leading plus (+) signs are omitted.
4. Leading minus (−) signs are printed and use one position of the specified field.
5. Digits appearing to the right of the decimal have been rounded rather than truncated.

As with integers, if a field width is specified that is too small, most versions of C++ will default to the minimum width required to present all digits to the left of the decimal as well as the specified digits to the right of the decimal. Real numbers in floating-point form can also be used in a formatted output statement. Table 2.8 illustrates how output using data of type **double** can be formatted.

▼ Table 2.8

Samples of formatted
data of type **double**

Program Statement	Output
`cout << setprecision(3) << setw(10) << 765.432;`	`***765.432`
`cout << setprecision(2) << setw(10) << 23.14;`	`****23.14`
`cout << setprecision(2) << setw(10) << 65.50`	`*****65.50`
`cout << setprecision(2) << setw(10) << +341.2;`	`****341.20`
`cout << setprecision(2) << setw(10) << -341.2;`	`***-341.20`
`cout << setprecision(2) << setw(10) << 16.458;`	`*****16.46`
`cout << setprecision(4) << setw(10) << 0.00456;`	`****0.0046`
`cout << setprecision(2) << setw(6) << 136.51;`	`136.51`

Formatting Strings

Strings and string constants can be formatted by using **setw** to specify field width. The string will be right justified in the field. Unlike real numbers, strings are truncated when necessary. Thus,

```
cout << "field" << setw(10) << "width" << setw(15) << "check" << endl;
```

would produce

```
field*****width**********check
```

and

```
cout << setw(4) << "check" << endl;
```

would produce

```
chec
```

Test Programs

test program: A short
program written to
provide an answer to a
specific question.

Programmers should develop the habit of using **test programs** to improve their knowledge and programming skills. Test programs should be relatively short and written to provide an answer to a specific question. Test programs allow you to play with the computer. You can answer "what if" questions by adopting a "try it and see" attitude. This is an excellent way to become comfortable with your computer and the programming language you are using.

■ Exercises 2.3

1. Which of the following are valid **int** constants? Explain why the others are invalid.
   a. `521`
   b. `-32.0`
   c. `5,621`
   d. `+00784`
   e. `+65`
   f. `6521492183`
   g. `-0`

2. Which of the following are valid **double** constants? Explain why the others are invalid.
   a. `26.3`
   b. `+181.0`
   c. `-.14`
   d. `492.`
   e. `+017.400`
   f. `43E2`
   g. `-0.2E-3`
   h. `43,162.3E5`
   i. `-176.52E+1`
   j. `1.43000E+2`

3. Change the following fixed-point decimals to floating-point decimals with exactly one nonzero digit to the left of the decimal:
   a. `173.0`
   b. `743927000000.0`
   c. `-0.000000023`
   d. `+014.768`
   e. `-5.2`

4. Change the following floating-point decimals to fixed-point decimals:
   a. `-1.0046E+3`
   b. `4.2E-8`
   c. `9.020E10`
   d. `-4.615230E3`
   e. `-8.02E-3`

5. Indicate the data type for each of the following:
   a. `-720`   e. `"150"`
   b. `-720.0`   f. `"23.4E2"`
   c. `150E3`   g. `23.4E-2`
   d. `150`

6. Write and run test programs for each of the following:
   a. Examine the output for a decimal number without field width specified; for example,

      ```
      cout << 2.31;
      ```

   b. Try to print a message without using quotation marks for a character string; for example,

      ```
      cout << Hello;
      ```

7. For each of the following, write a program that would produce the indicated output.

    a. ```
    Score
    86
    82
    79
    ```

    where "**S**" is in column 10.

    b. ```
    Price
    $ 19.94
    $100.00
    $ 58.95
    ```

    where "**P**" is in column 50.

8. Assume the hourly wages of five students are 3.65, 4.10, 2.89, 5.00, and 4.50. Write a program that produces the following output, where the "**E**" of **Employee** is in column 20.

    ```
    Employee            Hourly Wage

        1               $   3.65
        2               $   4.10
        3               $   2.89
        4               $   5.00
        5               $   4.50
    ```

9. What is the output from the following segment of code on your printer or terminal?

```
cout << "My test average is" << 87.5;
cout << setw(20) << "My test average is" << setw(10) << 87.5;
cout << setw(25) << "My test average is" << setprecision(2) << setw(10)
     << 87.5;
cout << setw(25) << "My test average is" << setprecision(2) << setw(6)
     << 87.5;
```

10. Write a program that produces the following output. Start **Student** in column 20 and **Test** in column 40.

    ```
    Student Name            Test Score

    Adams, Mike             73

    Conley, Theresa         86

    Samson, Ron;            92

    O'Malley, Colleen       81
    ```

11. The Great Lakes Shipping Company is going to use a computer program to generate billing statements for their customers. The heading of each bill is as follows:

```
              GREAT LAKES SHIPPING COMPANY
              SAULT STE. MARIE, MICHIGAN

    Thank you for doing business with our company. The
    information listed below was used to determine your
    total cargo fee. We hope you were satisfied with our
    service.

        CARGO      TONNAGE      RATE/TON      TOTAL DUE
```

Write a complete C++ program that produces the heading above.

12. What output is produced by each of the following statements or sequence of statements when executed by the computer?
    a. `cout << 1234 << setw(8) << 1234 << setw(6) << 1234;`
    b. `cout << setw(4) <<12 << setw(4) << -21 << setw(4)`
       `<< 120;`
    c. `cout << "FIGURE AREA PERIMETER";`
       `cout << "";`
       `cout << endl;`
       `cout << "SQUARE" << setw(5) << 16 << setw(12) <<16;`
       `cout << endl;`
       `cout << "RECT " << setw(5) << 24 << setw(12) << 20;`

13. Write a complete program that produces the following table:

    ```
    WIDTH          LENGTH          AREA
     4              2              8


    21              5              105
    ```

14. What output is produced when each of the following is executed?
    a. `cout << setprecision(2) << setw(15) << 2.134;`
    b. `cout << setprecision(2) << setw(5) << 423.73;`
    c. `cout << setprecision(3) << setw(8) << -42.1;`
    d. `cout << setprecision(2) << setw(2) << -4.21E3;`
    e. `cout << 10.25;`
    f. `cout << 1.25 << setprecision(2) << setw(6) << 1.25`
       `<< setprecision(1) << setw(2) << 1.25;`

15. Write a complete program that produces the following output:

    ```
    Hourly Wage        Hours Worked         Total
       5.00                20.0            100.00
       7.50                15.25           114.375
    ```

16. What type of data would be used to print each of the following?
    a. your age
    b. your grade-point average
    c. your name
    d. a test score
    e. the average test score
    f. your grade

A Note of Interest

The ACM Code of Ethics

The Association for Computing Machinery (ACM) is the flagship organization for computing professionals. The ACM supports publications of research results and new trends in computer science, sponsors conferences and professional meetings, and provides standards for computer scientists as professionals. The standards concerning the conduct and professional responsibility of computer scientists have been published in the <u>ACM Code of Ethics</u>. The code is intended as a basis for ethical decision making and for judging the merits of complaints about violations of professional ethical standards.

The code lists several general moral imperatives for computer professionals:

♦ Contribute to society and human well-being.
♦ Avoid harm to others.
♦ Be honest and trustworthy.
♦ Be fair and take action not to discriminate.
♦ Honor property rights including copyrights and patents.
♦ Give proper credit for intellectual property.
♦ Respect the privacy of others.
♦ Honor confidentiality.

The code also lists several more specific professional responsibilities:

♦ Strive to achieve the highest quality, effectiveness, and dignity in both the process and products of professional work.
♦ Acquire and maintain professional competence.
♦ Know and respect existing laws pertaining to professional work.
♦ Accept and provide appropriate professional review.
♦ Give comprehensive and thorough evaluations of computer systems and their impacts, including analysis of possible risks.
♦ Honor contracts, agreements, and assigned responsibilities.
♦ Improve public understanding of computing and its consequences.
♦ Access computing and communication resources only when authorized to do so.

In addition to these principles, the code offers a set of guidelines to provide professionals with explanations of various issues contained in the principles.

The complete text of the <u>ACM Code of Ethics</u> is available at the ACM's World Wide Web site, http://www.acm.org.

2.4 Graphics

Objectives

♦ to understand the basic conceptual framework for computer graphics
♦ to learn to set the graphics mode for drawing images
♦ to learn how to use some basic graphics operations for drawing line segments

Thus far in this chapter, we have been developing programs that output text. Every modern computer supports the display of graphical images as well. For example, it is often useful to see a table of data displayed in the form of a bar graph or pie chart. It is very likely that you have played a video game or used a Macintosh or a PC with Windows. If so, you have used a graphical user interface (GUI). A GUI allows users to interact with a computer not just by entering characters at a keyboard, but also by aiming a pointing device at icons on the screen. An icon is an image that represents a computational object, such as a data file or an application, or a real object, such as a trash can. Even the characters that are displayed by these systems are "painted" with a graphics application.

Pixels, Points, and Coordinate Systems

To display an image on a computer screen, a computer maintains a two-dimensional grid of tiny dots called **pixels** or picture elements. Each pixel has a horizontal and vertical position in the grid. A pixel can be set to values that

pixel: A picture element or dot of color used to display images on a computer screen.

represent different colors or shades of gray. Graphics programs draw images on a computer screen by manipulating pixels at the appropriate positions.

C++ has no standard for graphics operations, but most C++ compilers support a graphics library. The basic principles of graphics are platform independent, and the graphics operations in most versions of C++ are similar. The graphics applications discussed in this book were developed with Turbo C++ 3.0, which provides a **graphics** library. If you have a different compiler, consult Appendix 5 of this book or your compiler's manual for suggestions about dealing with the portability of the code.

coordinate system: A grid in which a point in space or a pixel on a computer screen can be located.

One thing that is standard on most computers is the **coordinate system** for the grid of pixels. The position of a pixel in the grid is specified just like a point in a coordinate system, using the notation (**<horizontal>**, **<vertical>**) or (**<x>**, **<y>**). The position of the pixel at the upper left corner of the grid is (0, 0). This is unlike the situation with standard algebra, where the origin is located in the center of the coordinate system. Figure 2.9 shows the origin and three other points in the two coordinate systems. When dealing with a computer's coordinate system, it is important to remember that the position of a point or pixel on the y axis gets larger as we go down the screen from the top, and the position on the x axis gets larger as we move from left to right.

Graphics Operations

Every programming language that supports graphics has a set of simple graphics operations. These operations commonly assume the existence of a virtual pen. When an application starts up, this pen is located at a default position, usually (0, 0). The operations then move the pen to a new position without drawing anything, or move the pen to a new position and change some pixels to

◆ Figure 2.9

Some points in two coordinate systems

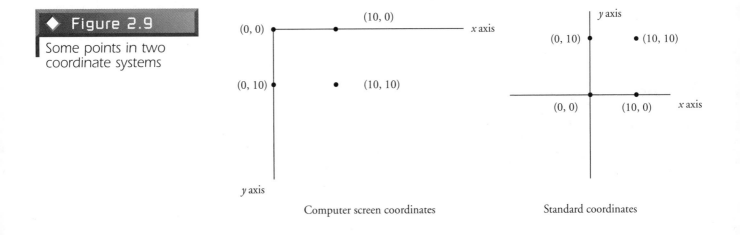

Computer screen coordinates   Standard coordinates

draw an image. There might be a few dozen graphics operations, including ones that draw geometric shapes such as rectangles and ellipses. A table of these is given in Appendix 5.

The two most commonly used operations are **moveto** and **lineto**. **moveto** is used when we wish to move the pen from its current position to a new position without drawing anything. **lineto** is used to draw a line segment from the pen's current position to a new position.

Assume that the current position of the pen is at the origin. The following program segment would draw a diagonal line segment from the origin to the point (100, 100) on the screen (see Figure 2.10):

```
lineto(100, 100);
```

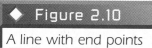

◆ Figure 2.10

A line with end points (0, 0) and (100, 100)

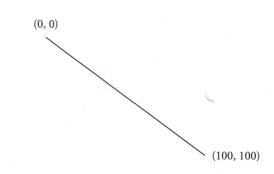

As a continuation of the previous code segment, the following code segment would draw a line segment from the point (50, 50) to the point (50, 0) (see Figure 2.11):

```
moveto(50, 50);
lineto(50, 0);
```

◆ Figure 2.11

A continuation of the image in Figure 2.10

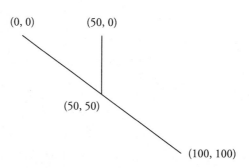

As you can see, the way that we specify a point for a graphics operation is to use the form

<operation name>(<horizontal>, <vertical>)

When the operation is completed, the designated point becomes the new position of the pen.

The **outtext** operation is used for displaying a string of text. The following program segment would display the string **"Hello world!"** between two parallel lines (see Figure 2.12):

```
moveto(50, 50);
lineto(150, 50);
moveto(55, 100);
outtext("Hello world!");
moveto(50, 130);
lineto(150, 130);
```

The form for using **outtext** is

outtext(<string>)

◆ **Figure 2.12**

A graphic greeting

Hello world!

Setting the Graphics Mode

Most programming languages require the programmer to set the graphics mode. This command tells the computer that the application is about to perform graphics operations. This usually involves the call of a special function to initialize the screen or a window for drawing. At the end of the process, these settings are closed with another command. Thus, most graphics programs have the following form:

1. Set the graphics mode.
2. Perform graphics operations to draw images.
3. Close the graphics mode.

A driver program for testing graphics commands is shown next. You might want to keep a copy of this program as a template for any new graphics program that you write.

```
// Program file: graphdr.cpp
// Sample graphics test driver program

#include <graphics.h>
```

```
int main()
{
    // Set the graphics mode

    int graphdriver = DETECT, graphmode;
    initgraph(&graphdriver, &graphmode, "c:..\\bgi");

    // Draw an image

    // Close the graphics mode

    closegraph();
    return 0;
}
```

The commands to set and close the graphics mode vary from platform to platform. In addition to the commands discussed earlier, it is useful to provide a way for the program to pause to allow the user to view the image and signal the program to continue. The **getch()** function from the **conio** library pauses the program until the user strikes any key on the keyboard:

```
#include <conio.h>

// Pause until the user strikes a key

getch();
```

Example 2.2

The Müller-Lyer illusion is caused by an image that consists of two parallel line segments. One line segment looks like an arrow with two heads, and the other line segment looks like an arrow with two tails. Although the line segments are of exactly the same length, they appear to be unequal (see Figure 2.13). The following complete program displays this illusion:

```
// Program file: muller.cpp

// Displays the image that causes the Muller-Lyer illusion

#include <conio.h>
#include <graphics.h>
```

◆ **Figure 2.13**

The Müller-Lyer illusion

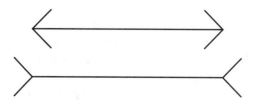

```
int main()
{
        // Set the graphics mode

        int graphdriver = DETECT, graphmode;
        initgraph(&graphdriver, &graphmode, "c:..\\bgi");

        // Draw the two-headed arrow

        moveto(30, 30);
        lineto(180, 30);
        moveto(30, 30);
        lineto(60, 0);
        moveto(30, 30);
        lineto(60, 60);
        moveto(180, 30);
        lineto(150, 0);
        moveto(180, 30);
        lineto(150, 60);

        // Draw the two-tailed arrow

        moveto(30, 100);
        lineto(180, 100);
        moveto(30, 100);
        lineto(0, 70);
        moveto(30, 100);
        lineto(0, 130);
        moveto(180, 100);
        lineto(210, 70);
        moveto(180, 100);
        lineto(210, 130);

        // Label the drawing

        moveto(0, 250);
        outtext("The Muller-Lyer illusion");

        // Pause for a key to be pressed

        moveto(200, 300);
        outtext("Strike any key to continue");
        getch();

        // Close the graphics mode

        closegraph();
        return 0;
}
```

Exercises 2.4

1. Draw pictures of the images produced by the following code segments:

   a. `moveto(0, 0);`
      `lineto(100, 0);`
      `moveto(50, 0);`
      `lineto(50, 100);`

   b. `moveto(0, 0);`
      `lineto(50, 50);`
      `lineto(100, 0);`

   c. `moveto(50, 50);`
      `lineto(100, 50);`
      `lineto(50, 100);`
      `lineto(100, 100);`

2. Write code segments that would produce images of the following types:

   a. a square
   b. a right triangle
   c. an isosceles triangle
   d. a pentagon

3. Write a code segment that would draw an image of a YIELD sign. The sign should look like this:

Summary

Key Terms

comment	main block	software engineering
constant and type definition section	main program heading	software system life cycle
	module	standard output stream
coordinate system	module specifications	statement section
data type	object-oriented design	stepwise refinement
declaration section	pixel	string
effective statement	preprocessor directives	string constant
executable statement	programmer-supplied identifiers	structure chart
fixed-point form		syntax
floating-point form	pseudocode	test program
format manipulator	reserved words	top-down design
keywords	simple type	
library identifiers		

Keywords

char	**float**	**short**
const	**int**	**unsigned**
double	**long**	

⚿ Key Concepts

◆ Six steps toward problem solving include the following: analyze the problem, develop an algorithm, document the program, write code for the program, run the program, and test the results against answers manually computed with paper and pencil.

◆ Top-down design is a process of dividing tasks into subtasks until each subtask can be readily accomplished.

◆ Stepwise refinement refers to refinements of tasks into subtasks.

◆ A structure chart is a graphic representation of the relationship between modules.

◆ Software engineering is the process of developing and maintaining large software systems.

◆ The software system life cycle consists of the following phases: analysis, design, coding, testing/verification, maintenance, and obsolescence.

◆ Valid identifiers must begin with a letter or underscore and they can contain only letters, digits, and underscores.

◆ The five components of a simple C++ program are preprocessor directives, constant and type definitions, program heading, declaration section, and executable statement section.

◆ Semicolons are used to terminate most executable statements.

◆ Extra spaces and blank lines are ignored in C++.

◆ Output is generated by using **cout** and **<<**.

◆ Strings are formatted using the manipulator **setw** with a positive integer that specifies the total field width, for example,

```
cout << setw(30) << "This is a string";
```

◆ The following table summarizes the use of the data types **int**, **double**, and **char**.

Data Type	Permissible Data	Formatting
int	Numeric	**setw** (an integer); for example `cout << setw(6) << 25;`

double	Numeric	**setiosflags(ios::fixed |ios::showpoint)**, **setprecision** (an integer), and **setw** (an integer); for example,
		
		`cout << setiosflags(ios::fixed |`
		`        ios::showpoint)`
		`    << setprecision(2)`
		`    << setw(8) << 1234.5;`

char	Character	**setw** (an integer); for example `cout << setw(6) << 'A';`

Chapter Review Exercises

1. List the six steps in developing a program.

For Exercises 2–6, write pseudocode showing the tasks needed for solving each problem.

2. Determine the weekly salary of an employee.
3. Find the batting average of a baseball player.
4. Find the slope of a line. (Remember that slopes can be undefined.)
5. Determine the letter grade earned on a test.
6. Find the smallest number from a set of 50 numbers.

For Exercises 7–12, state whether or not the identifiers are valid. If not, explain why.

7. **C**
8. **Chapter2**
9. **for**
10. **alpha**
11. **6weeks**
12. **here-and-there**

For Exercises 13–16, write constant definitions for the information requested.

13. the current year
14. the FICA tax rate for employees (7.5%, expressed in decimal form)
15. 30, the number of students in the class
16. $2500, the amount allowed as a personal exemption

Programming Problems and Activities

Write and run a short program for each of the following:

1. A program to print your initials in block letters. Your output could look like this:

```
JJJJJ              A                CCC
    J            A  A            C      C
    J           A    A          C
    J           AAAAAAA         C
J   J          A        A        C      C
 JJJ           A        A          CCC
```

2. Design a simple picture and print it using output statements. If you plan the picture using a sheet of graph paper, keeping track of spacing will be easier.
3. Write and run a program that prints your mailing address.
4. Our Lady of Mercy Hospital prints billing statements for patients when they are ready to leave the hospital. Write a program that prints a heading for each statement as follows:

```
/////////////////////////////////////////////////
/                                               /
/                                               /
/            Our Lady of Mercy Hospital         /
/                                               /
/                                               /
/                                               /
/                                               /
/                1306 Central City              /
/                                               /
/                                               /
/              Phone (416) 555-3333             /
/                                               /
/                                               /
/                                               /
/////////////////////////////////////////////////
```

5. Your computer science teacher wants course and program information included as part of every assignment. Write a program that can be used to print this information. Sample output should look like this:

```
*******************************************
*                                         *
*        Author:        Mary Smith        *
*        Course:        CPS-150           *
*        Assignment:    Program #3        *
*                                         *
*        Due Date:      September 18      *
*        Teacher:       Mr. Samson        *
*                                         *
*******************************************
```

6. As part of a programming project that will compute and print grades for each student in your class, you have been asked to write a program that produces a heading for each student report. The columns in which the various headings should be are as follows:

The border for the class name starts in column 30
Student Name starts in column 20
Test Average starts in column 40
Grade starts in column 55

Write a program to print the heading as follows:

```
*************************
*                       *
*   CPS 150      C++     *
*                       *
*************************
```

Student Name   **Test Average**   **Grade**

7. Mr. Fixit's bill for the repair of a leaking roof looks like this:

```
Fixit Roof Repair Service

Date: July 20, 1998

Cost of labor:          $150.00
Cost of materials:        53.00
Tax:                       7.21
                        -------
Total cost:             $210.21
```

Write a program that produces this output.

 8. Modify the program of Example 2.2 so that it draws two new vertical line segments. Each of the new line segments should connect the end points of the two parallel line segments that cause the Müller-Lyer illusion. Does the illusion go away when you display the new figure?

9. Modify the program of Example 2.2 so that the parallel line segments do not produce the Müller-Lyer illusion. You can do this by making one of the line segments shorter than the other. How much shorter (number of pixels) does this line segment have to be so that both line segments appear to be equal?

Communication in Practice

1. Obtain a copy of the complete ACM Code of Ethics (see the **Note of Interest** earlier in this chapter). Read the guideline pertaining to the principle "Respect the privacy of others," and prepare a written report on this topic to present to your class.

2. Exchange complete programs with a classmate and critique the use of descriptive identifiers. Offer positive suggestions as to what would help others read and understand the program.

3. Discuss the issue of using descriptive identifiers with each of the following:
   a. another student in your class
   b. a senior or college student in computer science
   c. a computer science teacher (not your own)
   d. a professional programmer

   Prepare a written report of your conversations with these people, and present the results to your class.

Chapter

3

Arithmetic, Variables, Input, Constants, and Library Functions

Chapter Outline

3.1 Arithmetic in C++

Objectives

◆ to understand what an expression is in C++

◆ to be able to evaluate arithmetic expressions using data of type **int** and of type **double**

◆ to understand the order of operations for evaluating expressions

◆ to be able to identify and evaluate mixed-mode expressions

◆ to be able to distinguish between valid and invalid mixed-mode expressions

Y ou have probably used a pocket calculator. Pocket calculators provide a set of built-in arithmetic functions. Many pocket calculators also provide built-in constants, such as **PI**, and users can program them to perform a series of functions that share data with variables. In this chapter we discuss all of these concepts, including arithmetic operations, using data in a program, obtaining input, and using constants and variables. We also discuss the use of functions to perform standard operations such as finding a square root or raising a number to a given power.

Basic Operations for Integers

Integer arithmetic in C++ allows the operations of addition, subtraction, multiplication, division, and modulus (remainder) to be performed. The notation for these operations is shown in Table 3.1.

In a standard integer division problem, there is a quotient and a remainder. In C++, the slash (/) produces the quotient and **%** produces the integer remainder. For example, in the problem 17 divided by 3, **17 / 3** produces 5, and **17 % 3** produces 2. Avoid using **/ 0** (zero) and **% 0**. Division by zero will cause a run-time error. Note that **%** in C++ means modulus or remainder, not percent.

▼ Table 3.1

Integer arithmetic operations

Symbol	Operation	Example	Value
+	Addition	**3 + 5**	8
–	Subtraction	**43 – 25**	18
*	Multiplication	**4 * 7**	28
/	Division	**9 / 2**	4
%	Modulus	**9 % 2**	1

Several integer expressions and their values are shown in Table 3.2. Notice that when 3 is multiplied by −2, the expression is written as **3 * (-2)** rather than **3 * -2**. The parentheses make the expression more readable, but are not required.

▼ Table 3.2

Values of integer expressions

Expression	Value
-3 + 2	−1
2 - 3	−1
-3 * 2	−6
3 * (-2)	−6
-3 * (-2)	6
17 / 3	5
17 % 3	2
17 / (-3)	−5
-17 / 3	−5
-17 % 7	−3
-17 / (-3)	5

Order of Operations for Integers

Expressions involving more than one operation are frequently used when writing programs. When this happens, it is important to know the order in which these operations are performed. The order of operations is referred to as the *precedence rule*. The priorities for these are as follows:

1. All expressions within a set of parentheses are evaluated first. If there are parentheses within parentheses (the parentheses are nested), the innermost expressions are evaluated first.
2. The operations, *, %, and / are evaluated next in order from left to right.
3. The operations + and – are evaluated last from left to right.

These operations are similar to algebraic operations; they are summarized in Table 3.3.

▼ Table 3.3	Expression or Operation	Priority
Integer arithmetic priority	**( )**	1. Evaluate from inside out.
	*, %, /	2. Evaluate from left to right.
	+, –	3. Evaluate from left to right.

To illustrate how expressions are evaluated, consider the values of the expressions listed in Table 3.4. As expressions get more elaborate, it can be helpful to list partial evaluations in a manner similar to the order in which the computer performs the evaluations. For example, suppose the expression

$$(3 - 4) + 18/5 + 2$$

is to be evaluated. If we consider the order in which subexpressions are evaluated, we get

```
(3 - 4) + 18 / 5 + 2
-1 + 18 / 5 + 2
-1 + 3 + 2
2 + 2
4
```

▼ Table 3.4	Expression	Value
Priority of operations	**3 - 4 * 5**	−17
	3 - (4 * 5)	−17
	(3 - 4) * 5	−5
	3 * 4 - 5	7
	3 * (4 - 5)	−3
	17 - 10 - 3	4
	17 - (10 - 3)	10
	(17 - 10) - 3	4
	-42 + 50 % 17	−26

Using Modulus and Division

Modulus and division can be used when it is necessary to perform conversions within arithmetic operations. For example, consider the problem of adding two weights given in units of pounds and ounces. This problem can be solved by converting both weights to ounces, adding the ounces, and then converting the total ounces to pounds and ounces. The conversion from ounces to pounds can be accomplished by using modulus and division. If the total number of ounces is 243, then

> `243 / 16`

yields the number of pounds (15), and

> `243 % 16`

yields the number of ounces (3).

Representation of Integers

Computer representation of integers is different from what we see when we work with integers. Integers are stored in *binary notation,* and the operations performed on them are those of *binary arithmetic.* Thus, the integer 19, which can be written as

$$19 = 16 + 0 + 0 + 2 + 1$$
$$= 1 * 2^4 + 0 * 2^3 + 0 * 2^2 + 1 * 2^1 + 1 * 2^0$$

word: A unit of memory consisting of one or more bytes. Words can be addressed.

is stored as 1 0 0 1 1. This binary number is actually stored in a **word** in memory, which consists of several individual locations called bits, as mentioned in Chapter 1. The number of bits used to store an integer is machine dependent. If you use a 16-bit machine, then 19 is

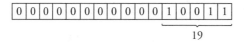

In this representation, the leftmost bit is reserved for the sign of the integer (1 meaning negative, 0 meaning positive).

We can make two observations regarding the storage and mechanics of the operations on integers. First, integers produce exact answers; numbers are stored exactly (up to the limits of the machine). Second, a maximum and a minimum number can be represented. In a 16-bit machine, these numbers are

| 0 | 1 | 1 | 1 | 1 | 1 | 1 | 1 | 1 | 1 | 1 | 1 | 1 | 1 | 1 | 1 |

where the leftmost 0 represents a positive number equaling 32,767, and

| 1 | 0 | 0 | 0 | 0 | 0 | 0 | 0 | 0 | 0 | 0 | 0 | 0 | 0 | 0 | 0 |

where the leftmost 1 represents a negative number equaling −32,768. To find out what the minimum and maximum integer values for your particular system are, you can use the C++ library constants discussed in Section 3.5.

integer overflow: A condition in which an integer value is too large to be stored in the computer's memory.

If a program contains an integer operation that produces a number outside of your machine's range, this is referred to as **integer overflow,** which means that the number is too large or too small to be stored. Ideally, an error message would be printed when such a situation arises. However, many systems merely store an unpredictable value and continue with the program. In Section 5.3, we will discuss how to protect a program against this problem.

Basic Operations for Real Numbers

The operations of addition, subtraction, and multiplication are the same for data of type **double** as for integers. Additionally, real division is now permitted. Modulus is restricted to data of type **int**. The symbol for division of data of type **double** is **/**. The *real arithmetic operations* are shown in Table 3.5.

▼ **Table 3.5**

Real arithmetic operations

Symbol	Operation	Example	Value
+	Addition	`4.2 + 19.36`	23.56
–	Subtraction	`19.36 - 4.2`	15.16
*	Multiplication	`3.1 * 2.0`	6.2
/	Division	`54.6 / 2.0`	27.3

Division is given the same priority as multiplication when arithmetic expressions are evaluated by the computer. The rules for order of operation are the same as those for evaluating integer arithmetic expressions. A summary of these operations is shown in Table 3.6. Some example calculations using data of type **double** are shown in Table 3.7.

▼ **Table 3.6**

Real arithmetic priority

Expression or Operation	Priority
( )	1. Evaluate from inside out.
*, /	2. Evaluate from left to right.
+, –	3. Evaluate from left to right.

▼ **Table 3.7**

Type **double** calculations

Expression	Value
`-1.0 + 3.5 + 2.0`	4.5
`-1.0 + 3.5 * 2.0`	6.0
`2.0 * (1.2 - 4.3)`	−6.2
`2.0 * 1.2 - 4.3`	−1.9
`-12.6 / 3.0 + 3.0`	−1.2
`-12.6 / (3.0 + 3.0)`	−2.1

As expressions get a bit more complicated, it is again helpful to write out the expression and evaluate it step by step. For example,

$$18.2 + (-4.3) * (10.1 + (72.3 / 3.0 - 4.5))$$
$$18.2 + (-4.3) * (10.1 + (24.1 - 4.5))$$
$$18.2 + (-4.3) * (10.1 + 19.6)$$
$$18.2 + (-4.3) * 29.7$$
$$18.2 + (-127.71)$$
$$-109.51$$

Representation of Real Numbers

As with integers, real numbers are stored and operations are performed using binary notation. Unlike integers, however, the storage and representation of real numbers frequently produce answers that are not exact. For example, an operation such as

```
1 / 3.0
```

produces the repeating decimal .3333. . . . At some point, this decimal must be truncated or rounded so that it can be stored. Such conversions produce **round-off errors.**

Now let's consider some errors that occur when working with real numbers. A value very close to zero may be stored as 0. Thus, you may think you are working with

$$1.23 * 10^{-20} = .00000000000000000000123$$

but, in fact, this value may have been stored as a zero. This condition is referred to as **underflow.** Generally, this would not be a problem because replacing numbers very close to zero with 0 does not affect the accuracy of most answers. However, sometimes this replacement can make a difference; therefore, you should be aware of the limitations of the system on which you are working.

Because operations with real numbers are not stored exactly, errors referred to as **representational errors** can be introduced. To illustrate, suppose we are using a machine that only yields three digits of accuracy (most machines exhibit much greater accuracy) and we want to add the three numbers 45.6, −45.5, and .215. The order in which we add these numbers makes a difference in the result we obtain. For example, −45.5 + 45.6 yields .1. Then, .1 + .215 yields .315. Thus, we have

$$(-45.5 + 45.6) + .215 = .315$$

However, if we consider 45.6 + .215 first, then the arithmetic result is 45.815. Since our hypothetical computer only yields three digits of accuracy, this result will be stored as 45.8. Then, −45.5 + 45.8 yields .3. Thus, we have

$$-45.5 + (45.6 + .215) = .3$$

This operation produces a representational error.

round-off error: A condition in which a portion of a real number is lost because of the way it is stored in the computer's memory.

underflow: If a value is too small to be represented by a computer, the value is automatically replaced by zero.

representational error: A condition in which the precision of data is reduced because of the order in which operations are performed.

A Note of Interest

Herman Hollerith

Herman Hollerith (1860–1929) was hired by the U.S. Census Bureau in 1879 at the age of 19. Since the 1880 census was predicted to take a long time to complete (it actually took until 1887), Hollerith was assigned the task of developing a mechanical method of tabulating census data. He introduced his census machine in 1887. It consisted of four parts:

1. A punched paper card that represented data using a special code (Hollerith code)
2. A card punch apparatus
3. A tabulator that read the punched cards
4. A sorting machine with 24 compartments.

The punched cards used by Hollerith were the same size as cards still in use until the 1980s.

Using Hollerith's techniques and equipment, the 1890 census tabulation was completed in one-third the time required for the previous census tabulation. This included working with data for 12 million additional people.

Hollerith proceeded to form the Tabulating Machine Company (1896), which supplied equipment to census bureaus in the United States, Canada, and Western Europe. After a disagreement with the census director, Hollerith began marketing his equipment in other commercial areas. Hollerith sold his company in 1911. It was later combined with 12 others to form the Computing-Tabulating-Recording Company, a direct ancestor of International Business Machines Corporation.

In the meantime, Hollerith's successor at the census bureau, James Powers, redesigned the census machine. He then formed his own company, which subsequently became Remington Rand, then Sperry Univac, and finally Unisys.

Another form of representational error occurs when numbers of substantially different size are used in an operation. For example, consider the expression

2 + .0005

We would expect this value to be 2.0005, but stored to only three digits of accuracy, the result would be 2.00. In effect, the smaller of the two numbers disappears or is canceled from the expression. This form of error is called a **cancellation error.**

cancellation error: A condition in which data are lost because of differences in the precision of the operands.

Although representational and cancellation errors cannot be avoided, their effects can be minimized. Operations should be grouped in such a way that numbers of approximately the same magnitude are used together before the resulting operand is used with another number. For example, all very small numbers should be summed before adding them to a large number.

Attempting to store very large real numbers can result in *real overflow*. In principle, real numbers are stored with locations reserved for the exponents. An oversimplified illustration using base 10 digits is

1 2 3 + 0 8

mixed-mode expression: An expression containing data of different types; the values of these expressions will be of either type, depending on the rules for evaluating them.

for the number $123 * 10^8$. Different computers place different limits on the size of the exponent that can be stored. An attempt to use numbers outside the defined range causes overflow in much the same way that integer overflow occurs, with results that depend on the particular run-time system.

Mixed-Mode Expressions

Arithmetic expressions using data of two or more types are called **mixed-mode expressions.** In a mixed-mode expression involving both **int** and **double** data types, the value will be of type **double**. When formatting output of mixed-mode expressions, always format for real numbers. Note that you should avoid using **%** with mixed-mode expressions. The way in which C++ deals with mixed-mode expressions in general is fairly complex and is discussed in detail in Section 3.7. You may wish to avoid using mixed-mode expressions until you read that section.

Exercises 3.1

1. Find the value of each of the following expressions:
   a. `17 - 3 * 2`
   b. `-15 * 3 - 4`
   c. `123 % 5`
   d. `123 / 5`
   e. `5 * 123 / 5 - 123 % 5`
   f. `-21 * 3 * (-1)`
   g. `14 * (3 - 18 / 4) - 50`
   h. `100 - (4 * (3 - 2)) * (-2)`
   i. `-56 % 3`
   j. `14 * 8 % 5 - 23 / (-4)`

2. Find the value of each of the following expressions:
   a. `3.21 - - 5.02 - 6.1`
   b. `6.0 / 2.0 * 3.0`
   c. `6.0 / (2.0 + 3.0)`
   d. `-20.5 * (2.1 + 2.0)`
   e. `-2.0 * ((56.8 / 4.0 + 0.8) + 5.0)`
   f. `1.04E2 * 0.02E3`
   g. `800.0E-2 / 4.0 - 15.3`

3. Which of the following are valid expressions? For those that are valid, indicate whether they are of type **int** or **double**.
   a. `18 - (5 * 2)`
   b. `(18 - 5) * 2`
   c. `18 - 5 * 2.0`
   d. `25 * (14 % 7.0)`
   e. `1.4E3 * 5`
   f. `28 / 7`
   g. `28.0 / 4`
   h. `10.5 + 14 / 3`
   i. `24 / 6 / 3`
   j. `24 / (6 / 3)`

4. Evaluate each of the valid expressions in Exercise 3.

5. What is the output produced by the following program?

```
#include <iostream.h>
#include <iomanip.h>

int main()
{
```

```
        cout << setiosflags(ios::showpoint | ios::fixed)
            << setprecision(3);
        cout << endl << "Expression Value" << endl;
        cout << "----------------" << endl << endl;
        cout << " 10 / 5" << setw(12) << 10/5 << endl;
        cout << " 2.0+7 * (-1)" << 2.0 + 7 * (-1)
            << endl << endl;
        return 0;
    }
```

6. Explain why the second operand for the **/** and **%** operators cannot be zero.
7. Explain why more memory is needed to store a real number than is needed to store an integer in a computer.

Memory Locations

It is frequently necessary to store values for later use. This is done by putting the value into a **memory location** and using a symbolic name to refer to this location. If the contents of the location are to be changed during a program, the symbolic name is referred to as a **variable;** if the contents are not to be changed, it is referred to as a **constant.**

A graphic way to think about memory locations is to envision them as boxes; each box is named and a value is stored inside. For example, suppose a program is written to add a sequence of numbers. If we name the memory location to be used **sum**, initially we have

| ? |
sum

which depicts a memory location that has been reserved and can be accessed by a reference to **sum**. If we then add the integers 10, 20 , and 30 and store them in **sum**, we have

| 60 |
sum

It is important to distinguish between the name of a memory location (**sum**) and the value or contents of a memory location (**60**). The name does not change during a program, but the contents can be changed as often as necessary. (Contents of memory locations that are referred to by constants cannot be changed.) If 30 were added to the contents in the previous example, the new value stored in **sum** could be depicted as

| 90 |

sum

Those symbolic names representing memory locations whose values will be changing must be declared before they are used (as indicated in Section 2.4); for example,

```
int sum;
```

Those that represent memory locations whose values will not be changing must also be defined before they are used.

Assignment Statements

We now examine how the contents of variables are manipulated. When variables are declared in a C++ program, they contain values. However, a programmer does not know what these values are. Henceforth, we denote these system-supplied values with a question mark (?). The programmer may put a value into a memory location with an **assignment statement** in the form of

assignment statement: A method of putting values into memory locations.

```
<variable name> = <value>;
```

or

```
<variable name> = <expression>;
```

where **<variable name>** is the name of the memory location. For example, if **sum** has an unknown value, then

```
sum = 30;
```

changes

| ? |
sum

to

| 30 |
sum

Some important rules concerning assignment statements follow:
1. The assignment is always made from right to left (←).
2. Constants cannot be on the left side of the assignment symbol.
3. The expression can be a constant, a constant expression, a variable that has previously been assigned a value, or a combination of variables and constants.
4. Normally, values on the right side of the assignment symbol are not changed by the assignment.
5. The variable and expression must be of compatible data types.
6. Only one value can be stored in a variable's memory location at a time, so the previous value of a variable is thrown away.

One common error that beginners make is trying to assign from left to right.

Repeated assignments can be made. For example, if **sum** is an integer variable, the statements

```
sum = 50;

sum = 70;

sum = 100;
```

produce first 50, then 70, and finally 100, as shown.

```
50 70 100
```
sum

In this sense, memory is destructible in that it retains only the last value assigned.

C++ variables are symbolic addresses that can hold values. When a variable is declared, the type of values it will store must be specified (declared). Storing a value of the wrong type in a variable leads to a program error. This means that data types must be compatible when using assignment statements. For now, consider all of the basic data types—**char**, **int**, and **double**—as compatible with each other. This means that assignments of values to variables are allowed for any possible combination of these types on both sides of an assignment statement. Type compatibility and type conversion are discussed in Section 3.7.

Assignments of character constants to a character variable require that the constant be enclosed in single quotation marks. For example, if **letter** is of type **char** and you want to store the letter C in **letter**, use the assignment statement

```
letter = 'C';
```

This could be pictured as

```
C
```
letter

Furthermore, only one character can be assigned or stored in a character variable at a time.

Expressions

Actual use of variables in a program is usually more elaborate than what we have just seen. Variables may be used in any manner that does not violate their type declarations. This includes both arithmetic operations and assignment statements. For example, if **score1**, **score2**, **score3**, and **average** are **double** variables, then

```
score1 = 72.3;

score2 = 89.4;
```

```
score3 = 95.6;

average = (score1 + score2 + score3) / 3.0;
```

is a valid fragment of code.

Now consider the problem of accumulating a total. Assuming **new_score** and **total** are integer variables, the following code is valid:

```
total = 0;
new_score = 5;
total = total + new_score;
new_score = 7;
total = total + new_score;
```

As this code is executed, the values of memory locations for **total** and **new_score** could be depicted as

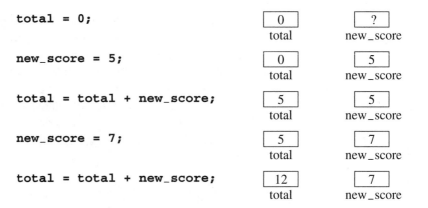

Compound Assignment

Consider the expression **x = x + y**. This expression

1. adds the value of **x** and the value of **y**, and then
2. stores the sum in **x**.

This kind of expression occurs so often in programs that C++ provides a shorthand form of it called **compound assignment.** Using this form, the expression

```
x = x + y
```

can be rewritten as

```
x += y
```

compound assignment: An assignment operation that performs a designated operation, such as addition, before storing the result in a variable.

Although these two expressions look different, they mean exactly the same thing. The clue for interpreting this compound expression is that the **+** sign comes before the **=** sign in the operator **+=**. This means that the values of **x** and **y** are added before the result is stored in **x**.

As Table 3.8 shows, C++ supports compound assignment operators for each of the standard arithmetic operations. For readability, we will continue to use the longer form of these expressions throughout this text.

▼ Table 3.8	Operator	Form for Use	Equivalent Longer Form
	+=	x += y	x = x + y
The compound assignment operators	-=	x -= y	x = x - y
	*=	x *= y	x = x * y
	/=	x /= y	x = x / y
	%=	x %= y	x = x % y

Output

Variables and variable expressions can be used when creating output. When used in an output statement, they perform the same function as a constant. For example, if the assignment statement

```
age = 5;
```

has been made, these two statements

```
cout << 5;
cout << age;
```

produce the same output. If **age1**, **age2**, **age3**, and **sum** are integer variables and the assignments

```
age1 = 21;
age2 = 30;
age3 = 12;
sum = age1 + age2 + age3;
```

are made, then

```
cout << "The sum is" << 21 + 30 + 12;
cout << "The sum is" << age1 + age2 + age3;
cout << "The sum is" << sum;
```

all produce the same output.

Formatting of variables and variable expressions in output statements follows the same rules presented in Chapter 2 for formatting constants. The statements needed to write the sum of the problem we just saw in a field width of four are

```
cout << "The sum is" << setw(4) << 21 + 30 + 12;
cout << "The sum is" << setw(4) << age1 + age2 + age3;
cout << "The sum is" << setw(4) << sum;
```

Example 3.1

Suppose you want a program to print data about the cost of three textbooks and the average price of the books. A complete program for this task could be written as follows:

```cpp
// Program file: books.cpp

#include <iostream.h>
#include <iomanip.h>

int main()
{
    // Variable declarations

    double math_text, bio_text, comp_sci_text, total, average;

    // Variable initializations

    math_text = 23.95;
    bio_text = 27.50;
    comp_sci_text = 19.95;
    total = math_text + bio_text + comp_sci_text;
    average = total / 3;

    // Output of variables

    cout << setiosflags(ios::fixed | ios::showpoint | ios::right);
    cout << setprecision(2) << endl;
    cout << "Text                Price" << endl;
    cout << "----                ----" << endl;
    cout << endl;
    cout << "Math" << setw(18) << math_text << endl;
    cout << "Biology" << setw(15) << bio_text << endl;
    cout << "CompSci" << setw(15) <<  comp_sci_text << endl;
    cout << endl;
    cout << "Total" << setw(17) << total << endl;
    cout << endl;
    cout << "The average price is" << setw(7) << average
        << endl;
    return 0;
}
```

The output would be

```
Text                      Price
----                      -----

Math                      23.95

Biology                   27.50

CompSci                   19.95

Total                     71.40

The average price is      23.80
```

Software Engineering

self-documenting code: Code that is written using descriptive identifiers.

The communication aspect of software engineering can be simplified by judicious choices of meaningful identifiers. Systems programmers must be aware that over time many others will need to read and analyze their code. Some extra time spent thinking about and using descriptive identifiers provides great time savings during the testing and maintenance phases. Code that is written using descriptive identifiers is referred to as **self-documenting code.**

■ Exercises 3.2

1. Assume the variable declaration section of a program is

```
int age, IQ;
double income;
```

Indicate which of the following are valid assignment statements. If a statement is invalid, give the reason why.
   a. `age = 21;`
   b. `IQ = age + 100;`
   c. `IQ = 120.5;`
   d. `age + IQ = 150;`
   e. `income = 22000;`
   f. `income = 100 * (age + IQ);`
   g. `age = IQ / 3;`
   h. `IQ = 3 * age;`

2. Write and run a test program to illustrate what happens when values of one data type are assigned to variables of another type.

3. Suppose **a**, **b**, and **temp** have been declared as integer variables. Indicate the contents of **a** and **b** at the end of each of the following sequences of statements:
   a. `a = 5;`
       `b = -2;`
       `a = a + b;`
       `b = b - a;`

```
b. a = 31;
   b = 26;
   temp = a;
   a = b;
   b = temp;
c. a = 0;
   b = 7;
   a = a + b % 2 * (-3);
   b = b + 4 * a;
d. a = -8;
   b = 3;
   temp = a + b;
   a = 3 * b;
   b = a;
   temp = temp + a + b;
```

4. Suppose **x** and **y** are real variables and the assignments

```
x = 121.3;
y = 98.6;
```

have been made. What output statements would cause the following output?
   a. **The value of x is 121.3**
   b. **The sum of x and y is 219.9**
   c. **x =   121.3**
      y =   98.6

      Total =   219.9

5. Assume the variable declaration section of a program is

```
int age, height;
double weight;
char gender;
```

What output would be created by the following program fragment?

```
age = 23;
height = 73;
weight = 186.5;
gender = 'M';
cout << setprecision(1);
cout << "Gender" << setw(10) << gender << endl;
cout << "Age" << setw(14) << age << endl;
cout << "Height" << setw(11) << height << " inches" << endl;
cout << "Weight" << setw(14) << weight << " lbs" << endl;
```

6. Write a complete program that allows you to add five integers and then print
   a. the integers.
   b. their sum.
   c. their average.

7. Assume the declarations **char ch** and **int age**. What output is produced by the following?

```
ch = 'M';
age = 21;
cout << setw(40) << "******************************" << endl;
cout << setw(11) << "*" << setw(29) << "*" << endl;
cout << setw(11) << "*"<< setw(7) << "Name" << setw(9) << "Age";
cout << setw(6) << "Gender" << setw(4) << "*" << endl;
cout << setw(11) << "*" setw(7) << "____" << setw(9)
     << "____" << setw(9) << "____" << setw(4) << "*" << endl;
cout << endl;
cout << setw(11) << "*" << setw(8) << "Jones" << setw(8)
     << age << setw(9) << ch << setw(4) << "*" << endl;
cout << endl;
cout << setw(11) << "*" << setw(29) << "*" << endl;
cout << setw(40) << "******************************" << endl;
```

8. Assume the variable declaration section of a program is

```
int weight1, weight2;
double average_weight;
```

and the following assignment statements have been made:

```
weight1 = 165;
weight2 = 174;
average_weight = (weight1 + weight2) / 2;
```

a. What output would be produced by the following section of code?

```
cout << "Weight" << endl;
cout << "_____" endl;
cout << endl;
cout << weight1 << endl;
cout << weight2 << endl;
cout << endl;
cout << "The average weight is" << (weight1 + weight2) / 2
     << endl;
```

b. Write a segment of code to produce the following output (use **average_weight**):

```
          weight
          ------
           165
           174
           ---
Total      339
```

The average weight is 169.5 pounds.

9. Assume the variable declaration section of a program is

```
char letter;
```

and the following assignment has been made:

```
letter = 'A';
```

What output is produced from the following segment of code?

```
cout << setw(40) << "This reviews string formatting" << endl;
cout << "When a letter" << letter << "is used" << endl;
cout << setw(14) << "Oops!" << setw(20)
     << "I forgot to format." << endl;
cout << setw(22) << "When a letter" << setw(2)
     << letter << setw(9) << "is used" << endl;
cout << setw(38) << "it is a string of length one." << endl;
```

10. Explain why it is a good idea to assign a value to a variable as soon as it is declared.

3.3 Input

Objectives

◆ to be able to use the standard input stream and its operator to get data for a program

◆ to be able to design a program that supports interactive input of data

Earlier, "running a program" was subdivided into the three general categories of getting the data, manipulating it appropriately, and printing the results. Our work thus far has centered on creating output and manipulating data. We are now going to focus on how to get data for a program.

Input Statements

Data for a program are usually obtained from an input device, which can be a keyboard or disk. When such data are obtained from the keyboard, the standard input stream, **cin**, normally is associated with one of these input devices.

The standard input stream, **cin**, is used in a similar way to the standard output stream, **cout**. **cin** behaves like an intelligent agent that knows how to take input from the keyboard and pass it back to a program. To make **cin** available to a program, you must include the C++ library header file **iostream.h**:

```
#include <iostream.h>
```

extractor: The standard input operator **>>**.

inserter: The standard output operator **<<**.

To obtain input from the standard input stream, you direct it into a variable with the **extractor** operator **>>** (note that the arrows point in the opposite direction from the **inserter** operator **<<**). For example, assume that **length** is a variable of type **int**. Then the following statement takes input from the keyboard and stores it in **length**:

```
cin >> length;
```

When an input statement is used to get data, the value of the data item is stored in the indicated memory location. Data read into a program must match the type of variable specified. To illustrate, if a variable declaration section includes

```
int age;
double wage;
```

and the data items are

```
21    5.25
```

then

```
cin >> age >> wage;
```

results in

```
┌──────┐    ┌──────┐
│  21  │    │ 5.25 │
└──────┘    └──────┘
  age         wage
```

Interactive Input

Interactive input refers to entering values from the keyboard while the program is running. An input statement causes the program to halt and wait for data items to be typed. For example, if you want to enter three scores at some point in a program, you can use

```
cin >> score1 >> score2 >> score3;
```

as program statements. At this point, you must enter at least three integers, separated by at least one blank space, and press **<Enter>**. The remaining part of the program is then executed. To illustrate, the following program reads in three integers and prints the integers and their average as output.

```
// Program file: input.cpp
// This program illustrates the use of input statements.

#include <iostream.h>
#include <iomanip.h>

int main ()
{

    int score1, score2, score3;
    double average;

    cin >> score1 >> score2 >> score3;
    average = (score1 + score2 + score3) / 3.0;
```

```
cout << setiosflags(ios::fixed | ios::showpoint | ios::right);
cout << endl;
cout << setw(10) << "The numbers are" << setw(4)
     << score1 << setw(4) << score2 << setw(4) << score3
     << endl;
cout << endl;
cout << setprecision(2);
cout << "Their average is "
     << average << endl;
return 0;
}
```

When the program runs, if you type in

```
89 90 91
```

and press **<Enter>**, output is

```
The numbers are  89  90  91

Their average is 90.00
```

Interactive programs should have a prompting message to the user so the user knows what to do when the program pauses for input. For example, the problem in the previous example can be modified by the line

```
cout >> "Please enter 3 scores separated by spaces, ";
cout >> "and then press <Enter>. ";
```

before the line

```
cin >> score1 >> score2 >> score3;
```

The screen will display the message

```
Please enter 3 scores separated by spaces and then press <Enter>.
```

when the program is run. Another method for getting the three inputs mentioned above is to prompt the user for each one on a separate line. Clearly stated screen messages to the person running a program are what make a program *user-friendly*.

Example 3.2

Pythagorean triples are sets of three integers that satisfy the Pythagorean theorem. That is, integers a, b, and c such that $a^2 + b^2 = c^2$. The integers 3, 4, and

5 make up such a triple because $3^2 + 4^2 = 5^2$. Formulas for generating Pythagorean triples are $a = m^2 - n^2$, $b = 2mn$, and $c = m^2 + n^2$, where m and n are positive integers such that $m > n$. The following interactive program allows the user to enter values for m and n and then have the Pythagorean triple printed:

```cpp
// Program file: triples.cpp
// This program illustrates Pythagorean triples.

#include <iostream.h>
#include <iomanip.h>

int main ()
{

    int m, n, a, b, c;

    cout << "Enter a positive integer and press <Enter>. ";
    cin >> n;
    cout << "Enter a positive integer greater than "
         << n << endl;
    cout << "and press <Enter>. ";
    cin >> m;
    a = (m * m) - (n * n);
    b = 2 * m * n;
    c = (m * m) + (n * n);
    cout << endl;
    cout << "For m = " << m << " and n = " << n << endl;
    cout << "the Pythagorean triple is ";
    cout << setw(5) << a << setw(5) << b << setw(5)
         << c << endl;
    return 0;

}
```

Sample runs of this program (using data 1, 2 and 2, 5) produce the following:

```
Enter a positive integer and press <Enter>. 1
Enter a positive integer greater than 1 and press <Enter>. 2

For m = 2 and n = 1 the Pythagorean triple is 3 4 5


Enter a positive integer and press <Enter>. 2
Enter a positive integer greater than 2 and press <Enter>. 5

   For m = 5 and n = 2 the Pythagorean triple is 21 20 29
```

Reading Numeric Data

Reading numeric data into a program is reasonably straightforward. At least one character of whitespace must be used to separate numbers. Whitespace characters are typed by hitting the space bar, the **<Tab>** key, or the **<Enter>** key.

Character Sets

Before we look at reading character data, we need to examine the way in which character data are stored. In the **char** data type, each character is associated with an integer. Thus, the sequence of characters is associated with a sequence of integers. The particular sequence used by a machine for this purpose is referred to as the **collating sequence** for that **character set.** The principal sequence currently in use is the American Standard Code for Information Interchange (ASCII).

The collating sequence contains an ordering of the characters in a character set and is listed in Appendix 4. For programs in this text, we use the ASCII code. As shown in Table 3.9, 52 of these characters are letters, 10 are digits, and the rest are special characters.

Reading Character Data

Reading characters from the standard input stream using **>>** is much the same as reading numeric data. If you want to read in a student's initials followed by three test scores, the following code will do that:

```
char first_initial, middle_initial, last_initial;
int score1, score2, score3;

cin >> first_initial >> middle_initial >> last_initial
    >> score1 >> score2 >> score3;
```

When program execution is halted, you would type in something like

```
J D K 89 90 91
```

and press **<Enter>**.

Debugging Output Statements

A frequently used technique for debugging programs is to insert an output statement to print the values of variables. Once you have determined that the desired values are obtained, you can delete the output statements. For example, if your program segment is supposed to read in three scores and three initials, you could write

```
// for debugging
cin >> score1 >> score2 >> score3;
cout << score1 << " " << score2 << " " << score3;
// for debugging
cin >> first_initial >> middle_initial >> last_initial;
cout << first_initial << " " << middle_initial
        << " " <<last_initial;
```

collating sequence: The particular order sequence for a character set used by a machine.

character set: The list of characters available for data and program statements.

▼ Table 3.9

ASCII ordering of a character set

Ordinal	Character	Ordinal	Character	Ordinal	Character	Ordinal	Character
0	NUL	32	SP	64	@	96	`
1	SOH	33	!	65	A	97	a
2	STX	34	"	66	B	98	b
3	ETX	35	#	67	C	99	c
4	EOT	36	$	68	D	100	d
5	ENQ	37	%	69	E	101	e
6	ACK	38	&	70	F	102	f
7	BEL	39	'	71	G	103	g
8	BS	40	(	72	H	104	h
9	HT	41	)	73	I	105	i
10	LF	42	*	74	J	106	j
11	VT	43	+	75	K	107	k
12	FF	44	'	76	L	108	l
13	CR	45	-	77	M	109	m
14	SO	46	.	78	N	110	n
15	SI	47	/	79	O	111	o
16	DLE	48	0	80	P	112	p
17	DCI	49	1	81	Q	113	q
18	DC2	50	2	82	R	114	r
19	DC3	51	3	83	S	115	s
20	DC4	52	4	84	T	116	t
21	NAK	53	5	85	U	117	u
22	SYN	54	6	86	V	118	v
23	ETB	55	7	87	W	119	w
24	CAN	56	8	88	X	120	x
25	EM	57	9	89	Y	121	y
26	SUB	58	:	90	Z	122	z
27	ESC	59	;	91	[	123	{
28	FS	60	<	92	\	124		
29	GS	61	=	93	]	125	}
30	RS	62	>	94	^	126	~
31	US	63	?	95	__	127	DEL

Note: Codes 00–31 and 127 are nonprintable control characters.

These debugging lines might be left in until the program has been sufficiently tested for input.

■ Exercises 3.3

1. Discuss the difference between **cin** and **cout**.
2. Assume the following variable declaration section:

```
int num1, num2;

double num3;

char ch;
```

You enter these data:

```
15 65.3 -20
```

Explain what results from each of the following statements. Also indicate what values are assigned to appropriate variables.

a. `cin >> num1 >> num3 >> num2;`
b. `cin >> num1 >> num2 >> num3;`

```
c. cin >> num1 >> num2 >> ch >> num3;
d. cin >> num2 >> num3 >> ch >> num2;
e. cin >> num2 >> num3 >> ch >> ch >> num2;
f. cin >> num3 >> num2;
g. cin >> num1 >> num3;
h. cin >> num1 >> ch >> num3;
```

3.   Write a program statement that prints a message to the screen directing the user to enter data in the form used for Exercise 2. Write an appropriate program statement (or statements) to produce a screen message and write an appropriate input statement for each of the following:
   a. Desired input is number of hours worked and hourly pay rate.
   b. Desired input is three positive integers followed by −999.
   c. Desired input is price of an automobile and the state sales tax rate.
   d. Desired input is the game statistics for one basketball player. (Check with a coach to see what must be entered.)
   e. Desired input is a student's initials, age, height, weight, and gender.

4.   Assume variables are declared as in Exercise 2. If an input statement is

```
cin >> num1 >> num2 >> ch >> num3;
```

   indicate which lines of the following data do not result in an error message. For those that do not, indicate the values of the variables. For those that produce an error, explain what the error is.
   a. **83 95 100**
   b. **83 95.0 100**
   c. **83-72 93.5**
   d. **83-72   93.5**
   e. **83.5**
   f. **70 73-80.5**
   g. **91 92 93 94**
   h. **-76-81-16.5**

5.   Why is it a good idea to print values of variables that have been read into a program?

6.   Write a complete program that will read your initials and five test scores. Your program should then compute your test average and print all information in a reasonable form with suitable messages.

7.   List several ways in which a program can be made more "user-friendly."

3.4 String Variables

The **apstring** data type is defined in the C++ **apstring** library. This data type can be used to declare string variables. Before declaring a string variable, you must include the library header file, **apstring.h**, at the beginning of the program. The following program fragment declares a string variable, assigns it a value, and outputs it on the screen:

```
#include "apstring.h"

apstring name;
```

```
name = "John Doe";
cout << name;
```

String Input with >>

A string variable can also receive input from the standard input stream, as in the following example:

```
#include "apstring.h"

apstring name;

cout << "Enter your last name: ";
cin >> name;
```

As with numbers, the **>>** operator ignores leading whitespace characters (a space, a tab, or a carriage return) and then reads nonblank characters up to the next whitespace character. The user is allowed to erase any input characters with the backspace or delete key until the trailing whitespace key is struck. When the user strikes the trailing whitespace key, the computer allocates memory for the string and stores the nonblank input characters in this memory.

String Input with getline

The **>>** operator cannot be used to enter a string containing spaces. Thus, the string "John Doe" cannot be input into a string variable with the **>>** operator. To solve this problem, the **apstring** library provides the function **getline**. As the name implies, this function reads characters, including the tab and space characters, from an input stream into a string variable, until a newline (**'\n'**) character is detected. The newline character is not stored in the string variable.

---
getline(<input stream>, <string variable>)

Recall that **cin** is the name of the standard input stream for reading characters from the keyboard. Thus, the following code segment could obtain the string "John Doe" from the keyboard:

```
#include "apstring.h"

apstring name;

cout << "Enter your full name: ";
getline(cin, name);
```

Because **getline** does not ignore leading whitespace characters, you should take special care when using it in conjunction with **>>**. Consider the following example:

```
#include "apstring.h"

apstring name;
int age;

cout << "Enter your age: ";
cin >> age;
cout << "Enter your full name: ";
getline(cin, name);
cout << name ", you are " << age << endl;
```

This program segment will allow the user to enter the age. It then prompts for the name but displays the results immediately without pausing for the input of the name. The reason for this is that **>>** reads and stores characters up to the newline character in **age**. **getline** then detects this newline character as the first character "in" the input of the name, so it returns with an empty string before the user can enter any characters. There are two ways to avoid this problem:

1. Reverse the order of the inputs, with **getline** being called before **>>**. In general, if you adopt this method, a call to **getline** can come after another call to **getline**, but never after a call to **>>**. A correct code segment thus would be

    ```
    #include "apstring.h"

    apstring name;
    int age;

    cout << "Enter your full name: ";
    getline(cin, name);
    cout << "Enter your age: ";
    cin >> age;
    cout << name ", you are " << age << endl;
    ```

2. In cases where at least one call of **>>** must come before a call of **getline**, you must "consume" the trailing newline character first. A simple way to do this would be to declare a dummy string variable and and run **getline** with it after the **>>** operation. This would have the effect of "throwing away" the extra newline character before the next call to **getline**. A correct code segment that uses this method would be

    ```
    #include "apstring.h"

    apstring name, dummy;
    int age;

    cout << "Enter your age: ";
    cin >> age;
    getline(cin, dummy); // Consume the trailing newline
    ```

```
cout << "Enter your full name: ";
getline(cin, name);
cout << name ", you are " << age << endl;
```

To summarize, we use **>>** when we want to read a single word into a string variable, and we use **getline** when we want to read an entire line of words into a string variable.

Example 3.3

Faculty at the local college are categorized by name, rank, and number of years of service. The following complete program uses string variables to take this information as input and display it as output:

```
// Program faculty.cpp
// This program echoes the name, rank, and number of years of
// service of a college professor.

#include <iostream.h>
#include "apstring.h"

int main()
{
        apstring name, rank;
        char middle_initial;
        int years_of_service;

        cout << "Enter the full name: ";
        getline(cin, name);
        cout << "Enter the rank (Assistant, Associate, or Full): ";
        cin >> rank;
        cout << "Enter the number of years of service: ";
        cin >> years_of_service;
        cout << endl << endl;
        cout << "Name: " << name << endl;
        cout << "Rank: " << rank << " Professor" << endl;
        cout << "Years of service: " << years_of_service << endl;
        return 0;
}
```

A sample interaction with this program is

```
Enter the name: Albert H. Einstein
Enter the rank (Assistant, Associate, or Full): Full
Enter the number of years of service: 25


Name: Albert H. Einstein
Rank: Full Professor
Years of service: 25
```

Memory for String Variables

The computer manages memory for string variables and numeric variables differently. Memory for a numeric variable is always of a fixed size, though the actual size varies with the numeric type. When a string variable is declared, no memory for the character data is initially provided. During an assignment statement or an input statement, the computer automatically adjusts the memory for a string variable to accommodate the number of characters to be stored there. For example, suppose that the following code segment has just run:

```
int num1, num2;
apstring word1, word2;

num1 = 10;
num2 = 100;
word1 = "Hi there";
word2 = "Hello";
```

The memory allocated for these variables can be visualized in this way:

10

num1

100

num2

H	i		t	h	e	r	e

word1

H	e	l	l	o

word2

Note that the memory cells for the two integers are the same size, even though the integer values stored there are of different sizes. But the memory cells for the two strings are of different sizes, in order to accommodate string values containing different numbers of characters.

The **length** function returns the number of characters currently stored in a string variable. The form for calling **length** is different from that of ordinary function calls, so it will take some getting used to:

```
<string variable>.length()
```

Thus, the following code segment

```
cout << "Length of " << word1 << " = " << word1.length() << endl;
cout << "Length of " << word2 << " = " << word2.length() << endl;
```

produces the output

```
Length of Hi there = 8
Length of Hello = 5
```

The Empty String

Although no memory is allocated for character data when a string variable is declared, the computer considers the variable to contain the empty string. The empty string is represented in C++ as the literal **""** (two consecutive double quotes). Thus, the memory allocated for the string variable in the following code segment does not change:

```
apstring word;

cout << word.length() << endl;
word = "";
cout << word.length() << endl;
```

The output produced by this code segment would be

```
0
0
```

String Concatenation

concatenation: An operation in which the contents of one data structure are placed after the contents of another data structure.

An important operation on strings is **concatenation.** Concatenation puts two objects together in such a way that the second one follows the first one in a new object. One version of this operation copies the characters in two strings to a third string. The following code segment concatenates the strings "Hi" and " there" to form the string "Hi there", and then displays this string on the screen:

```
apstring first, second, third;

first = "Hi";
second = " there";
third = first + second;
cout << third;
```

The concatenation operator for strings is **+**. Note that when used with numbers, **+** means *add,* but when used with strings, **+** means *concatenate.*

The + operator can also be used to append a character to the end of a string. For example, the following code segment displays the string "fishes" on the screen:

```
string singular;

singular = "fish";
cout << singular + 'e' + 's';
```

Note that the concatenation operations in this example are performed from left to right. The first operation builds the string "fishe" from "fish" and 'e'. The second operation builds the string "fishes" from "fishe" and 's'. Note also that the concatenation operator does not change the contents of its operands. It builds a new string with the contents of its operands and returns this string as a value.

Compound Assignment with Strings

Another form of string concatenation occurs when the compound assignment operator **+=** is used. Recall from Section 3.2 that in the context of numbers, the expression **x += y** means the same thing as **x = x + y**. In the context of strings, where **x** is a string and **y** is a string, the two expressions are equivalent also, but **+** now means concatenation. For example, the following code segment

```
apstring x, y;

x = "Hi ";
y = "there.";
x += y;
cout << x << endl;
```

would display the string

```
Hi there.
```

Note that the expression **x + y** builds and returns a new string but does not change **x** and **y**. However, the expression **x += y** builds a new string from **x** and **y** and then stores this string in the variable **x**.

The compound assignment operator can also be used to concatenate a character value to the left operand, as follows:

```
apstring x;
char y;

x = "rose";
y = 's';
x += y;
```

However, the expression **y += x** is invalid, because the resulting string cannot be stored in the character variable **y**.

For readability, we will continue to use the long form, **x = x + y**, for assignment with string concatenation in this text.

■ Exercises 3.4

1. Assume a user has entered the strings "The" and "rain" into the string variables **first** and **second**, respectively. Write program statements that use these variables to perform the following tasks:
   a. Output the string "The rain".
   b. Store the string "The rain" in a new string variable, **third**.
   c. Reset the value of each variable to an empty string.
   d. Prompt the user for new strings to be entered into the variables and input them.

2. Explain why the **>>** operator can only read one word at a time from an input stream.

3. Suppose a user types the string " 567 is a small number" at the keyboard, followed by a carriage return. **word1** and **word2** are string variables and **number** is an **int**. Describe the contents of the variables when the following statements are run to receive this input:
   a. `cin >> word1;`
   b. `getline(cin, word1);`
   c. `cin >> number;`
   d. `cin >> number >> word1;`
   e. `cin >> number;`
      `getline(cin,  word1);`
   f. `cin >> number;`
      `getline(cin, word1);`
      `getline(cin, word2);`

4. Draw a picture that shows how the character data for the string "Computer Science" might be stored in a string variable named **department**. Then draw another picture that shows what might happen to this memory when the variable **department** is reset to "French".

5. Indicate which of the following expressions are valid. If an expression is valid, describe the value returned. If an expression is invalid, explain why.
   a. `"Hi" + "there"`
   b. `"Hi" + 's'`
   c. `"Hi" + 4`
   d. `'H' + 'i' + 's'`
   e. `"H" + 'i' + 's'`

6. Write an expression that concatenates the character values 'H', 'i', and 's' to form the string "His". (*Hint:* You must use a special string value in the expression.)

7. Write a complete, interactive program that inputs your name, address, and telephone number into string variables and displays them on the screen. Be sure to issue the appropriate prompts for the input information.

8. Explain why the **+** operator is used for addition of numbers and concatenation of strings.

3.5 Using Constants

Objectives

- to be aware of the appropriate use of constants
- to be able to use constants in programs
- to be able to format constants

The word *constant* has several interpretations. In this section, we distinguish between a symbolic constant, like **PI**, and a literal constant, like **3.14**. Symbolic constants are defined by giving them the values of literal constants. Recall that a C++ program consists of preprocessor directives, an optional constant and type definition section, a program heading, an optional variable declaration section, and an executable section. We now examine uses for constants.

Rationale for Uses

There are many reasons to use constants in a program. If a number is to be used frequently, the programmer may wish to give it a descriptive name in the constant definition subsection and then use the descriptive name in the executable section, thus making the program easier to read. For example, if a program included a segment that computed a person's state income tax, and the state tax rate was 6.25% of taxable income, the constant section might include:

```
const double STATE_TAX_RATE = 0.0625;
```

This defines both the value and type for **STATE_TAX_RATE**. In the executable portion of the program, the statement

```
state_tax = income * STATE_TAX_RATE;
```

computes the state tax owed. Or suppose you wanted a program to compute areas of circles. Depending on the accuracy you desire, you could define π as

```
const double PI = 3.14159;
```

You could then have a statement in the executable section such as

```
area = PI * radius * radius;
```

where **area** and **radius** are appropriately declared variables.

Perhaps the most important use of constants is for values that are currently fixed but subject to change for subsequent updates of the program. If these are defined in the constant section, they can be used throughout the program. If the value changes later, only one change need be made to keep the program current. This prevents the need to locate all uses of a constant in a program. Some examples might be

```
const double MINIMUM_WAGE = 4.25;
const int SPEED_LIMIT = 65;
const double PRICE = 0.75;
const double STATE_TAX_RATE = 0.0625;
```

Software Engineering

The appropriate use of constants is consistent with principles of software engineering. Communication between teams of programmers is enhanced when

A Note of Interest

Defined Constants and Space Shuttle Computing

An excellent illustration of the utilization of defined constants in a program was given by J. F. ("Jack") Clemons, former manager of avionics flight software development and verification for the space shuttle on-board computers. In an interview with David Gifford, editor for <u>Communications of the ACM</u>, Clemons was asked: "Have you tried to restructure the software so that it can be changed easily?"

His response was, "By changing certain data constants, we can change relatively large portions of the software on a mission-to-mission basis. For example, we've designed the software so that characteristics like atmospheric conditions on launch day or different lift-off weights can be loaded as initial constants into the code. This is important when there are postponements or last-minute payload changes that invalidate the original inputs."

program constants have been agreed on. Each team should have a list of these constants for use as they work on their part of the system.

The maintenance phase of the software system life cycle is also aided by use of defined constants. Clearly, a large payroll system is dependent on being able to perform computations that include deductions for federal tax, state tax, social security taxes, Medicare, health insurance, retirement options, and so on. If appropriate constants are defined for these deductions, system changes are easily made as necessary. For example, if the salary limit for deducting social security taxes is $53,400, an amount that changes regularly, one could define

```
const double SS_LIMIT = 53400.00;
```

Program maintenance is then simplified by changing the value of this constant as the law changes.

Library Constants

Some constants are provided in C++ libraries. For example, it is often necessary to determine the range of integer values allowed by a particular computer system, or the range of real number values, or the number of digits of precision supported by the system. The C++ library header files **limits.h** and **float.h** define constants for each of these important values for your particular system. When you include these files at the beginning of your source program, each of the constants appearing in Table 3.10 will be available for use.

▼ Table 3.10	Library Constant	Meaning
Library constants for maximum numeric values	**INT_MAX**	The maximum allowable positive integer value
	INT_MIN	The maximum allowable negative integer value
	DBL_MAX	The maximum allowable positive double value
	DBL_MIN	The maximum allowable negative double value
	DBL_DIG	The maximum number of digits of precision

Formatting Constants

Formatting of symbolic constants is identical to formatting of real and integer values as discussed in Section 2.3.

■ Exercises 3.5

1. Write a short program that includes the **limits** and **float** libraries and displays the values of the constants listed in Table 3.10.
2. Why is the use of symbolic constants preferable to literal constants?
3. Write C++ code to define the following symbolic constants:
   a. **PI**
   b. The number of degrees to be added to a centigrade temperature to produce a Fahrenheit temperature.
   c. The number of degrees in a right angle.
   d. The last letters (uppercase and lowercase) in the alphabet.

3.6 Library Functions

Objectives

♦ to understand the reasons for having library functions

♦ to be able to use library functions in a program

♦ to be able to use appropriate data types for the arguments of library functions

argument: A value or expression passed in a function call.

Programmers often use standard operations such as squaring numbers and finding square roots of numbers. Because these operations are so basic, C++ provides built-in *library functions* for them. Different versions of C++ and other programming languages have differing library functions available, so you should always check which functions your compiler supplies. Appendix 2 sets forth many of those available in most versions of C++.

A function can be used in a program if it appears in the following form:

<function name> (<argument list>)

where **argument** is a value or variable with an assigned value. When a function appears in this manner, it is said to be *called* or *invoked*. A function is invoked by using it in a program statement. After the function performs its work, it may *return a value*. If, for example, you want to raise 3 to the fourth power, you include the **math.h** library header file and then

```
cout << pow(3, 4) << endl;
```

produces the desired result and returns it as a value to the caller.

Many functions operate on numbers, starting with a given number and returning some associated value. Table 3.11 shows five math library functions, each with its argument type, data type of return, and an explanation of the value returned. A more complete list of library functions can be found in Appendix 2. Several examples of specific function expressions together with the value returned by each expression are depicted in Table 3.12.

▼ Table 3.11

Some math library functions

Function Declaration	Action of Function
`double fmod(double x, double y);`	Returns floating-point remainder of x / y
`double log(double x);`	Returns natural logarithm of x
`double pow(double x, double y);`	Returns x raised to power of y
`double sqrt(double x);`	Returns square root of x
`double cos(double x);`	Returns cosine of x

▼ Table 3.12

Values of function expressions

Expression	Value
`pow(2, 4)`	16
`pow(2.0, 4)`	16.0
`pow(-3, 2)`	9
`fmod(5.3, 2.1)`	1.1
`sqrt(25.0)`	5.0
`sqrt(25)`	5
`sqrt(0.0)`	0.0
`sqrt(-2.0)`	Not permissible

Using Functions

When a function is invoked, it produces a value in much the same way that 3 + 3 produces 6. Thus, use of a function should be treated similarly to use of constants or values of an expression. Typical uses are in assignment statements,

```
x = sqrt(16.0);
```

output statements,

```
cout << setw(20) << pow(2, 5);
```

or arithmetic expressions,

```
hypotenuse = sqrt(pow(base, 2) + pow(height, 2));
```

Arguments of functions can be expressions, variables, or constants.

Member Functions

class: A description of the attributes and behavior of a set of computational objects.

Some library functions are associated with C++ data types called **classes.** The **apstring** data type is one of these classes. The functions defined for strings are called **member functions.** A member function behaves just like a standard C++ function, but is invoked with a different syntax. As you have seen, the **apstring** member function **length** examines a string and returns the number of characters currently stored in it.

```
string word;

cout << word.length();
word = "Hello";
cout << word.length();
```

Note that the syntax used to call this function is different from that of other, more conventional function calls that you have seen. Instead of the form

member function: An operation defined for a class of objects.

> <conventional function name> (<variable name>)

we have

> <variable name>.<member function name> ()

In either case, the important point is not the syntax but what the function does.

Random Numbers

Many applications require the use of random numbers. For example, a computerized game of backgammon requires the roll of two dice on each move. The results can be computed by selecting two random numbers between 1 and 6. C++ provides a library function, **rand**, that returns an integer between 0 and the compiler-dependent constant **RAND_MAX**, inclusive. Both the function and the constant are declared in the library header file **stdlib.h**. Unfortunately, the numbers generated by **rand** are not as random as we would like. The reason for this is that the number returned by **rand** depends on an initial value, called a

seed: An initial value used by a random number generator.

seed, that is the same for each run of a program. Thus, the sequence of random numbers generated by a program that uses this method will be exactly the same on each run of the program.

To help solve this problem, another function, **srand(seed)**, also declared in **stdlib.h**, allows an application to specify the initial value used by **rand** at program startup. Using this method, two runs of a program that use different values for **seed** will thus receive different sequences of random numbers. The problem then becomes one of providing an arbitrary seed value. Rather than force a user to enter this value interactively, most applications obtain it by reading the current time from the computer's internal clock. The C++ data type **time_t** and the function **time**, both declared in the **time.h** library header file, can be used to obtain the current time on the computer's clock. When converted to an unsigned integer, the current time can serve as a fairly arbitrary seed for a random number generator in most programs.

To summarize the discussion so far, the following program would display three random numbers between 0 and **RAND_MAX**, depending on the current time on the computer's clock at program startup:

```
// Program file: randtest.cpp

// Displays three random numbers

#include <iostream.h>
#include <stdlib.h>
#include <time.h>

int main()
{
     time_t seconds;

     time(&seconds);
     srand((unsigned int) seconds);
     cout << rand() << endl;
     cout << rand() << endl;
     cout << rand() << endl;
     return 0;
}
```

Users of a random number generator might desire a narrower or a wider range of numbers than **rand** provides. Ideally, a user would specify the range with integer values representing the lower and upper bounds. To see how we might use **rand** to accomplish this, first consider how to generate a number between 0 and an arbitrary upper bound, **high**, inclusive. For any two integers, *a* and *b, a % b* is between 0 and *b* − 1, inclusive. Thus, the expression **rand() % high + 1** would generate a random number between 0 and **high**, inclusive, where **high** is less than or equal to **RAND_MAX**. To place a lower bound other than 0 on the result, we can generate a random number between 0 and **high - low + 1**, and then add **low** to the result. Thus, the complete expression for computing a random number between a lower bound and an upper bound would be **rand() % (high - low + 1) + low**.

Example 3.4

The following complete program uses constants and random numbers to display the results of two rolls of dice:

```
// Program file: dice.cpp
// This program displays the results of two rolls of dice.
```

```cpp
#include <iostream.h>
#include <stdlib.h>
#include <time.h>

const int LOW = 1;
const int HIGH = 6;

int main()
{
        int first_die, second_die;
        time_t seconds;

        time(&seconds);
        srand((unsigned int) seconds);
        first_die = rand() % (HIGH - LOW + 1) + LOW;
        second_die = rand() % (HIGH - LOW + 1) + LOW;
        cout << "Your roll is (" << first_die << ", "
             << second_die << ")" << endl << endl;
        first_die = rand() % (HIGH - LOW + 1) + LOW;
        second_die = rand() % (HIGH - LOW + 1) + LOW;
        cout << "My roll is (" << first_die << ", "
             << second_die << ")" << endl << endl;
        return 0;
}
```

A sample run might produce the following output:

```
Your roll is (1, 4)

My roll is (6, 6)
```

Note that the use of constants and the complete expressions for computing random numbers are not really necessary for this program. We could have used the expression **rand() % 6 + 1** for simplicity.

■ Exercises 3.6

1. Write a short program that displays the square root of an input number. Test the program with input values whose square roots are whole numbers and whose square roots are not whole numbers.
2. Test the program from Exercise 1 with a negative input value. How does your computer respond?
3. Explain the facts that a programmer must know about a function in order to use it properly.
4. Suppose that a programmer wants to generate a random real number between 0 and 1. Suggest an algorithm for accomplishing this.
5. Write a program to test your suggestion in Exercise 4.

3.7 Type Compatibility and Type Conversion

Objectives

- to be able to understand how different data types are related to each other
- to be able to understand how one data type can be converted to another

type promotion: The process of converting a less inclusive data type, such as **int**, to a more inclusive data type, such as **double**.

ordinal data type: A data type ordered in some association with the integers.

We mentioned in Section 3.2 that the operands of arithmetic expressions and assignment statements must be of compatible data types. For example, we saw that we can not only add an integer to an integer, but we can also add an integer to a real number. In the latter case, the computer automatically converts the type of the integer operand before performing the addition, and then returns a real number as the sum. This kind of type conversion is also referred to as **type promotion,** in that the value of a less inclusive type, **int**, is elevated to a value of a more inclusive type, **double**.

Automatic type conversion also occurs when an integer value is assigned to a variable of type **double**. In this case, a copy of the integer value is placed in the real number's storage location, and then promoted by adding to it a fractional part of zero. For example, assuming that **real_number** is of type **double**, the following lines of code would produce an output of 3.00:

```
real_number = 3;
cout << setiosflags(ios::fixed | ios::showpoint)
     << setprecision(2) << real_number << endl;
```

Conversely, when you assign a real number to a variable of type **int**, the computer drops or truncates a copy of the real number's value before placing it in the integer's storage location. Thus, the following two lines of code would display the value 5, assuming that **whole_number** is an **int**:

```
whole_number = 5.76;
cout << whole_number << endl;
```

The Character Set Once Again

It turns out that characters and integers are also compatible types in C++. This means that character values can be assigned to integer variables, integer values can be assigned to character variables, and integers can be added to characters. Moreover, each of these operations involves an implicit type conversion. To make sense of this apparently strange phenomenon, we must consider the character set once more.

Ordering of a character set requires association of an integer with each character. Data types ordered in some association with the integers are known as **ordinal data types.** Each integer is the ordinal of its associated value. Character sets are considered to be an ordinal data type, as shown in Table 3.9. In each case, the ordinal of the character appears to the left of the character. Using ASCII, as shown in Table 3.9, the ordinal of a capital a ('A') is 65, the ordinal of the character representing the Arabic number one ('1') is 49, the ordinal of a blank ('ｂ') is 32, and the ordinal of a lowercase a ('a') is 97.

Once we realize that characters are really represented as integers in a computer, we can begin to see how we can perform mixed-mode operations on these two data types. When a character value is assigned to an integer variable, the run-time system copies the character's ordinal into the integer's storage location. Thus, assuming an ASCII representation and our **whole_number** variable of type **int**, the following two lines of code would display the number 65:

```
whole_number = 'A';
cout << whole_number << endl;
```

Conversely, assuming that **letter** is of type **char**, the following two lines of code would display the letter 'A':

```
letter = 65;
cout << letter << endl;
```

When arithmetic operations are performed on characters (either two character values or one character and one integer), each character value is first promoted to a more inclusive type, namely, an integer. Then the system performs the operation, and the result returned is an integer. For example, the following two lines of code below would display the value 66:

```
whole_number = 'A' + 1;
cout << whole_number << endl;
```

It turns out that since the decimal digits are in the collating sequence from '0' to '9' in the character set, the integer value of a given digit can be computed quite easily with *character arithmetic*. For example, assuming that digit is of type **int**, the following two lines of code compute and display the integer value of the digit '5':

```
digit = '5' - '0'
cout << digit << endl;
```

In the next example, we show how to use character arithmetic to convert an uppercase letter to lowercase.

Example 3.5

To show how character arithmetic can be used to convert an uppercase letter to lowercase, let's assume that our task is to convert the letter **'H'** into the letter **'h'**. We first subtract **'A'** from **'H'** to obtain

```
'H' - 'A'
```

which is

```
72 - 65 = 7
```

We now add **'a'** to get

```
'H' - 'A' + 'a'
```

which yields

```
72 - 65 + 97 = 104
```

This is the ordinal of **'h'**. It can be converted to the letter by assigning it to a variable of type **char**. Thus,

```
letter = 'H' - 'A' + 'a';
```

places the letter **'h'** in the variable **letter**, where **letter** is of type **char**.

In general, the following is sufficient for converting from uppercase to lowercase, where **lower_case** and **upper_case** are of type **char**:

```
lower_case = upper_case - 'A' + 'a';
```

Note that if you always use the same ASCII ordering,

```
-'A' + 'a'
```

could be replaced by the constant 32. If you choose to do this, 32 should be given a name. A typical definition is

```
const int UPPER_TO_LOWER_SHIFT = 32;
```

You would then write the lowercase conversion as

```
lower_case = upper_case + UPPER_TO_LOWER_SHIFT;
```

Type Casts

Occasionally, we would like to force the conversion of a value from one type to another without resorting to an assignment statement. For example, the expression **whole_number % real_number** will generate an error, because the modulus operator is not defined for real numbers. We would like to convert the real number to an integer within the expression, rather than complicate matters by declaring an extra integer variable, assigning the real number to it, and then using the integer variable.

type cast: An operation that a programmer can invoke to convert the type of a data object.

explicit type conversion: The use of an operation by a programmer to convert the type of a data object.

C++ provides a set of operators called **type casts** for performing **explicit type conversions** of this sort. You can think of a type cast as a function whose name is the name of the type to which you wish to convert a value. The argument of this function is the value to be converted, and the value returned by the function is the converted value. For example, the following line of code uses the type cast for integers to display the integer value 3:

```
cout << int(3.14) << endl;
```

Our method of converting an uppercase letter to lowercase can make good use of the type cast for characters:

```
cout << char(upper_case - UPPER_TO_LOWER_SHIFT) << endl;
```

The form of a type cast that we will use in this text is

> <type name> (<expression>)

where **<type name>** is the name of the target type and **<expression>** evaluates to a type of value that the cast is capable of converting. In some rare cases, such as a conversion to type **long int**, the following form of type cast should be used:

> (<type name>) <expression>

For example, the following statement converts an integer value to a **long int** for output:

```
cout << (long int) an_integer;
```

Writing styles and suggestions are gathered for quick reference in the following style tip summary. These tips are intended to stimulate rather than terminate your imagination.

Communication and Style Tips

1. Use descriptive identifiers. Words—**sum**, **score**, **average**—are easier to understand than letters—**a**, **b**, **c**, or **x**, **y**, **z**.
2. The decimal points in the output of a column of reals should be aligned:
   ```
     14.32
    181.50
     93.63
   ```
3. Output can be made more attractive by using columns, left and right margins, underlining, and blank lines.
4. Extra output statements at the beginning and end of the executable section will separate desired output from other messages.
   ```
   cout << endl;
     .
     . (program body here)
     .
   cout << endl;
   ```

A Note of Interest

Computer Ethics: Copyright, Intellectual Property, and Digital Information

For hundreds of years, copyright law has existed to regulate the use of intellectual property. At stake are the rights of authors and publishers to a return on their investment in works of the intellect, which include printed matter (books, articles, etc.), recorded music, film, and video. More recently, copyright law has been extended to include software and other forms of digital information. For example, the software on the disk provided to your teacher is protected by copyright law. This prohibits the purchaser from reproducing the software for sale or free distribution to others. If the software is stolen or "pirated" in this way, the perpetrator can be prosecuted and punished by law. However, copyright law also allows for "fair use"—the purchaser may make backup copies of the software for personal use. When the purchaser sells the software to another user, the seller thereby relinquishes the right to use it and the new purchaser acquires this right.

When they design copyright legislation, governments try to balance the rights of authors and publishers to a return on their work against the rights of the public to fair use. In the case of printed matter and other works that have a physical embodiment, the meaning of fair use is fairly clear. Without fair use, borrowing a book from a library or playing a CD at a high school dance would be unlawful.

With the rapid rise of digital information and its easy transmission on networks, different interest groups—authors, publishers, users, and computer professionals—are beginning to question the traditional balance of ownership rights and fair use. For example, is browsing a copyrighted manuscript on a network service an instance of fair use? Or does it involve a reproduction of the manuscript that violates the rights of the author or publisher? Is the manuscript a physical piece of intellectual property when browsed, or just a temporary pattern of bits in a computer's memory? Users and technical experts tend to favor free access to any information placed on a network. Publishers and, to a lesser extent, authors tend to worry that their work, when placed on a network, will be resold for profit.

Legislators struggling with the adjustment of copyright law to a digital environment face many of these questions and concerns. Providers and users of digital information should also be aware of the issues. For a detailed discussion, see Pamela Samuelson, "Regulation of technologies to protect copyrighted works," Communications of the ACM, Volume 39, Number 7, July 1996, pp. 17–22.

■ Exercises 3.7

1. Find the value of each of the following expressions:
   a. **sqrt(15.51)**
   b. **pow(-14.2, 3)**
   c. **4 * 11 % sqrt(16)**
   d. **pow(17 / 5 * 2, 2)**
   e. **-5.0 + sqrt(5 * 5 - 4 * 6) / 2.0**
2. Write a test program that illustrates what happens when an inappropriate argument is used with a function. Be sure to include something like **sqrt(-1)**.
3. Two standard algebraic problems come from the Pythagorean theorem and the quadratic formula. Assume variables a, b, and c have been declared in a program. Write C++ expressions that allow you to evaluate the following:
   a. The length of the hypotenuse of a right triangle:

$$\sqrt{a^2 + b^2}$$

b. Both solutions to the quadratic formula:

$$\frac{-b \pm \sqrt{b^2 - 4ac}}{2a}$$

4. Indicate whether the following are valid or invalid expressions. Find the value of those that are valid; explain why the others are invalid.
   a. `-6 % (sqrt(16))`
   b. `8 / sqrt(65)`
   c. `sqrt(63 % (2))`
   d. `-sqrt(pow(3, 2) - 7)`
   e. `sqrt(16 / (-3))`
   f. `sqrt(pow(-4, 2))`

5. Using ASCII (Table 3.9), find the values of each of the following expressions:
   a. `13 + 4 % 3`
   b. `'E'`
   c. `'E' + 1`
   d. `5`
   e. `'5'`
   f. `'+'`
   g. `40`

6. Assume the variable declaration section of a program is

   ```
   double x; int a; char ch;
   ```

   What output is produced by each of the following program fragments?
   a. ```
   x = -4.3;
   cout << setprecision(2) << setw(6) << x << int(x) << endl;
   ```
   b. ```
   x = -4.3;
   a = x;
   cout << a << int('a');
   ```
   c. ```
   ch = char(76);
   cout << setw(5) << ch << setw(5) << char(ch - 1);
   ```

7. Write a complete program to print the first five uppercase letters of the alphabet and their ordinals in the collating sequence used by your machine's version of C++.

8. Using ASCII, show how each of the following conversions can be made:
   a. A lowercase letter converted into its uppercase equivalent
   b. A digit entered as a **char** value into its indicated numeric value

## 3.8 Graphics

### Objectives

- to be able to use input values to specify the position and size of an image
- to learn how to use graphics operations with relative coordinates
- to learn how to use operations that draw geometric shapes
- to be able to change the foreground color, background color, and line style
- to be able to determine the screen size

### Using Variables to Specify Coordinates

In Chapter 2, we examined several code segments and short programs for displaying images. Those examples all used constants to specify the end points of line segments or text drawn on the screen. More interesting graphics applications use variables for these purposes:

1. To allow the user to enter information that determines the position and size of the images.

2. To allow the program to perform calculations for purposes of layout, movement, and so forth.
   ```

The following example illustrates these points.

Example 3.6

Suppose we wish to allow the user to specify the location and size of a rectangle to be drawn on the screen. The user can provide this information by entering four integer values. The first two values are the coordinates of the upper left corner of the rectangle. This point specifies the rectangle's position in the coordinate system. The second two values are the rectangle's width and height. These values specify its size. As an intermediate step, the program uses the input values to compute the coordinates of the lower right corner point of the rectangle and save them in integer variables. The program uses these coordinates to draw the four line segments that are the sides of the rectangle.

A top-level pseudocode design for this program follows:
1. Obtain the coordinates of upper left corner and the values of the height and width from the user.
2. Compute the coordinates of the lower right corner of the rectangle.
3. Set the graphics mode.
4. Draw the line segments that make up the rectangle.
5. Wait for the user to signal to continue.
6. Close the graphics mode.

The following interactive program prompts the user for this information and displays the desired rectangle:

```cpp
// Program file: rect.cpp

// Displays a rectangle whose position and size are
// specified by the user.

#include <conio.h>
#include <graphics.h>
#include <iostream.h>

int main()
{
        int upper_x, upper_y, width, height, lower_x, lower_y;

        // Obtain input information from the user

        cout << "Enter the upper left x coordinate: ";
        cin >> upper_x;
        cout << "Enter the upper left y coordinate: ";
        cin >> upper_y;
        cout << "Enter the width: ";
        cin >> width;
        cout << "Enter the height: ";
        cin >> height;

        // Compute the coordinates of the lower right corner
```

```
lower_x = upper_x + width;
lower_y = upper_y + height;

// Set the graphics mode

int graphdriver = DETECT, graphmode;
initgraph(&graphdriver, &graphmode, "c:..\\bgi");

// Draw the rectangle

moveto(upper_x, upper_y);
lineto(lower_x, upper_y);
lineto(lower_x, lower_y);
lineto(upper_x, lower_y);
lineto(upper_x, upper_y);

// Pause for a key to be pressed

moveto(100, 250);
outtext("Strike any key to continue");
getch();

// Close the graphics mode
closegraph();
return 0;
}
```

Note how the coordinates of the lower right corner are computed by using the coordinates of the upper left corner and the height and width. When the user enters the values 50, 50, 100, and 200, the image displayed would look like this (the coordinates have been added for clarity):

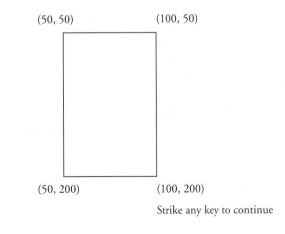

Strike any key to continue

Relative Coordinates

The **lineto** and **moveto** commands expect as parameters the coordinates of the destination point of the operation. Sometimes it would be more convenient to specify the horizontal and vertical distances to move or draw from the current position. For example, the program in Example 3.6 computed the end points for the **lineto** commands. The following code segment uses the **linerel** command to draw the same rectangle using the input height and width:

```
moveto(upper_x, upper_y);
linerel(width, 0);
linerel(0, height);
linerel(- width, 0);
linerel(0, - height);
```

Each **linerel** command uses the current position of the pen and the horizontal and vertical distance (the parameters) to compute the destination point of the line to be drawn. Because the two distances are relative to the current position, they are sometimes called **relative coordinates.** When the new coordinates are specified directly, as in the **lineto** command, they are called **absolute coordinates.** Note in the code segment that a negative width indicates an x coordinate of a point to the left of the current position, and a negative height indicates a y coordinate of a point above the current position.

moverel uses relative coordinates also, but it moves the pen without drawing anything. The forms for using **linerel** and **moverel** are

> **linerel**(<horizontal distance>, <vertical distance>)

> **moverel**(<horizontal distance>, <vertical distance>)

relative coordinates:
The use of horizontal and vertical distances to specify a new point in relation to an existing point.

absolute coordinates:
The specification of a point in terms of x and y coordinates.

The advantage of using these commands with relative coordinates is that you do not have to compute the destination points. All you have to specify are the horizontal and vertical distances; then the commands compute the destination points for you.

Geometric Shapes

Every set of graphics operations has commands for drawing commonly used geometric shapes, such as rectangles, circles, ellipses, and arcs. Remember that a rectangle requires at least two defining points: an upper left corner and a lower right corner. The **rectangle** command takes the four coordinates of these two points as parameters. Thus, assuming that **upper_x**, **upper_y**, **lower_x**, and **lower_y** are the coordinates of these corners, the following function call would draw a rectangle:

```
rectangle(upper_x, upper_y, lower_x, lower_y)
```

Note that the coordinates passed to this function must be absolute coordinates. However, the **rectangle** function saves the programmer the work of drawing the line segments. Figure 3.1 shows the rectangle produced by the command **rectangle(30, 30, 100, 200)**.

◆ Figure 3.1

The output of
rectangle(30, 30, 100, 200)

To specify a circle, we need to know three things: the coordinates of its center point and the size of its radius. The function **circle** takes these three integer parameters and draws the specified circle. Thus, assuming that **center_x** and **center_y** are the coordinates of a circle's center point, and **radius** is its radius, the following function call would draw a circle:

```
circle(center_x, center_y, radius)
```

Figure 3.2 shows the image produced by the command **circle(100, 100, 50)**. Note that the radius and pairs of coordinates are drawn just as comments.

◆ Figure 3.2

The output of
circle(100, 100, 50)

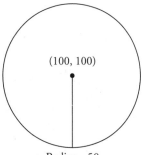

Example 3.7

This program allows the user to enter the position and size of a square and a circle. The positions of the two shapes are relative to a single center point. The sizes of the two shapes are the width of the square and the diameter of the circle. Thus, when they are displayed on the screen, the circle appears enclosed within the square. When the user strikes a key, the shapes are also displayed 200 points to the right.

```cpp
// Program file: sqarcirc.cpp

// Displays a square and a circle whose position and size are
// specified by the user. Copies them 200 points to the right
// when the user strikes a key.

#include <conio.h>
#include <graphics.h>
#include <iostream.h>

int main()
{
    int center_x, center_y, size;
    int upper_x, upper_y, lower_x, lower_y;

    // Obtain input information from the user

    cout << "Enter the center x coordinate: ";
    cin >> center_x;
    cout << "Enter the center y coordinate: ";
    cin >> center_y;
    cout << "Enter the size: ";
    cin >> size;

// Compute the coordinates of the square's corners

    upper_x = center_x - size / 2;
    upper_y = center_y - size / 2;
    lower_x = center_x + size / 2;
    lower_y = center_x + size / 2;

    // Set the graphics mode

    int graphdriver = DETECT, graphmode;
    initgraph(&graphdriver, &graphmode, "c:..\\bgi");

    // Draw the square and the circle

    rectangle(upper_x, upper_y, lower_x, lower_y);
    circle(center_x, center_y, size / 2);

    // Pause for a key to be pressed
```

```
    moveto(100, 250);
    outtext("Strike any key to draw again");
    getch();

    // Redraw the shapes in the new positions

    rectangle(upper_x + 200, upper_y, lower_x + 200, lower_y);
    circle(center_x + 200, center_y, size / 2);

    // Pause for user to signal to continue

    moveto(100, 300);
    outtext("Strike any key to continue");
    getch();

    // Close the graphics mode

    closegraph();
    return 0;
}
```

An arc is a portion of a curve in two dimensions. We can specify an arc with the following values:

1. The coordinates of the center point of the circle of which the arc is a portion
2. The initial angle on the circle in degrees
3. The terminal angle on the circle in degrees
4. The radius of the circle.

Thus, assuming that the parameter names are meaningful, the following function call would draw an arc:

arc(center_x, center_y, start_angle, terminal_angle, radius)

Figure 3.3 shows the image of an arc resulting from the command **arc(100, 100, 0, 90, 50)**. To draw the arc displayed in this figure, the pen travels from the position of the start angle, at 0 degrees, to the position of the end angle, at 90 degrees, thus moving in a counterclockwise direction. Figure 3.4 shows a map of the angles for specifiying arcs.

Changing Foreground and Background Colors

Every set of graphics operations allows the programmer to change the colors used for drawing. On a monochrome system, the palette of colors may contain just black and white or several shades of gray. Color systems have varying numbers of colors. The programmer can set both the foreground color, with which the pen draws lines and text, and the background color, which is used to fill shapes or even the screen itself.

◆ **Figure 3.3**

The output of
`arc(100, 100, 0, 90, 50)`

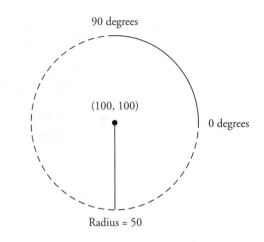

The two commands to perform these tasks are **setcolor** and **setbkcolor**. Each command takes a parameter specifying the desired color. The parameter can be either an integer value or a symbolic constant. A list of these values is shown in Table 3.13.

Suppose we change the program of Example 3.7 such that it erases the shapes before redrawing them at their new positions. This could be accomplished by redrawing the shapes at their first positions in the background color. We assume that the default background color is black, and the default foreground color is white. The following code segment expresses the required changes:

```
// Change foregound color to background color
setcolor(BLACK);

// Draw images, effectively erasing them
rectangle(upper_x, upper_y, lower_x, lower_y);
circle(center_x, center_y, size / 2);

// Return to original foreground color for further drawing
setcolor(WHITE);
```

◆ **Figure 3.4**

Angles for arcs

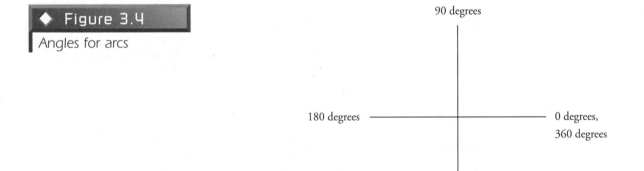

▼ Table 3.13	As an Integer	As a Symbol
Color values expressed as integers and symbols	0	BLACK
	1	BLUE
	2	GREEN
	3	CYAN
	4	RED
	5	MAGENTA
	6	BROWN
	7	LIGHTGRAY
	8	DARKGRAY
	9	LIGHTBLUE
	10	LIGHTGREEN
	11	LIGHTCYAN
	12	LIGHTRED
	13	LIGHTMAGENTA
	14	YELLOW
	15	WHITE

Clearing the Screen

Occasionally, a program must erase all of the images on the screen. A convenient way to do this is to clear the screen with the **cleardevice** command. The following line of code would erase the two images and any text messages from the screen in Example 3.7:

```
cleardevice();
```

This command does not change the foreground color or the background color.

Setting the Line Width and Style

The **setlinestyle** command allows the programmer to specify a line width and a line style for drawing. The form of this command is

```
setlinestyle(<width>, <pattern>, <style>)
```

where **<width>** specifies the line width, **<pattern>** is 0, and **<style>** specifies the line style.

There are two possible widths: 1 (or the symbolic value **NORMALWIDTH**) for a width of one pixel, and 3 (or the symbolic value **THICKWIDTH**) for a width of 3 pixels. The set of possible line styles is listed in Table 3.14.

▼ Table 3.14

Line style values
expressed as integers
and symbols

As an Integer	As a Symbol	Effect
0	SOLID_LINE	────────────
1	DOTTED_LINE	· · · · · · · · · · · · · · · · ·
2	CENTER_LINE	── ─ ── ─ ── ─ ──
3	DASHED_LINE	─ ─ ─ ─ ─ ─ ─ ─
4	USERBIT_LINE	Effect varies

As an example, the following code would display the shapes from Example 3.7 as a square with dotted sides and a circle with a solid, but thick circumference.

```
setlinestyle(1, 0, DOTTED_LINE);
rectangle(upper_x, upper_y, lower_x, lower_y);
setlinestyle(3, 0, SOLID_LINE);
circle(center_x, center_y, size / 2);
```

Determining the Screen Size

It is sometimes useful to know the screen size. For example, one might wish to draw a circle whose center point is the center point of the screen. The coordinates of this point could be computed by dividing the height and width of the screen by 2. The **graphics** library functions **getmaxx** and **getmaxy** return the maximum distances of the screen relative to its origin. Thus, because the origin is the point (0, 0), the point at the lower right corner of the screen would be **(getmaxx(), getmaxy())**.

Example 3.8

The center point and radius of a circle whose diameter is one-half the width of the screen can be computed with the following algorithm:

Set the graphics mode
Set **max_x** to **getmaxx()**
Set **max_y** to **getmaxy()**
Set **center_x** to **max_x / 2**
Set **center_y** to **max_y / 2**
Set **radius** to **max_x / 4**

A complete C++ program for drawing this circle follows:

```
// Program file: centcirc.cpp

// Displays a circle whose diameter is 1/2 the
// width of the screen at the center of the screen.

#include <conio.h>
#include <graphics.h>
```

```
int main()
{
        int center_x, center_y, radius;

        // Set the graphics mode

        int graphdriver = DETECT, graphmode;
        initgraph(&graphdriver, &graphmode, "c:..\\bgi");

        // Compute center point and radius

        center_x = getmaxx() / 2;
        center_y = getmaxy() / 2;
        radius = getmaxx() / 4;

        // Draw the circle

        circle(center_x, center_y, radius);

        // Pause for a key to be pressed

        moveto(100, 250);
        outtext("Strike any key to continue");
        getch();

        // Close the graphics mode

        closegraph();
        return 0;
}
```

■ Exercises 3.8

1. Explain the difference between relative and absolute coordinates. Give examples of graphics commands that use each kind of coordinates.

2. Assume that the current pen position is (50, 65). Translate the following commands to equivalent ones that use relative coordinates:
   a. `moveto(100, 120)`
   b. `lineto(60, 30)`
   c. `moveto(30, 30)`
   d. `lineto(45, 100)`

3. Assume that the current pen position is (50, 65). Translate the following commands to equivalent ones that use absolute coordinates:
   a. `moverel(100, 120)`
   b. `linerel(60, 30)`
   c. `moverel(-30, 30)`
   d. `linerel(45, -20)`

4. Write a code segment that takes an input radius and center point coordinates and draws three concentric circles. The inputs should specify the most deeply enclosed circle (the smallest one). The diameter of each enclosing circle should be half again the size of the the circle it encloses.

5. Modify the code segment of Exercise 4 so that each circle is a randomly chosen color (use the random number generator discussed in Section 3.6).

6. Draw pictures of the images that would be displayed by the following commands:
   a. `rectangle(20, 20, 100, 100)`
   b. `arc(100, 100, 0, 180)`
   c. `arc(100, 100, 90, 270, 50)`

7. Write a code segment that displays an image of a wagon wheel. The wheel should have six evenly spaced spokes, a hub, and be thick around the rim.

8. Write a code segment that causes a rectangle to be displayed using the default line style and then redisplayed using a dotted line style. The color should remain the same. You may assume that the coordinates of the corners are already specified by the variables **x1**, **y1**, **x2**, and **y2**.

The Case Study sections contain complete programs to illustrate concepts developed in the chapter. In each case, a typical problem is stated, a solution is developed in pseudocode and illustrated with a structure chart, and module specifications are written for the appropriate modules.

Focus on Program Design: Case Study

Computing the Cost of Pizza

Write a complete program to find the unit price for a pizza. Input for the program consists of the price and size of the pizza. Size is the diameter of the pizza ordered. Output consists of the price per square inch. A first-level development is

1. Get the data
2. Perform the computations
3. Print the results

A structure chart for this problem is given in Figure 3.5. Module specifications for the main modules are

Module: Get data
Task: Get cost and size of pizza from the user at the keyboard.
Output: The cost and size

Module: Compute price per square inch
Task: Compute the price per square inch of pizza.
Input: Cost and size of pizza
Output: Price per square inch

Module: Print results
Task: Print the price per square inch.
Input: Price per square inch

A further refinement of the pseudocode produces

◆ Figure 3.5

Structure chart for the pizza problem

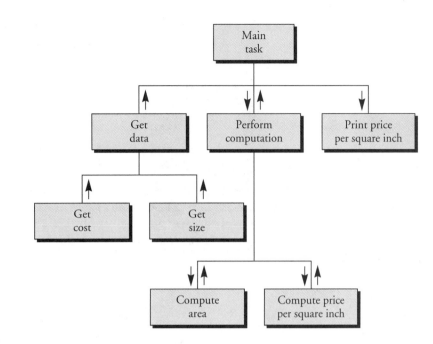

1. Get the data
   1.1 Get price
   1.2 Get size
2. Perform the computations
   2.1 Compute area
   2.2 Calculate unit price

Step 3 of the pseudocode, "Print the results," only requires printing the price per square inch, so no further development is required.

A complete program for this problem follows:

```cpp
// Program file: pizza.cpp

#include <iostream.h>
#include <iomanip.h>
#include <math.h>

const double PI = 3.14;

int main ()
{

    double size, radius, cost, area, price_per_square_inch;

    // This module gets the data.
```

```cpp
cout << "Enter the pizza price and press <Enter>. ";
cin >> cost;
cout << "Enter the pizza size and press <Enter>. ";
cin >> size;
```

1

```
// This module computes the unit price.
```

```
radius = size / 2;
area = PI * pow(radius, 2);
price_per_square_inch = cost / area;
```
2

```
// This module prints the results.
```

```
cout << setiosflags(ios::fixed | ios::showpoint | ios::right)
     << setprecision(2) << endl;
cout << "The price per square inch is $" << setw(4)
     << price_per_square_inch << endl;
```
3

```
return 0;
}
```

A sample run of this program yields

```
Enter the pizza price and press <Enter>. 10.50
Enter the pizza size and press <Enter>. 16
The price per square inch is $0.05
```

Summary

🔑 Key Terms

absolute coordinates	input	real arithmetic operations:
argument	inserter	+, −, *, /
assignment statement	integer arithmetic	real overflow
binary arithmetic	operations: +, −,	relative coordinates
binary notation	*, /, %	representational error
cancellation error	integer overflow	round-off error
character arithmetic	interactive input	seed
character set	invoke (call)	self-documenting code
class	library (built-in) function	type cast
collating sequence: ASCII	member function	type promotion
compound assignment	memory location	underflow
concatenation	mixed-mode expression	user-friendly
constant	ordinal data type	variable
explicit type conversion	precedence rule	word
extractor		

🔑 Key Concepts

◆ Operations and priorities for data of type **int** and **double** are summarized as follows:

Data Type	Operations	Priority
int	*, %, /	1. Evaluate in order from left to right.
	+, −	2. Evaluate in order from left to right.
double	*, /	1. Evaluate in order from left to right.
	+, −	2. Evaluate in order from left to right.

◆ Mixed-mode expressions involving **int** and **double** values return values of type **double**.

◆ Priority for order of operations on mixed-mode expressions is

1. *, /, in order from left to right
2. +, − in order from left to right.

◆ Overflow is caused by a value too large for computing on a particular machine.

◆ Underflow is caused by a value too small (close to zero) for computing. These numbers are automatically replaced by zero.

◆ A memory location can have a name that can be used to refer to the contents of the location.

◆ The name of a memory location is different from the contents of the memory location.

◆ Self-documenting code is code that is written using descriptive identifiers.

◆ Assignment statements are used to assign values to memory locations; for example,

```
sum = 30 + 60;
```

◆ Compound assignment can be used as shorthand for a calculation and assignment; for example,

```
sum += a;
```

◆ Variables and variable expressions can be used in output statements.

◆ **cin** is used to get data; the correct form is

```
cin >> <variable 1> >> <variable 2> ··· >> <variable n>;
```

◆ **cin** >> **<variable>;** causes a value to be transferred to the variable location.

◆ Interactive input expects data items to be entered from the keyboard at appropriate times during execution of the program.

◆ Data types for variables in an input statement should match data items read as input.

◆ The **apstring** library defines the **apstring** type. The programmer can declare string variables of this type. Among the operations defined for **apstring** variables are **>>**, **<<**, **=**, **getline**, and **length**.

◆ Appropriate uses for constants in the declaration section include frequently used numbers; current values subject to change over time; for example, **(MINIMUM_WAGE = 4.25)**.

◆ Five math library functions available in C++ are **pow**, **sqrt**, **sin**, **cos**, and **tan**.

◆ Functions can be used in assignment statements, for example,

```
x = sqrt(16.0);
```

in output statements,

```
cout << pow(-8, 2);
```

and in arithmetic expressions,

```
x = sqrt(3.78) + pow(5, 5);
```

◆ The **stdlib** library function **rand** returns a random number between 0 and the **stdlib** library constant **RAND_MAX**.

◆ The **stdlib** library function **srand** can be used to initialize the seed value for random numbers to a programmer-specified value.

◆ The library function **time** returns the current time on the computer's clock. This value can be converted to an integer and used to initialize the seed for a sequence of random numbers.

◆ Type casts can be used to convert one type of value to another type; for example,

```
int(3.14)
```

Chapter Review Exercises

For Exercises 1–3, write variable declarations.
1. An integer called **a**.
2. Real numbers named **number1**, **number2**, and **number3**.
3. A character variable called **first** and a real number called **second**.

For Exercises 4–13, if **a** is an **int**, **b** is a **double**, and **c** is a **char**, what is the type of value returned by each expression?
4. **a - b**
5. **a / 3.0**
6. **a / 3**
7. **a + c**
8. **int(c)**
9. **int(b)**
10. **sqrt(a * b)**
11. **c % a**
12. **char(a)**
13. **sqrt(a)**

Write constant definitions for Exercises 14–16.
14. The number of miles you live from your school

15. The number of ounces in a pound
16. The room number of your computer science class
17. Explain the difference between the input of character data and the input of numeric data

For Exercises 18–21, suppose the data line

```
AB 5 6.7 C
```

is entered into a program that uses the following variables:

```
int x, y;
double j, k;
char m, n, p;
```

Explain what happens when each statement is executed.
18. `cin >> m >> n >> x >> j >> p;`
19. `cin >> m >> n >> a >> b;`
20. `cin >> m >> n >> j >> p;`
21. `cin >> m >> n >> p >> j >> k;`

For Exercises 22–25, find the value of the expression.
22. `sqr(4) - abs(-12) * round(0.6)`
23. `sqrt(abs(-25)) - sqr(5.2)`
24. `34 % 10`
25. `int(char(67))`

Programming Problems and Activities

Write a complete C++ program for each of the following problems. Each program should use one or more input statements to obtain the necessary values. Each input statement should be preceded by an appropriate prompting message.
1. Susan purchases a computer for $985. The sales tax on the purchase is 5.5%. Compute and print the total purchase price.
2. Find and print the area and perimeter of a rectangle that is 4.5 feet long and 2.3 feet wide. Print both rounded to the nearest tenth of a foot.
3. Compute and print the number of minutes in a year.
4. Light travels at 3×10^8 meters per second. Compute and print the distance a light beam would travel in one year. (This is called a light-year.)
5. The 1927 New York Yankees won 110 games and lost 44. Compute their winning percentage and print it rounded to three decimal places.
6. A 10-kilogram object is traveling at 12 meters per second. Compute and print its momentum (momentum is mass times velocity).
7. Convert 98.0 degrees Fahrenheit to degrees Celsius.
8. Given a positive number, print its square and square root.
9. The Golden Sales Company pays its salespeople $0.27 for each item they sell. Given the number of items sold by a salesperson, print the amount of pay due.
10. Given the length and width of a rectangle, print its area and perimeter.
11. The kinetic energy of a moving object is given by the formula $KE = (1/2)mv^2$. Given the mass (m) and the speed (v) of an object, find its kinetic energy.

12. Matthew Moneypenny wants a program to enable him to balance his checkbook. He wishes to enter a beginning balance, five letters for an abbreviation for the recipient of the check, and the amount of the check. Given this information, write a program that will find the new balance in his checkbook.

13. A supermarket wants to install a computerized weighing system in its produce department. Input to this system will consist of a single-letter identifier for the type of produce, the weight of the produce purchase (in pounds), and the cost per pound of the produce. A typical input screen would be

```
Enter each of the following:

Description <Enter> A
Weight <Enter> 2.0
Price/lb. <Enter> 1.98
```

Print a label showing the input information along with the total cost of the purchase. The label should appear as follows:

```
%%%%%%%%%%%%%%%%%%%%%%%%%%%%%%%%%%%%%%%%%

          Penny Spender Supermarket
             Produce Department

    ITEM        WEIGHT        COST/lb        COST

    A           2.0 lb        $1.98          $3.96

             Thank you!

%%%%%%%%%%%%%%%%%%%%%%%%%%%%%%%%%%%%%%%%%
```

14. The New Wave Computer Company sells its product, the NW-PC, for $675. In addition, they sell memory expansion cards for $69.95, disk drives for $198.50, and software for $34.98 each. Given the number of memory cards, disk drives, and software packages desired by a customer purchasing an NW-PC, print a bill of sale that appears as follows:

```
***************************

        New Wave Computers

        ITEM                        COST
1 NW-PC                           $675.00
2 Memory card                      139.90
1 Disk drive                       198.50
4 Software                         139.92

        TOTAL                     $1153.32
```

15. Write an interactive program that allows you to see the characters contained within the character set of your computer. Given a positive integer as input, you can use the **char** type cast to determine the corresponding character. On most computers, only integers less than 256 are valid for this. Also, remember that most character sets contain some unprintable characters such as ASCII values less than 32. Print your output in the following form:

```
Character number nnn is x.
```

16. Mr. Vigneault, a coach at Shepherd High School, is working on a program that can be used to assist cross-country runners in analyzing their times. As part of the program, a coach enters elapsed times for each runner given in units of minutes, seconds, and hundredths. In a 5000-meter (5K) race, elapsed times are entered at the one-mile and two-mile marks. These elapsed times are then used to compute "splits" for each part of the race; that is, the time it took a runner to run each of the three race segments. Write a complete program that will accept as input three times given in units of minutes, seconds, and hundredths and then produce output that includes the split for each segment. Typical input would be

```
Runner number    234

Mile times:   1   5:34.22

              2   11:21.67

Finish time:      17:46.85
```

Typical output would be

```
Runner number    234

Split one        5:34.22

Split two        5:47.45

Split three      6:25.18

Finish time      17:46.85
```

17. The Swim-More Pool Installation Company installs rectangular swimming pools surrounded by a cement edge that extends three feet from each side of the pool. The cement is poured to a uniform depth of four inches. Write a program that accepts as input the dimensions of the pool and then provides as output the number of cubic yards of cement needed along with the total cost of the cement. Use a constant to define the price per yard. Contact a local cement company to obtain the current price.

18. Rewrite the program of Example 2.1 (the Müller-Lyer illusion) using two colors to draw the line segments. The two parallel line segments should be one color,

and the remaining line segments should be the other color. Test the program to see if the image still causes the illusion of unequal line segments.

19. Rewrite the program of Problem 18 so that it uses two randomly generated colors to draw the different sets of line segments. Run the program several times to determine which pairs of colors make the line segments seem most equal or most unequal in length.

20. Write a complete program that draws four circles. The radius of each circle should be one-eighth of the size of the screen. The center of each circle should be the center of a separate quadrant of the screen.

21. Write a complete program that displays the image of a stick figure.

22. Modify the program of Problem 21 so that the user can input the coordinates of the center point of the stick figure. The figure's center point should be a point halfway between the top of the figure's head and the bottom of the figure's legs.

23. Modify the program of Problem 22 so that the user can specify the size of the stick figure. The size of the figure should be the height and width of the rectangular area that bounds the figure's image.

Communication in Practice

1. Read at least two articles on the issue of copyright and digital information (see the **Note of Interest** on copyright in this chapter), and prepare a report on this topic to present to your class.

2. Modify one of the programs you have written for this chapter by changing all constant and variable identifiers to single-letter words. Exchange your modified program with another student who has done the same thing. After reading the exchanged program, discuss the use of meaningful identifiers with the other student. Suggest identifiers for the program that you have read.

3. Many (but not all) teachers in beginning computer science courses encourage their students to use meaningful identifiers in writing code. It is natural to wonder to what extent this practice is followed outside the educational world. Investigate this issue by contacting several programmers who work for nearby companies. Prepare a complete written report of your conversations for distribution to class members. Include charts that summarize your findings.

Subprograms: Functions for Problem Solving

R ecall from Section 2.1 the process of solving a problem by top-down design and stepwise refinement of tasks into subtasks. The structure of a top-down design can be reflected in a C++ program that uses **subprograms.**

The concept of a subprogram is not difficult to understand. It is a program within a program and is provided by most programming languages. Each subprogram should complete some task, the nature of which can range from simple to complex. You could have a subprogram that prints only a line of data, or you could rewrite an entire program as a subprogram. To extend the metaphor of the programmable pocket calculator introduced in Chapter 3, we create a subprogram by giving a name to a sequence of program statements. We then specify the data that this sequence will take as inputs and return as outputs. Next, we store this name with the built-in functions in the calculator. Finally, we use the name as if it were a built-in function wherever it is appropriate in any program.

4.1 Program Design

Objectives

◆ to understand the concepts of modularity and bottom-up testing

◆ to be aware of the use of structured programming

Modularity

We have previously discussed and illustrated the process of solving a problem by top-down design. Using this method, we divide the main task into major subtasks, and then continue to divide the subtasks (stepwise refinement) into smaller subtasks until all subtasks can be easily performed. Once an algorithm for solving a problem has been developed using top-down design, the programmer then writes code to translate the general solution into a C++ program.

127

A Note of Interest

Structured Programming

From 1950 to the early 1970s programs were designed and written on a linear basis. Programs written and designed on such a basis can be called **unstructured programs.** These programs consist of long linear sequences of statements. Control flows from each statement in the sequence to the next statement, unless it is transferred by means of a **GOTO** statement. Structured programming, on the other hand, organizes a program around separate semi-independent modules that are linked by a single sequence of simple commands, including structured control statements for selection and iteration (see Chapters 5 and 6).

In 1964, mathematicians Corrado Bohm and Guiseppe Jacopini proved that any program logic, regardless of complexity, can be expressed by using the control structures of sequencing, selection, and iteration. This result is termed the **structure theorem.** This theorem, combined with the efforts of Edger W. Dijkstra, led to a significant move toward structured programming and away from the use of **GOTO** statements.

In fact, in a letter to the editor of <u>Communications of the ACM</u> (Volume 11, March 1968), Dijkstra stated that the **GOTO** statement "should be abolished from all 'higher level' programming languages . . . . [The **GOTO** statement] is just too primitive; it is too much an invitation to make a mess of one's program."

Structured programming concepts were applied to a large-scale data processing application the first time in the IBM Corporation's "New York Times Project," which ran from 1969 to 1971. Using these techniques, programmers posted productivity figures from four to six times higher than those of the average programmer. In addition, the error rate was a phenomenally low 0.0004 per line of coding.

---

subprogram: A program within a program.

abstract data type (ADT): A class of objects, a defined set of properties of those objects, and a set of operations for processing the objects.

modularity: The organization of a program into independent units.

bottom-up testing: Independent testing of modules.

As you have seen, code written to perform one well-defined subtask can be referred to as a module. One should be able to design, code, and test each module in a program independently from the rest of the program. In this sense, a module is a subprogram containing all definitions and declarations needed to perform the indicated subtask. Everything required for the subtask (but not needed in other parts of the program) can be created in the subprogram. Consequently, the definitions and declarations have meaning only when the module is being used.

At the lowest level in a programming language like C++, a module is a single function. However, one can also think, at a higher level in a design, of a module as consisting of several functions and related data. One important kind of higher level module of this sort is known as an **abstract data type.** The design and construction of abstract data type modules are discussed in some detail in Chapters 9, 10, and 11. You have already been using some standard abstract data type modules whenever you have used the operations on integers, real numbers, and characters in your C++ programs.

A program that has been created using modules to perform various tasks is said to possess **modularity.** In general, modular programs are easier to test, debug, and correct than programs that are not modular because each independent module can be tested by running it from a test driver. Then, once the modules are running correctly, they can become part of a longer program. This independent testing of modules is referred to as **bottom-up testing.** A modular program is also easier to maintain than a nonmodular program, because we can replace one module without modifying the other modules at all. For example, a new version of the C++ compiler might provide faster operations for floating-point arithmetic in the module that defines these operations. All you would have to do to maintain your system is to recompile your program.

Structured Programming and Design

Structured programming is the process of developing a program where emphasis is placed on the flow of control between independent modules. **Structured design** is the process of organizing communication between modules. Connections between these modules are specified in parameter lists and are usually controlled by the main program. Structured programming and design are especially suitable to large programs being worked on by teams. By carefully designing the modules and specifying what information is to be received by and returned from the module, a team of programmers can independently develop a module and then connect it to the complete program.

The remainder of this chapter is devoted to seeing how subprograms can be written to accomplish specific tasks. Subprograms in C++ are called *functions*. We discussed library functions in Section 3.6. We will now learn how to write our own functions.

structured programming: Programming that parallels a solution to a problem achieved by top-down design.

structured design: A method of designing software by specifying modules and the flow of data among them.

4.2 User-Defined Functions

Objectives

- to understand the need for user-defined functions
- to be able to use correct syntax when declaring and implementing a function
- to be able to use stubs and drivers to test functions

User-defined functions resemble the library functions **sqrt** and **pow** that were introduced in Section 3.6. To review briefly, note the following concepts when using these functions:

1. An argument is required for each; thus, **sqrt(y)** and **pow(2, 5)** are appropriate.
2. Functions can be used in expressions; for example,

   ```
   x = sqrt(y) + sqrt(z);
   ```

3. Functions can be used in output statements; for example,

   ```
   cout << setw(8) << setprecision(2) << sqrt(3);
   ```

Need for User-Defined Functions

It is relatively easy to envision the need for functions that are not on the list of library functions available in C++. For example, if you must frequently cube numbers, it would be convenient to have a function named **cube** that would allow you to make an assignment such as

```
x = cube(y);
```

Other examples from mathematics include computing a factorial (*n*!), computing a discriminant ($b^2 - 4ac$), and finding roots of a quadratic equation:

$$\frac{-b \pm \sqrt{b^2 - 4ac}}{2a}$$

In business, a motel might need to have available a function to determine a customer's bill given the number in the party, the length of stay, and any telephone charges. Similarly, a hospital might like a function to compute the room charge for a patient given the type of room (private, ward, and so on) and various other options, including telephone (yes or no) and television (yes or no). Functions such as these are not library functions. However, in C++, we can create **user-defined functions** to perform these tasks. The following diagram illustrates the components of a simple C++ program that has one user-defined function:

user-defined function:
A new function introduced and defined by the programmer.

```
#include <iostream.h>

// Function: cube
// Computes the cube of a number
//
// Input: a number
// Output: a number representing the cube of the input

double cube (double x);

int main()
{
    double number;

    cout << "Enter a number followed by <Enter>. "
    cin >> number;
    cout << "The cube of " << number << " is "
        << cube(number) << endl;
    return 0;
}

double cube(double x);
{
    return x * x * x;
}
```

Function Declarations

In the previous two chapters of this text, you learned how to import library functions from library files with the **#include** directive, and then how to invoke or call these functions in your application program. An important point to remember is that you do not know anything about how these functions are written or *implemented*. All you know is the *declaration* of a function. A **function declaration** consists of the function's name, the number and kind of arguments it expects when you invoke it, and the type of value, if any, that it returns when its job is done. A function's declaration gives you all the information you need to know in order to use the function, and no more. For example, the declaration of the library function **pow** might be written as follows:

function declaration:
A form that contains a function's name, parameter declarations, and return type.

```
double pow(double base, double exponent);
```

The first word in this expression, **double**, tells us the type of value returned by the function. The second word, **pow**, is the name of the function. The words enclosed in the parentheses and separated by commas denote the types of arguments expected when the function is invoked, that is, two arguments of type **double**. Note that the names used for these arguments, **base** and **exponent**, also serve to document the role that they play in the function.

The general form for a function declaration is

<return type> <function name> (<list of argument specifiers>) **;**

to which the following comments apply:

1. **<function name>** is any valid identifier.
2. The function name should be descriptive.
3. **<return type>** declares the data type for the function name. This indicates what type of value, if any, will be returned to the caller.

It is good programming practice to supply with a declaration some comments that describe the inputs or data received by the function (its *arguments*) and the output or information returned (its *value* or *result*). In addition, we might specify any assumptions about the function's arguments that must be satisfied so that the function can perform its task correctly. For example, the function **sqrt** assumes that its argument is not just any **double**, but a nonnegative **double**. Therefore, we supply a comment about the function's arguments and value:

```
// Function: sqrt
// Compute the square root of a double-precision floating-point number
//
// Input: a nonnegative double-precision floating-point number
// Output: a nonnegative double-precision floating-point number
// representing the square root of the data received

double sqrt(double x);
```

Note that we have given the reader no information about *how* the function performs its task. Nonetheless, the reader has enough information to invoke or use the function. This is the kind of function declaration and comment that we will use in examples of user-defined functions throughout this text. Hereafter, when we say "function declaration," we mean a C++ function declaration and any supporting comments. Writing out all of your function declarations in this way will encourage you to think in terms of the uses for your functions before you become immersed in their implementation details.

Declaring Functions in a Program

Before you can use functions that you write yourself, you must provide declarations for them. All function declarations, if there are any, should appear in the region of your source program file between the global data declarations and the main program heading:

```
[ preprocessor directives

[ global data declarations

 ┌ function declaration 1
 │ .
 │ .
 └ function declaration n

 ┌ int main()
 │ {
 │       main program data declarations
 │
 │       statements
 │ }
 └

 ┌ function implementation 1
 │ .
 │ .
 └ function implementation n
```

Implementing Functions in a Program

After you have decided how your functions will be used and what their declarations will be, and after you have written a main program that will call them, you can turn to the job of implementing or writing them. A **function implementation** describes in detail how the function performs its task. Simply put, a function implementation is a complete, brief program that produces some effects if certain assumptions about the arguments to the function are satisfied. For example, let's assume that the data value **x** is a number. Then the following expression produces the square of the number:

function implementation: A detailed, complete, and executable description of a function.

```
x * x
```

We can use this expression to implement a function **sqr(x)**, where **x** is any number, as follows:

```
double sqr(double x)
{
        return x * x;
}
```

function heading: The portion of a function implementation containing the function's name, parameter declarations, and return type.

You will note that the first line of the implementation, called the **function heading,** looks almost like a function declaration. The only difference is that the semicolon following the right parenthesis is omitted. The rest of the implementation after the heading is a little program block. Like the main program block, this block contains optional data declarations and at least one executable statement. The single statement in our example says that the block will return (as the value of the function) the result of multiplying **x** (the argument of the function) by itself. The form for a function implementation is

---

<function heading>
{
                            <optional data declarations>
                            <executable statements>
}

Function Headings

A function heading in a C++ program must match up with a corresponding function declaration. The return type and the function name must be the same in the heading as they are in the declaration, and the types of the arguments must match in the same positions. In addition, each type in the argument list of a function heading must be followed by an argument name, usually called a **formal parameter.** The number of formal parameters must be the same as the number of arguments (usually called **actual parameters**) used when the function is called. Thus, if you are writing a function to compute the area of a rectangle and you want to call the function from the main program by

formal parameter:
A name, declared and used in a function declaration, that is replaced by an actual parameter when the function is called.

actual parameter
(synonym: **argument**):
A variable or expression contained in a function call and passed to that function.

```
rect_area = area(width, length);
```

the function implementation might have

```
int area (int w, int l)
```

as a heading. The two formal parameters, **w** and **l**, correspond to the actual parameters, **width** and **length**. In general, you should make sure the formal parameter list and actual parameter list match up as indicated:

```
(int w, int l)
(width, length)
```

A function to compute the cube of an integer could use the following as a heading:

```
int cube(int x)
```

The general form for a function heading is

<return type> <function name> (<list of formal parameters>)

Using this general form, we note the following:
1. **<function name>** is any valid identifier.
   a. The function name should be descriptive.
   b. If it is expected, some value should be returned in the executable section of the function.
2. **<return type>** declares the data type for the function name. This indicates what type of value will be returned to the caller, if expected.
3. The list of formal parameters consists of a series of pairs of names, where the first name in the pair is the name of a data type, and the second name is the name of a formal parameter. The pairs in the list must be separated by commas.

Hereafter in this chapter, when we say *heading*, we mean a C++ function heading.

The types of the formal parameters in a function heading must also match the types of the arguments used when the function is called. The compiler uses the same type checking rules for matching the types of formal and actual parameters as it does for matching the operands of an assignment statement. When an actual parameter passed to a function is not exactly the same type as the formal parameter in its position, the compiler checks to see whether or not the actual parameter's type can be automatically converted to the type of the formal parameter. For example, an integer value passed to a function that expects a **double** would be converted to a **double** before being processed in the function. Conversely, a **double** that is passed to a function expecting an **int** would be automatically truncated to an **int**.

Data and Executable Statements in a Function Implementation

As in the main program, a function does not have to have a declaration section, but when there is one, only constants and variables needed in the function should be declared. Further, the section is usually not very elaborate because the purpose of a function is normally a small, single task.

The executable statement section of a function's implementation has the same form as the executable statement section of the main program. Remember that at least one statement, of the form **return <expression>**, should return the value of the function if a returned value is expected.

We now illustrate user-defined functions with several examples.

Example 4.1

Implement a function to compute the cube of an integer. First, consider what a typical call to this function from the main program will look like:

```
a = cube(5);
```

Then decide what the assumptions about the arguments are, what the effects of the function will be, and write down a function declaration:

```
// Function: cube
// Computes the cube of an integer
```

```
//
// Input: a number
// Output: a number representing the cube of the input

double cube (double x);
```

To match this declaration, we have as an implementation

```
double cube (double x)
{
      return x * x * x;
}
```

Example 4.2

Let's write a function to perform the task of computing unit cost for pizza. Data sent to the function are size and cost. The function returns the unit cost. Formal parameters are cost and size. We invoke the function, using the name **price_per_square_inch** as follows:

```
unit_cost = price_per_square_inch(cost, price);
```

Therefore, we write the declaration

```
// Function: price_per_square_inch
// Computes the price per square inch of pizza
//
// Input: two positive real numbers representing the cost
// in dollars and cents and the diameter in inches of a pizza
// Output: a real number representing the price, in dollars
// and cents, per square inch of pizza

double price_per_square_inch(double cost, double size);
```

The implementation then is

```
double price_per_square_inch(double cost, double size)
{
      double radius, area;

      radius = size / 2.0;
      area = PI * sqr(radius);
      return cost / area;
}
```

locally declared data:
Data declared within a block, usually the block of the main program or a function.

You should note that this function has some **locally declared data.** The variables **radius** and **area** are declared within the local block of the function, because they are needed only for computing the area of a pizza. In general, data that are not needed elsewhere in a program should be declared locally within functions. You should also note that there are two important, unstated assumptions made by this implementation: first, the constant **PI** must be defined; and second, the function **sqr** must be declared. These names can be defined or declared in the area above the main program. The function **sqr** must then also be implemented, along with the function **price_per_square_inch**, after the main program.

Example 4.3

We want to implement a function that converts digits to integer values. Our version of the function, called **char_to_int**, has the following declaration:

```
// Function: char_to_int
// Computes the integer value of a digit
//
// Input: a digit
// Output: the integer value represented by the digit

int char_to_int(char ch);
```

The implementation uses the method we developed in Chapter 3:

```
int char_to_int(char ch)
{
      return ch - '0';
}
```

Use in a Program

Now that you have seen several examples of user-defined functions, let us consider their use in a program. Once they are written, they can be used in the same manner as library functions. This usually means in one of the following forms.

1. Assignment statements:

```
a = 5;

b = cube(a);
```

2. Arithmetic expressions:

```
a = 5;

a = 3 * cube(a) + 2;
```

3. Output statements:

```
    a = 5;
    cout << setw(17) << cube(a) << endl;
```

Using Stubs

stub programming:
The process of using incomplete functions to test data transmission among them.

As programs get longer and incorporate more subprograms, a technique frequently used to get the program running is **stub programming.** A stub program is a no-frills, simple version of what will be a final program. It does not contain details of output and full algorithm development. It does contain declarations and rough implementations of each subprogram. When the stub version runs, you know your logic is correct and values are appropriately being passed to and from subprograms. Then you can fill in the necessary details to get a complete program.

Using Drivers

main driver: The main program when subprograms are used to accomplish specific tasks.

The main program is sometimes referred to as the **main driver.** When subprograms are used in a program, this driver can be modified to check subprograms in a sequential fashion. For example, you can start with a main driver that gets some input data:

```
// Program file: driver.cpp

#include <iostream.h>

int main()
{
    int data;

    cout << "Enter an integer: ";
    cin >> data;
    return 0;
}
```

You can think of this driver as a "function factory" for building and testing functions. First, you add a function declaration, and then a rough implementation of the function that simply returns a value, usually, the value of one of the arguments of the function. You test this function stub by placing a call to the function, with an input value, inside of an output statement in the main driver. If you were building the **sqr** function, your next version of the program would look like this:

```
// Program file: driver.cpp

#include <iostream.h>

// Function: sqr
// Computes the square of a number
//
```

```
// Input: a double-precision floating-point number
// Output: a double-precision floating-point number
// representing the square of the input

double sqr(double x);

int main()
{
        int data;

        cout << "Enter an integer: ";
        cin >> data;
        cout <<"The square is " << sqr(data) << endl;
        return 0;
}

double sqr(double x)
{
        return x;
}
```

Once you are sure that a subprogram is running and that data are being transmitted properly to it, you can proceed to fill in the rest of the details of its implementation. In the case of the **sqr** function, you merely substitute **x * x** for **x** in the **return** statement, and test the driver again. As you complete the implementation, you can be more confident that the function will return the values expected.

Functions Without Returned Values (void Functions)

Some functions require data to do their work, but return no values to their callers. For example, displaying several values with their labels to the terminal screen is such a task. This function might be called as follows:

```
display_results(result1, result2, result3);
```

The implementation of this function would probably send the parameter values and the appropriate string labels to the standard output stream. Note that the function call appears all by itself in a complete C++ statement. That is, a value is not assigned to a variable or passed on as an intermediate value within a more complex expression. Functions of this sort are called **void functions** because they return no values. The example function is declared as follows:

void function: A function that returns no value.

```
void display_results(int result1, int result2, int result3);
```

The reserved word **void** indicates that the function is not meant to return a value. When a **void** function is implemented, it need not end with a return statement:

```
void display_results(int result1, int result2, int result3)
{
    cout << "The first result is " << result1 << endl;
    cout << "The second result is " << result2 << endl;
    cout << "The third result is " << result3 << endl;
}
```

The declarations of **void** functions have the following form:

---

void <function name> (<list of argument specifiers>) ;

Functions Without Parameters

Occasionally, a function is needed to do some work without receiving any data from the caller. It may or may not return a value as well. An example of such a function is one whose task is that of displaying a chunk of text as a header for a table of output data. One might invoke this function as follows:

```
display_header();
```

This function takes no data from parameters, and returns no value to the caller. Its sole purpose is to display some text on the terminal screen. Its declaration is

```
void display_header();
```

Its implementation might display a header for a table of names and grades:

```
void display_header()
{
    cout << "GRADES FOR COMPUTER SCIENCE 110" << endl;
    cout << endl;
    cout << "Student Name                      Grade" << endl;
    cout << "------------                      -----" << endl;
}
```

Another example of this kind of function would display a sign-on or greeting at the start of a program.

An example of a function that takes no parameters, but still returns a result to the caller, would be a function that controls interactive input. The function prompts the user for input, reads the input value, and then returns it to the caller. The function might be used as follows:

```
data = get_integer();
```

Note that since this function returns a value, the value should be used by the caller. In this example, the value is stored in a variable with an assignment statement. A declaration for the function is

```
int get_integer();
```

Its implementation would prompt the user for an integer value, read it in from the standard input stream, and then return it as the value of the function. Because a place is needed to store the value during input, we declare a local variable for this purpose within the function:

```
int get_integer()
{
    int data;

    cout << "Enter an integer value, followed by <Enter>. ";
    cin >> data;
    return data;
}
```

Functions with Strings

Often it is useful to write functions that take strings as parameters. For example, we could rewrite the **get_integer** function so that the prompt could be passed as a string parameter. The following code segment shows how this version of **get_integer** could be called to present the user with two different prompts:

```
int length, width;

length = get_integer("Enter the length: ");
width = get_integer("Enter the width: ");
```

The caller provides the exact form of the prompt to be displayed, and the function takes care of displaying it and reading the data. The declaration of this function would be

```
int get_integer(apstring prompt);
```

The implementation displays the string parameter with an output statement.

```
int get_integer(apstring prompt)
{
    int data;

    cout << prompt;
    cin >> data;
    return data;
}
```

Communication and Style Tips

It is considered good programming practice to design a function that is as **general** as possible. General functions solve a **class** of problems rather than a particular problem. For example, separate functions to prompt for and input the length and the width solve particular problems, whereas a single function to get any integer value solves both of these particular problems, as well as others. You should strive to make your functions as general as those you find in the C++ libraries. Designing general functions from scratch is not an easy thing to do. Frequently, you will not spot the need for a general function until you have written several more specialized functions that reveal a common or redundant pattern of code. When that happens, you can take two steps to design a more general function. First, write a single function that contains the common pattern of code that you see in the more specialized functions. Second, add parameters that will allow the callers of the new function to use it for their more specialized purposes.

Note that the use of parameters makes this version of **get_integer** more general than the first version of **get_integer**. In the first version, the programmer specifies a particular prompt in the body of the function. The use of other prompts would require other function definitions. By making the prompt a parameter of the function in the second version, the same function can be defined once and invoked with many different particular prompts.

A similar function could be developed to obtain a string as input and return it as a value.

```
apstring get_string(apstring prompt)
{
        apstring data;

        cout << prompt;
        cin >> data;
        return data;
}
```

Exercises 4.2

1. Indicate which of the following are valid function declarations. Explain what is wrong with those that are invalid.
    a. `round_tenth (double x);`
    b. `double make_change (X, Y);`
    c. `int max (int x, int y, int z);`
    d. `char sign (double x);`
    e. `void output_string(apstring s);`

2. Find all errors in each of the following functions:
   a.
```
int average (int n1, int n2);
{
        return N1 + N2 / 2;
}
```
   b.
```
int total (int n1, int n2)
{
        int sum;
        return 0;
        sum = n1 + n2;
}
```

3. Write a function for each of the following:
   a. Round a real number to the nearest tenth.
   b. Round a real number to the nearest hundredth.
   c. Convert degrees Fahrenheit to degrees Celsius.
   d. Compute the charge for cars at a parking lot; the rate is 75 cents per hour or fraction thereof.

4. Write a program that uses the function you wrote for Exercise 3.d. to print a ticket for a customer who parks in the parking lot. Assume the input is in minutes.

5. Use the functions **sqr** and **cube** to write a program to print a chart of the integers 1 to 5 together with their squares and cubes. Output from this program should be as follows:

Number	Number Squared	Number Cubed
1	1	1
2	4	8
3	9	27
4	16	64
5	25	125

6. Write a program that contains a function that allows the user to enter a base (a) and exponent (x) and then have the program print the value of a^x.

7. What role do parameters play in a function?

8. Explain the difference between formal parameters and actual parameters.

9. Why is it a good idea to write functions that are as general as possible?

4.3 Parameters

Objectives

◆ to be able to understand the need for and appropriate use of parameters in functions

◆ to be able to understand the difference between value and reference parameters

Value Parameters

We have seen that parameters are used so that data values can be transmitted, or passed, from the caller to a function. Several different **parameter modes,** or ways of transmitting data to a function, are available. If values are to be passed *only* from the caller to a function, the parameters are called **value parameters.** The following program demonstrates the use of value parameters:

```cpp
// Program file: area.cpp

#include <iostream.h>

// Function: area
// Computes the area of a rectangle
//
// Inputs: two integers representing the length and the width
// of the rectangle
// Outputs: an integer representing the area of the rectangle

int area(int length, int width);

int main()
{
    int this_length, this_width;

    cout << "Enter the length: ";
    cin >> this_length;
    cout << "Enter the width: ";
    cin >> this_width;
    cout << "The area is " << area(this_length, this_width)
        << endl;
    return 0;
}

int area(int length, int width)
{
    return length * width;
}
```

parameter mode:
The way in which a parameter is passed, such as by value or by reference.

value parameter:
A formal parameter that is local to a subprogram. Values of these parameters are not returned to the calling program.

In this program, the formal parameters **length** and **width** are used for one-way transmission of values to the function **area**. When the function is called, the values of the actual parameters, **this_length** and **this_width**, are copied into separate memory locations for the formal parameters **length** and **width**. The fact that there are separate memory locations for the formal and actual parameters guarantees that any changes to the formal parameters will leave the actual parameters unchanged.

Suppose that the user enters 8 for **this_length** and 7 for **this_width**. The state of the machine is now

| 8 |
this_length

| 7 |
this_width

Note that the only memory locations visible to the program are those for the variables **this_length** and **this_width**. The function is then called to compute the area. The system *allocates* memory locations for the formal parameters **length** and **width**. These names and their memory locations now become visible to the block of statements within the function. The system then places copies of the values 8 and 7 into the memory locations for **length** and **width**. This is why value parameters are said to be *passed by value*. The state of the machine is now

8

this_length

7

this_width

8

length

7

width

When the function returns from its call, the system *deallocates* the memory locations for **length** and **width**. Also, because the function is no longer active, its formal parameters are no longer visible to the program. The values of **this_length** and **this_width**, which are still visible, have not changed. A value parameter always indicates a *local copy* of the value transmitted to the function.

Reference Parameters

You will frequently want a function to return more than one value to a caller. A good example of a task that calls for more than one value to be returned is the interaction with the user for two input values in the program that computes the area of a rectangle. The C++ code for this task reads integer values from the keyboard into two variables:

```
cout << "Enter the length: ";
cin >> this_length;
cout <<"Enter the width: ";
cin >> this_width;
```

We could document this task as follows:

```
// Prompts the user for two input integers representing
// the length and width of a rectangle
```

reference parameter:
A formal parameter that requires the address of the actual parameter to be passed to a subprogram. The value of the actual parameter can be changed within the subprogram.

We can represent information to be returned with **reference parameters** in the parameter list of a C++ function. In a function declaration, reference parameters are declared by using the symbol **&** before the appropriate formal parameters. The form of a reference parameter declaration in a function declaration is

> <type name> &<formal parameter name>

The C++ declaration for a function **get_data** to perform this task can be added to the documentation:

```
// Function: get_data
// Prompts the user for two input integers representing
// the length and width of a rectangle
//
// Outputs: two integers representing the length and
// width of a rectangle

void get_data(int &length, int &width);
```

Note that the parameter and type names look the same as they would in declarations of functions that would use the parameters to receive data. However, in this function they will be used to return information to the caller, as is indicated by the **&** symbol.

The form of a reference parameter declaration in the heading of a function implementation is

> <type name> &<formal parameter name>

Our **get_data** function can now be implemented as follows:

```
void get_data(int &length, int &width)
{
      cout << "Enter the length: ";
      cin >> length;
      cout << "Enter the width: ";
      cin >> width;
}
```

When reference parameters are declared, values appear to be sent from the function to the caller. Actually, when reference parameters are used, values are not transmitted at all. Reference parameters in the function heading are merely **aliases** for actual variables used by the caller. Thus, variables are said to be *passed by reference* rather than by value. When reference parameters are used, any change of values in the function produces a corresponding change of values in the caller's block.

The notion of aliasing can be seen during a run of the program where the user enters the values 8 and 7 as inputs. Just before the function **get_data** returns, the state of the machine is as follows:

alias: A situation in which two or more identifiers in a program refer to the same memory location.

```
    ┌─────┐
    │  8  │
    └─────┘
this_length
length
```

```
    ┌─────┐
    │  7  │
    └─────┘
this_width
width
```

Note that there are only two memory locations for data in the program thus far. However, each location has two different names associated with it, which means that an assignment to either of the two names, say, **this_width** or **width**, will change the value stored in the corresponding memory location.

Technically, **length** and **width** do not exist as variables. They contain pointers to the same memory locations as **this_length** and **this_width**, respectively. Thus, a statement in the function such as

```
length = 5;
```

causes the memory location reserved for **length** to receive the value 5. That is, it causes the net action

```
this_length = 5;
```

Thus, constants cannot be used when calling a function with reference parameters. For example,

```
get_data(8, 7);
```

produces an error because 8 and 7 are passed in the positions of reference parameters.

An error would also occur if we tried to pass the value of an expression in the position of a reference parameter. For example, the following call would generate an error for the second parameter:

```
get_data(this_length, this_width + 1);
```

In general, the only legitimate actual parameter to pass by reference is a variable or the name of another function's parameter. The reason for this is that only names of this sort can refer to memory locations capable of being aliased by a reference parameter.

The next example also shows a useful function that requires reference parameters.

Example 4.4

Many problems call for a function that will exchange the values of data in two variables. For any two variables **a** and **b**, the effect of calling the function **swap(a, b)** will be to replace the value of **a** with the value of **b**, and to replace the value of **b** with the value of **a**. Clearly, a function that returns a single value cannot accomplish this task. We will assume that the values to be swapped are real numbers. Two parameters will be used both to receive data from the caller and to return information as well. Thus, the function's declaration can be written as follows:

```
// Function: swap
// Exchanges the values of the two input variables
//
// Inputs: two real numbers
// Outputs: the two real numbers in reversed order

void swap(double &a, double &b);
```

The function's implementation will use a temporary variable to save one of the input values during the exchange:

```
void swap(double &a, double &b)
{
        double temp;

        temp = a;
        a = b;
        b = temp;
}
```

Note that this function itself returns no value to the caller. This is not unusual for functions that have reference parameters.

Constant Reference Parameters

Recall from Section 3.4 that a string variable requires a chunk of computer memory large enough to accommodate all of the characters in the string. When a string variable is passed by value to a function, all of the characters in the variable must be copied to temporary memory locations for the parameter. This process can be costly in time (to copy the characters) and memory (to store them) for large strings. To cut these costs, one might decide to pass all string parameters by reference. However, this move would be unsafe, because unintended changes to the original string variables might occur.

As a solution to this problem, C++ provides a third parameter passing mode called **constant reference.** A constant reference parameter is passed by reference, so it has the efficiency of reference parameters. However, the C++ compiler disallows all assignments to a constant reference parameter within the body of the function where it is declared. Thus, a constant reference parameter is also as safe as a value parameter.

The form of a constant reference parameter declaration is just like a reference parameter declaration, except that it is prefixed by the reserved word **const**:

constant reference:
A method of declaring a formal parameter so that the actual parameter is passed by reference but will not change in a function.

A Note of Interest

The History of Parameter Passing

The use of parameters to communicate information among subprograms is almost as old as the use of subprograms. As soon as subprograms became available in high-level programming languages, programmers realized that subprograms would be virtually useless without parameters. The inclusion of parameters in programming languages allowed programmers to design better code in two respects. First, the use of parameters made code more readable. The parameters of a subprogram module gave it a manifest interface for receiving information from and sending it to other modules. Second, the use of parameters made subprograms more general. Before parameters became available, each subprogram's operations were restricted to a particular problem involving particular data. The addition of parameters allowed programmers to generalize their solutions to manipulate whole classes of data.

The design of different parameter passing mechanisms has been an important chapter in the history of programming languages. Each major step in this process has reflected both the vision of computer scientists about what they consider important in a programming context and the limitations of the available hardware and software technology.

When the use of parameters first appeared in the mid-1950s in the programming language FORTRAN, the focus of programmers was on efficiency. FORTRAN was used primarily to perform mathematical and scientific computations (the acronym stands for **FOR**mula **TRAN**slation language). This kind of application demanded high processing speed and large amounts of memory. But early processors were slow, and memory was expensive. With these resources at a premium, John Backus, the designer of FORTRAN, decided that all parameters in the language would be passed by reference. Pass by reference is less expensive than pass by value, because no extra memory needs to be allocated for a local copy of the actual parameter, and no extra processing time is needed to copy it. Because FORTRAN subprograms always manipulated the actual arguments passed to them by reference, the subprograms ran very quickly even when large data structures were passed. The use of a single parameter passing mode also made the language easy to learn and the compiler for it easy to write.

Needless to say, the early FORTRAN programs were not safe. Programmers discovered this to be true especially for large programs that passed many parameters among subprograms. Unintended side effects were numerous. Because of the way that constant symbols were represented, even constants could be changed if they were passed as parameters to FORTRAN subprograms!

After a few years of experience with FORTRAN, John McCarthy, a mathematician at the Massachusetts Institute of Technology, designed LISP. LISP, short for **LIS**t **P**rocessing Language, was intended for processing lists of symbols and was based on a theory of computation known as the recursive lambda calculus. According to this theory, programs should consist of functions that receive zero or more arguments and return a single value. In the process, these functions should not change the arguments themselves. To enforce this requirement, McCarthy designed a pass-by-value mechanism for parameters. In cases where an actual argument was a simple data type, like a number, functions worked on a local copy of the actual argument, so that no side effects were possible. Efficiency was not important, because LISP was a highly interactive and interpreted language. Thus, the time taken to allocate the extra memory for a formal parameter and copy the value of the actual parameter to it was insignificant when compared to the time taken to interpret LISP expressions generally. In cases where an actual argument was a structured data type, such as a string or a list of numbers, a copy of a pointer to the argument was passed for reasons of efficiency. The parameter passing mechanism of LISP thus reflected concerns of both safety and efficiency.

The primary teaching language in computer science for the last 20 years until recently has been Pascal. Named after the French mathematician, Pascal was designed by Niklaus Wirth. Pascal has two parameter passing modes. Pass by value worked like pass by value in LISP. However, Wirth extended pass by value to structured data values as well, making this mode expensive to use at run time. Pass by reference worked as in FORTRAN, except that constants and expressions were disallowed as actual reference parameters. Pascal also allows subprograms to be passed as parameters. This is an important development in our story, in that subprograms can be generalized still further by being parameterized for more specific subprograms. The following example of a general summation function in Pascal illustrates this point:

(continued)

```
function sum(low, high : integer;
        function f(x : integer) : integer) : integer;
        var
            i, accum : integer;
        begin
        accum := 0;
        for i := low to high do
            accum := accum + f(i);
        sum := accum;
        end;


begin
writeln(sum(1, 10, square));
end.
```

The syntax of Pascal is fairly close to that of C++. Assuming that the function **square** had been defined elsewhere, the **sum** function would return the summation of the **squares** of all of the integers between 1 and 10 in this example. The name **square** substitutes for **f** inside of the function at run time. The summation function will work with any function parameter of one integer argument that returns an integer value. As you can see, passing functions as parameters is a powerful way to generalize functions and reduce the redundancy of code in programs. C++ also allows functions to be passed as parameters.

```
const <type name> &<parameter name>
```

The **get_ string** function developed in Section 4.2 is a good candidate for the use of a constant reference parameter. Its new declaration would be

```
apstring get_string(const apstring &prompt);
```

Except for the change in the heading, the implementation of the function would be the same as that of the earlier version.

Rules of Thumb for Choosing a Parameter Mode

Choosing the appropriate mode when declaring a parameter for a function takes practice. Here are some rules of thumb to keep in mind:

1. When the value of the original variable (the actual parameter) must be changed by the function, declare the formal parameter as a reference parameter.

2. When the value of the original variable should not be changed by the function and the size of these data is relatively small (an **int**, a **double**, or a short string), declare the formal parameter as a value parameter.

3. When the value of the original variable should not be changed by the function and the size of these data is relatively large (a long string), declare the formal parameter as a constant reference parameter.

■ Exercises 4.3

1. Find the errors in the following function declarations:

a. ```
// Function: get_data
// Prompts user for two integer input values
//
// Outputs: two integers

void get_data(int length, int width);
```

b. ```
// Function: area
// Computes the area of a rectangle
//
// Inputs: two integers representing the length
// and the width of the rectangle
// Outputs: an integer representing the area
// of the rectangle

int area(int length, int &width);
```

c. ```
// Function: circle_attributes
// Computes the diameter and area of a circle
//
// Input: a real number representing the radius
// of the circle
// Outputs: two real numbers representing
// the diameter and area of the circle

void circle_attributes(double &radius,
    double &diameter, double &area);
```

2. Write and test a function **int_divide** that receives two integer values and two integer variables from the caller. When the function completes execution, the values in these variables should be the quotient and the remainder produced by dividing the second value by the first value. Be sure to name your parameters descriptively so as to aid the reader of the function.

3. Explain the differences between value parameters, reference parameters, and constant reference parameters.

## 4.4 Functions as Subprograms

Functions can be used as subprograms for a number of purposes. Two significant uses are to facilitate the top-down design philosophy of problem solving and to avoid having to write repeated segments of code.

Functions facilitate problem solving. Recall the Case Study in Chapter 3. In that problem, you were asked to compute the unit cost for a pizza. The main modules were
```

- to understand how functions can be used to design programs
- to be able to use functions to get data for programs
- to be able to use functions to perform required tasks in programs
- to be able to use functions for output

1. Get the data
2. Perform the computations
3. Print the results

A function can be written for each of these tasks and the program can then call each function as needed. Thus, the statement portion of the program would have the form

```
data = get_data();
results = perform_computations(data);
print_results(results);
```

This makes it easy to see and understand the main tasks of the program.

Once you develop the ability to write and use subprograms, you will usually write programs by writing the main program first. Your main program should be written so it can be easily read by a nonprogrammer but still contain enough structure to enable a programmer to know what to do if asked to write code for the tasks. In this sense, it is not necessary for a person reading the main program to understand *how* a subprogram accomplishes its task; it need only be apparent *what* the subprogram does.

When you design subprograms, you should also consider the problem of data flow. The most difficult aspect of learning to use subprograms is handling transmission of data with parameters. Recall from the structure charts shown earlier that arrows were used to indicate whether data were received by and/or sent from a module. Also, each module specification indicated if data were received by that module and if information was sent from it. Since a subprogram will be written to accomplish the task of each module, we must be able to transmit data as indicated. Once you have developed this ability, using functions becomes routine.

Using Subprograms

Use of subprograms facilitates the writing of programs for problems whose solutions have been developed using top-down design. A function can be written for each main task.

How complex should a function be? In general, functions should be relatively short and perform a specific task. Some programmers prefer to limit functions to no more than one full screen of text. If longer than a page or screen, the task might need to be subdivided into smaller functions.

Cohesive Subprograms

The term "cohesive" means hanging together in a unified way. The cohesion of a subprogram is the degree to which the subprogram performs a single task. A subprogram that is developed in such a way is called a **cohesive subprogram.** As you use subprograms to implement a design based on modular development, you should always try to write cohesive subprograms.

The property of cohesion is not well defined. Subtask complexity varies in the minds of different programmers. In general, if the task is unclear, the corresponding subprogram will not be cohesive. The resulting subprogram might look like it

cohesive subprogram:
A subprogram designed to accomplish a single task.

does too many different things. When this happens, you should subdivide the task until a subsequent development allows cohesive subprograms.

To illustrate briefly the concept of cohesion, consider the first-level design of a problem to compute grades for a class. Step 3 of this design could be

3.   Process grades for each student

Clearly, this is not a well-defined task. Thus, if you were to write a subprogram for this task, the subprogram would not be cohesive. Consider the subsequent development:

3.   Process grades for each student.
      While not end of input
          3.1 Get a line of data
          3.2 Compute average
          3.3 Compute letter grade
          3.4 Print data
          3.5 Compute totals

Here we see that functions to accomplish subtasks 3.1, 3.2, 3.3, and 3.4 would be cohesive because each subtask consists of a single task. The final subtask, compute totals, may or may not result in a cohesive subprogram. More information is needed before you can decide what is to be done at this step.

Functional Abstraction

The purpose of using functions is to simplify reasoning. The term *abstract* means simple, and the term *abstraction* means simplification. During the design stage, as a problem is subdivided into tasks, the problem solver (you) should have to consider only what a function is to do and not be concerned about details of the function. Instead, the function name and comments at the beginning of the function should be sufficient to inform the user as to what the function does. Developing functions in this manner is referred to as **functional abstraction** (this notion is also called *procedural abstraction,* because some languages support subprograms known as *procedures* that are similar to functions).

Functional abstraction is the first step in designing and writing a function. The list of parameters and comments about the action of the function should precede development of the body of the function. This forces clarity of thought and aids design. Use of this method might cause you to discover that your design is not sufficient to solve the task and that a redesign is necessary. Therefore, you could reduce design errors and save time when writing code.

Functional abstraction becomes especially important when teams work on a project. Each member of the writing team should be able to understand the purpose and use of functions written by other team members without having to analyze the body of each function. This is analogous to the situation in which you use a predefined function without really understanding how the function works.

Functional abstraction is perhaps best formalized in terms of preconditions and postconditions. A **precondition** is a comment that states precisely what is true before a certain action is taken. A **postcondition** states what is true after the action has been taken. Carefully written preconditions and postconditions used

functional abstraction: The process of considering only what a function is to do rather than details of the function.

precondition: A statement of what is true before a certain action is taken.

postcondition: A statement of what is true after a certain action is taken.

Computer Ethics: Hacking and Other Intrusions

A famous sequence of computer intrusions has been detailed by Clifford Stoll. The prime intruder came to Stoll's attention in August 1986, when an intruder attempted to penetrate a computer at Lawrence Berkeley Laboratory (LBL). Instead of denying the intruder access, management at LBL went along with Stoll's recommendation that they attempt to unmask the intruder, even though the risk was substantial because the intruder had gained system-manager privileges.

The intruder, Markus H., a member of a small group of West Germans, was unusually persistent, but no computer wizard. He made use of known deficiencies in the half-dozen or so operating systems, including UNIX, VMS, VM-TSO, and EMBOS, with which he was familiar, but he did not invent any new modes of entry. He penetrated 30 of the 450 computers then on the network system at LBL.

After Markus H. was successfully traced, efforts were instituted to make LBL's computers less vulnerable. To ensure high security, it would have been necessary to change all passwords overnight and recertify each user. This and other demanding measures were deemed impractical. Instead, deletion of all expired passwords was instituted; shared accounts were eliminated; monitoring of incoming traffic was extended, with alarms set in key places; and education of users was attempted.

The episode was summed up by Stoll as a powerful learning experience for those involved in the detection process and for all those concerned about computer security. That the intruder was caught at all is testimony to the ability of a large number of concerned professionals to keep the tracing effort secret.

In a later incident, an intruder left the following embarrassing message in the computer file assigned to Clifford Stoll: "The cuckoo has egg on his face." The reference was to Stoll's book, The Cuckoo's Egg, which tracked the intrusions of the West German hacker just described. The embarrassment was heightened by the fact that the computer, owned by Harvard University with which astronomer Stoll is now associated, was on the Internet network. The intruder, or intruders, who goes by the name of Dave, also attempted to break into dozens of other computers on the same network—and succeeded.

The **nom de guerre** of "Dave" was also used by one or more of three Australians recently arrested by the federal police down under. The three, who at the time of their arrest were respectively 18, 20, and 21 years of age, successfully penetrated computers in both Australia and the United States.

The three Australians went beyond browsing to damage data in computers in their own nation and the United States. At the time they began their intrusions in 1988 (when the youngest was only 16), there was no law in Australia under which they could be prosecuted. It was not until legislation making such intrusions prosecutable was passed that the police began to take action.

with functions enhance the concept of functional abstraction. (Additional uses of preconditions and postconditions are discussed in Sections 5.6 and 6.5.)

In summary, functional abstraction means that, when writing or using functions, you should think of them as single, clearly understood units, each of which accomplishes a specific task.

information hiding:
A condition in which the user of a module does not know the details of how it is implemented and the implementer of a module does not know the details of how it is used.

Information Hiding

Information hiding can be thought of as the process of hiding the implementation details of a subprogram. This is just what we do when we use a top-down design to solve a problem. We decide which tasks and subtasks are necessary to solve a problem without worrying about how the specific subtasks will be accomplished. In the sense of software engineering, information hiding is what allows teams to work on a large system: It is only necessary to know what another team is doing, not how they are doing it.

Interface and Documentation

interface: A formal statement of how communication occurs between the user of a subprogram and its implementer.

Independent subprograms need to communicate with the main program and other subprograms. A formal statement of how such communication occurs is called the **interface** of the subprogram. This usually consists of comments at the beginning of a subprogram and includes all the documentation the reader will need to use the subprogram. We have seen examples of subprogram interfaces in the function declarations and headings that have appeared in this chapter.

Software Engineering

Perhaps the greatest difference between beginning students in computer science and "real-world" programmers is how they perceive the need for documentation. Typically, beginning students want to make a program run; they view anything that delays this process as an impediment to progress. Thus, some students consider using descriptive identifiers, writing variable dictionaries, describing a problem as part of program documentation, and using appropriate comments throughout a program as a nuisance. In contrast, system designers and programmers who write code for a living often spend up to 50 percent of their time and effort on documentation. There are at least three reasons for this difference in perspective.

First, real programmers work on large, complex systems with highly developed logical paths. Without proper documentation, even the person who developed an algorithm will have difficulty following its logic six months later. Second, communication among teams is required as systems are developed. Complete, clear statements about what the problems are and how they are being solved are essential. Third, programmers know they can develop algorithms and write the necessary code. They are trained so that problems of searching, sorting, and file manipulation are routine. Knowing that they can solve a problem thus allows them to devote more time and energy to documenting how the solution has been achieved.

We close this section with a revision of the program from Chapter 3 that found the unit cost for a pizza. The original program was designed using module specifications, but implemented in C++ as a long sequence of statements in the main program section. The revision will implement each module of the design as a C++ function to be called from the main program section. The structure chart is shown in Figure 4.1.

The module specifications are

Module: Get data
Task: Get cost and size of pizza from the user at the keyboard.
Output: The cost and size

Module: Compute price per square inch
Task: Compute the price per square inch of pizza.
Input: Cost and size of pizza
Output: Price per square inch

Module: Print results
Task: Print the price per square inch.
Input: Price per square inch

◆ **Figure 4.1**

Structure chart for the pizza problem

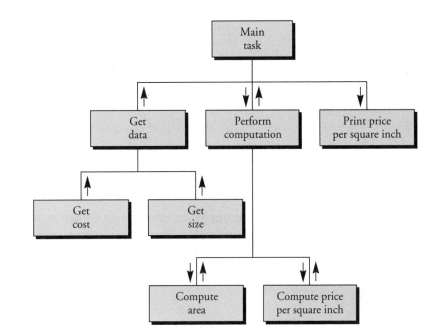

The module for getting the data receives no data, but returns two data values to the caller. The C++ function declaration specifies a function named **get_data** and two reference parameters, **cost** and **size**, in which the input data are returned to the caller:

```
// Function: get_data
// Gets cost and size of pizza from the user at the keyboard
//
// Outputs: The cost and size

void get_data(double &cost, int &size);
```

The C++ function implementation prompts the user for the cost and then for the size of the pizza, and returns the two input values in the reference parameters:

```
void get_data(double &cost, int &size)
{
     cout << "Enter the pizza price and press <Enter>. ";
     cin >> cost;
     cout << "Enter the pizza size and press <Enter>. ";
     cin >> size;
}
```

We next write a function for performing the desired computations. This function receives the cost and size and then returns the price per square inch. Thus, cost and size are parameters and the price per square inch is the returned value of the function. If we name the function `price_per_square_inch`, we can write its declaration as follows:

```
// Function: compute price per square inch
// Compute the price per square inch of pizza
//
// Input: cost and size of pizza
// Output: price per square inch

double price_per_square_inch(double cost, int size);
```

The implementation of this function also requires variables for the radius and area to be declared in the data declaration section of the function. Assuming **PI** has been defined as a constant and **sqr** has been defined as a function, the function's implementation is

```
double price_per_square_inch(double cost,
      int size)
{
      double radius, area;
      radius = size / 2;
      area = PI * sqr(radius);
      return cost / area;
}
```

A function to print the results receives the unit cost. A declaration for the function is

```
// Function: print results
// Print the price per square inch
//
// Input: price per square inch

void print_results(double price_per_sq_inch);
```

The function's implementation is:

```
void print_results(double price_per_sq_inch)
{
      cout << setiosflags(ios::fixed | ios::showpoint)
          << setprecision(2) << endl;
      cout << "The price per square inch is $";
      cout << setw(6) << price_per_sq_inch << endl;
}
```

The complete program for this problem is as follows:

```cpp
// Program file: pizza.cpp

#include <iostream.h>
#include <iomanip.h>

const double PI = 3.14159;

// Function: get_data
// Gets cost and size of pizza from the user at the keyboard
//
// Outputs: The cost and size

void get_data(double &cost, int &size);

// Function: compute price per square inch
// Compute the price per square inch of pizza
//
// Input: cost and size of pizza
// Output: price per square inch

double price_per_square_inch(double cost, int size);

// Function: print results
// Print the price per square inch
//
// Input: price per square inch

void print_results(double price_per_sq_inch);

// Function: sqr
// Computes the square of a number
//
// Input: a real number
// Output: a real number representing the square of the input

double sqr(double x);

int main()
{
    int size;
    double cost, price;

    get_data(cost, size);
    price = price_per_square_inch(cost, size);
```

```
        print_results(price);
        return 0;
}
```

```
    void get_data(double &cost, int &size)
    {
        cout << "Enter the pizza price and press <Enter>. ";
        cin >> cost;
        cout << "Enter the pizza size and press <Enter>. ";
        cin >> size;
    }
```
1

```
    double price_per_square_inch(double cost, int size)
    {
        double radius, area;
        radius = size / 2;
        area = PI * sqr(radius);
        return cost / area;
    }
```
2

```
    void print_results(double price_per_sq_inch)
    {
        cout << setiosflags(ios::fixed | ios::showpoint)
             << setprecision(2) << endl;
        cout << "The price per square inch is $";
        cout << setw(6) << price_per_sq_inch << endl;
    }
```
3

```
double sqr(double x)
{
    return x * x;
}
```

Note the way in which the use of subprograms has simplified the structure of the main program compared to the original version in Chapter 3. Sample runs of this program produce the following output:

```
Enter the pizza price and press <Enter>. 10.50
Enter the pizza size and press <Enter>. 16

The price per square inch is $ 0.05
```

Enter the pizza price and press <Enter>. 8.75
Enter the pizza size and press <Enter>. 14

The price per square inch is $ 0.06

■ **Exercises 4.4**

1. Draw a structure chart for a program that prompts the user for an integer, computes its square root, and displays this result with an informative label on the terminal screen. Your chart should contain three modules: one for getting the data, one for computing the result, and one for printing the result. Be sure to label the data flow between the modules with arrows.

2. Construct a main program module in C++, and add to it the declarations of three functions that will carry out the tasks of the modules from the previous exercise.

3. Implement and test each of the functions from Exercise 2. You will have to declare at least one integer variable to pass the data from module to module.

4.5 Scope of Identifiers

Objectives

- to understand what is meant by global identifiers
- to understand what is meant by local identifiers
- to understand the scope of an identifier
- to recognize the appropriate and inappropriate uses of global identifiers
- to be able to understand and control side effects in programs
- to be able to use appropriate names for identifiers

block: The area of program text within a compound statement that contains statements and optional data declarations.

subblock: A block structure for a subprogram.

Global and Local Identifiers

Identifiers used to declare variables in the declaration section of a program can be used throughout the entire program. For purposes of this section, we will think of the global text of the program file as a **block** and the main program and each subprogram as a **subblock** for the main program or subprogram. Each subblock may contain a parameter list, a local declaration section, and the body of the block. A program file block can be envisioned as shown in Figure 4.2. Furthermore, if **x1** is a variable in the main program block, we will indicate this as shown in Figure 4.3, where an area in memory has been set aside for **x1**. When a program contains a subprogram, a separate memory area within the memory area for the program is set aside for the subprogram to use while it executes. Thus, if the program file contains a function named **subprog**, we can envision this as shown in Figure 4.4. If **subprog** contains the variable **x2**, we have the program shown in Figure 4.5. This could be indicated in the program by

```
const double PI = 3.14;

double subprog(double x2);

int main()
{
    double x1;

    subprog(x1);
    .
    .
```

The **scope of an identifier** refers to the area of the program text in which it can be used. When subprograms are used, each identifier is available to the block in which it is declared and any nested blocks. Identifiers are not available outside their blocks.

◆ **Figure 4.2**

Program file block

scope of identifier: The largest block in which the identifier is available.

global identifier: A name that can be used by the main program and all subprograms in a program.

local identifier: A name that is restricted to use within a subblock of a program.

Identifiers that are declared before the main block are called **global identifiers;** identifiers that are restricted to use within the main block or subblock are called **local identifiers.** Constant **PI** in Figure 4.5 can be used throughout the main program and in the function **subprog**; therefore it is a global identifier. Variable **x1** can be used in the main program but not in the function **subprog**; it is a local identifier. Variable **x2** can only be used within the function where it is declared; it is a local identifier. Any attempt to reference **x2** outside the function will result in an error. Lastly, function **subprog** can be used either in the main program block, within another function's block, or within its own block. This last use is a recursive one, which we will discuss in Chapter 12.

As a matter of C++ syntax, function names must be declared as global identifiers. Constant, variable, and type names can be declared either globally or locally. However, as a matter of good programming style, constant and type names are usually declared globally, and variable names are declared locally.

Let us now examine an illustration of local and global identifiers. Consider the following program and function declaration:

```cpp
const int A = 10;

subprog(int a1);

int main()
{
        int x, y;
        .
        .
}
```

◆ **Figure 4.3**

Variable location in main block

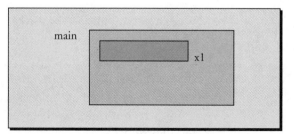

◆ **Figure 4.4**

An illustration of a subblock

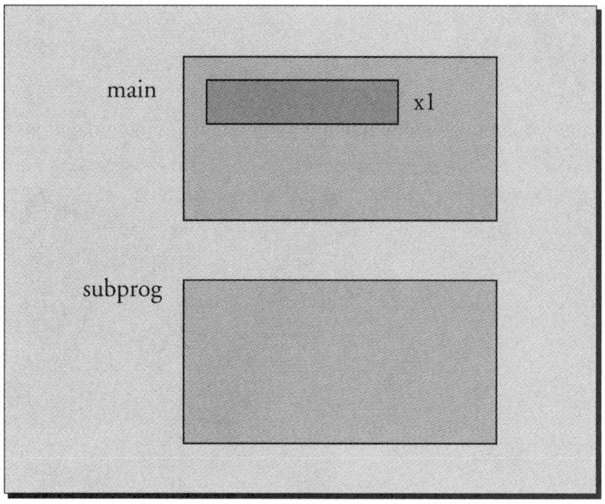

```
int subprog(int a1)
{
      double x;
      .
      .
```

Blocks for this program can be envisioned as shown in Figure 4.6. Because **A** is global, the statement

```
cout << A << a1 << x << endl;
```

could be used in the function **subprog**, although **A** has not been specifically declared there. However,

◆ **Figure 4.5**

Variable location within a subblock

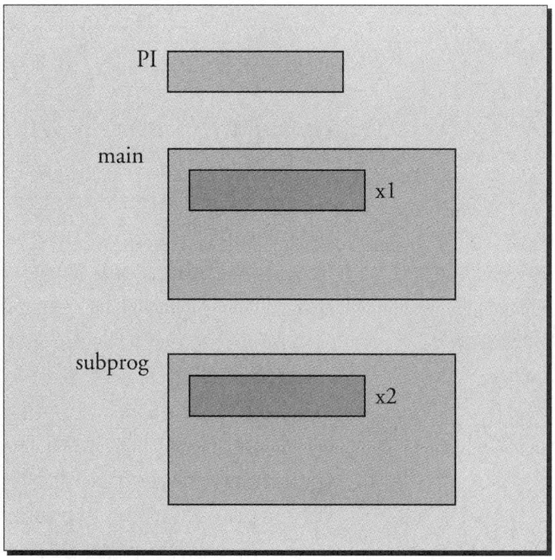

◆ **Figure 4.6**

Scope of identifiers

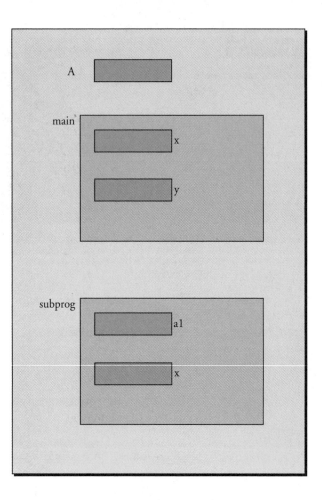

```
cout << A << a1 << x << endl;
```

could not be used in the main program because **a1** is local to the function **subprog**.

Using Global Identifiers

In general, it is not good practice to refer to global variables within functions. A **side effect** is a change in a nonlocal variable that is the result of some action taken in a program. The use of locally defined variables in functions and in the main program block helps to avoid unexpected side effects and protects your programs. In addition, locally defined variables facilitate debugging and top-down design and enhance the portability of functions. This is especially important if different people are working on different functions for a program.

The use of global constants is different. Because the values cannot be changed by a function, it is preferred that constants be defined in the data declaration section before the main program block and then be used whenever needed by any subprogram. This is especially important if the constant is subject to change over time, for example, **STATE_TAX_RATE**. When a change is necessary, one change

side effect: A change in a variable that is the result of some action taken in a program, usually from within a function.

in the main program is all that is needed to make all subprograms current. If a constant is used in only one function, some programmers prefer to have it defined near the point of use. Thus, they would define it in the subprogram in which it is used.

Side Effects and Parameters

Unintentional side effects are frequently caused by the misuse of reference parameters. Since any change in a reference parameter causes a change in the corresponding actual parameter in the calling program or function, you should use reference parameters only when your intent is to produce such changes. In all other cases, use value parameters or constant reference parameters. For example, the following program would produce a syntax error, because a function attempts to access a variable declared in the main block:

```
void bad_square();

int main()
{
        int main_data = 2;

        bad_square();
        return 0;

}

void bad_square();
{
        main_data = main_data * main_data;
}
```

If we move the declaration of **main_data** outside of the main block, we can extend its scope into the local block of the function, unless the name is redeclared within the function as a parameter or local variable:

```
int main_data = 2;

void bad_square();

int main()
{

        bad_square();
        return 0;
}

void bad_square();
{
        main_data = main_data * main_data;
}
```

We have named the function **bad_square** to indicate that the assignment that occurs in the function is bad programming practice, even though the result might be intended by the programmer. Not only does the use of this function result in a serious side effect, but there is no indication in the function's declaration or in the function's call that the function will modify the global variable. Keeping the declarations of these variables inside the main program block will help to guard against this problem.

A better version of this program moves the declaration of the global variable back into the main block and passes the variable as a reference parameter to the function:

```
void better_square(int &x);

int main()
{
        int main_data = 2;

        better_square(main_data);
        return 0;
}

void better_square(int &x)
{
        x = x * x;
}
```

manifest interface:
The property of a function such that, when the function is called, the reader of the code can tell clearly what information is being transmitted to it and what information is being returned from it.

The function **better_square** improves on **bad_square** in two respects. First, the function now has a **manifest interface.** A function has a manifest interface if we can see, just from looking at the function's declaration and the function's call, exactly what data the function is manipulating, and that they will be subject to change within the function. In other words, we are given clear notice that a side effect will occur in the function, and a clear indication of what that side effect will be. Second, the function can be used to take the square of any variable passed to it as an actual parameter. We have indicated this by using **x** to name the formal parameter of the function. Thus, **better_square** is more general than **bad_square**, which could take the square of just one variable.

While **better_square** is an improvement on **bad_square**, we can write a still better version of this function:

```
int best_square(int x);

int main()
{
        int main_data = 2;

        main_data = best_square(main_data);
        return 0;
}
```

```
int best_square(int x)
{
        return x * x;
}
```

This version of the function is the best one for two reasons. First, it has a manifest interface. The caller knows exactly what data will be used by the function. Second, the function produces no side effects. The caller passes the function a value to be squared, and the square of this value is returned to the caller. In particular, if the caller passes a variable to this function, the caller can be sure that the function will not change the variable. If the caller wants to set a variable to the value returned by the function, then this assignment must be explicitly done by the caller after the function returns its value.

The last three versions of the function in this example are technically correct, in that they accomplish the task intended by the programmer. However, as the example demonstrates, whenever possible, it is best to write functions that have manifest interfaces and that produce no side effects.

Names of Identifiers

Because separate areas in memory are set aside when subprograms are used, it is possible to have identifiers with the same name in both the main program and a subprogram. Thus,

```
int main()
{
        int age;
        .

        .
}

int subprog(int age)
```

can be envisioned as shown in Figure 4.7. When the same name is used in this manner, any reference to this name results in action being taken as locally as possible. Thus, the assignment statement

```
age = 20;
```

made in the function **subprog** assigns 20 to **age** in the function but not in the main program (see Figure 4.8).

Now that you know you can use the same name for an identifier in a subprogram and the main program, the question is "Should you?" There are two schools of thought regarding this issue. If you use the same name in the functions, it facilitates matching parameter lists and independent development of functions.

◆ **Figure 4.7**

Relation of identifiers

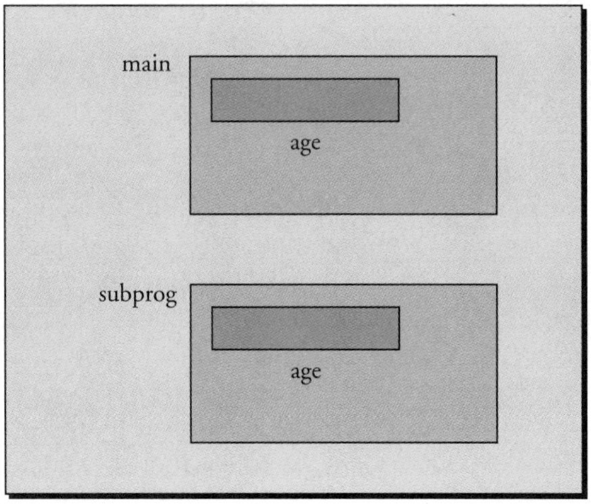

However, this practice can be confusing when you first start working with subprograms. Thus, some instructors prefer using different, but related, identifiers. For example,

```
display_data(score1, score2);
```

in the main program could have a function heading of

```
void display_data(int sc1, int sc2);
```

In this case, the use of **sc1** and **sc2** is obvious. Although this may facilitate better understanding in early work with subprograms, it is less conducive to portability and independent development of functions. Both styles are used in this text.

◆ **Figure 4.8**

Assigning values in subprograms

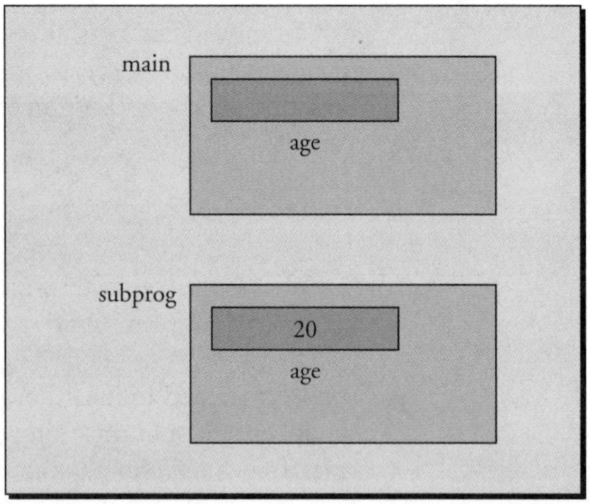

A Note of Interest

John Backus

You have read about John Backus, the inventor of FORTRAN, in a **Note of Interest** on program libraries in Chapter 2 and we also mentioned him earlier in this chapter. Backus has had a long and distinguished career as a computer scientist with IBM. During the late 1950s, he sat on a committee that developed ALGOL, the first **block-structured** programming language. The block structure of ALGOL represented a significant advance over FORTRAN. A block in ALGOL is a set of related data declarations and executable statements. The data declared in a block are visible only within it. This greatly enhances program security, readability, and maintenance. Most modern programming languages developed after ALGOL, including C++, have been block structured.

In 1977, Backus was given the Turing Award for his contributions to computer science at the annual meeting of the Association for Computing Machinery. Each recipient of this annual award presents a lecture. Backus discussed a new discipline in his talk called **function-oriented programming.** This style of programming was developed to address concerns about the reliability and maintainability of large software systems. One of the principal causes of errors in large programs is the presence of side effects and unintentional modifications of variables. These modifications can occur anywhere in a program with assignment statements whose targets are global variables. Backus proposed that function-oriented programming could eliminate side effects by eliminating the assignment statement and keeping global variables to a minimum. Function-oriented programs consist of sets of function declarations and **function applications.** A function application simply evaluates the arguments to a function, applies the function to these values, and returns a result to the caller. No assignment statements to global variables are allowed within a function. No side effects occur.

The philosophy of function-oriented programming has motivated the design of function-oriented languages. These languages do not allow the programmer to perform assignments to global variables within functions. Though C++ allows programmers to declare and use functions, the language does not forbid this kind of side effect. However, by exercising some discipline, C++ programmers can still emulate a function-oriented style to prevent side effects from occurring in their programs.

Communication and Style Tips

1. Adopt a convention of listing all of the value parameters in a function declaration and heading before you list any of the reference parameters. This will aid in reading the function. For example, the following declaration has six parameters, three of which are value parameters and three of which are reference parameters:

```
void process_data(double a, double b, int x,
    double &c, double &d, int &y);
```

2. In most cases where a function returns a single value to the caller, you should use value parameters only. You should use reference parameters only where you wish to return more than one value to the caller.

3. Most functions that use reference parameters should be **void** functions. This will avoid confusion about how many values are returned.

4. To help minimize side effects, declare all variables used by the main program within the main program block.

◆ **Figure 4.9**

Multiple function blocks

FUNCTION A

FUNCTION B

FUNCTION C

Multiple Functions

More than one function can be used in a program. When this occurs, all of the previous uses and restrictions of identifiers apply to each function. Blocks for multiple functions can be depicted as shown in Figure 4.9. Identifiers in the main program can be accessed by each function. However, local identifiers in the functions cannot be accessed outside their blocks.

When a program contains several functions, they can be called from the main part of the program in any order.

◆ **Figure 4.10**

Identifiers in multiple subprograms

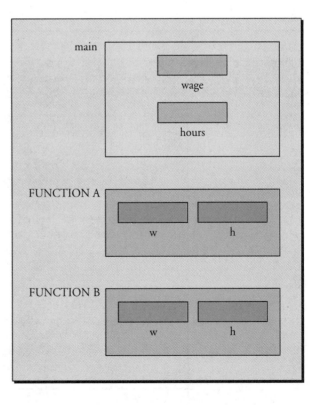

The same names for identifiers can be used in different functions. Thus, if the main program uses variables **wage** and **hours**, and both of these are used as arguments in calls to different functions, you have the situation shown in Figure 4.10. Using the same names for identifiers in different functions makes it easier to keep track of the relationship between variables in the main program and their associated parameters in each subprogram.

■ Exercises 4.5

1. Explain the difference between local and global identifiers.
2. State the advantages of using local identifiers.
3. Discuss some appropriate uses for global identifiers. List several constants that would be appropriate global definitions.
4. What is meant by the scope of an identifier?
5. Write a test program that will enable you to answer the following questions:
   a. What happens when an attempt is made to access an identifier outside of its scope?
   b. How do the values change as a result of assignments in the subprogram and the main program when the same identifier is used in the main program and a subprogram?
6. Review the following program:

```
int main()
{
       int a, b;
       double x;
       char ch;

       .
       .

}
int sub1(int a1)
{
       int b1;

       .
       .

}

int sub2(int a1, int b1)
{
       double x1;
       char ch1;

       .
       .

}
```

   a. List all global variables.
   b. List all local variables.
   c. Indicate the scope of each identifier.
7. Provide a schematic representation of the program and all subprograms and variables in Exercise 6.

Figure 4.11

Scope diagram for
Exercise 8

a

b

void sub1

a

void sub2

b

8. Using the program with variables and subprograms as depicted in Figure 4.11, state the scope of each identifier.

9. What is the output from the following program?

```cpp
#include <iostream.h>

void sub1 (int a);

int main()
{
    int a;
    a = 10;

    cout << a << endl;
    sub1 (a);
    cout << a << endl;
    return 0;
}

void sub1 (int a)
{
    a = 20;
    cout << a << endl;
}
```

◆ Figure 4.12

Scope diagram for
Exercise 10

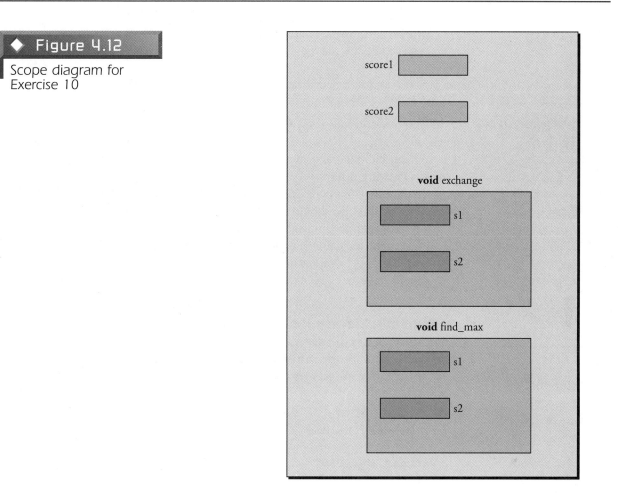

10. Write appropriate headings and declaration sections for the program and
    subprograms illustrated in Figure 4.12.
11. Find all errors in the following program:

```
int main()
{
        double x, y;
        x = 10;
        y = 2 * x;
        cout << x << y << endl;
        sub1(x);
        cout << x1 << x << y <<endl;
        return 0;
}

void sub1 (int x1)
{
        cout << x1 << x << y << endl;
}
```

12. Discuss the advantages and disadvantages of using the same names for identifiers in a subprogram and the main program.

4.6 Programmer-Defined Libraries

Objectives

- to be able to define libraries
- to distinguish between library header files and library implementation files

library header file:
A file of source code, usually having an **.h** suffix, containing data and function declarations.

library implementation file:
A file of source code, usually having a **.cpp** suffix, containing function implementations.

As you develop functions, you will find that some of them are useful in a wide range of programs. It is convenient to create your own libraries of functions so that you can include them in any program where they are needed. There are two steps for creating a library:

1. Declare the functions and save this code in a **library header file.** The name of this file should have an **.h** extension, and will be included by any program needing these functions.
2. Implement the same functions and save this code in a **library implementation file.** For many C++ compilers, the name of this file should have a **.cpp** extension.

An Example Library Header File

Let us create a library of interactive input functions. The two functions, **get_integer** and **get_string**, were discussed in Section 4.2. The declarations of the functions go in a header file named **myinput.h**. The text of this file follows:

```
// Library header file: myinput.h

#ifndef MY_INPUT

#include "apstring.h"

// Function: get_integer
// Prompts user for an integer, inputs it, and returns it
//
// Input: A string representing the prompt
// Output: The integer input by the user

int get_integer(apstring prompt);

// Function: get_string
// Prompts user for a string, inputs it, and returns it
//
// Input: A string representing the prompt
// Output: The string input by the user

apstring get_string(apstring prompt);

#define MY_INPUT

#endif
```

Note that comments documenting the functions go with the declarations in the header file. The header file serves as the communication link between the implementers of the library and its users. Thus, it is very important to maintain adequate documentation of all library functions in this file.

Note also the use of the preprocessor directives **#ifndef**, **#define**, and **#endif**. These directives are used to prevent the preprocessor from including a library file more than once in an application at compile time. For example, the header file **apstring.h** is included in this file, so that the identifier **apstring** will have a definition. But the same header file would also be included in the main program, which would use it to declare string variables. The new directives work to prevent multiple inclusions from occurring as follows:

1. The first directive, **#ifndef**, asks if a file identifier has been defined. If it has, that means that the library file has already been preprocessed, so the preprocessor skips the current inclusion by jumping to **#endif** at the end of the file.

2. If the file identifier has not been defined, the preprocessor will reach the **#define** directive after preprocessing the library file. This directive then makes visible a global file identifier, so that the next inclusion after this one will behave as in step 1.

In general, every library header file should use these directives to avoid compilation errors. The basic form of a header file is

```
#ifndef <file identifier>

<function declarations>

#define <file identifier>
#endif
```

An Example Library Implementation File

The implementation file for the **myinput** library contains the function implementations, and is named **myinput.cpp**.

```
// Library implementation file: myinput.cpp

#include "myinput.h"

int get_integer(apstring prompt)
{
    int data;

    cout << prompt;
    cin >> data;
    return data;
}
```

```
apstring get_string(apstring prompt)
{
        apstring data;

        cout << prompt;
        cin >> data;
        return data;
}
```

The implementation file includes the header file before defining the functions. This order is necessary for the compiler to check that the function declarations in the header file match the headings in the implementation file. Note that the file name used with the **#include** directive is enclosed in double quotes rather than angle brackets. You have already seen this notation used with the **apstring** library, and is typical for programmer-defined libraries.

Example Use of a Programmer-Defined Library

The following driver program tests the functions defined in the **myinput** library:

```
// Program file: testmyin.cpp

#include <iostream.h>
#include "apstring.h"
#include "myinput.h"

int main()
{
        int age;
        apstring name;

        name = get_string("Enter your first name: ");
        age = get_integer("Enter your age: ");
        cout << "Name = " << name << endl;
        cout << "Age = " << age << endl;
        return 0;
}
```

Note the use of double quotes to enclose the file name rather than angle brackets. In general, names of programmer-defined libraries will appear this way when they are included in example programs in this text. Names of standard libraries will continue to appear in angle brackets.

■ Exercises 4.6

1. Why is it a good idea to put commonly used functions in a program library?
2. Discuss the difference between a library header file and a library implementation file. What are the roles and responsibilities of each file?

3. Discuss how C++ preprocesses code in library files before compilation. Be sure to address the role of the directives **#include**, **#ifndef**, **#define**, and **#endif** in this process.
4. Create a program library named **mymath**. This library should define functions for computing the areas of rectangles, circles, and triangles.

4.7 Graphics

Objectives

♦ to learn how to define a graphics function

♦ to learn how to set the fill pattern and fill color

♦ to learn how to develop functions for drawing filled shapes

Defining a Graphics Function

As you know, the basic graphics commands that you learned in Chapters 2 and 3 are C++ **graphics** library functions. Commands such as **lineto(30, 40)** and **circle(100, 100, 50)** are named to reflect the kind of image being drawn. These functions also expect parameters that specify the position and size of the object in the coordinate system. We can easily extend this toolbox of graphics operations by defining similar functions of our own. As always, we must be sure to take these steps:

1. Pick a name that describes the purpose of the function.
2. Specify the inputs and outputs of the function in terms of parameters and returned value.
3. Test the function with various actual parameters during implementation.

Example 4.5

Different applications require a function that draws triangles. We can name this function **triangle**. A triangle can be completely specified by its three vertices. These three pairs of coordinates will be the six input parameters to the **triangle** function. The function draws the triangle and returns no value. The function might be used as follows:

```
// Draw a right isosceles triangle

triangle(10, 10, 110, 10, 110, 110);

// Draw a scalene triangle

triangle(200, 10, 250, 100, 240, 50);
```

The function's declaration, with documentation, is

```
// Function: triangle
// Draws a triangle at the specified coordinates
//
// Inputs: Six integers specifying the coordinates of the
//         vertices of the triangle

void triangle(int x1, int y1, int x2, int y2, int x3, int y3);
```

The implementation of the **triangle** function uses **moveto** and **linerel** commands to position the pen and draw the line segments that connect the vertices.

```
void triangle(int x1, int y1, int x2, int y2, int x3, int x4)
{
        moveto(x1, y1);
        linerel(x2, y2);
        linerel(x3, y3);
        linerel(x1, y1);
}
```

Example 4.6

Cartoons require operations to draw smiling faces and sad faces. These images occur so often that functions for drawing them are highly desirable. The user of these functions specifies the center point of the face and its size (radius). The functions might be invoked as follows:

```
smiling_face(100, 100, 50);
sad_face(200, 100, 50);
```

with the output

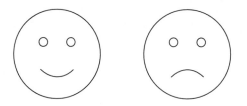

The following function implementations draw simple smiling and sad faces:

```
void smiling_face(int center_x, int center_y, int size)
{
        // Draw outline of head

        circle(center_x, center_y, size);

        // Draw left eye

        circle(center_x - size / 4, center_y - size / 4, 2);

        // Draw right eye

        circle(center_x + size / 4, center_y - size / 4, 2);

        // Draw smiling mouth

        arc(center_x, center_y + size / 5, 200, 340,
            size / 2);
}
```

```
void sad_face(int center_x, int center_y, int size)
{
    // Draw outline of head

    circle(center_x, center_y, size);

    // Draw left eye

    circle(center_x - size / 4, center_y - size / 4, 2);

    // Draw right eye

    circle(center_x + size / 4, center_y - size / 4, 2);

    // Draw sad mouth

    arc(center_x, center_y + size - size / 4, 20, 160,
        size / 2);
}
```

Example 4.7

An experienced programmer will spot a redundant pattern of code in the two functions in Example 4.6. The code to draw the outline of the head and the two eyes is the same in both functions; only the code to draw the mouth is different. There may be other functions for drawing other kinds of faces that exhibit this same pattern as well. We can save some code by writing a single general function, **face**, that draws the common features of all faces.

```
void face(int center_x, int center_y, int size)
{
    // Draw outline of head

    circle(center_x, center_y, size);

    // Draw left eye

    circle(center_x - size / 4, center_y - size / 4, 2);

    // Draw right eye

    circle(center_x + size / 4, center_y - size / 4, 2);
}
```

Note that this function draws every feature of a face but the mouth. We then call this function at the beginning of each function that draws a particular kind of face.

```
void smiling_face(int center_x, int center_y, int size)
{
    // Draw outline of face
```

```
        face(center_x, center_y, size);

        // Draw smiling mouth

        arc(center_x, center_y + size / 5, 200, 340,
            size / 2);
}

void sad_face(int center_x, int center_y, int size)
{
        // Draw outline of face

        face(center_x, center_y, size);

        // Draw sad mouth

        arc(center_x, center_y + size - size / 4, 20, 160,
            size / 2);
}
```

Fill Patterns

Occasionally, we need to fill a closed region. For example, the eyes of the faces in Example 4.6 might look better if they were filled in rather than empty. The most general steps used to fill a bounded region are as follows:

1. Set the pattern and color of the interior.
2. Fill the region.

The graphics function **setfillstyle** is used to set the pattern and the color of an interior region. For example, the following call would set the fill pattern to a solid color and set the fill color to white:

```
setfillstyle(SOLID_FILL, WHITE);
```

The form for using **setfillstyle** is

setfillstyle(<fill pattern >, <fill color>)

where **<fill pattern>** is one of the integers or symbols in Table 4.1 and **<fill color>** is one of the values in Table 3.13.

After the fill pattern and fill color have been set, an enclosed region can be filled by calling the **floodfill** function. The form for using **floodfill** is

floodfill(<x coordinate>, <y coordinate>, <border color>)

where **(<x coordinate>, <y coordinate>)** is a point within the interior region of the shape to be filled and **<border color>** is the color of the shape's

▼ Table 4.1

Fill pattern values expressed as integers and symbols

As an Integer	As a Symbol	Effect
0	EMPTY_FILL	Background color
1	SOLID_FILL	Solid fill with fill color
2	LINE_FILL	———————————
3	LTSLASH_FILL	///////////// (light)
4	SLASH_FILL	///////////// (thick)
5	BKSLASH_FILL	\\\\\\\\\\\\ (thick)
6	LTBKSLASH_FILL	\\\\\\\\\\\\ (light)
7	HATCH_FILL	
8	XHATCH_FILL	
9	INTERLEAVE_FILL	
10	WIDE_DOT_FILL	
11	CLOSE_DOT_FILL	
12	USER_FILL	Effect varies

boundary. The computer fills the region with the current fill pattern and fill color by starting at the specified point and painting the pixels outward from there to the colored border.

For example, the following code segment draws a red circle, sets the fill pattern and fill color, and then fills the region within the circle:

```
setcolor(RED);
circle(100, 100, 50);
setfillstyle(SOLID_FILL, RED);
floodfill(100, 100, RED);
```

Note that the coordinates passed to **floodfill** must be within a region whose boundary is closed and drawn with the border color. Otherwise, the entire exterior will be filled. If the coordinates lie on the border itself, nothing will happen.

Drawing Filled Shapes

The task of drawing filled shapes can be simplified by developing functions for drawing each shape. For example, the **fill_circle** and **fill_rectangle** functions would be similar to the **circle** and **rectangle** functions, in that they draw circles and rectangles, respectively. The difference would be that the fill functions would expect extra parameters for the fill pattern, fill color, and border color and would fill the shape appropriately. Examples of their use are

```
fill_circle(100, 100, 50, SOLID_FILL, WHITE, RED);
fill_rectangle(200, 100, 300, 200, SLASH_FILL, BLUE, WHITE);
```

where the two colors in the parameter list are the fill color and the border color, respectively.

Note that these functions must change the current pen color. This change represents a side effect that might cause problems for the rest of an application. To minimize these side effects, a function can save the current pen color before it performs its task, and then restore that color when the task is completed. The graphics function **getcolor** returns the current pen (foreground) color. Thus, code of the following form will save and restore the pen color during the execution of a function:

```
// Function heading goes here.
{
    int color = getcolor();        // Save current color

    // Task of function goes here.

    setcolor(color);               // Restore color
}
```

Example 4.8

The functions **fill_circle** and **fill_rectangle** set the fill pattern, fill color, and border color to the values specified by the caller, and draw the corresponding filled images.

The implementation of **fill_rectangle** is

```
void fill_rectangle (int x1, int y1, int x2, int y2,
    int fill_pattern, int fill_color, int border_color);
{
    int color = getcolor();        // Save current color

    setcolor(border_color);
    rectangle(x1, y1, x2, y2);
    setfillstyle(fill_pattern, fill_color);
    floodfill(x1 + (x2 - x1) / 2, y1 + (y2 - y1) / 2,
        border_color);

    setcolor(color);               // Restore color
}
```

Note how the implementation of **fill_rectangle** guarantees that the **flood-fill** function will work correctly, in that the starting point is in the interior of the rectangle and the border color is the color of the rectangle's perimeter. The development of **fill_circle** is left as an exercise.

Example 4.9

Any computer game that uses dice (Example 3.4) should display the results of a roll graphically. Let's write a function named **display_three** that draws an image of a die whose face has three dots. The image looks like a white square on a black background, with three black dots on a diagonal.

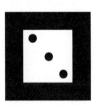

The input data passed to the function are the coordinates of the upper left corner of the die and its height and width (all integers). Thus, it might be invoked as follows:

```
display_three(100, 100, 100, 100);
```

The function assumes that the background color is black. Its declaration is

```
// Function: display_three
// Displays the face of a die having three dots
// Assumes that the background color is black

void display_three(int left, int top, int width, int height);
```

The implementation of **display_three** must draw a filled white rectangle and three filled black circles on a diagonal within the rectangle. The function first calculates the center point of the interior of the rectangle to use as a reference point for drawing the circles. The function then calculates the horizontal and vertical offset distances for use in separating the circles. The function finally draws the rectangle and the circles at the appropriate positions, using the functions **fill_rectangle** and **fill_circle** discussed earlier.

```
void display_three(int left, int top, int height, int width)
{
        int center_x = left + width / 2;
        int center_y = top + height / 2;
        int x_offset = width / 4;
        int y_offset = height / 4;
        int dot_width = 6;
```

```
fill_rectangle(left, top, left + width, top + height
        SOLID_FILL, WHITE, WHITE);
fill_circle(center_x - x_offset, center_y - y_offset, DOT_WIDTH,
        SOLID_FILL, BLACK, BLACK);
fill_circle(center_x, center_y, DOT_WIDTH,
        SOLID_FILL, BLACK, BLACK);
fill_circle(center_x + x_offset, center_y + y_offset, DOT_WIDTH,
        SOLID_FILL, BLACK, BLACK);
}
```

Note the expressions used as parameters for each call of **fill_circle.** The calls draw the filled circles on a diagonal from the upper left of the rectangle to its lower right.

■ Exercises 4.7

1. Design, implement and test a function for drawing parallelograms. Like a triangle, a parallelogram can be specified with three points.
2. Design, implement, and test a function for drawing stick figures. The function should expect parameters specifying the figure's center point and size. The function should call the **smiling_face** function to draw the head of the figure.
3. Design, implement, and test a function for drawing rectangles that uses relative coordinates. The function should expect parameters that specify the coordinates of one corner and the rectangle's height and width.
4. Design, implement and test the **fill_circle** function described in Example 4.8.
5. Rewrite the **face** function of Example 4.7 so that it draws the eyes as filled circles.
6. State two reasons why the development of programmer-defined graphics functions is beneficial.

Focus on Program Design: Case Study

E-Z Parking

To encourage people to shop downtown, the Downtown Businesses Association partially subsidizes parking. They have established the E-Z Parking parking lot where customers are charged $0.75 for each full hour of parking. There is no charge for part of an hour. Thus, if someone has used the lot for less than an hour, there would be no charge.

The E-Z Parking parking lot is open from 9:00 A.M. until 11:00 P.M. When a vehicle enters, the driver is given a ticket with the entry time printed in military style. Thus, if a car entered the lot at 9:30 A.M., the ticket would read 930. If a vehicle entered at 1:20 P.M., the ticket would read 1320. When the vehicle leaves, the driver presents the ticket to the attendant and the amount due is computed.

Let us now develop a solution and write a program to assist the attendant. Input consists of a starting and ending time. Output should be a statement to the customer indicating the input information, the total amount due, a heading, and a closing message. Sample output for the data 1050 (10:50 A.M.) and 1500 (3:00 P.M.) follows:

```
Please enter the time in and press <Enter>. 1050
Please enter the time out and press <Enter>. 1500

                    E - Z Parking

            Time in: 1050 Time out: 1500

        Amount due       $ 3.00

    Thank you for using E - Z Parking

                    BUCKLE UP
                and DRIVE SAFELY
```

A first-level development for this problem is

1. Get the data
2. Compute amount
3. Print results

A structure chart for this problem is given in Figure 4.13. (Recall, an arrow pointing into a module indicates data are being received, whereas an arrow pointing out indicates data are being sent from the module.)

Module specifications for the three main modules are

Module: Get data
Task: Prompt user for and inputs entry time and exit time.
Output: Integers representing entry time and exit time

Module: Compute amount
Task: Compute the amount due in dollars and cents.

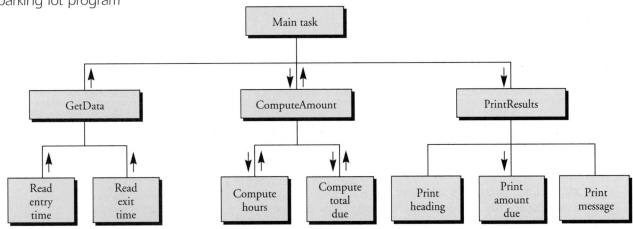

◆ Figure 4.13

Structure chart for the parking lot program

Input: Integers representing entry time and exit time
Output: A real number representing the amount due

Module: Print results
Task: Print heading, entry and exit times, amount due, and closing message.
Input: Integers representing entry time and exit time and a real number representing the amount due

By examining the module specifications, we see that **get_data** needs two parameters, **compute_amount** needs two parameters, and **print_results** needs three parameters.

A second-level pseudocode development is

1. Get the data
   1.1 Prompt user for time entered
   1.2 Read time entered
   1.3 Prompt user for time exited
   1.4 Read time exited
2. Compute amount
   2.1 Compute number of hours
   2.2 Compute amount due
3. Print results
   3.1 Print a heading
   3.2 Print amount due
   3.3 Print a closing message

A complete program for this pseudocode follows:

```
// This program prints statements for customers of the E-Z
// Parking lot. Interactive input consists of entry
// time and exit time from the lot. Output consists of a
// customer statement. Emphasis is placed on using
// functions to develop the program.

// Program file: parking.cpp

#include <iostream.h>
#include <iomanip.h>

const double HOURLY_RATE = 0.75;

// Function: get_data
// Prompts user for and inputs entry time and exit time

// Outputs: integers representing entry time and exit time

void get_data(int &entry_time, int &exit_time);

// Function: compute_amount
// Computes the amount due in dollars and cents
```

```
//
// Inputs: integers representing entry time and exit time
// Output: a real number representing the amount due

double compute_amount(int entry_time, int exit_time);

// Function: print_results
// Prints heading, entry and exit times, amount due,
// and closing message
//
// Inputs: integers representing entry time and exit time
// and a real number
// representing the amount due

void print_results(int entry_time, int exit_time,
     double amount_due);

// Function: print_heading
// Print a heading for the ticket

void print_heading();

// Function: print_message
// Print a closing message for the ticket

void print_message();

int main()
{
     int entry_time;        // Time of entry into parking lot
     int exit_time;         // Time of exit from parking lot
     double amount_due;     // Cost of parking in lot

     get_data(entry_time, exit_time);
     amount_due = compute_amount(entry_time, exit_time);
     print_results (entry_time, exit_time, amount_due);
     return 0;
}
```

```
void get_data(int &entry_time, int &exit_time)
{
     cout << "Please enter the time in 24 hour notation "
         << "and press <Enter>. ";
     cin >> entry_time;
     cout << "Please enter the time out and press <Enter>. ";
     cin >> exit_time;
}
```

1

```
double compute_amount (int entry_time, int exit_time)
{
        int number_of_hours;

        number_of_hours = (exit_time - entry_time) / 100;
        return number_of_hours * HOURLY_RATE;
}
```

2

```
void print_heading()
{
        cout << endl;
        cout << setw(25) << "E - Z Parking" << endl;
        cout << endl;
}

void print_message()
{
        cout << endl;
        cout << setw(4)
             << "Thank you for using E - Z Parking" << endl;
        cout << endl;
        cout << setw(21) << "BUCKLE UP" << endl;
        cout << setw(25) << "and DRIVE SAFELY";
        cout << endl;
}

void print_results (int entry_time, int exit_time,
        double amount_due)
{
        cout << setiosflags(ios::fixed | ios::showpoint | ios::right)
             << setprecision(2);
        print_heading();
        cout << setw(13) << "Time in: "
             << setw(5) << entry_time;
        cout << " Time out:"
             << setw(5) << exit_time << endl;
        cout << endl;
        cout << setw(17) << "Amount due $"
             << setw(6) << amount_due << endl;
        print_message();
}
```

3

A sample run using the data 930 as entry time and 1320 as exit time produces

```
Please enter the time in and press <Enter>. 930
Please enter the time out and press <Enter>. 1320
```

```
                    E - Z Parking

            Time in: 930 Time out: 1320

            Amount due      $ 2.25

        Thank you for using E - Z Parking

                    BUCKLE UP
                and DRIVE SAFELY
```

Running, Debugging, and Testing Hints

1. Each subprogram can be tested separately to see if it is producing the desired result. This is accomplished by a main program that calls and tests only the subprogram in question.
2. You can use related or identical variable names in the parameter lists. For example,

   ```
   double compute (int n1, int n2);
   ```

   or

   ```
   double compute (int number1, int number2);
   ```

   could be called by

   ```
   compute (number1, number2);
   ```

3. Be sure the type, order, and purpose of actual parameters and formal parameters agree. You can do this by listing them one below the other. For example,

   ```
   void display_data (char init1, char init2, int sc);
   ```

   could be called by

   ```
   display_data ('a', 'b', 9);
   ```

4. Be sure that you really need to use a reference parameter in a function before you declare it. If a function returns only one value to the caller, use no reference parameters.
5. If a function does not seem to return a value to the caller as expected, perhaps a parameter has not been declared as a reference parameter. Check the function's heading and declaration to be sure that the symbol **&** is associated with the desired output parameter.

Summary

🔑 Key Terms

abstract data type
actual parameter
   (arguments)
alias
block
bottom-up testing
cohesive subprogram
constant reference
formal parameter
function declaration
function heading
function implementation
functional abstraction
global identifier

information hiding
interface
library header file
library implementation
   file
local copy
local identifier
locally declared data
main driver
manifest interface
modularity
parameter mode
pass by reference
pass by value

postcondition
precondition
procedural abstraction
reference parameter
scope of identifier
side effect
structured design
structured programming
stub programming
subblock
subprogram
user-defined function
value parameter
void function

🔑 Keywords

return   **void**

🔑 Key Concepts

◆ A subprogram is a program within a program; functions are subprograms.
◆ Subprograms can be utilized to perform specific tasks in a program. Functions are often used to initialize variables, get data, print headings (no parameters needed), perform computations, and print data.
◆ The general form for a function declaration is

> <type identifier> <name> (<parameter list>);

◆ A **void** return type is used when a function returns no value to its caller.
◆ A typical parameter list is

```
void display_data(int n1, int n2, double x, double y);
```

◆ A formal parameter is one listed in the subprogram heading; it is like a blank waiting to receive a value from the calling program:

formal parameters

```
void arithmetic (char sym, int n1, int n2);
```

◆ An actual parameter is a variable listed in the subprogram call in the calling program:

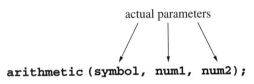

actual parameters

```
arithmetic(symbol, num1, num2);
```

◆ The formal parameter list in the subprogram heading must match the number and types of actual parameters used in the main program when the subprogram is called:

```
void arithmetic(char sym, int n1, int n2);
arithmetic(symbol, num1, num2);
```

◆ The type of an actual parameter being passed to a function must be compatible with the type of the formal parameter in its position in a function heading; the computer makes automatic type conversions whenever possible.

◆ If the symbol **&** appears in a formal parameter declaration, then the formal parameter is a reference parameter; otherwise, the formal parameter is a value parameter.

◆ For value parameters, a copy of the actual parameter's value is passed to a function when it is called.

◆ Pass by value is safe; the value of the actual parameter does not change during the call of the function.

◆ For reference parameters, the address of the actual parameter is passed to the function when it is called.

◆ Pass by reference is not safe; it should be used with caution and only when side effects are intended.

◆ Global identifiers can be used by the main program and all subprograms.

◆ Local identifiers are available only to the main program block or the subprogram block in which they are declared.

◆ Each identifier is available to the block in which it is declared.

◆ Identifiers are not available outside their blocks.

◆ The scope of an identifier refers to the area of text in which the identifier is available.

◆ Understanding the scope of identifiers is aided by graphic illustration of blocks in a program; thus, the following program

```
const double PI = 3.14;

double sub1(double x1);
double sub2(double x1);

int main()
{
     double x, y, z;

          .
          .

}

double sub1(double x1)
{
```

```
        double x2;
        .
        .
}

double sub2(double x1)
{
        double z2;
        .
        .
}
```

◆ can be visualized as shown in Figure 4.14. A user-defined function is a subprogram that performs a specific task.

◆ The form for a user-defined function is

<type identifier> <function name> (<parameter list>)
{
    <data declarations>
    <executable statements>
}

◆ **Figure 4.14**

Scope diagram for a program

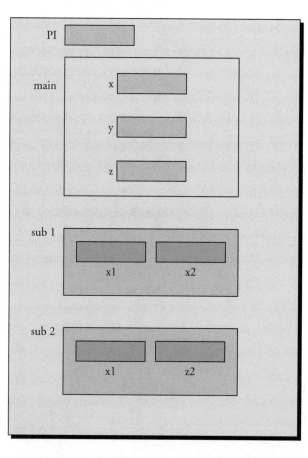

◆ A programmer-defined library is a useful way to organize the definitions of related functions. A library consists of a header file and an implementation file.

◆ The form of a library header file is

#ifndef <file identifier>

<function declarations>

#define <file identifier>
#endif

Chapter Review Exercises

1. Explain the difference between a value parameter and a reference parameter. Give an example of how each is used.
2. Explain the difference between an actual parameter and a formal parameter.
3. A function is declared as

   ```
   void sample_func(int a, double &b, char c);
   ```

   Which parameters in this declaration are reference parameters and which are value parameters?

In Exercises 4–12, assume that the **sample_func** function is being called. Which function calls are valid? (**int1** represents an integer variable, **double1** represents a real number, and **ch1** represents a character.) If the call is invalid, explain why.

4. ```
   sample_func(int1, double1, ch1);
   ```
5. ```
   sample_func;
   ```
6. ```
   sample_func();
   ```
7. ```
   sample_func(int int1, double double1, char ch1);
   ```
8. ```
   sample_func(int1, double1);
   ```
9. ```
   sample_func(int, double, char);
   ```
10. ```
    sample_func(10, double1, 'A');
    ```
11. ```
    sample_func(10.5, double1, 66);
    ```
12. ```
    sample_func(10, 10.5, 'A');
    ```
13. Write a function to display the following:

    ```
    <<<<<<<<<<<<<<<<<<<<<<<<<<<<>>>>>>>>>>>>>>>>>>>>>>>>>>>>
                      Programming in C++

                        is GREAT!
    ```

14. Write a main program to display the message from Exercise 13 five times.

In Exercises 15–21, indicate if the statement is a valid function declaration. Explain the problem for those that are invalid.

15. ```
    void exercise15(int a, double y);
    ```
16. ```
    void exercise16(&a, double y);
    ```
17. ```
    int exercise17(int &a, int &b);
    ```
18. ```
    int (int &a, char b);
    ```
    ```

19. `void exercise19(int &a, int &b);`
20. `int exercise20(int a, char &b);`
21. `double exercise 21(int &a, char &b);`

For Exercises 22–26, write a statement that can be used to call each of the following functions:

22. `void exercise22(int &a, int &b, double c);`
23. `double exercise23(int &a, double b);`
24. `char exercise24();`
25. `char exercise25(double a);`
26. `bool exercise26(int a, int b, int c);`
27. Why are reference parameters used in a function designed to initialize variables?

Programming Problems and Activities

The following programming problems will be run on a very limited set of data. In later chapters, as you build your programming skills, you will run these problems with larger databases and subprograms for various parts. *Be sure to package coherent tasks in functions wherever possible.*

1. Write a program to get the coefficients of the quadratic equation

$$ax^2 + bx + c = 0$$

from the keyboard and then print the value of the discriminant $b^2 - 4ac$. A sample display for getting input is

```
Enter coefficients a, b, and c for the quadratic equation

ax² + bx + c = 0

a = ?
b = ?
c = ?
```

Run this program at least three times using test data that result in $b^2 - 4ac = 0$, $b^2 - 4ac > 0$, and $b^2 - 4ac < 0$.

2. Write a program to compute the cost for carpeting a room. Input should consist of the room length, room width, and carpet price per square yard. Use constants for the pad charge and installation charge. Include a heading as part of the output.
   A typical input screen would be:

```
What is the room length in feet? <Enter> ?
What is the room width in feet? <Enter> ?
What is the carpet price/square yard? <Enter> ?
```

Output for a sample run of this program (without a heading) could be

```
Dimensions of the room (in feet) are 17 × 22.
The area to be carpeted is 41.6 square yards.
The carpet price is $11.95 per yard.
```

Room dimensions	17 × 22
Carpet required	41.6 square yards
Carpet price/yard	$11.95
Pad price/yard	$2.95
Installation cost/yard	$ .95
Total cost/yard	$15.85
Total cost	$659.36

3. Williamson's Paint and Papering Store wants a computer program to help them determine how much paint is needed to paint a room. Assuming a room is to have four walls and the ceiling painted, input for the program should be the length, width, and height of the room. Use a constant for the wall height (usually 8 feet). One gallon of paint should cover 250 square feet. Cost of paint for the walls and ceiling should be entered by the user. Output should be the amount and cost for each kind of paint, and the total cost.

4. The Fairfield College faculty recently signed a three-year contract that included salary increments of 7%, 6%, and 5%, respectively, for the next three years. Write a program that allows a user to enter the current salary and then prints the compounded salary for each of the next three years.

5. Several teachers use various weights (percentage of the final grade) for test scores. Write a program that allows the user to enter three test scores and the weight for each score. Output should consist of the input data, the weighted score for each test, and the total score (sum of the weighted scores).

6. The Roll-Em Lanes bowling team would like to have a computer program to print the team results for one series of games. The team consists of four members whose names are Weber, Fazio, Martin, and Patterson. Each person on the team bowls three games during the series; thus, the input will contain three lines, each with four integer scores. Your output should include all input data, individual series totals, game average for each member, team series, and team average. Sample output is

NAME	GAME 1	GAME 2	GAME 3	TOTAL	AVERAGE
Weber	212	220	190	622	207.3
Fazio	195	235	210	640	213.3
Martin	178	190	206	574	191.3
Patterson	195	215	210	620	206.7

Team Total: 2456

Team Average: 818.7

7. The Natural Pine Furniture Company has recently hired you to help them convert their antiquated payroll system to a computer-based model. They know you are still learning, so all they want right now is a program that will print a one-week pay report for three employees. You should use the constant definition section for the following:
   a. Federal withholding tax rate   18%
   b. State withholding tax rate   4.5%
   c. Hospitalization $25.65
   d. Union dues $7.85

   Each line of input will contain the employee's initials, the number of hours worked, and the employee's hourly rate. Your output should include a report for each employee and a summary report for the company files. A sample employee form follows:

```
Employee:           JIM
Hours Worked:          40.00
Hourly Rate:            9.75
Total Wages:          390.00

Deductions:
Federal Withholding    70.20
State Withholding      17.55
Hospitalization        26.65
Union Dues              7.85
                       -----
Total Deductions      122.25

Net Pay             $267.75
```

   Output for a summary report could be

```
            Natural Pine Furniture Company
                   Weekly Summary

Gross Wages:

Deductions:
        Federal Withholding
        State Withholding
        Hospitalization
        Union Dues
        Total Deductions

        Net Wages
```

8. The Child-Growth Encyclopedia Company wants a computer program that will print a monthly sales chart. Products produced by the company, prices, and sales commissions for each are
   a. Basic encyclopedia, $325.00; 22%
   b. Child educational supplement, $127.50; 15%

c. Annual update book, $ 18.95; 20%

Monthly sales data for one region consist of a two-letter region identifier (such as MI) and three integers, representing the number of units sold for each product listed above. A typical input screen would be:

```
What is your sales region? MI
How many Basic Encyclopedias were sold? 150
How many Child Supplements were sold? 120
How many Annual Updates were sold? 105
```

Write a program that will get the monthly sales data for two sales regions and produce the desired company chart. The prices may vary from month to month and should be defined in the constant definition section. The commissions are not subject to change. Typical output could be:

MONTHLY SALES CHART

		Basic Encyclopedia	Child Supplement	Annual Update
Region				
Units sold	MI	150	120	105
(by region)	TX	225	200	150
Total units sold:		375	320	255
Price/unit		$325.00	$127.50	$18.95
Gross Sales:		$121875.00	$40800.00	$4832.25
Commission rate		22%	15%	20%
Commissions paid:		$26812.50	$6120.00	$966.45

9. The Village Variety Store is having its annual Christmas sale. They would like you to write a program to produce a daily report for the store. Each item sold is identified by a code consisting of one letter followed by one digit. Your report should include data for three items. Each of the three lines of data will include item code, number of items sold, original item price, and reduction percentage. Your report should include a chart with the input data, sale price per item, and total amount of sales per item. You should also print a daily summary. Sample input is

```
A1 13     5.95 15

A2 24     7.95 20

A3 80     3.95 50
```

Typical output could be in this form:

Item Code	# Sold	Original Price	Reductions	Sale Price	Income
A1	13	$5.95	15%	$5.06	$65.78

Daily Summary

    Gross Income:

10. The Holiday-Out Motel Company, Inc., wants a program that will print a statement for each overnight customer. Each line of input will contain room number (integer), number of nights (integer), room rate (real), telephone charges (real), and restaurant charges (real). You should use the constant definition section for the date and current tax rate. Each customer statement should include all input data, the date, tax rate and amount, total due, appropriate heading, and appropriate closing message. Test your program by running it for two customers. The tax rate applies only to the room cost. A typical input screen is

```
Room number? 135
Room rate? 39.95
Number of nights? 3
Telephone charges? 3.75
Meals? 57.50
```

A customer statement form is

Holiday-Out Motel Company, Inc.

Date:	XX-XX-XX
Room #	135
Room Rate:	$39.95
Number of Nights:	3
Room Cost:	$119.85
Tax: XXX%	4.79
Subtotal:	$124.64
Telephone:	3.75
Meals:	57.50
TOTAL DUE	$185.89

Thank you for staying at Holiday-Out
        Drive safely
       Please come again

11. As a part-time job this semester, you are working for the Family Budget Assistance Center. Your boss has asked you to write and execute a program that will analyze data for a family. Input for each family will consist of

```
Family ID number (int)
Number in family (int)
Income (double)
Total debts (double)
```

Your program should output the following:

a. An appropriate header.

b. The family's identification number, number in family, income, and total debts.

c. Predicted family living expenses ($3000 times the number in family).

d. The monthly payment necessary to pay off the debt in one year.

e. The amount the family should save (the family size times 2% of the income minus debt—**fam_size * 0.02 * (income - debt))**.

f. Your service fee (0.5% of the income).

Run your program for the following two families:

Identification Number	Size Income	Debt
51	18,000.00	4800.00
4	26,000.00	3200.00

Output for the first family could be:

```
        Family Budget Assistance Center
               March 1989
          Telephone: (800)555-1234

Identification number          51
Family size                    4
Annual income                  $ 18000.00
Total debt                     $  2000.00
Expected living expenses       $ 12000.00
Monthly payment                $   166.67
Savings                        $  1280.00
Service fee                    $    90.00
```

12. The Caswell Catering and Convention Service has asked you to write a computer program to produce customers' bills. The program should read in the following data:

a. The number of adults to be served.

b. The number of children to be served.

c. The cost per adult meal.

d. The cost per child's meal (60% of the cost of the adult's meal).

e. The cost for dessert (same for adults and children).

f. The room fee (no room fee if catered at the person's home).

g. A percentage for tip and tax (not applied to the room fee).

h. Any deposit should be deducted from the bill.

Write a program and test it using data sets 2, 3, and 4 from the following table:

Set	Child Count	Adult Count	Adult Cost	Dessert Cost	Room Cost	Tip/Tax Rate	Deposit
1	7	23	12.75	1.00	45.00	18%	50.00
2	3	54	13.50	1.25	65.00	19%	40.00
3	15	24	12.00	0.00	45.00	18%	75.00
4	2	71	11.15	1.50	0.00	6%	0.00

Note that data set 1 was used to produce the following sample output.

```
            Caswell Catering and Convention Service
                         Final Bill

Number of adults:                             23
Number of children:                            7
Cost per adult without dessert:    $     12.75
Cost per child without dessert:    $      7.65
Cost per dessert:                  $      1.00
Room fee:                          $     45.00
Tip and tax rate:                      0.18

Total cost for adult meals:        $    293.25
Total cost for child meals:        $     53.55
Total cost for dessert:            $     30.00
Total food cost:                   $    376.80
Plus tip and tax:                  $     67.82
Plus room fee:                     $     45.00
Less deposit:                      $     50.00

Balance due:                       $    439.62
```

13. The Maripot Carpet Store has asked you to write a computer program to calculate the amount a customer should be charged. The president of the company has given you the following information to help in writing the program.
    a. The carpet charge is equal to the number of square yards purchased times the carpet cost per square yard.
    b. The labor cost is equal to the number of square yards purchased times the labor cost per square yard. A fixed fee for floor preparation is added to some customers' bills.
    c. Large-volume customers are given a percentage discount but the discount applies only to the carpet charge, not the labor costs.
    d. All customers are charged 4% sales tax on the carpet; there is no sales tax on the labor cost.

Write the program and test it using the following data sets for customers 2, 3, and 4.

Customer	Sq. yds.	Cost per sq. yd.	Labor per sq. yd.	Prep. Cost	Discount
1	17	18.50	3.50	38.50	0.02
2	40	24.95	2.95	0.00	0.14
3	23	16.80	3.25	57.95	0.00
4	26	21.25	0.00	80.00	0.00

Note that the data for customer 1 were used to produce the following sample output:

```
Square yards purchased:              17
       Cost per square yard:    $    18.50
      Labor per square yard:    $     3.50
    Floor preparation cost:    $    38.50
             Cost for carpet:    $   314.50
              Cost for labor:    $    98.00
         Discount on carpet:    $     6.29
              Tax on carpet:    $    12.33
         Charge to customer:    $   418.54
```

14. The manager of the Croswell Carpet Store has asked you to write a program to print customers' bill. The manager has given you the following information:

The store expresses the length and width of a room in terms of feet and tenths of a foot. For example, the length might be reported as 16.7 feet.

The amount of carpet purchased is expressed as square yards. It is found by dividing the area of the room (in square feet) by nine.

The store does not sell a fraction of a square yard. Thus, square yards must always be rounded up.

The carpet charge is equal to the number of square yards purchased times the carpet cost per square yard. Sales tax equal to 4% of the carpet cost must be added to the bill.

All customers are sold a carpet pad at $2.25 per square yard. Sales tax equal to 4% of the pad cost must be added to the bill.

The labor cost is equal to the number of square yards purchased times $2.40, which is the labor cost per square yard. No tax is charged on labor.

Large volume customers may be given a discount. The discount may apply only to the carpet cost (before sales tax is added), only to the pad cost (before sales tax is added), only to the labor cost, or to any combination of the three charges.

Each customer is identified by a five-digit number and that number should appear on the bill. The sample output follows:

```
              Croswell Carpet Store
                    Invoice

      Customer number :           26817

                   Carpet :       574.20
                     Pad :         81.00
                   Labor :         86.40

               Subtotal :         741.60
          Less discount :          65.52

               Subtotal :         676.08
               Plus tax :          23.59
                  Total :         699.67
```

Write the program and test it for the following three customers:

a. Mr. Wilson (customer 81429) ordered carpet for his family room, which measures 25 feet long and 18 feet wide. The carpet sells for $12.95 per square yard and the manager agreed to give him a discount of 8% on the carpet and 6% on the labor.

b. Mr. and Mrs. Adams (customer 04246) ordered carpet for their bedroom, which measures 16.5 feet by 15.4 feet. The carpet sells for $18.90 per square yard and the manager granted a discount of 12% of everything.

c. Ms. Logan (customer 39050) ordered carpet that cost $8.95 per square yard for her daughter's bedroom. The room measures 13.1 by 12.5 feet. No discounts were given.

15. Each week Abduhl's Flying Carpets pays its salespeople a base salary plus a bonus for each carpet they sell. In addition, they pay a commission of 10% of the total sales by each salesperson. Write a program to compute a salesperson's salary for the month by inputting the base, bonus, quantity, and sales, and making the necessary calculations. Use the following test data:

Salesperson	Base	Bonus	Quantity	Commission	Sales
1	250.00	15.00	20	10%	1543.69
2	280.00	19.50	36	10%	2375.90

The commission figure is 10%. Be sure you can change this easily if necessary. Sample output follows:

```
          Salesperson :           1
                 Base :         250.00
                Bonus :          15.00
             Quantity:          20
          Total Bonus :         300.00
```

```
    Commission :          10%
         Sales :       1543.69
Total Commission :       154.37
           Pay :        704.37
```

16. Write a program to help people convert their height and weight from inches and pounds to centimeters and kilograms. The program should take keyboard input of a person's height (in feet and inches) and weight (rounded to the nearest pound). Output should consist of the height and weight in metric units.

17. Reread the material in Section 4.4 concerning functional abstraction. Then, from Problems 5, 7, 8, and 11, select one that you have not yet worked. Develop a structure chart and write module specifications for each module required for the problem you have chosen. Also, write a main driver for your program and write complete documentation for each subprogram including comments about all parameters.

18. The design of the functions to draw faces (Example 4.7) divides tasks among three functions, **face**, **smiling_face**, and **sad_face**. Marjorie Seeplus, an expert programmer, says that the task of drawing a face can be subdivided even further, into the subtasks of drawing eyes, head, sad mouth, and smiling mouth. Each of these subtasks should be represented as a new module or function. Carry out this new design proposal in the following steps:
   a. Draw structure charts for the functions **smiling_face** and **sad_face**, showing the modules (functions) that are used and the transmission of data between them.
   b. Write module specifications for all of these functions.
   c. Code the functions in a **faces** library. The function declarations should go in the file **faces.h**, and the function implementations should go in the file **faces.cpp**.
   d. Write a driver program that includes the **faces** library and test the top-level **smiling_face** and **sad_face** functions.

19. Any computer game that uses dice (Example 4.9) should display the results of a roll graphically. Write a **dice** library defining six functions (named **display_one**, **display_two**, etc.) that draw images of the six faces of a die:

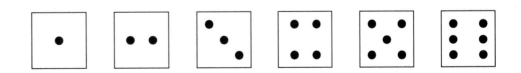

Each function should expect four parameters: the coordinates of the upper left corner and the height and width of the die. The border color and the fill color of a dot are both black and the border and fill colors of the rest of the die are white. Write a driver program that includes the **dice** library and test the functions.

20. An interesting optical illusion is caused by a phenomenon known as *induced contrast*. Induced contrast occurs when two images of the same shade are placed on backgrounds of different shades, as shown in the following picture:

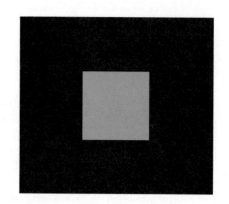

One image appears darker than the other, even though they are exactly the same shade. Use the **fill_rectangle** function developed in Example 4.8 to write a program that generates such an illusion.

Communication in Practice

1. Reread the **Note of Interest** on hacking and other intrusions in this chapter. Then search in the ACM Code of Ethics (see **Note of Interest** in Chapter 2) for principles that apply to these problems. Prepare a written report on your findings to present to your class.

2. Discuss the issue of documenting subprograms with teachers of computer science, college students majoring in computer science, and some of your classmates. Prepare a report for your class on this issue. Your report should contain information about different forms of documentation, the perceived need for documentation by various groups, the significance of documenting data transmission, and so forth. If possible, use specific examples to illustrate good documentation of subprograms versus poor documentation of subprograms.

3. Modify one of your programs from this section by saving only the documentation, constant definitions, variable declarations, function declarations, and main driver. Exchange your modified program with a student who has prepared a similar version. Using the modified version, reconstruct the tasks of the program. Discuss your results with the student who wrote the program.

4. Pick a problem from this section and solve it as a team project for a four-member team with one project director. The project director is responsible for the final design of the main program and must set up an adequate division of responsibilities and communication for the other team members. Each of the team members should develop complete documentation for a subtask. The final project should include a report that contains the main driver, a description of the subtask for each team member, and a summary of the communication required for the team to work together.

Chapter 5

Selection Statements

Chapter Outline

5.1 Boolean Expressions

Objectives

- to understand the need for a Boolean data type
- to be able to use relational operators
- to understand the hierarchy for evaluating simple Boolean expressions
- to be able to use the logical operators that express AND, OR, and NOT
- to be able to use compound Boolean expressions
- to understand the short-circuit evaluation of compound Boolean expressions

The previous chapters set the stage for using computers to solve problems. You have seen how programs in C++ can be used to get data, perform computations, and print results. You should be able to write complete, short programs, so it is now time to examine other aspects of problem solving.

Let us review the metaphor of the programmable pocket calculator that we have been using in the last two chapters. Our calculator allows us to solve some simple and complex problems by using built-in functions or by creating and using functions of our own. However, the calculator is limited in that it can only take input, calculate results, and display them as output. We would like the calculator to be more flexible, to be able to respond in different ways to different inputs or changes in its environment.

A major feature of a full-fledged computer, as opposed to our calculator, is the ability to make decisions. For example, a condition is examined and a decision is made as to which program statement is executed next. Statements that permit a computer to make decisions are called **selection statements.** Selection statements are examples of **control structures** because they allow the programmer to control the flow of execution of program statements.

Before looking at decision making, we need to examine the logical constructs in C++, which include a new data type called **Boolean.** This data type allows you to represent something as true or false. Although this sounds relatively simple (and it is), this is a very significant feature of computers.

selection statement:
A control statement that selects some particular logical path based on the value of an expression.

control structure:
A structure that controls the flow of execution of program statements.

Boolean: An expression whose value is either true or false.

type definition:
The introduction of a synonym for an existing data type.

Defining Boolean Constants and a Boolean Data Type

Thus far we have used only three data types, **int**, **double**, and **char**. In any C++ program, the value 0 means *false,* and any other value means *true.* Instead of having to remember these associations, it would be convenient to use the names **TRUE** and **FALSE** to denote the Boolean constants, as well as to use the name **bool** when we wish to refer to the data type itself. For example, we might like to declare a variable **b** of type **bool**, and assign it an initial value of **TRUE**:

```
bool b = TRUE;
```

You might have an older version of C++ that does not provide **bool** as a standard data type. In that case, so that C++ programs can use these names properly, we define the constants **FALSE** and **TRUE** to have the values 0 and 1, respectively:

```
const int FALSE = 0;
const int TRUE = 1;
```

To create a new type name for declaring variables, function parameters, and function returns of these values, we use a C++ **type definition:**

```
typedef int bool;
```

typedef is a reserved word in C++. The general form of a type definition is

```
typedef <data type> <new type name>;
```

where data type is any C++ data type. All our **typedef** example does is create a synonym, **bool**, for a built-in type name, **int**.

Some C++ compilers may have already defined the words **TRUE** and **FALSE** for system use. In that case, you can override these definitions by using the preprocessor directive **#undef**, as follows:

```
#undef FALSE
#undef TRUE

const int FALSE = 0;
const int TRUE = 1;
```

If we define the new names above the main program, Boolean variables can be declared anywhere in the program and manipulated according to the scope rules:

```
#undef FALSE
#undef TRUE
```

```
const int FALSE = 0;
const int TRUE = 1;

typedef int bool;

int main()
{
      bool a, b;

      a = FALSE;
      b = TRUE;
      .
      .
```

As with other data types, if two variables are of type **bool**, the value of one variable can be assigned to another variable as

```
b = TRUE;
a = b;
```

and can be envisioned as

```
TRUE
 a
TRUE
 b
```

Once again, if your version of C++ provides a built-in **bool** data type, you can simply use it and the values **TRUE** and **FALSE** without defining them.

Saving a New Type Definition in a Library File

The Boolean values **TRUE** and **FALSE** and the type name **bool** will be mentioned in many applications. Entering the same five lines of code by hand to define these names in every new source program will be an annoying task. Instead, we can place the definitions in a library header file to be included in every program file that uses them. The file is named **bool.h** and contains our definitions:

```
// Library file: bool.h

// Defines Boolean constants and a type name for any application.

#ifndef BOOL_H

#undef FALSE
#undef TRUE
```

```
const int FALSE = 0;
const int TRUE = 1;

typedef int bool;

#define BOOL_H
#endif
```

This file can then be included in any source program by means of the following line of code:

```
#include "bool.h"
```

Placing the definitions of a new data type in a library file is another example of information hiding. Programmers who use the **bool.h** library need not be concerned with the representation of Boolean values as integers, any more than they have already been concerned with the representation of integers as bit patterns. All that we need to know about Boolean values, aside from their names, is how they can be used to make decisions in programs.

Relational Operators and Simple Boolean Expressions

relational operator: An operator used for comparison of data items of the same type.

simple Boolean expression: An expression in which two numbers or variable values are compared using a single relational operator.

In arithmetic, integers and reals can be compared for the relationships of equality, inequality, less than, and greater than. C++ also provides for the comparison of numbers or values of variables. The operators used for comparison are called **relational operators.** Their arithmetic notation, C++ notation, and meaning are given in Table 5.1.

When two numbers or variable values are compared using a single relational operator, the expression is referred to as a **simple Boolean expression.** Each simple Boolean expression has the Boolean value **TRUE** or **FALSE** according to the arithmetic validity of the expression. In general, data of most of the built-in types can be compared. For example, when a character value is compared to an integer, the ASCII value of the character is used. When comparing reals, however, the computer representation of a real number might not be the exact real number intended. Table 5.2 sets forth several Boolean expressions and their respective Boolean values, assuming the assignment statements **a = 3** and **b = 3** have been made.

▼ Table 5.1

Relational operators

Arithmetic Operation	Relational Operator	Meaning
=	==	Is equal to
<	<	Is less than
>	>	Is greater than
≤	<=	Is less than or equal to
≥	>=	Is greater than or equal to
≠	!=	Is not equal to

▼ Table 5.2	Simple Boolean Expression	Boolean Value
Values of simple Boolean expressions	7 == 7	TRUE
	-3.0 == 0.0	FALSE
	4.2 > 3.7	TRUE
	-18 < -15	TRUE
	13 < 0.013	FALSE
	-17.32 != -17.32	FALSE
	a == a	TRUE

Arithmetic expressions can also be used in simple Boolean expressions. Thus,

```
4 < (3 + 2)
```

has the value **TRUE**. When the computer evaluates this expression, the parentheses dictate that **(3 + 2)** be evaluated first and then the relational operator. Sequentially, this becomes

```
4 < (3 + 2)
4 < 5
TRUE
```

What if the parentheses had not been used? Could the expression be evaluated? This type of expression necessitates a priority level for the relational operators and the arithmetic operators. The following table summarizes the priorities of these operations:

Expression	Priority
( )	1
*, /, %	2
+, -	3
==, <, >, <=, >=, !=	4

Thus, we see that the relational operators are evaluated last. As with arithmetic operators, these are evaluated in order from left to right. Thus, the expression

```
4 < 3 + 2
```

could be evaluated without parentheses and would have the same Boolean value.

The following example illustrates the evaluation of a somewhat more complex Boolean expression.

| Example 5.1 | Indicate the successive steps in the evaluation of the following Boolean expression: |

```
10 % 4 * 3 - 8 <= 18 + 30 / 4 - 20
```

The steps in this evaluation are

```
10 % 4 * 3 - 8 <= 18 + 30 / 4 - 20
 ↓
2 * 3 - 8 <= 18 + 30 / 4 - 20
 ↓
6 - 8 <= 18 + 30 / 4 - 20
 ↓
-2 <= 18 + 30 / 4 - 20
              ↓
-2 <= 18 + 7 - 20
-2 <= 25 - 20
          ↓
-2 <= 5
 ↓
TRUE
```

As shown in Example 5.1, even though parentheses are not required when using arithmetic expressions with relational operators, it is usually a good idea to use them to enhance the readability of the expression and to avoid using an incorrect expression.

Comparing Strings

When a programmer includes the **apsring.h** header file, all of the comparison operators in Table 5.1 can be used with strings. For example, a string variable can be compared with a string literal as follows:

```
#include "apstring.h"

apstring fruit;

cout << "Enter the name of a fruit: ";
cin >> fruit;
cout << fruit == "apple" << endl;
```

If the user enters "apple" as input, the output would be 1 (indicating **TRUE**); otherwise, the output would be 0 (indicating **FALSE**).

In general, each string has some lexicographic relationship to any other string, as defined by the collating sequence of characters within the strings. For example, the strings "hi", "there", and "Jane" are in the lexicographic relationship "Jane" < "hi" < "there" (note that J precedes h as an ASCII value).

A special case occurs when one string is shorter than the other string, but every character in the two strings is the same up to the end of the shorter string. In this case, the shorter string is considered less than the longer string. For example, the following program segment would output the value 1:

```
#include "apstring.h"

apstring string1, string2;

string1 = "William";
string2 = "Williams";
cout << string1 < string2 << endl;
```

Confusing = and ==

Note that the equality operator in C++ is ==, not =. As you know, = means assignment in C++. The equality operator does not change the values of its operands, whereas the assignment operator changes the value of its left operand. Unfortunately, the assignment operator also returns a value, and can be used in a C++ program wherever the == operator is used. This can be the source of some frustrating errors. Consider the following code segment:

```
int x = 1;
int y = 0;

cout << "x equals " << x << endl;
cout << "y equals " << y << endl;
cout << "Boolean for x equals y: "
     << x = y << endl;
cout << "Boolean for x not equal to y: "
     << x != y << endl;
cout << "x equals " << x << endl;
cout << "y equals " << y << endl;
```

The output of this code would be

```
x equals 1
y equals 0
Boolean for x equals y: 0
Boolean for x not equal to y: 0
x equals 0
y equals 0
```

After displaying the values of **x** and **y**, this code outputs the Boolean results of comparing **x** and **y** for equality and inequality. The Boolean values should be 0 and 1, but they are both 0. Here is what really happens:

1. The programmer has omitted the second = of the equality operator.
2. The computer interprets the single = as an assignment operator.
3. As a result, the value of **y** is stored in **x**.
4. This value, 0, is returned from the assignment operation.

5. The output statement displays the 0, so we think that **x** and **y** are not equal.
6. The next output statement also displays a 0, so we think that **x** and **y** are equal.
7. The second output of **x** shows a change from the previous output of **x**.

To make a long story short, the omission of the second **=** from the equality operator has caused an unwelcome side effect on a variable.

In general, the value returned by an assignment operation is the value of the expression on its right side. If this value is zero, it will be considered **FALSE** in a Boolean expression. If this value is any value other than zero, it will be considered **TRUE** in a Boolean expression. The C++ compiler will not protect you from this kind of mistake. Thus, be careful not to use **=** in C++ when you mean "equals."

Boolean Functions

Suppose we want a function called **even** that takes an integer as an argument and returns the value **TRUE** if the integer is even and **FALSE** otherwise. We compare the remainder of dividing the argument by 2 to 0. We then return this result:

```
bool even(int x)
{
        return x % 2 == 0;
}
```

Logical Operators and Compound Boolean Expressions

Boolean values may also be generated by using **logical operators** with simple Boolean expressions. The logical operators used by C++ are **&&** (meaning AND), **||** (meaning OR), and **!** (meaning NOT). Operators **&&** and **||** are used to connect two Boolean expressions in the relationships of **conjunction** and **disjunction,** respectively. **!** is used to negate the Boolean value of an expression; hence, it is sometimes referred to as **negation.** When one of these connectives or negation is used to generate Boolean values, the complete expression is referred to as a **compound Boolean expression.**

If **&&** is used to join two simple Boolean expressions, the resulting compound expression is true only when both simple expressions or conjuncts are true. If **||** is used, the result is true if either or both of the expressions or disjuncts are true. These relationships are summarized as follows:

logical operator: Either logical connective (**&&**, **||**) or negation (**!**).

conjunction: The connection of two Boolean expressions using the logical operator **&&** (AND), returning FALSE if at least one of the expressions is FALSE, or TRUE if they are both TRUE.

disjunction: The connection of two Boolean expressions using the logical operator **||** (OR), returning TRUE if at least one of the expressions is TRUE, or FALSE if they are both FALSE.

negation: The use of the logical operator **!** (NOT) with a Boolean expression, returning TRUE if the expression is FALSE, and FALSE if the expression is TRUE.

compound Boolean expression: Refers to the complete expression when logical connectives and negation are used to generate Boolean values.

Expression 1 (E1)	Expression 2 (E2)	E1 && E2	E1 || E2
TRUE	TRUE	TRUE	TRUE
TRUE	FALSE	FALSE	TRUE
FALSE	TRUE	FALSE	TRUE
FALSE	FALSE	FALSE	FALSE

As previously indicated, ! merely produces the logical complement of an expression as follows:

Expression (E)	!E
TRUE	**FALSE**
FALSE	**TRUE**

Illustrations of the Boolean values generated using logical operators are given in Table 5.3.

▼ Table 5.3	Expression	Boolean Value
Values of compound Boolean expressions	`(4.2 >= 5.0) && (8 == (3 + 5))`	**FALSE**
	`(4.2 >= 5.0) || (8 == (3 + 5))`	**TRUE**
	`(-2 < 0) && (18 >= 10)`	**TRUE**
	`(-2 < 0) || (18 >= 0)`	**TRUE**
	`(3 > 5) && (14.1 == 0.0)`	**FALSE**
	`(3 > 5) || (14.1 == 0.0)`	**FALSE**
	`! (18 == (10 + 8))`	**FALSE**
	`! (- 4 > 0)`	**TRUE**

Complex Boolean expressions can be generated by using several logical operators in an expression. The priority for evaluating these operators follows:

Operator	Priority
!	1
&&	2
||	3

When complex expressions are being evaluated, the logical operators, arithmetic operators, and relational operators are evaluated during successive passes through the expression. The priority list is now as follows:

Expression or Operation	Priority
( )	Evaluate from inside out.
!	Evaluate from left to right.
*,/,%	Evaluate from left to right.
+,-	Evaluate from left to right.
<<=, > , >=, ==, !=	Evaluate from left to right.
&&	Evaluate from left to right.
||	Evaluate from left to right.

As a matter of style, it is useful to parenthesize any comparison that is used as an operand for a logical operator. The following examples illustrate evaluation of some complex Boolean expressions.

Example 5.2

```
(3 < 5) || (21 < 18) && (-81 > 0)
(3 < 5) || FALSE && (-81 > 0)   (parentheses first, then &&)
(3 < 5) || FALSE && FALSE
(3 < 5) || FALSE
TRUE || FALSE
TRUE
```

Example 5.3

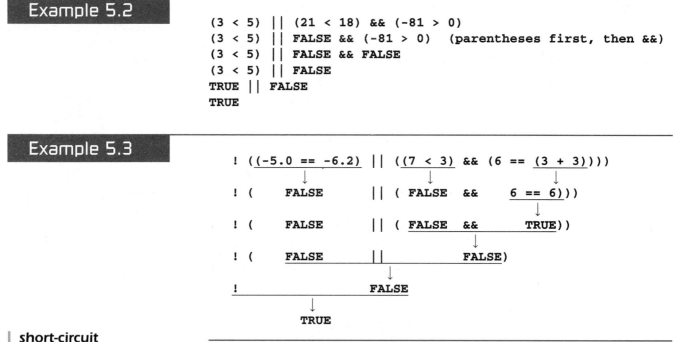

short-circuit
evaluation: The
process whereby a
compound Boolean
expression halts
evaluation and returns
the value of the first
subexpression that
evaluates to **TRUE**, in the
case of ||, or **FALSE**, in
the case of **&&**.

Short-Circuit Evaluation of Boolean Expressions

Whenever two Boolean expressions are separated by a logical operator in C++, either **&&** or ||, the run-time system uses **short-circuit evaluation.** The rules for this kind of evaluation are as follows:

1. In compound Boolean expressions connected by ||, stop and return **TRUE** at the first Boolean expression that returns **TRUE**. Evaluate the next Boolean expression only if the current one returns **FALSE**. This rule captures the notion that a disjunction is **TRUE** only if at least one of the disjuncts is **TRUE**, and **FALSE** only if all of the disjuncts are **FALSE**.

2. In compound Boolean expressions connected by **&&**, stop and return **FALSE** at the first Boolean expression that returns **FALSE**. Evaluate the next Boolean expression only if the current one returns **TRUE**. This rule captures the notion that a conjunction is **FALSE** only if at least one of the conjuncts is **FALSE**, and **TRUE** only if all of the conjuncts are **TRUE**.

Short-circuit evaluation can enhance the efficiency of programs. For example, C++ actually evaluates the expression in Example 5.2 in three lines rather than six:

```
(3 < 5) || (21 < 18) && (-81 > 0)
              ↓
(3 < 5) || FALSE
    ↓
TRUE
```

Short-circuit evaluation can also be used to make some simple decisions. For example, one might guard against division by zero as follows:

```
(y != 0) && (x / y == 2)
```

Note that if **y** equals zero, the second expression, which divides a number by **y**, will not be evaluated in C++.

■ Exercises 5.1

1. Assume the variable declaration section of a program is

```
bool flag1, flag2;
```

What output is produced by the following segment of code?

```
flag1 = TRUE;
flag2 = FALSE;
cout << flag1 << " " << TRUE << " " << flag2 << endl;
flag1 = flag2;
cout << flag2 << endl;
```

2. Assume the variable declaration section of a program is

```
char ch;
bool flag;
```

Indicate whether each of the following assignment statements is valid or invalid:
a. `flag = "true";`
b. `flag = T;`
c. `flag = TRUE;`
d. `ch = flag;`

    e. `ch = true;`
    f. `ch = 'T';`
3. Evaluate each of the following expressions:
    a. `(3 < 7) && (2 < 0) || (6 == 3 + 3)`
    b. `((3 < 7) && (2 < 0)) || (6 == 3 + 3)`
    c. `(3 < 7) && ((2 < 0) || (6 == 3 + 3))`
    d. `! ((-4.2 < 3.0) && (10 < 20))`
    e. `(! (-4.2 < 3.0)) || (! (10 < 20))`
4. For each of the following simple Boolean expressions, indicate whether it is **TRUE, FALSE**, or invalid:
    a. `-3.01 <= -3.001`
    b. `-3.0 == -3`
    c. `25 - 10 < 3 * 5`
    d. `42 % 5 < 42 / 5`
    e. `-5 * (3 + 2) > 2 * (-10)`
    f. `10 / 5 < 1 + 1`
    g. `3 + 8 % 5 == 6 - 12 % 2`
5. For each of the following expressions, indicate whether it is valid or invalid. Evaluate those that are valid.
    a. `3 < 4 || 5 < 6`
    b. `! 3.0 == 6 / 2`
    c. `! (TRUE || FALSE)`
    d. `! TRUE || FALSE`
    e. `! TRUE || ! FALSE`
    f. `! (18 < 25) && || (-3 < 0)`
    g. `8 * 3 < 20 + 10`
6. Assume the variable declaration section of a program is

```
int int1, int2;
double fl1, fl2;
bool flag1, flag2;
```

and the values of the variables are

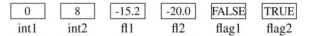

0	8	-15.2	-20.0	FALSE	TRUE
int1	int2	fl1	fl2	flag1	flag2

Evaluate each of the following expressions:
    a. `(int1 <= int2) || ! (fl2 == fl1)`
    b. `! (flag1) || ! (flag2)`
    c. `! (flag1 && flag2)`
    d. `((fl1-fl2) < 100/int2) && ((int1 < 1) && ! (flag2))`
    e. `! ((int2 - 16 / 2) == int1) && flag1`
7. DeMorgan's laws state the following:
    a. `! (A || B) is equivalent to (! A) && (! B)`
    b. `! (A && B) is equivalent to (! A) || (! B)`
    Write a test program that demonstrates the validity of each of these equivalent statements.
8. Indicate which of the following string comparisons are **TRUE** or **FALSE** using the full ASCII character set:

A Note of Interest

George Boole

George Boole was born in 1815 in Lincoln, England. Boole was the son of a small shopkeeper and his family belonged to the lowest social class. In an attempt to rise above his station, Boole spent his early years teaching himself Latin and Greek. During this period, he also received elementary instruction in mathematics from his father.

At the age of 16, Boole worked as a teacher in an elementary school. He used most of his wages to help support his parents. At the age of 20 (after a brief, unsuccessful attempt to study for the clergy), he opened his own school. As part of his preparation for running the school, he had to learn more mathematics. This activity led to the development of some of the most significant mathematics of the nineteenth century.

Boole's major contributions were in the field of logic. An indication of his genius is given by the fact that his early work included the discovery of invariants. The mathematical significance of this is perhaps best explained by noting that the theory of relativity developed by Albert Einstein would not have been possible without the previous work on invariants.

Boole's first published contribution was The Mathematical Analysis of Logic, which appeared in 1848 while he was still working as an elementary teacher and was the sole source of support for his parents. In 1849, he was appointed professor of mathematics at Queen's College in Cork, Ireland. The relative freedom from financial worry and time constraints the college appointment provided allowed him to pursue his work in mathematics. His masterpiece, An Investigation of the Laws of Thought, on which Are Founded the Mathematical Theories of Logic and Probabilities, was published in 1854. Boole was then 39, relatively old for such original work. According to Bertrand Russell, pure mathematics was discovered by Boole in this work.

The brilliance of Boole's work laid the foundation for what is currently studied as formal logic. The data type Boolean is named in honor of Boole because of his contribution to the development of logic as part of mathematics. Boole died in 1864. His early death resulted from pneumonia contracted by keeping a lecture engagement when he was soaked to the skin.

a. "Mathematics" less than "CompScience"
b. "Jefferson" less than "Jeffersonian"
c. "Smith Karen" less than "Smithsonian"
d. "Tom" greater than "apple"
e. "#45" less than or equal to "$45"
f. "Hoof in mouth" less than "Foot in door"
g. "453012" greater than "200000"

9. Write a test program that allows you to examine the following Boolean expressions:
   a. "William Joe" < "Williams Bo"
   b. "James" > "Jameson"

10. Explain how short-circuit evaluation of logical expressions with **&&** and **||** works.

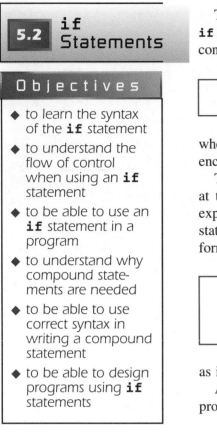

The first decision-making statement we will examine is the **if** statement. An **if** statement is used to make a program do something only when certain conditions are used. The form and syntax for an **if** statement are

---
if (<Boolean expression>)
      <statement>

---

where **<statement>** represents any C++ statement. Note that the parentheses enclosing the Boolean expression are required.

The Boolean expression can be any valid expression that is either true or false at the time of evaluation. If it is **TRUE**, the statement following the Boolean expression is executed. If it is **FALSE**, control is transferred to the first program statement following the complete **if** statement. In general, code would have the form

---
<statement 1>
if (<Boolean expression>)
      <statement 2>
<statement 3>

---

as illustrated in Figure 5.1.

As a further illustration of how an **if** statement works, consider the following program fragment:

```
sum = 0.0;
cin >> num;
if (num > 0.0)
        sum = sum + num;
cout << setios flags(ias:: fixed|ias:: showpoint)
        << setprecision(2) << setw(10) << sum << endl;
```

If the value read is 75.85, prior to execution of the **if** statement, the contents of **num** and **sum** are

75.85

num

0.0

sum

The Boolean expression **num > 0.0** is now evaluated and, since it is **TRUE**, the statement

```
sum = sum + num;
```

is executed and we have

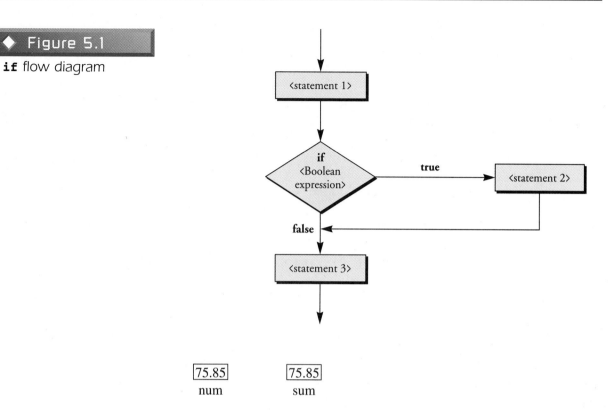

◆ Figure 5.1

if flow diagram

num   sum

The next program statement is executed and produces the output

75.85

However, if the value read is –25.5, the variable values are

–25.5   **0.0**
num   sum

The Boolean expression **num > 0.0** is **FALSE** and control is transferred to the line

```
cout << setiosflags(ios:: fixed|ios:: showpoint)
     << setprecision(2) << setw(10) << sum << endl;
```

Thus, the output is

0.00

Now, let's suppose you want a program in which one objective is to count the number of zeros in the input. Assuming suitable initialization and declaration, a program fragment for this task could be

```
cin >> num;
if (num == 0)
        zero_count = zero_count + 1;
```

One writing style for using an **if** statement calls for indenting the program statement to be executed if the Boolean expression is **TRUE**. This, of course, is not required. The following code

```
if (num == 0)
        zero_count = zero_count + 1;
```

could be written

```
if (num == 0)   zero_count = zero_count + 1;
```

However, the indenting style for simple **if** statements is consistent with the style used for more elaborate conditional statements.

Compound Statements

The last concept needed before looking further at selection in C++ is that of a **compound statement.** In a C++ program, simple statements end with a semicolon. Thus,

compound statement:
Uses the symbols **{** and **}** to group several statements as a unit.

```
cin >> a >> b;
a = 3 * b;
cout << b;
```

are three simple statements.

In some instances, it is necessary to perform several simple statements when some condition is true. For example, you may want the program to do certain things if a condition is true. In this situation, several simple statements that can be written as a single compound statement would be helpful. In general, several C++ constructs require compound statements. A compound statement is created by using the symbols **{** and **}** at the beginning and end, respectively, of a sequence of simple statements. Correct syntax for a compound statement is

```
{
        <statement 1>
        <statement 2>
           .

           .

           .

        <statement n>
}
```

Simple statements within a compound statement end with semicolons. The end of the compound statement is not followed by a semicolon.

When a compound statement is executed within a program, the entire segment of code between { and } is treated as a single action. This is referred to as a **statement block.** It is important that you develop a consistent, acceptable writing style for writing compound statements. What you use will vary according to your teacher's wishes and your personal preferences. Examples in this text will align each statement within the compound statement with the enclosing symbols. Thus,

statement block (synonym: **compound statement**): A form by which a sequence of statements can be treated as a unit.

```
{
        cin >> a >> b;
        a = 3 * b;
        cout << b;
}
```

is a compound statement in a program; what it does is easily identified.

Using Compound Statements

As you might expect, compound statements can be (and frequently are) used as part of an **if** statement. The form and syntax for this are

```
if (<Boolean expression>)
{
        <statement 1>
        .
        .
        <statement n>
}
```

Program control is exactly as before depending on the value of the Boolean expression. For example, suppose you are writing a function that keeps track of and computes fees for vehicles in a parking lot where separate records are kept for senior citizens. A segment of code in the procedure could be

```
if (customer == 'S')
{
        senior_count = senior_count + 1;
        amount_due = senior_citizen_rate;
}
```

Confusing == and = Again

In Section 5.1, we discussed the errors caused by using **=** instead of **==** in a Boolean expression. When a Boolean expression is used to control an **if** statement, these errors can be even more harmful to a program. For example, consider what would happen if **==** were replaced by **=** in the code segment above:

```
if (customer = 'S')
{
        senior_count = senior_count + 1;
        amount_due = senior_citizen_rate;
}
```

The use of the assignment operator causes two bad things to happen:
1. The value of **customer** is changed to **'S'**, a side effect.
2. The statements inside the **if** statement execute, even if **customer** did not have the value **'S'** to begin with.

As you can see, you must take great care to use **==** when you mean equality in C++.

if **Statements with Functions**

The next example designs a program to solve a problem using an **if** statement with a function.

Example 5.4

Let's write a program that reads two integers and prints them in the order of larger first, smaller second. The first-level pseudocode solution is

1. Read numbers
2. Determine the larger
3. Print results

A structure chart for this is given in Figure 5.2. Reading the numbers and printing the results require no further discussion of their design or implementation. Our strategy for determining the larger of the two numbers will be to maintain three variables, **min**, **max**, and **temp**. Step 2 assumes that the numbers have been read in to the variables **min** and **max**. We will compare the values, and if **min** is greater than **max**, we will use the variable **temp** to help swap the values of **min** and **max**. Thus, step 2 will have the effect of placing the larger value in **max** and the smaller value in **min**. The pseudocode for step 2 is

    if min > max
        assign min to temp
        assign max to min
        assign temp to max

◆ **Figure 5.2**

Structure chart for ordering two numbers

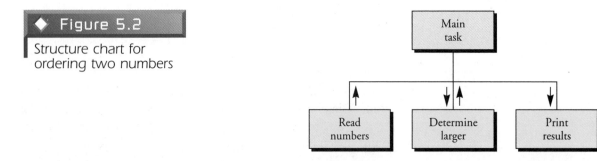

This algorithm translates to the following C++ function:

```
// Function: determine_larger
// Enforces the ordering relation min <= max between two integer variables
//
// Inputs: two integer variables in random order
// Outputs: min will contain the smaller of the two inputs, and max the larger

void determine_larger(int &min, int &max)
{
      int temp;

      if (min > max)
      {
           temp = min;
           min = max;
           max = temp;
      }
}
```

A complete program for this follows:

```
// Program file: minmax.cpp

#include <iostream.h>
#include <iomanip.h>

// Function: get_data
// Prompts for and obtains two integers from user
//
// Outputs: two integers

void get_data(int &first, int &second);

// Function: determine_larger
// Enforces the ordering relation min <= max between two integer variables
//
// Inputs: two integer variables in random order
// Outputs: min will contain the smaller of the two inputs, and max the larger

void determine_larger(int &min, int &max);

// Function: print_results
// Displays results on screen
//
// Inputs: two integers, the smaller in min, the larger in max

void print_results(int min, int max);
```

```cpp
int main()
{
     int min, max;

     get_data(min, max);
     determine_larger(min, max);
     print_results(min, max);
     return 0;
}

void get_data(int &first, int &second)
{
     cout << "Enter the first number and press <Enter>. ";
     cin >> first;
     cout << "Enter the second number and press <Enter>. ";
     cin >> second;
}

void determine_larger(int &min, int &max)
{
     int temp;

     if (min > max)
     {
          temp = min;
          min = max;
          max = temp;
      }
}

void print_results(int min, int max)
{
     cout << setiosflags(ios::right) << endl;
     cout << setw(19) << "Larger number"
          << setw(15) << "Smaller number" << endl;
     cout << setw(19) << "-------------"
          << setw(15) << "--------------" << endl;
     cout << endl;
     cout << setw(15) << max << setw(15) << min << endl;
}
```

Sample runs of this program produce the following output:

```
Enter the first number and press <Enter>. 35
Enter the second number and press <Enter>. 115

          Larger number Smaller number
          ------------- --------------

               115            35
```

```
Enter the first number and press <Enter>. 85
Enter the second number and press <Enter>. 26

    Larger number Smaller number
    ------------ --------------

        85              26
```

Note that two runs of this program are required to test the logic of the **if** statement.

■ Exercises 5.2

1. What is the output from each of the following program fragments? Assume the following assignment statements precede each fragment:

```
a = 10;
b = 5;
```

a.
```
if (a <= b)
        b = a;
cout << a << endl << b << endl;
```
b.
```
if (a <= b)
    {
        b = a;
        cout << a << endl << b << endl;
    }
```
c.
```
if (a < b)
        temp = a;
    a = b;
    b = temp;
    cout << a << endl << b endl;
```
d.
```
if (a < b)
    {
        temp = a;
        a = b;
        b = temp;
    }
    cout << a << endl << b << endl;
```
e.
```
if ((a < b) || (b - a < 0))
    {
        a = a + b;
        b = b - 1;
        cout << a << endl << b << endl;
    }
    cout << a << endl << b << endl;
```
f.
```
if ((a < b) && (b - a < 0))
    {
        a = a + b;
```

```
            b = b - 1;
            cout << a << endl << b << endl;
    }
    cout << a << endl << b << endl;
```

2. Write a test program to illustrate what happens when a semicolon is inadvertently inserted after a Boolean expression in an **if** statement. For example,

```
if (a > 0);
        sum = sum + a;
```

3. Find and explain the errors in each of the following program fragments. Assume all variables have been suitably declared.

  a. ```
  if (a == 10)
          cout << a << endl;
  ```

  b. ```
  x = 7;
  if (3 < x < 10)
  {
        x = x + 1;
        cout << x << endl;
  }
  ```

  c. ```
  count = 0;
  sum = 0;
  a = 50;
  if (a > 0)
          count = count + 1;
  sum = sum + a;
  ```

  d. ```
  cin >> ch;
  if (ch = 'a' || 'b')
          cout << ch << endl;
  ```

4. What is the output from each of the following program fragments? Assume variables have been suitably declared.

  a. ```
  j = 18;
  if (j % 5 == 0)
          cout << j << endl;
  ```

  b. ```
  a = 5;
  b = 90;
  b = b / a - 5;
  if (b > a)
          b = a * 30;
  cout << a << endl << b << endl;
  ```

5. Can a simple statement be written using a { ... } block? Write a short program that allows you to verify your answer.

6. Discuss the differences in the following programs. Predict the output for each program using sample values for num.

  a. ```
  int main()
  {
        int num;
        cout << "Enter an integer and press <Enter>. ";
        cin >> num;
  ```
  ```

```
            if (num > 0)
                    cout << endl;
            cout << setw(22) << "The number is" << setw(6)
                << num << endl;
            cout << endl;
            cout << setw(30) << "The number squared is"
                << setw(6) << num * num << endl;
            cout << setw(28) << "The number cubed is"
                << setw(6) << num * num * num << endl;
            cout << endl;
            return 0;
        }
b.  int main()
    {
        int num;
        cout << "Enter an integer and press <Enter>. ";
        cin >> num;
        if (num > 0)
        {
            cout << endl;
            cout << setw(22) << "The number is"
                << setw(6) << num << endl;
            cout << endl;
            cout << setw(30) << "The number squared is"
                << setw(6) << num * num << endl;
            cout << setw(28) << "The number cubed is"
                << setw(6) << num * num * num << endl;
            cout << endl;
        }
        return 0;
    }
```

7. Discuss writing style and readability of compound statements.
8. Find all errors in the following compound statements.

a.
```
    {
        cin >> a
        cout << a << endl
    }
```

b.
```
    {
        sum = sum + num
    };
```

c.
```
    {
        cin >> size1 >> size2;
        cout << setw(8) << size1 << setw(8) << size2
            << endl
    }
```

d.
```
    {
        cin << age << weight;
        total_age = total_age + age;
        total_weight = total_weight + weight;
        cout << setw(8) << age << weight << endl;
```

9. Write a single compound statement that will do the following:
   a. Read three integers from the keyboard.
   b. Add them to a previous total.
   c. Print the numbers on one line.
   d. Skip a line (output).
   e. Print the new total.
10. Write a program fragment that reads three reals, counts the number of positive reals, and accumulates the sum of positive reals.
11. Write a program fragment that reads three characters and then prints them only if the letters have been read in alphabetical order (for example, print "boy" but do not print "dog").
12. Given two integers, **A** and **B**, **A** is a divisor of **B** if **B % A = 0**. Write a complete program that reads two positive integers **A** and **B** and then, if **A** is a divisor of **B**,
    a. Print **A**.
    b. Print **B**.
    c. Print the result of **B** divided by **A**.
    For example, the output could be

    ```
    A is 14

    B is 42

    B divided by A is 3
    ```

5.3 if...else Statements

Objectives

◆ to learn the syntax of **if...else** statements

◆ to understand the flow of control when using **if...else** statements

◆ to be able to use an **if...else** statement in a program

◆ to be able to design programs using **if...else** statements

Form and Syntax

The previous section discussed the one-way selection statement **if**. The second selection statement we will examine is the two-way selection statement **if . . . else**. Correct form and syntax for **if . . . else** are

```
if (<Boolean expression>)
        <statement>
else
        <statement>
```

Flow of control when using an **if . . . else** statement is as follows:
1. The Boolean expression is evaluated.
2. If the Boolean expression is **TRUE**, the statement following is executed and control is transferred to the first program statement following the complete **if . . . else** statement.
3. If the Boolean expression is **FALSE**, the statement following **else** is executed and control is transferred to the first program statement following the **if . . . else** statement.

A flow diagram is given in Figure 5.3.

◆ Figure 5.3

if . . . else flow
diagram

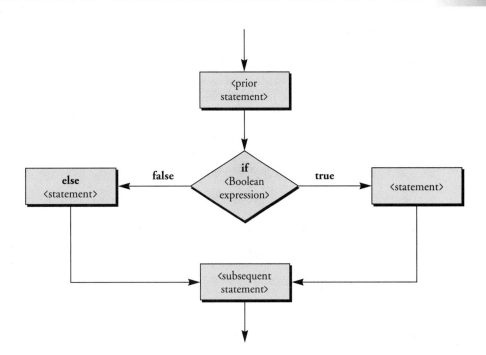

A few points follow that you should remember concerning **if . . . else**
statements:
1. The Boolean expression can be any valid expression having a value of
   TRUE or **FALSE** at the time it is evaluated.
2. The complete **if . . . else** statement is one program statement and
   is separated from other complete statements by a semicolon whenever
   appropriate.
3. Writing style should include indenting within the **else** option in a
   manner consistent with indenting in the **if** option.

Example 5.5

Let us write a program fragment to keep separate counts of negative and
nonnegative numbers entered as data. Assuming all variables have been suitably
declared and initialized, an **if . . . else** statement could be used as follows:

```
cout << "Please enter a number and press <Enter>.";
cin >> num;
if (num < 0)
      neg_count = neg_count + 1;
else
      non_neg_count = non_neg_count + 1;
```

Using Compound Statements

Program statements in both the **if** option and the **else** option can be
compound statements. When using compound statements in these options, you
should use a consistent, readable indenting style; remember to use **{ . . . }** for
each compound statement and do not put a semicolon after **}**.

Example 5.6

Suppose you want a program to read a number, count it as negative or nonnegative, and print it in either a column of nonnegative numbers or a column of negative numbers. Assuming all variables have been suitably declared and initialized, the fragment might be

```
cout << "Please enter a number and press <Enter>.";
cin >> num;
if (num < 0)
{
     neg_count = neg_count + 1;
     cout << setw(15) << num << endl;
}
// end of if option
else
{
     non_neg_count = non_neg_count + 1;
     cout << setw(30) << num << endl;
}
// end of else option
```

We next consider an example of a program fragment that requires the use of compound statements within an **if . . . else** statement.

Example 5.7

We want to write a function that computes gross wages for an employee of the Florida OJ Canning Company. Input includes hours worked and the hourly rate. Overtime (more than 40 hours) pay is computed as time-and-a-half. A function would be

```
const double WEEKLY_HOURS = 40.0;
const double TIME_AND_A_HALF = 1.5;

double compute_wages (double hours, double pay_rate)
{
     double overtime;
     if (hours <= WEEKLY_HOURS )
          return hours * pay_rate;
     else
     {
          overtime = TIME_AND_A_HALF *
               (hours - WEEKLY_HOURS ) * pay_rate;
          return WEEKLY_HOURS * pay_rate + overtime;
     }
}
```

Robust Programs

If a program is completely protected against all possible crashes from bad data and unexpected values, it is said to be **robust.** The preceding examples have all assumed that desired data would be accurately entered from the keyboard. In actual practice, this is seldom the case. The **if . . . else** statements can be used to guard against bad data entries. For example, if a program is designed to use positive numbers, you could guard against negatives and zeros by

```
cout << "Enter a positive number and press <Enter>. ";
cin >> number;
if (number <= 0)
      cout << "You entered a nonpositive number." << endl;
else

      .

    . (code for expected action here)

      .
```

robust: The state in which a program is protected against most possible crashes from bad data and unexpected values.

This program protection can be used anywhere in a program. For example, if you are finding square roots of numbers, you could avoid a program crash by using this code:

```
if (num < 0)
        cout << "The number " << num
             << " is negative" << endl;
else

      .

    . (rest of action here)

      .
```

In actual practice, students need to balance robustness against amount of code and efficiency. An overemphasis on making a program robust can detract from time spent learning new programming concepts. You should discuss this with your teacher and decide what is best for your situation. Generally, there should be an agreement between the programmer and the customer regarding the level of robustness required. For most programs and examples in this text, it is assumed that valid data are entered when requested.

| Example 5.8 | Callers of functions that take input would like to be signaled that it is within a given lower and upper bound. For example, a function that inputs the age of an employee might check to see that the integer value entered by the user is greater than 17 and less than 70 (assuming these are conventional age limits for |

employable persons). In this example, the function would return **TRUE** if the age is greater than 17 and also less than 70, or **FALSE** otherwise. The caller of the function takes care of prompting the user for information and of error recovery, such as an error message and a loop for more input. The function, named **get_valid_data**, is passed the values of the lower and the upper bounds, and variables for the data and a Boolean flag indicating a valid input value. One might invoke the function as follows:

```
bool age_ok;
int age;

cout << "Enter the employee's age: ";
get_valid_data(17, 70, age, age_ok);
if (! age_ok)
      cout << "Age must be greater than 17 and less than 70"
            << endl;
else
      <process the age, etc.>
```

A declaration of the function is therefore

```
// Function: get_valid_data
// Takes an input integer from the user and checks it
// for validity
//
// Inputs: two integers representing the lower and
// upper bounds of valid input
// Outputs: an integer representing the input and a Boolean
// value representing its validity

void get_valid_data(int low, int high, int &data,
      bool &data_ok);
```

The function does not prompt the user; it simply reads data. The function then compares the data to the limits. If the data are within the limits, the flag is set to **TRUE**; if not, the flag is set to **FALSE**.

```
void get_valid_data(int low, int high, int &data,
      bool &data_ok)
{
      cin >> data;
      if ((data > low) && (data < high))
            data_ok = TRUE;
      else
            data_ok = FALSE;
}
```

Guarding Against Overflow

As we discussed in Chapter 3, integer overflow occurs when the absolute value of an integer exceeds a maximum and real overflow occurs when a value is obtained that is too large to be stored in a memory location. Both of these values vary according to the compiler being used. The maximum value of an integer is named by the constant **INT_MAX**, and the maximum value of a real number is named by the constant **DBL_MAX**. Both constants become available to a C++ program by including the library header files **limits.h** and **float.h**.

One method that is used to guard against integer overflow is based on the principle of checking a number against some function of **INT_MAX**. Thus, if you want to multiply a number by 10, you would first compare it to **INT_MAX / 10**. A typical segment of code could be

```
if (num > INT_MAX / 10)
        (overflow message)
else
{
        num = num * 10;
        (rest of action)
}
```

We can now use this same idea with a Boolean-valued function. For example, consider the function

```
bool near_overflow (int num)
{
        return num > INT_MAX / 10;
}
```

This could be used in the following manner:

```
if (num > near_overflow(num))
        (overflow message)
else
{
        num = num * 10;
        (rest of action)
}
```

■ Exercises 5.3

1. What output is produced from each of the following program fragments? Assume all variables have been suitably declared.

    a. ```
        a = -14;
        b = 0;
        if (a < b)
                cout << a << endl;
        ```
        ```

```
        else
                cout << a * b << endl;
b.  a = 50;
    b = 25;
    count = 0;
    sum = 0;
    if (a == b)
            cout << a << b << endl;
    else
    {
            count = count + 1;
            sum = sum + a + b;
            cout << a << b << endl;
    }
    cout << count << sum << endl;
c.  temp = 0;
    a = 10;
    b = 5;
    f (a > b)
            cout << a << b << endl;
    else
            temp = a;
    a = b;
    b = temp;
    cout << a << b << endl;
```

2. Find all errors in the following program fragments:

```
a.  if (ch < '.')
            char_count = char_count + 1;
            cout << ch << endl;
    else
            period_count = period_count + 1;
b.  if (age < 20)
    {
            young_count = young_count + 1;
            young_age = young_age + age;
    };
    else
    {
            old_count = old_count + 1;
            old_age = old_age + age;
    };
c.  if (age < 20)
    {
            young_count = young_count + 1;
            young_age = young_age + age
    }
    else
            old_count = old_count + 1;
    old_age = old_age + age;
```

3. Write a program to balance your checkbook. Your program should get an entry from the keyboard, keep track of the number of deposits and checks, and keep a

Artificial Intelligence

Artificial intelligence (AI) research seeks to understand the principles of human intelligence and apply those principles to the creation of smarter computer programs. The original goal of AI research was to create programs with human-like intelligence and capabilities, yet after many years of research, little progress has been made toward this goal.

In recent years, however, AI researchers have pursued much more modest goals with much greater success. Programs based on AI techniques are playing increasingly important roles in such down-to-earth areas as medicine, education, recreation, business, and industry. Such programs come nowhere near achieving human levels of intelligence, but they often have capabilities that are not easily achieved with non-AI programs.

The main principles of AI can be summarized as follows:

Search: A method whereby the computer solves a problem by searching through all logically possible solutions.
Rules: Knowledge about what actions to take in particular circumstances is stored as rules; each rule has the form **if** situation **then** action or conclusion.
Reasoning: Programs can use reasoning to draw conclusions from the facts and rules available to the program.
Planning: The control program plans the actions that must be taken to accomplish a particular goal, then modifies the plan if unexpected obstacles are encountered; this is most widely used in robot control.
Pattern recognition: Important for rule-based systems, the **if** part of a rule specifies a particular pattern of facts; the rule is to be applied when that pattern is recognized in the facts known to the program.
Knowledge bases: Storage of the facts and rules that govern the operation of an AI program.

running balance. The data consist of a character, D (deposit) or C (check), followed by an amount.

4. Discuss the concept of robustness in programs. Be sure to compare the advantages and disadvantages of adding this feature to a program.

Objectives

- to learn the syntax of nested **if** statements
- to know when to use nested **if** statements
- to be able to use extended **if** statements
- to be able to trace the logic of nested **if** statements
- to develop a consistent writing style when using nested **if** statements

Multiway Selection

Sections 5.2 and 5.3 examined one-way (**if**) and two-way (**if . . . else**) selection. Because each of these is a single C++ statement, either can be used as part of a selection statement to achieve multiple selection. In this case, the multiple selection statement is referred to as a **nested if statement.** These nested statements can be any combination of **if** or **if . . . else** statements.

To illustrate, let's write a program fragment to issue interim progress reports for students in a class. If a student's score is below 50, the student is failing. If the score is between 50 and 69 inclusive, the progress is unsatisfactory. If the score is 70 or above, the progress is satisfactory. The first decision to be made is based on whether the score is below 50 or not; the design is

```
if score >= 50
        .

    . (progress report here)

        .
```

nested if statement:
A selection statement used within another selection statement.

```
                              else
                                  cout << setw(34)
                                          << "You are currently failing." << endl;
```

We now use a nested **if . . . else** statement for the progress report for students who are not failing. The complete fragment is

```
if score >= 50
      if score > 69
          cout << setw(38) << "Your progress is satisfactory."
                  << endl;
      else

          cout << setw(40) << "Your progress is unsatisfactory."
                  << endl;
else
    cout << setw(34) << "You are currently failing." << endl;
```

extended if statement: Nested selection where additional **if . . . else** statements are used in the **else** option.

One particular instance of nesting selection statements requires special development. When additional **if . . . else** statements are used in the **else** option, we call this an **extended if statement** and use the following form:

```
if (<condition 1>)

        .

        . (action 1 here)

        .

else if (<condition 2>)

        . (action 2 here)

        .

else if (<condition 3>)

        . (action 3 here)

        .

else    .

        . (action 4 here)

        .
```

Using this form, we could redesign the previous fragment that printed progress reports as follows:

```
if (score > 69)
     cout << setw(38) << "Your progress is satisfactory."
          << endl;
else if (score >= 50)
     cout << setw(40) << "Your progress is unsatisfactory."
          << endl;
else
     cout << setw(34) << "You are currently failing." << endl;
```

If you trace through both fragments with scores of 40, 60, and 80, you will see they produce identical output.

Another method of writing the nested fragment is to use sequential selection statements as follows:

```
if (score > 69)
     cout << setw(38) << "Your progress is satisfactory."
          << endl;
if ((score <= 69) && (score >= 50))
     cout << setw(40) << "Your progress is unsatisfactory."
     <    < endl;
if (score < 50)
     cout << setw(34) << "You are currently failing."
          << endl;
```

However, there are two reasons why this is not considered good programming practice. First, this is less efficient because the condition of each **if** statement is evaluated each time through the program. Second, only one of the three conditions can be true; they are said to be *mutually exclusive*. In general, mutually exclusive conditions are most accurately represented with nested **if** . . . **else** statements. You should generally avoid using sequential **if** statements if a nested statement can be used.

Tracing the flow of logic through nested or extended **if** statements can be tedious. However, it is essential that you develop this ability. For practice, let us trace through the following example.

Example 5.9

Consider the nested statement

```
if (a > 0)
     if (a % 2 == 0)
          sum1 = sum1 + a;
     else
          sum2 = sum2 + a;
else if (a == 0)
```

```
             cout << setw(18) << "a is zero" << endl;
      else
             neg_sum = neg_sum + a;
      cout << setw(17) << "All done" << endl;
```

We will trace through this statement and discover what action is taken when **a** is assigned 20, 15, 0, and −30, respectively. For **a = 20**, the expression **a > 0** is **TRUE**, hence

```
   a % 2 == 0
```

is evaluated. This is **TRUE**, so

```
   sum1 = sum1 + a;
```

is executed and control is transferred to

```
   cout << setw(17) << "All done" << endl;
```

For **a = 15, a > 0** is **TRUE**,

```
   a % 2 == 0
```

is evaluated. This is **FALSE**, so

```
   sum2 = sum2 + a;
```

is executed and control is again transferred out of the nested statement to

```
   cout << setw(17) << "All done" << endl;
```

For **a = 0, a > 0** is **FALSE**, thus

```
   a == 0
```

is evaluated. Since this is **TRUE**, the statement

```
   cout << setw(18) << "a is zero" << endl;
```

is executed and control is transferred to

```
   cout << setw(17) << "All done" << endl;
```

Finally, for **a = -30, a > 0** is **FALSE**, thus

```
    a == 0
```

is evaluated. This is **FALSE**, so

```
    neg_sum = neg_sum + a;
```

is executed and control is transferred to

```
    cout << setw(17) << "All done" << endl;
```

Note that this example traces through all possibilities involved in the nested statement. This is essential to guarantee that your statement is properly constructed.

Designing solutions to problems that require multiway selection can be difficult. A few guidelines can help. If a decision has two courses of action and one is complex and the other is fairly simple, nest the complex part in the **if** option and the simple part in the **else** option. This method is frequently used to check for bad data. An example of the program design for this could be:

```
    .  (get the data)

        .

if (data_ok)
        .

            .  (complex action here)

            .

    else  (message about bad data)
```

This method could also be used to guard against dividing by zero in computation. For instance, we could have

```
    divisor = <value>;
    if (divisor != 0)
        .

            .  (proceed with action)

            .

    else
            cout << "division by zero" << endl;
```

When there are several courses of action that can be considered sequentially, an extended **if . . . else** should be used. To illustrate, consider the program fragment of Example 5.10.

Example 5.10

Let's write a program fragment that allows you to assign letter grades based on students' semester averages. Grades are to be assigned according to the following scale:

100 >= X >= 90	A
90 > X >= 80	B
80 > X >= 70	C
70 > X >= 55	D
55 > X	F

Extended **if** statements can be used to accomplish this as follows:

```
if (average >= 90)
      grade = 'A';
else if (average >= 80)
      grade = 'B';
else if (average >= 70)
      grade = 'C';
else if (average >= 55)
      grade = 'D';
else
      grade = 'F';
```

Because any average of more than 100 or less than 0 would be a sign of some data or program error, this example could be protected with a statement as follows:

```
if ((average <= 100) && (average >= 0))
    .

    . (compute letter grade)

    .


else
      cout << setw(38) << "There is an error. Average is"
           << setw(8) << average << endl;
```

Protecting parts of a program in this manner will help you avoid unexpected results or program crashes. It also allows you to identify the source of an error.

Form and Syntax

The rule for matching **else**s in nested selection statements is:

*When an **else** is encountered, it is matched with the most recent **if** in the same block that has not yet been matched.*

Matching **if**s with **else**s is a common source of errors. When designing programs, you should be very careful to match them correctly. For example, consider the following situation, which can lead to an error:

```
if (<condition 1>)
       .
     . (action 1)
       .

else   .
     . (action 2)
       .
```

where action 1 consists of an **if** statement. Specifically, suppose you want a fragment of code to read a list of positive integers and print those that are perfect squares. A method of protecting against negative integers and zero could be:

```
cin >> num;
if (num > 0)
       .
     . (action 1 here)
       .

else
       cout << num << " is not positive." << endl;
```

If we now develop action 1 so that it prints only those positive integers that are perfect squares, we get

```
if (sqrt(num) == int(sqrt(num)))
       cout << num << endl;
```

Nesting this selection statement in our design, we have

```
    cin >> num;
    if (num > 0)
          if (sqrt(num) == int(sqrt(num))
                cout << num << endl;
          else
                cout << num << " is not positive." << endl;
```

If you now use this segment with input of 20 for **num**, the output is

```
20 is not positive.
```

Thus, this fragment is not correct to solve the problem. The indenting is consistent with our intent, but the actual execution of the fragment treated the code as

```
cin >> num;
if (num > 0)
      if (sqrt(num) == int(sqrt(num)))
            cout << num << endl;
else
      cout << num << " is not positive." << endl;
```

because the **else** is matched with the most recent **if**. This problem can be resolved by redesigning the fragment as follows:

```
cin >> num;
if (num <= 0)
      cout << num << " is not positive." << endl;
else if (sqrt(num) == int(sqrt(num)))
      cout << num << endl;
```

We conclude this section with an example that uses nested **if** statements.

| Example 5.11 |

Write a program that computes the gross pay for an employee of the Clean Products Corporation of America. The corporation produces three products: A, B, and C. Supervisors earn a commission of 7 percent of sales and representatives earn 5 percent. Bonuses of $100 are paid to supervisors whose commission exceeds $300 and to representatives whose commission exceeds $200. Input is in the form

```
S 18 15 10
```

where the first position contains an **S** or **R** for supervisor or representative, respectively. The next three integers include the number of units of each of the products sold. Because product prices may vary over time, the constant definition section will be used to indicate the current prices. The constants for this problem will be

```
const double SUPER_RATE = 0.07;
const double REP_RATE = 0.05;
```

Communication and Style Tips

It is very important to use a consistent, readable writing style when using nested or extended **if** statements. The style used here for nested **if** statements is to indent each nested statement a single tab stop. Also, each **else** of an **if . . . else** statement is in the same column as the **if** of that statement. This allows you to see at a glance where the **else**s match with the **if**s. For example,

```
if
        if
        else
else
```

An extended **if** statement has all the **else**s on the same indenting level as the first **if**. This reinforces the concept of an extended **if**. For example,

```
if
else if
else if
else
```

```
const double A_PRICE = 13.95;
const double B_PRICE = 17.95;
const double C_PRICE = 29.95;
```

A first-level pseudocode development for this problem is
1.   Get the data
2.   Compute commission and bonus
3.   Print heading
4.   Print results

The structure chart for this is given in Figure 5.4. Module specifications for each of the main modules follow:

Module: Get the data
Task: Read input data from the keyboard.
Output: Employee classification and sales of products A, B, and C

Module: Compute commission and bonus
Task: If a supervisor
             Compute total commission
             Compute bonus
     Else
             Compute total commission
             Compute bonus.
Input: Classification, a_sales, b_sales, c_sales
Output: a_commission, b_commission, c_commission, total_commission, bonus

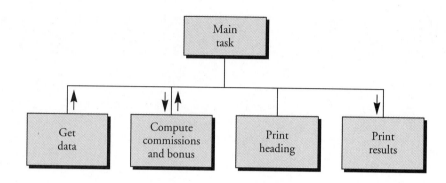

Module: Print heading
Task: Print a heading for the report.

Module: Print results
Task: Print the employee's report.
Input: classification b_commission
   a_sales c_commission
   b_sales total_commission
   c_sales bonus
   a_commission

Modules for "Get data," "Print heading," and "Print results" are similar to those previously developed. The module "Compute the commission and bonus" requires some development. Step 2 of the pseudocode becomes

2.   Compute commission and bonus
   2.1 If employee is supervisor
         Compute supervisor's earnings
      Else
         Compute representative's earnings

where "Compute supervisor's earnings" is refined to

2.1.1 Compute commission from sales of A
2.1.2 Compute commission from sales of B
2.1.3 Compute commission from sales of C
2.1.4 Compute total commission
2.1.5 Compute supervisor's bonus
   2.1.5.1 If total commission > 300
         Bonus is 100.00
      Else
         Bonus is 0.00

A similar development follows for computing a representative's earnings. Step 3 will be an appropriate function to print a heading. Step 4 will contain whatever you feel is appropriate for output. It should include at least the number of sales, amount of sales, commissions, bonuses, and total compensation.

The main program for this problem is

```cpp
int main()
{
        int a_sales, b_sales, c_sales;
// Sales of Products A, B, C
        double a_comm, b_comm, c_comm;
// Commission on sales of A, B, C
        double bonus;
// bonus, if earned
        double total_commission;
// Commission on all products
        char classification;
// S-Supervisor or R-Representative

        get_data(classification, a_sales, b_sales, c_sales);
        compute_commission_and_bonus(classification, a_sales,
                b_sales, c_sales, a_comm, b_comm,
                c_comm, total_commission, bonus);
        print_heading(classification);
        print_results(classification, a_sales, b_sales, c_sales,
                a_comm, b_comm, c_comm, total_commission, bonus);
        return 0;

}
```

A complete program for this is

```cpp
// This program computes gross pay for an employee.
// Note the use of constants and selection.

// Program file: sales.cpp

#include <iostream.h>
#include <iomanip.h>

const double SUPER_RATE = 0.07;
const double REP_RATE = 0.05;
const double A_PRICE = 13.95;
const double B_PRICE = 17.95;
const double C_PRICE = 29.95;

// Function: get_data
// gets input data from the user
//
// Outputs: Outputs: employee classification and sales
// of products A, B, and C

void get_data(char &classification, int &a_sales,
        int &b_sales, int &c_sales);

// Function: compute_commission_and_bonus
// If a supervisor
```

```
//                compute total commission
//                compute bonus
//        else
//                compute total commission
//                compute bonus
// Inputs: classification, a_sales, b_sales, c_sales
// Outputs: a_commission, b_commission, c_commission,
// total_commission, bonus

void compute_commission_and_bonus(char classification, int a_sales,
        int b_sales, int c_sales, double &a_commission, double& b_commission,
        double &c_commission, double &total_commission, double &bonus);

// Function: print_results
// Prints employee's report
//
// Inputs:       classification
//               a_sales
//               b_sales
//               c_sales
//               a_commission
//               b_commission
//               c_commission
//               total_commission
//               bonus

void print_results(char classification, int a_sales, int b_sales,
        int c_sales, double a_comm, double b_comm, double c_comm,
        double total_commission, double bonus);

// Function: print_heading
// Print heading for results
//
// Input: classification

void print_heading(char classification);

int main()
{
        int a_sales, b_sales, c_sales;
// Sales of Products A, B, C
        double a_comm, b_comm, c_comm;
// Commission on sales of A, B, C
        double bonus;
// bonus, if earned
        double total_commission;
// Commission on all products
        char classification;
// S-Supervisor or R-Representative
```

```
        get_data(classification, a_sales, b_sales, c_sales);
        compute_commission_and_bonus(classification, a_sales,
                b_sales, c_sales, a_comm, b_comm,
                c_comm, total_commission, bonus);
        print_heading(classification);
        print_results(classification, a_sales, b_sales,
                c_sales, a_comm, b_comm, c_comm,
                total_commission, bonus);
        return 0;
}
```

```
void get_data(char &classification, int &a_sales,
        int &b_sales, int &c_sales)
{
        cout << "Enter S or R for classification: ";
        cin >> classification;
        cout << "Enter a_sales, b_sales, c_sales: ";
        cin >> a_sales >> b_sales >>c_sales;
}
```

1

```
void compute_commission_and_bonus(char classification, int a_sales,
        int b_sales, int c_sales,  double &a_commission, double& b_commission,
        double &c_commission, double &total_commission, double &bonus)
{
        if (classification == 'S')
        // Supervisor
        {
                a_commission = a_sales * A_PRICE * SUPER_RATE;
                b_commission = b_sales * B_PRICE * SUPER_RATE;
                c_commission = c_sales * C_PRICE * SUPER_RATE;
                total_commission = a_commission + b_commission
                        + c_commission;
                if (total_commission > 300.0)
                        bonus = 100.0;
                else
                        bonus = 0.0 ;
        }
        else
        // Representative
        {
                a_commission = a_sales * A_PRICE * REP_RATE;
                b_commission = b_sales * B_PRICE * REP_RATE;
                c_commission = c_sales * C_PRICE * REP_RATE;
                total_commission = a_commission + b_commission
                        + c_commission;
                if (total_commission > 200.0)
                        bonus = 100.0;
                else
                        bonus = 0.0;
        }
}
```

2

```
void print_heading(char classification)
{
    cout << setiosflags(ios::fixed | ios::showpoint | ios::right);
    cout << endl;
    cout << setw(29)
        << "Clean Products Corporation of America" << endl;
    cout << endl;
    cout << setw(29) << "Sales Report for" << setw(11)
        << "June" << endl;
    cout << endl;
    cout << setw(27) << "classification";
    if (classification == 'S')
        cout << setw(18) << "Supervisor"<< endl;
    else
        cout << setw(18) << "Representative"<< endl;
    cout << endl;
    cout << setw(44)
        << "Product    Sales       Commission" << endl;
    cout << setw(44)
        << "-------    -----       ----------" << endl;
    cout << endl;
}
```

3

```
void print _results(char classification, int a_sales, int b_sales,
    int c_sales, double a_comm, double b_comm, double c_comm,
    double total_commission, double bonus)

{
    cout << setprecision(2);
    cout << setw(15) << "A" << setw(13) << a_sales
        << setw(14) << a_comm << endl;
    cout << setw(15) << "B" << setw(13) << b_sales
        << setw(14) << b_comm << endl;
    cout << setw(15) << "C" << setw(13) << c_sales
        << setw(14) << c_comm << endl;
    cout << endl;
    cout << setw(31) << "Subtotal"<< setw(3) << "$" << setw(9)
        << total_commission << endl;
    cout << endl;
    cout << setw(31) << "Your bonus is:" << setw(3) << "$"
        << setw(9) << bonus << endl;
    cout << endl;
    cout << setw(31) << "Total Due" << setw(3) << "$"
        << setw(9) << total_commission + bonus << endl;
}
```

4

A sample run produces the following output:

```
Enter R or S for classification: S
Enter a_sales, b_sales, c_sales: 1100 990 510

          Clean Products Corporation of America

          Sales Report for              June

          Classification               Supervisor

          Product     Sales            Commission
          -------     -----            ----------

          A           1100             1074.15

          B            990             1243.93

          C            510             1069.21

                 Subtotal              $3387.30

                 Your bonus is:        $100.00

                 Total Due             $3487.30
```

Program Testing

In actual practice, a great deal of time is spent testing programs in an attempt to make them run properly when they are installed for some specific purpose. Formal program verification is briefly discussed in Section 5.6 and is developed more fully in subsequent course work. However, examining the issue of which data are minimally necessary for program testing is appropriate when working with selection statements.

As you might expect, test data should include information that tests every logical branch in a program. Whenever a program contains an **if . . . else** statement of the form

```
if (<condition>)
        (action 1 here)
else
        (action 2 here)
```

the test data should guarantee that both the **if** and the **else** options are executed.

Nesting and use of extended **if** statements require a bit more care when selecting test data. In general, a single **if . . . else** statement requires at least two data items for testing. If an **if . . . else** statement is nested within the **if** option, at least two more data items are required to test the nested selection statement.

For purposes of illustration, let's reexamine the module "Compute commission and bonus" from Example 5.11. This module contains the logic

```
if (classification == 'S')

    •


    •

        if (total_commission > 300.00)

            •

            •

        else

            •

            •

else

    •

    •

if (total_commission > 200.00)

    •

    •

else

    •

    •
```

To see what data should minimally be used to test this function, consider the following table:

Classification	Total Commission
S	400.00
S	250.00
R	250.00
R	150.00

It is a good idea to also include boundary conditions in the test data. Thus, the previous table could also have listed 300.00 as the total commission for **S** and 200.00 as the total commission for **R**.

In summary, you should always make sure every logical branch is executed when running the program with test data.

Exercises 5.4

1. Consider the program fragment

```
if (x >= 0.0)
        if (x < 1000.00)
        {
                y = 2 * x;
                if (x <= 500)
                        x = x / 10;
        }
         else
                y = 3 * x;
else
        y = abs(x);
```

Indicate the values of **x** and **y** after this fragment is executed for each of the following initial values of **x**:
a. `x = 381.5;`
b. `x = -21.0;`
c. `x = 600.0;`
d. `x = 3000.0;`

2. Write and run a test program that illustrates the checking of all branches of nested **if . . . else** statements.

3. Rewrite each of the following fragments using nested or extended **if** statements without compound conditions.

```
a. if ((ch == 'M') && (sum > 1000))
        x = x + 1;
   if ((ch == 'M') && (sum <= 1000))
        x = x + 2;
   if ((ch == 'F') && (sum > 1000))
        x = x + 3;
   if ((ch == 'F') && (sum <= 1000))
        x = x + 5;
b. cin >> num;
   if ((num > 0) && (num <= 10000))
   {
        count = count + 1;
        sum = sum + num;
   }
   else
        cout << setw(27) << "Value out of range" << endl;
```

c. ```
if ((a > 0) && (b > 0))
        cout << setw(22) << "Both positive" << endl;
   else
        cout << setw(22) << "Some negative" << endl;
```
d. ```
if (((a > 0) && (b > 0)) || (c > 0))
        cout << setw(19) << "Option one" << endl;
   else
        cout <<setw(19) << "Option two" << endl;
```

4. Consider each of the following program fragments:

a. ```
if (a < 0)
        if (b < 0)
            a = b;
        else
            a = b + 10;
cout << a << b << endl;
```
b. ```
if (a < 0)
   {
        if (b < 0)
            a = b;
   }
   else
        a = b + 10;
cout << a << b << endl;
```
c. ```
if (a == 0)
        a = b + 10;
   else if (b < 0)
        a = b;
cout << a << b << endl;
```
d. ```
if (a >= 0)
        a = b + 10;
   if (b < 0)
        a = b;
cout << a << b << endl;
```

Indicate the output of each fragment for each of the following assignment statements:

```
i.   a = -5;
     b = 5;
ii.  a = -5;
     b = -3;
iii. a = 10;
     b = 8;
iv.  a = 10;
     b = -4;
```

5. Look back to Example 5.10, in which we assigned grades to students, and rewrite the grade assignment fragment using a different nesting. Could you rewrite it without using any nesting? Should you?

6. Many nationally based tests report scores and indicate in which quartile the score lies. Assuming the following quartile designation,

Score	Quartile
100–75	1
74–50	2
49–25	3
24–0	4

write a program to read a score from the keyboard and report in which quartile the score lies.

7. What are the values of **a**, **b**, and **c** after the following program fragment is executed?

```
a = -8; b = 21;
c = a + b;
if (a > b)
{
        a = b;
        c = a * b;
}
else if (a < 0)
{
        a = abs(a);
        b = b - a;
        c = a * b;
}
else
        c = 0;
```

8. Create minimal sets of test data for each part of Exercise 4 and for Exercise 7. Explain why each piece of test data has been included.

9. Discuss a technique that could be used as a debugging aid to guarantee that all possible logical paths of a program have been used.

5.5 switch Statements

Objectives

◆ to learn the syntax of the **switch** statement

◆ to understand how **switch** statements can be used as an alternate method for multiway selection

◆ to be able to use **switch** statements in designing programs

Thus far, this chapter has examined one-way selection, two-way selection, and multiway selection. Section 5.4 illustrated how multiple selection can be achieved using nested and extended **if** statements. Because multiple selection can sometimes be difficult to follow, C++ provides an alternative method of handling this concept, the **switch** statement.

Form and Syntax

switch statements can often be used when several options depend on the value of a single variable or expression. The general structure for a **switch** statement follows:

```
switch (<selector>)
{
        case <label 1> :        <statements 1>
                                    break;
        case <label 2> :        <statements 2>
                                    break;

                    .       .

        case <label n> :        <   statements n >
                                    break;
        default:                <   statements>}
```

This structure is shown graphically in Figure 5.5. The words **switch**, **case**, **break**, and **default** are reserved. The selector can be any variable or expression whose value is any data type we have studied previously except for **double** (only ordinal data types can be used). Values of the selector constitute the labels. Thus, if **age** is an integer variable whose values might be 18, 19, and 20, we could have

```
switch (age)
{
        case 18 :        <statement 1>
                            break;
        case 19 :        <statement 2>
                            break;
        case 20 :        <statement 3>
                            break;
        default :        <default statement>
}
```

When this program statement is executed, the value of **age** will determine to which statement control is transferred. More specifically, the program fragment

```
age = 19;
switch (age)
{
      case 18 :      cout << "I just became a legal voter." << endl;
                     break;
      case 19 :      cout << "This is my second year to vote." << endl;
                     break;
      case 20 :      cout << "I am almost twenty-one." << endl;
                     break;
      default :      if (age > 20)
                         cout << "I have all of the privileges of adulthood."
                              << endl;
                     else
                         cout << "I have no privileges at all." << endl;
}
```

◆ Figure 5.5

The **switch** statement flow diagram

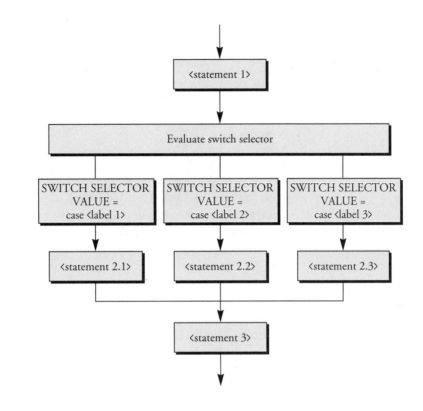

produces the output

> **This is my second year to vote.**

Before considering more examples, several comments are in order. The flow of logic within a **switch** statement is as follows:

1. The value of the selector is determined.
2. The first instance of value is found among the labels.
3. The statements following this value are executed.
4. **break** statements are optional. If a **break** statement occurs within these statements, then control is transferred to the first program statement following the entire **switch** statement; otherwise, execution continues. In general, even though they are optional, you should end every case with a **break** statement anyway.

The selector can have a value of any type previously studied except **double** and **apstring**. Only ordinal data types may be used.

Several cases may be associated with an alternative action. For example, if **<statement 1>** should be run when **age** has the integer value 10 or 100, the **switch** statement could appear as

```
switch (age)
{
    case 10:
```

```
        case 100 :        <statement 1>
                            break;
        case 19 :         <statement 2>
                            break;
        case 20 :         <statement 3>
                            break;
        default :         <default statement>
    }
```

All possible values of the **switch** selector do not have to be listed. However, if a value that is not listed is used, subtle logic errors can occur. Consequently, it is preferable to use a *default option*. If certain values require no action, the program will finish executing the **switch** statement by running the default as the last option; for example,

```
switch (age)
{
    case 10  :
    case 100 :        <statement 1>
                        break;
    case 19  :        <statement 2>
                        break;
    case 20  :        <statement 3>
                        break;
    default  :        cout << "There is no case for " << age << endl;
}
```

Like the **break** statement, the **default** statement is optional.

At this stage, we will consider several examples that illustrate various uses of **switch** statements. Because our purpose is illustration, the examples are somewhat contrived. Later examples will serve to illustrate how these statements are used in solving problems.

Example 5.12

Suppose the selector of a **switch** statement can have a value of type **char** and the ordinal of the character determines the option. Thus, the label list of the **switch** statement must contain the appropriate characters in single quotation marks. If **grade** has values **'A'**, **'B'**, **'C'**, **'D'**, or **'F'**, a **switch** statement could be

```
    switch (grade)
    {
        case 'A' : points = 4.0;
                    break;
        case 'B' : points = 3.0;
                    break;
        case 'C' : points = 2.0;
                    break;
```

```
        case 'D' :        points = 1.0;
                          break;
        case 'F' :        points = 0.0;
}
```

Communication and Style Tips

Writing style for a **switch** statement should be consistent with your previously developed style. The lines containing options should be indented. Thus, a typical **switch** statement is

```
switch (score)
{
     case 10:
     case  9:
     case  8: cout <<"Excellent" <<endl;
          break;
     case  7:
     case  6:
     case  5: cout <<"Fair" <<endl;
          break;
     case  4:
     case  3:
     case  2:
     case  1:
     case  0: cout <<"Failing <<endl;
          break;
     default: cout <<"Error in switch statement"
                    <<score <<endl;
}
```

Example 5.13

Let's rewrite the following program fragment using a **switch** statement:

```
if ((score == 10) || (score == 9))
     grade = 'A';
else if ((score == 8) || (score == 7))
     grade = 'B';
else if ((score == 6) || (score == 5))
     grade = 'C';
else
     grade = 'F';
```

If we assume **score** is an integer variable with values 0, 1, 2, . . . , 10, we could use a **switch** statement as follows:

```
switch (score)
{
      case 10:
      case  9: grade = 'A';
              break;
      case  8:
      case  7: grade = 'B';
              break;
      case  6:
      case  5: grade = 'C';
              break;
      case  4:
      case  3:
      case  2:
      case  1:
      case  0: grade = 'F';
}
```

Use in Problems

The **switch** statements should not be used for relational tests involving large ranges of values. For example, if one wanted to examine a range from 0 to 100 to determine test scores, nested selection would be better than a **switch** statement. We close this section with some examples that illustrate how **switch** statements can be used in solving problems.

| Example 5.14 |

Suppose you are writing a program for a gasoline station owner who sells four grades of gasoline: regular, premium, unleaded, and super unleaded. Your program reads a character (R, P, U, S) that designates which kind of gasoline was purchased and then takes subsequent action. The outline for this fragment is

```
cin >> gas_type;
switch (gas_type)
{
      case 'R' :        <action for regular>;
                        break;
      case 'P' :        <action for premium>;
                        break;
      case 'U' :        <action for unleaded>;
                        break;
      case 'S' :        <action for super unleaded>;
                        break;
}
```

Equivalent of Extended if Statements

As previously indicated, **switch** statements can sometimes (ordinal data types) be used instead of extended **if** statements when multiple selection is required for solving a problem. The following example illustrates this use.

Example 5.15

An alternative method of assigning letter grades based on integer scores between 0 and 100 inclusive is to divide the score by 10 and assign grades according to some scale. This idea could be used in conjunction with a **switch** statement as follows:

```
new_score = score / 10;
switch (new_score)
{
        case 10:
        case  9: grade = 'A';
                break;
        case  8: grade = 'B';
                break;
        case  7: grade = 'C';
                break;
        case  6:
        case  5: grade = 'D';
                break;
        case  4:
        case  3:
        case  2:
        case  1:
        case  0: grade = 'F';
}
```

■ Exercises 5.5

1. Discuss the need for program protection when using a **switch** statement.
2. Show how the following **switch** statement could be protected against unexpected values:

```
switch (age / 10)
{
    case 10:
    case  9:
    case  8:
    case  7: cout << setw(40) << "These are retirement years" << endl;
        break;
    case  6:
    case  5:
    case  4: cout << setw(40) << "These are middle age years" << endl;
        break;
    case  3:
    case  2: cout << setw(40) << "These are mobile years" << endl;
        break;
    case  1: cout << setw(40) << "These are school years" << endl;
}
```

3. Find all errors in the following statements:

a.
```
switch (a)
        case 1  :

                          break;
        case 2  :         a = 2 * a
                          break;
        case 3  ;         a = 3 * a;
                          break;
        case 4; 5; 6 :    a = 4 * a;
}
```

b.
```
switch (num)
   {
        case 5            num = num + 5;
                          break;
        case 6:
        case 7: ;         num = num + 6;
                          break;
        case 7, 8, 9, 10 : num = num + 10;
   }
```

c.
```
switch (age)
   {
        15, 16, 17 :      y_count = y_count + 1;
                          cout << age << y_count << endl;
        case 18:
        case 19:
        case 20:          m_count = m_count + 1;
        case 21:          cout << age endl;
   }
```

d.
```
switch (ch)
   {
        a :      points =       4.0;
                 break;
        b :      points =       3.0;
                 break;
        c :      points =       2.0;
                 break;
        d :      points =       1.0;
                 break;
        e:       points =       0.0
   }
```

e.
```
switch (score)
   {
        case 5: grade = 'A';
                break;
        case 4: grade = 'B';
                break;
        case 3: grade = 'C';
                break;
        case 2:
        case 1:,
```

```
                           case 0 :         grade = 'F';
               }
        f. switch (num / 10)
               {
                           case 1 :         num = num + 1;
                                            break;
                           case 2 :         num = num + 2;
                                            break;
                           case 3 :         num = num + 3;
               }
```

4. What is the output for each of the following program fragments?

```
a. a = 5;
   power = 3;
   switch (power)
   {
           case 0: b = 1;
                   break;
           case 1: b = a;
                   break;
           case 2: b = a * a;
                   break;
           case 3: b = a * a * a;
   }
   cout << a << power << b << endl;
b. gas_type = 'S';
   cout << "You have purchased ";
   switch (gas_type)
   {
           case 'R':         cout << "Regular";
                             break;
           case 'P':         cout << "Premium";
                             break;
           case 'U':         cout << "Unleaded";
                             break;
           case 'S':         cout << "Super Unleaded";
   }
   cout << "gasoline" << endl;
c. a = 6;
   b = -3;
   switch (a)
   {
           case 10:
           case 9:
           case 8: switch b
                        {
                                case -3:
                                case -4:
                                case -5:         a = a * b;
                                                 break;

                                case 0:
```



```
                                   case -1:
                                   case -2:          a = a + b;
                         }
                         break;
          case 7:
          case 6:
          case 5: switch (b)
                       {
                                   case -5:
                                   case -4:  a = a * b;
                                             break;
                                   case -3:
                                   case -2:  a = a + b;
                                             break;
                                   case -1:
                                   case 0:   a = a - b;
                       }
          }
          cout << a << b << endl;
      d. symbol = '-';
         a = 5;
         b = 10;
         switch (symbol)
         {
             case '+' :          num = a + b;
             case '-' :          num = a - b;
             case '*' :          num = a * b;
         }
         cout << a << b << num << endl;
```

5. Rewrite each of the following program fragments using a **switch** statement:

a.
```
if (power = 1)
num = a;
if (power = 2)
      num = a * a;
if (power = 3)
      num = a * a * a;
```

b. Assume **score** is an integer between 0 and 10.

```
if (score > 9)
      grade = 'A'
else if (score > 8)
      grade = 'B'
else if (score > 7)
      grade = 'C'
else if (score > 5)
      grade = 'D'
else
      grade = 'E';
```

A Software Glitch

The software glitch that disrupted AT&T's long-distance telephone service for nine hours in January 1990 dramatically demonstrates what can go wrong even in the most reliable and scrupulously tested systems. Of the roughly 100 million telephone calls placed with AT&T during that period, only about half got through. The breakdown cost the company more than $60 million in lost revenues and caused considerable inconvenience and irritation for telephone-dependent customers.

The trouble began at a "switch"—one of 114 inter-connected, computer-operated electronic switching systems scattered across the United States. These sophisticated systems, each a maze of electronic equipment housed in a large room, form the backbone of the AT&T long-distance telephone network.

When a local exchange delivers a telephone call to the network, it arrives at one of these switching centers, which can handle up to 700,000 calls an hour. The switch immediately springs into action. It scans a list of 14 different routes it can use to complete the call, and at the same time hands off the telephone number to a parallel, signaling network, invisible to any caller. This private data network allows computers to scout the possible routes and to determine whether the switch at the other end can deliver the call to the local company it serves.

If the answer is no, the call is stopped at the original switch to keep it from tying up a line, and the caller gets a busy signal. If the answer is yes, a signaling-network computer makes a reservation at the destination switch and orders the original switch to pass along the waiting call—after that switch makes a final check to ensure that the chosen line is functioning properly. The whole process of passing a call down the network takes 4 to 6 seconds. Because the switches must keep in constant touch with the signaling network and its computers, each switch has a computer program that handles all the necessary communications between the switch and the signaling network.

AT&T's first indication that something might be amiss appeared on a giant video display at the company's network control center in Bedminster, New Jersey. At 2:25 P.M. on Monday, January 15, 1990, network managers saw an alarming increase in the number of red warning signals appearing on many of the 75 video screens showing the status of various parts of AT&T's worldwide network. The warnings signaled a serious collapse in the network's ability to complete calls within the United States.

To bring the network back up to speed, AT&T engineers first tried a number of standard procedures that had worked in the past. This time, the methods failed. The engineers realized they had a problem they'd never seen before. Nonetheless, within a few hours, they managed to stabilize the network by temporarily cutting back on the number of messages moving through the signaling network. They cleared the last defective link at 11:30 P.M. that night.

Meanwhile, a team of more than 100 telephone technicians tried frantically to track down the fault. Because the problem involved the signaling network and seemed to bounce from one switch to another, they zeroed in on the software that permitted each switch to communicate with the signaling-network computers.

The day after the slowdown, AT&T personnel removed the apparently faulty software from each switch, temporarily replacing it with an earlier version of the communications program. A close examination of the flawed software turned up a single error in one line of the program. Just one month earlier, network technicians had changed the software to speed the processing of certain messages, and the change had inadvertently introduced a flaw into the system.

From that finding, AT&T could reconstruct what had happened.

Assume **measurement** is either **'M'** or **'N'**.

```
if (measurement == 'M')
{
    cout << setw(37) << "This is a metric measurement." << endl;
    cout <<  setw(42) << "It will be converted to nonmetric." << endl;
    length = num * CM_TO_INCHES;
}
else
{
    cout << setw(40) << " This is a nonmetric measurement. << endl;
    cout << setw(39) << "It will be converted to metric." << endl;
    length = num * INCHES_TO_CM;
}
```

6. Show how a **switch** statement can be used in a program to compute college tuition fees. Assume there are different fee rates for undergraduates (U), graduates (G), foreign students (F), and special students (S).

7. Use nested **switch** statements to design a program fragment to compute postage for domestic (noninternational) mail. The design should provide for four weight categories for both letters and packages. Each can be sent first, second, third, or fourth class.

5.6 Assertions

Objectives

◆ to know how to use assertions as preconditions

◆ to know how to use assertions as postconditions

assertion: Special comments used with selection and repetition that state what you expect to happen and when certain conditions will hold.

An **assertion** is a statement about what we expect to be true at the point in the program where the assertion is placed. For example, if you wish to compute a test average by dividing the **sum_of_scores** by **number_of_students**, you could state your intent that **number_of_students** is not equal to zero with a comment:

```
// assert that (number_of_students != 0)
class_average = sum_of_scores/ number_of_students;
```

Assertions are usually Boolean-valued expressions and typically concern program action. In the preceding example, the assertion that appears in a comment would remind the programmer that a certain condition must be true before an action is taken. Modern programming languages such as C++ provide a way of executing an assertion at run time. The computer verifies that the assertion is true, and if it is false, the computer halts program execution with an error message. To use this kind of feature in C++, you must include the **assert.h** library header file:

```
#include <assert.h>
```

Then you can state your assertion by calling the function **assert** with the Boolean expression as a parameter. The previous example might now look like this:

```
assert(number_of_students != 0);
class_average = sum_of_scores / number_of_students;
```

At execution time, this program would halt with an error message before an attempt to divide by zero.

Assertions frequently come in pairs: one preceding program action and one following the action. In this format, the first assertion is a precondition and the second is a postcondition.

To illustrate preconditions and postconditions, consider the following segment of code:

```
if (num1 < num2)
{
        temp = num1;
        num1 = num2;
        num2 = temp;
}
```

The intent of this code is to have **num1** be greater than or equal to **num2**. If we intend for both **num1** and **num2** to be positive, we can write

```
assert((num1 >= 0) && (num2 >= 0));    // Precondition
if (num1 < num2)
{
        temp = num1;
        num1 = num2;
        num2 = temp;
}
assert((num1 >= num2) && (num2 >= 0)); // Postcondition
```

As a second example, consider a **switch** statement used to assign grades based on quiz scores.

```
switch (score)
{
        case 10:        grade = 'A';
                        break;
        case  9:
        case  8:        grade = 'B';
                        break;
        case  7:
        case  6:        grade = 'C';
                        break;
        case  5:
        case  4:        grade = 'D';
                        break;
        case  3:
        case  2:
        case  1:
        case  0:        grade = 'F';
}
```

Assertions can be used as preconditions and postconditions in the following manner:

```
assert((score >= 0) && (score <= 10));              // Precondition
switch (score)
{
     case 10:          grade = 'A';
                       break;
     case 9:
     case 8:           grade = 'B';
                       break;
     case 7:
     case 6:           grade = 'C';
                       break;
     case 5:
     case 4:           grade = 'D';
                       break;
     case 3:
     case 2:
     case 1:
     case 0:           grade = 'F';
}
assert(((score = 10) && (grade = 'A')) ||           // Postcondition
     ((score = 9) && (grade = 'B'))    ||
     ((score = 8) && (grade = 'B'))    ||
     ((score = 7) && (grade = 'C'))    ||
     ((score = 6) && (grade = 'C'))    ||
     ((score = 5) && (grade = 'D'))    ||
     ((score = 4) && (grade = 'D'))    ||
     (((score >= 0) && (score <= 3)) && (grade = 'F')));
```

program proof: An analysis of a program that attempts to verify the correctness of program results.

Assertions can be used in **program proofs.** Simply put, a program proof is an analysis of a program that attempts to verify the correctness of program results. A detailed study of program proofs is beyond the scope of this text. If, however, you use assertions as preconditions and postconditions now, you will better understand them in subsequent courses. They are especially useful for making a program safer, even if you cannot be sure that their use will guarantee that the program is correct. If you do choose to use assertions in this manner, be aware that the postcondition of one action is the precondition of the next action.

5.7 Graphics

Objectives

◆ to be able to use selection statements in graphics applications

◆ to understand the use of Boolean conditions in graphics applications

Responding to Changes

Graphics applications detect and respond to conditions just like any other computer application—by using selection statements. A typical example is in game-playing programs, where images are drawn or erased in response to changes in user input or internal program state. The following example makes use of these ideas in a program that displays a roll of dice.

Example 5.16

Recall from Section 3.6 that a random number generator can be used to simulate the roll of a pair of dice. In Chapter 4, Programming Problem 19, you developed a library of functions for displaying each face of a die (see also Example 4.9). In this example, we put these two modules together to display the roll of a pair of dice.

The new code consists of a driver program and four new library functions, **init_dice**, **roll_dice**, **display_die**, and **display_dice**. These functions can be added to the **dice** library. Their declarations are as follows:

```
// Function: init_dice
// Sets up the dice library by seeding
// the random number generator

void init_dice();

// Function: roll_dice
// Generates two random numbers between 1 and 6
//
// Outputs: Two random numbers between 1 and 6

void roll_dice(int &first_die, int &second_die);

// Function: display_dice
// Displays two dice of specified size, position,
// and values
//
// Inputs: 2 integers for the values of the dice,
//         2 integers for the center point of the display,
//         and 2 integers for the height and width of dice

void display_dice(int first_die, int second_die,
     int center_x, int center_y,
     int height, int width);

// Function: display_die
// Displays a die of specified size, position,
// and value
//
// Inputs: An integer for the value of the die,
//         2 integers for the corner point of the die,
//         and 2 integers for the height and width of die

void display_die(int die, int left, int top,
     int height, int width);
```

The main program file includes the **dice** library, initializes the data, rolls the dice, and displays the results.

```cpp
// Program file: rolldice.cpp
// This program displays the results of one roll of dice.
#include <graphics.h>
#include <conio.h>
#include "dice.h"

int main()
{
    // Set up the dice library

    init_dice();

    // Set the graphics mode

    int graphdriver = DETECT, graphmode;
    initgraph(&graphdriver, &graphmode, "c:..\\bgi");

    // Compute the position and size of the dice.

    int center_x = getmaxx() / 2;
    int center_y = getmaxy() / 2;
    int height = 100;
    int width = 100;
    int first_die, second_die;

    // Roll the dice and display the results.

    roll_dice(first_die, second_die);
    display_dice(first_die, second_die,
         center_x, center_y, height, width);

    // Close the graphics mode.

    moveto(0, 0);
    outtext("Strike any key to continue");
    getch();
    closegraph();
    return 0;
}
```

Because the **dice** library will have to use a random number generator, it will have to include the **time** and **stdlib** libraries discussed in Section 3.6.

The implementation of **init_dice** seeds the random number generator used to roll the dice. This is a task that must be run at program startup. However, the main program that uses the dice library should "know" nothing about how the random number generator is seeded. Thus, the **dice** library hides the implementation of this task in the **init_dice** function. The seed is derived from the **time** library function **time**, as discussed in Section 3.6.

```
void init_dice()
{
      time_t seconds;

      time(&seconds);
      srand((unsigned int) seconds);
}
```

The implementation of **roll_dice** uses the expression for generating a random number between two bounds discussed in Section 3.6.

```
void roll_dice(int &first_die, int &second_die)
{
      // Generate two random numbers between
      // 1 and 6

      first_die = rand() % 6 + 1;
      second_die = rand() % 6 + 1;
}
```

The implementation of **display_dice** computes the positions of the dice and calls **display_die** to draw each die.

```
void display_dice(int first_die, int second_die,
      int center_x, int center_y,
      int height, int width)
{

      // Compute size of trough separating the dice.

      int trough = width / 4;

      // Display the die on the left.

      display_die(first_die, center_x - width - trough,
            center_y - height / 2, height, width);

      // Display the die on the right.

      display_die(second_die, center_x + trough,
            center_y - height / 2, height, width);
}
```

The implementation of **display_die** uses a **switch** statement to examine the number of dots on the die and call the appropriate **dice** library display function.

```
void display_die(int die, int left, int top,
    int height, int width)
{
    switch (die)
    {
        case 1: display_one(left, top, height, width);
                break;
        case 2: display_two(left, top, height, width);
                break;
        case 3: display_three (left, top, height, width);
                break;
        case 4: display_four(left, top, height, width);
                break;
        case 5: display_five(left, top, height, width);
                break;
        case 6: display_six(left, top, height, width);
    }
}
```

Clipping Rectangles

As you saw in Chapter 3, the coordinate system of the computer's screen is bounded by the points (0, 0) and (**getmaxx()**, **getmaxy()**). Thus far, we have not had to worry about the possibility of drawing images whose coordinates extend beyond these boundaries. However, consider the following code segment:

```
// Get end point coordinates as inputs.

cout << "Enter the x coordinate: ";
cin >> x;
cout << "Enter the y coordinate: ";
cin >> y;

// Set the graphics mode

int graphdriver = DETECT, graphmode;
initgraph(&graphdriver, &graphmode, "c:..\\bgi");

// Draw a line segment

lineto(x, y);
```

If the user enters values for **x** or **y** that are less than zero or greater than the maximum values defined by the computer, the computer will draw a line segment up to the edge of the screen and then "clip" the line at this point. In general, the area within which images are drawn before they are clipped in this way is called a **clipping rectangle.** The last line of the code segment could be changed to detect the fact that the end point of the desired line segment is beyond this boundary and display an error message:

clipping rectangle:
An area within which a graphical image is drawn.

```
// Draw a line segment if within the screen boundaries;
// otherwise, display an error message.

if ((x >= 0) && (x <= getmaxx())
        && (y >= 0) && (y <= getmaxy())))
        lineto(x, y);
else
        outtext("Error: point outside screen");
```

Example 5.17

It would be useful to have a function that tests a point to see whether or not it is within the area bounded by a rectangle. This function, **point_in_rect**, would return a Boolean value and would expect the coordinates of the point and the corners of the rectangle as parameters. The function could be used in the previous code segment as follows:

```
// Draw a line segment if within the screen boundaries;
// otherwise, display an error message.

if (point_in_rect(x, y, 0, 0, getmaxx(), getmaxy()))
        lineto(x, y);
else
        outtext("Error: point outside screen");
```

The implementation of **point_in_rect** hides the detail of the compound Boolean expression.

```
bool point_in_rect(int x, int y, int left, int top,
        int right, int bottom)
{
        return ((x >= left) && (x <= right)
                && (y >= top) && (y <= bottom));
}
```

■ Exercises 5.7

1. We have been assuming that the coordinate parameters passed to **rectangle** are in the order left, top, right, bottom. Test this function by ordering the parameters differently, and explain the output.
2. Write a function **safe_rectangle** that draws a rectangle only when the coordinate parameters are in the order left, top, right, bottom. If this is not the case, the function should display an error message.
3. Discuss the use of a clipping rectangle in computer graphics.
4. Write a function **rect_in_rect** that determines whether or not a specified rectangle is within another specified rectangle.
5. Discuss the possibility of using a programmer-defined clipping rectangle in a graphics application. What would be the consequences of using this rectangle when images such as line segments, circles, and triangles are drawn?

6. Write a function **clip_line** that draws only the portion of a line segment that lies within a specified clipping rectangle.

Focus on Program Design: Case Study

The Gas-N-Clean Service Station

The Gas-N-Clean Service Station sells gasoline and has a car wash. Fees for the car wash are $1.25 with a gasoline purchase of $10.00 or more and $3.00 otherwise. Three kinds of gasoline are available: regular at $1.149, unleaded at $1.199, and super unleaded at $ 1.289 per gallon. Write a program that prints a statement for a customer. Input consists of number of gallons purchased, kind of gasoline purchased (R, U, S, or, for no purchase, N), and car wash desired (Y or N). Use the constant definition section for gasoline prices. Your output should include appropriate messages. Sample output for these data is

```
Enter number of gallons and press <Enter>. 9.7
Enter gas type (R, U, S, or N) and press <Enter>. R
Enter Y or N for car wash and press <Enter>. Y

          ****************************************
          *                                      *
          *      Gas-N-Clean Service Station     *
          *                                      *
          *             July 25, 1998            *
          *                                      *
          ****************************************
          Amount of gasoline purchased        9.700 Gallons
          Price per gallon              $    1.149
          Total gasoline cost           $   11.15
          Car wash cost                 $    1.25
                    Total due           $   12.40

                  Thank you for stopping

                  Please come again

             Remember to buckle up and drive safely
```

A first-level pseudocode development is
1. Get data
2. Compute charges
3. Print results

A structure chart for this problem is given in Figure 5.6. Module specifications for the main modules follow:

Module: Get the data
Task: Get information interactively from the keyboard.

◆ Figure 5.6

Structure chart for the
Gas-N-Clean Service
Station problem

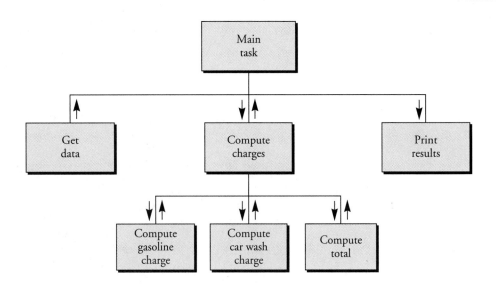

Output: Number of gallons purchased, type of gasoline, a choice as to whether or not
a car wash is desired

Module: Compute the charges
Task: Compute the gas cost, wash cost, and total cost.
Input: Number of gallons, gas type, wash option
Output: Gas cost, wash cost, total cost

Module: Print the results
Task: Print the results.
Input: Number of gallons purchased, type of gasoline, gas cost, wash cost, total cost

Further refinement of the pseudocode produces

1. Get data
    1.1 Read number of gallons
    1.2 Read kind of gas purchased
    1.3 Read car wash option
2. Compute charges
    2.1 Compute gasoline charge
    2.2 Compute car wash charge
    2.3 Compute total
3. Print results
    3.1 Print heading
    3.2 Print information in transaction
    3.3 Print closing message

Module 2 consists of three subtasks. A refined pseudocode development of this step is

2. Compute charges
    2.1 Compute gasoline charge
        2.1.1 switch gas_type
          'R'
          'U'
          'S'
          'N'

2.2 Compute car wash charge
2.2.1 If WashOption is yes
Compute charge
Else
Charge is 0.0
2.3 Compute total
2.3.1 Total is GasCost plus WashCost

A C++ program for this problem follows:

```cpp
// This program is used to compute the amount due from a
// customer of the Gas-N-Clean Service Station. Constants
// are used for gasoline prices. Note the use of nested
// selection to compute cost of the car wash.

//Program file: gas.cpp

#include <iostream.h>
#include <iomanip.h>

const double REGULAR_PRICE = 1.149;
const double UNLEADED_PRICE = 1.199;
const double SUPER_UNLEADED_PRICE = 1.289;

// Function: print_heading
// Prints a signon message for program

void print_heading();

// Function: get_data
// Get information interactively from the keyboard.
// Outputs: number of gallons purchased, type of gasoline,
// a choice as to whether or not a car wash is desired

void get_data(double &num_gallons, char &gas_type,
        char &wash_option);

// Function : compute_charges
// Computes the gas cost, wash cost, and total cost
// Inputs: number of gallons, gas type, wash option
// Outputs: gas cost, wash cost, total cost

void compute_charges(double num_gallons, char gas_type,
        char wash_option, double &gas_cost, double &wash_cost,
        double &total_cost);

// Function: print_message
// Prints a signoff message for program

void print_message();

// Function: print_results
// Print the results
```

```cpp
//
// Inputs: number of gallons purchased, type of gasoline,
// gas cost, wash option, wash cost, total cost

void print_results (double num_gallons, char gas_type,
        char wash_option, double gas_cost, doubt wash_cost,
        double total_cost);

int main ()
{
        char gas_type;              //     Type of gasoline purchased (R,U,S,N)
        char wash_option;           //     Character designating option (Y,N)
        double num_gallons;         //     Number of gallons purchased
        double gas_cost;            //     Computed cost for gasoline
        double wash_cost            //     Car wash cost
        double total_cost;          //     Total amount due

        get_data(num_gallons, gas_type, wash_option);
        compute_charges(num_gallons, gas_type, wash_option,
                gas_cost, wash_cost, total_cost);
        print_results (num_gallons, gas_type, wash_option,
                gas_cost, wash_cost, total_cost);
        return 0;
}

 void print_heading()
{
        cout << setiosflags(ios::right) << endl;
        cout << setw(55)
             << "*************************************"
             << endl;
        cout << setw(55)
             << "*                                   *"
             << endl;
        cout << setw(55)
             << "*     Gas-N-Clean Service Station     *"
             << endl;
        cout << setw(55)
             << "*                                   *"
             << endl;
        cout << setw(55)
             << "*           July 25, 1998           *"
             << endl;
        cout << setw(55)
             << "*                                   *"
             << endl;
        cout << setw(55)
             << "*************************************"
             << endl;
        cout << endl;
}
```

```
void get_data(double &num_gallons, char &gas_type,
    char &wash_option)
{
    cout << "Enter number of gallons and press <Enter>. ";
    cin >> num_gallons;
    cout << "Enter gas type (R, U, S, or N) and press <Enter>. ";
    cin >> gas_type;
    cout << "Enter Y or N for car wash and press <Enter>. ";
    cin >> wash_option;
}

void compute_charges(double num_gallons, char gas_type,
    char wash_option, double &gas_cost, double &wash_cost,
    double &total_cost)
{
    switch (gas_type)
    {
        case 'R':   gas_cost = num_gallons * REGULAR_PRICE;
                    break;
        case 'U':   gas_cost = num_gallons * UNLEADED_PRICE;
                    break;
        case 'S':   gas_cost = num_gallons * SUPER_UNLEADED_PRICE;
                    break;
        case 'N':   gas_cost = 0.0;
    }
    // Compute car wash cost
    if (wash_option == 'Y')
        if (gas_cost >= 10.0)
            wash_cost = 1.25;
        else
            wash_cost = 3.0;
    else
        wash_cost = 0.0;
    total_cost = gas_cost + wash_cost;
}

void print_message()
{
    cout << endl;
    cout << setw(48) << "Thank you for stopping" << endl;
    cout << endl;
    cout << setw(43) << "Please come again" << endl;
    cout << endl;
    cout << setw(55)
        << "Remember to buckle up and drive safely"
        << endl;
    cout << endl;
}
```

```
void print_results (double num_gallons, char gas_type,
     char wash_option, double gas_cost, double wash_cost,
     double total_cost)

{
     print_heading();
     cout << setiosflags(ios::fixed | ios::showpoint);
     cout << setw(43) << "Amount of gasoline purchased"
          << setw(12) << setw(6) << setprecision(3)
          << num_gallons << " Gallons" << endl;
     cout << setw(31) << "Price per gallon"
          << setw(22) << "$";
     switch (gas_type)
     {
          case 'R':   cout << setw(7) << REGULAR_PRICE << endl;
                      break;
          case 'U':   cout << setw(7) << UNLEADED_PRICE << endl;
                      break;
          case 'S':   cout << setw(7) << SUPER_UNLEADED_PRICE
                              << endl;
                      break;
          case 'N':   cout << setw(7) << 0.0 << endl;
     }
     cout << setw(34) << "Total gasoline cost"
              << setw(19) << "$"
              << setw(6) << setprecision(2) << gas_cost
              << endl;
     if (wash_cost > 0)
          cout << setw(28) << "Car wash cost"
               << setw(25) << "$"
               << setw(6) << wash_cost << endl;
     cout << setw(31) << "Total due"
          << setw(22) << "$" << setw(6)
          << total_cost << endl;
     print_message();
}
```

Running, Debugging, and Testing Hints

1. **if . . . else** is a single statement in C++.
2. A misplaced semicolon used with an **if** statement can be a problem. For example,

Incorrect:

```
if (a > 0) ;
        cout << a << endl;
```

(continued)

Correct:

```
if (a > 0)
      cout << a << endl;
```

3. Be careful with compound statements as options in an **if . . . else** statement. They must be in a **{ . . . }** block, and a trailing **}** must not be followed by a semicolon.

Incorrect:

```
if (a >= 0)
      cout << a << endl;
      a = a + 10;
else
      cout << a << " is negative" << endl;
```

Correct:

```
if (a >= 0)
{
     cout << a << endl;
     a = a + 10;
}
else
      cout << a << " is negative" << endl;
```

4. Your test data should include values that will check both options of an **if . . . else** statement.
5. An **if . . . else** statement can be used to check for other program errors. In particular,
   a. Check for bad data by

```
   cin >> <data>;
   if (<bad data>)
```
          .
             . (error message)
          .
```
   else
```
          .
             . (proceed with program)
          .

(continued)

   b. Check for reasonable computed values by

```
if (<unreasonable values>)
        .
            . (error message)
        .
    else
        .
            . (proceed with program)
        .
```

For example, if you were computing a student's test average, you could have

```
if ((test_average > 100) || (test_average < 0))
        .
            . (error message)
        .
else
        .
            . (proceed with program)
        .
```

  6. Be careful with Boolean expressions. You should always keep expressions reasonably simple, use parentheses, and minimize the use of **!**.

  7. Be careful to match **else**s with **if**s properly in nested **if . . . else** statements. Indenting levels for writing code are very helpful.

```
if (<condition 1>)
      if (<condition 2>)
        .
            . (action here)
        .
```

(continued)

```
    else    .

                .

            .  (action here)

                .

    else

                .

            .  (action here)

                .
```

8. The form for using extended **if** statements is

```
    if (<condition 1>)
                .

            .  (action 1 here)

                .

    else if (<condition 2>)
                .

            .  (action 2 here)

                .

    else
                .

            .  (final option here)

                .
```

9. Be sure to include **break** statements and a **default** option where necessary in a **switch** statement.

Summary

Key Terms

assertion
Boolean expression
clipping rectangle
compound Boolean
    expression
compound statement
conjunction
control structure
default option

disjunction
extended **if** statement
logical operators: **&&,**
    ||, !
mutually exclusive
negation
nested **if** statement
program proof

relational operator
robust
selection statement
short-circuit evaluation
simple Boolean
    expression
statement block { ... }
type definition

Keywords

break	else	switch
case	if	typedef
default		

Key Concepts

◆ Boolean constants have the values **1 = TRUE** and **0 = FALSE**. To make these values obvious in programs, one can define them as symbolic constants. Because some C++ compilers use the symbols **TRUE** and **FALSE** for other purposes, one can "undefine" them with the preprocessor directive **#undef** before reusing them, as follows:

```
#undef TRUE
#undef FALSE

const int TRUE = 1;
const int FALSE = 0;
```

◆ Data types can be given more descriptive names by using a **typedef**. For example, a data type for Boolean variables can be defined with

```
typedef int bool;
```

and variables can then be declared with

```
bool done = FALSE;
```

◆ Frequently used data definitions, such as those for the **bool** type, can be placed in a program library and included in application programs. For example, the library file **bool.h** can be included with

```
#include "bool.h"
```

◆ Relational operators are **==, >, <, >=, <=, !=**.
◆ Logical operators **&&** (AND), **||** (OR), and **!** (NOT) are used as operators on Boolean expressions.

◆ Boolean expressions will be interpreted during execution as having the value 1 (meaning true) or 0 (meaning false).

◆ A complete priority listing of arithmetic operators, relational operators, and logical operators follows:

Expression or Operation	Priority
( )	Evaluate from inside out.
!	Evaluate from left to right.
*,/,%	Evaluate from left to right.
+,−	Evaluate from left to right.
<,<=,>,>=,==,!=	Evaluate from left to right.
&&	Evaluate from left to right.
||	Evaluate from left to right.

◆ The values of compound Boolean expressions connected by || or **&&** are computed by using short-circuit evaluation. In the case of ||, evaluation stops at the first operand that returns **TRUE**; in the case of **&&**, evaluation stops at the first operand that returns **FALSE**.

◆ A selection statement is a program statement that transfers control to various branches of the program.

◆ A compound statement is sometimes referred to as a **{ . . . }** block; when it is executed, the entire segment of code between the **{** and **}** is treated like a single statement.

◆ **if . . . else** is a two-way selection statement.

◆ If the Boolean expression in an **if . . . else** statement is **TRUE**, the command following **if** is executed; if the expression is **FALSE**, the command following **else** is executed.

◆ Multiple selections can be achieved by using decision statements within decision statements; this is termed multiway selection.

◆ An extended **if** statement is a statement of the form

if (<condition 1>)

  .

  . (action 1 here)

  .

else if (<condition 2>)

  .

  . (action 2 here)

  .

```
else if (<condition 3>)
    .
    . (action 3 here)
    .

else
    .
    . (action 4 here)
    .
```

♦ Program protection can be achieved by using selection statements to guard against unexpected results.
♦ **switch** statements can sometimes be used as alternatives to multiple selection.
♦ **default**, a reserved word in C++, can be used to handle values not listed in the **switch** statement.

Chapter Review Exercises

In Exercises 1–8, indicate if the Boolean expressions are **TRUE**, **FALSE**, or invalid.

1. `5 < (7 - 2)`
2. `((8 + 7) < 12) || ((12 + 6) > 10)`
3. `((8 + 7) < 12) && ((12 + 6) > 10)`
4. `8 + 7 > 4 | 6 + 3 > 5`
5. `! (12 > (5 + 9))`
6. `(18 != (4 + 5 * 2)) && (! (16 == (5 * 4)))`
7. `15 % 8 > 6 % 3`
8. `! (8.3 < 5.4) || (4.5 > -3.5)`

For Exercises 9–15, write a valid C++ statement.

9. Add 4 to the integer variable **a** if **c** is greater than 5.4.
10. Display the value of **h** if the Boolean **g** is **TRUE**.
11. Display either "zero" or "nonzero" based on the value of the **double** variable **d**.
12. Add 5 to the value of **a** and display this new value if the integer **h** is negative.
13. Display the letter *A* if **g** > 90, *B* if **g** is between 80 and 90, or *C* if **g** is less than 80.
14. Input new values for **a** or **b** if either of them is less than 0.0.
15. Skip three lines if the value of the integer variable **line_count** is greater than 64.

Write Exercises 16 and 17 with nested **if** statements.

16. If the value of the integer variable **a** is 2, square it. If it is 3, input a new value for **a**. If it is 4 or 5, multiply it by 3 and display the new value.
17. **g** is a character variable. If it contains either **'A'** or **'D'**, display the letter. If it contains **'B'**, display the value of the **double** variable **h** using a 10-character field with three places of precision. If it is **'c'**, display the value of **g**.
18. Rewrite Exercise 16 using a **switch** statement.
19. Rewrite Exercise 17 using a **switch** statement.

Programming Problems and Activities

The first 13 problems listed here are relatively short, but to complete them you must use concepts presented in this chapter. Some of the remaining programming problems are used as the basis for writing programs for subsequent chapters as well as for this chapter. In this chapter, each program is run on a very limited set of data. Material in later chapters permits us to run the programs on larger databases.

1. A three-minute telephone call to Scio, New York, costs $1.15. Each additional minute costs $0.26. Given the total length of a call in minutes, calculate and print the cost.

2. When you first learned to divide, you expressed answers using a quotient and a remainder rather than a fraction or decimal quotient. For example, if you divided 7 by 2, your answers would have been given as 3 r. 1. Given two integers, divide the larger by the smaller and print the answer in this form. Do not assume that the numbers are entered in any order.

3. Revise Problem 2 so that, if there is no remainder, you print only the quotient without a remainder or the letter r.

4. Given the coordinates of two points on a graph, find and print the slope of a line passing through them. Remember that the slope of a line can be undefined.

5. Mr. Lae Z. Programmer wishes to computerize his grading system. He gives five tests, then averages only the four highest scores. An average of 90 or better earns a grade of A; 80–89, a grade of B; and so on. Write a program that accepts five test scores and prints the average and grade according to this method.

6. Given the lengths of three sides of a triangle, print whether the triangle is scalene, isosceles, or equilateral.

7. Given the lengths of three sides of a triangle, determine whether or not the triangle is a right triangle using the Pythagorean theorem. Do not assume that the sides are entered in any order.

8. Given three integers, print only the largest.

9. The island nation of Babbage charges its citizens an income tax each year. The tax rate is based on the following table:

Income Tax	Tax Rate
$ 0–5000	0
5001–10,000	3%
10,001–20,000	5.5%
20,001–40,000	10.8%
Over $40,000	23.7%

Write a program that, when given a person's income, prints the tax owed rounded to the nearest dollar.

10. Many states base the cost of car registration on the weight of the vehicle. Suppose the fees are as follows:

Weight	Cost
0–1500 pounds	$23.75
1501–2500 pounds	$27.95
2501–3000 pounds	$30.25
Over 3000 pounds	$37.00

Given the weight of a car, find and print the cost of registration.

11. The Mapes Railroad Corporation pays an annual bonus as part of its profit sharing plan. This year all employees who have been with the company for 10 years or more receive a bonus of 12 percent of their annual salary, and those who have worked at Mapes from 5 through 9 years will receive a bonus of 5.75 percent. Those who have been with the company less than 5 years receive no bonus.

Given the initials of an employee, the employee's annual salary, and the number of years employed with the company, find and print the bonus. All bonuses are rounded to the nearest dollar. Output should be in the following form:

```
MAPES RAILROAD CORP.

Employee xxx
Years of service nn
Bonus earned: $ yyyy
```

12. A substance floats in water if its density (mass/volume) is less than 1 g/cm^3. It sinks if it is 1 or more. Given the mass and volume of an object, calculate and print whether it will sink or float.

13. Mr. Arthur Einstein, your high school physics teacher, wants a program for English-to-metric conversions. You are given a letter indicating whether the measurement is in pounds (P), feet (F), or miles (M). Such measures are to be converted to newtons, meters, and kilometers, respectively. (There are 4.9 newtons in a pound, 3.28 feet in a meter, and 1.61 kilometers in a mile.) Given an appropriate identifying letter and the size of the measurement, convert it to metric units. Print the answer in the following form:

```
3.0 miles = 4.83 kilometers.
```

14. The Caswell Catering and Convention Service (Chapter 4, Problem 12) has decided to revise its billing practices and is in need of a new program to prepare bills. The changes Caswell wishes to make follow.
   a. For adults, the deluxe meals will cost $15.80 per person and the standard meals will cost $11.75 per person, dessert included. Children's meals will cost 60 percent of adult meals. Everyone within a given party must be served the same meal type.
   b. There are five banquet halls. Room A rents for $55.00, room B rents for $75.00, room C rents for $85.00, room D rents for $100.00, and room E

rents for $130.00. The Caswells are considering increasing the room fees in about six months and this should be taken into account.

A surcharge, currently 7 percent, is added to the total bill if the catering is to be done on a weekend (Friday, Saturday, or Sunday).

d. All customers will be charged the same rate for tip and tax, currently 18 percent. It is applied only to the cost of food.

e. To induce customers to pay promptly, a discount is offered if payment is made within 10 days. This discount depends on the amount of the total bill. If the bill is less than $100.00, the discount is 0.5 percent; if the bill is at least $100.00 but less than $200.00, the discount is 1.5 percent; if the bill is at least $200.00 but less than $400.00, the discount is 3 percent; if the bill is at least $400.00 but less than $800.00, the discount is 4 percent; and, if the bill is at least $800.00, the discount is 5 percent.

Test your program on each of the following three customers:

Customer A: This customer is using room C on Tuesday night. The party includes 80 adults and 6 children. The standard meal is being served. The customer paid a $60.00 deposit. *Customer B:* This customer is using room A on Saturday night. Deluxe meals are being served to 15 adults. A deposit of $50.00 was paid. *Customer C:* This customer is using room D on Sunday afternoon. The party includes 30 children and 2 adults, all of whom are served the standard meal.

Output should be in the same form as that for Problem 12, Chapter 4.

15. State University charges $90.00 for each semester hour of credit, $200.00 per semester for a regular room, $250.00 per semester for an air-conditioned room, and $400.00 per semester for food. All students are charged a $30.00 matriculation fee. Graduating students must also pay a $35.00 diploma fee. Write a program to compute the fees that must be paid by a student. Your program should include an appropriate warning message if a student is taking more than 21 credit hours or fewer than 12 credit hours. A typical line of data for one student would include room type (R or A), student number (in four digits), credit hours, and graduation status (T or F).

16. Write a program to determine the day of the week a person was born given his or her birth date. The following steps should be used to find the day of the week corresponding to any date in this century.

a. Divide the last two digits of the birth year by 4. Put the quotient (ignoring the remainder) in **total**. For example, if the person was born in 1983, divide 83 by 4 and store 20 in **total**.

b. Add the last two digits of the birth year to **total**.

c. Add the last two digits of the birth date to **total**.

d. Using the following table, find the "month number" and add it to **total**.

January	= 1
February	= 4
March	= 4
April	= 0
May	= 2
June	= 5
July	= 0

August   = 3
September = 6
October   = 1
November = 4
December = 6

e. If the year is a leap year and if the month you are working with is either January or February, then subtract 1 from the **total**.

f. Find the remainder when **total** is divided by 7. Look up the remainder in the following table to determine the day of the week the person was born. Note that you should not use this procedure if the person's year of birth is earlier than 1900.

1 = Sunday
2 = Monday
3 = Tuesday
4 = Wednesday
5 = Thursday
6 = Friday
0 = Saturday

Typical input is

5-15 78

where the first entry (**5-15**) represents the birth date (May 15) and the second entry (**78**) represents the birth year. An appropriate error message should be printed if a person's year of birth is before 1900.

17. Community Hospital needs a program to compute and print a statement for each patient. Charges for each day are as follows:
    a. room charges: private room, $125.00; semiprivate room, $95.00; ward, $75.00
    b. telephone charge: $1.75
    c. television charge: $3.50
    Write a program to get a line of data from the keyboard, compute the patient's bill, and print an appropriate statement. Typical input is

5PNY

where **5** indicates the number of days spent in the hospital, **P** represents the room type (**P**, **S**, or **W**), **N** represents the telephone option (**Y** or **N**), and **Y** represents the television option (**Y** or **N**). A statement for the data given follows:

```
                  Community Hospital

            Patient Billing Statement

Number of days in hospital: 5 Type of room: Private

Room charge                  $ 625.00
```

```
Telephone charge      $    0.00

Television charge      $   17.50

       TOTAL DUE       $  642.50
```

18. Write a program that converts degrees Fahrenheit to degrees Celsius and degrees Celsius to degrees Fahrenheit. In the input, the temperature is followed by a designator (F or C) indicating whether the given temperature is Fahrenheit or Celsius.

19. The city of Mt. Pleasant bills its residents for sewage, water, and sanitation every three months. The sewer and water charge is figured according to how much water is used by the resident. The scale is

Amount (gallons)	Rate (per gallon)
Less than 1000	$0.03
1000–1999	$30 + $0.02 for each gallon over 1000
2000 or more	$50 + $0.015 for each gallon over 2000

The sanitation charge is $7.50 per month.

Write a program to read the number of months for which a resident is being billed (1, 2, or 3) and how much water was used; then print a statement with appropriate charges and messages. Use the constant definition section for all rates and include an error check for incorrect number of months. Typical input is

3 2175

20. Al Derrick, owner of the Lucky Wildcat Well Corporation, wants a program to help him decide whether or not a well is making money. Data for a well will consist of one or two lines. The first line contains a single character (D for a dry well, O for oil found, and G for gas found) followed by a real number for the cost of the well. If an "O" or "G" is detected, the cost will be followed by an integer indicating the volume of oil or gas found. In this case, there will also be a second line containing an "N" or "S" indicating whether or not sulfur is present. If there is sulfur, the "S" will be followed by the percentage of sulfur present in the oil or gas. Unit prices are $5.50 for oil and $2.20 for gas. These should be defined as constants. Your program should compute the total revenue for a well (reduce output for sulfur present) and print all pertinent information with an appropriate message to Mr. Derrick. A gusher is defined as a well with profit in excess of $50,000. Typical input is

G 8000.00 20000 S 0.15

21. The Mathematical Association of America hosts an annual summer meeting. Each state sends one official delegate to the section officer's meeting at this

summer session. The national organization reimburses the official state delegates according to the following scale:

Round-trip Mileage	Rate
0–500 miles	15 cents per mile
501–1000 miles	$75.00 plus 12 cents for each mile over 500
1001–1500 miles	$135.00 plus 10 cents for each mile over 1000
1501–2000 miles	$185.00 plus 8 cents for each mile over 1500
2001–3000 miles	$225.00 plus 6 cents for each mile over 2000
3001 or more miles	$285.00 plus 5 cents for each mile over 3000

Write a program that will accept as input the number of round-trip miles for a delegate and compute the amount of reimbursement.

22. Mr. Lae Z. Programmer (Problem 5) wants you to write a program to compute and print the grade for a student in his class. The grade is based on three examinations (worth a possible 100 points each), five quizzes (10 points each), and a 200-point final examination. Your output should include all scores, the percentage grade, and the letter grade. The grading scale is

90 <= average	<= 100	A
80 <= average	< 90	B
70 <= average	< 80	C
60 <= average	< 70	D
0 <= average	< 60	E

Typical input is

80 93 85 (examination scores)
9 10 8 7 10 (quiz scores)
175 (final examination)

23. Mr. Lae Z. Programmer now wants you to modify Problem 22 by adding a check for bad data. Any time an unexpected score occurs, you are to print an appropriate error message and terminate the program.

24. A quadratic equation is one of the form

$$ax^2 + bx + c = 0$$

where $a \neq 0$. Solutions to this equation are given by

$$x = \frac{-b \pm \sqrt{b^2 - 4ac}}{2a}$$

where the quantity $(b^2 - 4ac)$ is referred to as the discriminant of the equation. Write a program to read three integers as the respective coefficients (a, b, and c), compute the discriminant, and print the real number solutions. Use the following rules:

    a. discriminant = 0 –> single root.
    b. discriminant < 0 –> no real number solution.
    c. discriminant > 0 –> two distinct real solutions.

25. Write an interactive program that receives as input the lengths of three sides of a triangle. Output should first identify the triangle as scalene, isosceles, or equilateral. The program should use the Pythagorean theorem to determine whether or not scalene or isosceles triangles are right triangles. An appropriate message should be part of the output.

26. The sign on the attendant's booth at the Pentagon parking lot is

PENTAGON VISITOR PARKING	
Cars:	
First 2 hours	Free
Next 3 hours	0.50/hour
Next 10 hours	0.25/hour
Trucks:	
First 1 hour	Free
Next 2 hours	1.00/hour
Next 12 hours	0.75/hour
Senior Citizens:	No charge

Write a program that will accept as input a one-character designator (C, T, or S) followed by the number of minutes a vehicle has been in the lot. The program should then compute the appropriate charge and print a ticket for the customer. Any part of an hour is to be counted as a full hour.

27. Some businesses use attention-getting telephone numbers with an 800 prefix (for example, 1-800-STARTUP) so more customers will become familiar with the business telephone numbers. Write an interactive program that allows the user to enter a seven-letter telephone message and then have the corresponding telephone number printed. Typical input will consist of seven letters. Typical output will consist of the message and the associated telephone number.

28. Write a program that will add, subtract, multiply, and divide fractions. Input will consist of a single line representing a fraction arithmetic problem as follows: integer/integer operation integer/integer. For example, a line of input might be

    2/3 + 1/2

Your program should do the following:
a. Check for division by zero.
b. Check for proper operation symbols.
c. Print the problem in its original form.
d. Print the answer.
e. Print all fractions in horizontal form.

Your answer need not be in lowest terms. For the sample input

    2/3 + 1/2

sample output is

```
2/3 + 1/2 = 7/6
```

29. Write an interactive program that permits the user to print various recipes. Write a function for each recipe. After the user enters a one-letter identifier for the desired recipe, a **switch** statement should be used to call the appropriate function. Part of the code could be

```
cin >> selection;
switch (selection)
{
        case 'J':        jambalaya;
                         break;
        case 'S':        spaghetti;
                         break;
        case 'T':        tacos;
}
```

30. The force of gravity is different for each of the nine planets in our solar system. For example, on Mercury it is only 0.38 times as strong as on Earth. Thus, if you weigh 100 pounds (on Earth), you would weigh only 38 pounds on Mercury. Write an interactive program that allows you to enter your Earth weight and your choice of planet to which you would like your weight converted. Output should be your weight on the desired planet together with the planet name. The screen message for input should include a menu for planet choice. Use a **switch** statement in the program for computation and output. The relative forces of gravity are

Earth	1.00
Jupiter	2.65
Mars	0.39
Mercury	0.38
Neptune	1.23
Pluto	0.05
Saturn	1.17
Uranus	1.05
Venus	0.78

31. Cramer's rule is a method for solving a system of linear equations. If you have two equations with variables x and y written as

$$ax + by = c$$

$$dx + ey = f$$

then the solution for x and y can be given as

$$x = \frac{\begin{vmatrix} c & b \\ f & e \end{vmatrix}}{\begin{vmatrix} a & b \\ d & e \end{vmatrix}}$$

$$y = \frac{\begin{vmatrix} a & c \\ d & f \end{vmatrix}}{\begin{vmatrix} a & b \\ d & e \end{vmatrix}}$$

Using this notation,

$$\begin{vmatrix} a & b \\ d & e \end{vmatrix}$$

is the determinant of the matrix

$$\begin{bmatrix} a & b \\ d & e \end{bmatrix}$$

and is equal to $ae - bd$. Write a complete program that will solve a system of two equations using Cramer's rule. Input will be all coefficients and constants in the system. Output will be the solution to the system. Typical output is

For the system of equations

x + 2y = 5

2x - y = 0

we have the solution

x = 1

y = 2

Use an **if . . . else** statement to guard against division by zero.

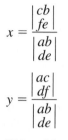

32. Extend the program of Example 5.16 so that it plays an interactive game of dice with you. The program should display one roll of the dice, pause for you to strike a key, and then display a second roll of the dice. When the second roll is displayed, the program should pause and display a message about the winner ("You win!" or "I win!" or "We tie!"). The first roll of dice will be "your" roll, and the second roll of dice will be "my" (the computer's) roll.

33. Develop a menu-driven program that allows the user to select a shape to be drawn. The user can choose from a list containing rectangle, triangle, circle, and line segment. The program should also prompt the user for the appropriate shape specifiers (vertices, etc.) when a shape is chosen.

Communication in Practice

1. Reread the **Note of Interest** in this chapter on a software glitch. Then read the sections of the ACM Code of Ethics that deal with designing and testing reliable computer systems. Prepare a written report to present to your class on the way in which the ACM code deals with this issue.

2. Using a completed program from this chapter, remove all documentation pertaining to selection statements. Exchange this version with another student who has prepared a similar vesion. Write documentation for all selection statements in the other student's program. Compare your results with the program author's original version. Discuss the differences and similarities with your class.

3. Contact a programmer and discuss the concept of robustness in a program. Prepare a report of your conversation for class. Your report should include a list of specific instances that illustrate how programmers make programs robust.

4. Conduct an unscientific survey of at least two people from the following groups: students in college computer science courses, teachers of computer science, and programmers working in industry. Your survey should attempt to ascertain the importance of robustness. Discuss similarities and differences of your findings with those of other classmates.

5. Selecting appropriate test data for a program that uses nested selection is not an easy task. Create diagrams that allow you to trace the flow of control when nested selection is used. Use your diagrams to draw conclusions about the minimal test data required to test all the branches of a program that uses nested selection at various levels.

6

Repetition Statements

Chapter Outline

T he previous chapter on selection introduced you to a control structure that takes advantage of a computer's ability to make choices. We now study a second major control structure that takes advantage of a computer's ability to repeat the same task many times. The control structures for selection and repetition allow us to specify any algorithm we need to solve a problem with a computer.

This chapter examines the different methods C++ permits for performing a process repeatedly. For example, as yet, we cannot conveniently write a program that solves the simple problem of adding the integers from 1 to 100 or processing the grades of 30 students in a class. By the end of this chapter, you will be able to solve these problems three different ways. The three forms of repetition (loops) are

1. **for** <a definite number of times> <do an action>
2. **while** <condition is true> <do an action>
3. **do** <action> **while** <condition is true>

Each of these three loops contains the basic constructs necessary for repetition:
1. A variable is assigned some value.
2. The variable value changes at some point in the loop.
3. Repetition continues until the variable reaches some predetermined value. When the predetermined value (or Boolean condition) is reached, repetition is terminated and program control moves to the next executable statement.

6.1 Classifying Loops

Objectives

◆ to understand the difference between a pretest loop and a post-test loop

◆ to understand what fixed repetition and variable condition loops are

◆ to understand when to use a fixed repetition loop

Pretest and Post-Test Loops

A loop that uses a condition to control whether or not the body of the loop is executed before going through the loop is a **pretest** or **entrance-controlled loop.** The testing condition is the **pretest condition.** If the condition is **TRUE**, the body of the loop is executed. If the condition is **FALSE**, the program skips to the first line of code following the loop. The **for** loop and the **while** loop are pretest loops.

A loop that examines a Boolean expression after the loop body is executed is a **post-test** or **exit-controlled loop.** This is the **do . . . while** loop.

Fixed Repetition Versus Variable Condition Loops

Fixed repetition (iterated) loops are used when it can be determined in advance how often a segment of code needs to be repeated. For instance, you might know that you need a predetermined number of repetitions of a segment of code for a program that adds the integers from 1 to 100 or for a program that uses a fixed number of data lines, for example, game statistics for a team of 12 basketball players. The number of repetitions need not be constant. For example, a user might enter information during execution of a program that would determine how often a segment should be repeated. In this chapter, we introduce a class of **for** loops that are fixed repetition loops.

Variable condition loops are needed to solve problems for which conditions change within the body of the loop. These conditions involve sentinel values, Boolean flags, arithmetic expressions, or end-of-line and end-of-file markers (see Chapter 9). A variable condition loop provides more power than a fixed repetition loop. The **while** and **do . . . while** loops are variable condition loops.

6.2 The for Loop

Objectives

♦ to understand how the loop control variable is used in a loop

♦ to understand the flow of control when using a fixed repetition loop in a program

♦ to be able to use a **for** loop in a program

♦ to be able to use a **for** loop that counts down in a program

---

The **for** loop is a pretest loop. Although one can write variable condition **for** loops in C++, we will discuss only fixed repetition **for** loops.

In the following example, a **for** loop displays all of the numbers between 1 and 10:

```
for (i = 1; i <= 10; i = i + 1)        // Heading of loop
    cout << i << endl;                 // Body of loop
```

A **for** loop is considered to be a single executable statement. The information contained within the parentheses is referred to as the heading of the loop. The actions performed in the loop are referred to as the body of the loop.

The heading of a **for** loop consists of three parts:

1. *Initialization expression:* In fixed repetition **for** loops, this part sets a *control variable* to an initial value. This variable will control the number of times that the body of the loop is executed.

2. *Termination condition:* This part normally consists of a comparison of the control variable to a value. The body of the loop will execute while this condition is **TRUE**.

3. *Update expression:* This part normally consists of a statement that makes the value of the control variable approach the value specified in the termination condition. In **for** loops that count up, this part increments the control variable by some value; in **for** loops that count down, this part decrements the control variable by some value.

The typical form of a **for** loop is

> for (<initialization expression>; <termination condition>; <update expression>)
>   <statement>

pretest loop (synonym: **entrance-controlled loop**): A loop where the control condition is tested before the loop is executed.

pretest condition: A condition, tested at the top of the loop, that controls whether the body of the loop is executed.

post-test loop (synonym: **exit-controlled loop**): A loop where the control condition is tested after the loop is executed.

fixed repetition loop (synonym: **iterated loop**): A loop used when the number of times that a segment of code needs to be repeated is known in advance.

variable condition loop: A repetition statement in which the loop control condition changes within the body of the loop.

The internal logic of a **for** loop that counts up is as follows:

1. The control variable is assigned an initial value in the initialization expression.
2. The termination condition is evaluated.
3. If the termination condition is **TRUE** then
   a. the body of the loop is executed and
   b. the update expression is evaluated.
4. If the termination condition is **FALSE** then control of the program is transferred to the first statement following the loop.

As you can see, this **for** loop proceeds by counting up from a lower bound to an upper bound. A flow diagram for this example is given in Figure 6.1.

We have discussed only a typical form of the **for** loop, one that counts up. We look at variations on this form, such as **for** loops that count from an upper bound down to a lower bound, or count by some factor other than one, in later sections of this chapter.

The Increment and Decrement Operators

C++ has a pair of operators that increment or decrement variables. These operators are very concise and handy to use in loops. The increment operator, **++**, can precede or follow a variable in a complete C++ statement. For example, the statement

```
++x;
```

would increment (add one to) the variable **x**. It has the same effect as the assignment statement

```
x = x + 1;
```

Thus, the example **for** statement could be rewritten more concisely as

```
for (i = 1; i <= 10; ++i)
    cout << i << endl;
```

When the increment operator precedes a variable, it is called a *prefix operator;* when it follows a variable, it is called a *postfix operator.*

◆ Figure 6.1

Flow of control of a **for** loop

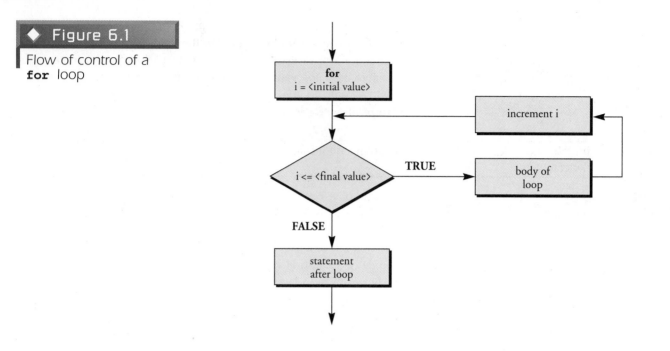

The decrement operator, **--**, can precede or follow a variable in a complete C++ statement. The operator has the effect of subtracting one from the variable and storing the result in it.

In general, we use the prefix versions of these operators in this text. You might see the postfix versions in other books or in C++ code. The primary difference between the two versions is that the prefix operator may execute faster on most machines than the postfix operator.

You should avoid using the increment or decrement operator in fancy statements such as the following:

```
y = ++x / z;
y = x++ / z;
```

Because of the difference in priority, these statements mean different things. The first one increments and changes **x** before the division or assignment operations. The second one waits to increment and change **x** until after all of the other operations are completed. In general, you should treat an increment or decrement operation as a complete statement to avoid confusion.

Accumulators

accumulator: A variable used for the purpose of summing successive values of some other variable.

The problem of adding the integers from 1 to 100 needs only one statement in the body of the loop. This problem can be solved by code that constructs an **accumulator.** An accumulator merely sums values of some variable. In the following code, the loop control variable, **lcv**, successively assumes the values 1, 2, 3, . . . , 100.

```
sum = 0;

for (lcv = 1; lcv <= 100; ++lcv)

        sum = sum + lcv;
```

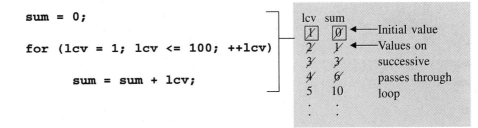

This program segment contains an example of graphic documentation. Throughout the text, these insets will be used to help illustrate what the code is actually doing. The insets are not part of the program; they merely show what some specific code is trying to accomplish.

To see how **sum** accumulates these values, let us trace through the code for several values of **lcv**. Initially, **sum** is set to zero by

```
    sum = 0;
```

When **lcv** is assigned the value 1,

```
    sum = sum + lcv;
```

produces

1		Ø 1
lcv		sum

For **lcv = 2**, we get

2		X 3
lcv		sum

and **lcv = 3** yields

3		X 6
lcv		sum

Note that **sum** has been assigned a value equal to $1 + 2 + 3$. The final value for **lcv** is 100. Once this value has been assigned to **sum**, the value of **sum** will be 5050, which is the sum of $1 + 2 + 3 + \cdots + 100$.

Accumulators are frequently used in loops. The general form for this use is

```
accumulator = 0;
for (lcv = <initial value>; lcv <= <final value>; ++lcv)
        accumulator = accumulator + lcv;
```

Scope of a Loop Control Variable

In general, the loop control variable of a **for** loop must be declared before it is used in the loop. In accordance with the scope rules of C++, the scope of this variable will be the program block within which it is declared. However, on many occasions, a loop control variable will only be used within a loop. In these cases, using a variable whose scope extends beyond a loop opens the program to serious side effects. To minimize these, the loop control variable can be declared when it is initialized within the loop. The visibility of the variable will be restricted to the body of the loop. For example, the following loop performs the equivalent task of our first example, but its loop control variable cannot be accessed outside of the body of the loop:

```
// References to i are not allowed here.

for (int i = 1; i <= 10; ++i)
     cout << i << endl;

// References to i are not allowed here (except in older versions of C++).
```

In older versions of C++, the scope of **i** would extend below the loop. In general, it is safe programming practice to restrict the scope of variables to only those areas of a program in which it is necessary to access them.

Some comments concerning the syntax and form of **for** loops are now necessary.

1. The loop control variable must be declared as a variable. We will usually declare this variable as part of the loop heading.
2. The loop control variable can be any valid identifier.
3. The loop control variable can be used within the loop just as any other variable except that the value of the variable should not be changed by the statements in the body of the loop.
4. The initial and final values can be constants or variable expressions with appropriate values.
5. The loop will be repeated for each value of the loop control variable in the range indicated by the initial and final values.

At this point you might try writing some test programs to see what happens if you do not follow these rules. Then consider the following examples, which illustrate the features of **for** loops.

Example 6.1	

Write a segment of code to list the integers from 1 to 10 together with their squares and cubes. This can be done by

```
for (int j = 1; j <= 10; ++j)
     cout << j << setw(10) << j * j << setw(8) << j * j * j << endl;
```

This segment produces

```
    1              1       1

    2              4       8
```

3	9	27
4	16	64
5	25	125
6	36	216
7	49	343
8	64	512
9	81	729
10	100	1000

Example 6.2

Write a **for** loop to produce the following design.

Assuming the first asterisk is in column 20, the following loop will produce the desired result. Note carefully how the output is formatted.

```
for (int j = 1; j <= 5; ++j)
        cout << setw(21 - j) << '*' << setw(2 * j - 1)
                << '*' << endl;
```

Example 6.3

When computing compound interest, it is necessary to evaluate the quantity $(1 + R)^N$, where R is the interest rate for one time period and N is the number of time periods. A **for** loop can be used to perform this computation. If we declare a variable **base**, this can be solved by

```
base = 1;

for (int j = 1; j <= n; ++j)

    base = base * (1 + r);
```

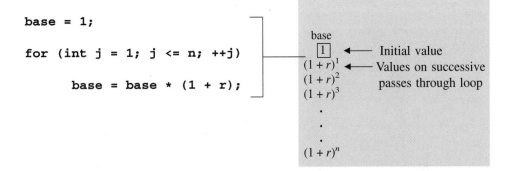

for **Loops that Count Down**

A variation of the pretest, fixed repetition loop is a **for** loop that counts down. This loop does exactly what you expect; it is identical to a **for** loop that counts up, except the loop control variable is decreased by one instead of increased by one each time through the loop. This is referred to as **decrementing.** The test is loop control value **>=** final value. The loop terminates when the loop control value is less than the final value. The decrement operator is used to adjust the loop control variable on each pass through the loop. Proper form and syntax for a loop of this type are the same as that of **for** loops that count up; however, the contents of the statements within the loop heading will be the opposite of those of **for** loops that count up:

1. The initialization part sets the control variable to an upper bound rather than a lower bound.
2. The termination part consists of a comparison to see whether the control variable is greater than or equal to a value that is the lower bound of the loop.
3. The update part decrements rather than increments the control variable by some value.

We now consider an example of a **for** loop that counts down.

decrement: To decrease the value of a variable.

Example 6.4

Illustrate the control values of a **for** loop that counts down by writing the control value during each pass through the loop. The segment of code for this could be

```
for (int k = 20; k >= 15; --k)
    cout << "K =" << setw(4) << k << endl;
```

and the output is

```
K =   20
K =   19
K =   18
K =   17
K =   16
K =   15
```

Loops that Count by Factors Other than One

Thus far, we have examined **for** loops that count up or count down. They do this by incrementing or decrementing a loop control variable by one. There are some occasions when we would like to count by a factor of two or more. One example is the problem of adding all of the even numbers between a lower and an upper bound. For this problem, the loop should count up or down by twos. The following example solves this problem for the numbers 2 through 10 by incrementing the loop control variable by two in an assignment expression:

```
        sum = 0;
        for (int j = 2; j <= 10; j = j + 2)
                sum = sum + j;
        cout << sum << endl;
```

Writing Style for Loops

As you can see, writing style is an important consideration when writing code using loops. There are three features to consider. First, the body of the loop should be indented. Compare the following two pieces of code:

```
// Code segment #1
for (int j = 1; j <= 10; ++j)
{
        cin >> num >> amt;
        total1 = total1 + amt;
        total2 = total2 + num;
        cout << "The number is" << setw(6) << num << endl;
}
cout << "The total amount is" << setiosflags(ios::fixed | ios::showpoint)
        << setw(8) << setprecision(2) << total1 << endl;
average = total2 / 10.0;


// Code segment #2
for (int j = 1; j <= 10; ++j)
{
cin >> num >> amt;
total1 = total1 + amt;
total2 = total2 + num;
cout << "The number is" << setw(6) << num << endl;
}
cout << "The total amount is" << setiosflags(ios::fixed | ios::showpoint)
        << setw(8) << setprecision(2) << total1 << endl;
average = total2 / 10.0;
```

The indenting in the first segment makes it easier to determine what is contained in the body of the loop than does the second segment, without any indenting.

Second, blank lines can be used before and after a loop for better readability. Compare the following:

```
    // Code segment #1
    cin >> x >> y;
    cout << setiosflags(ios:: fixed|ios:: showpoint);
    cout << setw(6) << setprecision(2) << x << setw(6)
            << y << endl;
    cout << endl;

    for (int j = -3; j <= 5; ++j)
            cout << setw(3) << j << setw(5) << '*' << endl;
```

```
sum = sum + x;
cout << setw(10) << setprecision(2) << sum << endl;

// Code segment #2
cin >> x >> y;
cout << setiosflags (ios:: fixed|ios:: showpoint);
cout << setw(6) << setprecision(2) << x << setw(6)
     << y << endl;
cout << endl;
for (int j = -3; j <= 5; ++j)
     cout << setw(3) << j << setw(5) << '*' << endl;
sum = sum + x;
cout << setw(10) << setprecision(2) << sum << endl;
```

Again, the first segment is a bit more clear because it emphasizes that the entire loop is a single executable statement and makes it easy to locate the loop.

Third, comments used within loops make them more readable. In particular, a comment could accompany the end of a compound statement that is the body of a loop. The general form for this is

```
// Get a test score
for (int j = 1; j <= 50; ++j)
{
     .

     .    (body of the loop)

     .

} // end of for loop
```

We close this section with an example that uses a **for** loop to solve a problem.

Example 6.5   Suppose you have been asked to write a segment of code to compute the test average for each of 30 students in a class and the overall class average. Data for each student consist of the student's initials and four test scores.

A first-level pseudocode development is

1.   Print a heading
2.   Initialize total
3.   Process data for each of 30 students
4.   Compute class average
5.   Print a summary

A **for** loop could be used to implement step 3. The step could first be refined to

3.   Process data for each of 30 students
     3.1   Get data for a student
     3.2   Compute average
     3.3   Add to total
     3.4   Print student data

Communication and Style Tips

You may wish to incorporate three features as you work with **for** loops. First, loop limits can be defined as constants or declared as variables and then have assigned values. Thus, you could have

```cpp
const int LOOP_LIMIT = 50;
```

Second, the loop control variable could be declared as

```cpp
int lcv;
```

The loop could then be written as

```cpp
for (lcv = 1; lcv <= LOOP_LIMIT; ++lcv)
        .
        .  (body of the loop here)
        .
```

Third, a loop limit could be declared as a variable and then the user would enter a value during execution.

```cpp
int loop_limit;
        .
        .
        .
cout << "How many entries? ";
cin >> loop_limit;
for (lcv = 1; lcv <= loop_limit; ++lcv)
```

The code for this step is

```cpp
for (int lcv = 1; lcv <= CLASS_SIZE; ++lcv)
{
    cout << "Enter three initials and press <Enter>. ";
    cin >> init1 >> init2 >> init3;
    cout << "Enter four test scores and press <Enter>. ";
    cin >> score1 >> score2 >> score3 >> score4;
    average = (score1 + score2 + score3 + score4) / 4.0;
    total = total + average;
    cout << endl;
    cout << setw(4) << init1 << init2 << init3;
    cout << setw(6) <<score1 << setw(6) <<score2
```

```
              << setw(6) << score3 << setw(6) <<score4;
    cout << setprecision(2) << setw(10) << average
              << endl;
}
```

1. What is the output from each of the following segments of code?

   a. ```
      for (k = 3; k <= 8; ++k)
              cout << setw(k) << '*'<< endl;
      ```

   b. ```
      for (j = 1; j <= 10; ++j)
              cout << setw(4) << j << " :" << setw(5)
                  << (10 - J) << endl;
      ```

   c. ```
      a = 2;
      for (j = (3 * 2 - 4); j <= 10 * a; ++j)
              cout << setw(4) << j << endl;
      ```

   d. ```
      for (j = 50; j >= 30; --j)
              cout << setw(5) << (51 - j) << endl;
      ```

2. Write a test program for each of the following:

   a. Illustrate what happens when the loop control variable is assigned a value inside the loop.

   b. Demonstrate how an accumulator works. For this test program, sum the integers from 1 to 10. Your output should show each partial sum as it is assigned to the accumulator.

3. Write segments of code using a loop that counts up and a loop that counts down to produce the following designs. Start each design in column 2.

   a.
   ```
    *
    *
    *
    *
   ```

   b.
   ```
    ***
     ***
      ***
       ***
        ***
         ***
          ***
           ***
   ```

   c.
   ```
        *
       * *
      *   *
     *     *
    ***   ***
     *     *
      *   *
       *****
   ```

   d.
   ```
    *********
     *******
      *****
       ***
        *
   ```

4. Which of the following segments of code do you think accomplish their intended task? For those that do not, what changes would you suggest?

a.
```
for (k = 1; k <= 5; ++k);
     cout << k << endl;
```

b.
```
sum = 0;
for (j = 1; j <= 10; ++j)
     cin >>a;
sum = sum + a;
cout << setw(15) << sum << endl;
```

c.
```
     sum = 0;
for (j = -3; j <= 3; ++j)
     sum = sum + j;
```

d.
```
a = 0;
for (k = 1; k <= 10; ++k)
{
     a = a + k;
     cout << setw(5) << k << setw(5)<< a setw(5)
          << (a + k) << endl;
}
cout << setw(5) << k << setw(5) << a << setw(5)
     << (a + k) << endl;
```

5. Produce each of the following outputs using a loop that counts up and a loop that counts down:

a. `1 2 3 4 5`

b.
```
*
   *
      *
         *
            *
```

6. Rewrite the following segment of code using a loop that counts down to produce the same result:

```
sum = 0;
for (k = 1; k <= 4; ++k)
{
     cout << setw(21 + k) << endl;
     sum = sum + k;
}
```

7. Rewrite the following segment of code using a loop that counts up to produce the same result:

```
for (j = 10; j >= 2; --j)
     cout << setw(j) << j << endl;
```

8. Write a complete program that produces a table showing the temperature equivalents in degrees Fahrenheit and degrees Celsius. Let the user enter the starting and ending values. Use the following formula:

```
cels_temp = 5.0/9.0 (faren_temp - 32.0)
```

A Note of Interest

Charles Babbage

The first person to propose the concept of the modern computer was Charles Babbage (1791–1871), a man truly ahead of his time. Babbage was a professor of mathematics at Cambridge University, as well as an inventor. As a mathematician, he realized the time-consuming and boring nature of constructing mathematical tables (squares, logarithms, sines, cosines, and so on). Because the calculators developed by Pascal and Leibniz could not provide the calculations required for these more complex tables, Babbage proposed the idea of building a machine that could compute the various properties of numbers, accurate to 20 digits.

With a grant from the British government, he designed and partially built a simple model of the difference engine. However, the lack of technology in the 1800s prevented him from making a working model. Discouraged by his inability to materialize his ideas, Babbage imagined a better version, which would be a general purpose, problem-solving machine—the analytical engine.

The similarities between the analytical engine and the modern computer are amazing. Babbage's analytical engine, which was intended to be a steam-powered device, had four components:

1. A "mill" that manipulated and computed the data
2. A "store" that held the data
3. An "operator" of the system that carried out instructions
4. A separate device that entered data and received processed information via punched cards.

After spending many years sketching variations and improvements for this new model, Babbage received some assistance in 1842 from Ada Augusta Byron (see the next **Note of Interest**).

6.3 while Loops

Objectives

- to understand when variable repetition should be used in a program
- to understand why **while** is a variable repetition loop
- to understand the flow of control when using a **while** loop
- to be able to use a counter in a **while** loop
- to be able to use a **while** loop in a program

9. Write a complete program to produce a chart consisting of the multiples of 5 from −50 to 50 together with the squares and cubes of these numbers. Use a function to print a suitable heading and user-defined functions for square and cube.

10. The formula $A = P(1 + R)^N$ can be used to compute the amount due (A) when a principal (P) has been borrowed at a monthly rate (R) for a period of N months. Write a complete program that will read in the principal, annual interest rate (divide by 12 for monthly rate), and number of months and then produce a chart that shows how much will be due at the end of each month.

In Section 6.2, we studied **for** loops in which the body of the loop is repeated a fixed number of times. For some problems, this kind of loop is inappropriate, because a segment of code may need to be repeated an unknown number of times. The condition controlling the loop must be variable rather than constant. C++ provides two repetition statements that are especially well suited to handle variable control conditions, one with a pretest condition and one with a post-test condition.

A useful pretest loop with variable conditions in C++ is the **while** loop. The condition controlling the loop is a Boolean expression written between parentheses. Correct form and syntax for such a loop are

```
while ( <Boolean expression> )
          <statement>
```

Note that the parentheses enclosing the Boolean expression are required. The flow diagram for a **while** loop is given in Figure 6.2. Program control, when using a **while** loop, is in order as follows:

1. The loop condition is examined.
2. If the loop condition is **TRUE**, the entire body of the loop is executed before another check is made.
3. If the loop condition is **FALSE**, control is transferred to the first statement following the loop. For example,

```
a = 1;
while (a < 0)
{
     num = 5;
     cout << num << endl;
     a = a + 10
}
cout << a << endl;
```

produces the single line of output

```
1
```

◆ Figure 6.2

Flow of control of a
while loop

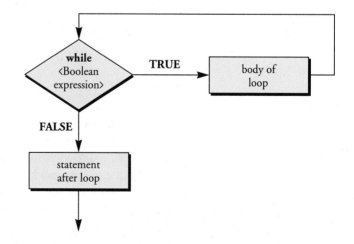

Before analyzing the components of the **while** statement, we should consider a short example.

| Example 6.6 | This example prints some powers of two. |

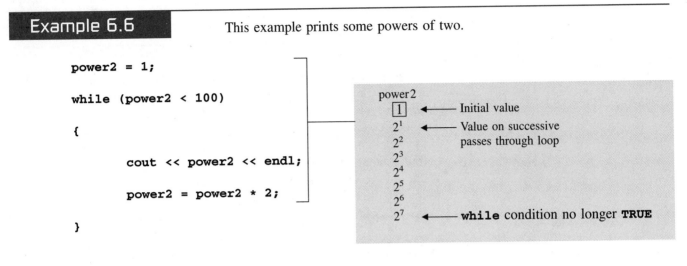

```
power2 = 1;

while (power2 < 100)

{

        cout << power2 << endl;

        power2 = power2 * 2;

}
```

The output from this segment of code is

```
        1
        2
        4
        8
       16
       32
       64
```

With this example in mind, let us examine the general form for using a **while** loop.

1. The condition can be any expression that has a Boolean value. Standard examples include relational operators and Boolean variables; thus, each of the following would be appropriate:

```
while (j < 10)
while (a < b)
while (! done)
```

2. The Boolean expression must have a value prior to entering the loop.
3. The body of the loop can be a simple statement or a compound statement.
4. Provision must be made for appropriately changing the loop control condition in the body of the loop. If no such changes are made, the following could happen.

   a. If the loop condition is **TRUE** and no changes are made, a condition called an **infinite loop** is caused. For example,

```
a = 1;
while (a > 0)
{
```

infinite loop: A loop in which the controlling condition is not changed in such a manner as to allow the loop to terminate.

```
                num = 5;
                cout<< num << endl;
        }
        cout << a << endl;
```

The condition **a > 0** is **TRUE**, the body is executed, and the condition is retested. However, because the condition is not changed within the loop body, it will always be **TRUE** and will cause an infinite loop. It will not produce a compilation error but, when you run the program, the output will be a column of fives.

b. If the loop condition is **TRUE** and changes are made, but the condition never becomes **FALSE**, you again have an infinite loop. An example of this is

```
power3 = 1;
while (power3 != 100)
{
        cout << power3 << endl;
        power3 = power3 * 3
}
```

Since the variable **power3** never is assigned the value 100, the condition **power3 != 100** is always **TRUE**. At run time, the computer will continue to multiply **power3** by 3 until an integer overflow error occurs.

Sentinel Values

sentinel value:
A special value that indicates the end of a set of data or of a process.

The Boolean expression of a variable control loop is frequently controlled by a **sentinel value.** For example, a program might require the user to enter numeric data. When there are no more data, the user will be instructed to enter a special (sentinel) value. This then signifies the end of the process. Example 6.7 illustrates the use of such a sentinel.

| Example 6.7 |

Here we write a segment of code that allows the user to enter a set of test scores and then print the average score.

```
num_scores = 0;
sum = 0;
cout << "Enter a score and press <Enter>, -999 to quit. ";
cin >> score;
while (score != -999)
{
        num_scores = num_scores + 1;
        sum = sum + score;
        cout << "Enter a score and press <Enter>, -999 to quit. ";
        cin >> score;
```

```
     }
     if (num_scores > 0)
     {
           average = sum / double(num_scores);
           cout << endl;
           cout << "The average of " << setw(4) << num_scores
                << " scores is "
                << setiosflags(ios::fixed | ios::showpoint);
                << setw(6) << setprecision(2) << average << endl;
     }
     else
           cout << "No scores were entered" << endl;
```

Writing Style

Writing style for **while** loops should be similar to that adopted for **for** loops; that is, indenting, skipped lines, and comments should all be used to enhance readability.

Using Counters

Because **while** loops may be repeated a variable number of times, it is a common practice to count the number of times the loop body is executed. This is accomplished by declaring an appropriately named integer variable, initializing it to zero before the loop, and then incrementing it by one each time through the loop. For example, if you use count for your variable name, Example 6.6 (in which we printed some powers of two) could be modified to

```
count = 0;
power2 = 1;

while (power2 < 100)
{
      cout << power2 << endl;
      power2 = power2 * 2;
      count = count + 1;
}

cout << "There are" << setw(4) << count
      << " powers of 2 less than 100." << endl;
```

The output from this segment of code is

```
1
2
4
8
16
32
64

There are 7 powers of 2 less than 100.
```

counter: *A variable used to count the number of times some process is completed.*

Although the process is tedious, it is instructive to trace the values of variables through a loop where a **counter** is used. Therefore, let us consider the segment of code we have just seen. Before the loop is entered, we have

count

power2

The loop control is **power2 < 100 (1 < 100)**. Since this is **TRUE**, the loop body is executed and the new values become

| 1 |
count

power2

Prior to each successive time through the loop, the condition **power2 < 100** is checked. Thus, the loop produces the following sequence of values:

count	power2
1	2
2	4
3	8
4	16
5	32
6	64
7	128

Although **power2** is 128, the remainder of the loop is executed before checking the loop condition. Once a loop is entered, it is executed completely before the loop control condition is reexamined. Because **128 < 100** is **FALSE**, control is transferred to the statement following the loop.

Compound Conditions

All previous examples and illustrations of **while** loops have used simple Boolean expressions. However, because any Boolean expression can be used as a loop control condition, compound Boolean expressions can also be used. For example,

```
cin >> a >> b;
while ((a > 0) && (b > 0))
{
```

```
                        cout << a << " " << b << endl << endl;
                        a = a - 5;
                        b = b - 3;
               }
```

will go through the body of the loop only when the Boolean expression **(a > 0)**
&& (b > 0) is **TRUE**. Thus, if the values of **a** and **b** obtained from the keyboard
are

```
       17  8
```

the output from this segment of code is

```
       17  8

       12  5

       7  2
```

Compound Boolean expressions can be as complex as you wish to make them.
However, if several conditions are involved, the program can become difficult to
read and debug; therefore, you may wish to redesign your solution to avoid this
problem.

■ Exercises 6.3

1. Compare and contrast **for** loops with **while** loops.
2. Write a test program that illustrates what happens when you have an infinite
   loop.
3. What is the output from each of the following segments of code?

   a.
```
      k = 1;
      while (k <= 10)
      {
           cout << k << endl;
           k = k + 1;
      }
```

   b.
```
      a = 1;
      while (17 % a < 5)
      {
           cout << a << 17 % a << endl;
           a = a + 1;
      }
```

   c.
```
      a = 2;
      b = 50;
      while (a < b)
           a = a * 3;
      cout << a << b << endl;
```

   d.
```
      count = 0;
      sum = 0;
```

```
        while (count < 5)
        {
            count = count + 1;
            sum = sum + count;
            cout << "The partial sum is" << setw(4)
                << sum << endl;
        }
        cout<< "The count is" << setw(4) << count << endl;
    e.  x = 3.0;
        y = 2.0;
        while (x * y < 100)
            x = x * y;
        cout<< setprecision(2) << setw(10) << x setw(10) << y
            << endl;
```

4. Indicate which of the following are infinite loops and explain why they are infinite:

```
    a.  j = 1;
        while (j < 10)
            cout << j;
            j = j + 1;
    b.  a = 2;
        while (a < 20)
        {
            cout << a << endl;
            a = a * 2;
        }
    c.  a = 2;
        while (a != 20)
        {
```

```
            cout << a << endl;
            a = a * 2;
      }
  d.  b = 15;
      while (b / 3 == 5)
      {
            cout << b << b / 5 << endl;
            b = b - 1;
      }
```

5. Write a **while** loop for each of the following tasks:
    a. Print a positive real number, **num**, and then print successive values where each value is 0.5 less than the previous value. The list should continue as long as values to be printed are positive.
    b. Print a list of squares of positive integers as long as the difference between consecutive squares is less than 50.

6. Write a segment of code that reads a positive integer and prints a list of powers of the integer that are less than 10,000.

6.4 do . . . while Loops

Objectives

◆ to understand that a **do . . . while** loop is a post-test loop

◆ to understand the flow of control using a **do . . . while** loop

◆ to be able to use a **do . . . while** loop in a program

◆ to be able to use **do . . . while** loops with multiple conditions

The previous two sections discussed two kinds of repetition. We looked at fixed repetition using **for** loops and variable repetition using **while** loops. C++ provides a second form of variable repetition, a **do . . . while** loop, which is a *post-test,* or *exit-controlled, loop.*

The basic form and syntax for a **do . . . while** loop are

```
do
{
      <statement>
} while (<Boolean expression>);
```

A flow diagram for a **do . . . while** loop is given in Figure 6.3. Prior to examining this form, let us consider the following fragment of code:

```
count = 0;
do
{
      count = count + 1;
      cout << count << endl;
} while (count < 5);
cout << "All done" << endl;
```

The output for this fragment is

```
1
2
3
4
5
All done
```

◆ Figure 6.3

Flow of control of a
do . . . while loop

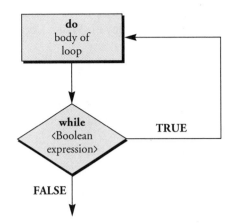

With this example in mind, the following comments concerning the use of a
do . . . while loop are in order:

1. The Boolean expression must have a value before it is used at the end of the loop.
2. The loop must be entered at least once because the Boolean expression is not evaluated until after the loop body has been executed.
3. When the Boolean expression is evaluated, if it is **TRUE**, control is transferred back to the top of the loop; if it is **FALSE**, control is transferred to the next program statement.
4. Provision must be made for changing values inside the loop so that the Boolean expression used to control the loop will eventually be **FALSE**. If this is not done, you will have an infinite loop, as shown here:

```
j = 0;
do
{
    j = j + 2;
    cout << j << endl;
} while (j != 5);
```

5. Writing style for using **do . . . while** loops should be consistent with your style for other loop structures.

There is one important difference between **while** and **do . . . while** loops. A **do . . . while** loop must be executed at least once, but a **while** loop can be skipped if the initial value of the Boolean expression is **FALSE**. Because of this, **do . . . while** loops are generally used less frequently than **while** loops.

Example 6.8

An early method of approximating square roots was the Newton-Raphson method. This method consisted of starting with an approximation and then getting successively better approximations until the desired degree of accuracy was achieved. Writing code for this method, each **new_guess** is defined to be

```
new_guess = 1/2.0 * (old_guess + number / old_guess)
```

Thus, if the number entered was 34 and the first approximation was 5, the second approximation would be

```
1/2.0 * (5 + 34 / 5)      (5.9)
```

and the third approximation would be

```
1/2.0 * (5.9 + 34 / 5.9)      (5.83135593)
```

Let's see how a **do . . . while** loop can be used to obtain successively better approximations until a desired degree of accuracy is reached.

Assume **number** contains the number whose square root we wish to approximate, **old_guess** contains a first approximation, and **DESIRED_ACCURACY** is a defined constant. A loop used in the solution of this problem is

```
cout << setprecision(8) << setw(12) << new_guess << endl;
do
{
     old_guess = new_guess;
     new_guess = 1/2.0 * (old_guess + number / old_guess);
     cout << setw(12) << new_guess << endl;
} while (abs(new_guess - old_guess) >= DESIRED_ACCURACY);
```

If **DESIRED_ACCURACY** is 0.0001, **number** is 34, and **new_guess** is originally 5, the output from this segment is

```
5.00000000

5.90000000

5.83135593

5.83095191

5.83095189
```

Example 6.9   Interactive programming frequently requires the use of a menu to give the user a choice of options. For example, suppose you want a menu like this one:

```
Which of the following recipes do you wish to see?

        (T) acos
        (J) ambalaya
        (G) umbo
        (Q) uit

Enter the first letter and press <Enter>.
```

This screen message could then be written as a function **menu** and the main program could use a **do . . . while** loop as follows:

```
do
{
        menu();
        cin >> selection;
        switch (selection)
        {
                case 'T' :        tacos();
                                  break;
                case 'J' :        jambalaya();
                                  break;
                case 'G' :        gumbo();
                                  break;
                case 'Q' :        goodbye_message();
        }
} while (selection != 'Q');
```

where **tacos**, **jambalaya**, **gumbo**, and **goodbye_message** are each separate functions with appropriate messages.

Compound Conditions

The Boolean expression used with a **do . . . while** loop can be as complex as you choose to make it. However, as with **while** loops, if the expression gets too complicated, you might enhance program readability and design by redesigning the algorithm to use simpler expressions.

Choosing the Correct Loop

"Which type of loop should I use?" is a question often faced by programmers. A partial answer is easy. If a loop is to be repeated a predetermined number of times during execution, a **for** loop is preferable. If the number of repetitions is not known, one of the variable control loops is preferable.

The more difficult part of the answer is deciding which variable control loop is appropriate. Simply stated, if a control check is needed before the loop is executed, use a **while** loop. If the check is needed at the end of the loop, use a **do . . . while** loop. Remember, however, that a **do . . . while** loop must always be executed at least once. Therefore, if there is a possibility that the loop will not be executed, a **while** loop must be used. For example, when reading data (especially from files, see Chapter 7), if there is a possibility of no data, a **while** loop must be used with a prompting input statement or other control check prior to the loop. Thus, you could have

```
cout << "Enter a score, -999 to quit. ";
cin << score;
while (score != -999)
{
        .

        . (process data)

        .

        cout << "Enter a score, -999 to quit. ";
        cin << score;
}
```

In the event either variable control loop can be used, the problem itself might help with the decision. Does the process need to be repeated until something happens, or does the process continue as long as (while) some condition is true? If either of these is apparent, use the code that most accurately reflects the solution to the problem.

Data Validation

Variable condition loops can be used to make programs more robust. In particular, suppose you are writing an interactive program that expects positive integers to be entered from the keyboard, with a sentinel value of −999 to be entered when you wish to quit. You can guard against bad data by using the following:

```
do
{
        cout << "Enter a positive integer; <-999> to quit. ";
        cin >> num;
} while ((num > 0) && (num != -999));
```

data validation: The process of examining data prior to its use in a program.

This process of examining data prior to its use in a program is referred to as **data validation,** and loops are useful for such validation. A second example of using a loop for this purpose follows.

Example 6.10

One problem associated with interactive programs is guarding against typing errors. This example illustrates how a **do . . . while** loop can be used to avoid having something entered other than the anticipated responses. Specifically, suppose users of an interactive program are asked to indicate whether or not they wish to continue by entering either a **Y** or **N**. The screen message could be

```
Do you wish to continue? <Y or N>
```

You wish to allow any of **Y**, **y**, **N**, or **n** to be used as an appropriate response. Any other entry is considered an error. This can be accomplished by the following:

```
do
{
    cout << "Do you wish to continue? <Y or N> ";
    cin >> response;
    good_response = (response == 'Y') || (response == 'y') ||
    (response == 'N') || (response == 'n');
} while (! good_response);
```

Any response other than those permitted as good data (**Y**, **y**, **N**, **n**) results in **good_response** being **FALSE** and the loop being executed again.

■ Exercises 6.4

1. Explain the difference between a pretest loop and a post-test loop.
2. Indicate what the output will be from each of the following code fragments:

   a.
   ```
   a = 0;
   b = 10;
   do
   {   a = a + 1;
       b = b - 1;
       cout << a << b << endl;
       } while (a <= b);
   ```

   b.
   ```
   power = 1;
   do
   {
       power = power * 2;
       cout << power << endl;
   } while (power <= 100);
   ```

   c.
   ```
   j = 1;
   do
   {
       cout << j << endl;
       j = j + 1;
   } while (j <= 10);
   ```

   d.
   ```
   a = 1;
   do
   {
       cout << a << 17 % a << endl;
       a = a + 1;
   } while (17 % a != 5);
   ```

3. Indicate which of the following are infinite loops and explain why:

a.
```
j = 1;
do
{
      cout << j << endl;
} while (j <= 10);
j = j + 1;
```

b.
```
a = 2;
do
{
      cout << a << endl;
      a = a * 2;
} while (a <= 20);
```

c.
```
a = 2;
do
{
      cout << a << endl;
      a = a * 2;
} while (a != 20);
```

d.
```
b = 15;
do
{
      cout << b << b / 5 << endl;
      b = b - 1;
} while (b / 3 >= 5);
```

4. Write a **do . . . while** loop for each of the following tasks:

a. Print a positive real number, **num**, and then print successive values where each value is 0.5 less than the previous value. The list should continue as long as values to be printed are positive.

b. Print a list of squares of positive integers as long as the difference between consecutive squares is less than 50.

5. Discuss whether or not a priming read is needed before a **do . . . while** loop that is used to get data.

6. Give an example of a situation that would require a predetermined number of repetitions.

7. In mathematics and science, many applications require a certain level or degree of accuracy obtained by successive approximations. Explain how the process of reaching the desired level of accuracy would relate to loops in C++.

8. Write a program that utilizes the algorithm for approximating a square root as shown in Example 6.8. Let the defined accuracy be 0.0001. Input should consist of a number whose square root is desired. Your program should guard against bad data entries (negatives and zero). Output should include a list of approximations and a check of your final approximation.

9. Compare and contrast the three repetition structures previously discussed in this chapter.

6.5 Loop Verification

Loop verification is the process of guaranteeing that a loop performs its intended task. Such verification is part of program testing and correctness to which we referred in Chapter 5.

Objectives

◆ to understand how input assertions and output assertions can be used to verify loops

◆ to understand how loop invariants and loop variants can be used to verify loops

loop verification: The process of guaranteeing that a loop performs its intended task.

input assertion: A precondition for a loop.

output assertion: A postcondition for a loop.

Some work has been done on constructing formal proofs to determine that loops are "correct." We now examine a simplified version of loop verification; a complete treatment of the issue is the topic of subsequent course work.

Preconditions and Postconditions with Loops

Preconditions and postconditions can be used with loops. Loop preconditions are referred to as **input assertions.** They state what can be expected to be true before the loop is entered. Loop postconditions are referred to as **output assertions.** They state what can be expected to be true when the loop is exited.

To illustrate input and output assertions, we consider the mathematical problem of summing the proper divisors of a positive integer. For example, we have these integers:

Integer	Proper Divisors	Sum
6	1, 2, 3	6
9	1, 3	4
12	1, 2, 3, 4, 6	16

As part of a program that takes a positive integer as input, and displays as output a determination of whether the integer is perfect **(sum = integer)**, abundant **(sum > integer)**, or deficient **(sum < integer)**, it is necessary to sum the divisors. The following loop performs this task:

```
divisor_sum = 0;
for (trial_divisor = 1; trial_divisor <= num / 2; ++trial_divisor)
    if (num % trial_divisor == 0)
        divisor_sum = divisor_sum + trial_divisor;
```

An input assertion for this loop is

```
Precondition:    1. num is a positive integer.
                 2. divisor_sum = 0.
```

An output assertion is

```
Postcondition: divisor_sum is the sum of all proper
divisors of num.
```

When these are placed with the previous code, we have

```
divisor_sum = 0;
assert((num > 0) && (divisor_sum > 0));
```

```
for (trial_divisor = 1; trial_divisor <= num / 2; ++trial_divisor)
if (num % trial_divisor == 0) then
        divisor_sum = divisor_sum + trial_divisor;
// Postcondition: divisor_sum is the sum of all proper divisors of num.
```

Note that we pass the precondition to the **assert** function of C++, so that the run-time system actually establishes the truth of that assertion. However, we cannot do this with the postcondition, because the sum of all the proper divisors of a number is just what we are computing in the **for** loop!

loop invariant: An assertion that expresses a relationship between variables that remains constant throughout all iterations of the loop.

Invariant and Variant Assertions

A loop invariant is an assertion that expresses a relationship between variables that remains constant throughout all iterations of the loop. In other words, it is a statement that is true both before the loop is entered and after each pass through the loop. An invariant assertion for the preceding code segment could be

```
divisor_sum is the sum of proper divisors of num that are less than or equal to
trial_divisor.
```

loop variant: An assertion whose truth changes between the first and final execution of the loop.

A loop variant is an assertion whose truth changes between the first and final execution of the loop. The loop variant expression should be stated in such a way that it guarantees the loop is exited. Thus, it contains some statement about the loop variable being incremented (or decremented) during execution of the loop. In the preceding code, we could have

```
trial_divisor is incremented by 1 each time through the loop. It eventually exceeds
the value num / 2, at which point the loop is exited.
```

Variant and invariant assertions usually occur in pairs.

We now use four kinds of assertions—input, output, variant, and invariant—to produce the formally verified loop that follows:

```
divisor_sum = 0;
// Precondition:      1. Num is a positive integer.    (input assertion)
//                    2. divisor_sum = 0.

assert((num > 0) && (divisor_sum == 0));

for (trial_divisor = 1; trial_divisor <= num / 2; ++trial_divisor)

// trial_divisor is incremented by 1 each time         (variant assertion)
// through the loop. It eventually exceeds the
// value (num / 2), at which point the loop is exited.

    if (num % trial_divisor == 0)
        divisor_sum = divisor_sum + trial_divisor;
```

```
// divisor_sum is the sum of proper divisors of        (invariant assertion)
// num that are less than or equal to trial_divisor.

// Postcondition: divisor_sum is the sum of            (output assertion)
// all proper divisors of num.
```

In general, code that is presented in this text does not include formal verification of the loops. This issue is similar to that of robustness. In an introductory course, a decision must be made regarding the trade-off between learning new concepts and writing robust programs with formal verification of loops. We encourage the practice, but space and time considerations make it inconvenient to include such documentation at this level. We close this discussion with another example illustrating loop verification.

Example 6.11

Consider the problem of finding the greatest common divisor (**gcd**) of two positive integers. To illustrate, we have this information:

num1	num2	gcd (num 1, num2)
8	12	4
20	10	10
15	32	1
70	40	10

A segment of code to produce the **gcd** of two positive integers after they have been ordered as **small**, **large**, is

```
trial_gcd = small;
gcd_found = FALSE;
while (! gcd_found)
    if ((large % trial_gcd == 0) && (small % trial_gcd == 0))
    {
        gcd = trial_gcd;
        gcd_found = TRUE;
    }
    else
        trial_gcd = trial_gcd - 1;
```

Using assertions as previously indicated, this code would appear as

```
trial_gcd = small;
gcd_found = FALSE;
```

```
// Precondition:   1. small <= large
//                 2. trial_gcd (small) is the first candidate for gcd
//                 3. gcd_found is FALSE

assert((small <= large) && (small == trial_gcd) && ! gcd_found);

while (! gcd_found)

// trial_gcd assumes integer values ranging from small
// to 1. It is decremented by 1 each time through the
// loop. When trial_gcd divides both small and large,
// the loop is exited. Exit is guaranteed since 1
// divides both small and large.

if ((large % trial_gcd == 0) && (small % trial_gcd == 0))

// When trial_gcd divides both large and small,
// then gcd is assigned that value.

{

    assert((large % trial_gcd == 0) && (small % trial_gcd == 0));

    gcd = trial_gcd;
    gcd_found = TRUE;
}
else
    trial_gcd = trial_gcd - 1;

// Postcondition: gcd is the greatest common
// divisor of small and large.
```

■ Exercises 6.5

1. Write appropriate input assertions and output assertions for each of the following loops:

    a. ```
        cin >> score;
        while (score != -999)
        {
            num_scores = num_scores + 1;
            sum = sum + score;
            cout << "Enter a score; -999 to quit. ";
            cin >> score;
        }
        ```

    b.  ```
        count = 0;
        power2 = 1;
        while (power2 < 100)
        {
            cout << power2 << endl;
        ```

```
              power2 = power2 * 2;
              count = count + 1;
      }
```

c. (From Example 6.8)

```
do
{
    old_guess = new_guess;
    new_guess = 1/2 * (old_guess + number / old_guess);
    cout << setprecision(8) << setw(10)
            << new_guess << endl;
} while (abs(new_guess - old_guess) <
DESIRED_ACCURACY);
```

2. Write appropriate loop invariant and loop variant assertions for each of the loops in Exercise 1.

3. Consider the following loop. The user enters a number, **guess**, and the computer then displays a message indicating whether the guess is correct, too high, or too low. Add appropriate input assertions, output assertions, loop invariant assertions, and loop variant assertions to the following code.

```
correct = FALSE;
count = 0;
while ((count < MAX_TRIES) && (! correct))
{
    count = count + 1;
    cout << "Enter choice number " << count << endl;
    cin >> guess;
    if (guess == choice)
    {
        correct = TRUE;
        cout << "Congratulations!" <<endl;
    }
    else if (guess < choice)
        cout << "Your guess is too low" <<end;
    else
        cout << "Your guess is too high" << endl;
}
```

6.6 Nested Loops

In this chapter, we have examined three loop structures. Each of them has been discussed with respect to syntax, semantics, form, writing style, and use in programs. But remember that each loop is treated as a single C++ statement. In this sense, it is possible to have a loop as one of the statements in the body of another loop. When this happens, the loops are referred to as **nested loops.**

Loops can be nested to any depth; that is; a loop can be within a loop within a loop, and so on. Also, any of the three types of loops can be nested within any

nested loop: A loop as one of the statements in the body of another loop.

loop. However, a programmer should be careful not to design a program with nesting that is too complex. If program logic becomes too difficult to follow, you might be better off redesigning the program, perhaps by splitting off the inner logic into a separate subprogram.

Flow of Control

As a first example of using a loop within a loop, consider

```
for (k = 1; k <= 5; ++k)
    for (j = 1; j <= 3; ++j)
        cout << (k + j) << endl;
```

When this fragment is executed, the following happens:
1. **k** is assigned a value.
2. For each value of **k**, the following loop is executed:

```
for (j = 1; j <= 3; ++j)
    cout << (k + j) << endl;
```

Thus, for **k = 1**, the "inside," or nested, loop produces the output

```
2
3
4
```

At this point, **k = 2** and the next portion of the output produced by the nested loop is

```
3
4
5
```

The complete output from these nested loops is

```
2
3 from k = 1
4

3
4 from k = 2
5

4
5 from k = 3
6
```

```
5
6 from k = 4
7


6
7 from k = 5
8
```

As you can see, for each value assigned to the index of the outside loop, the inside loop is executed completely. Suppose you want the output to be printed in the form of a chart as follows:

```
2   3   4

3   4   5

4   5   6

5   6   7

6   7   8
```

The pseudocode design to produce this output is

1.   For (k = 1; k <= 5; ++k)
        Produce a line

A refinement of this is

1.   For (k = 1; k <= 5; ++k)
        1.1 Print on one line
        1.2 Advance the printer

The C++ code for this development becomes

```cpp
for (k = 1; k <= 5; ++k)
{
    for (j = 1; j <= 3; ++j)    // print on one line
        cout << setw(4) << (k + j);
    cout << endl;               // advance the printer
}
```

Our next example shows how nested loops can be used to produce a design.

Example 6.12

Use nested **for** loops to produce the following output:

```
*
**
***
****
*****
```

The left asterisks are in column 10. The first-level pseudocode to solve this problem could be

1. For (k = 1; k <= 5; ++k)
        Produce a line

A refinement of this could be

1. for (k = 1; k <= 5; ++k)
        1.1 Print on one line
        1.2 Advance the printer

Step 1.1 is not yet sufficiently refined, so our next level could be

1. For (k = 1; k <= 5; ++k)
        1.1 Print on one line
            1.1.1 Put a blank in column 9
            1.1.2 Print k asterisks
        1.2 Advance the printer

We can now write a program fragment to produce the desired output as follows:

```
for (k = 1; k <= 5; ++k)
{
        cout << setw(9) << ' ';
        for (j = 1; j <= k; ++j)
             cout << '*';
        cout << endl;
}
```

A significant feature has been added to this program fragment. Note that the upper bound for the inner loop is the loop control variable of the outer loop.

Communication and Style Tips

When working with nested loops, use line comments to indicate the effect of each loop control variable. For example,

```
for (k = 1; k <= 5; ++k)        // Each value produces a
                                // line
{
        cout << setw(9) << ' ';
        for (j = 1; j <= k; ++j) // This moves across
             cout << '*';        // one line
        cout << endl;
}
```

Thus far, nested loops have been used only with **for** loops, but any of the loop structures can be used in nesting. Our next example illustrates a **do . . . while** loop nested within a **while** loop.

Example 6.13

Trace the flow of control and indicate the output for the following program fragment:

```
a = 10;
b = 0;
while (a > b)
{
        cout << setw(5) << a << endl;
        do
        {
                cout << setw(5) << a << setw(5)
                        << b << setw(5) << (a + b) << endl;
            a = a - 2;
        } while (a > 6);
        b = b + 2;
}
cout << endl;
cout << setw(20) << "All done" << endl;
```

The assignment statements produce

and **a > b** is **TRUE**; thus, the **while** loop is entered. The first time through this loop the **do . . . while** loop is used. Output for the first pass is

```
10
10   0   10
```

and the values for **a** and **b** are

The Boolean expression **a > 6** is **TRUE** and the **do . . . while** loop is executed again to produce the next line of output

```
8   0   8
```

and the values for **a** and **b** become

a

b

At this point, **a > 6** is **FALSE** and control transfers to the line of code

```
b = b + 2;
```

Thus, the variable values are

a

b

and the Boolean expression **a > b** is **TRUE**. This means the **while** loop will be repeated. The output for the second time through this loop is

```
6
6   2   8
```

and the values for the variables are

a

b

Now **a > b** is **FALSE** and control is transferred to the line following the **while** loop. Output for the complete fragment is

```
10
10   0   10
8    0   8
6
6    2   8
```

All done

This example is a bit contrived and tracing the flow of control somewhat tedious. However, it is important for you to be able to follow the logic involved in using nested loops.

Writing Style

As usual, you should be aware of the significance of using a consistent, readable style of writing when using nested loops. There are at least three features you should consider.

1. *Indenting:* Each loop should have its own level of indenting. This makes it easier to identify the body of the loop. If the loop body consists of a compound statement, the **{** and **}** should start in the same column. Using our previous indenting style, a typical nesting might be

```
for (k = 1; k <= 10; ++k)
{
        while (a > 0)
        {
                do
                {
                        .



                        .



                        .

                } while (<condition>);
                // end of do . . . while loop
                <statement>
        }
        // end of while loop
            <statement>
}
// end of for loop
```

   If the body of a loop becomes very long, it is sometimes difficult to match the **{**'s with the proper **}**'s. In this case, you should either redesign the program (for example, write a separate subprogram) or be especially careful.

2. *Using comments:* Comments can precede a loop and explain what the loop will do, or they can be used with statements inside the loop to explain what the statement does. They should be used to indicate the end of a loop where the loop body is a compound statement.

3. *Skipping lines:* This is an effective way of isolating loops within a program and making nested loops easier to identify.

A note of caution is in order with respect to writing style. Program documentation is important; however, excessive use of comments and skipped lines can detract from readability. You should develop a happy medium.

Statement Execution in Nested Loops

Using nested loops can significantly increase the number of times statements get executed in a program. To illustrate, suppose a program contains a **do . . . while** loop that gets executed six times before it is exited, as illustrated here:

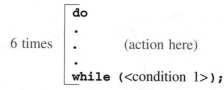

If one of the statements inside this loop is another loop, the inner loop will be executed six times. Suppose this inner loop is repeated five times whenever it is entered. This means each statement within the inner loop will be executed 6 × 5 = 30 times when the program is run. This is illustrated by

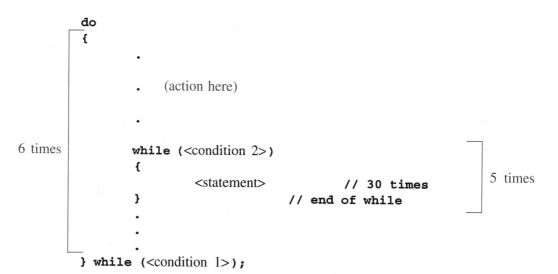

When a third level of nesting is used, the number of times a statement is executed can be determined by the product of three factors, $n_1 * n_2 * n_3$, where n_1 represents the number of repetitions of the outside loop, n_2 represents the number of repetitions for the first level of nesting, and n_3 represents the number of repetitions for the innermost loop.

We close this section with an example of a program that uses nested loops to print a multiplication table.

Example 6.14

This example presents a complete program whose output is the multiplication table from 1 × 1 to 10 × 10. A suitable heading is part of the output.

```
// Program file: multab.cpp

#include <iostream.h>
#include <iomanip.h>

// Function: print_heading
// Print a heading for multiplication table
```

```cpp
void print_heading();

// Function: print_table
// Print multiplication table

void print_table();

int main()
{
      print_heading();
      print_table();
      return 0;
}

void print_heading()
{
      cout << setiosflags(ios::right) << endl;
      cout << setw(28)
           << "Multiplication Table" << endl;
      cout << setw(28)
           << "--------------------" << endl;
      cout << "(  Generated by nested for loops  )"
           << endl;
      cout << endl;
}

void print_table()
{
      int row, column;

      //Print the column heads

      cout << "     ";
      for (int i = 1; i <=10; ++i)
           cout << setw(4) << i;
      cout << endl;
      cout << "---!------------------------------------"
           << endl;

      // Now start the loop

      for (row = 1; row <= 10; ++row)
      {
           // print one row
           cout << setw(2) << row << " !";
           for (column = 1; column <= 10; ++column)
                cout << setw(4) << (row * column);
           cout << endl;
      }   // end of each row
      cout << endl;
}
```

The output from this program is

```
                  Multiplication Table
                  --------------------
          (   Generated by nested for loops   )

               1   2   3   4   5   6   7   8   9  10
       ---!----------------------------------------
        1 !   1   2   3   4   5   6   7   8   9  10
        2 !   2   4   6   8  10  12  14  16  18  20
        3 !   3   6   9  12  15  18  21  24  27  30
        4 !   4   8  12  16  20  24  28  32  36  40
        5 !   5  10  15  20  25  30  35  40  45  50
        6 !   6  12  18  24  30  36  42  48  54  60
        7 !   7  14  21  28  35  42  49  56  63  70
        8 !   8  16  24  32  40  48  56  64  72  80
        9 !   9  18  27  36  45  54  63  72  81  90
       10 !  10  20  30  40  50  60  70  80  90 100
```

■ Exercises 6.6

1. Write a program fragment that uses nested loops to produce each of the following designs:

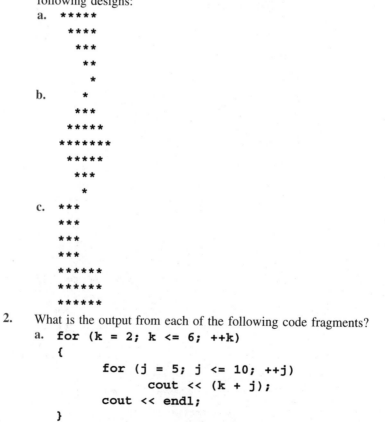

a.
```
*****
 ****
  ***
   **
    *
```

b.
```
   *
  ***
 *****
*******
 *****
  ***
   *
```

c.
```
***
***
***
***
******
******
******
```

2. What is the output from each of the following code fragments?
   a.
```
for (k = 2; k <= 6; ++k)
{
        for (j = 5; j <= 10; ++j)
                cout << (k + j);
        cout << endl;
}
```

A Digital Matter of Life and Death

The radiation-therapy machine, a Therac 25 linear accelerator, was designed to send a penetrating x ray or electron beam deep into a cancer patient's body to destroy embedded tumors without injuring skin tissue. But in three separate instances in 1985 and 1986, the machine failed. Instead of delivering a safe level of radiation, the Therac 25 administered a dose that was more than 100 times larger than the typical treatment dose. Two patients died and a third was severely burned.

The malfunction was caused by an error in the computer program controlling the machine. It was a subtle error that no one had picked up during the extensive testing the machine had undergone. The error surfaced only when a technician happened to use a specific, unusual combination of keystrokes to instruct the machine.

The Therac incidents and other cases of medical device failures caused by computer errors have focused attention on the increasingly important role played by computers in medical applications. Computers or machines with built-in microprocessors perform functions that range from keeping track of patients to diagnosing ailments and providing treatments.

"The impact of computers on medical care and the medical community is the most significant factor that we have to face," says Frank E. Samuel Jr., president of the Health Industry Manufacturers Association (HIMA), based in Washington, DC. "Health care will change more dramatically in the next 10 years because of software driven products than for any other single cause." Samuel made his remarks at a recent HIMA-sponsored conference on the regulation of medical software.

At the same time, reports of medical devices with computer-related problems are appearing more and more frequently. In 1985, the Food and Drug Administration (FDA) reported that recalls of medical devices because of computer faults had roughly doubled over the previous five years. Since then, the number of such complaints has risen further.

The FDA, in its mandated role as guardian of public health and safety, is now preparing to regulate the software component of medical devices. The agency's effort has already raised questions about what kinds of products, software, and information systems should be regulated.

```
b.  for (k = 2; k <= 6; ++k)
    {
            for (j = 5; j <= 10; ++j)
                    cout << (k + j);
            cout << endl;
    }
c.  sum = 0;
    a = 7;
    while (a < 10)
    {
            for (k = a; k <= 10; ++k)
                    sum = sum + k;
            a = a + 1;
    }
    cout << sum << endl;
d.  sum = 0;
    for (k = 1; k <= 10; ++k)
            for (j = (10 * k - 9); j <= (10 * k); ++j)
                    sum = sum + J;
    cout << sum << endl;
```

3. What output is produced from the following segment of code?

```
a = 4;
b = 7;
do
{
   num = a;
   while (num <= b)
   {
     for (k = a; k <= b; ++k)
          cout << setw(4) << num;
     cout << endl;
     num = num + 1;
   } // end of while
   cout << endl;
   a = a + 1;
}
while (a != b); // end of do . . . while loop
```

4. Write a program fragment that uses nested loops to produce the following output:

2	4	6	8	10
3	6	9	12	15
4	8	12	16	20
5	10	15	20	25

6.7 Repetition and Selection

Objectives

- to be able to use a selection statement within the body of a loop
- to be able to use a loop within an option of a selection statement

Selection Within Repetition (Loops)

In Chapter 5 we discussed the use of selection statements. In this chapter we have discussed the use of three different types of loops. It is now time to see how they are used together. We will first examine selection statements contained within the body of a loop.

Example 6.15

Write a program fragment that computes gross wages for employees of the Florida OJ Canning Company. The data consist of three initials, the total hours worked, and the hourly rate; for example,

JHA 44.5 12.75

Overtime (more than 40 hours) is computed as time-and-a-half. The output should include all input data and a column of gross wages.

A first-level pseudocode development for this program is

1. While more__employees
   1.1 Process one employee
   1.2 Print results

This could be refined to

1. While more_employees
    1.1 Process one employee
        1.1.1 Get data
        1.1.2 Compute wage
    1.2 Print results

Step 1.1.2 can be refined to

        1.1.2 Compute wage
            1.1.2.1 If Hours <= 40.0
                    Compute regular time
                Else
                    Compute time-and-a-half

and the final algorithm for the fragment is

1. While more__employees
    1.1 Process one employee
        1.1.1 Get data
        1.1.2 Compute wage
            1.1.2.1 if Hours <= 40.0
                    Compute regular time
                Else
                    Compute time-and-a-half
    1.2 Print results

The code for this fragment follows:

```
cout << setiosflags(ios::fixed | ios::showpoint);
cout << "Any employees? <Y> or <N> ";
cin >> choice;
more_employees = (choice == 'Y') || (choice == 'y');
while (more_employees)
{
    cout << endl;
    cout << "Enter initials, hours, and payrate. ";
    cin >> init1 >> init2 >> init3 >> hours >> pay_rate;
    if (hours <= 40.0)
        total_wage = hours * pay_rate;
    else
    {
        overtime = 1.5 * (hours - 40.0) * pay_rate;
        total_wage = 40 * pay_rate + overtime;
    }
    cout << endl;
    cout << setw(5) << init1 << init2 << init3;
    cout << setprecision(2) << setw(10) << hours
         << setw(10) << pay_rate;
    cout << setw(10) << '$' << setw(7) << total_wage;
    cout << endl;
    cout << "Any more employees? <Y> or <N> ";
```

```
        cin >> choice;
        more_employees = (choice == 'Y') || (choice == 'y');
}
```

Repetition (Loops) Within Selection

The next example illustrates the use of a loop within an **if** statement.

Example 6.16

Write a program fragment that allows you to read an integer from the keyboard. If the integer is between 0 and 50, you are to print a chart containing all positive integers less than the integer, their squares, and their cubes. Thus, if 4 is read, the chart is

```
1    1    1

2    4    8

3    9    27
```

The design for this problem has a first-level pseudocode development of

1.   Input num
2.   If (num > 0) && (num < 50)
        2.1 Print the chart

Step 2.1 can be refined to

2.1   Print the chart
        2.1.1 For (k = 1; k <= (num − 1); ++k)
            2.1.1.1 Print each line

We can now write the code for this fragment as follows:

```
cin >> num;
if ((num > 0) && (num < 50))
    for (k = 1; k <= num - 1; ++k)
        cout << k << (k * k) << (k * k * k) << endl;
```

Exercises 6.7

1.   Find and explain the errors in each of the following program fragments. Assume all variables have been suitably declared.
     a.
```
a = 25;
flag = TRUE;
while (flag == TRUE)
    if (a >= 100)
    {
        cout << a << endl;
        flag = FALSE;
    }
```

```
b. for (k = 1; k <= 10; ++k)
            cout << k << (k * k) << endl;
         if (k % 3 == 0)
         {
               cout << k;
               cout << " is a multiple of three" << endl;
         }
```

2. What is the output from each of the following program fragments? Assume variables have been suitably declared.

```
a. for (k = 1; k <= 100; ++k)
         if (k % 5 == 0)
               cout << k << endl;
```

```
b. j = 20;
   if (j % 5 == 0)
         for (k = 1: k <= 100; ++k)
               cout << k << endl;
```

```
c. a = 5;
   b = 90;
   do
   {
         b = b / a - 5;
         if (b > a)
               b = a + 30;
   } while (b >= 0);
   cout << a << b << endl;
```

```
d. count = 0;
   for (k = -5; k <= 5; ++k)
         if (k % 3 == 0)
         {
               cout << "k = " << setw(4) << k << " output ";
               while (count < 10)
               {
                     count = count + 1;
                     cout << setw(4) << count << endl;
               }
               count = 0;
               cout << endl;
         }
```

```
e. a = 5;
   b = 2;
   if (a < b)
         for (k = a; k <= b; ++k)
               cout << k << endl;
   else
         for (k = a; k >= b; --k)
               cout << k << endl;
```

```
f. for (k = -5; k <= 5; ++k)
   {
         cout << "k = " << setw(4) << k " output ";
         a = k;
```

```
                            if (k < 0)
                                // k = -5, -4, -3, -2, -1
                                do
                                {
                                        cout << setw(5) << (-2 * a) << endl;
                                        a = a + 1;
                                } while (a > 0);
                            else // K = 0, 1, 2, 3, 4, 5
                                while (a % 2 == 0)
                                {
                                        cout << a << endl;
                                        a = a + 1;
                                }
                            cout << endl;
                    }
```

3. Write a program fragment that reads reals from the keyboard, counts the number of positive reals, and accumulates their sum.

4. Given two integers, **a** and **b**, **a** is a divisor of **b** if **b % a = 0**. Write a complete program that reads a positive integer **b** and then prints all the positive divisors of **b**.

6.8	Graphics

Objectives

- to learn how to create animations of images
- to learn how to affect the speed and smoothness of the movement of an image

Animations

Thus far in the text, we have seen how to use graphics operations to draw "still" images. Many applications require that these images be animated. For example, a video game might move figures around in response to user's input. The basic technique underlying animation is to enter a loop in which we draw an image, erase it, and update its coordinates. This process continues until the image reaches a desired location or orientation on the screen. To become familiar with the use of loops with graphics operations, we first provide an example of a blinking image.

Example 6.17

A blinking circle can be created with the following algorithm:

Draw the circle
For a definite number of iterations do
    Pause a specified time
    Erase the circle
    Pause a specified time
    Draw the circle

The circle is erased by drawing it with the background color. Note that execution pauses after drawing and after erasing. Most computers perform these operations so quickly that the naked eye cannot see an image being erased. In general, the larger and more complex the image, the briefer the time required for a pause between erasing and redrawing. The function **delay**, which expects an integer argument denoting the number of milliseconds, is defined in the **dos** library for Turbo C++. Other C++ compilers usually support a similar library function.

The following C++ program allows the user to input the radius of the circle, the number of blinks, and the time delay between blinks:

```cpp
// Program file: blink.cpp
// This program displays a blinking circle of
// radius specified by the user. The number
// of blinks and time delay between blinks are
// also user inputs.

#include <iostream.h>
#include <graphics.h>
#include <conio.h>
#include <dos.h>

int main()
{
        int radius, blinks, time_delay;

        // Obtain radius, number of blinks,
        // and time delay from the user.

        cout << "Enter the radius: ";
        cin >> radius;
        cout << "Enter the number of blinks: ";
        cin >> blinks;
        cout << "Enter the time delay: ";
        cin >> time_delay;

        // Set the graphics mode

        int graphdriver = DETECT, graphmode;
        initgraph(&graphdriver, &graphmode, "c:..\\bgi");

        // Compute the center of the circle
        // and get the default colors

        int center_x = getmaxx() / 2;
        int center_y = getmaxy() / 2;
        int fore_color = getcolor();
        int back_color = getbkcolor();

        // Blink the circle

        circle(center_x, center_y, radius);
        for (int i = 1; i <= blinks; ++i)
        {
                delay(time_delay);
                setcolor(back_color);
                circle(center_x, center_y, radius);
                delay(time_delay);
```

```
            setcolor(fore_color);
            circle(center_x, center_y, radius);
    }
    // Close the graphics mode.

    moveto(0, 0);
    outtext("Strike any key to continue");
    getch();
    closegraph();
    return 0;

}
```

Horizontal Motion and Vertical Motion

The appearance of a moving image on a computer screen differs from that of a blinking image in two ways:

1. The image changes position at regular intervals.
2. Though the image is erased and redrawn during the process, the observer sees only the appearance of continuous motion.

The basic algorithm for describing the movement of an image is

Draw the image
While the image is not at its destination point
  Pause a specified time
  Erase the image
  Update the image's position
  Draw the image

Note that this algorithm differs from that for blinking an image (Example 6.17) in three ways:

1. The loop termination condition is a test for the destination point of the image rather than an arbitrary number of blinks.
2. The body of the loop changes the position of the image on each pass. This change is invisible when it occurs, but becomes visible when the image is redrawn on the next step.
3. The process is paused only once, immediately before the image is erased, rather than twice, after erasing as well.

When just the x coordinates of the image are changed, the image appears to move horizontally. When just the y coordinates of the image are changed, the image appears to move vertically.

The motion of an image has two important properties, speed and smoothness. These qualities depend on the size of the image, the distance it moves when its position is changed, and the duration of the time delay on each pass of the loop.

The horizontal and vertical distances that an image moves when it changes position can be expressed in terms of the quantities **delta_x** and **delta_y**. In the case of simple horizontal motion, expressions of the form

```
x_coordinate = x_coordinate + delta_x
```

would be required to update all of the relevant *x* coordinates of the image. The *y* coordinates would remain unchanged. Simple vertical motion would keep the *x* coordinates fixed, but change the *y* coordinates with expressions of the form

```
y_coordinate = y_coordinate + delta_y
```

Example 6.18

The following C++ program moves a square horizontally from the center point of the screen to the right border. The program allows the user to input the width of the square, the **delta_x** factor, and the time delay.

```
// Program file: mvsquare.cpp
// This program displays a square moving horizontally
// from the center of the screen to the right edge of
// the screen. User inputs are the width of the square,
// the delta_x factor, and the time delay.

#include <iostream.h>
#include <graphics.h>
#include <conio.h>
#include <dos.h>

int main()
{
        int width, delta_x, time_delay;

        // Obtain width, delta_x,
        // and time delay from the user.

        cout << "Enter the width: ";
        cin >> width;
        cout << "Enter the delta_x factor: ";
        cin >> delta_x;
        cout << "Enter the time delay: ";
        cin >> time_delay;

        // Set the graphics mode

        int graphdriver = DETECT, graphmode;
        initgraph(&graphdriver, &graphmode, "c:..\\bgi");

        // Compute the starting and ending points of
        // the animation and get the default colors

        int end_x = getmaxx() - width;
        int x1 = getmaxx() / 2;
        int y1 = getmaxy() / 2;
        int x2 = x1 + width;
        int y2 = y1 + width;
```

```
int fore_color = getcolor();
int back_color = getbkcolor();

// Move the square

rectangle(x1, y1, x2, y2);
while (x2 <= end_x)
{
      delay(time_delay);
      setcolor(back_color);
      rectangle(x1, y1, x2, y2);
      x1 = x1 + delta_x;
      x2 = x2 + delta_x;
      setcolor(fore_color);
      rectangle(x1, y1, x2, y2);
}

// Close the graphics mode.

moveto(0, 0);
outtext("Strike any key to continue");
getch();
closegraph();
return 0;
}
```

Linear Motion

Linear motion generalizes the simple motions discussed above so that both the x and y coordinates are updated on each pass through the loop. In other words, expressions of the form

```
x_coordinate = x_coordinate + delta_x;
y_coordinate = y_coordinate + delta_y;
```

would appear in the loop, causing the position of the image to change along a line of any slope. Horizontal and vertical motion would be special cases of this kind of transformation, where **delta_y = 0** and **delta_x = 0**, respectively.

Unlike the cases of simple horizontal and vertical motion, a loop that controls linear motion must test both the x and y coordinates of the image against upper or lower bounds. One form of this test would be

```
while ((x < end_x) && (y < end_y))
```

Nonlinear Motion

Nonlinear motion can be described mathematically by stating an equation wherein the change in the y coordinates varies as a nonlinear function of the change in the x coordinates. For example, a parabolic pattern of movement is described by the equation $y = x^2$. The coordinate transformations for this equation would be expressed as

```
x_coordinate = x_coordinate + delta_x;
y_coordinate = y_coordinate + x * x;
```

Example 6.19

The following C++ program draws a parabola from the bottom of the screen to its top edge. The user inputs the **delta_x** value. The **delta_y** value is computed by function **delta_y**, which uses a factor of 0.01 to enhance the parabolic nature of the curve. The **graphics** library function **putpixel** expects the x and y coordinates and the color of a pixel as arguments and displays the pixel.

```cpp
// Program file: parabola.cpp
// This program displays parabola running
// from the bottom of the screen to its top
// edge. The user inputs the delta_x factor.

#include <iostream.h>
#include <math.h>
#include <graphics.h>
#include <conio.h>

// Function: delta_y
// Computes change in y as a function of x
//
// Input: the current value of x
// Output: the corresponding value of y,
//         in this case, .01 times the square
//         of x

int delta_y(int x);

int main()
{
    int delta_x;

    // Obtain delta_x from the user.

    cout << " Enter the delta_x factor: " ;
    cin >> delta_x;

    // Set the graphics mode

    int graphdriver = DETECT, graphmode;
    initgraph(&graphdriver, &graphmode, "c:..\\bgi");

    // Compute the starting and ending points of
    // the drawing and get the forecolor
```

```cpp
        int end_x = getmaxx();
        int end_y = 0;
        int x = 0;
        int y = getmaxy();
        int forecolor = getcolor();

        // Draw the parabola

        while ((x < end_x) && (y > end_y))
        {
            putpixel(x, y, forecolor);
            x = x + delta_x;
            y = y - delta_y(x);
        }

        // Close the graphics mode.

        moveto(0, 0);
        outtext("Strike any key to continue");
        getch();
        closegraph();
        return 0;
}

int delta_y(int x)
{
        return int(.01 * (x * x));
}
```

| Example 6.20 |

The following C++ program moves a filled circle in a parabolic pattern from the bottom of the screen to its top edge. The user inputs the radius of the circle, the **delta_x** value, and the time delay. The **graphics** library function **fillellipse** expects center point coordinates and the *x* and *y* radii and displays a filled ellipse in the current fill color and fill pattern.

```cpp
// Program file: paracirc.cpp
// This program moves a filled circle in
// a parabolic pattern from the bottom of
// the screen to its top edge.
// The user inputs the radius, the
// delta_x value, and the time delay.

#include <iostream.h>
#include <math.h>
#include <graphics.h>
#include <conio.h>
#include <dos.h>
```

```
// Function: delta_y
// Computes change in y as a function of x
//
// Input: the current value of x
// Output: the corresponding value of y,
//         in this case, .01 times the square
//         of x

int delta_y(int x);

int main()
{
      int radius, delta_x, time_delay;

      // Obtain delta_x from the user.

      cout << "Enter the radius: ";
      cin >> radius;
      cout << "Enter the delta_x factor: ";
      cin >> delta_x;
      cout << "Enter the time delay: ";
      cin >> time_delay;

      // Set the graphics mode

      int graphdriver = DETECT, graphmode;
      initgraph(&graphdriver, &graphmode, "c:..\\bgi");
      // Compute the starting and ending points of
      // the animation and get the default colors

      int end_x = getmaxx() - radius;
      int end_y = radius;
      int x = radius;
      int y = getmaxy() - radius;
      int forecolor = getcolor();
      int backcolor = getbkcolor();

      // move the circle

      setfillstyle(SOLID_FILL, forecolor);
      fillellipse(x, y, radius, radius);
      while ((x < end_x) && (y > end_y))
      {
            delay(time_delay);
            setfillstyle(SOLID_FILL, backcolor);
            fillellipse(x, y, radius, radius);
            x = x + delta_x;
            y = y - delta_y(x);
            setfillstyle(SOLID_FILL, forecolor);
            fillellipse(x, y, radius, radius);
```

```
        }

        // Close the graphics mode.

        moveto(0, 0);
        outtext("Strike any key to continue");
        getch();
        closegraph();
        return 0;
}

int delta_y(int x)
{
        return int(.01 * (x * x));
}
```

■ Exercises 6.8

1. Discuss the ways in which the time delay, the **delta_x** and **delta_y** quantities, and the size of an image affect the quality of its motion during a computer animation.
2. Describe how several images could be moved at once during a computer animation.
3. Write an algorithm for animating the transformation of a smiling face to a sad face (see Example 4.6). The smiling mouth should appear to bend down to the shape of a sad mouth during the animation.
4. Write an algorithm that would make a stick figure jump and return to its original position.
5. Write a function, **parabola**, that expects the starting x, starting y, and ending x coordinates as arguments. The function should display a parabola covering this range, but also within the bounds of the screen.
6. Explain why filled images have a major impact on animations.

Focus on Program Design: Case Study 6.1

Finding Prime Numbers

This program illustrates the combined use of repetition and selection statements. This is the problem statement: Write a program that allows positive integers to be entered from the keyboard and, for each such entry, list all primes less than or equal to the number. The program should include a check for bad data and use of a sentinel value to terminate the process. Typical output for the integer 17 is

```
Enter a positive integer; <-999> to quit.17

The number is 17. The prime numbers
less than or equal to 17 are:

                            2
                            3
                            5
                            7
                           11
                           13
                           17

Enter a positive integer; <-999> to quit.-999
```

For purposes of this program, note the mathematical property that a number *k* is prime if it has no divisors (other than 1) less than its square root. For example, because 37 is not divisible by 2, 3, or 5, it is prime. Thus, when we check for divisors, it is only necessary to check up to **sqrt(k).** Also note that 1 is not prime by definition.

A first-level pseudocode development for this problem is

1.   Get a number
        While more_data
2.   Examine the number
3.   Get a number

A structure chart for this problem is shown in Figure 6.4. The module specifications for the main modules are

Module: Get a number
Task: Get an entry from the keyboard.
Output: A number

Module: Examine the number
Task:
 If the number is 1
        Print a message
 Else
        Print a heading.
        Print list of all primes less than or equal to the integer read.
Input: The integer read

A second-level development is

1.   Get a number
        1.1 Get entry from the keyboard
        1.2 Check for valid entry
        While more_data
            2. Examine the number
                If number is 1
                    2.1 Print a message for 1
                Else list the primes
                    2.2 Print a message
                    2.3 Check for primes less than or equal to number
            3. Get a number
                3.1 Get entry from the keyboard
                3.2 Check for valid entry

Step 2.3 can be refined to

                    2.3 Check for primes less than or equal to number
                        For (k = 2; k <= number; ++k)
                            2.3.1 Check to see if k is prime
                            2.3.2 If k is prime
                        Print k in list of primes

Instead of maintaining **more_data** as a simple Boolean flag, we will write a function that takes the number as a parameter, determines whether or not the number is the sentinel value, and returns **TRUE** or **FALSE** depending on what it finds. The pseudocode for this function is

  Make sure it is a valid entry or the sentinel value for terminating the process.
  If it is the sentinel value, return **FALSE**; otherwise, return **TRUE**.

◆ Figure 6.4

Structure chart for
prime numbers
program

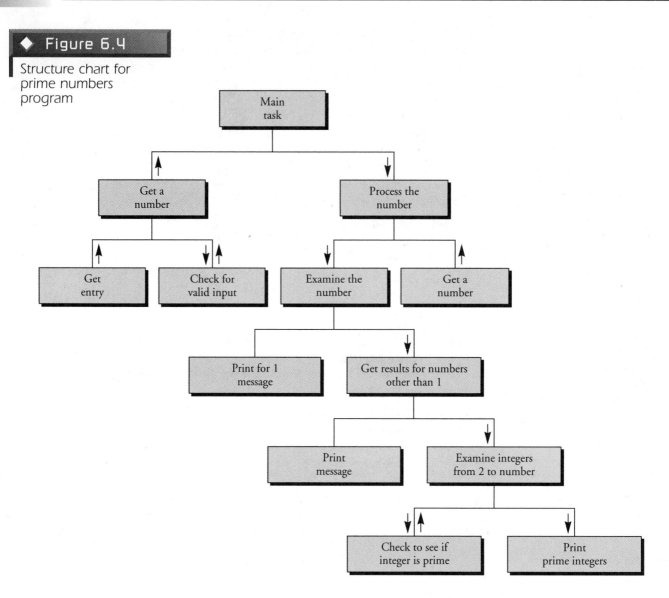

Thus, the complete pseudocode development is
1.   Get a number
        1.1 Get entry from the keyboard
        1.2 Check for valid entry
        While more_data
            2. Examine the number
                If number is 1
                    2.1 Print a message for one
                Else list the primes
                    2.2 Print a message
                    2.3 Check for primes less than or equal to number
                        For (k = 2; k <= number; ++k)
                            2.3.1 Check to see if k is prime

              2.3.2 If k is prime
                    Print k in list of primes
       3. Get a number
          3.1 Get entry from the keyboard
          3.2 Check for valid entry

With this pseudocode development, the main program would be

```
num = get_a_number();
while (more_data(num))
{
        examine_the_number(num);
        num = get_a_number();
}
```

The complete program for this problem follows:

```cpp
// Program file: primes.cpp

#include <iostream.h>
#include <iomanip.h>
#include <math.h>
#include "bool.h"

// Function: get_a_number();
// Obtain valid number from the user
//
// Output: the integer read

int get_a_number();

// Function: print_one_message
// Print a message for 1

void print_one_message();

// Function: print_message
// Print a heading for the output
//
// Input: the integer read

void print_message(int number);

// Function: list_all_primes
// Print list of all primes less than or equal
// to the integer read
//
// Input: the integer read

void list_all_primes(int number);
```

```
// Function: examine_the_number
// If integer read is one,
// then print a message for one
// else
// Print list of all primes less than or equal
// to the integer read
//
// Input: the integer read

void examine_the_number(int number);

// Function: more_data
// Determines whether number = -999
// (the sentinel for end of input)
// Input: the integer read
// Output: TRUE, if the input is not
// the sentinel, FALSE otherwise

bool more_data(int number);

int main()
{
    int number;

    cout << setiosflags(ios::right);
    number = get_a_number ();
    while (more_data(number))
    {
        examine_the_number (number);
        number = get_a_number ();
    }
    return 0;
}
```

```
int get_a_number()
{
    int number;
    bool done;

    do
    {
        cout << endl;
        cout << "Enter a positive integer; <-999> to quit.";
        cin >> number;
        done = (number == -999) || (number >= 0);
    } while (! done);               // assumes valid data
    return number;
}
```

1

```cpp
void print_one_message()
{
      cout << endl;
      cout << "1 is not prime by definition." << endl;
}


void print_message(int number)
{
      cout << endl;
      cout << "The number is " << number
           << ". The prime numbers" << endl;
      cout << "less than or equal to "<< number
         << " are:" << endl;
      cout << endl;
}


void list_all_primes(int number)
{
      bool prime;
      int candidate, divisor;
      double limit_for_check;

      for (candidate = 2; candidate <= number; ++candidate)
      {
            prime = TRUE;
            divisor = 2;
            limit_for_check = sqrt(candidate);
            while ((divisor <= limit_for_check) && prime)
                  if (candidate % divisor == 0)
                         prime = FALSE;
                  // candidate has a divisor
                  else
                         divisor = divisor + 1;
            if (prime)
      //Print list of primes
                  cout << setw(35) << candidate << endl;
      }
}
```

```cpp
void examine_the_number(int number)
{
      if (number == 1)
            print_one_message();
      else
      {
            print_message(number);
            list_all_primes (number);
      }
}
```

2

```
bool more_data(int number)
{
        return number != -999;
}
```

Sample runs of this program produce this output:

```
Enter a positive integer; <-999> to quit.10

The number is 10. The prime numbers
less than or equal to 10 are:

                                        2
                                        3
                                        5
                                        7

Enter a positive integer; <-999> to quit.17

The number is 17. The prime numbers
less than or equal to 17 are:

                                        2
                                        3
                                        5
                                        7
                                        11
                                        13
                                        17

Enter a positive integer; <-999> to quit.1

1 is not prime by definition.

Enter a positive integer; <-999> to quit.25

The number is 25. The prime numbers
less than or equal to 25 are:

                                        2
                                        3
                                        5
                                        7
                                        11
                                        13
                                        17
                                        19
                                        23

Enter a positive integer; <-999> to quit.-3

Enter a positive integer; <-999> to quit.2
```

```
The number is 2. The prime numbers
less than or equal to 2 are:

                                    2

Enter a positive integer; <-999> to quit.-999
```

More efficient algorithms than what we used here do exist. However, the purpose of this program was to see how loops can be used to solve a problem.

Focus on Program Design: Case Study 6.2

A Sentence Analyzer
Good writing style traditionally has emphasized short- to medium-length words and sentences. An important part of text evaluation is obtaining statistics on word and sentence length. This kind of computation is now a standard tool provided with word processing packages. Let us design a small text analysis system that works on individual sentences entered at the keyboard. The program will proceed interactively as follows:

1. The user is prompted for a sentence, which is a series of words ending with a word that is terminated by a period (.).
2. The system computes and displays statistics about the number of words in the sentence and the average length of a word. It also displays the longest word in the sentence.
3. The user is asked whether another input is desired with a yes/no prompt. If the answer is **Y**, the program repeats steps 1 and 2; if **N**, the program terminates.

A sample session with this program follows:

```
Enter a sentence [terminating with a period ('.')]: Hi there.

Number of words: 2
Number of characters: 8
Average length of a word: 4
Longest word: there.

Run once more? [Y/N]: y
Enter a sentence [terminating with a period ('.')]: This is a longer
sentence, going down to the next line.

Number of words: 11
Number of characters: 45
Average length of a word: 4
Longest word: sentence,

Run once more? [Y/N]: n
```

The top-level module runs a simple query driver loop:

Module: main program
Do
    Prompt for a sentence

Analyze a sentence
Query for further input
While query does not equal N

Here is a C++ main program that represents this main program module:

```cpp
int main()
{
    char query;
    do
    {
        cout << "Enter a sentence [terminating with a period ('.')]: ";
        analyze_sentence();
        cout << "Run once more? [Y/N]: ";
        cin >> query;
    } while ((query == 'Y') || (query == 'y'));
    return 0;
}
```

The module to analyze a sentence is responsible for taking input from the keyboard, computing the statistics and displaying them. This process can be described by a loop that reads individual words from the keyboard, until a word terminated by a period is entered:

Module: Analyze a sentence
Task: Read words from keyboard and update statistics, until word ending with '.' is reached.

Initialize the data
Do
        Input a word
        Update the statistics
While the word does not end with '.'
Display the statistics

The statistics will consist of the number of words, the total number of characters in the words, the average length of a word, and the longest word in the sentence. Therefore, this module will need two integer variables and two string variables to maintain the data. The integer data are locally declared, initialized to 0, and simply passed to the other modules for further processing. That leaves us with the problem of detecting a period (.) at the end of an input word. The **apstring** library provides an operator, **[ ]**, that can be used to access a character at a position in a string variable. The form for using this operator is

---

<string variable> **[**<position>**]**

---

where **<position>** is an integer value ranging from 0 to the length of the string minus one. Thus, the expression **word[0]** would return the first character in the string, while the expression **word[word.length() - 1]** would return the last character in the string, assuming that **word.length()** is greater than or equal to 1.

```
void analyze_sentence()
{
    apstring word, longest_word;
    int word_count, char_count;

    word_count = 0;
    char_count = 0;
    do
    {
        cin >> word;
        update_statistics(word, longest_word, word_count,
            char_count);
    } while (word[word.length() - 1] != '.');
    display_statistics(longest_word, word_count, char_count);
}
```

The module for updating the statistics is responsible for increasing the count of characters and words, and changing the value of the longest word if necessary.

Module: Update statistics
Task: Adjust character count and word count and adjust longest word if necessary.
Inputs: The current input word, the longest word so far, word count, character count

If the length of current input word > length of longest word so far then
    Set longest word so far to current input word
Increment the word count by one
Increment the character count by the length of the input word

Updating statistics compares the length of the current input word to the length of the longest word seen so far. If the new word is longer, it becomes the longest word.

```
void update_statistics(apstring word, apstring &longest_word,
    int &word_count, int &char_count)
{
    int length = word.length();

    if (length > longest_word.length())
        longest_word = word;
    ++word_count;
    char_count = char_count + length;
}
```

The display of statistics module computes the average length of a word as a function of the word count and the character count. Then it displays the labeled statistics on the terminal screen:

```
void display_statistics(apstring longest_word, int word_count,
    int char_count)
{
```

```
                    cout << endl << "Number of words: " << word_count << endl;
                    cout << "Number of characters: " << char_count << endl;
                    cout << "Average length of a word: "
                         << char_count / word_count << endl;
                    cout << "Longest word: " << longest_word << endl << endl;
          }
```

Our program will use the **apstring** library. The main C++ program is

```
// Program file: stats.cpp

#include <iostream.h>

#include "apstring.h"

// <function declarations>

int main()
{
      char query;
      do
      {
             cout << "Enter a sentence [terminating with a period ('.')]: ";
             analyze_sentence();
             cout << "Run once more? [Y/N]: ";
             cin >> query;
      } while ((query == 'Y') || (query == 'y'));
      return 0;
}

// <function implementation discussed earlier>
```

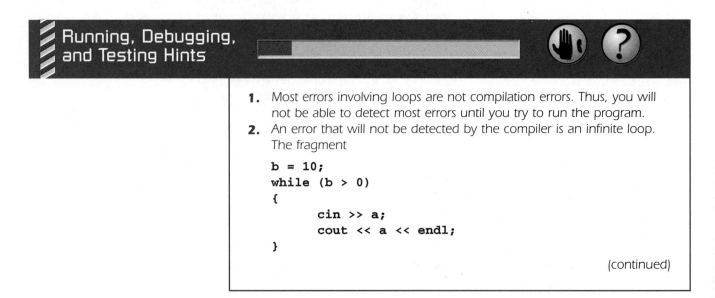

Running, Debugging, and Testing Hints

1. Most errors involving loops are not compilation errors. Thus, you will not be able to detect most errors until you try to run the program.
2. An error that will not be detected by the compiler is an infinite loop. The fragment

```
b = 10;
while (b > 0)
{
       cin >> a;
       cout << a << endl;
}
```

(continued)

will loop forever, because **b** never becomes zero inside the loop.
3. Carefully check entry conditions for each loop.
4. Carefully check exit conditions for each loop. Make sure the loop is exited (not infinite) and that you have the correct number of repetitions.
5. Loop entry, execution, and exit can be checked by
   a. pencil and paper check on initial and final values
   b. count of the number of repetitions
   c. use of debugging output statements:
      i. Boolean condition prior to loop
      ii. variables inside loop
      iii. values of the counter in loop
      iv. Boolean values inside the loop
      v. values after loop is exited

Summary

Key Terms

accumulator	infinite loop	post-test (exit-controlled) loop
control variable	input assertion	
counter	loop invariant	pretest condition
data validation	loop variant	pretest (entrance-controlled) loop
decrement	loop verification	
fixed repetition (iterated) loop	nested loop	sentinel value
	output assertion	variable condition loop

Keywords

do   **for**   **while**

Key Concepts

◆ The following table provides a comparison summary of the three repetition structures discussed in this chapter:

Traits of Loops	for Loop	while Loop	do...while Loop
Pretest loop	Yes	Yes	No
Post-test loop	No	No	Yes
{...}for compound statements	Required	Required	Required
Repetition	Fixed/variable	Variable	Variable

◆ A fixed repetition loop is to be used when you know exactly how many times something is to be repeated.

◆ The basic form of a **for** loop is

```
for (j = 1; j <= 5; ++j)
      <statement>
```

◆ A **while** loop is a pretest loop that can have a variable loop control; a typical loop is

```
score = 0;
sum = 0;
more_data = TRUE;
while (more_data)
{
      sum = sum + score;
      cout << "Enter a score; -999 to quit. ";
      cin >> score;
      more_data = (score != -999);
}
```

◆ A counter is a variable whose purpose is to indicate how often the body of a loop is executed.
◆ An accumulator is a variable whose purpose is to sum values.
◆ An infinite **while** loop is caused by having a **TRUE** loop control condition that is never changed to **FALSE**.
◆ A post-test loop has a Boolean condition checked after the loop body has been completed.
◆ A **do . . . while** loop is a post-test loop; a typical loop is

```
do
{
    cout << "Enter a positive integer; <-999> to quit . ";
    cin >> num;
} while ((num > 0) && (num != -999));
```

◆ **do . . . while** and **while** are variable control loops; **for** is usually a fixed control loop.
◆ **while** and **for** are pretest loops; **do . . . while** is a post-test loop.
◆ Any one of these loops can be nested within any other of the loops.
◆ Indenting each loop is important for program readability.
◆ Several levels of nesting make the logic of a program difficult to follow.
◆ Loops and conditionals are frequently used together. Careful program design will facilitate writing code in which these concepts are integrated; typical forms are

```
    while (<condition1>)
    {
      .

      .

        if (<condition2>)
          .

          .

        else
         .

         .

         .

    } // end of while

    and

    if <condition>
    {
       .

       .

       .

        for (j = <value1>; j <= <valueN>; ++j)
        {
          .

          .

        } // end of for loop . . .
    } // end of if... else
       .

       .
```

Chapter Review Exercises

In Exercises 1–10, indicate if the loop heading is valid or invalid. If invalid, explain why.

1. `for (k = 1; k <= 10; ++k)`

```
2.  for (j = 1; j <= 5; j = j + 2)
3.  for (j = 10; j >= 1; --j)
4.  for (ch = 'a'; ch <= 'z'; ++ ch)
5.  for (k = a; k >= b; ++k)
6.  k = 1; k <= 10; ++k;
7.  while (j = 1)
8.  while (j == 1)
9.  while (ch != 'A')
10. while (! boolean_variable)
```

For Exercises 11–14, write a program to display a table of integers, their squares, and their square roots using integers running from 1 to 25.

11. Use a **for** loop that counts up.
12. Use a **for** loop that counts down.
13. Use a **while** loop that counts up.
14. Use a **do . . . while** loop that counts up.
15. Write a program that uses **for** loops to produce the following pattern:

16. Use nested loops to produce the following numbering on the screen:

```
1


1
2


1
2
3


1
2
3
4
```

17. Brian wants the following code to display a list of numbers and their cubes. What happens when it is executed? Can you correct it for him (if necessary)?

```
for (int k = 1; k <= 10; ++k)
    z = k * k * k;
    cout << setw(10) << k << setw(10) << z << endl;
```

18. Explain why it is important to use proper indentation, blank lines, and comments when writing programs that involve loops.

Programming Problems and Activities

1. The Caswell Catering and Convention Service (Problem 12, Chapter 4, and Problem 14, Chapter 5) wants you to upgrade their program so they can use it for all of their customers.

2. Modify your program for a service station owner (Case Study, Chapter 5) so that it can be used for an unknown number of customers. Your output should include the number of customers and all other pertinent items in a daily summary.

3. Modify the Community Hospital program (Problem 17, Chapter 5) so that it can be run for all patients leaving the hospital in one day. Include appropriate bad data checks and daily summary items.

4. The greatest common divisor (gcd) of two integers a and b is a positive integer c such that c divides a, c divides b, and for any other common divisor d of a and b, d is less than or equal to c. (For example, the gcd of 18 and 45 is 9.) One method of finding the gcd of two positive integers (a, b) is to begin with the smaller (a) and see if it is a divisor of the larger (b). If it is, then the smaller is the gcd. If not, find the next largest divisor of a and see if it is a divisor of b. Continue this process until you find a divisor of both a and b. This is the gcd of a and b.

   Write an interactive program that will accept two positive integers as input and then print their gcd. Enhance your output by printing all divisors of a that do not divide b. A sample run could produce

   Enter two positive integers. 42 72

   The divisors of 42 that do not divide 72 are:

   42
   21
   14
   7

   The gcd of 42 and 72 is 6.

5. The least common multiple (LCM) of two positive integers a and b is a positive integer c, such that c is a multiple of both a and b and for any other multiple m of a and b, c is a divisor of m. (For example, the LCM of 12 and 8 is 24.) Write an interactive program that allows the user to enter two positive integers and then print the LCM. The program should guard against bad data and should allow the user the option of "trying another pair" or quitting.

6. A perfect number is a positive integer such that the sum of the proper divisors equals the number. Thus, $28 = 1 + 2 + 4 + 7 + 14$ is a perfect number. If the sum of the divisors is less than the number, it is deficient. If the sum exceeds the number, it is abundant.

   a. Write an interactive program that allows the user to enter a positive integer and then displays the result, indicating whether the number entered is perfect, deficient, or abundant.

b. Write another interactive program that allows the user to enter a positive integer N and then displays all perfect numbers less than or equal to N. Your programs should guard against bad data and should allow the user the option of entering another integer or quitting.

7. In these days of increased awareness of automobile mileage, more motorists are computing their miles per gallon (mpg) than ever before. Write a program that will perform these computations for a traveler. Data for the program are entered as indicated by the following table:

Odometer Reading	Gallons of Fuel Purchased
18828 (start)	—
19240	9.7
19616	10.2
19944	8.8
20329	10.1
20769 (finish)	10.3

The program should compute the mpg for each tank and the cumulative mpg each time the tank is filled up. Your output should produce a chart with the following headings:

Odometer (begin)	Odometer (end)	Fuel (tank)	Miles (tank)	Fuel (trip)	Miles (trip)	Mpg (tank)	Mpg (trip)

8. Parkside's Other Triangle is generated from two positive integers, one for the size and one for the seed. For example,

Size 6, Seed 1	Size 5, Seed 3
1 2 4 7 2 7	3 4 6 9 4
3 5 8 3 8	5 7 1 5
6 9 4 9	8 2 6
1 5 1	3 7
6 2	8
3	

Size gives the number of columns. Seed specifies the starting value for column 1. Column n contains n values. The successive values are obtained by adding 1 to the previous value. When 9 is reached, the next value becomes 1.

Write a program that reads pairs of positive integers and produces Parkside's Other Triangle for each pair. The check for bad data should include checking for seeds between 1 and 9 inclusive.

9. Modify the sewage, water, and sanitation problem (Problem 19, Chapter 5) so that it can be used with data containing appropriate information for all residents of the community.

10. Modify the program for the Lucky Wildcat Well Corporation (Problem 20, Chapter 5) so that it can be run with data containing information about all of Al Derrick's wells.

11. Modify the program concerning the Mathematical Association of America (Problem 21, Chapter 5). There will be 50 official state delegates attending the next summer national meeting. The new data file will contain the two-letter state abbreviation for each delegate. Output should include one column with the state abbreviation and another with the amount reimbursed.

12. In Fibonacci's sequence, *0, 1, 1, 2, 3, 5, 8, 13,* ... , the first two terms are 0 and 1 and each successive term is formed by adding the previous two terms. Write a program that will read positive integers and then print the number of terms indicated by each integer read. Be sure to test your program with data that include the integers 1 and 2.

13. Mr. Lae Z. Programmer is at it again. Now that you have written a program to compute the grade for one student in his class (Problems 5, 22, and 23, Chapter 5), he wants you to modify this program so it can be used for the entire class. He will help you by making the first entry be a positive integer representing the number of students in the class. Your new version should compute an overall class average and the number of students receiving each letter grade.

14. Modify the Pentagon parking lot problem (Problem 26, Chapter 5) so that it can be used for all customers in one day. In the new program, time should be entered in military style as a four-digit integer. The lot opens at 0600 (6:00 A.M.) and closes at 2200 (10:00 P.M.). Your program should include appropriate summary information.

15. The Natural Pine Furniture Company (Problem 7, Chapter 4) now wants you to refine your program so that it will print a one-week pay report for each employee. You do not know how many employees there are, but you do know that all information for each employee is on a separate line. Each line of input will contain the employee's initials, the number of hours worked, and the hourly rate. You are to use the constant definition section for the following:

Federal withholding tax rate   18%
State withholding tax rate   4.5%
Hospitalization $25.65
Union dues $ 7.85

Your output should include a report for each employee and a summary report for the company files.

16. Orlando Tree Service, Inc., offers the following services and rates to its customers:
   a. Tree removal $500 per tree
   b. Tree trimming $80 per hour
   c. Stump grinding $25 plus $2 per inch for each stump whose diameter exceeds ten inches. The $2 charge is only for the diameter inches in excess of 10.

Write a complete program to allow the manager, Mr. Sorwind, to provide an estimate when he bids on a job. Your output should include a listing of each separate charge and a total. A 10 percent discount is given for any job whose total exceeds $1000. Typical data for one customer are

```
R 7
T 6.5
G 8   8   10   12   14   15   15   20   25
```

where **R**, **T**, and **G** are codes for removal, trimming, and grinding, respectively. The integer following **G** represents the number of stumps to be ground. The next line of integers represents the diameters of stumps to be ground.

17. A standard science experiment is to drop a ball and see how high it bounces. Once the "bounciness" of the ball has been determined, the ratio gives a bounciness index. For example, if a ball dropped from a height of 10 feet bounces 6 feet high, the index is 0.6 and the total distance traveled by the ball is 16 feet after one bounce. If the ball were to continue bouncing, the distance after two bounces would be 10 ft + 6 ft + 6 ft + 3.6 ft = 25.6 ft. Note that distance traveled for each successive bounce is the distance to the floor plus 0.6 of that distance as the ball comes back up.

   Write an interactive program that lets the user enter the initial height of the ball and the number of times the ball is allowed to continue bouncing. Output should be the total distance traveled by the ball. At some point in this process, the distance traveled by the ball becomes negligible. Use the constant section to define a "negligible" distance (for example, 0.00001 inches). Terminate the computing when the distance becomes negligible. When this stage is reached, include the number of bounces as part of the output.

18. Write a program that prints a calendar for one month. Input consists of an integer specifying the first day of the month (1 = Sunday) and an integer specifying how many days are in a month.

19. An amortization table shows the rate at which a loan is paid off. It contains monthly entries showing the interest paid that month, the principal paid, and the remaining balance. Given the amount of money borrowed (the principal), the annual interest rate, and the amount the person wishes to repay each month, print an amortization table. (Be certain that the payment desired is larger than the first month's interest.) Your table should stop when the loan is paid off, and should be printed with the following heads:

   MONTH NUMBER   INTEREST PAID   PRINCIPAL PAID   BALANCE

20. Computers work in the binary system, which is based on powers of 2. Write a program that prints the first 15 powers of 2 beginning with 2^0. Print your output in headed columns.

21. Print a list of the positive integers less than 500 that are divisible by either 5 or 7. When the list is complete, print a count of the number of integers found.

22. Write a program that reads in 20 real numbers, then prints the average of the positive numbers and the average of the negative numbers.

23. In 1626, the Dutch settlers purchased Manhattan Island from the Indians. According to legend, the purchase price was $24. Suppose that the Indians had invested this amount at 3 percent annual interest compounded quarterly. If the money had earned interest from the start of 1626 to the end of last year, how much money would the Indians have in the bank today? (*Hint:* Use nested loops for the compounding.)

24. Write a program to print the sum of the odd integers from 1 to 99.

25. The theory of relativity holds that as an object moves, it gets smaller. The new length of the object can be determined from the formula:

New length = Original length $* \text{sqrt}(1 - B^2)$

where B^2 is the percentage of the speed of light at which the object is moving, entered in decimal form. Given the length of an object, print its new length for speeds ranging from 0 to 99 percent of the speed of light. Print the output in the following columns:

```
Percent of Light        Speed       Length
----------------        -----       ------
```

26. Mr. Christian uses a 90 percent, 80 percent, 70 percent, 60 percent grading scale. Given a list of test scores, print out the number of A's, B's, C's, D's, and F's on the test. Terminate the list of scores with a sentinel value.

27. The mathematician Gottfried Leibniz determined a formula for estimating the value of π.

pi/4 = $1 - 1/3 + 1/5 - 1/7 + 1/9 - 1/11 + \cdots$

Evaluate the first 200 terms of this formula and print its approximation of π.

28. In a biology experiment, Carey finds that a sample of an organism doubles in population every 12 hours. If she starts with 1000 organisms, in how many hours will she have 1 million?

29. C++ does has a function that permits raising a number to a power. We can easily write a program to perform this function, however. Given an integer to represent the base number and a positive integer to represent the power desired, write a program that prints the number raised to that power.

30. Mr. Thomas has negotiated a salary schedule for his new job. He will be paid $0.01 the first day, with the daily rate doubling each day. Write a program that will find his total earnings for 30 days. Print your results in a table set up as follows:

Day Number	Daily Salary	Total Earned
1	.01	.01
2	.02	.03
3	.	.
.	.	.
.	.	.
.		
30		

31. Write a program to print the perimeter and area of rectangles using all combinations of lengths and widths running from 1 foot to 10 feet in increments of 1 foot. Print the output in headed columns.

32. Teachers in most school districts are paid on a salary schedule that provides a salary based on their number of years of teaching experience. Suppose that a beginning teacher in the Babbage School District is paid $21,000 the first year. For each year of experience after this up to 12 years, a 4 percent increase over the preceding value is received. Write a program that prints a salary schedule for teachers in this district. The output should appear as follows:

```
Years Experience              Salary

        0                     $21000

        1                     $21840

        2                     $22714

        3                     $23622

        .                        .

        .                        .

        .                        .

       12
```

(Actually, most teachers' salary schedules are more complex than this. As an additional problem, you might like to find out how the salary schedule is determined in your school district and write a program to print the salary schedule.)

33. The Euclidean algorithm can be used to find the greatest common divisor (gcd) of two positive integers (n_1, n_2). For example, suppose $n_1 = 72$ and $n_2 = 42$; you can use this algorithm in the following manner:
(1) Divide the larger by the smaller:

$$72 = 42 * 1 + 30$$

(2) Divide the divisor (42) by the remainder (30)

$$42 = 30 * 1 + 12$$

(3) Repeat this process until you get a remainder of zero:

$$30 = 12 * 2 + 6 \qquad 12 = 6 * 2 + 0$$

The last nonzero remainder is the gcd of n_1 and n_2.
   Write a program that lets the user enter two integers and then prints each step in the process of using the Euclidean algorithm to find their gcd.

34. Cramer's rule for solving a system of equations was given in Problem 31, Chapter 5. Add an enhancement to your program by using a loop to guarantee that the coefficients and constants entered by the user are precisely those that were intended.

35. Gaussian elimination is another method used to solve systems of equations. To illustrate, if the system is

$$x - 2y = 1$$
$$2x + y = 7$$

Gaussian elimination would start with the augmented matrix

$$\begin{bmatrix} 1 & -2 & 1 \\ 2 & 1 & 7 \end{bmatrix}$$

and proceed to produce the identity matrix on the left side

$$\begin{bmatrix} 1 & 0 & 3 \\ 0 & 1 & 1 \end{bmatrix}$$

At this stage, the solution to the system is seen to be $x = 3$ and $y = 1$.

Write a program in which the user enters coefficients for a system of two equations containing two variables. The program should then solve the system and display the answer. Your program should include the following:
   a. A check for bad data
   b. A solvable system check
   c. A display of partial results as the matrix operations are performed.

36. A Pythagorean triple consists of three integers A, B, and C such that $A^2 + B^2 = C^2$. For example, 3, 4, 5 is such a triple because $3^2 + 4^2 = 5^2$. These triples can be generated by positive integers m, n ($m > n$), where $a = m^2 - n^2$, $b = 2mn$, and $c = m^2 + n^2$. These triples will be primitive (no common factors) if m and n have no common factors and are not both odd. Write a program that allows the user to enter a value for m and then prints all possible primitive Pythagorean triples such that $m > n$. Use one function to find the greatest common factor of m and n, another to see if m and n are both odd, and another to guard against overflow. For the input value of $m = 5$, typical output would be

m	n	a	b	c	a^2	b^2	c^2
2	1	3	4	5	9	16	25
3	2	5	12	13	25	144	169
4	1	15	8	17	225	64	289
4	3	7	24	25	49	576	625
5	2	21	20	29	441	400	841
5	4	9	40	41	81	1600	1681

37. This chapter's first case study problem determined whether or not an integer was prime by checking for divisors less than or equal to the square root of the number. The check started with 2 and incremented trial divisors by 1 each time as seen by the code

```
prime = TRUE;
divisor = 2;
limit_for_check = sqrt(candidate);
while ((divisor <= limit_for_check) && prime)
        if (candidate % divisor == 0)
              prime = FALSE;
        else
              divisor = divisor + 1;
```

Other methods can be used to determine whether or not an integer N is prime. For example, you may

   a. Check divisors from 2 to $N - 1$ incrementing by 1.
   b. Check divisors from 2 to $(N - 1)/2$ incrementing by 1.
   c. Check divisor 2, 3, 5, ... $(N - 1)/2$ incrementing by 2.
   d. Check divisor 2, 3, 5, ... sqrt(N) incrementing by 2.

Write a program that allows the user to choose between these options in order to compare relative efficiency of different algorithms. Use a function for each option.

38. The prime factorization of a positive integer is the positive integer written as the product of primes. For example, the prime factorization of 72 is

$$72 = 2 * 3 * 3 * 4$$

Write a program that allows the user to enter a positive integer and then displays the prime factorization of the integer. A minimal main program could be

```
num = get_a_number ();
if (number_is_prime(num))
cout << num << " is prime" << endl;
else
print_factorization(num);
```

Enhancements to this program could include an error trap for bad data and a loop for repeated trials.

39. Write a menu-driven program that allows the user to select a function for plotting a curve and displaying it as a graphical image. The curves should correspond to the following equations:

$$y = x$$
$$y = x^2$$
$$y = x^n$$
$$y = 1.5^x$$

The user should input the starting value of x and the ending value of x for each function chosen from the menu.

40. Modify the **display_dice** function of the dice game (Problem 32, Chapter 5) so that, on each roll of the dice, the two dice appear to move from off the opposite edges of the screen toward a destination point at the center of the screen.

41. Modify the movement of dice in Problem 40 so that each die appears to tumble end over end as it moves toward the center of the screen.

Communication in Practice

1. Reread the **Note of Interest** in this chapter on computer reliability and medical devices. Then read the sections of the ACM Code of Ethics that deal with designing and testing reliable computer systems. Prepare a written report to present your class on the way in which the ACM code deals with this issue.

2. Using a completed program from this chapter, remove all documentation and replace all identifiers with one- or two-letter identifiers. Exchange this version with another student who has prepared a similar version of a different program. Add documentation and change identifiers to meaningful identifiers. Discuss the similarities and differences with your class.

3. As you might expect, teachers of computer science do not agree on whether a **while** loop or a **do...while** loop is the preferred variable control loop in C++. Interview the computer science teachers at your local college or university to determine what preference (if any) they have regarding these two forms of repetition. Prepare a class report based on your interviews. Include the advantages and disadvantages of each form of repetition.

4. Examine the repetition constructs of at least five other programming languages. Prepare a report that compares and contrasts repetition in each of the languages. Be sure to include information such as which languages provide for both fixed and variable repetition and which languages have more than one kind of variable repetition. Which language appears to have the most desirable form of repetition? Include your rationale for this decision in your report.

5. Examine some old computer science texts and talk to some computer science teachers who worked with the early languages to see how repetition was achieved in the "early days." Prepare a brief chronological chart for class display that depicts the various stages in the development of repetition in computer programming.

7

Files

Chapter Outline

H aving now completed six chapters, you've made significant steps in the process of learning to use a programming language for the purpose of solving problems. Thus far, however, it has been impossible to work with large amounts of data. To write programs that solve problems using large databases, it is necessary to be able to store, retrieve, and manage the data. Consider the relatively simple problem of using a computer to compute and print water bills for a community of 30,000 customers. If the data consist of a customer name, address, and amount of water used, you can imagine that entering this information interactively every billing period would involve an enormous amount of time. In addition to saving that time, it is often desirable to save information between runs of a program for later use. For example, in large software systems, the information output from one program might be the input to another program.

To avoid these problems, we can store data in some secondary storage device, usually magnetic tapes or disks. Data can be created by one program, stored on these devices, and then accessed by other programs when necessary. It is also possible to modify and save this information for other runs of the same program or for running another program using these same data. In this chapter, we look at storage and retrieval of data in another data structure called a **file.**

Before you can work with files, you need to become acquainted with the notion of a **stream.** You can think of a stream as a channel or conduit on which data are passed from senders to receivers. Data can be sent out on a stream, in which case, we are using an **output stream.** Or data can be received from a stream, in which case, we are using an **input stream.** Streams are connected to devices. For example, at program startup, the standard input stream, named **cin**, is connected to the keyboard device, and the standard output stream, named

7.1   Streams and Stream Processing

Objectives

◆ to understand the use of streams for obtaining input and output data

◆ to understand how streams are used to access data in files

◆ to be able to use loops with file streams

file: A data structure that resides on a secondary storage medium.

stream: A channel in which data are passed from sender to receiver.

output stream: A channel for sending output data.

input stream: A channel for receiving input data.

cout, is connected to the terminal screen. Thus, you can think of the keyboard as the *source device* from which data are received from an input stream, and think of the terminal screen as the *destination device* to which data are sent on an output stream.

The essential characteristic of stream processing is that data elements must be sent to or received from a stream one at a time, or in serial fashion, hence, the term *serial processing*. For example, if we have a collection of data elements to be printed on the terminal screen, they must be written one after the other, not all at once. When you think about the use of streams for interactive input and output, this restriction makes sense. For output, each character sent to the output stream must wait its turn to be displayed on a terminal screen. For input, the receiver in the program must wait for each character typed at the keyboard.

Stream processing requires at least five operations. First, the stream must be *opened* for use. If the stream has been opened for input, an operation is needed to *get* the next data item from the stream. In addition, an operation is needed to detect the *end of an input stream*, or the condition that there are no more data to be received from the stream. If the stream has been opened for output, an operation is needed to *put* the next data item into the stream. Finally, when the program is finished using a stream, an operation is necessary to *close* it.

The Standard Input and Output Streams

You are already familiar with the use of the standard input and output streams in C++. Let's take a look at how they work in more detail. These streams and the operations we perform on them become available to a program by including the **iostream.h** library header file. In the case of the standard input stream, a programmer obtains access to the variable **cin**, which names the stream, and the extractor operator **>>**, which is used to receive (or get) the next data item from the stream. In the case of the standard output stream, a programmer obtains access to the variable **cout**, which names the stream, and the inserter operator **<<**, which is used to send (or put) the next data item to the stream. The operations that open and close these streams are run automatically by the system when the program begins and finishes execution. Opening the streams simply connects each stream to its respective device, the keyboard or the terminal screen. Closing the streams disconnects them. The standard input and output streams and the devices to which they connect are depicted in Figure 7.1.

◆ Figure 7.1

The standard input and output streams and their devices

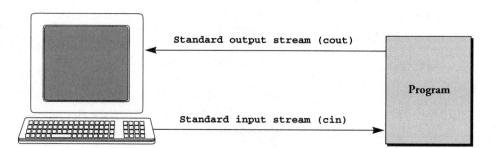

Standard output stream (cout)

Standard input stream (cin)

Program

File Streams

Files are data structures that are stored on a *disk device*. To work with a file, you must connect a stream to the file on a disk. The kind of stream used to receive input from a file is called an **input file stream.** The kind of stream used to send output to a file is called an **output file stream.** Input and output file streams and the device to which they connect are depicted in Figure 7.2. To create a file stream, you must first include the C++ library file **fstream.h**. After doing so, two new classes, **ofstream** (output file stream) and **ifstream** (input file stream), become available to a program.

Output File Streams

You can declare and open an output file stream as shown in the following example:

```
#include <fstream.h>
        .
        .
ofstream out_file;
        .
        .
out_file.open("myfile");
```

Syntactically, the second line of code is a C++ variable declaration. The class name, **ofstream**, appears on the left, followed by the variable name, **out_file**. The third line of code tells the system to connect the output file stream to a file on disk named **"myfile"**. The syntax of this statement is that used for expressing calls of member functions with objects, as introduced in Section 3.6. It consists of the name of the file stream, followed by a period (.), followed by a call to the **open** function with a string parameter. When this statement is executed, the following steps take place:

1. If a file named **"myfile"** exists on disk, it is opened for output and connected to the output stream **out_file**. If any data are in the file when it is opened, the data are erased from the file.
2. Otherwise, a file named **"myfile"** does not exist on disk. A new file with that name is created, opened for output, and connected to the output stream **out_file**.

input file stream:
An input stream that is connected to a file.

output file stream:
An output stream that is connected to a file.

◆ Figure 7.2

Input and output file streams and a disk device

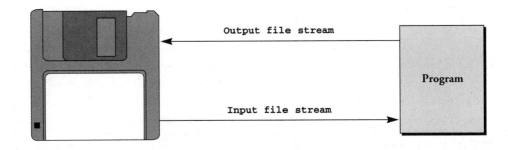

The general form for creating an output file stream is

```
ofstream <stream variable name>;

<stream variable name>.open(<file name>);
```

The stream variable name can be any legitimate C++ identifier. The file name must be a string that is consistent with the way files can be named on your particular implementation. You should consult your compiler's manual for the rules governing the naming of files.

When a program is finished using a file stream, it should be closed. Most computer systems close any data files when a program terminates execution. However, the **close** function can be run with the file stream to do this under program control. If **out_file** is an output file stream, the following statement will close the stream:

```
out_file.close();
```

Note that the name of the file does not appear as a parameter to this function, as it does with **open**.

Using String Variables to Name Files

Occasionally, we would like to obtain a file name interactively from the user before using it to open a file. To do this, we could prompt the user for the file name, take this name as input into a string variable, and attempt to pass this variable to the **open** function, somewhat as follows:

```
#include <fstream.h>
#include "apstring.h"

ofstream out_file;
apstring file_name;

cout << "Enter the output file name: ";
cin >> file_name;
out_file.open(file_name);
```

However, the C++ compiler will not accept the last statement. The **open** member function expects a string in C format. Fortunately, the **apstring** library defines a function, **c_str**, that converts a string variable to a string in C format. We can use this function in a corrected version of the previous program fragment:

```
#include <fstream.h>
#include "apstring.h"
```

```
ofstream out_file;
apstring file_name;

cout << "Enter the output file name: ";
cin >> file_name;
out_file.open(file_name.c_str());
```

Note that **file_name**, a string variable, is first run with the **c_str** member function. This function returns the equivalent string in C format. The C format string is then passed as a parameter to **open**, which opens an output file with that string as a file name.

Detecting Errors Opening and Closing Files

Occasionally, an error occurs when a program attempts to open or close a stream on a file. For example, a disk may be full and no more room exists for new data when a new file is requested. To detect these errors, C++ provides a fail function, **fail()**, for use with streams. The following code shows how to detect and respond to these errors in opening and closing an output file stream:

```
#include <fstream.h>
#include <assert.h>
   .
   .
ofstream out_file;
   .
   .
out_file.open("myfile");
assert(! out_file.fail());
      <send data to file>
out_file.close();
assert(! out_file.fail());
```

Using Output File Streams

Once a file stream has been opened for output, all of the familiar operations you use for terminal screen output can be used for file output. For example, assuming that the variable **out_file** names an output file stream, the following statement will write a line of text to the file:

```
out_file << "This is a test." << endl;
```

Note that this statement has exactly the same format as a statement to write the same data to the terminal screen using the standard output stream:

```
cout << "This is a test." << endl;
```

The output of integers and real numbers works the same way:

```
out_file << "The number ten is " << 10
         << " or " << 10.0 << endl;
```

If the C++ library for formatting output, **iomanip.h**, is included, you will be able to use familiar formatting commands with file output:

```
#include <iomanip.h>
    .
    .
out_file << setprecision(4);
out_file << setw(10) << 3.1416 << endl;
```

Note these two important points about output streams:

abstract: Simplified or partial; hiding detail.

1. The operations on output streams are **abstract.** It does not matter whether the destination of the output is a file on disk or the terminal screen. All we need to know is the name of the stream and the form of the statement to send data to the stream. Moreover, the results of sending data to output streams are similar, even when the destinations are different devices. The data saved in a disk file should "look the same" as the data displayed on a terminal screen. You can verify that this is the case by running our sample statements, and then examining the contents of your test file with a local text editor.

portable: Able to be transferred to different applications or computers without changes.

2. Programs that use output stream processing are **portable.** They can be written on one hardware system, transported to another hardware system, and then recompiled and run on the latter system without changes to the code. This will be true, even though the representation of files on a disk and data on a terminal screen tend to vary greatly from system to system. If we had to make changes to a program every time we wanted to move it to a new hardware system, we would have an enormous maintenance headache. The use of conventional output streams insulates a program from these machine dependencies in areas where they are most likely to occur.

Loops with Output File Streams

Most of the examples of sending data to an output file stream that we have seen thus far are unrealistic, in that only one or two data values are written. Programs typically output large amounts of data to files. One typical form of data processing with files takes input data from the user at the keyboard, processes the data, and writes the results to a file. A pseudocode algorithm for this process follows:

Open the output file
Read data from the keyboard
While data do not equal a sentinel value
    Process the data
    Write the result to the file, followed by a carriage return
    Read data from the keyboard
Close the output file

Note that each data value will be followed by a carriage return in the file. It is essential that a carriage return or a space character be used to separate the data values in the file. This will allow the data values to be recognized and read from the file subsequently.

Example 7.1

The following program uses a **while** loop to read integers from the keyboard and write them to a file until a sentinel is encountered:

```cpp
// Program file: kbdfile.cpp

#include <iostream.h>
#include <fstream.h>

const int SENTINEL = -999;

int main()
{
    int data;
    ofstream out_file;

    out_file.open("myfile");
    cout << "Enter an integer (-999 to end input): ";
    cin >> data;
    while (data != SENTINEL)
    {
        out_file << data << " ";
        cout << "Enter an integer (-999 to end input): ";
        cin >> data;
    }
    out_file.close();
    return 0;
}
```

Input File Streams

You can create an input file stream as in the following example:

```cpp
#include <fstream.h>
.
.
ifstream in_file;
.
.
in_file.open("myfile");
```

Syntactically, the first line of code is a C++ variable declaration. The class name, **ifstream**, appears on the left, followed by the variable name, **in_file**. The third line of code tells the system to connect the input file stream to a file on disk named **"myfile"**. The syntax of this statement is the same as that for output streams. When this statement is executed, the following steps take place:

1. If a file named **"myfile"** exists on disk, it is opened for input and connected to the input stream **in_file**.

2. Otherwise, a file named **"myfile"** does not exist on disk. On some implementations of C++, a new file with that name is created, opened for input, and connected to the input stream **in_file**.

The general form for creating an input file stream is

---

ifstream <stream variable name>**;**

<stream variable name>**.open(**<file name>**);**

The stream variable name can be any legitimate C++ identifier. The file name must be a string that is consistent with the way files can be named on your particular system.

Using Input File Streams

We have seen that programs can use the standard operator **<<**, called an *inserter,* to send data to the terminal screen or to an output file. Programs can also use the standard operator **>>**, called an *extractor,* to receive data from the keyboard or from an input file.

Let us review what happens when a program gets data from the keyboard or standard input stream:

1. The user types one or more characters at the keyboard, followed by a blank space or by a carriage return.

2. The computer converts the characters to the data value they represent. What the characters represent depends on the type of variable used for input. For example, the characters **'1'**, **'0'**, and **'4'** will be converted to the integer value 104 if the program's input statement is receiving the input data for an integer variable. Or the same characters will be placed into a string value **"104"** if the input statement is using a string variable.

3. The computer stores the data value from step 2 in the variable following the **>>** operator.

The success of an input operation from the keyboard thus depends on two things: the format of the data typed by the user, and the data type of the variable appearing in the input statement. For example, the code

```
int int_var;
double double_var;
string string_var;

cin >> int_var >> double_var >> string_var;
```

will run successfully if the user types a string of digits, followed by one or more whitespace characters, followed by a string of digits that may or may not contain a decimal point, followed by one or more whitespace characters, followed by a string of characters, followed by optional whitespace characters, and ending with a carriage return.

There are two important things to note about the standard input stream. First, at the source or keyboard, the data are individual characters. At the receiving end, however, these data are automatically converted to a type that the program can use, such as integers, real numbers, or strings.

Once we are aware of these two conditions, we can proceed to use an input file stream in the same way as we use the keyboard. For example, assuming that the file **"myfile"** contains a line of characters representing an integer, a real number, and a string, the following program will successfully read these data from the file and display them on the terminal screen:

```cpp
// Program file: filescr.cpp

#include <iostream.h>
#include <fstream.h>
#include <assert.h>
#include "apstring.h"

int main()
{
        int int_var;
        double double_var;
        apstring string_var;
        ifstream in_file;

        in_file.open("myfile");
        assert(! in_file.fail());
        in_file >> int_var >> double_var >> string_var;
        cout << int_var << endl;
        cout << double_var << endl;
        cout << string_var << endl;
        in_file.close();
        assert(! in_file.fail());
        return 0;
}
```

Communication and Style Tips

The use of the **<<** and **>>** operators in programs that process files enhances program maintenance. Because these operators work with integers, real numbers, and strings, programmers do not have to change the code of the input and output operations when the data type of the elements in the file is changed. In Chapter 9, you will see how to use the standard operators to define input and output operations for new classes to take advantage of this feature.

Loops with Input File Streams

The contents of an input file are almost never as precisely determined as those you just saw in the last example. Usually, all we know is the general format of a file and the type of data used to receive the input. The number of data values stored in the file is *indefinite*. There may be 2, 20, or 20,000 of them. Processing input file data will consist of reading each data value from the file stream, processing it, and halting when there are no more data to be read from the stream.

C++ provides a special function, **eof()**, that returns nonzero (meaning **TRUE**) when there are no more data to be read from an input file stream, and zero (meaning **FALSE**) otherwise. The general form for using this function is

<input file stream>**.eof()**

If we assume that **data** is the variable into which each data element of a file will be read, **in_file** is the input file stream, and **process_data(data)** is the specification of a function that processes the data, then the following code can serve as a model of input file processing in many C++ programs:

```
in_file >> data;
while (! in_file.eof())
{
      process(data);
      in_file >> data;
}
```

There are several important points to make about this model:

1. An attempt to read an initial datum from the file stream must be made *before* the **eof** function is executed. If the file contains no data initially, then **eof** will return **TRUE** after this initial input operation. This operation is sometimes called a **priming input statement.**

2. Placing the test for the end-of-file condition at the beginning of a **while** loop guards against processing data after the program has reached the end of the file stream.

3. Placing the next extraction operation at the bottom of the loop allows the loop to advance through the file to the end of the input data.

4. When this model is used, remember that **eof()** is **TRUE** when an attempt to read a value is made and there are no remaining values in the file.

priming input statement: An input statement that must be executed before a loop control condition is tested.

Example 7.2

The following program reads integers from an input file and displays them in a column on the terminal screen. The program assumes that the integers in the file are separated by one or more whitespace characters.

```
// Program file: intfile.cpp

#include <iostream.h>
#include <fstream.h>
```

```
int main()
{
      int data;
      ifstream in_file;

      in_file.open("myfile");
      in_file >> data;
      while (! in_file.eof())
      {
            cout << data << endl;
            in_file >> data;
      }
      in_file.close();
      return 0;
}
```

Some C++ implementations indicate that the end-of-input file has been reached when the file stream member function **fail()** returns **TRUE**. To guarantee that an input loop works on these implementations, you should use a compound condition, such as the following:

```
while (! in_file.fail() && ! in_file.eof())
```

Communication and Style Tips

1. Always test for the end-of-file condition before processing data read from an input file stream. This means:
a. Use a priming input statement before the loop.
b. Use an input statement at the bottom of the loop.

2. Use a **while** loop for getting data from an input file stream. (A **for** loop is desirable only when you know the exact number of data items in the file.)

Exercises 7.1

1. Assume that an input file stream, **in_file**, has been opened on a file containing two integers, and that **number** is an integer variable. Describe what happens when each of the following pieces of code is run:

a.
```
in_file >> number;
cout<< number << endl;
in_file >> number;
cout << number << endl;
in_file >> number;
cout << number << endl;
```

b.
```
in_file >> number;
while (! in_file.eof())
```

Career Opportunities in Computer Science

The list "Fastest Growing Occupations, 1990–2005," published by the Bureau of Labor Statistics, includes computer programmers and computer system analysts. During this time period, the number of these jobs is expected to increase by 78.9 percent. Computer scientists and systems analysts held about 828,000 jobs in 1994. Although they are found in most industries, the greatest concentration is in the computer and data processing services industry. In addition, tens of thousands of job openings will result annually from the need to replace workers who move into managerial positions or other occupations, or who leave the labor force. Employment of computer professionals is expected to grow much faster than the average of all occupations through the year 2005 (Occupational Outlook Handbook - 1996–1997).

A recent survey of employers was conducted to determine which academic disciplines were of greatest interest to employers. Of these, 60 percent mentioned computer science.

The relative ranking of the disciplines has remained very stable since 1980 when they were first compiled. The same three disciplines—computer science, electrical engineering, and mechanical engineering—have been on the top of the list, sought after by about two-thirds of the responding companies (Peterson, Job Opportunities).

Unemployment among computer specialists is traditionally exceptionally low, and almost all who enter the workforce find jobs. In 1994, the median annual income was about $44,000 for a system analyst. Computer scientists with advanced degrees generally earn more than systems analysts (Occupational Outlook Handbook - 1996–1997).

All able students—particularly women and minorities, who have been traditionally underrepresented in the sciences—are encouraged to consider computer science as a career.

```
        {
                cout << number << endl;
                in_file >> number;
        }
    c.  while (! in_file.eof())
        {
                in_file >> number;
                cout << number << endl;
        }
```

2. Write and test a program that allows you to input your name, address, and age from the keyboard (define a string type and variables for the first two inputs). Then save this information in an output file. Be sure to place separators, either spaces or carriage returns, between the data values in the file. Examine the file with a text editor to make sure that the data have been saved.

3. Write and test a program to input the data from the output file of Exercise 2 and display it on the terminal screen.

4. Extend the program of Exercise 2 so that you can input many names, addresses, and ages from the keyboard and then save them in a file (halt keyboard input when name is "done").

5. Extend the program of Exercise 3 so that it reads all of the names, addresses, and ages from a file and displays them on the terminal screen.

6. Write a program that copies integers from an input file to an output file. You should assume that the data in the input file are separated by spaces or carriage returns. Test the program with files containing 0, 1, and 10 data values. You can create test files with a text editor.

7. Extend the program of Exercise 6 so that it echoes the input data to the terminal screen as they are processed.

7.2 Using Functions with Files

Objectives

◆ to be able to design functions for use with file streams

◆ to be able to use file streams in conjunction with strings

◆ to understand the use of buffered input of data from file streams into strings

Now that you know how to create and use file streams, we will examine how to write functions that package some useful file handling operations. Consider the problem of opening a file. This process is seldom as simple as we have seen in our examples so far, where we have assumed that the only file being processed is named **"myfile"**. In many cases, the user will be asked for the name of the desired file to be opened for input or output. This task involves prompting the user for the file name, reading the name into a string variable, and passing the C format of the string to the **open** operation for the file stream. In addition, we might also check for a successful opening of the stream. We can hide these details in a pair of functions, **open_input_file** and **open_output_file**, that can be called in any application as follows:

```
open_input_file(in_file);
open_output_file(out_file);
```

In this code, **in_file** and **out_file** have been declared as input and output file streams, respectively.

Each function opens a stream on the file whose name the user specifies. The file stream is returned as a reference parameter. The declaration of **open_input_file** is

```
// Function: open_input_file
// Prompts user for a file name and opens
// input stream on the file
//
// Outputs: an input file stream

void open_input_file(ifstream &in_file);
```

The implementation of **open_input_file** is

```
void open_input_file(ifstream &in_file)
{
        apstring in_file_name;

        cout << "Enter the input file name: ";
        cin >> in_file_name;
        in_file.open(in_file_name.c_str());
        assert(! in_file.fail());
}
```

Note that the file stream is passed as a *reference* parameter. You should never try to pass a stream as a value parameter. This may be a syntax error in some implementations of C++. **open_output_file** has a similar declaration and implementation.

Another useful function copies the contents of a file of integers to another file. The function assumes that the two files have been successfully opened, one for input and one for output. Its declaration declares just the file stream parameters:

```
// Function: copy_integers
// Copies integers from one file to another
//
// Inputs: an opened input file wherein integers are
// separated by spaces and an opened output file
// Output: an output file containing the contents
//         of the input file

void copy_integers(ifstream &in_file, ofstream &out_file);
```

The implementation uses our standard **while** loop structure for input file processing:

```
void copy_integers(ifstream &in_file, ofstream &out_file)
{
    int data;

    in_file >> data;
    while (! in_file.eof())
    {
        out_file << data << " ";
        in_file >> data;
    }
}
```

Example 7.3

The following program uses the functions developed above to copy integers from an input file to an output file:

```
// Program file: intcopy.cpp

#include <iostream.h>
#include <fstream.h>
#include "apstring.h"
// Code for function declarations would go here
int main()
{
    int data;
    ifstream in_file;
    ofstream out_file;

    open_input_file(in_file);
    open_output_file(out_file);
```

```
        copy_integers(in_file, out_file);
        in_file.close();
        out_file.close();
        return 0;
    }
    // Code for function implementations would go here
```

Note that the **copy_integers** function assumes that the application will be opening and closing its files. File processing functions can be more general if they are not responsible for these details.

Files and Strings

File and string processing form the backbone of many word processing and database applications. In the following examples, we will use the **apstring** class defined in the C++ **apstring** library. Consider the problem of searching for a given word in a file. The user inputs the desired word and file name from the keyboard. The program searches for the first instance of the word in the file. If the word is found, the program displays the position of the word in the file and asks the user whether a search for the next instance is desired. If the word is not found, the program terminates with a message. An algorithm describing the top-level process is

Set position to 0
Open input file
Get word from user
Do
      Search file for next instance of word
      If word is found then
        Display position of word in file
        Ask user whether another search is desired
      Else
        Display message that word was not found
While word was found and another search is desired
Close input file

The main loop can be controlled by two Boolean flags, **word_found** and **another_search**. The process of searching a file for the next instance of a given word can be handled by a function, **search_for_word**. The function has four parameters: an opened input file stream, the desired word, the **word_found** flag, and the position of the word in the file. We can use the **open_input_file** function developed earlier in the chapter to open the file and detect an error. We can now translate the main algorithm to a main program in C++:

```
int main()
{
    apstring desired_word;
    bool word_found, another_search;
```

```
        char query;
        ifstream in_file;
        int position = 0;

        open_input_file(in_file);
        cout << "Enter the word you would like to find: ";
        cin >> desired_word;
        do
        {
              search_for_word(in_file, desired_word,
                    position, word_found);
              if (word_found)
              {
                    cout << "The word is at position "
                          << position << endl;
                    cout << "Search for the next instance?[Y/N] ";
                    cin >> query;
                    another_search = (query == 'Y')
                          || (query == 'y');
              }
              else
                    cout << "The word was not found." << endl;
        } while (word_found && another_search);
        in_file.close();
        return 0;
   }
```

The declaration of the function that performs the search is

```
// Function: search_for_word
// Searches for the next instance of a given word in a file
//
// Inputs: an opened input file stream, a word, and a position
// Outputs: the file stream and a Boolean flag that will be TRUE
// if the next instance of the word was found, or FALSE otherwise.
// If the word was found, its position in the file will be returned.
// If the word was not found, the file stream will be at its end.

void search_for_word(ifstream &in_file,
      const apstring &desired_word,
      int &position, bool &word_found);
```

On each call, the function advances through the file stream, until the next instance of the desired word is found or the end-of-file condition is reached. The function increments the position parameter after reading each word. If the function finds the word in the file, it sets the flag to **TRUE** and returns the word's position; otherwise, it sets the flag to **FALSE**. An algorithm describing the search process is

Read a word from the file
Increment the position

While not end of file and the input word does not equal the desired word do
  Read a word from the file
  Increment the position
Set **word_found** to not end of file

sequential search: The process of searching a list by examining the first component and then examining successive components in the order in which they occur.

Note that the loop stops when we hit the end of file (there are no more words to consider) or when we have found the next instance of the desired word. The loop describes a standard process called sequential search. In a sequential search, we begin at the first available data item, examine it, and continue until a match is found or we run out of items to consider. If the search terminates with no more items to consider, then we have not found a match, as the assignment to the flag at the end of the algorithm indicates. The translation of the algorithm into the C++ function is

```
void search_for_word(ifstream &in_file,
      const apstring &desired_word,
      int &position, bool &word_found)
{

      string input_word;

      in_file >> input_word;
      ++position;
      while (! in_file.eof() &&  (input_word != desired_word))
      {
            in_file >> input_word;
            ++position;
      }
      word_found = ! in_file.eof();
}
```

Note that the end-of-file condition is tested before the strings are compared in the **while** loop condition. The order of these two subexpressions within the Boolean expression is critical. If the end-of-file condition is **TRUE**, the next subexpression will be skipped, and the Boolean expression will return **FALSE**. This kind of process, known as short-circuit evaluation, was introduced in Chapter 5 and guards against errors such as comparing two strings when the data for one are not defined. In our example, if the two strings were compared before the end of file was tested and end of file happened to be **TRUE**, the program might produce mysterious and erroneous results.

The complete C++ program for searching for a word in a file is left as an exercise.

Buffered File Input

We frequently wish to take account of the line-by-line format of text in file processing. For example, we might want to count the number of lines in a file or copy the contents of one file to another with the same format. Unfortunately, the techniques we have seen thus far are inadequate for this purpose. As we saw in

Chapter 3, the standard **>>** operator for input streams treats the end-of-line character in a stream as a separator between words, not lines.

We also saw in Chapter 3 that the **apstring** library provides a **getline** function that allows us to input lines of text from an input stream. The form of a call to **getline** for reading a line of text is

---

getline(<input stream>, <string variable>)

---

where **getline** reads characters from the input stream and stores them into the string variable, until the number of characters equals a library-specifed value or the end-of-line character is reached in the stream. The end-of-line character is not stored in the variable. Because an input file stream is an input stream, **getline** can be used to input a line of text from a file as well.

For example, suppose we declared a string variable called **line** and we wished to read a line of text from a file stream called **in_file** into the variable. The following code declares the variable and inputs the text:

```
apstring line;
ifstream in_file;

// Code for opening the file stream would go here

getline(in_file, line);
```

The maximum number of characters that can be read with **getline** is 1024. This is not normally relevant during keyboard input, but a file might have longer lines of text.

buffered file input:
The input of large blocks of data from a file.

buffer: A block of memory into which data are placed for transmission to a program.

getline supports a process called **buffered file input.** This process utilizes a block of computer memory called a **buffer,** into which the data from a file are placed for transmission to a program. The main advantage of buffered file input is efficiency: Because the system reserves a block of memory of definite size for input data, the process can run very quickly. The main disadvantage is that some data may not be read if the data extend beyond the size of the buffer. Therefore, when we use **getline** for file processing, we must be careful to assume that the length of a line in a text file does not exceed this bound.

Example 7.4

In this example, we copy the contents of one text file to another, maintaining the line-by-line format. We assume that the maximum length of a line of text in the source file is 100 characters.

```
// Program file: buffcopy.cpp

#include <iostream.h>
#include <fstream.h>
#include <assert.h>
#include "apstring.h"
```

```cpp
// Function: open_input_file
// Prompts user for a file name and opens input stream on the file
//
// Outputs: an input file stream

void open_input_file(ifstream &in_file);

// Function: open_output_file
// Prompts user for a file name and opens output
// stream on the file
//
// Outputs: an output file stream

void open_output_file(ofstream &out_file);

// Function: copy_file
// Copies contents of one text file to another
//
// Inputs: opened input and output file streams

void copy_file(ifstream &in_file, ofstream &out_file);

int main()
{
      ifstream in_file;
      ofstream out_file;

      open_input_file(in_file);
      open_output_file(out_file);
      copy_file(in_file, out_file);
      in_file.close();
      out_file.close();
      return 0;
}

void open_input_file(ifstream &in_file)
{
      apstring in_file_name;

      cout << "Enter the input file name: ";
      cin >> in_file_name;
      in_file.open(in_file_name.c_str());
      assert(! in_file.fail());
}

void open_output_file(ofstream &out_file)
{
      apstring out_file_name;

      cout << "Enter the output file name: ";
      cin >> out_file_name;
```

Computer Ethics: Viruses

Tiny programs that deliberately cause mischief are epidemic among computers and are causing nervousness among those who monitor them.

Written by misguided or immature programmers, the "computer viruses" are placed on computer systems by piggybacking them on legitimate programs and messages. There, they may be passed along or instructed to wait until a prearranged moment to burst forth and destroy data.

At NASA headquarters in Washington, several hundred computers had to be resuscitated after being infected. NASA officials have taken extra precautions and reminded their machines' users to follow routine computer hygiene: Don't trust foreign data or strange machines.

Viruses have the eerie ability to perch disguised among legitimate data just as biological viruses hide among genes in human cells. They then spring out unexpectedly, multiplying and causing damage. Experts say that even when they try to study viruses in controlled conditions, the programs can get out of control and erase everything in a computer. The viruses can be virtually impossible to stop if their creators are determined enough.

"The only way to protect everybody against them is to do something much worse than the viruses: Stop talking to one another with computers," say William H. Murray, an information-security specialist at Ernst and Whinney financial consultants in Hartford, Connecticut.

Hundreds of programs and files have been destroyed by the viruses, and thousands of hours of repair or prevention time have been logged. Programmers have quickly produced antidote programs with such titles as Vaccine, Flu Shot, Data Physician, and Syringe.

Experts say known damage is minimal compared with the huge, destructive potential. They express the hope that the attacks will persuade computer users to minimize access to programming and data.

Viruses are the newest of evolving methods of computer mayhem. One type of virus is the Trojan horse: It looks and acts like a normal program but contains hidden commands that eventually take effect, ordering mischief. The "time bomb" explodes at a set time; the "logic bomb" goes off when the computer arrives at a certain result during normal computation. The "salami attack" executes barely noticeable small acts, such as shaving a penny from thousands of accounts.

A virus typically is written as perhaps only a few hundred characters in a program containing tens of thousands of characters. When the computer reads legitimate instructions, it encounters the virus, which instructs the computer to suspend normal operations for a fraction of a second. During that time, the virus instructs the computer to check for other copies of itself and, if none is found, to make and hide copies. Instruction to commit damage may be included.

Is Your Machine at Risk?

1. Computer viruses are actually miniature computer programs. Most were written by immature programmers intent on destroying information in computers for fun.

2. Those who write virus programs often conceal them on floppy disks that are inserted in the computer.

3. An immature programmer makes the disk available to others, saying it contains a useful program or game. These programs can be lent to others or put onto computerized "bulletin boards," where anyone can copy them for personal use.

4. A computer receiving the programs will "read" the disk and the tiny virus program at the same time. The virus may then order the computer to do a number of things:

   ◆ Tell it to read the virus and follow instructions.
   ◆ Tell it to make a copy of the virus and place it on any disk inserted in the machine today.
   ◆ Tell it to check the computer's clock, and on a certain date destroy all information that tells where data are stored on any disk: If an operator has no way of retrieving information, it is destroyed.
   ◆ Tell it not to list the virus programs when the computer is asked for an index of programs.

5. In this way, the computer will copy the virus onto many disks—perhaps all or nearly all the disks used in the infected machine. The virus may also be passed over the telephone, when one computer sends or receives data from another.

6. Ultimately hundreds or thousands of people may have infected disks and potential time bombs in their systems.

```
            out_file.open(out_file_name.c_str());
            assert(! out_file.fail());
    }

    void copy_file(ifstream &in_file, ofstream &out_file)
    {
            apstring line;

            while (! in_file.eof())
            {
                    getline(in_file, line);
                    out_file << line << endl;
            }
    }
```

Note that loop in the function **copy_file** tests for the end-of-file condition before the first input of text with **getline.** This order is different from a loop with the **>>** operator, because of the difference in the way that the two operations scan the input.

■ Exercises 7.2

1. Write a function that counts and displays on the screen the number of words in an input file. The program assumes that words in the file are separated by blank spaces or carriage returns. Test the program with files containing no words, one word, and several words.
2. Write a function that determines what the longest word in a file is. The function should display the longest word and its length on the terminal screen.
3. Write a function that finds and displays the average length of the words in a file.
4. Write a function that prompts the user for a word from the keyboard. Write a second function that counts the number of times that this word appears in a file. The program that uses this function should display the word count on the terminal screen.
5. Explain why it is a good idea to define functions for opening input and output files.

7.3 Character Input and Output

Many problems call for the input and output of individual characters with file streams. Consider the problems of counting the total number of characters in a file and counting the total number of lines of text in a file. If these data include individual space or carriage return characters, we cannot rely on formatting conventions and the use of the **>>** operator for input. Recall that the **>>** operator treats space or carriage return characters as separators between data values in an input stream. Therefore, the **>>** operator cannot be used to input whitespace characters as data values in their own right. C++ provides two lower level operators, **get** and **put**, for handling character-level operations on streams.

◆ to be able to obtain character data from input and output file streams

◆ to be able to distinguish character-level input and output from the input and output of other data types

Character Output with put

Character output with **put** is not much different than character output with **<<**. For example, the following three statements will have exactly the same effect on the file:

```
// Output a string with <<

out_file << "abcd";

// Output 4 characters with <<

for (char ch = 'a'; ch <= 'd'; ++ch)
     out_file << ch;

// Output 4 characters with put

for (char ch = 'a'; ch <= 'd'; ++ch)
     out_file.put(ch);
```

The form of a statement that uses **put** is

```
<output file stream>.put(<character value>);
```

where **put** is called as a function with a character value as its parameter. The function call is associated with the output stream by placing a period (.) between the name of the stream and the name of the function.

In general, **put** is defined such that it can work with any output stream. The loop

```
for (char ch = 'a'; ch <= 'd'; ++ch)
     cout.put(ch);
```

will print the string **"abcd"** on the terminal screen.

Character Input with get

Character input with **get** works in much the same way as character input with **>>**. One difference is that blank space and carriage return characters will be treated as character values in their own right.

The form of a statement that uses **get** is

```
<input stream>.get(<character variable>);
```

The following statement would get the first character in a file and place it in the character variable **ch**:

```
in_file.get(ch);
```

Detecting the End of File at the Character Level

A special character value is reserved to mark the end of a file of characters. In the case of an empty file, this character is the only character present in the file. It is important to detect this character during input, so that further input is not attempted. It turns out that after the end-of-file character has been read with **get**, the **eof** function will return **TRUE**. Otherwise, it will return **FALSE**.

<file stream>.eof() can be used to control a **while** loop for processing an entire stream of characters. A standard form of a loop for processing character-level input from a file stream is

```
<input stream name>.get(<character variable>);
while (! <input stream name>.eof())
      process_data(<character variable>);
      <input stream name>.get(<character variable>);
```

Note the order of the operations in this process. We get a character first, because there will be at least one character in the file. Then the condition in the **while** loop protects the program from attempting to get or process any more characters when the end-of-file condition becomes **TRUE**. The first step in the body of the loop is to process the character just read (either the initial one or the one from the previous pass through the loop). The second step in the loop is to get the next character, which eventually will be the end-of-file character.

The next three examples illustrate algorithms for counting the number of characters in a file, counting the number of lines in a file, and copying the contents of one file to another file.

Example 7.5

```cpp
// This program counts and displays the number of
// characters in a file.
// We don't count the end of file character as one of these

// Program file: charcnt.cpp

#include <iostream.h>
#include <fstream.h>

int main()
{
    ifstream in_file;
    char ch;
    int count;

    in_file.open("myfile");
    count = 0;
    in_file.get(ch);
    while (! in_file.eof())
    {
        ++count;
```

```
            in_file.get(ch);
      }
      cout << "The total number of characters in myfile is "
            << count << endl;
      in_file.close();
      return 0;
}
```

Example 7.6

To count the number of lines of text in a file, we can count the number of instances of the carriage return character denoted by **'\n'** in C++.

```
// This program counts and displays the number of
// lines in a file.

// Program file: linecnt.cpp

#include <iostream.h>
#include <fstream.h>

int main()
{
      ifstream in_file;
      char ch;
      int count;

      in_file.open("myfile");
      count = 0;
      in_file.get(ch);
      while (! in_file.eof())
      {
            if (ch == '\n')
                  ++count;
            in_file.get(ch);
      }
      in_file.close();
      cout << "The total number of lines in myfile is "
            << count << endl;
      return 0;
}
```

Example 7.7

```
// This program copies the contents of one file
// to another file.

// Program file: copyfile.cpp

#include <iostream.h>
#include <fstream.h>
```

```
int main()
{
        ifstream in_file;
        ofstream out_file;
        char ch;
        in_file.open("myfile");
        out_file.open("newfile");
        in_file.get(ch);
        while (! in_file.eof())
        {
                out_file.put(ch);
                in_file.get(ch);
        }
        in_file.close();
        out_file.close();
        return 0;
}
```

The last example calls for some comment. We copy every character from the input file to the output file, except for the input file's end-of-file character. This might lead you to think that the output file has no end-of-file character. However, the computer takes care of appending an end-of-file character to an output file whenever it is closed. Therefore, we were right to ignore the input file's end-of-file character. If we had copied it to the output file, this file would have contained two end-of-file characters, and would not have reflected the contents of the input file accurately.

■ Exercises 7.3

1. Assume that an input file stream, **in_file**, has been opened on a file, and that **ch** is a character variable. Describe what happens when each of the following pieces of code is run:

    a. ```
        in_file.get(ch);
        cout.put(ch);
        in_file.get(ch);
        cout.put(ch);
        in_file.get(ch);
        cout.put(ch);
        ```

    b.  ```
        in_file.get(ch);
        while (! in_file.eof())
        {
                cout.put(ch);
                in_file.get(ch);
        }
        ```

    c. ```
        while (! in_file.eof())
        {

                in_file.get(ch);
                cout.put(ch);
        }
        ```
        ```

A Note of Interest

Digital Video Disks

Technology is changing so rapidly that it is almost futile to comment on the current state of events. Nevertheless, we do so for two reasons. The first reason is to make you aware of rapidly changing technology; the second reason is that it is always interesting to mark a point in time from an historical perspective. Thus, we offer an observation about the current status of computer memory.

It is predicted that computer memory is about to undergo a tremendous revolution. Digital video disks (acronym DVDs) are the latest disks in the ever-changing world of data storage. They will be marketed as 4.75-inch disks, the same as current CDs. When recorded on two sides, they will hold up to 18 gigabytes (giga means billion). The basic entry-level DVD with only one side recorded will hold 4.7 gigabytes. That is as much as 7.5 ordinary CDs or 3450 3.5-inch high-density floppy disks. Potential computer applications are enormous. Current projections indicate that the DVD will come to market first as a read-only medium, like the current CD-

ROMs. By the end of 1997, rewritable DVDs should be marketed. By the year 2000, industry analysts project that 120 million DVDs will be marketed, a business expected to be worth more than $20 billion a year.

In its read-only format, a DVD will create memory able to hold not only encyclopedias but entire libraries. In rewritable configurations, a DVD will allow a personal computer to map the heavens or project accurate star maps from any perspective in the sky. DVD technology will reduce mainframe computer storage systems from rooms of disk drives to a few DVD players on a bookshelf. The potential for entertainment is immense. A single disk will be able to hold one movie of over two hours on a side with three audio tracks. Current projections claim that interactive players will allow a viewer to choose camera angles such as pan, scan, widescreen, and close-up, for as many as nine camera angles. DVD technology, high-definition television, and high-end audio equipment could create a multiple playback system that today is confined to recording studios.

2. Write a program that deletes all blanks from a file. Your program should save the revised file for later use (*Hint:* Copy the contents of the input file to another file, omitting the blanks).

3. Write a program using a **switch** statement to scramble a file by replacing all blanks with an asterisk (*), and interchanging all A's with U's and E's with I's. Your program should print the scrambled file and save it for subsequent use.

4. Write a program to update a file by numbering the lines consecutively as 1, 2, 3, ... The input file should not be modified.

5. Write a program to count the number of uppercase characters in a file.

6. Write a program to count the number of words in a text file. Assume that each word is followed by a blank or a period. The program should use **get** rather than **>>** to receive the input from the file.

7. Write a program to find the longest word in a file. Output should include the word and its length. The program should use **get** rather than **>>** to receive the input from the file.

8. Write a program to compute the average length of words in a file. The program should use **get** rather than **>>** to receive the input from the file.

9. Write a program that performs a search-and-replace operation on a file. The program will prompt the user for the word to search for and the word to use as a replacement. The program should replace all of the instances of the target word with the replacement word.

7.4 Graphics

Objectives

◆ to be able to save images to files

◆ to be able to load images from files

◆ to understand the cost of file operations with images in terms of memory and processing time

This chapter has focused on saving data to files. As you probably know, many graphical applications make use of files for storing images. For example, when a digital camera takes a photograph, a graphical image is saved in a file on a disk. The file can then be copied to the disks of other computers and displayed on a screen or printed on a printer. The techniques for saving images to files normally involve complex algorithms for compressing the data so as to save memory. In this section, we consider two very simple ways of saving images to files, leaving more sophisticated techniques for later computer science courses.

Saving Images as Data in a File

The most obvious way to save an image in a file is to save the information associated with each pixel in the image. A pixel is completely specified by its position on the screen and its color. Thus, this information consists of three integers—the x and y coordinates of the pixel and its color value.

An algorithm to save an image to a file would loop through all of the pixels in the image, writing their coordinates and color values to the file as integers. Assuming that the image is a rectangular area, the algorithm would be a nested **for** loop. The outer loop runs through all of the x coordinates or columns in the rectangle. The inner loop runs through all of the y coordinates or positions in a column. The inner loop uses a function, **get_pixel**, that returns the color value of the pixel at a given position.

For every x coordinate from lower x to upper x
   For every y coordinate from lower y to upper y
      Output **x**, **y**, and **get_pixel(x, y)** to the file

Conversely, an algorithm to load an image from a file and display it on the screen would read three integers on each pass through a **while** loop. The integers would be used as the x and y coordinates and the color for calling the **putpixel** function to draw the pixel. The loop would continue until the end of file is reached.

Input x, y, and color from the file
While not end of file
   put_pixel(x, y, color)
   Input x, y, and color from the file

Example 7.8

It would be useful to have a pair of functions, **save_image** and **load_image**, for transferring images to and from files. The functions might be invoked as follows:

```
load_image(in_file);

// Do some drawing here

save_image(out_file, 0, 0, 100, 100);
```

save_image expects as parameters an opened output file and the corner points of the rectangular area to be saved. The function uses the algorithm discussed earlier to write information about pixels in the rectangular area to the file.

```
void save_image(ofstream &out_file, int left, int top,
    int right, int bottom)
{
    for (int x = left; x <= right; ++x)
        for (int y = top; y <= bottom; ++y)
        {
        out_file << x << " ";
        out_file << y << " ";
        out_file << getpixel(x, y) << " ";
        }
}
```

load_image assumes that for each pixel in the image, three integers have been written to the file, separated by spaces and in the order *x, y,* color. The function takes one parameter, an opened input file. It uses the algorithm discussed earlier to read integers from the file and display the corresponding pixels.

```
void load_image(ifstream &in_file)
{
    int x, y, color;

    in_file >> x;
    in_file >> y;
    in_file >> color;
    while (! in_file.eof())
    {
        putpixel(x, y, color);
        in_file >> x;
        in_file >> y;
        in_file >> color;
    }
}
```

Saving Images as Operations in a File

The image saved in Example 7.8 is a rectangular area 101 pixels wide by 101 pixels high. This area totals 10,201 pixels. Because three integers represent the information for each pixel, 30,603 integers must be stored in the file. As you can see, saving large images can be costly, in terms of disk memory for the files. The process of saving can also be time intensive, in terms of the number of operations required to write data and the relatively long time for writing each datum to disk. For this reason, many computer scientists have devoted time to research on the topic of data compression techniques for files.

Occasionally, a much faster way of saving and loading images can be employed. Rather than save the data representing the individual picture elements of an image in a file, this method saves a description of the graphics operations (and their parameters) used to draw the images. For example, the following operations that draw a smiling face (see Example 4.6)

```
circle(100, 100, 50);
circle(12, 12, 2);
circle(37, 37, 2);
arc(100, 30, 200, 340, 25);
```

might be represented in a file as

```
circle 100 100 50
circle 12 12 2
circle 37 37 2
arc 100 30 200 340 25
```

The separate lines are not necessary, but are added for readability. Note that there is a close correspondence between the notation of the operations in the C++ program and their representation in the file. This format will enable the input operation to recognize the graphics operations and their parameters and execute them when the image is loaded.

Note also that the size of this file (about 75 characters) is considerably less than it would be if the pixels of the same image were saved instead (about 30,000 integers). The process of reading, recognizing, and running these operations will also be markedly faster than the alternative method of drawing each pixel.

The process of saving an image with this method is the same as saving a string corresponding to a graphics operation. For example, the first operation to draw the smiling face would be saved with

```
out_file << "circle 100 100 50" << endl;
```

Alternatively, one could type in the entire set of commands with a text editor and save this as a text file.

The process of loading the file is more complicated. It involves repeating the following three steps until the end of file is reached:

1. Read a word from the file.
2. Examine the word. Depending on the command that the word represents, read the appropriate number of arguments from the file into integer variables.
3. Run the appropriate graphics operation with the integer arguments.

As you can see, step 2 of this process involves a multiway selection statement that uses string comparisons. The actions of this statement require reading the appropriate number of integers from the file and then executing the appropriate graphics command with these integers as parameters. Because these actions are somewhat complex, it is best to delegate them to separate functions in the design. Example 7.9 shows how this is done in C++.

| Example 7.9 |

The design of the function for loading an image represented as graphics operations requires several modules. We develop three here. The top-level module, **load_image**, executes a loop that reads a command name and interprets it. Its implementation follows:

```
void load_image(ifstream &in_file)
{
        apstring command;

        in_file >> command;
        while (! in_file.eof())
        {
                interpret_command(in_file, command);
                in_file >> command;
        }
}
```

Note that the primary responsibility of this function is control of the loop. The task of recognizing a graphics command is hidden in the next lower module, **interpret_command**. This function receives the file stream and command name as parameters and selects the appropriate function to read the integer arguments from the file and execute the graphics operation.

```
void interpret_command(ifstream &in_file,
    const apstring &command)
{
        if (command == "circle")
            call_circle(in_file);
        else if (command == "rectangle")
            call_rectangle(in_file);
        else if (command == "lineto")
            call_lineto(in_file);
        else if (command == "moveto")
            call_moveto(in_file);
        else if (command == "setcolor")
            call_setcolor(in_file);
}
```

Note that the command interpreter can easily be extended by adding further comparisons and function calls. The lowest level modules read the integer arguments for a given command from the file and run the graphics operation with these arguments. **call_circle** does this for drawing circles:

```
void call_circle(ifstream &in_file)
{
      int center_x, center_y, radius;

      in_file >> center_x;
      in_file >> center_y;
      in_file >> radius;
      circle(center_x, center_y, radius);
}
```

Each of the lower level modules reads and processes the input data relevant to it. They either leave the next command in the input stream or reach the end of the stream.

■ Exercises 7.4

1. Discuss the problems posed by saving the entire graphics screen to a file using the method of saving pixels as integers.

2. Discuss the limitations of saving images to a file using the method of saving the graphics operations that drew them.

3. Simon Seeplus has suggested that we write a new library of graphics operations. Each operation runs one of the existing **graphics** library functions, and then saves a representation of this command, with its arguments, to a file. Each of the new operations has a **save** suffix. For example, **setcolor_save(out_ file, WHITE)** would both set the current foreground color to white and save the **setcolor** command and its argument in a file. Discuss the merits of this proposal, and write the code for the declaration and implementation of the **setcolor_save** function.

Focus on Program Design: Case Study

Analyzing a File of Sentences

The summary program for this chapter analyzes sentences in a file of text. It builds on a case study in Chapter 6, in which we analyzed single sentences typed in at the keyboard. That program displayed statistics about the number of characters and words in the sentence, and printed the longest word in the sentence as well.

The new program will prompt the user for a file name and open the file. If no error occurs, the program will compute and display statistics for

1. The total number of sentences in the file
2. The total number of words in the file
3. The average length of a sentence in the file
4. The length of the longest sentence in the file.

The program will recognize several kinds of sentences: those ending in a period ('**.**'), a question mark ('**?**'), and an exclamation point ('**!**'). Normally, a word ending with one of these characters will be treated as the last word in a sentence. As a special case, if one of these characters does not end the last word in the file, then that word is also treated as the last word in a sentence.

After the statistics are displayed, the program will ask the user if the analysis of another file is desired. If the answer is "Yes," the program will repeat the process; otherwise, the program will terminate execution.

Assume that a file named "test" contains the following text:

```
There are many words in this file.  A period follows some of
them.  My daughter is sitting in a chair watching a movie.
When I get thirsty, I get up to get a drink.  My baby daughter
is crying upstairs.  I guess she is hungry.  Well, I better
finish this book.
```

A session with the program would be as follows:

```
Enter the input file name: test

Statistics for the current file.

The number of words is 51.
The number of sentences is 7.
The average length of a sentence is 7.
The longest sentence had 11 words.

Analyze another file? [Y/N] n
```

A reasonable top-level module is

```
Do
      Open input file
      If there was no error opening the file then
          Initialize data
          Analyze sentences in file
          Close input file
          Display statistics
      Else
          Display error message
          Query user for another analysis
While answer to query = "Yes"
```

Before we can examine the submodules within this module, we must make explicit the data that are transmitted among them. The modules for opening and closing a file, and for analyzing sentences in the file, require a file stream. The modules for initializing data, analyzing sentences, and displaying statistics require three integers, which represent the total number of sentences, the total number of words, and the length of the longest sentence. The average sentence length of a sentence can be computed locally in the display statistics module as a function of the other data. This data flow is shown in the structure chart of Figure 7.3.

The main module translates to the following C++ main program:

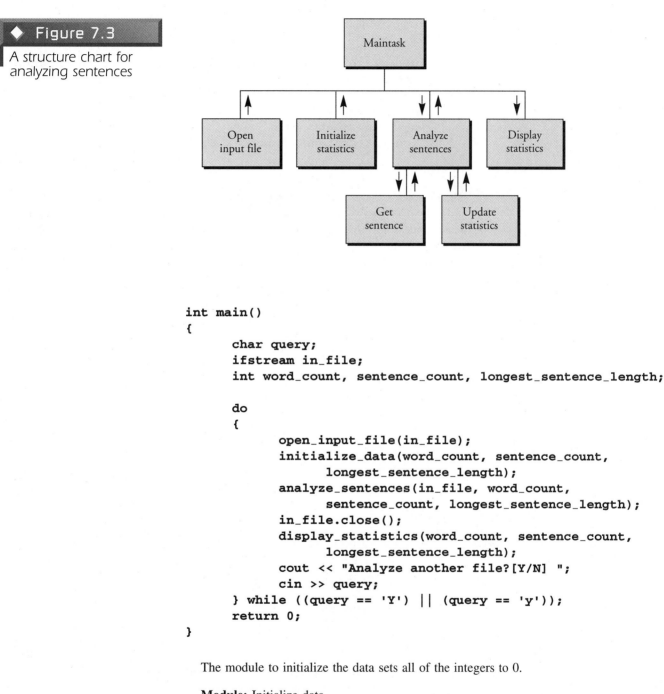

◆ Figure 7.3

A structure chart for analyzing sentences

```
int main()
{
      char query;
      ifstream in_file;
      int word_count, sentence_count, longest_sentence_length;

      do
      {
            open_input_file(in_file);
            initialize_data(word_count, sentence_count,
                  longest_sentence_length);
            analyze_sentences(in_file, word_count,
                  sentence_count, longest_sentence_length);
            in_file.close();
            display_statistics(word_count, sentence_count,
                  longest_sentence_length);
            cout << "Analyze another file?[Y/N] ";
            cin >> query;
      } while ((query == 'Y') || (query == 'y'));
      return 0;
}
```

The module to initialize the data sets all of the integers to 0.

Module: Initialize data
Task: Set all integers to 0.
Output: Integers representing the total number of sentences, the total number of
  words, and the length of the longest sentence

Set sentence count to 0
Set word count to 0
Set longest sentence length to 0

The C++ implementation is

```
void initialize_data(int &word_count, int &sentence_count,
        int &longest_sentence_length)
{
        word_count = 0;
        sentence_count = 0;
        longest_sentence_length = 0;
}
```

The module to analyze sentences must repeatedly invoke a process we developed in the program in Chapter 6 to analyze a single sentence. The difference here is that we read a sentence from a file and return just a word count. This value is then passed with the other data to a submodule that updates the statistics. The subprocesses are structured within a standard input file process.

Module: Analyze sentences
Task: Read sentences from a file and compute statistics.
Input: A file stream and integers representing the total number of sentences, the total number of words, and the length of the longest sentence
Output: The integers updated

Do
     Get a word count on an input sentence
     If the word count > 0 then
        Update statistics
While not end of file

Note that a sentence may have a word count of zero. This occurs only in the special case where the input file is empty. The C++ implementation maintains the word count of the current input sentence as a local variable, **current_count**:

```
void analyze_sentences(ifstream &in_file, int &word_count,
        int &sentence_count,
        int &longest_sentence_length)
{
        int current_count;

        do
        {
                get_sentence(in_file, current_count);
                if (current_count > 0)
                        update_statistics(current_count, word_count,
                                sentence_count, longest_sentence_length);
        } while (! in_file.eof());

}
```

The module to display statistics computes the average length of a sentence and displays the four integer values with descriptive labels. Here is the C++ implementation:

```
void display_statistics(int word_count, int sentence_count,
    int longest_sentence_length)
{
    cout << endl << "Statistics for the current file:"
        << endl << endl;
    cout << "The number of words is " << word_count
        << "." << endl;
    cout << "The number of sentences is " << sentence_count
        << "." << endl;
    cout << "The average length of a sentence is "
        << word_count / sentence_count << " words." << endl;
    cout << "The longest sentence had "
        << longest_sentence_length << " words."
        << endl << endl;
}
```

The get sentence module reads words from the file and maintains a count of them. This is an iterative process with two possible termination conditions: Either the end of file has been reached, or the last input word contains a sentence termination character (`'.'`, `'?'`, or `'!'`) at the end.

Module: Get sentence
Task: Read words from a sentence and maintain a count of words.
Input: An input file stream
Output: The count of words in the sentence; 0 words means no sentence at all

Set count to 0
Read a word from the file
If not end of file then
    Increment count by one
   While not end of file and word not at end of sentence do
    Read a word from the file
    Increment count by one

The initial test for an end of file guards against the case where the file is empty. The C++ implementation is

```
void get_sentence(ifstream &in_file, int &count)
{
    apstring word;

    count = 0;
    in_file >> word;
    if (! in_file.eof())
    {
        ++count;
        while (! in_file.eof() && ! end_of_sentence(word))
        {
            in_file >> word;
            ++count;
        }
    }
}
```

The update statistics module increments the word count and the sentence count and adjusts the length of the longest sentence if necessary.

Module: Update statistics
Task: Increment word and sentence counts and adjust length of longest sentence if necessary.
Input: Integers representing the number of words in the current sentence, the total number of sentences, the total number of words, and the length of the longest sentence
Output: The last three input integers updated

Increment the word count by the number of words in the current sentence
Increment the sentence count by one
If number of words in the current sentence > length of the longest sentence then
      Set length of the longest sentence to number of words in the current sentence

The C++ implementation is

```
void update_statistics(int current_count, int &word_count,
     int &sentence_count,
     int &longest_sentence_length)
{
     word_count = word_count + current_count;
     ++sentence_count;
     if (current_count > longest_sentence_length)
          longest_sentence_length = current_count;
}
```

At the lowest level of our design, the end-of-sentence module tests a word to see whether it marks the end of a sentence.

Module: End of sentence
Task: Determine whether a word marks the end of a sentence.
Input: A word
Output: **TRUE**, if the word ends with '.', '?', or '!'; **FALSE** otherwise

Here is the C++ implementation of the module:

```
bool end_of_sentence(const apstring &word)
{
     char last_ch = word[word.length()- 1];

     return(last_ch == '.') || (last_ch == '?')
          || (last_ch == '!');
}
```

Running, Debugging, and Testing Hints

1. **>>** treats an end-of-line marker and a blank space as input separators.
2. **get** treats an end-of-line marker and a blank space as character data.
3. Always test for the end-of-file condition after getting a character from an input file. If the condition is **TRUE**, do not attempt to process the most recently read character or to read more characters from the file.

Summary

Key Terms

abstract	file	priming input statement
buffer	input file stream	sequential search
buffered file input	input stream	serial processing
destination device	output file stream	source device
disk device	output stream	stream
end of input stream	portable	

Key Concepts

- Files can be used to store data between runs of a program.
- Access to file stream operations can be obtained by **#include <fstream.h>**.
- An input file stream can be declared by **ifstream** <stream name>**;**.
- An output file stream can be declared by **ofstream** <stream name>**;**.
- File streams must be opened before they can be written to or read from.
- A file stream can be opened by <stream name>**.open(**<file name>**);**.
- A file stream can be closed by <stream name>**.close();**.
- An error in connecting a stream to a file can be detected by <stream name>**.fail();**.
- For input data of most types, reading from a file stream can be accomplished by

  <input file stream name> **>>** <variable name> **. . .**
               >> <variable name>**;**

- For output data of most types, writing to a file stream can be accomplished by

  <output file stream name> **<<** <expression> **. . .**
               << <expression>**;**

- When reading data from a file stream with **>>**, the absence of more data in an input stream can be detected by reading a datum and then running <input stream name>**.eof()**.
- This condition will be **TRUE** if there is no more data to be read, and **FALSE** otherwise.

◆ When reading character-level input, the absence of more data in an input stream can be detected by reading a character and then running <input stream name>.**eof()**.

◆ A line of text can be read from an input stream by using the buffered input **apstring** function **getline**, as follows:

getline(<input stream name>, <string variable>);

◆ Character data can be read from an input stream by

<input stream name>.**get**(<character variable>);

◆ Character data can be written to an output stream by

<output stream name>.**put**(<character value>);.

◆ A file exists outside the program block in secondary storage.

Chapter Review Exercises

1. Show all of the data declarations that are necessary to create a file named exercise. Show how to put values into the file so that it looks like

   ```
   10F    16
   11M    8
   15F    7
   ```

   For Exercises 2–6, use the file from Exercise 1. Assume the variables are declared as follows:

   ```
   int a, b;
   char c, d;
   double e;
   string s;
   ```

   Indicate if the statements are valid. If so, indicate what values are read and where the input pointer in the file is after the statement is executed. Assume the pointer is at the beginning for each exercise.

2. `infile >> a >> c >> b;`
3. `infile >> a >> b >> c;`
4. `infile >> a >> c >> d;`
5. `infile >> a >> c >> e;`
6. `infile >> s >> a;`

7. Write a segment of code to write the integers 1 through 10 to a file.

Programming Problems and Activities

1. Write a program to print the contents of a text file omitting any occurrences of the letter *e* from the output.

2. A text file contains a list of integers in order from lowest to highest. Write a program to read and print the text file with all duplications eliminated.

3. Mr. John Napier, professor at Lancaster Community College, wants a program to compute grade-point averages. Each line of a text file contains three initials followed by an unknown number of letter grades. These grades are A, B, C, D, or F. Write a program that reads the file and prints a list of the students' initials and their grade-point averages. (Assume an A is 4 points, a B is 3 points, and so on.) Print an asterisk next to any grade-point average that is greater than 3.75.

4. An amortization table (Problem 19, Chapter 6) shows the rate at which a loan is paid off. It contains monthly entries showing the interest paid that month, the principal paid, and the remaining balance. Given the amount of money borrowed (the principal), the annual interest rate, and the amount the person wishes to repay each month, print an amortization table. (The payment desired must be larger than the first month's interest.) Your table should stop when the loan is paid off, and should be printed with the following heads:

   MONTH NUMBER   INTEREST PAID   PRINCIPAL PAID   BALANCE

   Create an enumerated data type for the month number. Limit this to require that the loan be paid back within 60 months.

5. Mr. Christian (Problem 26, Chapter 6) uses a 90 percent, 80 percent, 70 percent, 60 percent grading scale on his tests. Given a list of test scores, print the number of A's, B's, C's, D's, and F's on the test. Terminate the list of scores with a sentinel value.

6. Write a program to print the perimeter and area of rectangles using all combinations of lengths and widths running from 1 foot to 10 feet in increments of 1 foot. Print the output in columns with heads.

7. Write a program that can be used as a text analyzer. Your program should be capable of reading an input file and keeping track of the frequency of occurrence of each letter of the alphabet. There should also be a count of all characters (including blanks) encountered that are not in the alphabet. Your output should be the data file printed line by line followed by a histogram reflecting the frequency of occurrence of each letter in the alphabet. For example, the following histogram indicates five occurrences of a, two of b, and three of c:

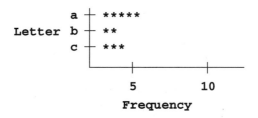

8. The Third Interdenominational Church has on file a list of all of its benefactors (a maximum of 20 names, each up to 30 characters) along with an unknown

number of amounts that each has donated to the church. You have been asked to write a program that does the following:

a. Print the name of each donor and the amount of any donations given by each.

b. Print the total amounts.

c. Print the grand total of all donations.

d. Print the largest single amount donated and the name of the benefactor who made this donation.

9. Read in a list of 50 integers from the data file **numberlist**. Place the even numbers into an output file called **even**, the odd numbers into an output file called **odd**, and the negatives into an output file called **negative**. Print all three files after all numbers have been read.

10. Ms. Alicia Citizen, your school's student government advisor, has come to you for help. She wants a program to total votes for the next student government election. Fifteen candidates will be in the election with five positions to be filled. Each person can vote for up to five candidates. The five highest vote getters will be the winners.

A data file called **votelist** contains a list of candidates (by candidate number) voted for by each student. Any line of the file may contain up to five numbers, but if it contains more than five numbers, it is discarded as a void ballot. Write a program to read the file and print a list of the total votes received by each candidate. Also, print the five highest vote getters in order from highest to lowest vote totals.

11. The data file **instructorlist** contains a list of the instructors in your school along with the room number to which each is assigned. Write a program that, given the name of the instructor, does a linear search to find and print the room to which the instructor is assigned.

12. Simon Seeplus has suggested a method for making the saving of images to a file more efficient. We assume that there is a single background color, say, black, in effect when an image is saved and when it is loaded. Thus, we need only save the pixels with nonbackground colors within the bounds of the image. Develop an algorithm that makes this improvement, write the corresponding C++ function, and test your design with an appropriate driver program.

13. Use the list of graphics operations in Appendix 5 to develop a complete set of descriptions of graphics commands that can be written to a file. Each description in your document should specify the name of the command and the number of integer arguments expected.

Communication in Practice

1. Reread the **Note of Interest** on computer viruses in this chapter. Then search in the ACM Code of Ethics for principles that apply to this problem. Prepare a written report on your findings to present to your class.

2. Select a problem that you have not done from the **Programming Problems and Activities** of this chapter. For that problem, write documentation that includes a complete description of

a. Required input

b. Required output

c. Required processing and computation

Exchange your documentation with another student who has been given the same assignment. Compare your results.

3. Using a completed program from this chapter, remove all documentation. Exchange this version with another student who has prepared a similar version. Write documentation for the exchanged program. Compare your results with the program author's original version. Discuss the differences and similarities with your class.

4. Select a team of three or four students and contact businesspeople who use computers for data storage. Find out exactly how they enter, store, and retrieve data. Discuss how they use their databases and how large the databases are. Ask them what they like and dislike about data entry and retrieval and if they have suggestions for modifying any aspect of working with their databases. Prepare a report for class that summarizes your findings.

Arrays

Chapter Outline

Thus far in this text, we have been able to store large amounts of data in files, but we have been unable to manipulate it in a convenient way. For example, we can write a program that allows the user to enter a long list of bank accounts interactively and save the list in a file. However, the file structure does not efficiently support functions to process the accounts in the list, such as searching for an account, updating information in it, or computing statistics on all of the accounts in the list. Other objects are difficult to represent at all with the data structures at our disposal. Consider the example of representing a student whose attributes are a name and a list of 10 quiz grades. Representing these attributes as 11 separate named variables is unwieldy.

Fortunately, C++ provides a structured data type called an **array** to facilitate solving problems that require working with large amounts of data. The use of arrays permits us to set aside a group of memory locations that we can then manipulate as a single entity or that gives us direct access to any component. For example, arrays can be used to develop strings. Other standard applications for arrays include creating tabular output (tables), alphabetizing a list of names, analyzing a list of test scores, and keeping an inventory.

In this chapter, we discuss the use of the array as a general data structuring mechanism.

Basic Idea and Notation

As previously mentioned, many instances arise in which several variables of the same data type are required. Let us at this point work with a list of five integers: 18, 17, 21, 18, and 19. Prior to this chapter, we would have declared five variables—**A**, **B**, **C**, **D**, and **E**—and assigned them appropriate values, or read them

---

8.1 Arrays

Objectives

- to understand the basic concept of an array

- to use correct notation for arrays

- to be able to declare arrays with variable declarations and with type definitions

- to be able to use array components with appropriate arithmetic operations

- to be able to use array components with appropriate input and output statements

array: A data structure whose elements are accessed by means of index positions.

from the keyboard. This would have produced five values in memory, each accessed by a separate identifier.

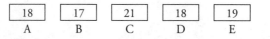

If the list was very long, this would be an inefficient way to work with these data; an alternative is to use an array. In C++, we declare a variable as an array variable using either of the following methods:

1. `int list[5];`
2. `typedef int list_type[5];`
   `list_type list;`

With either of these declarations, we now have five integer variables with which to work. They are denoted by

and each is referred to as a *component* (or *element*) *of the array.* A good way to visualize these variables is to assume that memory locations are aligned in a column on top of each other and the name of the column is `list`. If we then assign the five values of our list to these five variables, we have the following in memory:

list

18	list[0]
17	list[1]
21	list[2]
18	list[3]
19	list[4]

index (synonym: **subscript**): The relative position of the components of an array.

The components of an array are referred to by their relative position in the array. This relative position is called the **index**, or *subscript,* of the component. In the array of our five values, the component `list[2]` has an index of 2 and a value of 21. Note that an array index is always numbered from zero rather than one. The index of the last component in an array is always $N - 1$, where N is the number of elements in the array.

For the sake of convenience, you may choose to depict an array by listing only the index beside its appropriate component. Thus, `list` could be shown as

list

If you choose this method, remember that the array elements are referenced by the array name and the index, for example, `list[2]` for the third component. Whichever method you use, it is important to remember that each array component is a variable and can be treated exactly like any other declared variable of that base type in the program.

Declaring an Array

An earlier declaration of an array was

```
int list[5];
```

Let us now examine this declaration more closely. Several comments are in order.

1. The key word **int** indicates the data type for the components. This can, of course, be another data type such as **char**, as we have seen in our definition of a string type.
2. **[5]** is the syntax that indicates the array consists of five memory locations accessed by specifying each of the numbers 0, 1, 2, 3, and 4. We frequently say the array is of length five. The information inside the brackets must be an integer constant or an expression whose value can be computed at compile time. This value must lie in the range from 1 to an upper bound defined for the particular system on which you are running your programs. (You can look this value up in the manual for your system.) The integer constant can be expressed either literally (**[5]**) or as a named constant (**[MAX_LIST_SIZE]**). The latter form is preferred for better program maintenance.
3. **list**, the name of the variable, can be any valid identifier. As always, it is good practice to use descriptive names to enhance readability.

The form for declaring an array variable is

<component type> <variable name> [<integer value>] **;**

where **<component type>** is any predefined or user-defined data type and **<variable name>** is any valid identifier.

The following example illustrates another declaration of an array variable.

Example 8.1
Suppose you want to create a list of 10 integer variables for the hours worked by 10 employees as follows:

Employee Number	Hours Worked
0	35
1	40
2	20
3	38
4	25
5	40
6	25
7	40
8	20
9	45

Declare an array that has 10 components of type **int** and show how it can be visualized. A descriptive name for the variable could be **hours**. There are 10 items, so we will define a constant, **MAX_LIST_SIZE = 10**, and use this name in the array variable declaration. Because the data consist of integers, the component type will be **int**. An appropriate definition and subsequent declaration could be

```
const int MAX_LIST_SIZE = 10;
int hours[MAX_LIST_SIZE];
```

At this stage, the components can be visualized as

hours

	hours[0]
	hours[1]
	hours[2]
	hours[3]
	hours[4]
	hours[5]
	hours[6]
	hours[7]
	hours[8]
	hours[9]

After making appropriate assignment statements, **hours** can be visualized as hours

35	hours[0]
40	hours[1]
20	hours[2]
38	hours[3]
25	hours[4]
40	hours[5]
25	hours[6]
40	hours[7]
20	hours[8]
45	hours[9]

Other Element Types

The previous two arrays used element types that were integers. The following examples illustrate some array definitions with other element types.

Example 8.2

Declare an array that allows you to store the hourly price for a share of IBM stock. A descriptive name could be **stock_prices**. A price is quoted at each hour from 9:00 A.M. to 3:00 P.M., so we will use **MAX_LIST_SIZE = 7** in the declaration section. Because the data consist of real numbers, the data type must be **double**. A possible declaration could be

```
const int MAX_LIST_SIZE = 7;
double stock_prices[MAX_LIST_SIZE];
```

This would then allow us to store the 9:00 A.M. price in **stock_prices[0]**, the 1:00 P.M. price in **stock_prices[4]**, and so on.

Example 8.3

The declaration

```
const int MAX_LIST_SIZE = 6;
char alphas[MAX_LIST_SIZE];
```

will reserve six character components.

Example 8.4

The declaration

```
#include "bool.h"
const int MAX_LIST_SIZE = 4;
bool flags[MAX_LIST_SIZE];
```

will produce an array whose components are Boolean values.

| Example 8.5 | Declare an array that allows a program to store 20 strings. |

```
#include "apstring.h"
const int MAX_LIST_SIZE = 20;
apstring words[MAX_LIST_SIZE];
```

It is important to note that in each example, the array components will have no predictable values assigned until the program specifically makes some kind of assignment. Declaring an array does not assign values to any of the components.

Communication and Style Tips

The use of descriptive constants is not essential for creating arrays. However, programs that use this method are much easier to maintain than those that use declarations such as **int list[20];**. You will appreciate the use of symbolic constants and array type names better when you learn how to process arrays with loops and functions in the following sections of this chapter.

Assignment Statements

Suppose we have declared an array

```
constant int MAX = 5;
int a[MAX];
```

and we want to put the values 1, 4, 9, 16, and 25 into the respective components. We can accomplish this with these assignment statements:

```
a[0] = 1;
a[1] = 4;
a[2] = 9;
a[3] = 16;
a[4] = 25;
```

If variables **b** and **c** of type **int** are declared in the program, then the following are also appropriate assignment statements:

```
a[3] = b;
c = a[2];
a[2] = a[4];
```

If you want to interchange the values of two components (for example, exchange **a[2]** with **a[3]**), you could use a third integer variable:

```
b = a[2];
a[2] = a[3];
a[3] = b;
```

This exchange is frequently used in sorting algorithms, so let us examine it more closely. Assume **b** contains no previously assigned value, and **a[2]** and **a[3]** contain 4 and 9, respectively.

The assignment statement **b = a[2];** produces

4		4	a[2]
b		9	a[3]

The assignment statement **a[2] = a[3];** produces

4		9	a[2]
b		9	a[3]

and finally the assignment statement **a[3] = b;** produces

in which the original values of **a[2]** and **a[3]** have been interchanged.

Arithmetic

Components of an array can also be used in any appropriate arithmetic operation. For example, suppose **a** is the following array of integers:

a	
1	a[0]
4	a[1]
9	a[2]
16	a[3]
25	a[4]

and that the values of the components of the array are to be added. This could be accomplished by the statement

```
sum = a[0] + a[1] + a[2] + a[3] + a[4];
```

Each of the following would also be a valid use of an array component:

```
b = 3 * a[1];
c = a[4] % 3;
d = a[1] * a[4];
```

For the array **a** given earlier, these assignment statements produce

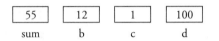

55	12	1	100
sum	b	c	d

Some invalid assignment statements and the reasons they are invalid follow:

```
a[6] = 7;
```

This statement will compile and run. However, because 6 is not a valid subscript for the array, the program may behave strangely.

```
a[2.0] = 3;
```

This statement will not compile, because a subscript of type **double** is not allowed.

Reading and Writing

Since array components are names for variables, they can be used in input and output statements. For example, if **scores** is an array of five integers and you want to input the scores 65, 43, 98, 75, and 83 from the keyboard, you could use the code

```
cin >> scores[0] >> scores[1] >> scores[2] >> scores[3] >> scores[4];
```

This would produce the array

scores

65	scores[0]
43	scores[1]
98	scores[2]
75	scores[3]
83	scores[4]

If you want to print the scores above 80, you could use the code

```
cout << setw(10) << scores[2] << setw(10) << scores[4] << endl;
```

to produce

```
    98      83
```

It is important to note that you cannot input or output values into or from an entire array by a reference to the array name. Statements such as **cout << a;** are legitimate, but will display the address of the array rather than its contents.

Out-of-Range Array References

You have seen that an array in C++ has index values in the range $0 .. N - 1$, where N is the number of cells for storing data in the array. For example, the data declarations

```
    const MAX_LIST_SIZE = 5;
    int week_days[MAX_LIST_SIZE];
```

range bound error:
The situation that occurs when an attempt is made to use an array index value that is less than 0 or greater than or equal to the size of the array.

cause the computer to allocate five cells of memory for an array whose index ranges from 0 to 4. The index values used in array references should also range from 0 to 4. If a programmer uses an index value outside of this range, a **range bound error** is said to occur. If the offending index is a variable, as in

```
    int i = 5;
    week_days[i] = 10;
```

the error will occur at run time, though the computer will not halt program execution with an error message that this error has occurred.

Even if the offending index is a constant, as in

```
    week_days[5] = 10;
```

the error will not be caught at compile time. C++ *does not do range bound error checking*. This means that the program will compile and execute, and the reference will be to some other area of memory than the cells allocated for the array. In the case of an assignment to that location, a serious side effect will occur and may cause the program to behave in very mysterious ways.

Range bound errors in C++ programs are most often caused by failure to remember that the upper bound on the array index is $N - 1$, where N is the number of cells in the array. One way to avoid range bound errors with arrays is to be careful always to use an index that satisfies the condition **0 <= index < N**, where **N** is the integer constant used to define the array type. You may wish to use the C++ assertion facility to place this precondition on array references in spots in a program where range bound errors are likely to occur.

In Chapter 10, we will develop an array type that supports range bound checking.

1. Using descriptive names, define an array type and declare subsequent variables for each of the following:
   a. A list of 35 test scores
   b. The prices of 20 automobiles
   c. The answers to 50 true or false questions
   d. A list of letter grades for the classes you are taking this semester

2. Write a test program in which you declare an array of three components, read values into each component, sum the components, and print the sum and value of each component.

3. Assume the array **list** is declared as

   ```
   int list[100];
   ```

   and that all other variables have been appropriately declared. Label the following as valid or invalid. Include an explanation for any that are invalid.
   a. `cin >> list[3];`
   b. `a = list[3] + list[4];`
   c. `cout << list;`
   d. `list[10] = 3.2;`
   e. `max = list[50];`
   f. `average = (list[0] + list[8]) / 2;`
   g. `cout << list[25, 50, 75];`
   h. `cout << list[10] + list[25];`
   i. `for (j = 0; j < 100; ++j)`
   `        cin >> list;`
   j. `list[36] = list[100];`
   k. `list_type[47] = 92;`
   l. `list[40] = list[41] / 2;`

4. Change each of the following so that a **typedef** is used to define the array type:
   a. `char letter_list[26];`
   b. `char company_name[30];`
   c. `double score_list[30];`

5. Consider the array declared by

   ```
   int waist_sizes[5]
   ```

   a. Sketch how the array should be envisioned in memory.
   b. After assignments

   ```
   waist_sizes[0] = 34;
   waist_sizes[1] = 36;
   waist_sizes[2] = 32;
   waist_sizes[3] = 2 * 15;
   waist_sizes[4] = (waist_sizes[0] + waist_sizes[2]) / 2;
   ```

   have been made, sketch the array and indicate the contents of each component.

Why Computer Scientists Number Things from Zero to N − 1

In Chapter 1, we mentioned that C++ incorporates features of high-level programming languages that make programs easy to read, modify, and maintain, and features of low-level programming languages that give programmers control over the structure and behavior of real computers. The numbering of array indices from zero rather than one is one of the low-level features of the language that calls for further comment.

An array index is numbered from zero in C++ because of the way in which the individual array cells are represented and accessed in the computer's memory. You can think of the computer's memory as a huge stack of cells or little boxes. Each cell has an address, which allows the computer to locate it and either fetch data from it or store data in it. Now, suppose that five of these cells have to be allocated for a new array variable in a program. The computer locates the next available contiguous block of five cells, and copies the address of the first cell into a sixth cell. This address will be the **base address** of the entire array. Suppose this base address is 276 in our example, and a programmer wishes to store data in the second cell of the array. The address of the second cell, or 277, can be computed by taking the base address of the array, or 276, from the sixth cell and adding 1 to it. The address of the third cell can be obtained by adding 2 to the base address, the address of the fourth cell by adding 3, and so on. In general, the address of the Nth cell in an array can be computed by adding N − 1 to the base address. The value N − 1 is called the **offset** of the Nth cell from the base address. The offset of the first cell in any array is zero, and the offset of the last cell is N − 1, where N is the total number of cells in the array.

There is also a more important reason why an array index is numbered from zero. The address of the first cell in the entire memory of a computer typically is zero. The address of the last cell in memory is then N − 1, where N is the total number of cells in memory. You might think

that computer scientists are a weird bunch, having set up computer systems so that their internal components are numbered in a way that is consistently off by 1 from the way that ordinary folks would number them. However, there is a very good reason to number things from zero to N − 1 in computers. Each address must itself be capable of being stored in a memory cell in the computer. As you know, a memory cell can store a number of finite size. The size of the number represented depends on the number of bits available in the memory cell. In general, numbers ranging from zero to $2^N - 1$ can be stored in a memory cell containing N bits. For example, numbers ranging from 0 to 255 and representing the ASCII character set can be stored in eight-bit memory cells.

Most computer scientists agree that it would be better to number an array index from 1 to N in a high-level programming language. This notation would be more intuitive and agree with common sense. Some languages, like Pascal, allow the programmer to specify the lowest and highest index values when an array type is defined, and a Pascal programmer typically will define an index from 1 to N. The compiler then takes care of translating a reference like `a[1]` to the underlying machine address `a[0]`.

You might then ask why the designers of C++ still made array indexing a low-level feature of the language. The reason is that programmers can then manipulate arrays not just with standard indexing, but with **pointer arithmetic.** Assume the reference `a[1]` in C++ adds 1 to the base address of the array **a**. Then the reference **a** by itself is to the base address of the array. Therefore, the reference `*(a + 1)` locates the same array cell in memory as the reference `a[1]`. Needless to say, pointer arithmetic is an even lower level feature of C++ than regular indexing, and is not recommended for novices!

---

6. Let the array **money** be declared by

        double money[3];

Let **temp**, **x**, and **y** be **double** variables and assume **money** has the following values:

money

19.26	money[0]
10.04	money[1]
17.32	money[2]

Assuming **money** contains the values indicated before each segment is executed, indicate what the array would contain after each of the following sections of code:

a.
```
temp = 173.21;
x = temp + money[1];
money[0] = x;
```
b.
```
if (money[1] < money[0])
{
        temp = money[2];
        money[1] = money[1];
        money[0] = temp;
}
```
c.
```
money[2] = 20.0 - money[2];
```

7. Let the array **list** be declared by

```
double list[10];
```

Write a program segment to initialize all components of **list** to 0.0.

8.2 Using Arrays

Objectives

♦ to be able to use loops to input data into an array

♦ to be able to use loops to output data from an array

♦ to be able to assign array values by component assignment

Loops for Input and Output

One advantage of using arrays is the small amount of code needed when **for** loops are used to manipulate array components. For example, suppose a list of 100 scores is to be used in a program. If an array is declared by

```
const int MAX_LIST_SIZE = 100;
int scores[MAX_LIST_SIZE];
```

the values can be read into the array using a **for** loop as follows:

```
for (j = 0; j < MAX_LIST_SIZE ; ++j)
{
    cout << "Enter a score: ";
    cin >> scores[j];
}
```

Note that the control variable is initialized to 0, and that the comparison in the termination condition is a simple less than operator (**<**). The reason for this is that the index positions in the array have been defined to range from 0 to 99, inclusive. Note also that the size of the array, **MAX_LIST_SIZE**, is used both in the array variable declaration and in the **for** loop. If we want to change the size of the array, we need only change the value 100 in the constant definition, and not in the array variable declaration or in the loop. As always, the use of symbolic constants greatly enhances program maintenance. Note finally that a statement such as **cin >> score** will not have the desired effect. You may only read data elements into individual components of the array.

Loops can be similarly used to produce output of array components. For example, if the array of test scores just given is to be printed in a column,

```
for (j = 0; j < MAX_LIST_SIZE; ++j)
        cout << scores[j] << endl;
```

will accomplish this. If the components of **scores** contain the values

scores

78	scores[0]
93	scores[1]
.	.
.	.
82	scores[99]

the loop for writing produces

```
78
93
.
.
.
82
```

Note that you cannot cause the array components to be printed by a statement such as **cout << scores**. You must refer to the individual components.

Loops for output are seldom this simple. Usually we are required to format the output in some manner. For example, suppose the array **scores** is as declared earlier and we wish to print 10 scores to a line, each with a field width of five spaces. The following segment of code would accomplish this:

```
for (j = 0; j < MAX_LIST_SIZE; ++j)
{
        cout << setw(5) << scores[j];
        if (j % 10 == 0)
                cout << endl;
}
```

Loops for Assigning

Loops can also be used to assign values to array components. In certain instances, you might wish to have an array contain values that are not read from the keyboard. The following examples show how loops can be used to solve such instances.

Example 8.6

Recall array **a** in Section 8.1 in which we made the following assignments:

```
a[0] = 1;
a[1] = 4;
a[2] = 9;
a[3] = 16;
a[4] = 25;
```

These assignments could have been made with the loop

```
for (j = 0; j < 4; ++j)
    a[j] = (j + 1) * (j + 1);
```

Example 8.7

Suppose an array is needed whose components contain the letters of the alphabet in order from **'A'** to **'Z'**. Assuming you are using the ASCII character set, the desired array could be declared by

```
const int MAX_LIST_SIZE = 26;
char alphabet[MAX_LIST_SIZE];
```

The array alphabet could then be assigned the desired characters by the statement

```
for (j = 0; j < MAX_LIST_SIZE; ++j)
    alphabet[j] = char(j + 'A');
```

If **j** equals 0, we have

```
alphabet[0] = char(0 + 'A');
```

Thus,

```
alphabet[0] = 'A';
```

Similarly, for **j** equals 1, we have

```
alphabet[1] = char(1 + 'A');
```

Eventually we obtain

alphabet

'A'	alphabet[0]
'B'	alphabet[1]
'C'	alphabet[2]
.	.
.	.
.	.
'Z'	alphabet[25]

Assignment of values from components of one array to corresponding components of another array is a frequently encountered problem. For example, suppose the arrays **a** and **b** are declared as

```
const int MAX_LIST_SIZE = 50;
double a[MAX_LIST_SIZE];
double b[MAX_LIST_SIZE];
```

If **b** has been assigned values and you want to put the contents of **b** into **a** component by component, you must use the loop

```
for (j = 0; j < MAX_LIST_SIZE; ++j)
        a[j] = b[j];
```

Now suppose you tried a shortcut, by assigning one whole array variable to another:

```
a = b;
```

This assignment does *not* cause 50 assignments to be made at the component level. In some implementations of C++, the assignment will cause the name **a** to be an alias for the array **b**. The reason for this is that references to array variables are really references to the addresses of the arrays. In other implementations of C++, the assignment is a syntax error. It would be good practice to write a function that copies components from one array to another so you can use it in various programs.

Processing with Loops

Loops are especially suitable for reading, writing, and assigning array components, and they can be used in conjunction with arrays to process data. The following examples illustrate additional uses of loops for processing data contained in array variables.

Example 8.8

Recall the problem earlier in this section in which we read 100 test scores into an array. Assume the scores have been read and you now wish to find the average score and the largest score. Assume variables **sum**, **max**, and **average** have been appropriately declared. The following segment will compute the average:

```
sum = 0;
for (j = 0; j < MAX_LIST_SIZE; ++j)
        sum = sum + scores[j];
average = sum / MAX_LIST_SIZE;
```

sum
~~235~~
310

	scores
0	80
1	65
2	90
j = 3	75
.	.
.	.
97	93
98	86
99	79

For example, on the fourth time through the **for** loop, **sum** would accumulate from 235 to 310.

The maximum score can be found by using the following segment of code:

```
max = scores[0];
for (j = 1; j < MAX_LIST_SIZE; ++ j)
    if (scores[j] > max)
        max = scores [j];
```

max

~~80~~
90

scores

0	80
1	65
2	90
j = 3	75
.	.
.	.
97	93
98	86
99	79

For example, when **j** is 2, **max** would be updated from 80 to 90.

Example 8.9

Write a segment of code to find the smallest value of array **a** and the index of the smallest value. Assume the variables have been declared as

```
const int MAX_LIST_SIZE = 100;
double a[MAX_LIST_SIZE];
double min;
int index;
```

and the values have been read into components of **a**. The following code will solve the problem:

```
index = 0;
for (j = 1; j < MAX_LIST_SIZE; ++ j)
    if (a[j] < a [index])
        index = j;
```

index

~~0~~
~~1~~
3

a

0	80
1	65
2	90
j = 3	62
.	.
.	.
97	93
98	86
99	79

For these data, when **j** is 3, **index** would be updated from 1 to 3.

A standard problem encountered when working with arrays is that of not knowing exactly how many components of an array will be needed. In C++, the standard array data type has a fixed size. Thus, you must decide some upper limit for the length of the array. A standard procedure is to declare a reasonable limit, keeping two points in mind:

1. The length must be sufficient to store all the data.
2. The amount of storage space should not be excessive; do not set aside excessive amounts of space that will not be used.

■ Exercises 8.2

1. Assume the following array declarations:

```
typedef int num_list_type[5];
typedef bool answer_list_type[10];
typedef char name_list_type[20];
num_list_type list, scores;
answer_list_type answers;
name_list_type initials;
```

Indicate the contents of the arrays after each segment of code.

a.
```
for (j = 0; j < 5; ++j)
        list[j] = j / 3;
```

b.
```
for (j = 1; j < 6; ++j)
{
        list[j - 1] = j + 3;
        scores[j - 1] = list[j - 1] / 3;
}
```

c.
```
for (j = 0; j < 10; ++j)
        if (j % 2 == 0)
                answers[j] = TRUE;
        else
                answers[j] = FALSE;
```

d.
```
for (j = 0; j < 20; ++j)
        initials[j] = char(j + 64);
```

2. Write a test program to illustrate what happens when you try to use an index that is not in the defined range for an array; for example, try to use the loop

```
for (j = 0; j < 10; ++j)
        cin >> a[j];
```

when **a** has been declared as **int a[5];**.

3. Let the array **best** be declared by

```
int best[30];
```

and assume that test scores have been read into **best**. What does the following section of code do?

```
count = 0;
for (j = 0; j < 30; ++j);
        if (best[j] > 90)
                ++count;
```

4. Declare an array and write a segment of code to do the following:
    a. Read 20 integer test scores into the array.
    b. Count the number of scores greater than or equal to 55.
5. Declare an array using a **typedef** and write a section of code to read a name of 20 characters from a line of input.
6. Let the array **list** be declared by **int list[7];** and assume the components have values of

list

−2	list[0]
3	list[1]
0	list[2]
−8	list[3]
20	list[4]
14	list[5]
−121	list[6]

Show what the array components would be after the following program segment is executed:

```
for (j = 0; j < 7; ++j)
      if (list[j] < 0)
            list[j] = 0;
```

7. Assume array **a** is declared as

```
double a[100];
```

Write a segment of code that uses a loop to initialize all components to zero.
8. Let the array **n** be declared as **char n[21];** and assume the array components have been assigned the values

J	O	H	N		S	M	I	T	H
n[0]	n[1]	n[2]	n[3]	n[4]	n[5]	n[6]	n[7]	n[8]	n[9]

What output is produced by the following?
a.
```
for (j = 0; j < 10; ++j)
      cout << n[j];
cout << endl;
```
b.
```
for (j = 0; j < 5; ++j)
      cout << n[j];
cout << ", ";
for (j = 0; j < 4; ++j)
      cout << n[j];
cout << endl;
```
c.
```
for (j = 9; j >= 0; --j)
cout << n[j];
```

9. Assume an array has been declared as

```
int test_scores[50];
```

Write a segment of code to print a suitable heading (assume this is a list of test scores) and then output a numbered list of the array components.

8.3 Array Parameters and Functions

Objectives

◆ to be able to use functions to process arrays

◆ to be able to pass arrays as parameters to functions

◆ to understand the difference between array parameters and parameters of other data types

Functions can be used with array parameters to maintain a structured design. Consider the problem of computing the mean of a list of test scores. We can represent the list of scores as an array that can be passed to several functions for processing. A first-level pseudocode development of a solution to this problem is as follows:

1. Get the scores (function `get_data`)
2. Compute the average (function `calc_mean`)
3. Print a header (function `print_header`)
4. Print the results (function `print_results`)

The functions `get_data`, `calc_mean`, and `print_results` all take an array parameter and an integer parameter representing the number of data elements currently stored in the array. Here are the declarations of these functions:

```
// Function: get_data
// Gets list of scores from the user at
// the keyboard until a sentinel is entered
//
// Inputs: length, representing the maximum
// physical size of the list
// Outputs: an array of integers representing
// the list and length, representing its logical size

void get_data(int list[ ], int &length);

// Function: calc_mean
// Computes the mean of the scores in the list
//
// Inputs: an array of integers and its length
// Output: a real number representing the
// mean of the integers in the array

double calc_mean(int list[ ], int length);

// Function: print_results
// Displays the scores and the mean score
//
// Inputs: an array of integers and the mean
// on the screen

void print_results(int list[ ], int length, double ave);
```

There are several things to note about these declarations:

1. None of the arrays appears to be passed by reference to the functions, but they all are. The address of an actual parameter of an array is always passed to a function. In the case of actual parameters that are array variables, the corresponding formal parameters in the function will serve as aliases for the variables. Therefore, changes to the array cells referenced by a formal array parameter will also be changes to the array cells referenced by the actual parameter.

2. The maximum size of each array does not appear to be specified in the formal parameter declarations, where we see a pair of empty square brackets (**[ ]**). Because the arrays are all passed by reference, the computer does not have to know how large the actual array will be when a function is called. Leaving the physical size of the array unspecified in the formal parameter declaration will allow a function to be called with arrays of different physical sizes, as long as the element type (in this case, **int**), is the same.

physical size: The number of memory units available for storing data items in a data structure.

3. The **length** parameter for **get_data** represents the **physical size** of the array parameter when the function is called, and it represents the **logical size,** or number of data elements input, when the function returns.

logical size: The number of data items actually available in a data structure at a given time.

4. Though the form **<element type> <parameter name> [ ]** is most commonly used to declare array parameters, other forms may specify the physical size of the array or may precede the array parameter name with an array type name.

The implementation of **get_data** is

```
void get_data(int list[ ], int &length)
{
    int data, logical_length;

    logical_length = 0;
    cout << "Enter an integer (" << INPUT_SENTINEL
        << " to end input): ";
    cin >> data;
    while ((logical_length < length) && ! end_of_input(data))
    {
        list[logical_length] = data;
        ++logical_length;
        cout << "Enter an integer (" << INPUT_SENTINEL
            << " to end input): ";
        cin >> data;
    }
    length = logical_length;
}
```

Using two different lists and their lengths, **get_data** could be called by

```
const int MAX1 = 10;
const int MAX2 = 20;
```

```
int list1[MAX1];
int list2[MAX2];

int length1 = MAX1;
int length2 = MAX2;

get_data(list1, length1);
get_data(list2, length2);
```

The average score in a list could be computed by the function **calc_mean**.

```
double calc_mean(int list[ ], int length)
{
      int sum = 0;

      for (int j = 0; j < length; ++j)
            sum = sum + list[j];
      return double(sum) / length;
}
```

A function to print a heading would be written in a manner similar to that which we have used previously. If we want the output to be

```
Test Scores
-----------
99
98
97
96
95

The average score on this test was 97.00.
```

the function for the heading could be

```
void print_header()
{
      cout << endl;
      cout << "Test Scores" << endl;
      cout << "-----------" << endl;
      cout << endl;
}
```

A function to print the results could be

```
void print_results(int list[ ], int length, double ave)
{
      for (int j = 0; j < length; ++j)
            cout << setw(5) << list[j] << endl;
      cout << endl << setiosflags(ios::fixed | ios::showpoint)
            << setprecision(2);
      cout << "The average score on this test was"
            << setw(6) << ave << endl;
}
```

This function could be called by

```
print_results(scores, length, ave);
```

where **ave** is found by

```
ave = calc_mean(scores, length);
```

The important thing to remember about array parameters is that they are treated very differently than parameters of other data types in C++. For reasons of efficiency, the address of a C++ array variable (which is actually identified by the array name and also is the address of the first data value in the array) is always passed to a function expecting an array parameter. The following rules of thumb will help in designing functions for processing arrays:

1.   Never use the **&** symbol when specifying a formal array parameter in a function declaration or heading.

2.   Specify a constant array formal parameter, of the form **const <base type> <parameter name> [ ]**, when you want to guarantee that no changes will be made to the array variable being passed to a function.

The special nature of array parameters in C++ can be a source of confusion for beginning programmers. In Chapter 10, we develop a new array class that allows array parameters to be treated like parameters of other data types in C++.

As a final example, consider an operation to convert a string of digits to the corresponding integer value. This function, named **string_to_int**, expects a string of digits as an argument and returns the integer that the string represents. Its declaration is

```
// Function: string_to_int
// Returns the integer represented by a string of digits
//
// Input: a string of digits
// Output: the integer value that the string represents

int string_to_int(const apstring &str);
```

The statement

```
cout << string_to_int("4532") + 3 << endl;
```

would convert the string to an integer, add the two integers, and display the output

4535

Like arrays, the **apstring** class provides the **[ ]** operator to access individual characters within the data structure. We assume that each character in the string is a digit. The integer value of the *i*th digit in the string is thus

```
int(str[i] - '0')
```

The function sets a running total to zero, and then loops from left to right through the digits in the string. On each pass, the running total is multiplied by 10 and then the integer value of the current digit is added to this total. When the loop terminates, the total is returned.

```
int string_to_int(const apstring &str)
{
     int total = 0;

     for (int i = 0; i < str.length(); ++i)
          total = 10 * total + int(str[i] - '0');
     return total;
}
```

Exercises 8.3

1. Assume the following declarations have been made in a program:

```
typedef int row_type[10];
typedef double column_type[30];
typedef char string20_type[21];

row_type list1, list2;
column_type aray;
string20_type name1, name2;
int a[10];
int b[10];
```

Indicate which of the following are valid function declarations. Write an appropriate line of code that will use each valid declaration. Include an explanation for those that are invalid.

a. `void new_list(row_type x, column_type y);`
b. `void new_list(row_type &x, column_type &y);`
c. `void new_list(int x[ ]);`
d. `void new_list(row_type &x, row_type &y);`
e. `void new_list(row_type &row_type);`

f. `void word_week(int days[7]);`

g. `void surname(name x);`

h. `void surnames(string20_type x, string20_type y);`

i. `void get_data(int x, name &y);`

j. `void table(row_type &x, row_type &y);`

2. When possible, use the declarations of Exercise 1 to write function declarations so that each of the following statements in the main program is an appropriate call to a function. Explain any inappropriate calls.

a. `old_list (list1, aray);`

b. `change_list (list1, name1, b);`

c. `scores (a, b);`

d. `surname (string20_type);`

3. Write an appropriate function declaration and a line of code to call the function for each of the following:

a. A function to input 20 test scores into an array

b. A function to count the number of occurrences of the letter **'A'** in an array of 50 characters

c. A function to input integer test scores from the keyboard, count the number of scores, count the number of scores greater than or equal to 90, and save this information for later use.

4. Assume the following declarations have been made:

```
typedef int column_type[10];
column_type list1, list2;
```

Indicate the contents of each array after the call to the corresponding function.

a.
```
void sample (column_type &list1, column_type list2)
{
        for (int j = 0; j < 10; ++j)
        {
                list1[j] = j *j;
                list2[j] = list1[j] % 2;
        }
}

for (int k = 0; k < 10; ++k)
{
        list1[k] = 0;
        list2[k] = 0;
}
sample (list1, list2);
```

b. Replace the function call with

```
sample (list2, list1);
```

c. Replace the function call with consecutive calls

```
sample (list1, list2);
sample (list2, list1);
```

5. Write a function to examine an array of integers and then return the maximum value, minimum value, and number of negative values to the main program.
6. Discuss some of the implementation details you would need in order to read a list of names into an array.
7. Develop a function **int_to_string** that expects an integer argument and returns the corresponding string representation of the integer. (*Hint:* Build a string by using the operators **%** and **/** to obtain a series of digits from the integer.)

<table>
<tr><td>8.4</td><td>Sorting and Searching an Array</td></tr>
</table>

Objectives

♦ to be able to sort an array using a selection sort

♦ to be able to search an array using a sequential search

selection sort: A sorting algorithm that sorts the components of an array in either ascending or descending order. This process puts the smallest or largest element in the top position and repeats the process on the remaining array components.

Sorting an Array

Arrays often need to be sorted in either ascending or descending order. We consider here one of the easier methods for doing this, the **selection sort;** we examine another method, the *quick sort,* in Chapter 12.

Suppose we have an array **a** of five integers that we wish to sort from smallest to largest. The values currently in **a** are as depicted on the left; we wish to end up with values as shown on the right:

a
6	a[0]
4	a[1]
8	a[2]
10	a[3]
1	a[4]

a
1	a[0]
4	a[1]
6	a[2]
8	a[3]
10	a[4]

The basic idea of a selection sort is

For each index position *I*
1. Find the smallest data value in the array from positions *I* through length − 1, where length is the number of data values stored.
2. Exchange the smallest value with the value at position *I*.

The first pass through the loop produces

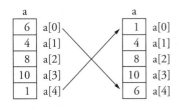

The second, third, and fourth passes produce

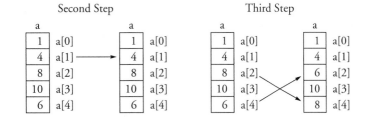

Fourth Step

a				a	
1	a[0]			1	a[0]
4	a[1]			4	a[1]
6	a[2]			6	a[2]
10	a[3]			8	a[3]
8	a[4]	→		10	a[4]

Notice that in the second pass, since the second smallest number was already in place, we did not exchange anything. Before writing the algorithm for this sorting procedure, note the following:

1. If the array is of length *n*, we need *n* − 1 steps.
2. We must be able to find the smallest number.
3. We need to exchange appropriate array components.

When the code is written for this sort, note that strict inequality (`<`) rather than weak inequality (`<=`) is used when looking for the smallest remaining value. The algorithm to sort by selection is

For each *j* from 0 to *n* − 1 do
    Find the smallest value among `a[j]`, `a[j + 1]`, ... `a[n - 1]` and store
       the index of the smallest value in **index**
    Exchange the values of `a[j]` and `a[index]`, if necessary

In Section 8.2, Example 8.9, we saw a segment of code required to find the smallest value of array **a**. With suitable changes, we incorporate this in the segment of code as a function, **find_minimum**, for the selection sort. We also develop a function, **swap**, that exchanges the elements in an array when necessary.

Using these two functions, the implementation of a **sort** function is

```
void sort(int a[ ], int length)
{
        int min_index = 0;

        for (int j = 0; j < length - 1; ++j)
        {
                min_index = find_minimum(a, j, length);
                if (min_index != j)
                        swap(a[j], a[min_index]);
        }
}
```

The function for finding the minimum value in an array takes three parameters: the array, the position to start the search, and the length or logical size of the array. The function returns the index position of the minimum element in the array. Its implementation uses a **for** loop:

```
int find_minimum(int a[ ], int first, int length)
{
      int min_index = first;

      for (int k = first + 1; k < length; ++k)
            if (a[k] < a[min_index])
                  min_index = k;
      return min_index;
}
```

The **swap** function exchanges the values of two integer variables:

```
void swap(int &x, int &y)
{
      int temp = x;
      x = y;
      y = temp;
}
```

Let us now trace this sort for the five integers in the array we sorted at the beginning of this section.

a
6	a[0]
4	a[1]
8	a[2]
10	a[3]
1	a[4]

For **j = 0**, **min_index = 0** (in **find_minimum**), and this produces

0

min_index

For the loop (in **find_minimum**) for **(k = 1; k < 5; ++k)**, we get successive assignments

k	min_index
1	1
2	1
3	1
4	4

The statements (in **swap**)

```
temp = a[j];
a[j] = a[min_index];
a[min_index] = temp;
```

produce the partially sorted array:

a

1	a[0]
4	a[1]
8	a[2]
10	a[3]
6	a[4]

Example 8.10

This example accomplishes these tasks:
1. Inputs real numbers from the keyboard.
2. Prints the numbers in a column of width six with two places to the right of the decimal.
3. Sorts the array from low to high.
4. Prints the sorted array using the same output format.

An expanded pseudocode development for this is
1. Print greeting (function **print_greeting**)
2. Read list (function **read_list**)
3. Output list of data (function **print_list**)
4. Sort list (function **sort_list**)
5. Output sorted list (function **print_list**)

```
// Program file: sort.cpp

// This program illustrates the use of a sorting algorithm
// with an array of reals.  Output includes data in both an
// unsorted and a sorted list.  The data are formatted and
// numbered to enhance readability.

#include <iostream.h>
#include <iomanip.h>
#include "bool.h"

const int MAX_LIST_SIZE = 5;
const double INPUT_SENTINEL = -999.0;

// Function: print_greeting
// Displays sign-on message about purpose of the program

void print_greeting();

// Function: read_list
// Reads data from keyboard into list
//
// Inputs: length represents physical size of list
// Outputs: a list of real numbers and its length,
// representing logical size of list

void read_list(double list[ ], int &length);
```

```
// Function: print_list
// Prints contents of list to terminal screen
//
// Inputs: a list of real numbers and its length

void print_list(double list[ ], int length);

// Function: sort_list
// Sorts contents of list into ascending order
//
// Inputs: a list of real numbers and its length
// Output: a sorted list of real numbers

void sort_list(double list[ ], int length);

// Function: end_of_input
// Informs caller whether or not input data
// is end-of-input sentinel
//
// Input: a real number
// Output: TRUE, if number is end of input sentinel,
// FALSE otherwise

// Function: find_minimum
// Finds position of minimum element in list between
// first and length
//
// Inputs: a list, the first position, and the length
// Output: the index position of the minimum element
// in the list

int find_minimum(double list[ ], int first, int length);

// Function: swap
// Exchanges two real numbers
//
// Inputs: two real number variables
// Outputs: the two variables, with their values exchanged

void swap(double &x, double &y);

bool end_of_input(double data);

int main()
{
    int length = MAX_LIST_SIZE;
    double list[MAX_LIST_SIZE];

    print_greeting();
    read_list(list, length);
    cout << endl;
```

```
        cout << "The original list is as follows:"
             << endl;
        print_list(list, length);
        sort_list(list, length);
        cout << endl;
        cout << "The sorted list is as follows:"
             << endl;
        print_list(list, length);
        return 0;
}

void print_greeting()
{
        cout << setiosflags(ios::fixed | ios::showpoint | ios::right);
        cout << setprecision(2);
        cout << endl;
        cout << "This sample program does the following:"
             << endl;
        cout << endl;
        cout << "1 Gets reals from the keyboard."
             << endl;
        cout << "2 Prints the data."
             << endl;
        cout << "3 Sorts the data from low to high."
             << endl;
        cout << "4 Prints a sorted list of the data."
             << endl;
        cout << endl;
}

void read_list(double list[ ], int &length)
{
        int logical_length = 0;
        double data;

        cout << "Enter a real number (-999 to stop input): ";
        cin >> data;
        while ((logical_length < length) && ! end_of_input(data))
        {
                list[logical_length] = data;
                ++logical_length;
                cout << "Enter a real number (-999 to stop input): ";
                cin >> data;
        }
        if (! end_of_input(data) && (logical_length == length))
                cout << "There is more data." << endl;
        length = logical_length;
}

void print_list(double list[ ], int length)
```

```
{
      cout << endl;
      for (int j = 0; j < length; ++j)
            cout << setw(12) << "<" << j + 1
                  << ">" << setw(6) << list[j] << endl;
}

void sort_list(double list[ ], int length)
{
      int min_index = 0;

      for (int j = 0; j < length - 1; ++j)
      {
            min_index = find_minimum(list, j, length);
            if (min_index != j)
                  swap(list[j], list[min_index]);
      }
}

int find_minimum(double list[ ], int first, int length)
{
      int min_index = first;

      for (int j = first + 1; j < length; ++ j)
            if (list[j] < list[min_index])
                  min_index = j;
      return min_index;
}

void swap(double &x, double &y)
{
      double temp = x;
      x = y;
      y = temp;
}

bool end_of_input(double data)
{
      return data == INPUT_SENTINEL;
}
```

The output for this program is

```
This sample program does the following:

    1 Gets reals from the keyboard.
    2 Prints the data.
    3 Sorts the data from low to high.
    4 Prints a sorted list of the data.
```

```
          The original data are as follows:

          <1>      34.56

          <2>      78.21

          <3>      23.30

          <4>      89.90

          <5>      45.00

     The sorted list is as follows:

          <1>      23.30

          <2>      34.56

          <3>      45.00

          <4>      78.21

          <5>      89.90
```

Searching an Array

The need to search an array for a value is a common problem. For example, you might wish to replace a test score for a student, delete a name from a directory or mailing list, or upgrade the pay scale for certain employees. These and other problems require you to be able to examine elements in some list until the desired value is located. When it is found, some action is taken.

The searching algorithm we examine is the most common method, a *sequential (linear) search*. We examined a similar search process for files in Section 7.2. This process is accomplished by examining the first element in some list and then proceeding to examine the elements in the order in which they appear until a match is found. Variations of this basic process include searching a sorted list for the first occurrence of a value, searching a sorted list for all occurrences of a value, and searching an unsorted list for the first occurrence of a value. We will look at another method, the *binary search,* in Chapter 12.

To illustrate a sequential search, suppose you have an array **list** of integers and you want to find the first occurrence of some particular target value. As you search the array, if the desired value is located, you want to return its position. If the value is not in the array, you return −1. The algorithm for such a search follows:

Set index to 0
Set found to FALSE
While **index < length** and not found do

> If **list[index]** is equal to target then
>> Set found to TRUE
>
> Else
>> Increment the index by 1
>
> If found then
>> Return index
>
> Else
>> Return −1

Note that the loop runs as long as the index can locate a value in the array and the target has not been found. A C++ sequential search function is

```cpp
int search(int target, int list[ ], int length)
{
        int index = 0;
        bool found = FALSE;
        while ((index < length) && ! found)
              if (list[index] == target)
                      found = TRUE;
              else
                      ++index;
        if (found)
              return index;
        else
              return -1;
}
```

Let's now consider some variations of this problem. Our code works for both sorted and unsorted lists. However, if we are searching a sorted list, the algorithm can be improved. For example, if the array components are sorted from low to high, we need to continue the search only until the value in an array component exceeds the value of **target**. At that point, there is no need to examine the remaining components. The only change required in the loop for searching is to add a middle alternative to the **if** statement.

```cpp
if (list[index] == target)
      found = TRUE;
else if (list[index] > target)        // Target not in list.
      index = length;
else
      ++index;
```

Note that the loop now terminates when the target "falls between" two data values in the sorted list.

A relatively easy modification of the sequential search is to return the number of occurrences of some value. To illustrate, if **list** is an array of integers and **target** has an integer value, we can search for the number of occurrences of **target** by

A Note of Interest

Computer Science and Women in Business

Among the rapid growth companies not to be overlooked are women-owned businesses. According to Peterson's Job Opportunities in Engineering and Technology, 1997, "There are six and one-half million women-owned businesses in the United States today. Virtually all of them have fewer than 250 employees. In each of the last five years, more than half of the three million businesses formed in the United States were started by a woman. Moreover, the gender profile of the personnel in a woman-owned company is typically two-thirds female."

Although women entrepreneurs are starting new businesses at a faster rate than their male counterparts, they have more difficulty attracting capital for new ventures. Thus, they tend to create businesses which substitute labor for capital.

Peterson continues by stating, "Women entrepreneurs have proven themselves heroines in the current United States economic recovery with the best and most expansive of [their businesses] growing from an average initial capital of $38,000 to an average valuation of $90 million in 15 years. They also are providing training grounds for their employees to leave and launch their own businesses, which creates an ever-widening circle of women hiring mostly women."

The Association for Computing Machinery (ACM) has taken an active role in promoting computer science as a career for women. The ACM Committee on the Status of Women has made the following recommendations:

◆ Ensure equal access to computers for young girls and boys and develop educational software appealing to both.
◆ Establish programs (such as science fairs, scouting programs, and conferences in which women speak about their careers in science and engineering) to encourage high school girls to continue with math and science.
◆ Develop programs to pair undergraduate women with women graduate students or faculty members who serve as role models, providing encouragement and advice.
◆ Provide women with opportunities for successful professional experiences (such as involvement in research projects) beginning as early as the undergraduate years.
◆ Establish programs that make women computer scientists visible to undergraduates and graduate students. Women can be invited to campuses to give talks or to serve as visiting faculty members (as, for example, in the National Science Foundation's Visiting Professorships for Women).
◆ Encourage men and women to serve as mentors for young women in the field.
◆ Maintain lists of qualified women computer scientists to increase the participation of women in influential positions such as program committees, editorial boards, and policy boards.
◆ Establish more reentry programs that enable women who have stopped their scientific training prematurely to retrain as computer scientists.
◆ Increase awareness of, and sensitivity to, subtle discrimination and its effects.
◆ Develop and enforce safety procedures on campus. Provide safe access at all hours to public terminal areas, well-lit routes from offices to parking lots, and services to escort those walking on campus after dark.
◆ Provide affordable, quality childcare.

To provide support for women computer professionals, several organizations have been established that focus on networking, including Systers, the Association for Women in Computing (AWC), and the International Network of Women in Technology (WITI).

```
int occurrences_of(int target, int list[ ], int length)
{
        count = 0;
        for (int index = 0; index < length; ++index)
            if (list[index] == target)
                 ++count;
        return count;
}
```

This code works for an unsorted list. A modification of the code for working with a sorted list is included as an exercise.

■ Exercises 8.4

1. Assume the array **column** is to be sorted from low to high using the selection sort.

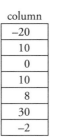

column

−20
10
0
10
8
30
−2

   a. Sketch the contents of the array after each of the first two passes.
   b. How many exchanges are made during the sort?

2. Write a test program that prints partially sorted arrays after each pass during a selection sort.

3. Change the code for the selection sort so it sorts an array from high to low.

4. Write a complete program to do the following:
   a. Read 10 reals into an array from the keyboard.
   b. If the first real is positive, sort the array from high to low; if it is negative, sort the array from low to high.
   c. Print a numbered column containing the sorted reals with the format of 10 columns of field width and two decimal places of precision.

5. Modify the selection sort by including a counter that counts the number of assignments of array elements made during a sort.

6. Using the modification in Exercise 5, sort lists of differing lengths that contain randomly generated numbers. Display the results of how many assignments were made for each sort on a graph. Use lists whose lengths are multiples of 10.

7. Suppose you have an array of student names and an array of these students' test scores. How would the array of names be affected if you sorted the test scores from high to low?

8.5 Two-Dimensional Arrays

Objectives

♦ to understand the need for representing the data for some problems as a two-dimensional grid

♦ to be able to represent this data structure as a two-dimensional array

♦ to be able to declare a two-dimensional array

♦ to be able to manipulate the components of a two-dimensional array

♦ to be able to use two-dimensional arrays with functions

Basic Idea and Notation

The arrays that we have been using thus far are **one-dimensional arrays,** in that we locate each data element in the array by specifying a single index position. However, suppose that we want to work with data that are best represented in tabular form. For example:

1. Box scores in baseball are reported with one player name listed for each row and one statistic listed for each column.

one-dimensional array: An array in which each data item is accessed by specifying a single index.

two-dimensional array: An array in which each data item is accessed by specifying a pair of indices.

2. A teacher's grade book lists one name for each row and an exam or lab score for each column.

In each of these cases, a multiple reference is needed for each data item. Other common computer applications, such as spreadsheets and bitmaps for graphics, also use tabular data with multiple reference.

In C++, multiple reference is accomplished with **two-dimensional arrays.** In these arrays, the row index precedes the column index. To illustrate, suppose we want to display the table

```
1   2   3   4
2   4   6   8
3   6   9   12
```

where we need to access both the row and column for a single data entry. The memory for this table could be produced by the following declaration:

```
int table[3] [4];
```

This memory can be visualized as three rows, each of which holds four integer variables. Thus, 12 memory cells have been reserved as shown:

table

The form for declaring two-dimensional arrays is

```
<item type> <array variable> [<rows>]  [<columns>]
```

A more maintainable declaration of this data structure would define the number of the rows and columns as symbolic constants and use a **typedef** to specify the type name for all tables.

```
// Define constants for bounds of tables

const int MAX_ROWS = 3;
const int MAX_COLS = 5;

// Define type for all tables
```

```
typedef int table_type[MAX_ROWS] [MAX_COLS];

// Declare two table variables

table_type table1, table2;
```

Now we have to consider how to access the data items in a two-dimensional array. As with one-dimensional arrays, C++ uses zero-based indexing to access data elements in a two-dimensional array. Thus, the first row is numbered 0, and the first column is numbered 0 also. Note that in the table

```
1    2    3    4
2    4    6    8
3    6    9   12
```

the 8 is in row 1, column 3. Therefore, in order to put an 8 in this position, we could use assignment statements, such as

```
row = 1;
col = 3;
table[row] [col] = 8;
```

Next, we could assign the values to the appropriate cells in **table** using 12 assignments, as follows:

```
table[0] [0] = 1;
table[0] [1] = 2;
table[0] [2] = 3;
table[0] [3] = 4;
table[1] [0] = 2;
table[1] [1] = 4;
table[1] [2] = 6;
table[1] [3] = 8;
table[2] [0] = 3;
table[2] [1] = 6;
table[2] [2] = 9;
table[2] [3] = 12;
```

As you can see, this is very tedious. Instead, we can note the relationship between the indices and the assigned values and use the variables **row** and **column** for the two indices. Each value to be assigned is then **(row + 1) * (column + 1)** and we can use nested loops to perform the assignments.

```
for (int row = 0; row < MAX_ROWS; ++row)
    for (int col = 0; col < MAX_COLS; ++col)
        table[row] [col] = (row + 1) * (col + 1);
```

Because two-dimensional arrays frequently require working with nested loops, let us examine what this segment of code does. When **row** equals 0, the loop

```
for (int col = 0; col < MAX_COLS; ++col)
        table[0] [col] = 1 * (col + 1);
```

is executed. This performs the four assignments

```
table[0] [0] = 1;
table[0] [1] = 2;
table[0] [2] = 3;
table[0] [3] = 4;
```

and we have the memory

table

1	2	3	4

Similar results hold for **row** equals 1 and **row** equals 2, and we produce a two-dimensional array that can be visualized as

table

1	2	3	4
2	4	6	8
3	6	9	12

Example 8.11

Declare a two-dimensional array and write a segment of code to produce the memory area and contents depicted.

0	1	2	3	4	5	6
1	2	3	4	5	6	7
2	3	4	5	6	7	8
3	4	5	6	7	8	9

An appropriate declaration is

```
const int MAX_ROWS = 4;
const int MAX_COLS = 7;

int table[MAX_ROWS] [MAX_COLS];
```

A segment of code to produce the desired contents is

```
for (int row = 0; row < MAX_ROWS; ++row)
        for (int col = 0; col < MAX_COLS; ++col)
                table[row] [col] = row + col;
```

Reading and Writing

Input and output with two-dimensional arrays resemble the same operations with one-dimensional arrays. In general, the forms to use are

---

<input stream> >> <array variable> [<row>] [<col>]

<output stream> << <array variable> [<row>] [<col>]

For example, consider the input and output of baseball statistics. Two arrays are required to represent the data. The first is a one-dimensional array of strings for the players' last names. The second is two-dimensional array of real numbers. Each row in this array contains the statistics for an individual player. Each column in the array represents a statistic. A very simple set of statistics might include at bats, hits, and batting average. When displayed, the data in these arrays might look like this:

Player	AB	HITS	AVE
Alomar	521	192	.369
Brett	493	180	.365
Canseco	451	160	.354
Dribble	590	205	.347
Hubble	501	167	.333
Marachino	485	156	.321
Noguchi	562	180	.320
Perez	499	159	.318
Sokoloski	480	149	.310
Tanenbaum	490	150	.306

It is clear that the two-dimensional array of statistics will need three columns. It will also need a number of rows that can accommodate the statistics for the maximum number of players allowed in the array of strings. Thus, the appropriate data declarations for these structures are

```
const int MAX_PLAYERS = 20;
const int MAX_ROWS = MAX_PLAYERS;
const int MAX_COLS = 3;

apstring players[MAX_PLAYERS];

double stats[MAX_ROWS] [MAX_COLS];

int num_players = 0;
```

Note the use of constants for maintainability. If the maximum number of players must be changed, the maximum number of player names in the array of strings and the maximum number of rows in the table of statistics will be updated automatically when the program is recompiled. The variable **num_players** maintains the number of players currently stored in the **players** array, which always equals the number of rows of data currently stored in the **stats** array.

When the **players** and **stats** arrays are initialized with the data in the tables, they can be visualized as

		0	1	2
Alomar	0	521	192	.369
Brett	1	493	180	.365
Canseco	2	451	160	.354
Dribble	3	590	205	.347
Hubble	4	501	167	.333
Marachino	5	485	156	.321
Noguchi	6	562	180	.320
Perez	7	499	159	.318
Sokoloski	8	480	149	.310
Tanenbaum	9	490	150	.306
players			stats	

To access a statistic for a player in the table, we use the index of the player in the **players** array as the row index and a number from 0 to 2 (0 = at bats, 1 = hits, 2 = average) as the column index. Thus, assuming that the index of Alomar is 0 and the column for average is 2, the average for Alomar can be look up with the expression

```
stats[0][2]
```

To output the contents of the arrays, we access the first array to display a player's name at the beginning of each line. We then loop through the corresponding row of numbers in the second array to display the player's statistics on the rest of the line. The code for this process follows:

```
// Display header of table

cout << "Player                        AB     HITS   AVE" << endl;

// Loop through number of players in array
```

```
for (int row = 0; row < num_players; ++row)
{

        // Output player's name

        cout << players[row];

        // Loop through numbers in a row

        for (int col = 0; col < MAX_COLS; ++col)
             cout << setw(10) << stats[row] [col];

        // Output end of line for row

        cout << endl;
}
```

Note that the number of rows occupied by data in the **stats** array may vary (depending on the number of players), but that each column in an occupied row always has data (every player has the same number of statistics).

The input process is slightly more complicated. We begin by prompting for a player's name. If the user enters a name containing just one character, this signals that the process is completed. Otherwise, we prompt for each statistic of the player, and enter the player's name into the **players** array and the statistics into their respective positions in the **stats** array. The code for this process follows:

```
num_players = 0;
cout << "Enter the player's name (or one letter to quit): ";
cin >> name;

// Halt process when name has 1 character or array is full

while((name.length() > 1) && (num_players < MAX_ROWS))
{
    // Store the name in the players array

    players[num_players] = name;

    // Enter the row of statistics for the player

    for (int col = 0; col < MAX_COLS; ++col)
    {
        switch (col)
        {
             case 0:  cout << "Enter at bats: ";
                      break;
             case 1:  cout << "Enter hits: ";
                      break;
             case 2:  cout << "Enter average: ";
        }
        cin >> stats[num_players] [col];
```

```
}

// Update the count of players and get the next name

++num_players;
cout << "Enter the player's name (or one letter to quit): ";
cin >> name;

}
```

Note the use of the **switch** statement to select the relevant prompt for a statistic.

We mentioned earlier that the maximum number of players allowed by this application can be changed easily. The number of statistics for each player is also fixed, but that too can be changed with a few modifications of our code segments. We first change the value of **MAX_COLS** in the constant definition section. Then, in the output process, we change the header to be displayed for the table to include the new names (such as **HR** for home runs). Note that no change is needed to output the new data values. Finally, we modify the **switch** statement in the input loop, so that the prompts for the new statistics appear in the appropriate order.

Manipulating Components

Once data have been stored in a two-dimensional array, they can be manipulated in much the same way as they are when they are stored in a one-dimensional array. For example, one might want to compute the average test score from a table of scores for students. Each row in the table contains an individual student's scores, and the number of rows equals the number of students in the class. Assuming that **table** is the name of this array, **num_students** names the current number of rows of data, and **num_scores** names the current number of scores in the table for each and every student, the following code segment would compute and output the average test score:

```
int sum = 0;
for (int row = 0; row < num_students; ++row)
     for (int col = 0; col < num_scores; ++col)
          sum = sum + table[row] [col];
cout << "The average score is "
     << sum / (num_students * num_scores) << endl;
```

As you can see, this process would move across each row in the table, adding the numbers in the row to the running total. When the additions are finished, the last line computes the total number of scores by multiplying the current number of rows by the current number of columns.

Another common manipulation of two-dimensional arrays involves placing the results of some computations in certain cells of the array. Spreadsheet applications are based on this idea. For example, in the case of a table of baseball statistics for players on one team, the cells in the last row of the table could be reserved for storing the totals of each column, except for the batting average column. In this last case, the average of all of the batting averages would be placed in the bottom cell. The table might be displayed as follows:

Player	AB	HITS	AVE
Alomar	521	192	.369
Brett	493	180	.365
Canseco	451	160	.354
Dribble	590	205	.347
Hubble	501	167	.333
Marachino	485	156	.321
Noguchi	562	180	.320
Perez	499	159	.318
Sokoloski	480	149	.310
Tanenbaum	490	150	.306
Totals	5072	1698	.335

The algorithm for computing a result for each column must traverse the two-dimensional array in a different order than we have seen in the examples thus far. The process starts at the top of a column and moves down that column to the last row of data, going row by row. To accomplish this pattern of movement, the outer loop of the algorithm uses the column as its control variable, and the inner loop uses the row as its control variable. Assuming that **table** is the name of this array and **num_players** names the current number of rows of data, the following code segment would describe the desired process:

```
int sum = 0;
for (int col = 0; col < MAX_COLS; ++col)
{
      sum = 0;
      for (int row = 0; row < num_players; ++row)
            sum = sum + table[row] [col];
      if (col == MAX_COLS - 1)
            table[MAX_ROWS - 1] [col] = sum / num_players;
      else
            table[MAX_ROWS - 1] [col] = sum;
}
```

Note how the **if** statement inside the loop handles the alternatives of storing a sum or storing an average, in the case of the column representing the batting averages.

In a real spreadsheet, not every result of every column needs to recalculated when a change of data occurs. In the case of the baseball statistics, if one player gets a hit, then all of the results will have to be recalculated. If the player gets an at bat with no hit, then only the results for at bats and batting average need to be recalculated.

Use with Functions

Two-dimensional arrays are passed as parameters to functions in the same way as other arrays. For example, we could package the code for displaying the table of baseball statistics in a function named **display_statistics**, and invoke it as follows:

```
display_statistics(players, table, num_players);
```

Note that the **players** and **table** arrays and the **num_players** integer variable are passed as arguments to this function. These data, and the global constants **MAX_ROWS** and **MAX_COLS**, represent all of the information that the function needs to perform its task. The function's declaration follows:

```
void display_statistics(apstring players[ ],
        double table[MAX_ROWS] [ ], int num_players);
```

Note the two different array parameter declarations. Recall that C++ allows the programmer to omit the physical size of a one-dimensional array when declaring the type of a formal array parameter, as follows:

```
void process_1d_array(int a[ ]);
```

When declaring the type of a formal two-dimensional array parameter in C++, the programmer must specify the physical size of the first dimension of the array. Thus, only the second of the following two function declarations is valid:

```
void process_2d_array(int a [ ] [ ]);

void process_2d-array (int a [MAX_ROWS][ ]);
```

The implementation of **display_statistics** displays the header for the table and then runs a nested loop to display the contents of each row:

```
void display_statistics(apstring players[ ],
        double table[MAX_ROWS] [ ], int num_players);
{
    // Display header of table

    cout << "Player              AB     HITS    AVE" << endl;

    // Loop through number of players in array

    for (int row = 0; row < num_players; ++row)
    {
        // Output player's name from the players array

        cout << players[row];

        // Loop through numbers in a row of the table array

        for (int col = 0; col < MAX_COLS; ++col)
            cout << setw(10) << stats[row] [col];

        // Output the end of line for the row

        cout << endl;
    }
}
```

Communication and Style Tips

1. Use descriptive identifiers when working with two-dimensional arrays. For example, row and col are appropriate identifiers for index variables, and **MAX_ROWS** and **MAX_COLS** are useful identifiers for specifying the upper bounds of an array type.

2. Remember that C++ does not report range bound errors with any arrays, so use care when indexing.

Exercises 8.5

For Exercises 1–3, declare a two-dimensional array for the tables described.

1. A table with real number entries that shows the prices for four different drugs charged by five different drug stores

2. A table with character entries that shows the grades earned by 20 students in six courses

3. A table with integer entries that shows the 12 quiz scores earned by 30 students in a class

4. Write a test program to read integers into a 3 × 5 array and then display the array components together with each row sum and column sum.

For Exercises 5–8, sketch the area of memory reserved for the data. In each case, state how many variables are available to the programmer.

5. ```
double shipping_cost_table[10] [4];
int grade_book_table[15] [6];
```

6. ```
type int matrix[3] [6];
matrix a, b;
```

7. ```
bool schedule[7, 3];
```

8. ```
const int QUESTIONS = 50;
const int ANSWERS = 5;
char table[QUESTIONS] [ANSWERS];
```

For Exercises 9–12, assume array **table** has been declared as follows:

```
int table3×5[3] [5];
```

Indicate the array contents produced by each of the following:

9. ```
for (int j = 0; j < 3; ++j)
        for (int k = 0; k < 5; ++k)
                table3x5[j] [k] = j - k;
```

10. ```
for (int j = 0; j < 3; ++j)
        for (int k = 0; k < 5; ++k)
                table3×5[j] [k] = j;
```

11. ```
for (int k = 0; k < 5; ++k)
        for (int j = 0; j < 3; ++j)
                table3×5[j] [k] = j;
```

12. ```
for (int j = 2; j >=0; --j)
        for (int k = 0; k < 5; ++k)
                table3×5[j] [k] = j % k;
```

For Exercises 13–15, let the two-dimensional array **table3×6** be declared by

```
int table3×6[3] [6];
```

Write nested loops to store the following values in **table3×6**:

13.

table3x6

3	4	5	6	7	8
5	6	7	8	9	10
7	8	9	10	11	12

14.

table3x6

0	0	0	0	0	0
0	0	0	0	0	0
0	0	0	0	0	0

15.

table3x6

2	2	2	2	2	2
4	4	4	4	4	4
6	6	6	6	6	6

16. Suppose you want to work with a table that has three rows and eight columns of integers.
   a. Declare an appropriate two-dimensional array for this table.
   b. Write a function that replaces all negative numbers in a table with zero.
   c. Show what is needed to call the function.

8.6 Graphics

Objectives

◆ to learn how to plot data using bar graphs and pie charts

◆ to learn how to construct an animation of an algorithm to visualize its behavior

Arrays are often used with graphics applications to hold data that are displayed as images. For example, the statistics for a company's sales for each quarter of a year might be stored in an array and displayed in a bar graph or a pie chart. Other applications use arrays in animations or to visualize the state of data in some system. In this section, we introduce the use of arrays in some graphics applications.

Bar Graphs

The basic graphics operation used in constructing bar graphs is the **bar** function. This function expects the coordinates of the upper left and lower right corners of the bar as arguments, and displays a solid rectangle whose fill color is the same as the border color. For example, the call

```
bar(10, 10, 40, 80)
```

does the same thing as

```
rectangle(10, 10, 40, 80);
floodfill(11, 11, getcolor());
```

The general form for calling the **bar** function is

```
bar(<left>, <top>, <right>, <bottom>)
```

It is possible to vary the color and pattern used to fill the interior of a bar. The **setfillstyle** function will do this. For example, the calls

```
setfillstyle(SLASH_FILL, RED);
bar(10, 10, 40, 80)
```

would fill the interior of a bar with red slashes.

Now suppose we want to plot the following array of grades for 30 students as a bar graph:

A—5
B—7
C—10
D—6
F—2

Before we develop an algorithm for drawing the graph, some issues must be considered:

1. What are the relative heights of the bars? That is, how many pixels per unit of data should we use? Because the range of our data is from 2 to 10, we choose 10 pixels per unit. Thus, the bar representing C's would be 100 pixels high.

2. Where do we want the bottom edges of the bars to be located? To center the graph vertically, we determine how much space is not being used by the tallest bar. Assuming that **list** is the name of the array and **find_maximum** is the name of a function that returns the largest value in an array of integers, then **find_maximum(list, 0, 5)** would return the value represented by the tallest bar. For the present graph, the tallest bar's height in pixels would be computed by

```
max_bar_height = getmaxy() - 10 * find_maximum(list, 0, 5)
```

To distribute half of these above and half below the graph, we would use the expression

```
bottom_edge = max_bar_height + (getmaxy() - max_bar_height) / 2
```

The *y* coordinate of the lower right corner of each bar would be **bottom_edge**. The *y* coordinate of the upper left corner of each bar would be **bottom_edge** minus the height of the bar in pixels.

3. How wide should our bars be? We pick an arbitrary width of 10 pixels.

4. How far apart should the bars be? Again, this depends on what looks nice. We use 10 pixels for the width of the trough here as well.

5. Where should the bars start? We can center the bars horizontally, or simply start at an arbitrary leftmost *x* coordinate. We opt for the latter course, picking 30 as the *x* coordinate of the upper left corner of the leftmost bar.

The following code segment pulls these ideas together:

```
num_bars = 5;
bar_width = 10;
trough = 10;
height_factor = 10;
max_bar_height = getmaxy() - height_factor
        * find_maximum(list, 0, 5);
bottom_edge = max_bar_height +
        (getmaxy() - max_bar_height) / 2;
left_edge = 30;
for (int i = 0; i <num_bars; ++i)
{
        bar(left_edge, bottom_edge - height_factor * list[i],
            left_edge + bar_width, bottom_edge);
        left_edge = left_edge + bar_width + trough;
}
```

The output of this code is depicted in Figure 8.1. The bar graph shown in this figure simplifies one of the important considerations in constructing bar graphs. That is, we allow our tallest bar to be 10 times the number of C's because the range of values is 2–10. In general, such easy choices are not available. A better method is to define the tallest bar to be a percentage, as an integer, of the vertical portion of the screen that you want to use. We call this percentage **height_factor**. For example, if the data values range from 100 to 1300 and one of the values is 685, the height in pixels for that bar would be

```
685 / 1300 * height_factor
```

An example using this method is included in the exercises for this section.

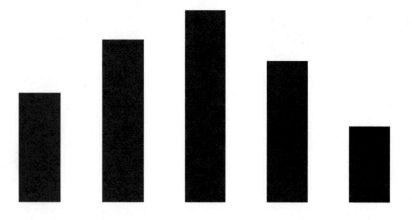

A bar graph of student grades

Pie Charts

The basic operation used in constructing a pie chart is the **pieslice** function. This function expects the same arguments as the **arc** function. **pieslice** displays a sector by drawing the specified arc and also connecting its end points to the center of the circle. For example, consider the statements

```
arc(100, 100, 0, 45, 50);

pieslice(100, 100, 0, 45, 50);
```

The images displayed by these statements are shown in Figures 8.2(a) and (b).

The general form for invoking **pieslice** is

pieslice(<center x>,<center y>, <start angle>, <end angle>, <radius>)

The sector is filled with the border color by default. The interior can be controlled by using **setfillstyle** to specify a particular pattern and color.

The size of the central angle of a sector in a pie chart corresponds to the height of a bar in a bar graph. To illustrate how to construct a pie chart, we can use the same data array of grades from the bar graph example. Because the total number of grades is 30, each grade must be represented by 360 / 30 (12) degrees. Thus, the central angle for representing the number of A's is 5 ∗ 12 (60) degrees. In general, the expression for computing the degree representation for each unit of data is

```
unit_angle_size = 360 / total_units
```

The central angle for each item is

```
central_angle = unit_angle_size * list[i]
```

◆ Figure 8.2(a)

The display produced
by **arc**
(100, 100, 0, 45, 50)

◆ Figure 8.2(b)

The display produced
by **pieslice**
(100, 100, 0, 45, 50)

The angles for the data in our example are listed in Table 8.1

We must next determine how to start and end each sector. The starting angle for the first sector is zero degrees:

```
start_angle = 0;
```

The ending angle for each sector is computed by adding its central angle to the current start angle:

```
central_angle = unit_angle_size * list[i];
end_angle = start_angle + central_angle;
```

To distinguish sectors, we use a different fill pattern for each one. The first pattern is a line fill:

```
pattern = LINE_FILL;
```

After each sector is drawn, the starting angle of the next sector is computed by setting it to the current ending angle. The next fill pattern is computed by incrementing it by one:

```
start_angle = end_angle;
++pattern;
```

▼ Table 8.1

Sizes of sectors in pie
chart for table of grades

Data Item	Number of Items	Sector Size in Degrees
A	5	60
B	7	84
C	10	120
D	6	72
F	2	24

A complete code segment to draw the pie chart uses a **for** loop like the one used for drawing the bar graph:

```
total_units = 30;
num_slices = 5;
center_x = getmaxx() / 2;
center_y = getmaxy() / 2;
radius = 100;
unit_angle_size = 360 / total_units;
start_angle = 0;
pattern = LINE_FILL;
for (int i = 0; i < num_slices; ++i)
{
        setfillstyle(pattern, getcolor());
        central_angle = unit_angle_size * list[i];
        end_angle = start_angle + central_angle;
        pieslice(center_x, center_y, start_angle,
                end_angle, radius);
        start_angle = end_angle;
        ++pattern;
}
```

Figure 8.3 shows the resulting pie chart.

Animating Sort Algorithms

Visualization of data is a very important application of graphics. For example, computer animations help scientists to visualize the behavior of subatomic particles.

To understand how visualization works, let us construct some animations of the selection sort algorithm discussed in Section 8.4. There are two ways in which the data might be displayed. The first visualizes the array of data as a row

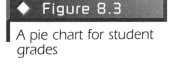

◆ Figure 8.3

A pie chart for student grades

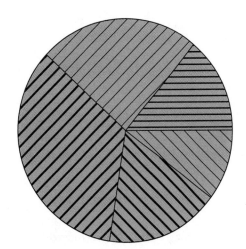

of rectangles containing the data values. The initial configuration of an array of six randomly positioned numbers might look like

When the algorithm runs and two values are exchanged, the rectangles move to their new positions on the screen. The directions of movement for the first exchange would be

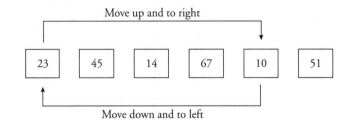

We develop a function called **display_list** to display the array before the algorithm starts. The function expects as arguments the array, the number of values currently stored in the array, the *x* and *y* coordinates of the upper left corner of the leftmost rectangle, the width of a rectangle, and the width of the trough separating the rectangles. We use the function **int_to_string**, developed in Exercise 7 of Section 8.3 to convert each integer data value to a string before it is drawn within a rectangle.

```
void display_list(int list[ ], int length,
     int left, int top, int rect_width, int trough)
{
     int right = left + rect_width;
     int bottom = top + rect_width;

     for (int i = 0; i < length; ++i)
     {
          rectangle(left, top, right, bottom);
          moveto(left + 2, top + (bottom - top) / 2);
          outtext(int_to_string(list[i]).c_str());
          left = right + trough;
          right = left + rect_width;
     }
}
```

The movement of two array cells during an exchange of data can be described by the following algorithm:
1. Move the smallest value down
2. Move the other value up

3. Move the smallest value to the left
4. Move the other value to the right
5. Move the smallest value up
6. Move the other value down

These movements are accomplished with four functions, **move_down**, **move_up**, **move_left**, and **move_right**. Each function expects as arguments the data value (as a string), its current index position in the array, its new index position, the rectangle's width, the trough's width, and the coordinates of the upper left corner of the leftmost rectangle. The functions **move_up** and **move_down** move the cell a distance of two cell widths.

Assuming that we are sorting a list of integers, the appropriate calls to the movement functions are added to the **sort_list** function. When two data values are exchanged on a pass through the main loop, the rectangle containing the smallest value is moved to the left; the rectangle containing the value at the beginning of the unsorted portion of the array is moved to the right.

```
void sort_list(int list[ ], int length,
     int left, int top, int rect_width, int trough)
{
     int min_index = 0;

     for (int j = 0; j < length - 1; ++j)
     {
          min_index = find_minimum(list, j, length);
          if (min_index != j)
          {
               // move smallest value down

               move_down(int_to_string(list[min_index]),
                    min_index, j,
                    left, top, rect_width, trough);

               // move other value up

               move_up(int_to_string(list[j]),
                    j, min_index,
                    left, top, rect_width, trough);

               // move smallest value left

               move_left(int_to_string(list[min_index]),
                    min_index, j,
                    left, top + rect_width * 2,
                    rect_width, trough);

               // move other value right

               move_right(int_to_string(list[j]),
                    j, min_index,
```

```
                    left, top - rect_width * 2,
                    rect_width, trough);

                // move smallest value up

                move_up(int_to_string(list[min_index]),
                        j, min_index,
                        left,top + rect_width * 2,
                        rect_width, trough);

                // move other value down

                move_down(int_to_string(list[j]),
                        min_index, j,
                        left, top - rect_width * 2,
                        rect_width, trough);

                // swap values in the array

                swap(list[j], list[min_index]);
            }
        }
}
```

Note the parameters that are passed to each of the movement functions. For example, in the call

```
    // move smallest value left

    move_left(int_to_string(list[min_index]),
            min_index, j,
            left, top + rect_width * 2,
            rect_width, trough);
```

the cell containing the smallest value has already been moved down. Therefore, we must compute the new y coordinate of its upper left corner (**top + rect_width * 2**) before passing this as a parameter to **move_left**. Then, by the time we move this cell up, its index position will be **j** rather than **min_index**, as shown in the call

```
    // move smallest value up

    move_up(int_to_string(list[min_index]),
            j, min_index,
            left,top + rect_width * 2,
            rect_width, trough);
```

The implementations of **move_up** and **move_left** follow:

```
void move_up(const apstring &value, int old_index, int new_index,
    int left, int top, int rect_width, int trough)
{
    // Compute initial coordinates of rectangle

    left = left + (rect_width + trough) * old_index;
    int right = left + rect_width;
    int bottom = top + rect_width;
    int forecolor = getcolor();
    int backcolor = getbkcolor();

    // Move up

    for (int k = 1; k <= rect_width * 2; ++k)
    {
        setcolor(backcolor);
        rectangle(left, top, right, bottom);
        moveto(left + 2, top + (bottom - top) / 2);
        outtext(value.c_str());
        --top;
        --bottom;
        setcolor(forecolor);
        rectangle(left, top, right, bottom);
        moveto(left + 2, top + (bottom - top) / 2);
        outtext(value.c_str());
    }
}

void move_left(const apstring &value, int old_index, int new_index,
    int left, int top, int rect_width, int trough)
{
    // Compute initial coordinates of rectangle

    left = left + (rect_width + trough) * old_index;
    int right = left + rect_width;
    int bottom = top + rect_width;
    int forecolor = getcolor();
    int backcolor = getbkcolor();

    // Move left

    int x_end = left - (rect_width + trough) *
        (old_index - new_index);
    for (int j = left; j > x_end; --j)
    {
        setcolor(backcolor);
        rectangle(left, top, right, bottom);
```

```
        moveto(left + 2, top + (bottom - top) / 2);
        outtext(value.c_str());
        --left;
        --right;
        setcolor(forecolor);
        rectangle(left, top, right, bottom);
        moveto(left + 2, top + (bottom - top) / 2);
        outtext(value.c_str());
    }
}
```

Each function begins by computing the initial position of the array cell, as a function of the input parameters. Each function then repeatedly erases the cell and its contents, computes their new position, and redraws them. The main program for testing this visualization would be similar to the one developed in Example 8.10.

```
// Program file: visual1.cpp

// Visualizes the sort of an array by
// displaying array cells as rectangles
// enclosing the values

#include <conio.h>
#include <graphics.h>
#include <iostream.h>

const int MAX_LIST_SIZE = 10;

int main()
{
        int length = MAX_LIST_SIZE;
        int list[MAX_LIST_SIZE];

        // Obtain data for list from user

        print_greeting();
        get_data(list, length);

        // Set the graphics mode

        int graphdriver = DETECT, graphmode;
        initgraph(&graphdriver, &graphmode, "c:..\\bgi");

        // Compute the position and size of the array

        int rect_width = 30;
        int trough = rect_width / 4;
        int left = (getmaxx() - length *
```

```
                        (rect_width + trough)) / 2;
        int top = getmaxy() / 2 - rect_width;

        // Display the array and pause for key to be pressed

        display_list(list, length, left,
                top, rect_width, trough);
        moveto(0, 0);
        outtext("Strike any key begin sorting");
        getch();

        // Animate the sort

        sort_list(list, length, left,
                top, rect_width, trough);

        // Pause for a key to be pressed

        moveto(0, 30);
        outtext("Strike any key to continue");
        getch();

        // Close the graphics mode

        closegraph();
        return 0;
}
```

scattershot diagram:
A plotting of points such that one coordinate represents a value and the other coordinate represents the index position of the value in a data structure.

The second method of visualizing the data being sorted is to plot the data as points on a two-dimensional grid, or **scattershot diagram.** Figure 8.4(a) shows the initial configuration of a sample data set of 250 values. Figure 8.4(b) shows the same data set halfway through a selection sort.

We allow data values only within the range of x and y coordinates in the two-dimensional grid. The y coordinate of a point in the grid is the data value being plotted. The x coordinate of a point is the data value's current index position in the array. Thus, when a data value reaches its final position in the array, the x coordinate of its point in the grid will be close to the data value itself. A completely sorted array can be visualized as a diagonal line running from the origin of the grid to its lower right corner. Note that the smallest values move to the upper right of the screen during the sort.

As in the previous example, we need to call two functions, **get_data** and **display_list**, before the sort process begins. Rather than allow the user to enter specific data values, **get_data** now randomly generates these from a range of values between 0 and one less than a user-specified upper bound.

```
void get_data(int list[ ], int &length)
{
        cout << "Enter the size of the list: ";
        cin >> length;
```

◆ Figure 8.4(a)

Initial configuration of unsorted array

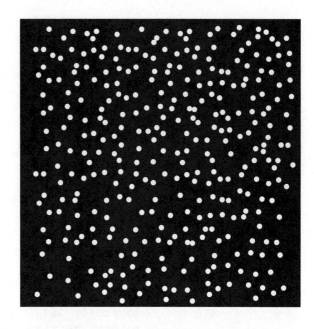

◆ Figure 8.4(b)

Configuration of array halfway through selection sort

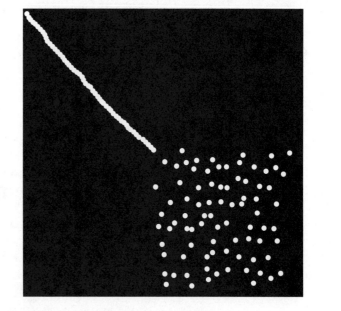

```
      if (length > MAX_LIST_SIZE)
            length = MAX_LIST_SIZE;
      for (int i = 0; i < length; ++i)
            list[i] = rand() % (length - 1) + 1;
}
```

Note that this function allows duplicate data values in the list. A modification to allow only unique data values is left as an exercise.

The function that initially displays the scattershot diagram uses `fillellipse` rather than `putpixel` to draw the points. We do this so that the viewer can easily see the points. The parameters `x_offset` and `y_offset` represent the dimensions of the points.

```
void display_list(int list[ ], int length,
      int x_offset, int y_offset)
{

      for (int i = 0; i < length; ++i)
            fillellipse(i + x_offset, list[i] + y_offset,
                  x_offset, y_offset);
}
```

The main program might define a default size of two pixels for each point. A more sophisticated method of sizing the points relative to the number of points plotted is left as an exercise.

When two data values are exchanged during the sort, the sort function first erases their points in the grid, swaps the data values in the array, and then redraws the points at their new positions.

```
void sort_list(int list[ ], int length,
      int x_offset, int y_offset)
{
      int min_index = 0;
      int forecolor = getcolor();
      int backcolor = getbkcolor();

      for (int j = 0; j <length - 1; ++j)
      {
            min_index = find_minimum(list, j, length);
            if (min_index != j)
            {

                  // Erase points at current positions

                  setfillstyle(SOLID_FILL, backcolor);
                  fillellipse(min_index + x_offset,
                        list[min_index] + y_offset,
                        x_offset, y_offset);
                  fillellipse(j + x_offset,
                        list[j] + y_offset,
                        x_offset, y_offset);
                  setcolor(backcolor);
                  circle(min_index + x_offset,
                        list[min_index] + y_offset,
                        x_offset);
                  circle(j + x_offset,
                        list[j] + y_offset,
```

```
                                        x_offset);
                          setcolor(forecolor);

                           // Move the values in the array

                           swap(list[j], list[min_index]);

                           // Draw points at new positions

                           setfillstyle(SOLID_FILL, forecolor);
                           fillellipse(min_index + x_offset,
                                list[min_index] + y_offset,
                                x_offset, y_offset);
                           fillellipse(j + x_offset,
                                list[j] + y_offset,
                                x_offset, y_offset);
                     }
                }
          }
```

The main program for this version of the sort animation resembles the previous version, except that the position of the grid need not be computed prior to running the algorithm.

```
// Program file: visual2.cpp

// Visualizes the sort of an array by
// displaying data values in a scattershot
// diagram

#include <conio.h>
#include <graphics.h>
#include <iostream.h>
#include <stdlib.h>
#include <time.h>

const int MAX_LIST_SIZE = 500;

int main()
{
      int length = MAX_LIST_SIZE;
      int list[MAX_LIST_SIZE];
      int x_offset = 2, y_offset = 2;

      // Initialize random number generator

      time_t seconds;
      time(&seconds);
      srand((unsigned int) seconds);
```

```
// Obtain data for list

print_greeting();
get_data(list, length);

// Set the graphics mode

int graphdriver = DETECT, graphmode;
initgraph(&graphdriver, &graphmode, "c:..\\bgi");

// Display the array and pause for key to be pressed

display_list(list, length, x_offset, y_offset);
moveto(0, getmaxy() - 30);
outtext("Strike any key begin sorting");
getch();

// Animate the sort

sort_list(list, length, x_offset, y_offset);

// Pause for a key to be pressed

moveto(0, getmaxy() - 20);
outtext("Strike any key to continue");
getch();

// Close the graphics mode

closegraph();
return 0;
}
```

Exercises 8.6

1. Review the discussion in this section about using relative bar heights where the tallest bar is defined to be of **max_bar_height**. Use this technique to write a segment of code to draw a bar graph of the values 120, 135, 180, 240, 290, and 345.

2. Find the average precipitation for the region in which your school is located. Write a code segment to enter these data into an array and display the results with a bar chart.

3. Write a code segment to display a color wheel using the **pieslice** function. The color should be changed every 45°.

4. How can colors and fill patterns be used to produce the outline of a sector? The interior should be the same as the screen background.

5. Discuss how the sectors of a pie chart can be labeled with text that describes the data displayed.

6. Write the function **move_right** for the algorithm animation discussed in this section.

7. The functions **move_left** and **move_right** discussed in this section both run code that moves images up and down a given number of pixels. Discuss how these operations might be packaged as functions.

8. The **get_data** function for initializing an array with randomly generated data values allows duplicate values. Modify this function so that only unique data values are stored in the array.

9. Modify the **sort_list** function so that the smallest data values are plotted in the lower left corner of the scattershot diagram.

Focus on Program Design: Case Study

The Home Sales Realty Company

The case study for this chapter features the use of arrays and functions. Because sorting an array is a common practice, it has been included as part of the case study. Suppose the Home Sales Realty Company wants to display a list of all sales for each month. Each sale amount is recorded on a separate line in a file. The number of homes sold is at most 20. Write a program to do the following:

1. Input the data from a file.
2. Display the data in the order in which it was read with a suitable header and format.
3. Display a sorted list (from high to low) of sales with a suitable header and format.
4. Display the total number of sales for the month, the total amount of the sales, the average sale price, and the company commission (7%).

Sample data would be

```
65000
56234
95100
78200
101750
56700
```

where each line represents the sale price of a home.

A first-level pseudocode development is

1. Get the list from the file (function **read_list**)
2. Display header for unsorted list (function **display_header**)
3. Display unsorted list (function **display_list**)
4. Sort the list (function **sort_list**)
5. Display header for sorted list (function **display_header**)
6. Display sorted list (function **display_list**)
7. Compute summary data (function **compute_summary**)
8. Display summary data (function **display_summary**)

Note that **display_list** and **display_header** are used twice.

Module specifications for the main modules are

Module: Read list
Task: Copy list of sales from file to array.

Input: A list of sales (real numbers), one per line, in a file
Output: An array of sales and the number of sales in the array

Module: Display list
Task: Display a numbered list of sales on terminal screen.
Input: A list of sales (real numbers) in an array and the number of sales

Module: Sort a list
Task: Sort a list of sales (real numbers) into descending order.
Input: A list of sales (real numbers) in an array and the number of sales
Output: A list of sales (real numbers) in an array, sorted into descending order

Module: Display header
Task: Display a header for the list of sales on the terminal screen.
Input: A string representing the header

Module: Compute summary
Task: Compute the total sales and the average sale.
Input: A list of sales (real numbers) in an array and the number of sales
Output: The total sales and the average sale, as real numbers

Module: Display summary
Task: Display the number of sales, total sales, the average sale on the terminal screen.
Input: The number of sales, total sales, the average sale

We represent the list of sales as an array of real numbers. The following data definitions simplify the declaration of variables and parameters for the list:

```
const int MAX_LIST_SIZE = 20;

typedef double list_type[MAX_LIST_SIZE];
```

We modify the selection sort function from Section 8.4 so that it finds the maximum value on each pass. This guarantees that the list is sorted in descending order. The **sort** function uses the helper functions **swap** and **find_maximum**.
The complete program for this problem is

```
// Program file: sales.cpp

// This program displays an unsorted and sorted list of
// sales for a month, followed by a summary that includes
// the number of sales, the total sales, and the average sale.

#include <iostream.h>
#include <iomanip.h>
#include <fstream.h>
#include "apstring.h"

const int MAX_LIST_SIZE = 20;
const double RATE = 0.07;
```

```
typedef double list_type[MAX_LIST_SIZE];

// Function name: read_list
// copy list of sales from file to array
//
// Input: a list of sales (real numbers),
// one per line, in a file
// Outputs: an array of sales and the
// number of sales in the array
void read_list(ifstream &in_file, list_type list,
      int &length);

// Function name: display_list
// Display a numbered list of sales on terminal screen
//
// Inputs: a list of sales (real numbers) in an array and
// the number of sales
void display_list(list_type list, int length);

// Function name: sort_list
// Sorts a list of sales (real numbers) into descending order
// Inputs: a list of sales (real numbers) in an array
// and the number of sales
// Output: a list of sales (real numbers) in an array,
// sorted into descending order
void sort_list(list_type list, int length);

// Function name display_header
// Display a header for the list of sales on the
// terminal screen
//
// Input: a string representing the header
void display_header(const apstring &header);

// Function name: compute_summary
// Compute the total sales, commission, and average sale
//
// Inputs: a list of sales (real numbers) in an array
// and the number of sales
// Outputs: the total sales, the average sale,
// and the commission as real numbers
void compute_summary(list_type list, int length,
      double &total_sales, double &average_sale,
      double &commission);

// Function name: display_summary
// Display the number of sales, total sales,
// commission, and average sale on the terminal screen
//
// Inputs: the number of sales, total sales,
```

```
// commission, and average sale
void display_summary(int length, double total_sales,
        double average_sale, double commission);

// Function name: find_maximum
// Find the index position of the maximum value
// in an array
//
// Inputs: a list of sales (real numbers) in an array
// and the first and last indexes bounding the search
// Output: the index position of the maximum value
int find_maximum(list_type list, int first, int length);

// Function name: swap
// Exchange the positions of two values
//
// Inputs: two variables
// Outputs: the variables with their values exchanged
void swap(double &x, double &y);

int main()
{
        ifstream in_file;
        apstring fname;
        list_type list;
        int length;
        double total_sales, average_sale, commission;

        cout << "Enter input file name: ";
        cin >> fname;
        in_file.open(fname.c_str());
        read_list(in_file, list, length);
        in_file.close();
        cout << setiosflags(ios::fixed | ios::showpoint | ios::right)
            << setprecision(2);
        display_header("An unsorted list of sales follows");
        display_list(list, length);
        sort_list(list, length);
        display_header("A sorted list of sales follows");
        display_list(list, length);
        compute_summary(list, length, total_sales,
            average_sale, commission);
        display_summary(length, total_sales,
            average_sale, commission);
        return 0;
}

void read_list(ifstream &in_file, list_type list,
        int &length)
{
```

```
        double data;

        length = 0;
        in_file >> data;
        while (! in_file.eof() && (length < MAX_LIST_SIZE))
        {
                list[length] = data;
                ++length;
                in_file >> data;
        }
}


void display_list(list_type list, int length)
{
        for (int i = 0; i < length; ++i)
                cout << setw(14) << "<" << setw(2) << i
                        << ">" << "$" << setw(11)
                        << list[i] << endl;
}


void sort_list(list_type list, int length)
{
        int max_index = 0;

        for (int j = 0; j < length - 1; ++j)
        {
                max_index = find_maximum(list, j, length);
                if (max_index != j)
                        swap(list[j], list[max_index]);
        }
}


void display_header(const apstring &header)
{
        cout << header << endl;
        for (int i = 1; i <= header.length(); ++i)
                cout << "-";
        cout << endl;
}


void compute_summary(list_type list, int length,
        double &total_sales, double &average_sale,
        double &commission)
{
        total_sales = 0.0;
        average_sale = 0.0;
        commission = 0.0;
        for (int i = 0; i < length; ++i)
                total_sales = total_sales + list[i];
        if (length > 0)
```

```
        {
                average_sale = total_sales / length;
                commission = total_sales * RATE;
        }
}


void display_summary(int length, double total_sales,
        double average_sale, double commission)
{
        cout << endl;
        cout << setw(10) << " " << "There were" << setw(3)
             << length << " sales." << endl << endl;
        cout << setw(10) << " " << "The total sales were $"
             << setw(12) << total_sales << endl << endl;
        cout << setw(10) << " " << "The average sale was $"
             << setw(12) << average_sale << endl << endl;
        cout << setw(10) << " " << "The company commission was $"
             << setw(11) << commission << endl << endl;
}


int find_maximum(list_type list, int first, int length)
{
        int max_index = first;

        for (int k = first + 1; k < length; ++k)
             if (list[k] > list[max_index])
                     max_index = k;
        return max_index;
}


void swap(double &x, double &y)
{
        double temp = x;
        x = y;
        y = temp;
}
```

Sample output from a run of this program is

```
        Enter input file name: salesdata
        An unsorted list of sales follows
        --------------------------------

                        < 0> $   65000.00
                        < 1> $   56234.00
                        < 2> $   95100.00
                        < 3> $   78200.00
                        < 4> $  101750.00
                        < 5> $   56700.00
```

```
A sorted list of sales follows
------------------------------

                < 0>  $ 101750.00
                < 1>  $  95100.00
                < 2>  $  78200.00
                < 3>  $  65000.00
                < 4>  $  56700.00
                < 5>  $  56234.00

         There were   6 sales.

         The total sales were $   452984.00

         The average sale was $   75497.33

         The company commission was $   31708.88
```

Running, Debugging, and Testing Hints

1. Do not attempt to use a subscript that is out of range. Suppose we have

   ```
   int list[6];
   ```

   An inadvertent reference such as

   ```
   for (int j = 0; j <= 6; ++j)
       cout << list[j];
   ```

   may produce mysterious results at run time.
2. Comparing array components to each other can lead to errors in using subscripts. Two common misuses are as follows:
   a. Attempting to compare **a[j]** to **a[j + 1]**. If this does not stop at **a[length − 2]**, then **j + 1** will be out of range.
   b. Attempting to compare **a[j − 1]** to **a[j]**. This presents the same problem at the beginning of an array. Remember, **j − 1** should have a value that is not less than zero.

   (continued)

3. Make sure the array index is correctly initialized, and that the termination condition evaluates all of the relevant subconditions. For example,

```
length = 0;
in_file >> data;
while ((length < MAX_ARRAY_SIZE) && ! in_file.eof())
{
        a[length] = data;
        ++length;
        in_file >> data
}
```

The first value is stored in **a[0]**, **a[length]** will not be referenced when **length == MAX_ARRAY_SIZE**, and **length** will indicate the number of data elements read when the loop is finished.

4. Make sure that all array elements referenced for their values have been initialized. Avoid using loops with **MAX_ARRAY_SIZE** as an upper bound, unless you are initializing an array. Use an integer variable, such as **length**, to maintain the number of data values currently stored in the array.

Summary

Key Terms

array

component (element) of
  an array

index (subscript)

logical size

one-dimensional array

physical size

range bound error

scattershot diagram

selection sort

sequential (linear) search

two-dimensional array

Key Concepts

◆ An array is a structured variable; a declaration of a single variable reserves several memory locations for data elements.

◆ It is good practice to use a symbolic constant to declare the size of array variables; for example,

```
const int MAX_ARRAY_SIZE = 10;
int list1[MAX_ARRAY_SIZE];
double list2[MAX_ARRAY_SIZE];
```

◆ Arrays can be visualized as lists; thus, the preceding arrays could be envisioned as

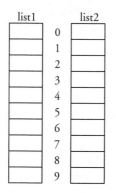

◆ Each component of an array is a variable of the declared type and can be used in the same way as any other variable of that type.

◆ Loops can be used to read data into arrays; for example,

```
length = 0;
in_file >> data;
while ((length < MAX_ARRAY_SIZE) && ! in_file.eof())
{
        a[length] = data;
        ++length;
        in_file >> data
}
```

◆ Loops can be used to print data from arrays; for example, if **scores** is an array of 20 test scores, the scores can be printed by

```
for (int j = 0; j < 20; ++j)
        cout << scores[j] << endl;
```

◆ Manipulating components of an array is generally accomplished by using the index as a loop variable; for example, assuming the preceding **scores** array, to find the smallest value in the array we can use

```
small = scores[0];
for (int j = 1; j < 20; ++j)
        if (scores[j] < small)
                small = scores[j];
```

◆ A selection sort is one method of sorting elements in an array from high to low or low to high. This sort repeatedly finds the minimum element in the unsorted portion of the array and exchanges it with the first element in that portion.

◆ C++ array parameters are always passed by reference and should not be declared as reference parameters.

◆ A sequential search of a list consists of examining the first item in a list and then proceeding through the list in sequence until the desired value is found or the end of the list is reached.

◆ Two-dimensional arrays may be specified by declaring a variable that has upper bounds on two indices:

```
int table[20] [10];
```

◆ References to cells in two-dimensional arrays specify the index of the row first and the index of the column second:

```
table[row] [col] = 125;
```

Chapter Review Exercises

Assume the following declarations are made:

```
int a [10];
char b [6];
double c [5];
int x = 7, y = 2,
double z = 0.0,
```

In Exercises 1–15, which are valid subscripted variables?
1. `a[0]`
2. `b[0]`
3. `c[0]`
4. `c[1.0]`
5. `b['a']`
6. `b[a]`
7. `a[x + y]`
8. `a[x % y]`
9. `b[x + y]`
10. `a[10]`
11. `c[10]`
12. `a[5]`
13. `a[x / z]`
14. `c[-1]`
15. `a[a[4]]`

For Exercises 16–21, assume that the array **a** defined in Exercises 1–15 contains the following values:

```
1  4  6  8  9  3  7  10  2  9
```

Indicate if the following are valid subscripts of **a** and, if so, find the value of the subscript. If invalid, explain why.
16. `a[2]`
17. `a[5]`
18. `a[a[2]]`
19. `a[4 + 7]`

20. `a[a[5] + a[2]]`
21. `a[sqrt(2)]`

For Exercises 22–26, write array declarations. Define array types using **typedef**, and declare the indicated variables.

22. **x**, an array of 5 integers
23. **z**, an array of 10 characters
24. **m**, an array of 100 real numbers
25. **t**, an array of 2 Booleans
26. **words**, an array of 20 strings

For Exercises 27–30, list the errors in the array declarations.

27. `int int_array[1.5];`
28. `bool boolean_array[int];`
29. `int int_matrix[10, 10];`
30. `double double_array[-10];`
31. Write a segment of code to store the first 10 even positive numbers into subscripts 1 through 10 of an array.
32. Write a segment of code that reads 20 integers from the keyboard and displays them in reverse order on the screen.

For Exercises 33–38, using the following table

table

5	8	12	9
4	6	1	10
11	2	7	3

indicate the value of each statement.

33. `table[2] [1]`
34. `table[0] [2]`
35. `table[2] [3]`
36. `table[1] [0]`
37. `table[2] [2]`
38. `table[0] [3]`
39. Write a declaration for **sample_table**.

sample_table

3	4	6	2	7
1	12	9	6	8

For Exercises 40–44, using **sample_table** from Exercise 39, write the proper expression for the table position that contains the value indicated.

40. 6
41. 2
42. 1
43. 12

44. 8
45. Suppose the contents of **sample_table** (Exercise 39) are read from the following input stream:

> 3 4 6 2 7 1 12 9 6 8

Write a fragment of code to input these data into the proper positions in **sample_table.**
46. Write a fragment of code to output **sample_table** (Exercise 39) in tabular form.
47. Write a fragment of code to add the values in columns 1 through 4 in each row of **sample_table** (Exercise 39) to the value in the column preceding it.
48. Write an appropriate function declaration to permit the passing of **sample_table** (Exercise 39) as a parameter to the function.

Programming Problems and Activities

1. Write a program to read an unknown number of integer test scores from the keyboard (assume at most 150 scores). Print the original list of scores, the scores sorted from low to high, the scores sorted from high to low, the highest score, the lowest score, and the average score.
2. Write a program to help you balance your checkbook. The input consists of the beginning balance and then a sequence of transactions, each followed by a transaction code. Deposits are followed by a "D"; withdrawals are followed by a "W." The output should consist of a list of transactions, a running balance, an ending balance, the number of withdrawals, and the number of deposits. Include an appropriate message for overdrawn accounts. Your program should represent the attributes and behavior of a transaction as a class.
3. One of the problems faced by designers of word processors is that of printing text without separating a word at the end of a line. Write a program to read several lines of text as input. Then print the message with each line starting in column 10 and no line exceeding column 70. No word should be separated at the end of a line.
4. Your local state university has to raise funds for an art center. As a first step, they are going to approach five previously identified donors and ask for additional donations. Because the donors wish to remain anonymous, only the respective totals of their previous donations are available for input. After the donors are contacted, the additional donations are listed at the end of input in the same order as the first 5 entries. Write a computer program to read the first 20 entries into one data structure and the second 5 entries into a second data structure. Compute the previous total donations and the new donations for the art center. Print the following:
   a. The list of previous donations
   b. The list of new donations
   c. An unsorted list of total donations
   d. A sorted list of total donations
   e. Total donations before the fund drive
   f. Total donations for the art center
   g. The maximum donation for the art center

5. Read in a list of 10 integers from the keyboard. Place the even numbers into an array called **even**, the odd numbers into an array called **odd**, and the negatives into an array called **negative**. Print all three arrays after all numbers have been read.

6. Read in 10 real numbers. Print the average of the numbers followed by all of the numbers that are greater than the average.

7. Read in the names of five candidates in a class election and the number of votes received by each. Print the list of candidates, the number of votes they received, and the percentage of the total votes they received sorted into order from the winner to the person with the fewest votes. You may assume that all names are 20 characters in length.

8. In many sports events, contestants are rated by judges with an average score being determined by discarding the highest and lowest scores and averaging the remaining scores. Write a program in which eight scores are entered, computing the average score for the contestant.

9. Given a list of 20 test scores (integers), print the score that is nearest to the average.

10. The game of Nim is played with three piles of stones. There are three stones in the first pile, five stones in the second, and eight stones in the third. Two players alternate taking as many stones as they like from any one pile. Play continues until someone is forced to take the last stone. The person taking the last stone loses. Write a program that permits two people to play the game of Nim using an array to keep track of the number of stones in each pile.

11. There is an effective strategy that can virtually guarantee victory in the game of Nim. Devise a strategy and modify the program in Problem 10 so that the computer plays against a person. Your program should be virtually unbeatable if the proper strategy is developed.

12. The median of a set of numbers is the value in the middle of the set if the set is arranged in order. The mode is the number listed most often. Given a list of 21 numbers, print the median and mode of the list.

13. The standard deviation is a statistic frequently used in education measurement. Write a program that, given a list of test scores, will find and print the standard deviation of the numbers. The standard deviation formula can be found in most statistics books.

14. Revise Problem 13 so that after the standard deviation is printed, you can print a list of test scores that are more than one standard deviation below the average and a list of the scores that are more than one standard deviation above the average.

15. The z-score is defined as the mean score earned on a test divided by the standard deviation. Given input data containing an unknown number of test scores (maximum of 100), print a list showing each test score (from highest to lowest) and the corresponding z-score.

16. Salespeople for the Wellsville Wholesale Company earn a commission based on their sales. The commission rates are as follows:

Sales	Commission (%)
$0–1000	3
1001–5000	4.5
5001–10,000	5.25
over 10,000	6

In addition, any salesperson who sells above the average of all salespeople receives a $50 bonus, and the top salesperson receives an additional $75 bonus.

Given the names and amounts sold by each of 10 salespeople, write a program that prints a table showing the salesperson's name, the amount sold, the commission rate, and the total amount earned. The average sales should also be printed.

17. Write a language translation program that permits the entry of a word in English, with the corresponding word of another language being printed. The dictionary words can be stored in parallel arrays, with the English array being sorted into alphabetical order prior to the first entry of a word. Your program should first sort the dictionary of words.

18. Elementary and middle school students are often given the task of converting numbers from one base to another. For example, 19 in base 10 is 103 in base 4 $(1 \times 4^2 + 0 \times 4^1 + 3 \times 4^0)$. Conversely, 123 in base 4 is 27 in base 10. Write an interactive program that allows the user to choose from the following:

```
<1>        Convert from base 10 to base A
<2>        Convert from base A to base 10
<3>        Quit
```

If option 1 or 2 is chosen, the user should then enter the intended base and the number to be converted. A sample run of the program would produce this output:

```
This program allows you to convert between bases. Which of the following would you
like?

<1>        Convert from base 10 to base A
<2>        Convert from base A to base 10
<3>        Quit

Enter your choice and press <Enter>. 1

Enter the number in base 10 and press <Enter>. 237

Enter the new base and press <Enter>. 4

The number 237 in base 4 is: 3231

Press <Enter> to continue

This program allows you to convert between bases. Which of the following would you
like?

<1>        Convert from base 10 to base A
<2>        Convert from base A to base 10
<3>        Quit

Enter your choice and press <Enter>. 2

What number would you like to have converted? 2332
```

```
Converting to base 10, we get:

2 * 1 = 2
3 * 4 = 12
3 * 16 = 48
2 * 64 = 128


The base 10 value is 190

Press <Enter> to continue

This program allows you to convert between bases. Which of the following would you
like?

<1>        Convert from base 10 to base A
<2>        Convert from base A to base 10
<3>        Quit

Enter your choice and press <Enter>. 3
```

19. You have been asked to write a program to grade the results of a true–false quiz and display the results in tabular form. The quiz consists of 10 questions. The data file for this problem consists of (1) correct responses (answer key) on line one, and (2) a four-digit student identification number followed by that student's 10 responses on each successive line. Thus, the data file would be of the form

    ```
    TFFTFTTFTT
    0461 TTFTTFTFTT
    3218 TFFTTTTFTT
      .
      .
    ```

    Your program should read the key and store it in the last row of a two-dimensional array. It should then read the remaining lines, storing the student identification numbers in a one-dimensional array and the corresponding responses in rows in the two-dimensional array. Output should consist of a table with three columns: one for the student identification number, one for the number of correct responses, and one for the quiz grade. Grade assignments are A (10 correct), B (9), C (8–7), D (6–5), F (4–0). Your output should also include the quiz average for the entire class.

20. Write a program to keep statistics for a basketball team consisting of 15 players. Statistics for each player should include shots attempted, shots made, and shooting percentage; free throws attempted, free throws made, and free throw percentage; offensive rebounds and defensive rebounds; assists; turnovers; and total points. Appropriate team totals should be listed as part of the output.

21. A magic square is a square array of positive integers such that the sum of each row, column, and diagonal is the same constant. For example,

16	3	2	13
5	10	11	8
9	6	7	12
4	15	14	1

is a magic square whose constant is 34. Write a program to input four lines of four positive integers from a data file. The program should determine whether or not the square is a magic square. Program efficiency should be such that computation ends as soon as two different sums have been computed.

22. Pascal's triangle can be used to recognize coefficients of a quantity raised to a power. The rules for forming this triangle of integers are such that each row must start and end with a 1, and each entry in a row is the sum of the two values diagonally above the new entry. Thus, four rows of Pascal's triangle are

```
            1
        1       1
     1      2      1
   1     3      3      1
```

This triangle can be used as a convenient way to get the coefficients of a quantity of two terms raised to a power (binomial coefficients). For example,

$$(a + b)^3 = 1 \times a^3 + 3a^2b + 1 \times b^3$$

where the coefficients 1, 3, 3, and 1 come from the fourth row of Pascal's triangle. Write a program to output Pascal's triangle for 10 rows.

23. The following table shows the total sales for salespeople of the Falcon Manufacturing Company:

Salesperson	Week 1	Week 2	Week 3	Week 4
Anna, Michael	30	25	45	18
Henderson, Marge	22	30	32	35
Johnson, Fred	12	17	19	15
Striker, Nancy	32	30	33	31
Ryan, Renee	22	17	28	16

The price of the product being sold is $1,985.95. Write a program that permits the input of the data in the table and displays both a replica of the table and a table showing the dollar value of sales for each individual during each week along with their total sales. Also, print the total sales for each week and the total sales for the company.

24. In the game of Penny Pitch, a two-dimensional board of numbers is laid out as follows:

```
1 1 1 1 1
1 2 2 2 1
1 2 3 2 1
1 2 2 2 1
1 1 1 1 1
```

A player tosses several pennies on the board, aiming for the number with the highest value. At the end of the game, the sum total of the tosses is returned. Develop a program that plays this game. The program should perform the following steps for a user-specified number of iterations:

Generate two random numbers for the row and column of the toss.
Add the number at this position to a running total.
Display the board, replacing the numbers with "P"s where the pennies land.

(*Hint:* you should use two two-dimensional arrays for this problem. The first array should contain the numbers shown above. The second array should contain Boolean values that indicate whether or not a penny has landed at a given position.)

25. Write an interactive program to display the grades for a class in the form of bar graphs and pie charts. The program should present the user with the following menu:

```
<1>        Enter grades
<2>        View bar graph
<3>        View pie chart
<4>        Quit
```

The program should insert grades entered by the user into an array. These data are displayed when the user selects menu choices **<2>** and **<3>**. Both the bar graph and the pie chart combine graphics and text in the display. The bar graph shows the letter grade below each bar. The pie chart should display a legend that explains the various shadings of the sectors. A title and continuation message should be part of each display.

26. Another method of displaying data in a graph is to plot the data as points in a coordinate system. The points are then connected by line segments. As in a bar graph, the data values correspond to vertical distances, with fixed horizontal distances between each point. The *y* axis is labeled with a description of the data being plotted and ticks indicating the data units. Add a module to Problem 25 that displays the data using this method.

Communication in Practice

1. One of the principles of good programming is that implementation details of data structures should be deferred to the lowest possible level. To illustrate, consider the following high-level design. A program requires you to work with a list of names and an associated list of numbers (student names and test scores). The first-level design follows:

   GetNames (function here);
   GetScores (function here);
   SortByName (function here);
   PrintNamesAndScores (function here);
   SortByScore (function here);

   Write complete documentation for each of these modules, including a description of all parameters and data structures required. Present your documentation to the class. Ask if your classmates have questions about the number or type of parameters, the data structures required, and/or the main tasks to be performed by each module.

2. Contact programmers at your local university and/or some businesses and discuss with them the use of lists as a data type. Ask what kinds of programming problems require the use of a list, how the programmers handle data entry (list length), and what operations they perform on the list (search, sort, and so on). Give an oral report of your findings to the class.

3. Contact someone who uses a spreadsheet as part of his or her daily work. Have the person show you several routine operations with the spreadsheet. In particular, find out how to adjust the size of the spreadsheet, sum rows, sum columns, and use functions to define entries for specfic locations. Give an oral report of your interview to your class. Explain how the various spreadsheet operations relate to what you have studied about two-dimensional arrays.

4. Select a programming problem from this chapter that you have not yet worked on. Construct a structure chart and write all documentary information necessary for the problem you have chosen. Do not write code. When you are finished, have a classmate read your documentation to see if precisely what is to be done is clear.

Building Structured Data: Structs and Classes

Chapter Outline

9.1 The Struct Data Type
9.2 Introduction to Classes
9.3 Object-Oriented Programming
     and Software Maintenance

     A Note of Interest: The Origins of the
     Object-Oriented Philosophy

9.4 A Rational Number Class

     A Note of Interest: Pure and Hybrid
     Object-Oriented Languages

9.5 Derived Classes and
     Inheritance

9.6 Graphics

T hus far in this text, you have been designing algorithms to solve problems, and coding your solutions in C++ using the major control structures of sequencing, selection, iteration, and functional abstraction. In the last two chapters, we began a shift in focus that will guide us through the rest of the text. We considered how to solve problems by structuring the data of a program appropriately, first with files (Chapter 7) and then with arrays (Chapter 8). In the present chapter, we continue this approach. We begin by examining a third kind of data structure provided by most programming languages. This data structure is called a *record* in some programming languages and a **struct** in C++. Unlike a file or array, which organizes data elements that are all of the same type, a struct organizes data elements that can be of different types. We then explore the development of some simple data structures using C++ **classes.** Classes are useful for building models of real-world objects. In the process, we begin the transition from a **procedural programming** style to an **object-oriented programming** style.

Basic Idea and Notation

Consider the problem of maintaining information for an employee of a company. This information might include a name, an address (street, city, state, and zip code), an age, and a salary. We could declare separate variables to store all of this information as follows:

```
apstring name, street, city, state, zip_code;
int age;
double salary;
```

9.1 The Struct Data Type

Objectives

◆ to understand the idea of a struct as a structured data type

◆ to be able to declare and use structs to represent and process information

◆ to be able to use functions with structs

◆ to be able to use structs to build more complex data structures

◆ to understand the benefits of data abstraction

◆ to be able to define abstract data types in libraries

struct: A data structure that can have components of different data types, accessible by name.

class: A description of the attributes and behavior of a set of computational objects.

procedural programming: A style of programming that decomposes a program into a set of functions or procedures.

object-oriented programming: A style of programming that decomposes a program into a set of communicating objects.

member: A component of a struct or class.

However, there are several problems with this way of representing the information:

1. We will have to repeat all of these declarations, using different variable names, for each employee used by an application.
2. If we want to add other kinds of information about an employee, such as length of service and job classification, we will have to add new variables for every employee in the application.
3. It might be useful to consider the information for an employee as one unit containing several items. For example, we might want to store several such units in an array of these units, or pass the unit as an argument to a function.

In C++, a convenient way to represent a collection of different data items as a unit is to use a struct. To return to our example of an employee's information, we could declare two struct variables, **employee1** and **employee2**, each of which contains the data elements for an employee, as follows:

```
struct
{
       apstring name, street, city, state, zip_code;
       int age;
       double salary;
} employee1, employee2;
```

When these struct variables are declared, the computer allocates memory for all of the components in both structs. These components are called *fields,* or members, of the struct. The form of a struct variable declaration is

```
struct
{
       <data type> <member name 1>;
       .
       .
       <data type> <member name n>;
} <list of struct variable names>;
```

The word **struct** is reserved. The members of a struct can be of any data type. There can be any number of members in a struct, but usually there are at least two.

The members of a struct are accessed by using a selector. A selector is formed by placing a period (.) between a struct variable and the name of a member. For example, the following code segment would initialize the members of the **employee1** variable to default values:

selector: The operator (.) used to access a member of a struct or class.

```
employee1.name = "John Doe";
employee1.street = "102 Maple Lane";
```

```
employee1.city = "York";
employee1.state = "PA";
employee1.zip_code = "12309";
employee1.age = 21;
employee1.salary = 10000.00;
```

The form for accessing a member of a struct variable is

<struct variable>.<member name>

After the statements in this code segment have executed, the memory for the **employee1** variable could be visualized as shown in Figure 9.1.

The important thing to note about a struct variable is that its name serves as a label for an entire group of data items, whereas each member name serves as a label for a data item contained in the struct variable.

◆ Figure 9.1

Visualization of a struct variable

```
                              employee1

               name      John Doe
               street    102 Maple Lane
               city      York
               state     PA
               zip_code  12309
               age       21
               salary    10000.00
```

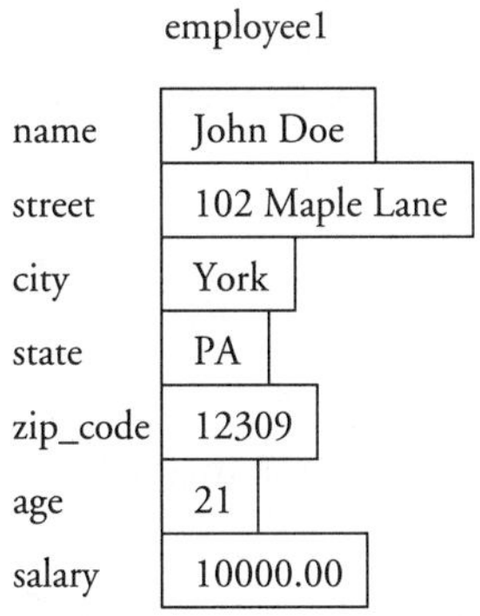

One manipulation of a struct variable as a unit is assignment. For example, the following statement would copy all of the members of **employee1** to **employee2**:

```
employee2 = employee1;
```

This statement would have the same effect as a series of assignments of all of the members.

```
employee2.name = employee1.name;
employee2.street = employee1.street;
employee2.city = employee1.city;
employee2.state = employee1.state;
employee2.zip_code = employee1.zip_code;
employee2.age = employee1.age;
employee2.salary = employee1.salary;
```

Note that the assignment of one struct variable to another struct variable has the desired effect of copying all of the data elements, whereas the assignment of one array variable to another array variable (see Chapter 8) does not.

As with arrays, it is often convenient to define a type name for a struct and use this name to declare struct variable names and struct function parameters. For example, the following code defines a struct type name, **employee_type**, and declares two variables of that type:

```
struct employee_type
{
        apstring name, street, city, state, zip_code;
        int age;
        double salary;
};

employee_type employee1, employee2;
```

The form for defining a struct type is

```
struct <new type name>
{
        <data type> <member name 1>;
        .
        .
        <data type> <member name n>;
};
```

Note that a semicolon (;) must immediately follow the right curly brace (}) at the end of the definition.

One advantage of this way of structuring the information is that an application has one place, the type definition, where the attributes of all employees are specified as members of a struct. Each variable of this type will then have its own memory allocated for its particular member values.

Another advantage of defining a type name for a struct is that this name can easily be used to build larger, more complex data structures. For example, an array could be declared to represent a list of 10 employees, as follows:

```
employee_type list[10];
```

Each component in this array would be a struct containing the members previously specified in the definition of **employee_type**. Thus, the expression

```
list[0]
```

accesses the first data element, an entire struct for an employee, within the array. The expression

```
list[0].name
```

accesses the **name** member of the first struct for an employee in the array.

The next three examples all assume the definition of **employee_type** as described earlier.

Example 9.1

Suppose that we wish to initialize an entire array of employee structures to default values. The following code segment sets the members of a temporary struct variable to these values, and then assigns the value of this variable to each location in the array.

```
// Declare a struct and an array of structs

employee_type employee;
employee_type list[10];

// Initialize the members of the struct
// to default values

employee.name = "John Doe";
employee.street = "102 Maple Lane";
employee.city = "York";
employee.state = "PA";
employee.zip_code = "12309";
employee.age = 21;
employee.salary = 10000.00;

// Copy the members of the struct into
// each struct in the array

for (int i = 0; i < 10; ++i)
        list[i] = employee;
```

Example 9.2

Assume that we wish to obtain information for each employee in the array from the user. A typical interaction for one employee in the series might be

```
Please enter information for employee 5

Enter the name: Simon Seeplus
Enter the street: 10 Hacker Lane
Enter the city: PCVille
Enter the state: WI
Enter the zip code: 34216
Enter the age: 19
Enter the salary: $40000.00
```

A code segment to perform this task would loop through the array and prompt the user for the input of each attribute of each employee.

```
employee_type list[10];
```

```
for (int i = 0; i < 10; ++i)
{
    cout << "Please enter information for employee "
        << i << endl << endl;
    cout << "Enter the name: ";
    getline(cin, list [i].name);
    cout << "Enter the street: ";
    getline(cin, list [i].street);
    cout << "Enter the city: ";
    getline(cin, list [i].city);
    cout << "Enter the state: ";
    cin >> list[i].state;
    cout << "Enter the zip code: ";
    cin >> list[i].zip_code;
    cout << "Enter the age: ";
    cin >> list[i].age;
    cout << "Enter the salary: $";
    cin >> list[i].salary;
}
```

Example 9.3

Suppose that we wish to display the information for each employee in the array in the following format:

```
Name:       John Doe
Address:    102 Maple Lane
            York, PA 12309
Age:        21
Salary:     $10000.00
```

Assuming that the application has declared and initialized the array **list** of 10 employees, a code segment for performing this task would be

```
for (int i = 0; i < 10; ++i)
{
    cout << "Name:      " << list[i].name << endl;
    cout << "Address:   " << list[i].street << endl;
    cout << "           " << list[i].city
        << "           " << list[i].state << " "
        << list[i].zip_code << endl;
    cout << "Age:       " << list[i].age << endl;
    cout << "Salary:    $" << list[i].salary << endl;
}
```

Another way in which a struct can be used to build more complex data structures is to use it to define another struct. For example, it might be convenient to treat the address of each employee as a single unit consisting of a street, a city, and a zip code. The following code segment defines a type name, **address_type**, to represent this information, and then uses this name to simplify the definition of the struct for an employee.

```
struct address_type
{
        apstring street, city, zip_code;
};

struct employee_type
{
        apstring name;
        address_type address;
        int age;
        double salary;
};

employee_type employee1, employee2;
```

The parts of an employee's address are now accessed by using more than one selector. For example, the expression

```
cout << "City: " << employee1.address.city << endl;
```

would output the **city** member (a string) contained in the **address** member (a struct) of the **employee1** variable (a struct).

Using Structs with Functions

In Chapter 8, we developed several functions for processing arrays. For example, the functions **read_list**, **sort_list**, and **print_list** expect

---

Communication and Style Tips

1. When working with complex information, try to simplify the way it is represented by grouping related data and treating them as a unit.
2. When the related data are of the same type and it is useful to access them in a definite order, use an array to group them.
3. When the related data are of different types and it is useful to access them by specifying names, use a struct to group them.
4. Like algorithms, data structures can be developed in a top-down fashion using stepwise refinement. Begin by defining the top-level data structure, such as a list of employees. Then work your way down (up in the program's text) to lower levels of data structures, such as the structure of an individual employee and the structure of an employee's address. This refinement will eventually lead you to a complete definition of the data structures necessary for an application.

arrays and their lengths as parameters. The functions perform the tasks of reading data into an array, sorting these data, and displaying them, respectively. The primary purpose of each function is to enable an application to treat a complex set of operations on the elements of an array as a single operation on a single data structure. This simplicity is evident in the following sequence of statements:

```
read_list(list, length);
sort_list(list, length);
print_list(list, length);
```

Functions can be used with structs in a similar way. Consider the code segments in Examples 9.1, 9.2, and 9.3. The code segments use loops to initialize an array of structs, input data into them, and display them. Most of the complexity of this code lies in the operations used to process an individual struct. Now assume that someone has provided functions named **init_employee**, **read_employee**, and **print_employee**. The first two functions return a value of type **employee _type**. The third function expects an argument of type **employee_type**. The following segment of code uses these functions to hide the detail of the tasks accomplished in the code segments of Examples 9.1 through 9.3:

```
// Declare the list of employees

employee_type list[10];

// Example 1: initialize the list of employees

for (int i = 0; i < 10; ++i)
    list[i] = init_employee();

// Example 2: input the list of employees

for (int i = 0; i < 10; ++i)
{
    cout << "Please enter information for employee "
        << i << endl << endl;
    list[i] = read_employee();
}

// Example 3: output the list of employees

for (int i = 0; i < 10; ++i)
    print_employee(list[i]);
```

Note that the reader of this application can now see what tasks are accomplished, for each employee, without having to read and understand how they are accomplished.

The use of types names for structs simplifies the declarations of functions that process them. The declarations of **init_employee** and **read_employee** expect no parameters and return a value of type **employee_type** (a struct).

```
// Function: init_employee
// Initializes the components of
// the structure of an employee
// to their default values
//
// Output: an employee structure

employee_type init_employee();

// Function: read_employee
// Prompts for and inputs the components
// of an employee structure
//
// Output: an employee structure

employee_type read_employee();
```

The implementations of these functions hide the details of setting the members of the employee's struct to the appropriate values. These details are similar to the code presented in Examples 9.1 and 9.2.

```
employee_type init_employee()
{
        employee_type employee;

        employee.name = "John Doe";
        employee.street = "102 Maple Lane";
        employee.city = "York";
        employee.state = "PA";
        employee.zip_code = "12309";
        employee.age = 21;
        employee.salary = 10000.00;
        return employee;
}

employee_type read_employee()
{
        employee_type employee;

        cout << "Enter the name: ";
        getline (cin, employee.name);
        cout << "Enter the street: ";
        getline (cin, employee.street);
        cout << "Enter the city: ";
        getline (cin, employee.city);
        cout << "Enter the state: ";
        cin >> employee.state;
        cout << "Enter the zip code: ";
        cin >> employee.zip_code;
        cout << "Enter the age: ";
        cin >> employee.age;
```

```
        cout << "Enter the salary: $";
        cin >> employee.salary;
        return employee;
    }
```

Note that each of these functions declares a local **employee_type** variable. This variable is used to store the values of the employee's attributes and is then returned as the value of the function.

The declaration of **print_employee** specifies a parameter of type **employee_type**.

```
    // Function: print_employee
    // Displays the components of the
    // structure an employee
    //
    // Input: an employee structure

    void print_employee(const employee_type &employee);
```

Note that the **employee** parameter is declared as a constant reference parameter. In C++, structs differ from arrays in that structs may be passed as value parameters, reference parameters, or constant reference parameters. When passed by value, all of the components of a struct (including array components) are copied into temporary storage locations. Therefore, to economize on memory, constant reference is the preferred parameter passing mode for structs when they have several members.

The implementation of **print_employee** is similar to the code shown in Example 9.3.

```
    void print_employee(const employee_type &employee)
    {
        cout << "Name:     " << employee.name << endl;
        cout << "Address:  " << employee.street << endl;
        cout << "          " << employee.city
            << " " << employee.state << " "
            << employee.zip_code << endl;
        cout << "Age:      " << employee.age << endl;
        cout << "Salary:   $" << employee.salary << endl;
    }
```

A final point to note about these functions is that they help to eliminate complex expressions, such as **list[i].age**, from a program. Instead, we see only expressions such as **employee.age** and **print_employee(list[i])**. In general, the presence of complex expressions, such as **list[i].age**, in a program is a sign that functions should be defined to manipulate the program's data structures.

Data Abstraction and Abstract Data Types

As a further step in our example of a list of employees, we might develop other functions for initializing, reading, and printing the entire list. The following function, **init_list**, is an example:

```
void init_list(employee_type list[ ])
{
        for (int i = 0; i < MAX_LIST_SIZE; ++i)
                list[i] = init_employee();
}
```

data abstraction: The separation between the conceptual definition of a data structure and its eventual implementation.

Note how the tasks of initializing a list of employees and initializing an individual employee have separate names and separate definitions. This separation of functions, whereby we associate a set of functions with each kind of data structure, is known as **data abstraction.** As you learned in Chapter 4, a function is an abstraction, in that it simplifies a complex task for its users. To simplify complex data for users, we need to provide two components:

1. A data structure, such as an array or a struct, preferably labeled with a type name

2. A set of functions that perform the operations on the data structure.

abstract data type (**ADT**): A class of objects, a defined set of properties of those objects, and a set of operations for processing the objects.

Data types that provide operations in this way are known as **abstract data types,** or ADTs. The primary benefits of an abstract data type are simplicity and ease of use. For example, the types **int**, **double**, and **apstring** are easy to understand and use because they are abstract—they come with sets of operations that literally say what they do without divulging the complex details of how they do it. We now provide a more formal definition of an abstract data type:

> *An abstract data type (ADT) consists of a set of values, a defined set of properties of these values, and a set of operations for processing the values.*

Note that the definition of an ADT makes no mention of how it is implemented, or even of the uses to which it may be put in a program.

Many ADTs in C++ are already defined in libraries. The library header file contains the type definitions for the data structures and the declarations of the functions for the ADT. The library implementation file contains the implementations of the functions. Thus, a programmer might provide some ADTs for other programmers by creating the appropriate library files.

As an example, an application that uses lists of employees would benefit by having library files for the **list_type** and **employee_type** ADTs. A very simple version of these ADTs might support just the operations for initializing, reading, and printing values that we explored earlier in this section.

Example 9.4

The header file for the **employee_type** ADT contains the definition of **employee_type** and the declarations of the functions **init_employee**, **read_ employee**, and **print_employee**. The file depends on the definition of the **apstring** ADT, so the **apstring.h** library header file is included.

```
// Library header file: employee.h

#ifndef EMPLOYEE_H

#include "apstring.h"

struct employee_type
{
        apstring name, street, city, state, zip_code;
        int age;
        double salary;
};

// Function: init_employee
// Initializes the components of
// the structure of an employee
// to their default values
//
// Output: an employee structure

employee_type init_employee();

// Function: read_employee
// Prompts for and inputs the components
// of an employee structure
//
// Output: an employee structure

employee_type read_employee();

// Function: print_employee
// Displays the components of the
// structure an employee
//
// Input: an employee structure

void print_employee(const employee_type &employee);

#define EMPLOYEE_H
#endif
```

Example 9.5

The header file for the **list_type** ADT contains the definitions of **MAX_LIST_SIZE** and **list_type** and the declarations of the functions **init_list**, **read_list**, and **print_list**. The file depends on the definition of the **employee_type** ADT, so it includes the header file **employee.h**.

```
// Library header file: list.h

#ifndef LIST_H
```

```
#include "employee.h"

const int MAX_LIST_SIZE = 100;

typedef employee_type list_type[MAX_LIST_SIZE];

// Function: init_list
// Initializes the list of employees
// to their default values
//
// Output: a list of employees

void init_list(list_type list);

// Function: read_list
// Prompts for and inputs the employees
// into the list
//
// Input: length, set to the maximum size of the list
// Outputs: length, set to the number of employees input
//          and the list of these employees

void read_list(list_type list, int &length);

// Function: print_list
// Displays the list of employees
//
// Inputs: a list of employees and its length

void print_list(list_type list, int length);

#define LIST_H
#endif
```

When designing ADTs for applications, the data can be organized in several ways. Sometimes, the advantage of one method, such as economy of memory or simplicity of code, is obvious when compared to other methods. Other times, the choice of organization depends on the personal taste of the programmer. The following example illustrates these points.

Example 9.6

The table of statistics for baseball players discussed in Section 8.5 is represented as a pair of arrays. The first array contains strings representing the players' names. The second array is two dimensional. Each column represents a kind of statistic (at bats, hits, batting average), and each row represents the set of statistics for a player. The two arrays are parallel, in that the index position of a player in the array of strings is used to locate the row of statistics for that player in the two-dimensional array.

An alternative plan for structuring these data places each player's name and statistics in an individual ADT called a player record. The table of player records is also an ADT, represented as a one-dimensional array of player records. The type definitions and a variable declaration for this design follow:

```
// Goes in library for player_record ADT

struct player_record
{
        apstring name;
        int at_bats, hits;
        double batting_average;
};

// Goes in library for table_type ADT

int MAX_PLAYERS = 20;

typedef player_record table_type[MAX_PLAYERS];

// Goes in main program file

table_type players_and_stats;
```

Note that in a real application, these definitions would not appear in the same file. Instead, the definitions of **player_record** and **table_type** would appear in separate library files for the respective ADTs. The declaration of the variable **players_and_stats** would appear in the main program file.

Communication and Style Tips

1. When designing a new data structure to solve a problem, begin by describing the operations that manipulate this structure. Declare these as C++ functions with the appropriate documentation.
2. Place the type definition of a new data structure and the function declarations for its operations in a library header file.
3. Implement the functions for a new data structure in a library implementation file.
4. Maintain a separate library for each new data structure that you develop.

■ Exercises 9.1

1. Explain the differences between arrays and structs as structured data types.
2. Use a **struct** to define a new type called **team_member**. This type should contain the components for a name, age, weight, height, and scoring average.

3. Use a **struct** to define a new type called **book**. This type should contain the components for a title, author, publication date, and price.

4. Use a **struct** to define a new type called **student**. This type should contain the components for a name, social security number, a list of four test scores, and the average of these scores.

For Exercises 5 and 6, draw a diagram of the memory allocated for the variables of the indicated types.

5. ```
   struct
   {
        apstring name, ssn;
        int num_of_dep;
        double wage;
   } employee;
   ```

6. ```
   struct
   {
        apstring location;
        int age, num_rooms, num_baths;
        double taxes, price;
   } house_info;
   ```

7. Assume that a new type has been defined as

   ```
   struct student
   {
        apstring name;
        int total_points;
        char letter_grade;
   };
   ```

   Write a function that computes a student's letter grade (A, B, C, or F) based on the cutoff levels of 90 percent, 80 percent, and 60 percent. Show how this function can be used in a program to set the appropriate member of a student structure.

8. Write a function named **equals** that takes two arguments of type **employee_type**, as defined in this section. The function should return a Boolean value indicating whether or not the **name** members in the two employee structures are the same.

9. Assume that a table of baseball statistics has been defined as in Example 9.6. Write a function to sort the data values in this table by ascending order of players' names.

10. Compare the two ways of structuring the data in Example 9.6, assessing their relative advantages and disadvantages.

11. Why is it a good idea to define a set of functions for each new data structure?

12. Write the type definitions that are necessary to represent a list of donors and their contributions, using an array of structs.

For Exercises 13–15, assume an array of structures as defined in Exercise 12. Write functions to solve each of the following problems.

13. Return the structure containing the maximum donation (or the first one encountered in the list if there are duplicates).

14. Return the average of all the donations.

15. Sort the list according to the size of the donation, with the largest one first.

16. Discuss the benefits of abstract data types, using examples.

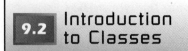

Introduction to Classes

Objectives

◆ to understand problems with data security that arise during the development of abstract data types

◆ to learn about implementing abstract data types as classes that guarantee data security

◆ to examine the implementation and use of an ADT as a class

Abstract Data Types and Data Security

Viewed as an abstract data type, the **employee_type** developed in the preceding section consists of a set of high-level operations, such as copying, comparisons, input, and output. Viewed as a C++ implementation, the **employee_type** consists of a **struct** type and several C++ function definitions. Though this implementation of the **employee_type** ADT is quite useful, it is not ideal. The primary problem is that the data in the implementation are not secure. There are too many ways in which users' modules can access the data and cause side effects. For example, the age in a given employee's structure should change only as a result of running certain employee processing functions, as follows:

```
init_employee(employee);      // Initialize all attributes

read_employee(employee);      // Input all attributes

increment_age(employee);      // Update the age attribute on
                              // the employee's birthday
```

However, given the scope rules of C++, nothing prevents the user of the **employee** variable from running statements like

```
employee.age = employee.age - 5;      // Makes employee younger
```

This statement is allowed by the language, but violates the intent of the programmers who provide the **employee_type** module. Errors due to side effects in large software systems are usually more subtle than this one. But the problem is quite general. What we would like to do is to develop a way of defining a data type that restricts the access that users have to the internal structure of the data to just those operations or functions provided by the data type. Program comments, warnings, and self-imposed restraint are not enough: These restrictions must be imposed by the compiler of the programming language. In other words, statements such as the last one should be prohibited outside of the module that implements the data type.

encapsulation: The process of hiding and restricting access to the implementation details of a data structure.

instance (synonym: **object**): A computational object bearing the attributes and behavior specified by a class.

Data Encapsulation, Classes, and Objects

An ADT should give users just a *logical view* of the data, in terms of the operations on it, so that users need not be concerned with the details of how the data are *represented*. For example, a string ADT might have operations for assignment, output, input, and comparisons. Ideally, the user of an individual string should not be able to access its component parts except by invoking these operations. If this is the case, the data are said to be **encapsulated.**

C++ allows programmers to define ADTs as classes. By defining an ADT as a class, we can restrict the access that users have to the data of any *objects*, or **instances,** of that class. An object is like an intelligent agent that takes a request for a service from a user and processes its own internal data to carry out the request.

We now show how to define and implement a class to represent bank accounts. Since this is our first opportunity to define and implement a C++ class, do not expect to master all of the details right away. However, we are not going to hide anything from you. We will develop other ADTs as classes in later chapters.

User Requirements for a Bank Account Class

The first step in developing a new class to solve a problem is to draw up a list of user requirements. These state the **attributes** and **behavior,** or operations, that users expect the class to have. A minimal set of attributes for a bank account might be the following:

1. A password (a string)
2. A balance (a real number)

The operations that users expect to perform on bank accounts follow:

1. Create a new account with default password and balance
2. Create a new account with user-specified password and balance
3. Change the password
4. Deposit money
5. Withdraw money
6. Observe the balance

These lists of attributes and operations can be visualized as shown in Figure 9.2.

attribute: A property that a computational object models, such as the balance in a bank account.

behavior: The set of actions that a class of objects supports.

◆ Figure 9.2

The attributes and operations of a bank account

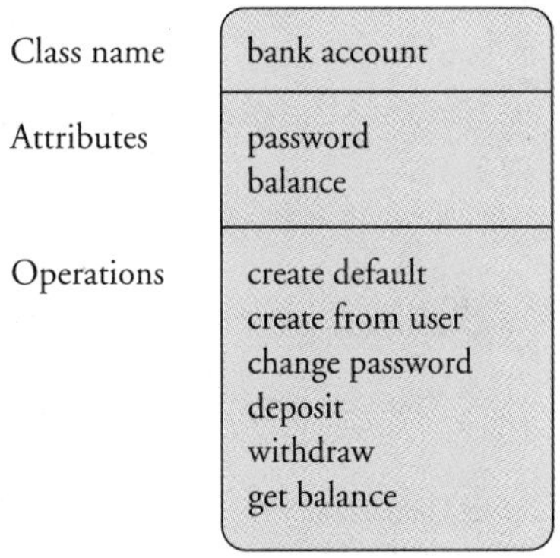

Class name	bank account
Attributes	password balance
Operations	create default create from user change password deposit withdraw get balance

Users expect the balance in an account to be secure. They do not want Smith's deposit going into Jones's account, unless it is a joint account. Access to an account's attributes cannot occur without knowledge of the owner's password. Thus, the owner's password must be passed as a parameter to the operations that observe or modify any of the attributes. Each of these operations will verify the validity of the password. If access is denied, each operation will return −1. Otherwise, some other value will be returned, such as the amount of the current balance. The withdrawal operation will return −2 if the user has insufficient funds.

Example 9.7

Assume that a class called **account** has been defined in a library file. The following driver program shows how to create and access a bank account object:

```cpp
// Program file: bankdriv.cpp

#include <iostream.h>
#include <iomanip.h>

#include "account.h"

int main()
{
    // Create two accounts and a dummy target

    account judy("beelzebub", 50.00);
    account jim("gadzooks", 100.00);
    account target;

    cout << setiosflags(ios::fixed | ios::showpoint)
         << setprecision(2);

    // Look up balances

    cout << "Judy's balance = $"
         << judy.get_balance("beelzebub") << endl;

    cout << "Jim's balance = $"
         << jim.get_balance("gadzooks") << endl;

    // An invalid password

    cout << "Result of invalid password = "
         << jim.get_balance("rosebud") << endl;

    // Make a deposit

    cout << "Depositing $20.00 to Jim, new balance = $"
         << jim.deposit("gadzooks", 20.00) << endl;

    // An attempted overdraft

    cout << "Result of overdraft from Judy ($51.00) = "
         << judy.withdraw("beelzebub", 51.00) << endl;

    // Copy to dummy target

    target = judy;
    cout << "Target's balance = $"
         << target.get_balance("beelzebub") << endl;
    return 0;
}
```

The output that this program produces is

```
Judy's balance = $50.00
Jim's balance = $100.00
Result of invalid password = -1.00
Depositing $20.00 to Jim, new balance = $120.00
Result of overdraft from Judy ($51.00) = -2.00
Target's balance = $50.00
```

Note the following points about this example:

1. The header file for the **account** class, **account.h**, is included like any other library header file.

2. Account objects are created by declaring them in much the same way as C++ variables. However, the parameters following the variable names in these declarations allow the programmer to set the values of the attributes of the objects when they are created. The form for this special kind of declaration is

> <class name> <variable name> (<parameter list>)

3. The operations on account objects use the syntax of member function calls that you learned in Section 3.6 and used with file streams in Chapter 7. Recall that the form of a member function call is

> <object name>.<function name> (<parameter list>)

and that member functions can expect parameters and return values like any other functions in C++.

Specifying the Operations

Once we have outlined the user requirements of a class, we can provide **formal specifications** for it. A formal specification describes the inputs, outputs, and any other assumptions about the data or the effects of an operation. We use preconditions and postconditions, as introduced in Chapter 5.

The names of the attributes of a bank account object are **my_password** and **my_balance**. The formal specifications of the bank account operations follow:

formal specification:
The set of preconditions and postconditions of a function.

Create operation (default values)

Preconditions : The account object is in an unpredictable state.

Postconditions: **my_balance** is set to 0.00, and **my_password** is set to an empty string in the account object.

Create operation (initial values specified)

Preconditions : The account object is in an unpredictable state, the parameter **password** is a string representing the password, and the parameter **balance** is a real number representing the initial amount to be deposited into the account.

(continued)

Postconditions: **my_password** is set to **password** and **my_balance** is set to **balance** in the account object.

Set password operation

Preconditions :   The account object is appropriately initialized, the parameter **password** is a string representing the password, and **new_password** is a string representing the new password.

Postconditions: If **password** and **my_password** are the same, **my_password** is set to **new_password**, and 1 is returned; otherwise, −1 is returned.

Deposit operation

Preconditions :   The account object is appropriately initialized, the parameter **password** is a string representing the password, and **amount** is the amount (a real number) to be deposited.

Postconditions: If the password is valid, then **my_balance** is increased by **amount**, and its value is returned; otherwise, −1 is returned.

Withdrawal operation

Preconditions :   The account object is appropriately initialized, the parameter **password** is a string representing the password, and **amount** is the amount (a real number) to be withdrawn.

Postconditions: If the password is valid, then if there are sufficient funds, **my_balance** is decreased by **amount**, and its value is returned. If the password is invalid, −1 is returned. If there are insufficient funds, then −2 is returned.

Get balance operation

Preconditions :   The account object is appropriately initialized, the parameter **password** is a string representing the password.

Postconditions: If the password is valid, then the value of **my_balance** is returned; otherwise, −1 is returned.

Assignment operation

Preconditions :   The target and source accounts are appropriately initialized.

Postconditions: The attributes of the source account have been copied into the target account, and a reference to the target account is returned.

As you can see, these specifications give users a precise idea of the assumptions that they must satisfy for the operations to run correctly. They also serve as a blueprint for declaring the operations as member functions of a C++ class.

Declaring a Bank Account Class

A description of an individual class in C++ consists of two parts, a **class declaration section** and a **class implementation section,** which are usually

class declaration section: An area of a program used to declare the data members and member functions of a class.

class implementation section: An area of a program used to implement the member functions of a class.

placed in separate files. This arrangement resembles the one we have used thus far for constructing a new library. The first file for our account class, called **account.h**, contains the declaration section of the class. Its text appears as follows:

```
// Class declaration file: account.h

#ifndef ACCOUNT_H

#include "apstring.h"

class account
{
        public:

        // Constructors

        account();
        account(const apstring &password, double balance);
        account(const account &a);

        // Accessor

        double get_balance(const apstring &password) const;

        // Modifiers

        int set_password(const apstring &password,
            const apstring new_password);
        double deposit(const apstring &password,
            double amount);
        double withdraw(const apstring &password,
            double amount);

        // Assignment

        const account& operator = (const account &a);

        private:

        // Data members

        apstring my_password;
        double my_balance;
};

#define ACCOUNT_H
#endif
```

The general form for writing a simple class declaration section in C++ is

```
<preprocessor directives>

<constant definitions>

class <class name>
{
        public:

        <public data declarations>
        <public function declarations>

        private:

        <private data declarations>
        <private function declarations>
};
```

data member: A data object declared within a class declaration module.

public member: A data member or member function that is accessible to any program component that uses the class.

private member: A data member or member function that is accessible only within the scope of a class declaration.

constructor: A member function used to create and initialize an instance of a class.

accessor: A member function used to examine an attribute of an object without changing it.

Several items call for comment:

1. The data and the functions belonging to a class are called its *members.* The data are called **data members,** and the functions are called *member functions.*
2. **Public members** can be referenced by any module that includes the class library. They should be restricted to the minimum necessary to serve users of the class.
3. **Private members** cannot be referenced directly by users of the class. Private member functions may be invoked indirectly by invoking public member functions, and private data members may be accessed indirectly by invoking public member functions.
4. The declarations of the member functions look exactly like the declarations of other functions in C++.
5. A semicolon must follow the right curly brace at the end of the class declaration.
6. The member functions belong to several categories, including
   a. **constructors,** which create objects of the class
   b. **accessors,** which return the values of attributes
   c. **modifiers,** which modify the values of attributes.
7. The operation to copy the attributes of one account to another account uses the assignment operator **=**.

Using a Class and Using a Struct

A good way to clarify what we have done in developing an account class is to compare its use with the use of a bank account represented as a struct. We could define a type for bank accounts with a struct as follows:

```
struct account_type
{
        apstring my_password;
        double my_balance;
};
```

modifier: A member function used to change the value of an attribute of an object.

Using this definition in the same program as the **account** class, we could run the following segment of code:

```
account first;                    // Create an object
account_type second;              // Create a struct

first.set_password("rosebud");    // Set members
first.deposit(50.00);             // of object

second.my_password = "shazzam";   // Set members
second.my_balance = 75.00;        // of struct
```

The state of the memory reserved for these variables after the code segment is run is shown in Figure 9.3. Note that the memory for the two variables seems to be represented in exactly the same way. However, the code for modifying the contents of the variables is quite different. **account** member functions must be used with the **account** object to modify its data members. Selectors can be used with the **account_type** (struct) variable to modify its members. Program statements of the following kind,

```
first.my_password = "rosebud";
first.my_balance = 50.00;
```

which use selectors to modify the data members of an **account** object, are illegal, unless the data members **my_password** and **my_balance** have been declared **public** in the **account** class.

◆ Figure 9.3

The state of the object and the state of the struct

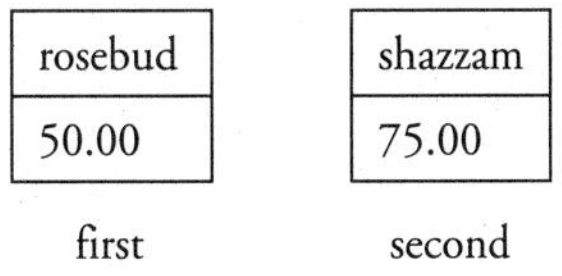

rosebud
50.00

first

shazzam
75.00

second

Implementing a Bank Account Class

The **account** class implementation file will have the form

```
// Class implementation file: account.cpp

<member function implementation 1>
    .
    .
<member function implementation n>
```

The headings of the function implementations must have the form

<return type> <class name>::<function name> (<optional parameter list>)

This form enables the compiler to resolve conflicts with the names of other, globally defined functions. Otherwise, data declarations and function implementations have the same syntax as those you have already seen in C++.

Creating Instances of a Bank Account Class with Constructors

Instances of a class, or objects, can be created in C++ in several ways. We can declare one or more instances as variables. If no constructors are provided in the class declaration, the computer creates the named instances and leaves their data members in an unpredictable state, just as with ordinary C++ variable declarations. To guarantee that new instances of a class always have their data members initialized, you should declare constructors for that purpose.

Default Constructors

Our **account** class declaration specifies three class constructors. The first constructor, **account()**, is run when a program declares account variables as in the following code:

```
account first, second;
account list[10];
```

default constructor:
A member function that creates and provides reasonable initial values for the data within an object.

This kind of constructor is called a **default constructor.** It should provide reasonable initial values for the attributes of an object when the user does not specify them. The implementation of the default constructor for an account sets the password to an empty string and the balance to zero:

```
account::account()
{
    my_password = "";
    my_balance = 0.00;
}
```

Note that the implementation references the data members for the account object even though they are not declared as parameters. The use of the prefix **account::** in a function heading allows the data members and other member functions of the **account** class to be visible in the function implementation. Note also that the constructor has no return type.

Constructors for Specifying Initial Values

The second constructor,

```
account(const apstring &password, double balance);
```

is run when users wish to declare an account variable with specified attributes, as in the code

```
account judy("beelzebub", 100.00);
```

The user appears to pass two values as parameters to the variable **judy**. In this example, what really happens is that the computer runs the second constructor. The implementation of this constructor assigns the values of the parameters to the corresponding data members of the account object.

```
account::account(const apstring &password,
    double balance)
{
    my_password = password;
    my_balance = balance;
}
```

Copy Constructors

copy constructor:
A member function defined by the programmer and automatically used by the computer to copy the values of objects when they are passed by value to functions.

The third constructor is called the **copy constructor** for the **account** class. This function is run whenever an account object is passed by value as a parameter to a function. Recall that when C++ passes data by value in a parameter, the data value is copied to a temporary memory location for the use of the function. If a class does not specify its own copy constructor, the computer performs what is known as a *shallow copy* of the object when it is passed by value. In a shallow copy, not all of the object's data members are necessarily copied into temporary memory locations. To guarantee a complete copy in all situations, we define a copy constructor that takes another account object as a parameter:

```
account::account(const account &a)
{
    my_password = a.my_password;
    my_balance = a.my_balance;
}
```

Note that the parameter, an account object, is passed by constant reference. The data members of the new account object, called the *receiver object,* are referenced by name. The data members of the account object to be copied, called the *parameter object,* are accessed by the selector notation used with C++ structs. In general, any of the data members of a parameter like this one can be accessed within a member function in the class implementation by using the form

```
<parameter name>.<data member name>
```

const function: A member function that does not allow changes to the attributes of an object.

Accessors and Modifiers

The role of accessor functions is to allow users to observe the attributes of an object without changing them. To guarantee that no changes occur, we can declare an accessor function as a **const function,** using the form

<return type> <function name> (<formal parameter declarations>) **const;**

The implementation of the accessor function for account objects, **get_balance**, follows:

```
double account::get_balance(const apstring &password) const
{
    if (password == my_password)
        return my_balance;
    else
        return -1;
}
```

The role of modifier functions is to set one or more of the attributes of an object to new values. We provide the implementation of the **withdraw** modifier function for account objects, and leave the rest as exercises.

```
double account::withdraw(const apstring &password,
    double amount)
{
    if (password == my_password)
        if ((amount >= 0) && (amount <= my_balance))
        {
            my_balance = my_balance - amount;
            return my_balance;
        }
        else
            return -2;   // Invalid amount
    else
        return -1;   // Invalid password
}
```

Note the logic of the nested **if** statements in this function. Two conditions must be satisfied to update the balance and return its value. Otherwise, the function returns different negative values to indicate an invalid amount or an invalid password.

The Assignment Operator, Polymorphism, and Overloading

polymorphism: The property of one operator symbol or function identifier having many meanings.

Many of the built-in operators in C++ are **polymorphic,** which means "many structures." For example, **+**, **==**, and **>>** are polymorphic for integers and real numbers. This means that the same operators designate the same general operations (arithmetic, comparions, input/output), even though the actual operations performed may vary with the type or structure of the operands. (Think of the difference between scanning input characters and converting them to an integer and doing the same thing for a real number, even though the symbol **>>** is used for both.)

C++ allows a programmer to reuse any built-in operator (or function name, also) to designate an operation on new data types. This process is called **overloading** an operation. For example, rather than use the named function

overloading: The process of using the same operator symbol or identifier to refer to many different functions.

```
copy(account1, account2)
```

programmers can use

```
account1 = account2
```

We begin by specifying the declaration of the member function to be overloaded:

```
const account& operator = (const account &a);
```

Note that **operator** is a reserved word in C++. The receiver object will be the left operand of the assignment, and the parameter object will serve as the right operand. The general form for specifying operators is

<return type> **operator** <standard operator symbol> (<parameter list>);

The implementation is written by placing a similar form in the function heading. If the target and the source objects are not the same object, the function copies the data members of the source object to the target object. The function returns a reference to the target object.

```
const account& account::operator = (const account &a)
{
        if (this != &a)
        {
                my_password = a.my_password;
                my_balance = a.my_balance;
        }
        return *this;
}
```

Note the following points:

1. The reserved word **this** always refers to the address of the receiver object. The expression **&a** returns the address of the parameter object **a**. Thus, the expression **(this != &a)** returns **TRUE** if the operands are addresses of different objects.

2. The assignment operator in C++ should normally return an **l-value**. An l-value is an object that can be the target of an assignment operation in C++. In the case of simple assignment statements such as **a = b;**, the l-value returned by the operation is not used. However, in the case of a *cascade* of assignments, such as **(a = b) = c;**, the expression

l-value: A computational object capable of being the target of an assignment statement.

(a = b) must return an l-value that can serve as the target of the value **c**. In this case, the value returned should be **a** as an l-value.

3. For this mechanism to work correctly, the return type of an assignment operator should be a constant reference to the class of the target object. The return type for our assignment operator for accounts is therefore specified as **const account&**.

4. The effect of the last line of code is to return the receiver object. To gain access to the object itself, we apply the *dereference operator* (∗) to **this**. The receiver object will be returned as an l-value because the return type is specified as a reference to a class.

Using a Class with Functions

There are many occasions for which we might want to include a class in a program and process its instances by means of functions. For example, consider the problem of interacting with the user for the input of the amount to withdraw from a bank account. A user interface function that performs this task follows:

```
void make_withdrawal(account &this_account)
{
        double amount, result;
        apstring password;

        cout << "Enter your password: ";
        cin >> password;
        cout << "Enter the amount to withdraw: ";
        cin >> amount;
        result = this_account.withdraw(password, amount);
        if (result >= 0)
                cout << "Thank you. Your new balance is "
                        << result << endl;
        else if (result == -1)
                cout << "Sorry, invalid password." << endl;
        else
                cout << "Sorry, insufficient funds."
                        << endl;
}
```

An alternative to this approach is to make this function a member of the **account** class. Then it could be invoked as

```
    this_account.make_withdrawal();
```

There are two problems with this second approach:

1. It makes more work for the developer, who must write new code for the **account** class rather than reuse existing code in the user interface module.

2. It makes application-specific components, such as the messages to
    the user in a particular context, part of a general class definition. This
    makes the **account** class less general and application independent than it
    should be.

As you can see, the processing of classes and their instances integrates very
easily with the more conventional style of programming in C++. This feature
enables developers to introduce objects and the object-oriented style into an
existing software system without redesigning and rewriting the entire system.

■ Exercises 9.2

1. Describe the differences between a class and a data structure, such as an array or
    a struct. Pay particular attention to the concepts of an abstract data type and data
    encapsulation.
2. Discuss the roles played by user requirements, formal specifications, class
    declaration, and class implementation in developing a C++ class.
3. Describe the differences between a default constructor, a constructor with
    user-specified initial values, and a copy constructor.

Exercises 4–7 ask you to add attributes or behavior to the bank account class we have
just discussed.

4. Add a data member for representing an account user's name. Add behavior so
    that each account is given a user's name when it is created.
5. Update the member functions **get_balance**, **deposit**, and **withdraw** so
    that each takes a user name and password as parameters. Perform the expected
    operations only if the name and password sent by the user match the name and
    password data members of the account. Otherwise, do nothing.
6. Add a data member to maintain a record of the number of times a user has failed
    to enter the correct name and password. It should be set to zero when the
    account is created and whenever the user successfully makes a deposit,
    withdrawal, or balance check. It should be incremented whenever these
    operations are unsuccessful.
7. Add a **private** member function that is run when the number of failed
    transactions becomes greater than 3. It should print a message that the user's
    ATM card is being confiscated.
8. Discuss the concept of overloading, which allows the assignment operator to be
    defined for the **account** class developed in this section.
9. Develop the user requirements and formal specifications for a new class, called
    employee, to represent the **employee_type** from Section 9.1.
10. Write a C++ class declaration file for the **employee** class of Exercise 9.
11. Write a code segment that illustrates the differences between the
    employee_type and the class **employee** from Exercises 9 and 10. Explain
    why the class would be better to use than the struct.

9.3 Object-Oriented Programming and Software Maintenance

You might be wondering why we went to all that trouble to define an **account**
class in the previous section, when we could have coded an **account** type as a
C++ struct. We have already stated one reason: data security. The members of a
struct are public, or visible, for access or modification to all parts of an

Objectives

◆ to understand the problems associated with software maintenance

◆ to understand the way in which reuse of software enhances software maintenance

◆ to become familiar with some basic terms of object-oriented programming

application. The private data members of a class are available for access or modification only by means of specially designated member functions.

There are other reasons for developing classes and using object-oriented methods. Through the study and development of large and complex software systems over the years, computer scientists have come to the conclusion that the techniques and tools that we have discussed through Section 9.1 are far from adequate for dealing with the challenges of building these systems. In this section, we explain why object-oriented programming should be added to our arsenal of tools and techniques for problem solving.

The Problem of Software Maintenance

Perhaps the most serious problem posed by a large software system is that of maintaining it over a period of years. After the initial release of a commercial system, users send complaints about errors and requests for additional features or functions to the developers almost immediately. Before a new version with corrections and additional features or functions can be released, the developers must search the system to fix the errors and add or remove features or functions. They must do so in such a way as not to disturb other parts of the system that are already working correctly. Moreover, the developers must divide up the maintenance tasks so that they can work independently and efficiently. Finally, some of the developers who maintain the software may not have been on the original development team. All of these factors add time and cost to the maintenance of large software systems.

The tools and techniques of structured programming and modular design go part of the way toward easing the software maintenance task. For example, if an error occurs in a particular function of a system, a programmer might locate the error in a C++ function within a particular library file and be able to fix the problem by changing a single line of code within the function. If an error occurs while the system is using a particular data structure such as a list, a programmer might find and correct the problem in the C++ library file where the list processing functions are implemented.

In Chapter 4, we saw that another kind of error, a side effect, is more difficult to track down. Many side effects are caused by allowing users too much access to the implementation of a module. We also saw that implementing a module as a class in C++ helps to control this kind of side effect by encapsulating or denying users direct access to the data.

Reuse of Software

Another major factor that adds to the cost of software maintenance is the need to rewrite entire modules to add features or functions to a system. For example, suppose that a module already exists in a bank management system for processing checking accounts. Savings accounts resemble checking accounts to a certain extent, as do the functions for processing each kind of account. However, using conventional structured programming techniques, developers must add a completely new module with a different set of data type definitions and functions for savings accounts. Much of this code will not only be redundant, but may also contain errors.

software reuse: The process of building and maintaining software systems out of existing software components.

server: A computational object that provides a service to another computational object.

client: A computational object that receives a service from another computational object.

sender: A computational object that requests a service from another computational object.

receiver: A computational object to which a request is sent for a service.

base class: The class from which a derived class inherits attributes and behavior.

derived class: A class that inherits attributes and behavior from other classes.

Developers should be able to reuse existing software modules to build new ones. In the example of savings and checking accounts, a developer could write a module for handling the structure and behavior that all accounts have in common. Other developers could then *specialize* this module, with extra data or functions, for more specific kinds of accounts. By reusing software components, developers can eliminate the redundancy and many of the errors that occur with more conventional methods. As we will see shortly, object-oriented programming provides a way of reusing software components in this manner.

The Client/Server Relationship

We can think of an object as a **server,** to which a user makes requests as a **client.** None of the data belonging to a server is accessible to a client, unless the client invokes a server-defined request to use or modify that data. In other words, the data belonging to an object are fully encapsulated. Figure 9.4 illustrates these concepts. Each object is an instance of a class that defines its data and behavior. The client of an object obtains its services by creating an instance of its class and then sending requests to this instance. The implementer of an object defines its services or behavior by defining the class to which the object belongs. An object that sends a request to another object is called the **sender** of the request; the object that receives the request is called the **receiver.**

Inheritance

The common behavior of several classes may be generalized by defining a **base class.** Each of the original, more specific classes can retain its own distinctive behavior as a **derived class.** Behavior can be added to a derived class to specialize it further, even if this behavior redefines the behavior already defined in the base class. The process of adding derived classes therefore allows developers to reuse existing software very easily.

Polymorphism and Overloading

The common behavior of several classes is also expressed by means of overloading the operations that define similar behavior. The operators that designate these operations are polymorphic or have many forms. A polymorphic operator, such as **<**, really has one general meaning when used by clients:

◆ Figure 9.4

Anatomy of objects as clients and servers

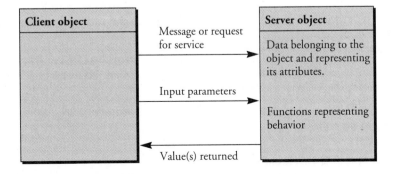

A Note of Interest

The Origins of the Object-Oriented Philosophy

We saw in an earlier note of interest that a philosophy can serve as the underpinning of a new approach to problem solving and software design. Such was the case with function-oriented programming. This approach was the direct result of efforts of two computer scientists, John McCarthy and John Backus, to bring a certain formal theory of computation, the recursive lambda calculus, to bear on the design of complex software systems. The object-oriented approach to problem solving and software design has a different kind of origin. In this case, there is no single theory of computation we can point to as the model for the approach. Object orientation in languages, programming style, and thinking has evolved over time and is the result of diverse sources and trends that eventually converged on a single body of ideas. However, there is one computer scientist in whose vision these sources

and trends have been brought together. This scientist, Alan Kay, recounts the history of the development of the object-oriented philosophy in "The Early History of Smalltalk," <u>ACM SIGPLAN Notices</u>, Volume 28, No. 3, March, 1993. Some of the important sources in the development of the object-oriented approach were

Ivan Sutherland's work on an interactive graphical programming environment called **Sketchpad.**

The development of Simula, a language for representing classes of objects.

Kay's work on Smalltalk, the first complete environment for object-oriented software development.

The work of Douglas Engelbart, Daniel Ingalls, Kay, and others at Xerox on WIMP (window, icon, mouse, pull-down menu) user interfaces.

9.4 A Rational Number Class

Objectives

◆ to be able to design a numeric class whose use and behavior are compatible with the use and behavior of built-in numeric data types

◆ to understand the use of overloaded operations in designing a numeric class with standard behavior

◆ to be able to use overloaded operations to implement mixed-mode operations on new classes and built-in data types

determine whether two objects are related by less than. However, it can have more than one specific meaning when implemented by different server classes, such as integers and strings, which carry out different operations on different data representations to determine the relation.

Our next example of the design of a class comes from pure mathematics, a different domain than that of finance and data processing. C++ has standard data types for representing real numbers and integers, but not rational numbers. In this section, we develop a new class, called **rational**, that allows applications to use rational numbers in much the same way as the other kinds of numbers are used.

User Requirements

A rational number has two attributes, a numerator and a denominator, both of which are integer values. One constructor operation for rational numbers should therefore take two integer parameters representing these attributes. For example, one might create the rational numbers ½ and ⅚ as follows:

```
rational one_half(1, 2);
rational five_sixths(5, 6);
```

Because rational numbers are expressed in the form

numerator
denominator

definitions of the form

```
rational <name>(<integer>, 0);
```

should not be allowed. Therefore, a precondition of the constructor is that the denominator can be any integer other than zero.

Access to the numerator and denominator is provided as in the following code segment:

```
rational seven_eighths(7, 8);
cout << "Numerator = " << seven_eighths.numerator() << endl;
cout << "Denominator = " << seven_eighths.denominator() << endl;
```

which produces the output

```
Numerator = 7
Denominator = 8
```

Users should be able to perform some standard arithmetic operations on rational numbers, and output the resulting values. For example, the following statement would output the sum of the two example numbers just defined to the screen:

```
cout << one_half + five_sixths << endl;
```

The output of this statement would be

```
4/3
```

Note that the sum of the two numbers is expressed in lowest terms.

Keyboard input of rational numbers would allow users to work with rational numbers interactively. To make the scanning of the input simple, we might require a definite format, such as

```
<integer>/<integer> <enter key>
```

Assignment of one rational number to another should also be provided, in the form

```
<rational number variable> = <rational number object>
```

where **<rational number object>** is the value returned by an expression.

Finally, users of rational numbers would like to compare them for the standard relationships of equality, less than, and greater than. The following code is an example of the use of the equality operator with two rational numbers:

```
rational one_half(1, 2);
rational number;

cout << "Enter a rational number: ";
cin >> number;
if (number == one_half)
    .
    .
```

Note that we have provided a second class constructor that takes no initial values for the numerator and the denominator. This constructor is used to create rational number objects that will be targets of subsequent input or assignment operations. These numbers can be given a default initial value of $1/1$.

Specifying the Operations

Now that clients' requirements have been discussed, we can present a formal specification of the desired operations for rational numbers. The attributes of a rational number are **my_numerator** and **my_denominator**.

Create operation (default value)
Preconditions :   The rational number is in an unpredictable state.
Postconditions: **my_numerator** is set to 1, and **my_denominator** is set to 1.

Create operation (initial values specified)
Preconditions :   The rational number is in an unpredictable state, **numerator** is an integer value, and **denominator** is an integer value other than zero.
Postconditions: **my_numerator** is set to **numerator**, and **my_denominator** is set to **denominator**. **my_numerator/my_denominator** is then reduced to lowest terms.

Numerator operation
Preconditions :   The rational number is appropriately initialized.
Postconditions: An integer representing the numerator of the rational number is returned.

Denominator operation
Preconditions :   The rational number is appropriately initialized.
Postconditions: An integer representing the denominator of the rational number is returned.

Addition operation
Preconditions :   The parameter objects are rational numbers appropriately initialized.
Postconditions: A rational number representing the sum of the two rational numbers is returned.

Subtraction operation
Preconditions :   The parameter objects are rational numbers appropriately initialized.
Postconditions: A rational number representing the difference of the two rational numbers is returned.

(continued)

Multiplication operation

Preconditions :   The parameter objects are rational numbers appropriately initialized.

Postconditions: A rational number representing the product of the two rational numbers is returned.

Division operation

Preconditions :   The parameter objects are rational numbers appropriately initialized, and the denominator of the parameter object does not equal zero.

Postconditions: A rational number representing the division of the two rational numbers is returned.

Equality operation

Preconditions :   The parameter objects are rational numbers appropriately initialized.

Postconditions: The Boolean value **TRUE** is returned if the two rational numbers are equal, and **FALSE** is returned otherwise.

Assignment operation

Preconditions :   Receiver and parameter objects are rational numbers appropriately initialized.

Postconditions: **my_numerator** and **my_denominator** of the parameter object are copied into the receiver object.

Input operation

Preconditions :   The receiver is an **istream** object appropriately initialized, and the parameter is a rational number appropriately initialized. The form of input to the stream should be <integer> /<integer> <enter key>

Postconditions: The numerator and the denominator in the rational number parameter are modified by the input values, and the **istream** object is returned.

Output operation

Preconditions :   The receiver is an **ostream** object appropriately initialized, and the parameter is a rational number appropriately initialized.

Postconditions: The rational number parameter is written to the stream in the form <my_numerator> /<my_denominator>, and the **ostream** object is returned.

Note that the specifications state that a rational number will not be created if the denominator is a zero, and that any new rational number will be reduced to lowest terms when it is created.

Declaring the Class

The class declaration module for rational numbers can now be presented:

```
// Class declaration file: rational.h

#ifndef RATIONAL_H

#include <iostream.h>
#include "bool.h"
```

```cpp
class rational
{
    public:

    // Constructors

    rational();
    rational(int numerator, int denominator);
    rational(const rational &r);

    // Accessors

    int numerator() const;
    int denominator() const;

    // Assignment

    const rational& operator = (const rational &rhs);

    private:

    // Data members

    int my_numerator, my_denominator;

    // Utility function

    void reduce();
};

// The following free (non-member) functions operate on
// rational numbers

// Arithmetic

rational operator + (const rational &lhs,
     const rational &rhs);
rational operator - (const rational &lhs,
     const rational &rhs);
rational operator * (const rational &lhs,
     const rational &rhs);
rational operator / (const rational &lhs,
     const rational &rhs);

// Comparison

bool operator == (const rational &lhs, const rational &rhs);

// Input and output
```

```
istream& operator >> (istream &is, rational &r);
ostream& operator << (ostream &os, const rational &r);
```

```
#define RATIONAL_H
#endif
```

Note two things about this class declaration module:
1. The module declares **reduce** as a **private** member function. This function will be run by the class implementation whenever a rational number object must be reduced to lowest terms.
2. Several **free functions** are declared. These are nonmember functions for manipulating rational numbers, and consist of several standard operators.

free function: *A function not declared within the scope of a class declaration module.*

Implementing the Class

The class implementation for rational numbers appears in the **rational.cpp** file. Here we present the portion of the file that defines the three class constructors:

```
// Class implementation file: rational.cpp

#include <assert.h>

#include "rational.h"
#include "gcd.h"

rational::rational()
{
     my_numerator = 1;
     my_denominator = 1;
}

rational::rational(int numerator, int denominator)
{
     assert(denominator != 0);
     my_numerator = numerator;
     my_denominator = denominator;
     reduce();
}

rational::rational(const rational &r)
{
     my_numerator = r.my_numerator;
     my_denominator = r.my_denominator;
}
```

Only the second constructor calls for comment. A precondition of the operation is that the **denominator** parameter must not be a zero. Therefore, the implementation verifies this condition with the C++ **assert** function. A post-condition of the operation is that the new rational number has been reduced to lowest terms. To achieve this result, we compute the greatest common divisor of the two parameters, and then reduce them by dividing by this factor. Here is the implementation of the **reduce** function:

```
void rational::reduce()
{
        int common_divisor = gcd(my_numerator, my_denominator);
        my_numerator = my_numerator / common_divisor;
        my_denominator = my_denominator / common_divisor;
}
```

The implementation of the **gcd** function, which was used in an example in Section 6.5, appears in the **gcd** library and is left as an exercise.

The development of the arithmetic operations for rational numbers depends on our knowledge of the rules of rational number arithmetic. These rules are specified by the following relations:

$$\frac{n_1}{d_1} + \frac{n_2}{d_2} = \frac{n_1 d_2 + n_2 d_1}{d_1 d_2}$$

$$\frac{n_1}{d_1} - \frac{n_2}{d_2} = \frac{n_1 d_2 - n_2 d_1}{d_1 d_2}$$

$$\frac{n_1}{d_1} * \frac{n_2}{d_2} = \frac{n_1 n_2}{d_1 d_2}$$

$$\frac{n_1/d_1}{n_2/d_2} = \frac{n_1 d_2}{d_1 n_2}$$

We present the implementation of the free function for the addition operation and leave the others as exercises:

```
rational operator + (const rational &lhs,
      const rational &rhs)
{
      int numerator = lhs.numerator() * rhs.denominator()
            + rhs.numerator() * lhs.denominator();
      int denominator = lhs.denominator() * rhs.denominator();
      rational sum(numerator, denominator);
      return sum;
}
```

The first two statements in this implementation use the rule for addition to compute the numerator and the denominator of the sum. Note the use of the member functions **numerator** and **denominator** to access the appropriate data members of the two rational numbers. Because **+** is a free function, we cannot access the data members of the rational numbers with the selector notation. The third line uses these values to construct a new rational number expressed in lowest terms. The last line returns the new rational number to the caller of the function.

The free function for the output operation writes a rational number to an output stream in the form **<numerator>/<denominator>**:

```
ostream& operator << (ostream &os, const rational &r)
{
    os << r.numerator() << "/" << r.denominator();
    return os;
}
```

Note the following:
1. We use the **ostream** class to declare the type of the output stream parameter and the return type. The use of this class allows our definition of **<<** to be used either with the standard output stream, **cout,** or with any output file stream.
2. We return a reference to an output stream. This allows output operations to one stream to be cascaded, as in the expression **cout << r1 << r2 << r3 << endl**.
3. We have been careful to write the data to the output stream in exactly the same form as it might appear for reading from an input stream. This technique allows correct processing of rational numbers with file streams.

The input operation expects data in the input stream to have the form **<integer>/<integer>**. Therefore, the implementation uses **assert** to enforce the use of this format:

```
istream& operator >> (istream &is, rational &r)
{
    char division_symbol;
    int numerator = 0, denominator = 0;

    is >> numerator >> division_symbol >> denominator;
    assert(division_symbol == '/');
    assert(denominator != 0);
    rational temp(numerator, denominator);
    r = temp;
    return is;
}
```

Note that the implementation also verifies that the denominator from the input stream is not a zero.

The implementations of the assignment and equality operations are left as exercises.

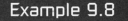

This example is a program that prompts the user for three rational numbers and outputs the result of an expression of the form **r1 + r2 * r3**.

```
// Program file: ratdriv.cpp

#include <iostream.h>

#include "rational.h"

int main()
{
    rational r1, r2, r3;

    cout << "Enter the first number (<integer>/<integer>): ";
    cin >> r1;
    cout << "Enter the second number (<integer>/<integer>): ";
    cin >> r2;
    cout << "Enter the third number (<integer>/<integer>): ";
    cin >> r3;
    cout << "The result of r1 + r2 * r3 is "
         << r1 + r2 * r3 << endl;
    return 0;
}
```

An example run of this program might produce the following output:

```
Enter the first number (<integer>/<integer>): 1/2
Enter the second number (<integer>/<integer>): 1/2
Enter the third number (<integer>/<integer>): 1/2
The result of r1 + r2 * r3 is 3/4
```

Note that the output is **3/4** rather than **1/2**. This means that the standard operator precedence of multiplication over addition is also enforced for rational numbers.

Mixed-Mode Operations

In Chapter 3, you were introduced to the notion of a mixed-mode operation. This kind of operation has two operands of different types, and performs a type conversion operation before computing a result value. For example, the addition operation promotes an integer operand to a real number before adding it to a real number operand. The result returned is then a real number.

When a rational number class is added to a software system, clients might be provided with a similar capability to perform mixed-mode operations on rational numbers and other kinds of numbers. For example, where the operands are an integer and a rational number, the integer would first be promoted to a rational number, and then rational number arithmetic would be performed. Where the operands are a real number and a rational number, the rational number would first be promoted to a real number, and then real number arithmetic would be performed. The following code and its output when executed illustrate some mixed-mode operations:

```
rational one_half(1, 2);
cout << setiosflags(ios::fixed | ios::showpoint);
```

```
cout << "Rational + integer = " << one_half + 2 << endl;
cout << "Rational + real = " << one_half + 3.4 << endl;

Rational + integer = 5/2
Rational + real = 3.9
```

Table 9.1 illustrates some operand and return types for addition:

▼ Table 9.1	Operand 1 Type	Operand 2 Type	Result Type
Types of data for mixed-mode addition	int	rational	rational
	rational	int	rational
	double	rational	double
	rational	double	double

We can provide mixed-mode operations for arithmetic with rational numbers by overloading. Let's consider just the case of addition, and leave the other operations for exercises. For the cases where the first operand is a rational number, we add free functions to the class declaration module of the rational number class:

```
rational operator + (const rational &lhs, int rhs);
double operator + (const rational &lhs, double rhs);
```

Each of these operations adds a number (an **int** or a **double**) to the first parameter, a rational.

To add an **int** to a rational number, we must promote the **int** to a rational number. We use the **int** parameter to create a new rational number object, and then add it (using the rational number operation named **+**) to the rational number parameter:

```
rational operator + (const rational &lhs, int rhs)
{
      rational new_operand(rhs, 1);
      return lhs + new_operand;
}
```

To add a **double** to a rational number, we must promote the rational number to a **double**. We cast the rational number's numerator as a **double**, divide the result by its denominator, and then add the result (using the real number operation **+**) to the **double** parameter:

```
double operator + (const rational &lhs, double rhs);
{
      return double(lhs.numerator()) / lhs.denominator()
            + rhs;
}
```

A Note of Interest

Pure and Hybrid Object-Oriented Languages

It is possible to classify programming languages in terms of the degree to which they possess object-oriented features. Older languages like FORTRAN, C, and standard Pascal have no object-oriented features at all. None of them supports classes, user-defined polymorphic operators, data encapsulation, or inheritance.

Smalltalk purports to be an object-oriented language in a "pure" sense. In this language, every data type is a class. All data values, including classes themselves, are objects. All subprograms and operators can be overloaded. Data can be fully encapsulated. Every operation on data comes about as a result of a request being sent to an object.

A third class of languages is a hybrid of object-oriented languages and older languages. Many of these are the older languages themselves, with object-oriented features grafted onto them. For example, C++ is an extension of C. Most current implementations of Pascal have object-oriented extensions. CLOS, or Common LISP Object System, is an object-oriented extension that comes with almost every Common LISP package.

The difference between hybrid languages and the pure object-oriented languages is that it is possible to write programs in a hybrid language that omit the object-oriented features entirely. For example, one could write a large program, or even a large software system consisting of many library modules, in C++ that would be indistinguishable from a C program. This possibility has led to a debate in the computer science community concerning the desirability of hybrid languages.

Proponents of the pure object-oriented languages argue that the object-oriented approach has superceded more traditional styles of programming. Therefore, one should use a language that enforces the superior approach, rather than a language that allows drift or slippage into inferior approaches. Moreover, proponents claim that the pure languages are better vehicles for training new computer scientists, because they enforce object-oriented thinking from the very beginning.

Proponents of the hybrid languages offer several counters to these points. First, it is not clear that object orientation is the best or most natural way to approach all problems. For example, problems in numerical analysis may find more natural solutions in terms of systems of functions, calling for a function-oriented approach. The notion of sending a request to a number to add one to itself seems somewhat silly from this perspective. A hybrid language offers object orientation as one possible approach among others that can be chosen when it is the most natural alternative.

Second, although object orientation might be the best possible approach to the design and maintenance of large software systems, smaller programs may be more easily designed and written using traditional techniques of structured programming.

Finally, a pure object-oriented language may not be the best vehicle for teaching programming. Beginning programmers start with simple problems, but pure object-oriented languages do not rest on a simple model of computation. Beginning programmers need to learn about the structure and behavior of real computers, about concepts such as memory, the distinction between an address and a data value, branching, and subprogram calls. Pure object-oriented languages tend to insulate a programmer from these features of real machines.

We suggest that you study and try out several of these languages, if they are available, and make your own judgments about the relative virtues of pure object-oriented and hybrid programming languages.

1. Complete the implementation of the rational number class and test it with a simple driver program. (*Hint:* Two rational numbers are equal if and only if $n_1 d_2 = n_2 d_1$.)

2. What is the total number of mixed-mode operations (**+**, **-**, *****, **/**) for the three data types **int**, **double**, and **rational**?

3. State a general formula for the total number of mixed-mode operations, where M is the number of operators and N is the number of data types.

4. The implementation of rational numbers presented in this section always reduces a rational number to lowest terms when it is created. Another method would be to wait until an output operation is executed to express a rational number in lowest terms. Assess the costs and benefits of these two strategies. (Be sure to take into account the speed of evaluating complex arithmetic operations and the possibility of integer overflow.)

5. Rational numbers such as 9/1 should be output as whole numbers, and used as whole numbers in arithmetic and comparison operations. Decide where to do this in the system and implement the change.

6. Simon Seeplus claims that it would be easier to represent a rational number as a struct with associated library functions, rather than as a class. Criticize the merits of this proposal.

9.5 Derived Classes and Inheritance

Objectives

◆ to understand how the behavior and attributes of a class can be reused by developing a derived class that inherits them

◆ to understand how to control access to data and behavior so that they are available to derived classes but protected from clients

One of the advantages of using classes and objects in a program is that they can be reused to develop new features. Consider the bank account example of Section 9.2. We defined a class to represent the kind of data and behavior that any account might possess, such as depositing into or withdrawing from a balance. Many more specialized kinds of bank accounts exist that have both this general sort of data and behavior and also other, more specific data and behavior. For example, a savings account will need data and operations to compute the interest on the balance. A timed savings account will not allow withdrawals before a certain date from the time of the deposit.

Instead of reinventing the wheel and defining a whole new class for each of these types of bank accounts, we can make each new kind of account a derived class of our abstract account class. Each class derived from **account** then *inherits* all of the common, more abstract data and behavior from the account class. To each derived class we need only add the data and behavior necessary to define it as a special class of account.

C++ provides support for defining derived classes. A derived class declaration is quite similar to a top-level class declaration. For example, here is a declaration of a **savings_account** class, with specific data and behavior for representing the computation of interest:

```
// Class declaration file: savings.h

#ifndef SAVINGS_H

#include "account.h"
```

```
class savings_account : public account
{
    public:

    // Constructors

    savings_account();
    savings_account(const apstring &password,
        double balance);
    savings_account(const savings_account &a);

    // Accessor

    double get_interest(const apstring &password) const;

    // Modifier

    void compute_interest(double rate);

    // Assignment

    const savings_account& operator = (const savings_account &a);

    private:

    // Data member

    double my_interest;
};

#define SAVINGS_H
#endif
```

The only difference in form between a derived class declaration and a top-level class declaration lies in the text immediately following the reserved word **class**. As before, we have the name of the new class. Then we see a colon (:), followed by an **access specifier,** followed by the name of the class from which the new class is being derived. The form for this is

class <new derived class name> : <access specifier> <parent class name>

access specifier:
A symbol (**public, protected,** or **private**) that specifies the kind of access that clients have to a server's data members and member functions.

The access specifier in this example is the reserved word **public**. This means that the public members of the base class are also public in the derived class. If this specifier were the reserved word **private**, then the public members of the base class would become private members in the derived class. Figure 9.5 is a *class hierarchy* diagram showing the relationship between the account class and the savings account class. Note that the member functions **set_password**, **deposit**, **withdraw**, and **get_balance** are not declared in the savings account

◆ Figure 9.5

The account and
savings account classes

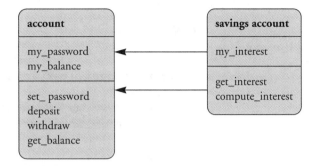

class. They are declared in the base class, **account**, but are still considered public members of the savings account class by inheritance. Note also that the assignment operation for savings accounts cannot be inherited from the base class. The reason for this is that the operation must copy an additional data member, **my_interest**, that is defined in **savings_account**.

The implementation file of the savings account class is

```cpp
// Class implementation file: savings.cpp

#include "savings.h"

savings_account::savings_account()
      : account()
{
      my_interest = 0.00;
}

savings_account::savings_account(const apstring &password,
      double balance)
      : account(password, balance)
{
      my_interest = 0.00;
}

savings_account::savings_account(const savings_account &a)
      : account(a)
{
      my_interest = a.my_interest;
}

const savings_account& savings_account::operator =
      (const savings_account &a)
{
      if (this != &a)
      {
            my_password = a.my_password;
            my_balance = a.my_balance;
            my_interest = a.my_interest;
```

```
        }
        return *this;
}

double savings_account::get_interest(const apstring &password) const
{
        if (password == my_password)
                return my_interest;
        else
                return -1;
}

void savings_account::compute_interest(double rate,
        const apstring &password)
{
        my_interest = get_balance(password) * rate;
}
```

The constructors for **savings_account** must first run the constructors for the base class, **account**, so that the data members belonging to the base class can be initialized. This is done by placing an expression of the form

---
: <base class constructor name> (<list of actual parameters>)
---

immediately after the heading of the constructor for the derived class. After this step, the data member **interest** belonging to the derived class is initialized.

Within the implementation of the member function **compute_interest**, we cannot refer directly to the savings account's balance. The reason for this is that access to private data members cannot be inherited from a base class. Therefore, we must access the savings account's balance indirectly, by invoking the base class public member function **get_balance**. As you might suppose, lack of direct access to the data members of a base class can make the implementation of derived classes inconvenient. We examine a way to remedy this problem shortly.

The following lines of code create and use a new instance of our savings account class:

```
savings_account my_account("rosebud", 50.00);
my_account.withdraw("rosebud", 20.00);
my_account.compute_interest(.025, "rosebud");
cout << setiosflags(ios::fixed | ios::showpoint) << setprecision(2);
cout << "Balance = $"
     << my_account.get_balance("rosebud") << endl;
cout << "Interest = $"
     << my_account.get_interest("rosebud") << endl;
```

The first line declares a new savings account called **my_account**. The computer runs the class constructor for savings accounts. This in turn runs the constructor in the base class, which gives **my_account** an initial balance of 50.00. The constructor in the derived class then sets the interest to a default value of 0.00.

The second line asks **my_account** to withdraw 20.00. Since this member function is also not defined for savings accounts, the computer locates and runs the function as defined in the base class.

The third line asks **my_account** to compute the interest, with a rate of .025. Because a member function is defined for this operation directly in the **savings_account** class, this function is invoked.

The last two lines of code ask **my_account** for the values of the balance and interest so they can be displayed to the user. The request for the balance has the effect of invoking a member function of the base class, whereas the request for the interest has the effect of invoking a member function of the derived class.

The rule that the computer uses for deciding which member function to run is fairly simple. If a member function exists in the defining class, then it is run. Otherwise, the computer searches for a member function in the base class, if one exists. This search continues until a member function is found in the next most immediate ancestor class, if one exists. If no member function is found, a syntax error occurs. The same search process occurs for **public** data member references as well.

As you can see, derived classes and inheritance provide powerful techniques for reusing software and eliminating redundant code.

Example 9.9

The following driver program tests the savings account class that we have just implemented:

```
// Program file: savedriv.cpp

#include <iostream.h>
#include <iomanip.h>
#include "savings.h"

int main()
{
    savings_account
            smith("narcissus", 0.00),
            jones("clio", 45.00);

    cout   << setiosflags(ios::fixed | ios::showpoint)
           << setprecision(2);
    cout   << "Smith's balance = $"
           << smith.get_balance("narcissus") << endl;
    cout   << "Jones's balance = $"
           << jones.get_balance("clio") << endl;
    smith.deposit("narcissus", 50.00);
    cout   << "Smith's balance = $"
           << smith.get_balance("narcissus") << endl;
    cout   << "Jones's balance = $"
           << jones.get_balance("clio") << endl;
```

```
        smith.withdraw("narcissus", 20.00);
        cout  << "Smith's balance = $"
              << smith.get_balance("narcissus") << endl;
        cout  << "Jones's balance = $"
              << jones.get_balance("clio") << endl;
        smith.compute_interest(.025, "narcissus");
        cout  << "Smith's interest = $"
              << smith.get_interest("narcissus") << endl;
        return 0;
    }
```

The program produces the output

```
    Smith's balance = $0.00
    Jones's balance = $45.00
    Smith's balance = $50.00
    Jones's balance = $45.00
    Smith's balance = $30.00
    Jones's balance = $45.00
    Smith's interest = $0.75
```

Inheritance and Protected Members

In the previous section, we mentioned that **private** data members of a base class cannot be directly referenced from a derived class. For example, the savings account class must invoke a **public** member function of the account class, such as **get_balance("clio")**, to access the value of the private data member **my_balance**. This kind of encapsulation is too restrictive. A derived class ought to be able to access frequently used and modified data members of a base class directly. A less restrictive type of encapsulation can be obtained by using the access specifier **protected** for certain data and member functions. A data or function member of a class is considered a protected member if it is visible to a derived class, but not visible to any other part of a program. Thus, **protected** members behave like **public** members for derived classes, but like **private** members for any other classes or modules in a software system.

The following code updates the account class by making the balance a **protected** data member rather than a **private** one:

protected member:
A data member or member function that is accessible only within the scope of a class declaration or within the class declaration of a derived class.

```
// Class declaration file: account.h

#ifndef ACCOUNT_H

#include "apstring.h"

class account
{
    public:

    // Constructors
```

```
        account();
        account(const apstring &password, double balance);
        account(const account &a);

        // Accessor

        double get_balance(const apstring &password) const;

        // Modifiers

        int set_password(const apstring &password,
            const apstring new_password);
        double deposit(const apstring &password,
            double amount);
        double withdraw(const apstring &password,
            double amount);

        // Assignment

        const account& operator = (const account &a);

    protected:

        // Data members

        apstring my_password;
        double my_balance;
};

#define ACCOUNT_H
#endif
```

We have replaced the reserved word **private** in the previous version with the reserved word **protected**. The implementation section of this module is the same as before. Once we have made this change in the account class declaration, we can refer to the data member **my_balance** in the savings account class implementation. For example, the member function **compute_interest** can be changed so that the balance is referenced directly:

```
void savings_account::compute_interest(double rate,
    const apstring &password)
{
    my_interest = my_balance * rate;
}
```

■ Exercises 9.5

1. Add members to the savings account class given in this section for maintaining a current interest rate.
2. A checking account is a special version of an account that requires data and behavior for maintaining the number of checks written. Write a derived class for account called **checking_account** that captures this information.

Communication and Style Tips

1. Data and function members that must be used by the entire system should be declared **public**. In general, there should be very few public data members of a class.
2. Data and function members that must be used by derived classes should be declared **protected**.
3. Data and function members that should be used only by the defining class should be declared **private**.

3. Draw a diagram showing the hierarchy of classes used in a system that manages checking and savings accounts.
4. Some checking accounts bear interest. Propose a strategy for reusing the existing classes in a bank management system to support checking accounts with interest. Draw a diagram of the new class hierarchy.
5. Unlike the other kinds of accounts, timed savings accounts may not permit access via a password. Explain how you would fit timed savings accounts into a bank management system as a new class, in such a way that the use of a password for these accounts would be disallowed. Draw a diagram of the new class hierarchy.

9.6 Graphics

Objectives

◆ to learn how to define classes for representing geo-metric shapes as objects

◆ to be able to use classes and objects in graphics applications

Thus far in this text, you have specified a geometric shape, such as a circle or a rectangle, as a set of coordinates passed as parameters to graphics functions for display. In many applications, it would be useful to treat a geometric shape as a distinct object with its own attributes and behavior. For example, we might first create a circle object with a specifed center point, radius, and color. Then we might draw it, erase it, enlarge it by a factor of two, and then redraw it. A code segment describing this process might look like

```
point center_point(100, 100);      // Create a center point
circl my_circle(center_point, 50);  // Create a circle

my_circle.draw();          // Draw the circle
delay(10000);              // Wait a moment
my_circle.erase();         // Erase the circle
my_circle.scale(2);        // Double the size of the circle
my_circle.draw();          // Redraw the circle
```

Note that we use two C++ classes in this code segment, **point** and **circl**, and that we use the syntax of object creation and member function calls discussed in Section 9.2. The details of drawing, erasing, and resizing the circle are hidden in the class implementations of **circl** and **point**. In addition, each object provides accessor functions that let us know its position and size. In the present section, we develop classes for points and circles.

The Class point

A point consists of an *x* coordinate and a *y* coordinate. The operations for a point are

1. Create with default coordinates of (0, 0)
2. Create with user-specified coordinates
3. Copy with assignment
4. Access the *x* coordinate
5. Access the *y* coordinate
6. Modify the *x* coordinate
7. Modify the *y* coordinate
8. Draw in the current color
9. Erase

The class declaration module, as contained in **point.h**, follows:

```
// Class declaration file: point.h

#ifndef POINT_H

class point
{
    public:

    // Constructors

    point();
    point(int x, int y);
    point(const point &p);

    // Accessors

    int x() const;
    int y() const;

    // Modifiers

    int set_x(int x);
    int set_y(int y);

    // Assignment

    const point& operator = (const point &rhs);

    // Output

    void draw();
    void erase();

    private:

    // Data members
```

```
                int my_x, my_y;
        };

        #define POINT_H
        #endif
```

The implementations of the **draw** and **erase** member functions use **putpixel** to draw or erase the point.

```
        void point::draw()
        {
                putpixel(my_x, my_y, getcolor());
        }

        void point::erase()
        {
                putpixel(my_x, my_y, getbkcolor());
        }
```

The rest of the implementation of the **point** class is left as an exercise.

Example 9.10

The following driver program tests the **point** class:

```
// Program file: ptdriv.cpp

// Tests the point class

#include <conio.h>
#include <graphics.h>
#include <dos.h>
#include <iostream.h>
#include "point.h"

const int DURATION = 10000;

int main()
{
        int x, y;

        // Obtain input information from the user

        cout << "Enter the x coordinate: ";
        cin >> x;
        cout << "Enter the y coordinate: ";
        cin >> y;
        // Set the graphics mode

        int graphdriver = DETECT, graphmode;
        initgraph(&graphdriver, &graphmode, "c:..\\bgi");
```

```
// Create and do some things with two points

point default_point, user_point(x, y);

default_point.draw();
user_point.draw();
delay(DURATION);
default_point.erase();
user_point.erase();
default_point = user_point;
default_point.draw();
delay(DURATION);
default_point.erase();
x = default_point.x();
y = default_point.y();
default_point.set_x(x + 50);
default_point.set_y(y + 25);
default_point.draw();

// Pause for a key to be pressed

moveto(100, 250);
outtext("Strike any key to continue");
getch();

// Close the graphics mode

closegraph();
return 0;
}
```

The Class circl

A circle consists of a center point and a radius. The operations for a circle are

1. Create with default values of
   a. center point at center of screen
   b. radius of ¼ screen width
2. Create with user-specified values for center point and radius
3. Copy with assignment
4. Access the center point
5. Access the radius
6. Scale
7. Translate
8. Draw
9. Erase

scaling: The modification of the size of an image by specified horizontal and vertical factors.

translation: The process of modifying the position of an image by a specified vertical and horizontal distance.

Note operations for modifying the center point and the radius of a circle are not provided. These changes occur when we **scale** or **translate** a circle. The **scale** operation for circles expects a real number as a parameter. This value serves as the factor by which the object is enlarged or reduced in the x and y dimensions.

For example, the expression

```
my_circle.scale(2)
```

would double the size of the radius of the circle, but leave the center point fixed. The expression

```
my_circle.scale(.33)
```

would reduce the size of the circle by ⅔.

Note that in each case, an attribute of the object is modified but the object is not redrawn on the screen. Code such as the following would update the display of the object after a change in its size:

```
my_circle.draw();
my_circle.erase();
my_circle.scale(.33);
my_circle.draw();
```

The **translate** operation for circles expects two integers as parameters. These values serve as the *x* and *y* distances by which the object is moved vertically and horizontally. Thus, the center point of the circle is modified, but the radius remains unchanged. For example, the following code segment would move the circle to a position 100 pixels to the right and 50 pixels up from its current position and redraw it:

```
my_circle.draw();
my_circle.erase();
my_circle.translate(100, -50);
my_circle.draw();
```

The class declaration module for the **circl** class follows:

```
// Class declaration file: circle.h

#ifndef CIRCL_H

#include "point.h"

class circl
{
        public:

        // Constructors

        circl();
        circl(const point &center_point,
                int radius);
        circl(const circl &c);
```

```
                // Accessors

                point center_point() const;
                int radius() const;

                // Modifiers

                void scale(double factor);
                void translate(int x_distance, int y_distance);

                // Assignment

                const circl& operator = (const circl &rhs);

                // Output

                void draw();
                void erase();

                private:

                // Data members

                int my_x, my_x, my_radius;
        };

        #define CIRCL_H
        #endif
```

Note that the names **draw** and **erase** are used to identify operations for both points and circles. This is a good example of the use of overloading to standardize the names of graphics operations.

We now examine the implementations of several **circl** member functions, and leave the rest as exercises. The second constructor extracts the coordinates from the **center_point** parameter and assigns them to the data members **my_x** and **my_y**.

```
    circl::circl(const point &center_point,
                    int radius)
    {
        my_x = center_point.x();
        my_y = center_point.y();
        my_radius = radius;
    }
```

The accessor **center_point** creates a point with the coordinates **my_x** and **my_y** and returns this point.

```
    point circl::center_point() const
```

```
    {
            point a_point(my_x, my_y);

            return a_point;
    }
```

The **scale** function multiplies **my_radius** by the **factor** parameter.

```
    void circl::scale(double factor)
    {
            my_radius = my_radius * factor;
    }
```

Note that the result of this multiplication, a real number, is converted to an integer automatically during its assignment to **my_radius**.

The **translate** function adds the x and y distance parameters to **my_x** and **my_y**, respectively.

```
    void circl::translate(int x_distance, int y_distance)
    {
            my_x = my_x + x_distance;
            my_y = my_y + y_distance;
    }
```

The **erase** function draws the circle in the current background color and then restores the foreground color for the application.

```
    void circl::erase()
    {
            int forecolor = getcolor();
            int backcolor = getbkcolor();

            setcolor(backcolor);
            draw();
            setcolor(forecolor);
    }
```

Note the call of the **circl** member function **draw** in this function.

Example 9.11

The following program creates a circle object and animates it. The circle begins its display in the lower left corner of the screen, and moves diagonally to the upper right corner of the screen. As the circle moves, it also grows in size, by a factor of 0.1 with every 8 pixels of movement.

```
// Program file: cirdriv.cpp
```

```cpp
// Tests the circle class

#include <conio.h>
#include <graphics.h>
#include <dos.h>
#include <iostream.h>
#include "point.h"
#include "circle.h"

const int TIME_DELAY = 20;

int main()
{

    // Set the graphics mode

    int graphdriver = DETECT, graphmode;
    initgraph(&graphdriver, &graphmode, "c:..\\bgi");

    // Set initial center point and create the circle

    int x = 10;
    int y = getmaxy() - 10;
    point center_point(x, y);
    circl our_circle(center_point, 10);

    // Draw the circle and animate it

    our_circle.draw();
    while (x < getmaxx())
    {
        delay(TIME_DELAY);
        our_circle.erase();
        our_circle.translate(1, -1);
        if (x % 8 == 0)
            our_circle.scale(1.1);
        our_circle.draw();
        ++x;
    }

    // Pause for a key to be pressed

    moveto(100, 250);
    outtext("Strike any key to continue");
    getch();

    // Close the graphics mode

    closegraph();
    return 0;
}
```

As you read the code of the main loop of this program, try to visualize how it would look if we tried to accomplish the same animation without the **circl** class.

1. Discuss why it is useful to represent geometric shapes as C++ classes.
2. Explain the benefits of using one name, **draw**, for the operation to draw any geometric shape.
3. Discuss the difference between scaling and translating a geometric shape.
4. Describe the changes needed to add a color attribute to the classes **point** and **circl**.
5. Write the user requirements and formal specifications for a **rectangl** class.
6. Write a C++ class declaration module for the **rectangl** class, and write a code segment to illustrate how a rectangle object might be used.
7. Explain how a class called **array_cell** could be used to simplify the design of the first sort animation example discussed in Section 8.6. List the attributes and behavior of this class.
8. Discuss the development of a class to represent line segments. A line segment is defined by two end points.
9. A polygon is a many-sided figure consisting of a set of line segments that enclose a region. Squares, rectangles, and triangles are all polygons. Discuss the development of a **polygon** class.

Focus on Program Design: Case Study

An ATM Machine

Thus far in this text, the end-of-chapter focus section has stated a problem, written out the top-level design of a solution as an algorithm, refined the design if necessary, and presented a complete program to solve the problem. In more recent chapters, we have had to focus more on the design of the appropriate data structures for solving a problem as well. Now that we are using object-oriented techniques, our focus must shift somewhat further away from top-down design and refinement of algorithms. In this section, we present part of a complete program, and leave the rest for the **Programming Problems and Activities** section. In fact, it would be in the object-oriented spirit if this project and those to follow were divided among students who form a team of programmers.

We begin as usual with a problem statement. But now we immediately consider how the behavior of certain classes of objects can help to solve the problem. If these classes have already been written, we can use them right away. If they do not quite fit the problem at hand, perhaps we can reuse them by creating a derived class for the desired behavior. Some algorithm and data structure design will still be necessary at the level of implementing a new class, but in general, there will be less work to do because there is less code to write. Rather than thinking in terms of data structures and algorithms, we can think in terms of clients and servers, many of which already exist and simply need to be hooked together in the appropriate way.

Consider the problem of simulating an automated teller machine (ATM). An ATM is a server that allows users to enter a name (on the card) and password to gain access to different kinds of bank accounts. The user can then select among various functions, each of which may request other inputs. A successful transaction results in output to the user, and may result in a change to an account. An unsuccessful transaction (using a bad password, for example) may lead to other outputs.

The ATM relies on other servers for support. Two of these are an **iostream** class and an account class. The role of the ATM is to serve as an interface handler that controls the communication between a user and his or her account. Put another way, you can think of an ATM class as both a model for an ATM machine and as an "application class" that drives the simulation.

To design an object-oriented system to solve this problem, we first take an inventory of existing classes to see how they can capture the desired behavior. Let's assume that we have an account class at our disposal. The account class has been extended to support user names and passwords.

Now that we know what we have, we can think about what we have to develop. The ATM can be represented as a new class. It will use, as servers, the **iostream** class and the account class. It will maintain the following data members:

1.   Master name and password (used to start up or shut down the system)
2.   Current account (the account currently being processed).

The ATM will serve users in two different modes:

1.   *Master user mode:* This mode allows an authorized bank employee to start up the machine in customer mode, to perform service functions such as entering a new account, and to shut the machine down.
2.   *Customer mode:* This mode allows an authorized customer to access an account to perform transactions.

Let's look at the abstract behavior that the ATM provides for each mode:

1.   Master mode
     1.1 Enter a new account
     1.2 Start customer mode
     1.3 Shut machine down
2.   Customer mode
     2.1 Get name and password
     2.2 If they belong to master mode then
     2.3   Run master mode
     2.4 Else if they belong to an account then
     2.5   Perform a transaction on the account
     2.6 Else handle user error

Many of the numbered items in both modes describe requests to which an ATM object can respond. Master mode really is a menu-driven command interpreter.

Let's develop code for the algorithm. First, when the request **master_mode** is sent to an ATM object, a member function should enter a command loop. The loop should display the master mode menu and wait for the user to enter the number of a command. When this occurs, the ATM runs the corresponding member function. After the function returns, the loop is entered once more. The following code might be an implementation of the **master_mode** member function:

```
void ATM::master_mode()
{
        int command;

        do
        {
                print_master_menu();
                command = get_command(1, 3);
                switch (command)
                {
```

```
                            case 1: enter_account();
                                    break;
                            case 2: customer_mode();
                                    break;
                            case 3: shut_down();
                }
        } while (command != 3);
}
```

Note that the manager launches customer mode by entering command 2 and shuts the machine down by entering command 3.

The member function **customer_mode** is

```
void ATM::customer_mode()
{
        string name, password;
        bool master_on = FALSE;

        do
        {
                cout << "Enter your name: ";
                cin >> name;
                cout << "Enter your password: ";
                cin >> password;
                if (master_account(name, password))
                        master_on = TRUE;
                else if (customer_account(name, password))
                        perform_transaction(password);
                else
                        cout << "Sorry, you entered an "
                             << "incorrect name or password."
                             << endl;
        } while (! master_on);
}
```

master_account is a member function that returns **TRUE** if the name and password match those of an authorized employee, and **FALSE** otherwise. The loop terminates when an authorized employee enters a name and password for master mode.

perform_transaction displays a menu of transaction options to the user, takes a command number, and performs the corresponding command:

```
void ATM::perform_transaction(const apstring &password)
{
        int command;

        print_transaction_menu();
        command = get_command(1, 3);
        switch (command)
        {
                case 1: get_balance(password);
                        break;
```

```
                              case 2: make_deposit(password);
                                      break;
                              case 3: make_withdrawal(password);
                      }
              }
```

As you can see, the ATM class that we have developed thus far is a large body of code, broken down into many small member functions (the use of classes does not free developers entirely from top-down design and algorithm development!). Most of these can be declared **private**, for the internal use of the ATM class only. A single member function, **master_mode**, can be declared **public**. This function can be invoked from a main program in C++, right after an ATM instance is declared. It would run master mode and wait for commands. The main program would be

```
// Program file: atmdriv.cpp

#include <iostream.h>
#include "apstring.h"
#include "atm.h"

int main()
{
        apstring name, password;

        cout << "Enter your name: ";
        cin >> name;
        cout << "Enter your password: ";
        cin >> password;
        ATM teller(name, password);
        teller.master_mode();
        return 0;
}
```

Here is the header file for the ATM class:

```
// Class declaration file: atm.h

#ifndef ATM_H

#include "bool.h"
#include "apstring.h"
#include "account.h"

// Declaration section

class ATM
{

        public:
```

```
        // Class constructors

        ATM(const apstring &n, const apstring &p);

        // Member functions

        void master_mode();

        private:

        // Data members

        //Used to start up or shut down the system
        apstring master_name, master_password;

        // The account currently being processed
        account current_account;

        // Member functions

        void customer_mode();
        bool master_account(const apstring &n, const apstring &p);
        bool customer_account(const apstring &n, const apstring &p);
        void perform_transaction(const apstring &password);
        void get_balance(const apstring &password);
        void make_deposit(const apstring &password);
        void make_withdrawal(const apstring &password);
        int get_command(int low, int high);
        void enter_account();
        void shut_down();
        void print_transaction_menu();
        void print_master_menu();

    };

#define ATM_H
#endif
```

The complete implementation file is left as an exercise.

Running, Debugging, and Testing Hints

1. Before you write a definition of a new class, write a description of the data members and abstract behavior that the class should exhibit.
2. Write a simple driver program to test each member function of a class.

Summary

⚷ Key Terms

abstract data type	data abstraction	parameter object
access specifier	data member	polymorphism
accessor	default constructor	private member
attribute	dereference operator	procedural programming
base class	derived class	protected member
behavior	encapsulation	public member
cascade	formal specification	receiver
class	free function	receiver object
class constructor	inheritance	scaling
class declaration section	instance (object)	selector
class hierarchy	l-value	sender
class implementation	member	server
section	member function	shallow copy
client	modifier	software reuse
const function	object-oriented	struct
constructor	programming	translation
copy constructor	overloading	

⚷ Keywords

class	**protected**	**struct**
private	**public**	**this**

⚷ Key Concepts

◆ A struct is a data structure that allows components of different types to be referenced by name. The form of a struct type definition is

```
struct <new type name>
{
        <data type> <member name 1>;
        .
        .
        <data type> <member name n>;
};
```

◆ The component parts of a struct are called members and are accessed by the selector notation according to the following form:

```
<struct variable>.<member name>
```

◆ Data abstraction is the process of separating a conceptual definition of a data structure from its implementation details.

◆ An abstract data type (ADT) consists of a class of objects, a defined set of properties for the objects, and a set of operations for processing the objects.

◆ Libraries for abstract data types can be created by specifying a header file and an implementation file.

◆ A class defines the abstract behavior and attributes belonging to an object.

◆ Objects provide services by responding to the requests sent by clients.

◆ Objects can be used to model or simulate objects in the real world, such as bank accounts, or computational objects, such as rational numbers.

◆ A class declaration specifies the public and private data and function members for a class of objects.

◆ A class implementation provides the implementations of the member functions for a class of objects.

◆ Polymorphic operators have the same general meaning, but can be used with data of different types or classes.

◆ Free (nonmember) functions are not declared within the scope of the class declaration.

◆ Classes can reuse data and behavior by inheriting them from a base class.

◆ Derived classes can specialize inherited behavior by extending it or overriding it.

◆ Data and operations can be hidden from all users by declaring them **private** within a class.

◆ Data and operations can be made available to all users by declaring them **public** within a class.

◆ Data and operations can be made available to derived classes but hidden from all other users by declaring them **protected** within a class.

Suggestions for Further Reading

Booch, Grady. *Object-Oriented Analysis and Design* (2nd ed.). Redwood City, CA: Benjamin/Cummings, 1994.

Coad, Peter, and Yourdon, Edward. *Object-Oriented Analysis* (2nd ed.). Englewood Cliffs, NJ: Yourdon Press, 1991.

Jacobson, I., Christerson, M., Jonsoon, P., and Overgaard, G. *Object-Oriented Software Engineering.* Reading, MA: Addison-Wesley, 1992.

Lambert, K., and Osborne, M. *Smalltalk in Brief: Introduction to Object-Oriented Software Development.* Boston: PWS Publishing Company, 1997.

Rumbaugh, J., et al., *Object-Oriented Modeling and Design.* Englewood Cliffs, NJ: Prentice Hall, 1991.

Chapter Review Exercises

For Exercises 1–5, use a struct containing the following information:

Student name (a string)
Homeroom number (an integer)
Class (a string)
Lab fees paid (a Boolean)
GPA (a real number)

1. Write a type definition and declare a variable of this type.

2. Draw a diagram of the memory reserved for the variable of Exercise 1.
3. Write a function to input data for this type.
4. Add a definition to create an array of 50 structs.
5. Write a function to display a list of names and homerooms of students who have not paid their fees.

For Exercises 6–17, refer to the following struct definition:

```
struct rec1
{
    int a[10];
    double b;
    int c[3] [5];
};

typedef rec1 arry[4];

rec1 x;
arry y;
```

Which of the following references are syntactically correct?
6. **x.b**
7. **y.b**
8. **x.a[0]**
9. **y.a[0]**
10. **x[0].b**
11. **y[0].b**
12. **y[1] .x[3]**
13. **y[2]**
14. **x.c[2] [3]**
15. **y[4].b**
16. **y.x.a**
17. **y.b**
18. Write a type definition of data structures that can be used to keep track of the names of nine starters on a baseball team, their positions, and their batting averages.
19. Include the struct definition in Exercise 18 in another struct to also keep the school names and nicknames of 10 high school baseball teams.
20. Write a function to check the struct defined in Exercise 19 and display the name of a team having a shortstop named Mapes.

For Exercises 21–24, develop a class called **student** with the following attributes:

Name (a string)
Homeroom number (an integer)
Class (a string)
Lab fees paid (a Boolean)
GPA (a real number)

21. Write the specifications of the operations for the **student** class. In addition to a create operation that sets all of the attributes of a student to reasonable default values, there should be an operation that returns the value of each attribute and an operation that modifies the value of each attribute. Each specification should describe the preconditions and postconditions of the operation.

22. Write declarations of the data members for all of the attributes. You may assume that a string class is available.

23. Write a default constructor that initializes the data members of a **student** object to reasonable default values.

24. Write member functions that return the values of the data members.

For Exercises 25–27, you will develop three classes called **baseball_player**, **pitcher**, and **batter**.

25. Write a class declaration module for the **baseball_player** class. A baseball player has a name, a height, and a weight. Each attibute can be observed or modified.

26. A pitcher has all of the attributes of a baseball player. A pitcher also has two other attributes: number of innings pitched and earned run average. Write a class declaration module for the **pitcher** class. This class should inherit all of the attributes and operations, in public mode, from the **baseball_player** class, and then provide the additional attributes and operations for a pitcher.

27. A batter has all of the attributes of a baseball player. A batter also has two other attributes: number of home runs and batting average. Write a class declaration module for the **batter** class. This class should inherit all of the attributes and operations, in public mode, from the **baseball_player** class, and then provide the additional attributes and operations for a batter.

28. Write an essay describing the difference between the public, protected, and private access modes used in C++ class declarations. Clarify how these modes help to control the flow of information between modules in a software system.

Programming Problems and Activities

1. Write a program to be used by the registrar of a university. The program should get information from the keyboard, and the data for each student should include student name, student number, classification (1 for freshman, 2 for sophomore, 3 for junior, 4 for senior, or 7 for special student), hours completed, hours taking, and grade-point average. You should design a class to represent a student as an abstract data type.

2. Robert Day, basketball coach at Indiana College, wants you to write a program to help him analyze information about his basketball team. He wants a record for each player containing the player's name, position played, high school graduated from, height, scoring average, rebounding average, grade-point average, and seasons of eligibility remaining. You should design a class to represent a player as an abstract data type.

   The program should read the information for each player from a data file. The output should include an alphabetized list of names together with other pertinent information, a list sorted according to scoring average, an alphabetized list of all players with a grade-point average above 3.0, and an alphabetized list of high schools together with an alphabetized list of players who graduated from each school.

3. Implement and extend the ATM class to handle user errors by confiscating a card after three unsuccessful attempts to gain access to an account.

4. Complex numbers are numbers of the form $a + bi$, where a and b are real and i represents sqrt(−1). Complex number arithmetic is defined by

Sum	$(a + bi) + (c + di) = (a + c) + (b + d)i$
Difference	$(a + bi) - (c + di) = (a - c) + (b - d)i$
Product	$(a + bi)(c + di) = (ac - bd) + (ad + bc)i$
Quotient	$(a + bi)/(c + di) = \dfrac{ac+bd}{c^2 + d^2} + \dfrac{(bd - ad)i}{c^2 + d^2}$

Write a program that will perform these calculations on two complex numbers. Each line of data consists of a single character designator (S, D, P, or Q) followed by four reals representing two complex numbers. For example, $(2+3i)+(5-2i)$ is represented by

`S2 3 5 - 2`

An instance of a class should be used for each complex number. The arithmetic operators should be overloaded to carry out the operations. Input and output should be in the form $a + bi$ (overload the input and output operators as well).

5. The Readmore Public Library wants a program to keep track of the books checked out. Information for each book should be kept in an object and the data members should include the author's name, a nonfiction designator (Boolean), the title, the library catalog number, and the copyright date. Each customer can check out at most 10 books. Develop an abstract data type for representing a book as a C++ class. There should be public member functions for returning each attribute of a book, and input and output operations for initializing and printing them as well.

6. Modify Problem 5 so that a daily printout is available that contains a summary of the day's transactions at the Readmore Public Library. You will need an object for each customer containing the customer's name and library card number. Be sure to make provision for books that are returned.

7. Write a program that uses objects to analyze poker hands. Each hand consists of five objects (cards). Each object should have one data member for the suit and one for the value. Rankings for the hands from high to low are

Straight flush
Four of a kind
Full house
Flush
Straight
Three of a kind
Two pair
One pair
None of the above

Your program should read data for five cards from the keyboard, evaluate the hand, and print the hand together with a message indicating its value.

8. Problem 7 can be modified in several ways. A first modification is to compare two different hands using only the ranking indicated. A second (more difficult)

modification is to also compare hands that have the same ranking. For example, a pair of eights is better than a pair of sevens. Extend Problem 7 to incorporate some of these modifications.

9. The university Biology Department has a Conservation Club that works with the state's Department of Natural Resources. Their project for the semester is to help capture and tag migratory birds. You have been asked to write a computer program to help them store information. In general, the program must have information for each bird tagged entered interactively in an object for subsequent use. For each bird tagged, you need a data member for the tag number, tagging site, sex, bird type, date, and name of the DNR officer doing the tagging. After all data have been entered, the program should print the contents of the object.

10. Mrs. Crown, your computer science instructor, wishes to keep track of the maintenance record of her computers and has turned to you for help. She wants to keep track of the type of machine, its serial number (up to 10 characters), the year of purchase, and a Boolean variable indicating whether the machine is under service contract. Write a program that permits the entry of this information and prints a record for a machine.

11. Write a program to read data containing the name, address, telephone number, and class of friend into an object and prints its contents.

12. The Falcon Manufacturing Company wishes to keep computerized structures of its telephone-order customers. They want the name, street address, city, state, and zip code for each customer. They include either a "T" if the customer is a business, or an "F" if the customer is an individual. A 30-character description of each business is also included. An individual's credit limit is in the structure.

    Write a program to read the information for the customer from the keyboard and print the information on the screen.

13. The **dice** library developed earlier (Problem 19, Chapter 4; Problem 32, Chapter 5; and Problem 40, Chapter 6) can be modified so that dice are represented as a C++ class. Each die has the following attributes:

    The number of dots
    A size (width in pixels)
    A position (upper left corner point)

    The default number of dots for a die is one. A die can be manipulated as follows:
    a. Create with specified size and position
    b. Roll, which modifies the number of dots
    b. Draw
    c. Erase
    d. Translate (as defined in Section 9.6)
    Develop the class for dice by writing formal specifications, declaring and implementing the code in C++, and testing it in the application from Problem 40, Chapter 6.

14. Develop the **polygon** class discussed in Section 9.6, Exercise 9. Test it with a driver program that creates triangles, squares, and pentagons with polygons.

15. Redo the dice class of Problem 13 so that the graphical image of a die is represented as a **polygon** object. Test the new implementation with the same application.

16. In the dice application, the dice appear to converge toward the center of the screen from its edges. A more realistic animation would rotate the dice as they

move horizontally. Describe how you might produce this effect by adding a member function **rotate** to the **polygon** class. This function expects the number of degrees (an integer) to rotate the object. A positive value causes counterclockwise rotation; a negative value causes clockwise rotation. (*Hint:* The image of a die has a center point by reference to which its corners and its dots are positioned.)

Communication in Practice

1. Interview some computer professionals in your region to determine whether they use object-oriented methods and programming languages in their work. Prepare a report for your class on your findings.

2. Interview some computer professionals in your region to determine how they make use of client/server relationships in their work. Prepare a report for your class on your findings.

3. Write an essay describing the importance of writing formal specifications for each abstract data type used in a program. Describe how this document can be used to enhance communication among programming team members.

4. Visit your local college's registrar, and discuss how information about students is represented and processed. Discover what data are kept on each student, how they are entered, and what the attributes are. Have the registrar explain what operations are allowed on each student. Prepare a written report for the class. Be sure to include a graphic that depicts how each student object can be envisioned.

5. Select an unworked problem from the **Programming Problems and Activities** for this chapter. Construct a structure chart and write all documentary information necessary for this problem. Do not write code. When finished, have a classmate read your documentation to see if precisely what is to be done is clear.

Chapter 10

Safe Arrays

Chapter Outline

T he C++ array is a useful data structure, but some features can cause inconvenience or, even worse, errors in users' programs. Perhaps the most serious problem is the absence of built-in range checking. Recall that references to data locations within an array must be specified by an index value that is within the range from zero (the first location) to **MAX_ARRAY_SIZE - 1** (the last location), where **MAX_ARRAY_SIZE** is the number of locations specified by the array variable declaration. Because range errors go undetected, they may cause undesirable behavior such as logic errors (unexpected output) or system crashes (side effects on the underlying operating system). Clearly, an array would be safer if it detected range errors and halted program execution with a message, rather than causing logic errors or crashes.

Several other features of C++ arrays are inconvenient:

1. A user ought to be able to copy the contents of one array to another by means of an assignment statement (**a = b**), but this is prohibited in most implementations of C++.

2. A user might want to copy the contents of one array into another of lesser or greater size. However, a standard C++ array cannot adjust its capacity to store data elements as needed.

3. Users might be confused about passing an array as a parameter to a function. They might prefer to see formal array parameters specified like other parameters, with the **&** symbol meaning pass by reference, and the absence of this symbol meaning pass by value. However, C++ arrays are always passed by reference, even when the **&** symbol is omitted in the parameter declaration.

In this chapter, we develop several C++ classes that solve these and other problems with the use of arrays.

10.1 Vectors

Objectives

◆ to be able to design and implement a new class that satisfies the requirements for a safe array

◆ to understand and implement a class template that allows users to specify the element type of a safe array

◆ to understand how dynamic storage allocation allows users to specify the size of a safe array and allows a safe array to adjust its size as needed

vector: A one-dimensional array that provides range checking and can be resized.

fill value: A value that is used to initialize every component in a data structure.

User Requirements

The first step in developing a new class to solve the problems with C++ arrays is to draw up a list of user requirements. These state the features and behavior that users or clients expect the class to have. We have seen that C++ arrays are both unsafe and inconvenient. Users would like the new class to retain the desirable features of arrays and avoid the undesirable ones. The list of features for the new class, called **vector,** follows:

1. Like arrays, vectors should support the subscript or indexing operation. This operation uses an integer index value to access a data element in constant time.
2. Indexing should be safe; range errors should be detected at run time.
3. Like arrays, vectors can contain data elements of any type, as long as the data elements in a given vector are all of the same type. The user specifies the type of element when a vector variable is declared.
4. Like arrays, vectors should have a fixed size or number of allowable data elements. This size can be specified when the user declares a vector variable, or it can be a default value of zero. The user should be able to examine and change the storage capacity of a vector.
5. Users should be able to specify a **fill value** to initialize the data elements in a vector when it is declared.
6. Vectors should support the standard assignment operation.
7. Vectors should adjust their size as needed during assignment operations.

To summarize, the use of instances of the vector class should resemble the use of standard C++ arrays, but be safer, cleaner, and more convenient. The following two examples compare the use of an array with the use of a vector to solve a problem.

Example 10.1

This program uses an array to obtain a user-specified number of integers as inputs. The program computes and displays the average of the integers in the array.

```
// Program file: arrayav.cpp

#include <iostream.h>

int const MAX_LIST_SIZE = 100;

int main()
{
    int list[MAX_LIST_SIZE];
    int count;

    cout << "Enter the number of integers: ";
    cin >> count;
    if (count > MAX_LIST_SIZE)
        cout << "Sorry, not enough memory" << endl;
    else
```

```
    {
            int i, data;
            for (i = 0; i < count; ++i)
            {
                    cout << "Enter the next integer: ";
                    cin >> data;
                    list[i] = data;
            }
            int sum = 0;
            for (i = 0; i < count; ++i)
                    sum = sum + list[i];
            cout << "The average is "
                << sum / count;
    }
    return 0;
}
```

Note that the user is limited by the size of the array defined by the program. If the user's count is greater than this size, the program quits with an error message. Also, if one of the loops is off by one, any range error will go undetected, possibly causing a system crash or a logic error.

| Example 10.2 |

The program of Example 10.1 is modified to use a vector rather than an array to store the input data. The program assumes that the vector class is implemented in the library file **apvector.cpp**. A complete definition of the **apvector** class appears in Appendix 6.

```
// Program file: vectorav.cpp

#include <iostream.h>

#include "apvector.cpp"

int main()
{
    int count;

    cout << "Enter the number of integers: ";
    cin >> count;

    apvector<int> list(count); // Create a vector of
                               // count integers
    int i, data;
    for (i = 0; i < count; ++i)
    {
            cout << "Enter the next integer: ";
            cin >> data;
            list[i] = data;
```

```
        }
        int sum = 0;
        for (i = 0; i < count; ++i)
              sum = sum + list[i];
        cout << "The average is "
              << sum / count;
        return 0;
    }
```

The most obvious change from the previous example is that the program defines the size of the vector with the user's count (a variable). In other words, the computer automatically allocates just the right amount of memory to store the user's data. Another change, in the syntax of the vector's declaration, is the use of the angle bracket **< >** notation to specify the element type of the vector. The least obvious change is that range errors may still occur in the loops, but the computer will detect them and halt execution with appropriate error messages.

The most important difference between vectors and standard C++ arrays is that vectors know about their size. They can use this knowledge to perform their own run-time range checking and to increase or decrease their capacity to hold data elements as needed.

Specifying the Operations for Vectors

Recall from previous chapters that these specifications take the form of preconditions and postconditions on all of the allowable operations for the class. The attributes of a vector are

1. **mySize** (the vector's capacity)
2. **myList** (the vector's data elements)
3. **itemType** (the vector's element type).

A formal specification of the vector class is

Create operation (default size)

Preconditions : The vector is in an unpredictable state.

Postconditions: **mySize** and **myList** are set to zero

Create operation (user-specified size)

Preconditions : The vector is in an unpredictable state.
                 size is an integer value **>= 0**.
                 There is memory available for creating a vector capable of storing **size** data elements.

Postconditions: Memory is reserved for a vector object capable of storing **size** data elements, and **mySize** is set to **size**.

(continued)

Create operation (user-specified size and fill value)

Preconditions :   The vector is in an unpredictable state.

`size` is an integer value `> 0`.

`fillValue` is a data element of the element type of the vector. There is memory available for creating a vector capable of storing `size` data elements.

Postconditions: Memory is reserved for a vector object capable of storing `size` data elements, `mySize` is set to `size`, and all of the cells in the vector are set to `fillValue`.

Destroy operation

Preconditions :   The vector is appropriately initialized.

Postconditions: The memory for the vector is made available to the computer for other applications.

Length operation

Preconditions :   The vector is appropriately initialized.

Postconditions: The value of `mySize` is returned.

Resize operation

Preconditions :   The vector is appropriately initialized.

`newSize` is an integer specifying the desired capacity of the vector.

Postconditions: The capacity of the vector is adjusted to the desired size, if memory is available, and `mySize` is set to `newSize`. Any data elements stored in the vector are copied to the resized vector. Some data may be lost if the new size is less than the old size.

Subscript operation (for observation or modification of a data element)

Preconditions :   The vector is appropriately initialized.

`index` is an integer value in the range `0 <= index < mySize`.

Postconditions: The location of a data element, which can be used either to observe or to store an object, is returned.

Subscript operation (for observation of a data element only)

Preconditions :   The vector is appropriately initialized.

`index` is an integer value in the range `0 <= index < mySize`.

Postconditions: The object at the index position is returned.

Assignment operation

Preconditions :   The target vector is appropriately initialized.

The source vector is appropriately initialized.

There is memory available for making the capacity of the target object equal to the capacity of the source object.

Postconditions: The capacity of the target object is adjusted to the capacity of the source object, and the contents of the source object are copied into the target object.

Note that these specifications include a *destroy* operation. We discuss the need for this operation shortly.

Declaring the Vector Class

To maintain consistency with the conventional uses of arrays, we use the standard operators for subscripting and assignment in the class declaration, and provide overloaded operations for them in the class implementation.

```
// Class declaration file: apvector.h

#ifndef _APVECTOR_H

template <class itemType> class apvector
{
    public:

    // constructors
    apvector();
    apvector(int size);
    apvector(int size, const itemType &fillValue);
    apvector(const apvector<itemType> &vec);

    // destructor

    ~apvector();

    // assignment

    const apvector<itemType>& operator =
            (const apvector<itemType> &rhs);

    // accessor

    int length() const;      // capacity of vector

    // indexing

    const itemType& operator [ ] (int index) const;
    itemType& operator [ ] (int index);

    // modifier

    void resize(int newSize);

    private:

    // Data members

    int mySize;             // # elements in array
    itemType *myList;       // array used for storage
```

```
};

#define _APVECTOR_H
#endif
```

Note that we declare two different subscript (`[ ]`) operations. The first subscript is declared as a constant operator that returns the value at the specified index position. This operation will be used in cases where the vector's contents cannot be changed, such as within functions that receive a vector as a constant parameter. The second subscript returns a reference to a memory cell in the vector, allowing either access to or modifications of the cell's contents. Note also the notation `itemType *myList` used to declare the array representing the data elements in a vector. We discuss this notation shortly.

Class Templates

A **class template** in C++ allows users to specify the component types in a class when instances of that class are created. In the case of the vector class, a user could create a vector of integers, a vector of real numbers, and a vector of strings, using the angle bracket notation shown earlier:

```
apvector<int> int_vector;
apvector<double> double_vector;
apvector<apstring> string_vector;
```

The angle brackets appear again in the class declaration, this time surrounding information about the component type. We use the notations `template <class itemType>` and `apvector<itemType>` to specify that the class can have any element type. The name `itemType` behaves like a formal type parameter in the class definition. It holds a place for any actual type parameter provided by the user, such as `int`, `double`, or `apstring`, when an instance of the class is created. Other than learning this new syntax and some special restrictions on included files (noted later), working with class templates should be about the same as working with ordinary C++ classes.

Pointers and Dynamic Memory

The data members for the **apvector** class are **mySize**, an integer, and **myList**, a pointer to an item type. We use a **pointer variable** in C++ when we cannot predict the size of a data structure. A pointer variable can hold the address of a chunk of **dynamic memory.** Dynamic memory is memory that the programmer can request when it is needed by an application. You do not have to have a complete understanding of these ideas to use them to implement vectors. We examine the syntax and behavior of pointers and dynamic memory in more detail in Chapter 11.

Constructing Vectors

The first member functions to be implemented are the creation operations or constructors. The default constructor sets the **mySize** data member to zero and the **myList** data member to zero:

class template: A kind of class that allows its component types to be specified as parameters.

pointer variable: A variable that contains the address of a memory location.

dynamic memory: Memory allocated under program control and accessed by means of pointers.

```
template <class itemType>
apvector<itemType>::apvector()
        : mySize(0), myList(0)
{
}
```

Note the following:

1. The notation : **mySize(0), myList(0)** is equivalent to the following pair of assignment statements:

```
mySize = 0;
myList = 0;
```

2. The special pointer value 0 is used to indicate an empty pointer, or the fact that no dynamic memory has yet been allocated to store data in **myList**.
3. There are no statements within the **{ }**.

The second constructor allows the user to specify the capacity of the vector with a parameter:

```
template <class itemType>
apvector<itemType>::apvector(int size)
{
        assert (size > 0);
        mySize = size;
        myList = new itemType[size];
        assert myList != 0;
}
```

This constructor asks for memory for the vector by running a statement of the form

---
<pointer variable> **= new** <item type> **[** <number of items> **];**

We use **new** in C++ to allocate memory for a data object dynamically, or as needed by a program. **new** is an operator that returns a pointer to a block of memory if memory is available. If memory is not available, **new** returns the pointer value 0. This block of memory, referenced by **myList** in a vector, behaves just like a standard C++ array. When working with **new** to allocate dynamic memory for arrays, remember these two important points:

1. The type and number of data elements should be specified.
2. You should verify that memory is available and has been allocated. We use the **assert** function for this throughout the class definition.

The difference between the two constructors can be illustrated as follows. Suppose that we have the declarations

```
apvector<int> v1;
apvector<int> v2(25);
```

Then the statements

```
cout << v1.length() << endl;
cout << v2.length() << endl;
```

will produce the output

```
0
25
```

If we then run the statement

```
v1.resize(25);
```

the vectors **v1** and **v2** will have the same size, because **resize** allocates dynamic memory for **v1**.

The Destructor for Vectors

The programmer is responsible for returning dynamic memory to the computer system when it is no longer needed. To help automate this process, C++ will run a special function called a **destructor** if it is in the class definition. C++ runs this function whenever locally declared pointer variables go out of scope, as in the following situation:

destructor: A member function that returns dynamic memory for an object to the system.

```
void lose_memory()
{
        apvector<int> local_vector(200);
}
```

This function appears to do nothing but declare a vector of 200 integers and return. However, unlike memory used for ordinary local variables, the dynamic memory allocated for the vector is not automatically returned to the system. If this function were called often enough, the program would run out of memory and crash.

If a destructor function is defined that returns the memory for the vector to the system, the computer will run the destructor automatically. The destructor for vectors follows:

```
template <class itemType>
apvector<itemType>::~apvector()
{
        delete [] myList;
}
```

The **delete** operator is the inverse of **new**. **delete** returns the memory pointed to by its operand to the system.

Remember that the destructor, **~apvector**, is run automatically and does not have to be invoked by the programmer.

Copy Constructor and Assignment

The copy constructor attempts to allocate memory for a copy of the data member **myList** of the vector parameter and to verify allocation. Then it iterates through the elements in this data member, copying the value of each element into the corresponding location in the data member of the receiver object.

```
template <class itemType>
apvector<itemType>::apvector(const apvector<itemType> &vec)
{
    mySize = vec.length();
    myList = new itemType [mySize];
    assert(myList != 0);
    for (int j = 0; j < mySize; ++j)
        myList[j] = vec.myList[j];
}
```

The assignment operation involves a similar process of memory allocation and copying. However, memory for the target object is first returned to the system, and a constant reference to the target object is returned at the end of the function.

```
template <class itemType>
const apvector& apvector<itemType>::operator =
    (const apvector<itemType> &rhs)
{
    if (this != &rhs)
    {
        delete [] myList;
        mySize = rhs.length();
        myList = new itemType [mySize];
        assert(myList != 0);
        for (int k = 0; k < mySize; ++k)
            myList[k] = rhs.myList[k];
    }
    return *this;
}
```

Note that both of these operations assume that an assignment operation exists for the element objects. Remember that complex objects (like bank accounts, strings, and safe arrays) should implement their own assignment operations, so that all of their data members are accurately copied.

Indexing

The indexing or subscript operations provide the primary benefit of a vector class: run-time range checking. The implementations use **assert** to enforce the preconditions governing the index value. If the value of the index parameter is out of range, the program will halt with an error message.

```
template <class itemType>
const itemType& apvector<itemType>::operator [ ] (int index) const
{
        assert((index >= 0) && (index < mySize));
        return myList[index];
}

template <class itemType>
itemType& apvector<itemType>::operator [ ] (int index)
{
        assert((index >= 0) && (index < mySize));
        return myList[index];
}
```

Example 10.3

The following program is a driver for testing many of the **apvector** operations:

```
// Program file: vectdriv.cpp

#include <iostream.h>

#include "apvector.cpp"

int main()
{
        apvector<int> a(10), b;
        int i;

// Test subscripts
        for (i = 0; i < a.length(); ++i)
                a[i] = i;

        cout<< "Values in vector a are: " << endl;
        for (i = 0; i < a.length(); ++i)
                cout << a[i] << " ";
        cout << endl;

// Test assignment
        b = a;

        cout<< "Values in vector b are: " << endl;
        for (i = 0; i < b.length(); ++i)
                cout << b[i] << " ";
        cout << endl;
```

```
            // Test range error check
                cout << a[10] << endl;
                return 0;
        }
```

The program produces the following output (the error message generated by **assert** may vary on different implementations):

```
Values in vector a are:
0 1 2 3 4 5 6 7 8 9
Values in vector b are:
0 1 2 3 4 5 6 7 8 9
vector.cpp:80 (index >= 0) && (index < size) -- assertion failed
abort -- terminating
```

Including Libraries of Class Templates

You might have noticed in Examples 10.2 and 10.3 that the programs include the class implementation file, **apvector.cpp**, rather than the header or declaration file, **apvector.h**. As a rule of thumb, any program module (the main program or another library header file) that uses a class template should include its implementation file rather than its header or declaration file. This unusual practice is required for the compiler to generate code for the templates when they are specialized for an element type in a module.

■ Exercises 10.1

1. Declare variables for the following data:
   a. A vector of 20 integers
   b. A vector of 100 characters, each initialized to **'a'**
   c. A vector of 50 persons (assume that class **person** is already defined)
   d. A vector of 20 vectors of 20 integers (*Hint:* your declaration will have nested angle brackets.)

2. Write and test a program that runs the following code with vectors and explain what happens:

   ```
   apvector<int> a;
   for (int i = 0; i <= 10; ++i)
         a[i] = i;
   ```

3. Describe the difference between the two indexing operations defined for vectors. What would happen if the constant indexing operation were not defined?

4. The assignment operation for vectors references every memory location in the source vector. Discuss any problems that might arise from these references. For example, predict what happens when you run the following pieces of code:
   a. ```
      apvector<int> a(100, 55);
         for (int i = 0; i < 100; ++i)
             cout << a[i] << endl;
      ```
      ```

b. ```
apvector<int> a(100);
for (int i = 0; i < 100; ++i)
    cout << a[i] << endl;
```
c. ```
apvector<int> a, b(100);
a = b;
for (int i = 0; i < 100; ++i)
    cout << a[i] << endl;
```

5. The assignment operation for vectors deletes and reallocates memory for the target vector, even if it has the same capacity as the source vector. Modify this member function in the implementation so that this unnecessary process will not occur.

10.2 Strings

Objectives

- to understand the requirements for a string
- to be able to design and implement a class that satisfies these requirements
- to understand and implement range checking for strings
- to understand the difference between the length of a string and the capacity of its underlying data structure

substring: A string that represents a segment of another string.

User Requirements

Throughout this text, we have been using a string class (**apstring**) to declare string variables and manipulate them with operations such as input (**>>**) and concatenation (**+**). As an abstract data type, the string class allows users to process strings without concern for the way in which the strings' data and operations are implemented. Viewed abstractly, a string is like a safe array, in that individual characters within the string can be accessed with a subscript operation, as long as the index is within a certain range. For example, in the following code segment, the first subscript operation, which returns the character **'i'**, is valid, but the second one produces an error:

```
apstring my_string;

my_string = "Hi there!";
cout << my_string[1] << endl;
cout << my_string[my_string.length()] << endl;
```

The valid index positions for this string are the integers 0 through 8. The length of the string, 9, is an invalid index position.

However, a string is unlike a safe array in that its length refers to the number of characters currently stored in the string, rather than the capacity (number of memory cells) of the underlying data structure. Users of strings are not aware of this distinction, but it may (and does) play a role in the implementation of a string class, as we see shortly.

In addition to the operations that we have seen thus far in this text, there are operations to search for given characters or **substrings** in a string and to access substrings at given positions.

Example 10.4

This program illustrates the use of the substring operations.

```
// Program file: substr.cpp

#include <iostream.h>
#include "apstring.h"
```

```
int main()
{
        apstring my_string;
        my_string = "Hi there!";

        // Output the index position of 't' (3)

        cout << my_string.find('t') << endl;

        // Output the starting index position
        // of "here" (4)

        cout << my_string.find("here") << endl;

        // Output the substring starting at position 0
        // and having a length of 2 ("Hi")

        cout << my_string.substr(0, 2) << endl;

        return 0;
}
```

Specifying the Operations for Strings

The attributes of a string are

1. **myCapacity** (the number of cells for storing characters)
2. **myLength** (the number of characters currently stored)
3. **myCString** (the string's characters).

We present formal specifications for only some of the string operations. A complete definition of the **apstring** class appears in Appendix 6.

Create operation (default)

Preconditions :   The string is in an unpredictable state.

Postconditions: **myCapacity** and **myLength** are set to zero.

Create operation (with string literal from user)

Preconditions :   The string is in an unpredictable state.

                The parameter **s** is a string literal.

                There is memory available for creating a string capable of storing **s**.

Postconditions: Memory is reserved for storing the characters in **s**, including the null character, which are copied into **myCString**.

                myCapacity is set to the size of this memory, and **myLength** is set to **myCapacity - 1**.

Destroy operation

Preconditions :   The string is appropriately initialized.

Postconditions: The memory for the string is made available to the computer for other applications.

(continued)

Length operation
Preconditions :   The string is appropriately initialized.
Postconditions: The value of **myLength** is returned.

Subscript operation (for observation of a data element only)
Preconditions :   The string is appropriately initialized.
                    index is an integer value in the range **0 <= index < myLength**.
Postconditions: The object at the index position is returned.

Assignment operation (another string object)
Preconditions :   The target string is appropriately initialized.
                    The source string is appropriately initialized.
                    There is memory available for making the capacity of the target object equal to the capacity of the source object.
Postconditions: If the capacity of the source object exceeds that of the target object, the capacity of the target object is adjusted to the capacity of the source object. The length of the target object is set to the length of the source object, and the contents of the source object are copied into the target object.

Assignment operation (a string literal)
Preconditions :   The target string is appropriately initialized.
                    The source string is a string literal.
                    There is memory available for making the capacity of the target object equal to the capacity of the source object.
Postconditions: The length of the target object is adjusted to the length of the source object, and the contents of the source object are copied into the target object.

Assignment operation (a character)
Preconditions :   The target string is appropriately initialized.
                    The source character is appropriately initialized.
                    There is memory available to create a target object whose capacity is 2.
Postconditions: The capacity of the target object is set to 2, its length is set to 1, and the source character is copied into **myCString** at the first position.

Find operation (a character)
Preconditions :   The string is appropriately initialized.
                    ch is the character to be found.
Postconditions: If the character is not in the string, -1 is returned. Otherwise, the index of the first instance of the character in the string is returned.

Find operation (a substring)
Preconditions :   The string is appropriately initialized.
                    str is the substring to be found.
Postconditions: If the substring is not in the string, -1 is returned. Otherwise, the starting index of the first instance of the substring in the string is returned.

                                                            (continued)

Substring operation

Preconditions :	The string is appropriately initialized.
	pos is the index of the first character of the substring, **len** is the length of the substring, and $0 \leq pos \leq pos + len - 1 < myLength$.
Postconditions:	Returns the substring of characters from position **pos** to position **pos + len - 1**.

C string operation

Preconditions :	The string is appropriately initialized.
Postconditions:	Returns an equivalent string as represented by the C language (actually, the attribute **myCString**).

Concatenate operation (two string objects)

Preconditions :	The string parameter is appropriately initialized.
	There is memory to create a string whose length equals the sum of the lengths of the parameter strings.
Postconditions:	Returns a new string representing the first parameter string followed by the second parameter string.

Note the following points:

1. Throughout the specifications, we distinguish between the capacity of a string and its length. A string's capacity is always at least one greater than its length. This allows for the storage of a null character (**'\0'**) at the end of the string. This character is used to mark the end of the string in the underlying data structure, but is not considered part of the string data from the user's perspective.
2. There is a constructor for creating a string object from a string literal. This constructor is used when string literals are passed as parameters to functions that expect string objects.
3. There are three assignment operations, allowing for the assignment of string objects, string literals, or individual characters to string variables.

Declaring the String Class

The class declaration file for the **apstring** class is

```
// Class declaration file: apstring.h

#ifndef _APSTRING_H
#define _APSTRING_H

#include <iostream.h>
#include "bool.h"

class apstring
{
        public:
```

```
// Constructors

apstring();
apstring(const char *s);
apstring(const apstring &str );

// Destructor

~apstring();

// Assignment

const apstring& operator =
      (const apstring &str );  // assign str
const apstring& operator =
      (const char *s );        // assign s
const apstring& operator =
      (char ch);               // assign ch

// Accessors

// number of chars

int length() const;

// index of first occurrence of str

int find(const apstring &str) const;

// index of first occurrence of ch

int find(char ch) const;

// substring of len chars starting at pos

apstring substr(int pos, int len) const;

// Conversion to type of string literal

const char* c_str() const;

// Indexing

char operator [ ](int index) const;
char& operator [ ](int index);

// Modifiers

const apstring& operator +=
      (const apstring &str);
```

```cpp
        const apstring& operator +=
                (char ch);

        private:

        // Data members

        int myLength;
        int myCapacity;
        char* myCstring;
};

// The following free (non-member)
// functions operate on strings

// I/O functions

ostream& operator << (ostream &os,
        const apstring &str);
istream& operator >> (istream &is,
        apstring &str);
istream& getline(istream &is,
        apstring &str);

// comparison operators:

bool operator == (const apstring &lhs,
        const apstring &rhs);
bool operator != (const apstring &lhs,
        const apstring &rhs);
bool operator < (const apstring &lhs,
        const apstring &rhs);
bool operator <= (const apstring &lhs,
        const apstring &rhs);
bool operator > (const apstring &lhs,
        const apstring &rhs);
bool operator >= (const apstring &lhs,
        const apstring &rhs);

// concatenation operator +

apstring operator + (const apstring &lhs,
        const apstring &rhs);
apstring operator + (char ch,
        const apstring &str);
apstring operator + (const apstring &str,
        char ch);

#endif
```

Constructing Strings

The data member **myCString** of the **apstring** class is declared as a pointer to a character. When a string object is created, memory is allocated for an array of characters and **myCString** is set to this memory, as is done with a vector object. However, in the case of a string, a single character, the null character (**'\0'**) is stored in this array:

```
apstring::apstring()
{
        myLength = 0;
        myCapacity = 1;
        myCString = new char[myCapacity];
        myCString[0] = '\0';
}
```

We use a null character at the end of **myCString** because this is how strings are represented in the C language. This language, which is a subset of C++, has a **string** library that defines several functions used by the implementation of the **apstring** class to manipulate **myCString**. The null character serves as a sentinel value that allows these functions to detect the end of a string within an array. Two **string** library functions, **strcpy** and **strlen**, are used in the next **apstring** constructor:

```
apstring::apstring(const char *s)
{
        myLength = strlen(s);
        myCapacity = myLength + 1;
        myCString = new char[myCapacity];
        strcpy(myCstring, s);
}
```

This function expects a C-style string (a string literal, for example) as a parameter. It performs the following steps:

1. Set the **myLength** data member to **strlen(s)**, which returns the length of the parameter **s**.
2. Set **myCapacity**, the physical size of **myCString**, to one greater than **myLength**, leaving room for the null character.
3. Allocate memory for **myCString**.
4. Run **strcpy(myCString, s)**, which copies all of the characters in **s**, including its null character, into **myCString**.

The implementation of the copy constructor is left as an exercise.

Conversion to a C-Style String

The use of a C-style string to represent the data within an **apstring** object is especially obvious in the implementation of the **c_str** function. This function returns the **myCString** data member, which is a C-style string:

```
const char* apstring::c_str() const
{
        return myCstring;
}
```

The **c_str** function serves as an accessor to the **myCstring** data member. However, because it is defined as a **const** function, the caller who receives the C-string as a returned value will not be allowed to modify its contents.

Substrings

There are two **find** functions. The first one returns the position of the first instance of a given character in a string, after a simple sequential search:

```
int apstring::find(char ch) const
{
        for (int k = 0; k < myLength; ++k)
            if (myCstring[k] == ch)
                    return k;
        return -1;
}
```

The second **find** function returns the starting position of the first instance of a given substring in the string. It uses the **string** library function **strncmp**. This function expects three parameters:

1. The string to be scanned (a C-style string)
2. A potential substring (a C-style string)
3. *n,* the number of characters to be compared

strncmp compares the first *n* characters in the two strings, and returns 0 if they are equal; otherwise, the function returns nonzero.

The implementation of **find** first computes the value of the third parameter as the difference between the lengths of the two strings. It then enters a loop that calls **strncmp** to test for the presence of a substring. The loop advances by adding the value of the loop control variable, **k**, to the address of the enclosing string. This operation has the effect of stripping a character off the beginning of the scanned string on each pass through the loop.

```
int apstring::find(const apstring &str) const
{
        int len = str.length();
        int last_index = length() - len;
        for (int k = 0; k <= last_index; ++k)
            if (strncmp(myCstring + k, str.c_str(), len) == 0)
                    return k;
        return -1;
}
```

The **substr** function returns a substring of a given length starting at a given index position. It begins by adjusting its parameters to fit the preconditions, if necessary. It then copies the characters in the given range from receiver object to a new string, and returns this string.

```
apstring apstring::substr(int pos, int len) const
{
        // start at front when pos < 0

        if (pos < 0)
              pos = 0;

        if (pos >= myLength)
              return "";    // empty string

        // last char's index (to copy)
        // off end of string?

        int last_index = pos + len - 1;
        if (last_index >= myLength)
              last_index = myLength - 1;

        apstring result(*this);

        int j, k;
        for (j = 0,k = pos; k <= last_index; ++j, ++k)
              result.myCstring[j] = myCstring[k];

        // properly terminate C-string

        result.myCstring[j] = '\0';

        // record length properly

        result.myLength = j;

        return result;
}
```

Assignment

The assignment operations must take into account the potential difference in length between the target string and the source string. If the target string is longer, then the characters from the source string, including its null character, are simply copied to the target's data member. Any extra memory in the target is retained as surplus capacity. If the source string is longer, then the target string's memory is deleted and new memory equal to the capacity of the source string is allocated for the target string before copying the characters.

```
const apstring& apstring::operator =
        (const apstring &rhs)
{
```

```
        if (this != &rhs)
        {
            // more memory needed?
            if (myCapacity < rhs.length() + 1)
            {
                delete[] myCstring;
                myCapacity = rhs.length() + 1;
                myCstring = new char[myCapacity];
            }
            myLength = rhs.length();
            strcpy(myCstring, rhs.myCstring);
        }
        return *this;
    }
```

The implementations of the remaining assignment operations are left as exercises.

Concatenation

The concatenation operation for two string objects first builds a copy of the left operand with a local variable. It then uses the compound assignment operator for strings to concatenate the right operand to this value, and finally returns this value as the result.

```
    apstring operator + (const apstring &lhs,
        const apstring &rhs)
    {
        apstring result(lhs);
        result += rhs;
        return result;
    }
```

Compound Assignment

The **+=** operator is used to concatenate the right operand string to the left operand string before assigning the result to the left operand string. Note the use of the function **strcpy** to copy the data from one C-style string to another.

```
const apstring& apstring::operator +=
    (const apstring &str)
{
    // Create a copy to avoid aliasing

    apstring copystring(str);

    // self + added string

    int newLength = length() + str.length();

    // index of '\0'

    int lastLocation = length();
```

```
        // check to see if local buffer not big enough

    if (newLength >= myCapacity)
    {
            myCapacity = newLength + 1;
            char* newBuffer = new char[myCapacity];
            strcpy(newBuffer, myCstring);// copy into new buffer
            delete [] myCstring;         // delete old string
            myLength = newLength;        // update information
            myCstring = newBuffer;
    }

    // now concatenate str (copystring) to end of myCstring

    strcpy(myCstring + lastLocation,
           copystring.c_str());

    return *this;
}
```

Input and Output

The input and output operations use the operators **>>** and **<<**, as we did with rational numbers in Section 9.4. This technique of overloading can be seen very clearly in the output operation, which runs the same operator on the string object's C-style string.

```
ostream& operator << (ostream &os, const apstring &str)
{
    return os << str.c_str();
}
```

The input operations make use of a large array as a buffer to hold the character data coming from the input stream. The size of this array, **MAX_LENGTH**, is a global constant defined in the class implementation file. This constant has a value of 1024. The first input operation behaves like the standard **iostream** operation for numbers. It ignores leading whitespace characters and accepts a string of characters terminated by a whitespace character.

```
istream& operator >> (istream &is, apstring &str)
{
    char buf[MAX_LENGTH];
    is >> buf;
    str = buf;
    return is;
}
```

Note that the capacity of **str**, as the result of the assignment statement, will not be 1024, but rather the number of input characters in **buf + 1**.

The second input operation is used to obtain a string of characters that might contain whitespace. The input operation in this case is terminated by the detection of an end-of-line character (`'\n'`).

```
istream& getline(istream &is, apstring &str)
{
    char buf[MAX_LENGTH];
    is.getline(buf, MAX_LENGTH);
    str = buf;
    return is;
}
```

Note that both input operations pass a C-style string as a parameter to a standard **iostream** operation. This is a good example of the use of overloading to make code easy to write and understand.

String Comparisons

The comparison operations for the **apstring** class depend on the use of the string library function **strcmp**. This function expects two C-style strings as parameters. It returns the following possible values:
1. 0, if the two parameters are equal
2. A negative number, if the left parameter is less than the right parameter
3. A positive number, if the left parameter is greater than the right parameter.

Only the `==` and `<` operations use the **strcmp** function directly. The other comparison operations can be defined in terms of `==` and `<`.

```
bool operator == (const apstring &lhs,
    const apstring &rhs)
{
    return strcmp(lhs.c_str(),
        rhs.c_str()) == 0;
}

bool operator < (const apstring &lhs,
    const apstring &rhs)
{
    return strcmp(lhs.c_str(),
        rhs.c_str()) < 0;
}
```

■ Exercises 10.2

1. Implement the remaining **apstring** class operations, and test them with a driver program.
2. Describe the differences between a string object and a vector object.
3. What is the difference between a string object and a C-style string?
4. Simon Seeplus proposes that we represent the **myCString** data member of the **apstring** class as a vector. Discuss the merits of this proposal.

5.   Write a free function, **make_uppercase**, that expects a string object as a parameter. The function should return a new string object that is a copy of the parameter, with all of its letters in uppercase.

Objectives

- ◆ to understand the difference between the physical size of an array and its logical size

- ◆ to be able to design and implement a new class that prohibits references to uninitialized data elements in an array

User Requirements

In almost any application that uses an array, the user must distinguish between the *physical size* of the array (its capacity or the number of memory locations available for data elements) and the *logical size* of the array (the number of data elements currently stored in the array). Failure to do this can cause errors when users attempt to access data locations in a vector where no data values have yet been stored. For example, an array **list** might be declared to store a maximum number of five integer elements, and three integers might be currently stored in positions 0 through 2. This situation is depicted in Figure 10.1. The data at index positions 3 and 4 are still unpredictable, so the references **list[3]** and **list[4]** for these values may cause errors.

In fact, references to uninitialized data may often occur during the execution of the copy constructor and the assignment operation for the vector class.

Users can keep track of the data within a physical array in two ways:

1.   The first method stores a special sentinel value at the index position immediately following the last data element currently in the array. This method is used by C++ to recognize the boundary of a string value (the null character) within an array of characters. The cost of this method is that one location in the array must be given up to store the sentinel value. Moreover, some data elements, such as bank account objects, might not be easily represented as sentinel values.

2.   The second method maintains a separate integer variable as a counter of the number of data elements currently stored in the array. We have seen this method used in many examples in Chapter 8, where a variable **length** maintains this value. When a new array is declared or reinitialized, **length** is set to zero, to reflect the fact that there are no data elements stored in the array. **length** is then passed with the array variable to any function that processes the array. Any subscript reference to a data element in an array, either for accessing or for storing a value, should use an index that satisfies the condition **0 <= index < length**. The costs of this method are that a separate variable or parameter must be maintained for the number of data elements in the array, and extra operations must be provided for adding or removing data elements.

◆ **Figure 10.1**

The logical size of a vector may be different from its physical size.

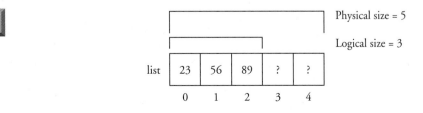

ordered collection:
A data structure that
behaves like a vector,
with the additional
capability of adding data
elements at the
beginning and the end.

We can use the second method to develop a new class or ADT called an
ordered collection. An ordered collection provides subscript access to just those
data locations where elements have been stored. It does this by maintaining its
own logical size as an attribute. A user can access the logical size of an ordered
collection, determine whether subscripting is allowed and, if so, what the
legitimate range of an index should be. Finally, a set of operations for adding or
removing data elements is provided by the ordered collection class. A piece of
code that illustrates the use of ordered collections of integers follows.

Example 10.5

The program of Example 10.2 is modified to use an ordered collection rather
than a vector to store the input data. The program assumes that the ordered
collection class is implemented in the library file **ordercol.cpp**.

```cpp
// Program file: orderav.cpp

#include <iostream.h>

#include "ordercol.cpp"

int main()
{
    // Create an empty ordered collection
    // of integers

    ordered_collection<int> list;

    // Use a sentinel-controlled loop
    // for input

    int data;
    cout << "Enter the next integer, "
         << "or -999 to quit: ";
    cin >> data;
    while (data != -999)
    {
        list.add_last(data);
        cout << "Enter the next integer, "
             << "or -999 to quit: ";
        cin >> data;
    }
    int sum = 0;
    for (int i = 0; i < list.length(); ++i)
        sum = sum + list[i];
    cout << "The average is "
         << sum / list.length();
    return 0;
}
```

Note the following points:

1. The ordered collection is created before the program has determined how many data values will be stored in it. A new ordered collection is always empty. When each input value is added to the collection, its logical size grows by one.
2. The program now uses a sentinel-controlled loop for input. The user does not have to specify how many data values are to be entered. A vector would not support this input strategy.
3. Range checking during indexing (in the second loop) prevents the program from accessing uninitialized memory cells in the collection. There are none, because the logical size of an ordered collection always equals its physical size.

To summarize, ordered collections provide the following features:

1. Range checking occurs during indexing.
2. The logical size of an ordered collection is always the same as its physical size. A newly created ordered collection always has a length of zero, and grows or shrinks with the needs of the application.
3. When a data element is added to the beginning of an ordered collection, the positions of the remaining elements shift up by one.
4. When a data element is removed from the beginning of an ordered collection, the positions of the remaining elements shift down by one.
5. The use of ordered collections is safer than the use of vectors, because references to uninitialized data elements are not allowed.

Specifying the Operations for Ordered Collections

The attributes of an ordered collection are

1. Its length (the number of data elements currently stored)
2. **myList** (the collection's data elements)
3. **itemType** (the collection's element type).

The formal specifications of the operations for an ordered collection follow:

Create operation
Preconditions :   The ordered collection is in an unpredictable state.
Postconditions: An ordered collection of length 0 is created.

Length operation
Preconditions :   The ordered collection is appropriately initialized.
Postconditions: The number of data elements in the ordered collection is returned.

Subscript operation (for observation or modification of a data element)
Preconditions :   The ordered collection is appropriately initialized.

(continued)

Postconditions: The **index** parameter is an integer value in the range **0 <= index <** length of the ordered collection.

The location of the data element, which can be used either to reference or to store a value, is returned.

Subscript operation (for observation of a data element only)

Preconditions : The ordered collection is appropriately initialized.

The **index** parameter is an integer value in the range **0 <= index <** length of the ordered collection.

Postconditions: The object at the index position is returned.

Assignment operation

Preconditions : The target is an ordered collection, appropriately initialized.

The source is an ordered collection, appropriately initialized.

Postconditions: The contents of the source object are copied into the target object, and the target's length is set to the source's length.

Add last operation

Preconditions : The ordered collection is appropriately initialized.

The parameter is an **itemType** object.

There is memory to store the new item in the collection.

Postconditions: The length of the ordered collection is incremented by one, and the parameter object is placed at the end of the ordered collection.

Remove last operation

Preconditions : The ordered collection is appropriately initialized, and the length of the ordered collection **> 0**.

Postconditions: **length** is decremented by one, and the last data element in the ordered collection is returned.

Add first operation

Preconditions : The ordered collection is appropriately initialized.

The parameter is an **itemType** object.

There is memory to store the new element in the collection.

Postconditions: The length of the ordered collection is incremented by one, the data elements in the ordered collection are shifted up by one index position, and the parameter element is placed in the first position in the ordered collection.

Remove first operation

Preconditions : The ordered collection is appropriately initialized, and the length of the ordered collection **> 0**.

Postconditions: **mySize** is decremented by one, the data elements in the ordered collection that come after the first element are shifted down by one index position, and the first element in the ordered collection is returned.

(continued)

Remove operation

Preconditions :	The ordered collection object is appropriately initialized.
	The parameter is the data element to be removed, the parameter must equal an element currently in the list, and the length of the ordered collection > 0.
Postconditions:	The length of the ordered collection is decremented by one, and the data elements in the ordered collection that come after the parameter element are shifted down by one index position.

Declaring the Ordered Collection Class

The class declaration module for the ordered collection class is

```
// Class declaration file: ordercol.h

#ifndef ORDERCOL_H

#include "bool.h"
#include "apvector.cpp"

template <class itemType> class ordered_collection
{
    public:

    // Constructors

    ordered_collection();
    ordered_collection(const ordered_collection<itemType> &oc);

    // Destructor

    ~ordered_collection();

    // Assignment

    const ordered_collection<itemType>& operator =
            (const ordered_collection<itemType> &rhs);

    // Accessor

    int length() const;

    // Indexing

    const itemType& operator [ ] (int index) const;
    itemType& operator [ ] (int index);

    // Modifiers

    void add_first(const itemType &item);
    void add_last(const itemType &item);
```

```
        itemType remove_first();
        itemType remove_last();
        void remove(const itemType &item);

    protected:

        // Data members

        apvector<itemType> myList;
};

#define ORDERCOL_H
#endif
```

Note that the data member for storing the data elements is a vector. The **length** function now returns the capacity of the vector, which always equals the number of data values accessible in the collection. We also declare the data member to be **protected**, so that any derived classes of **ordered_collection** will have direct access to it.

Constructing Ordered Collections

The default constructor seems to do nothing. In fact, the default constructor for a vector is run to set up **myList** as a vector of length zero.

```
        template <class itemType>
        ordered_collection<itemType>::ordered_collection()
        {
        }
```

There is no constructor that allows users to specify the physical size of an ordered collection. Memory for data elements in the vector will be allocated only when data are added to the collection, in the **add_first** and **add_last** operations described later.

The copy constructor assigns the vector contained in the parameter collection to **myList**.

```
        template <class itemType>
        ordered_collection<itemType>::ordered_collection
              (const ordered_collection<itemType> &oc)
        {
              myList = oc.myList;
        }
```

Examining the Length

An ordered collection does not need a **mySize** data member to maintain its length. Its length is the same as the length of the **myList** data member.

```
        template <class itemType>
        int ordered_collection<itemType>::length() const
```

```
    {
          return myList.length();
    }
```

Indexing Ordered Collections

The indexing operations for an ordered collection are the same as those for a vector. The only difference is that the logical size is used as an upper bound on the index value. The subscript operations enforce the precondition that the index parameter is greater than or equal to zero and less than the length of the collection.

```
    template <class itemType>
    itemType& ordered_collection< itemType>::operator
        [ ] (int index)
    {
          assert((index >= 0) && (index < length()));
          return myList[index];
    }

    template <class itemType>
    const itemType& ordered_collection< itemType>::operator
        [ ] (int index) const
    {
          assert((index >= 0) && (index < length()));
          return myList[index];
    }
```

Put another way, this code guarantees that users can index only the data elements currently available in the collection.

The implementation of the assignment operation has similar constraints and is left as an exercise.

Adding and Removing Elements

We have said that memory will be allocated for new data elements in an ordered collection on a strictly as-needed basis. A vector of data elements may already exist within a collection receiving a new data element. To add a new data element to the end of the collection, we must therefore perform the following steps:

1. Resize the vector to one greater than its current size.
2. Add the new data element to the last position in the vector.

add_last performs the necessary steps to add a data element to the end of the collection.

```
template <class itemType>
void ordered_collection<itemType>::add_last(const itemType &item)
{
      myList.resize(length() + 1); // Increase capacity by one
      myList[length() - 1] = item; // Add element at end of myList
}
```

To remove a data element from the end of the collection, we must perform the inverse steps:

1. Save a copy of the removed data element for return to the caller.
2. Resize the vector to one less than its current size.
3. Return the removed data element.

remove_last performs the necessary steps to remove a data element from the end of the collection.

```
template <class itemType>
itemType ordered_collection<itemType>::remove_last()
{
        assert(length() > 0);
        itemType removed_item = myList[length() - 1];
        myList.resize(length() - 1);
        return removed_item;
}
```

To add a new data element to the beginning of the collection, we must shift the existing data over one place to the right throughout the vector. Thus, we perform the following steps:

1. Resize the vector to one greater than its current size.
2. Move the data elements one position to the right, starting at the right and moving from right to left through the vector.
3. Add the new data element to the first position in the vector.

```
template <class itemType>
void ordered_collection<itemType>::add_first(const
itemType &item)
{
        myList.resize(length() + 1);

        // Copy old vector to new vector,
        // shifting elements to right by 1

        for (int i = length() - 1; i > 0; --i)
                myList[i] = myList[i - 1];

        // Add element at beginning of vector

        myList[0] = item;
}
```

Study the **for** loop in this function carefully to be sure that you understand the process of shifting the data in the vector.

To remove a data element from the beginning of an ordered collection, we must shift the existing data over one place to the left throughout the vector. Thus, we perform the following steps:

1. Save a copy of the removed data element for return to the caller.

2. Move the data elements one position to the left, starting at the left and moving from left to right through the vector.

3. Resize the vector to one less than its current size.

4. Return the removed data element.

```
template <class itemType>
itemType ordered_collection<itemType>::remove_first()
{
        assert(length() > 0);
        itemType removed_item = myList[0];
        for (int i = 0; i < length() - 1; ++i)
                myList[i] = myList[i + 1];
        myList.resize(length() - 1);
        return removed_item;
}
```

Note that the copying of data occurs before resizing. The implementation of the **remove** operation is left as an exercise.

The Hidden Costs of the Implementation

You might have noticed that the addition and removal operations incur two hidden costs: A new array of approximately the same size as the old array must be allocated, and existing data values must be copied from the old array to the new array. For users who perform frequent additions and removals with large collections, this implementation strategy is not the most efficient. An alternative implementation might fix the physical size of the collection at instance creation time, as with vectors, and allow the logical size of the collection to grow or shrink within this fixed storage capacity.

However, the primary benefit of the current implementation is that the physical size of the collection exactly mirrors its logical size. This arrangement tends to be economical for two reasons:

1. An application might initialize one or two large collections with data elements at start-up, and then simply access them with subscripting. A good example of this is a dictionary or table of words. In this case, all of the overhead occurs at the beginning of run time, so its impact on users is not significant.

2. We might underestimate or overestimate the memory requirements of an application. Sentinel-controlled input is a good example. Suppose we are reading data elements from a file into an ordered collection. A vector-like implementation of the collection must have a fixed size. But the size of a file is not known until all of the data elements have been input. Thus, our collection might not be able to accommodate all of the data coming in from the file, even though computer memory might be available. Or we might allocate memory for a collection of 100 elements and find that the file contains only 10. The current implementation of an ordered collection more adequately handles dynamic situations such as file input, where data elements can be added to the collection as long as computer memory is available.

Example 10.6

This example program inputs a series of bank account objects, as discussed in Chapter 9, from a file into an ordered collection. It then displays the contents of each account on the screen. The program assumes that the standard stream operations have been overloaded for account objects, and that the file **"myfile"** contains the accounts.

```cpp
// Program file: bankfile.cpp

#include <iostream.h>
#include <fstream.h>
#include "account.h"
#include "ordercol.cpp"

int main()
{
        ifstream in_file;
        ordered_collection<account> accounts;
        account new_account;

        in_file.open("myfile");
        in_file >> new_account;
        while (! in_file.eof())
        {
                accounts.add_last(new_account);
                in_file >> new_account;
        }
        in_file.close();
        for (int i = 0; i < accounts.length(); ++i)
                cout << accounts[i] << endl;
        return 0;
}
```

Exercises 10.3

1. Discuss the difference between the physical size of an array and its logical size.
2. State two reasons why ordered collections are safer and more convenient to use than vectors.
3. Users complain that halting the program with an error message is too severe a price to pay for attempting to remove a data element from an empty ordered collection. They argue that a Boolean flag could be returned instead, indicating the success or failure of the operation. Discuss the relative merits of these two approaches.
4. Someone has proposed using an ordered collection rather than an array to implement a string class. She claims that the new implementation will not have to waste a storage location on the null character. Discuss the merits of this proposal.
5. Implement the remaining operations for the ordered collection class, and test it with the sample code presented earlier in this section.

6. Add an operation, **index_of**, to the ordered collection class to search the collection for a given element. If the element is found, the index position of the first instance of this element in the ordered collection should be returned. Otherwise, −1 should be returned. You should use the sequential search algorithm developed in Section 8.4.

7. Add an operation to the ordered collection class to sort the data elements in the collection. You should use the selection sort algorithm developed in Section 8.4.

8. Add an operation for output of ordered collections, overloading the **<<** operator. Test the operation with an appropriate driver program.

9. Add an operation to concatenate two ordered collections. It should use the **+** operator in the same way as the **apstring** class.

10. Implement the vector-like version of the ordered collection class discussed in this section. Test this version with the driver program of Example 10.5.

10.4 Sorted Collections

Objectives

♦ to understand the difference between an ordered collection and a sorted collection

♦ to be able to design and implement a sorted collection class

User Requirements

Many applications demand that data values be kept in sorted order. For example, dictionaries and telephone books are two kinds of collections of data values that must be maintained in alphabetical order. One could use the ordered collection class to represent these kinds of data, as long as a sort operation is provided to alphabetize the data after each insertion into the collection. However, the sort operation can be very expensive to use with large collections. Clearly, an ordered collection that could maintain its contents in sorted form without resorting to a sort operation would be very desirable for these applications.

We can design a new class, called a **sorted collection,** that fulfills these requirements. The new class has many of the characteristics of an ordered collection, such as a length and subscripting to look up a data element's value. However, to keep its data elements sorted, a sorted collection prohibits insertions at given positions in the collection. The sorted collection permits only one insertion operation, and that operation always puts a data element in its proper place in the collection.

Example 10.7

sorted collection: A data structure that behaves like an ordered collection, but the data items are maintained in ascending order.

The following driver program allows the user to input an arbitrary number of integers in random order into a sorted collection. The program then displays the contents of the collection, which of course will be in sorted order:

```
// Program file: sortdriv.cpp

#include <iostream.h>
#include "sortcol.cpp"

int main()
{
        sorted_collection<int> list;

        // Get input values and insert
        // into the collection
```

```
                    int data;
                    cout << "Enter the next integer, "
                         << "or -999 to quit: ";
                    cin >> data;
                    while (data != -999)
                    {
                         list.add(data);
                         cout << "Enter the next integer, "
                              << "or -999 to quit: ";
                         cin >> data;
                    }

                    // Output values in the collection

                    for (int i = 0; i < list.length(); ++ i)
                         cout << i << " " << list[i] << endl;
                    return 0;
               }
```

Note the use of the operation **add** to insert a data element into the sorted collection. No position is specified, because the sorted collection figures this out automatically.

Specifying the Operations for Sorted Collections

Because a sorted collection has so many of the attributes and behaviors of an ordered collection, it will be convenient to specify it as a derived class of an ordered collection. The situation here is similar to that of the account and savings account classes discussed in Chapter 9. Sorted collections inherit all of the attributes of ordered collections—a length, **myList**, and **itemType**. We also assume that all of the operations on ordered collections can be used on sorted collections, except for adding a data element to the beginning or the end of the collection, and for indexing to modify a data element. We use an operation called **add** for insertions that enforce a sorted order in the collection. The formal specifications follow:

Create operation
Preconditions :   The sorted collection is in an unpredictable state.
Postconditions: A sorted collection of length 0 is created.

Length operation
Preconditions :   The sorted collection is appropriately initialized.
Postconditions: The number of data elements currently stored in the collection is returned.

Subscript operation (for observation of a data element only)
Preconditions :   The sorted collection is appropriately initialized.
                   The **index** parameter is an integer value in the range **0 <= index <** the length of
                   the collection.

(continued)

Postconditions: The object at the index position is returned.

Assignment operation

Preconditions :   The target is a sorted collection object, appropriately initialized.
The source is a sorted collection object, appropriately initialized.

Postconditions: The contents of the source object are copied into the target object, and the target's length is set to the source's length.

Add operation

Preconditions :   The sorted collection object is appropriately initialized, the parameter is an **itemType** object, and there is memory to store the new element in the collection.

Postconditions: The length of the collection is incremented by one, and the parameter object is placed in its proper position in the sorted collection.

Remove last operation

Preconditions :   The sorted collection is appropriately initialized, and the length of the collection
> 0.

Postconditions: The length of the collection is decremented by one, and the last data element in the sorted collection is returned.

Remove first operation

Preconditions :   The sorted collection is appropriately initialized, and the length of the collection
> 0.

Postconditions: The length of the collection is decremented by one, the data elements in the ordered collection that come after the first element are shifted down by one index position, and the first element in the sorted collection is returned.

Remove operation

Preconditions :   The sorted collection object is appropriately initialized.
The parameter is the data element to be removed, the parameter must equal an element currently in the list, and the length of the collection **> 0**.

Postconditions: The length of the collection is decremented by one, and the data elements in the sorted collection that come after the parameter element are shifted down by one index position.

Declaring the Sorted Collection Class

The class declaration module for the sorted collection class is

```
// Class declaration file: sortcol.h

#ifndef SORTCOL_H

#include "ordercol.cpp"

template <class itemType> class sorted_collection
      :protected ordered_collection<itemType>
   {
```

```
          public:

          // Constructors

          sorted_collection();
          sorted_collection(const sorted_collection<itemType> &sc);

          // Destructor

          ~sorted_collection();

          // These four are inherited from the base class

          ordered_collection<itemType>::length;
          ordered_collection<itemType>::remove_first;
          ordered_collection<itemType>::remove_last;
          ordered_collection<itemType>::remove;

          // These three are implemented here.

          // Assignment

          const sorted_collection<itemType>& operator =
                  (const sorted_collection<itemType> &rhs);

          // Indexing (access only)

          const itemType& operator [ ] (int index) const;

          // Modifier

          void add(const itemType &item);

          // Data member is defined in the base class
};

#define SORTCOL_H
#endif
```

Note several things about this class declaration:

1. The sorted collection class inherits its attributes and behavior from the ordered collection class in **protected** mode. This means that **public** and **protected** data members and member functions from the ordered collection can be used in the implementation of the sorted collection class, unless they are redefined by the sorted collection class. If inheritance were specified in **public** mode, all of the **public** members of the ordered collection class, such as **add_first**, would also be available to users of the sorted collection class as well. A derived class should be declared in **protected** mode whenever we wish to deny other users access to some of the public members of the base class.

2. Users of the sorted collection are given access to four member functions of the ordered collection class by listing them in the following form in the **public** section:

<class name>::<member name>;
---

access adjustment:
A method of changing the access mode of an inherited member from within a derived class. For example, a derived class may inherit all members from a base class in protected mode, and then make some members public by means of access adjustments.

This kind of declaration is called an **access adjustment.** In general, an access adjustment broadens the scope of access no wider than the mode of access specified by the base class.

3. The remaining three member function declarations specify operations to be implemented by the sorted collection class. Note that the assignment and subscript operations are not inherited from the base class. In the case of the assignment, we must return the address of an object of a specific class (sorted collection, in this case). In the case of the subscript, we prohibit the use of the returned element as an l-value by specifying the function as constant.

Implementing the Sorted Collection Class

The constructors for the sorted collection class invoke the corresponding constructors in the base class:

```
template <class itemType>
sorted_collection<E>::sorted_collection()
      : ordered_collection<itemType>()
{
}


template <class itemType>
sorted_collection<itemType>::sorted_collection
      (const sorted_collection<itemType> &sc)
      : ordered_collection<itemType>(sc)
{
}
```

The new operation to add a data element calls for some development. The logic of this operation faces three possibilities:

1. The collection is empty. The new data element goes at the end.
2. The new data element is greater than the last element in the collection. The new data element goes at the end.
3. The new data element is less than or equal to some data element in the collection. We search for this place, shift the data elements over to the right from there, and put the new data element in that place.

The implementation reflects these alternatives as follows:

```
template <class itemType>
void sorted_collection<itemType>::add(const itemType &item)
{
    if ((length() == 0)||(item > myList[length() - 1]))
        add_last(item);
    else
    {
        int place = 0;
        myList.resize(length() + 1);
        while (item > myList[place])
            ++place;
        for (int index = length() - 1; index > place; --index)
            myList[index] = myList[index - 1];
        myList[place] = item;
    }
}
```

Note that we use the **add_last** function from the ordered collection class if the data element should go at the end of the sorted collection. Note also that we resize the vector before running the sequential search for the position for the new data element.

The implementations of the assignment and subscript operations are left as exercises.

Contained Classes and Derived Classes

contained class:
A class that is used to define a data member of another class.

Our implementation of the ordered collection class uses a vector to define the **myList** data member. The vector class in this case is said to be a **contained class,** in that an object of this class is contained in any ordered collection object. By contrast, the sorted collection class is a derived class of the ordered collection class. Thus, the sorted collection declares no **myList** data member, but inherits this from its base class, ordered collection. When you design new classes to solve problems, you will often face the choice of defining a contained class or defining a derived class. For example, we could have defined the ordered collection as a derived class of the vector class. Then an ordered collection would inherit its **myList** data member from the vector class. Or we could have defined the sorted collection class to contain an ordered collection as its **myList** data member. We made our choices on the grounds that the two collection classes are fairly similar, whereas the ordered collection class and the vector class are somewhat different. The choice is not always so clear-cut, but as you acquire experience in object-oriented design, you will be able to make good judgments about these matters.

■ Exercises 10.4

1. Implement the assignment and subscript operations for sorted collections.
2. Design and test a program that attempts to use the subscript operator to assign a value to a position in a sorted collection. Explain the error that occurs.
3. Explain why the subscript operator for ordered collections cannot be used for sorted collections. What effect will this have on users of sorted collections?
4. Draw a class hierarchy diagram that describes the relationships among the array data type, the safe array class, the ordered collection class, and the sorted collection class.

5. Design and implement a class constructor for sorted collections that takes an ordered collection as a parameter. The constructor should add the data from the ordered collection to the sorted collection.

6. Design and implement a member function **merge** for sorted collections. **merge** expects a sorted collection as a parameter. The function should build and return a sorted collection that contains the elements in the receiver collection and the parameter collection.

10.5 Matrices

Objectives

◆ to understand the requirements for a safe two-dimensional array

◆ to be able to design and implement a new class that satisfies these requirements

User Requirements

In Section 8.5, we discussed the use of two-dimensional arrays in C++ programs. These arrays have all of the problems enumerated in Section 10.1. In addition, because two-dimensional arrays require two subscripts, the potential for range errors is twice as great as with one-dimensional arrays. A **matrix** class can solve these problems. Users can think of a matrix as a safe two-dimensional array. The capacity of a matrix is the product of the number of its rows and the number of its columns. The rows and columns can be specified, along with an initial fill value, when the matrix is created. A user can inspect the number of rows and the number of columns and resize a matrix by invoking the appropriate operations. Matrices can also be resized during assignment operations (with some data potentially being lost). Finally, a matrix supports two-dimensional indexing with range checking.

Example 10.8

The following driver program would test many of the user requirements for a matrix class. We assume that the class **apmatrix** has been defined in the implementation file **apmatrix.cpp**. A complete definition of the **apmatrix** class appears in Appendix 6.

matrix: A two-dimensional array that provides range checking and can be resized.

```
// Program file: matrdriv.cpp

#include <iostream.h>
#include "apmatrix.cpp"

int main()
{
    // Create a 4 X 4 matrix

    apmatrix<int> table(4, 4, 0);

    // Display number of rows and columns

    cout << "Rows = " << table.numrows() << endl;
    cout << "Columns = " << table.numcols() << endl;

    // Set contents of each cell to row * column

    for (int row = 0; row < table.numrows(); ++row)
```

```
                for (int col = 0; col < table.numcols(); ++col)
                        table[row] [col] = row * col;

        // Display positions and values

        for (int row = 0; row < table.numrows(); ++row)
                for (int col = 0; col < table.numcols(); ++col)
                        cout << row << " " << col << " "
                                << table[row] [col] << endl;
        // Resize the matrix

        table.resize(9, 4);

        // Cause a range error

        table[9][4] = 1;

        return 0;
}
```

This program produces the following output:

```
Rows = 4
Columns = 4
0 0 0
0 1 0
0 2 0
0 3 0
1 0 0
1 1 1
1 2 2
1 3 3
2 0 0
2 1 2
2 2 4
2 3 6
3 0 0
3 1 3
3 2 6
3 3 9
apmatrix.cpp:164 (row >= 0) && (row < myRows) -- assertion failed
abort -- terminating
```

Specifying the Operations for Matrices

The attributes of a matrix are

1. **myRows** (the number of rows)
2. **myCols** (the number of columns)
3. **myMatrix** (the data elements)
4. **itemType** (the matrix's element type).

The formal specifications of the operations for a matrix class are

---

Create operation (default size)

Preconditions :   The matrix is in an unpredictable state.

Postconditions: **myRows**, **myCols**, and **myMatrix** are set to zero.

Create operation (user specified rows and columns)

Preconditions :   The matrix is in an unpredictable state.

rows and cols are integer values >= 0.

There is memory available for creating a matrix capable of storing **rows * cols** data elements.

Postconditions: Memory is reserved for a vector object capable of storing **rows * cols** data elements, **myRows** is set to **rows**, and **myCols** is set to **cols**.

Create operation (user-specified rows, columns, and fill value)

Preconditions :   The matrix is in an unpredictable state.

rows and cols are integer values > 0.

fillValue is a data element of the element type of the matrix.

There is memory available for creating a vector capable of storing **size** data elements.

Postconditions: Memory is reserved for a matrix object capable of **rows * cols** data elements, **myRows** is set to **rows**, and **myCols** is set to **cols**, and all of the cells in the matrix are set to **fillValue**.

Destroy operation

Preconditions :   The matrix is appropriately initialized.

Postconditions: The memory for the matrix is made available to the computer for other applications.

Numrows operation

Preconditions :   The matrix is appropriately initialized.

Postconditions: The value of **myRows** is returned.

Numcols operation

Preconditions :   The matrix is appropriately initialized.

Postconditions: The value of **myCols** is returned.

Resize operation

Preconditions :   The matrix is appropriately initialized.

newRows and **newCols** are integers specifying the desired capacity of the matrix.

Postconditions: The capacity of the matrix is adjusted to the desired size, if memory is available, **myRows** is set to **rows**, and **myCols** is set to **cols**. Any data elements stored in the matrix are copied to the resized matrix. Some data may be lost if the new size is less than the old size.

(continued)

Subscript operation (for observation or modification of a data element)

Preconditions :	The matrix is appropriately initialized.
	row is an integer value in the range **0 <= row < myRows**.
	col is an integer value in the range **0 <= col < myCols**.
Postconditions:	The location of a data element, which can be used either to observe or to store an object, is returned.

Subscript operation (for observation of a data element only)

Preconditions :	The matrix is appropriately initialized.
	row is an integer value in the range **0 <= row < myRows**.
	col is an integer value in the range **0 <= col < myCols**.
Postconditions:	The object at the index positions is returned.

Assignment operation

Preconditions :	The target matrix is appropriately initialized.
	The source matrix is appropriately initialized.
	There is memory available for making the capacity of the target object equal to the capacity of the source object.
Postconditions:	The capacity of the target object is adjusted to the capacity of the source object, and the contents of the source object are copied into the target object.

Declaring the Matrix Class

The matrix class uses a vector of vectors to represent the data member for the two-dimensional array. Thus, the C++ declaration file must include the **apvector** library:

```cpp
// Class declaration file: apmatrix.h

#ifndef _APMATRIX_H
#define _APMATRIX_H

#include "apvector.cpp"

template <class itemType> class apmatrix
{
        public:

        // Constructors

        apmatrix( );
        apmatrix(int rows, int cols);
        apmatrix(int rows, int cols,
             const itemType& fillValue);
        apmatrix(const apmatrix<itemType> &mat);

        // Destructor
```

```
        ~apmatrix();

        // assignment

        const apmatrix& operator =
               (const apmatrix &rhs);

        // Accessors

        int numrows() const;
        int numcols() const;

        // Indexing

        const apvector<itemType>& operator [ ]
               (int row) const;
        apvector<itemType>& operator [ ]
               (int row);

        // Modifiers

        void resize(int newRows, int newCols);

        private:

        // Data members

        int myRows;
        int myCols;
        apvector<apvector<itemType> > myMatrix;
    };
    #endif
```

One unusual aspect of this code is the declaration

```
    apvector<apvector<itemType> > myMatrix;
```

This code says that the data member **myMatrix** is a vector of vectors of type **itemType**. Note that two type parameters are nested within the angle brackets, and that the two rightmost brackets are separated by a space. The space is merely a stylistic precaution to prevent the reader from mistaking this notation for the input operator >>.

Another point to note concerns the declarations of the indexing operations. They each specify a single [ ] operator, even though users invoke them with two consecutive [ ] operators. The computer executes the user's first [ ] operator as a matrix index operation. This operation returns a vector object (actually a row in the matrix). The computer then executes the user's second [ ] operator as a vector index operation. This operation returns the data or cell at the specified position in the vector.

Implementing the Matrix Class

The default constructor for the matrix class sets the data members for the rows and columns to zero. It then runs the constructor for vectors with the **myMatrix** data member, which creates a vector of size zero.

```
template <class itemType>
apmatrix<itemType>::apmatrix()
        : myRows(0),
        myCols(0),
        myMatrix(0)
{
}
```

The next constructor begins with a similar method, but with user-specified rows and columns. At the end of this portion of code, **myMatrix** is a vector of one or more empty vectors. The constructor then enters a **for** loop to resize each of these vectors to the size specified by the **cols** parameter. At the end of the entire process, **myMatrix** is a vector of **rows** vectors of **cols** cells of type **itemType**.

```
template <class itemType>
apmatrix<itemType>::apmatrix(int rows, int cols)
        : myRows(rows),
        myCols(cols),
        myMatrix(rows)
{
        for(int k = 0; k < rows; ++k)
                myMatrix[k].resize(cols);
}
```

To fill each cell of the matrix with an initial value, the next constructor extends the previous one with a nested **for** loop.

```
template <class itemType>
apmatrix<itemType>::apmatrix(int rows, int cols,
    const itemType & fillValue)
        : myRows(rows),
        myCols(cols),
        myMatrix(rows)
{
        for (int j = 0; j < rows; ++j)
        {
                myMatrix[j].resize(cols);
                for (int k = 0; k < cols; ++k)
                        myMatrix[j][k] = fillValue;
        }
}
```

The destructor for the matrix class appears to do nothing. However, the computer automatically invokes the destructor for the vector data member **myMatrix**. This call in turn results in further calls of this destructor for each of the vectors stored in **myMatrix**. In general, the destructor for any class that uses other classes with destructors can be written in this way.

```
template <class itemType>
apmatrix<itemType>::~apmatrix ()
{
// vector destructor frees everything
}
```

The index operations check the value of the row parameter against the range allowed by the vector **myMatrix**. They then invoke the **[ ]** operator with this vector, which does its own range checking for the second index value.

```
template <class itemType>
apvector<itemType>& apmatrix<itemType>::operator []
     (int row)
{
     assert((row >= 0) && (row < myRows));
     return myMatrix[row];
}
```

The implementations of the other matrix operations are left as exercises.

■ Exercises 10.5

1. Complete the implementations of the operations in the **apmatrix** class, and test this class with the driver program of Example 10.8.
2. Explain why the destructor for the **apmatrix** class appears to do nothing.
3. The indexing operations for the **apmatrix** class run **assert** to check the validity of the first index value. If this statement is removed from the implementation, would both index values still be checked and, if so, where?
4. Why is the data member **myMatrix** in the **apmatrix** class represented as a vector rather than a two-dimensional C++ array?
5. Write a function **sum** that returns the sum of all of the values in a matrix of integers. You should assume that the entire matrix is occupied by data.
6. Simon Seeplus complains that a matrix has the same problem as a vector: The logical size of a matrix is not necessarily the same as its physical size. Thus, errors can be caused by references to uninitialized cells in the data structure. He suggests a solution to this problem that is similar to the one provided by the ordered collection class. Each row of a matrix should be represented as an ordered collection. Four new matrix operations—**add_first**, **add_last**, **remove_first**, and **remove_last**—resemble those of the ordered collection class, but expect an integer parameter that specifies the row in the matrix to be modified. Discuss the merits of this proposal, and describe the changes that must be made to the current implementation.

10.6 Graphics

Objectives

- to understand the overhead associated with running animations
- to be able to design and implement an animation class that eliminates this overhead

An Animation Class

In Section 6.8, we introduced the idea of animating an image by repeatedly drawing, erasing, and changing the size and/or position of the image. The tasks of transforming the image and drawing it are interleaved in this process. However, sometimes it would be convenient or even necessary to compute all of the transformations of the image before any of the drawing takes place. For instance, an image might not appear to move rapidly enough with the original method, because the transformations take a bit of the time during the drawing process. A faster method would be to build a sequence of the images to be displayed and store them in a list. The display process then simply loops through the list, drawing and erasing each image as it goes.

In Section 9.6, we developed several classes for representing images, such as points and circles, as high-level objects with their own attributes and behavior. When we adopt an object-oriented perspective, it is natural to think of an animation as an object with its own attributes and behavior. There are two primary attributes of an animation object:

1. A list representing the sequence of images to be drawn
2. An integer representing the time delay factor

These attributes can be set when an animation is created. The user is responsible for creating the appropriate list of images to be passed to the constructor of the animation. The animation is then run with a simple command.

Example 10.9

The following program creates an animation that moves a circle from the upper left corner of the screen to its center, and then runs the animation. The program assumes that the classes **animation** and **circl** have been defined in the appropriate libraries.

```
// Program file: objanim.cpp
// This program moves a circle from the upper left
// corner of the screen to the center of the screen

#include <graphics.h>
#include <conio.h>
#include <dos.h>
#include "circle.h"
#include "ordercol.cpp"
#include "animate.cpp"

int main()
{
    // Set the graphics mode

    int graphdriver = DETECT, graphmode;
    initgraph(&graphdriver, &graphmode, "c:..\\bgi");

    // Create an empty list of circles

    ordered_collection<circl> images;
```

```
// Create the initial circle image

point center_point(10, 10);
circl a_circle(center_point, 10);

// Add translations of this
// circle to the collection

for (int i = 1; i <= getmaxx() / 2; ++i)
{
        images.add_last(a_circle);
        a_circle.translate(1, 1);
}

// Create an animation object with the
// collection of circles and a time delay

animation<circl> an_animation(images, 1);

// Run the animation

an_animation.run();

// Close the graphics mode.

moveto(0, 0);
outtext("Strike any key to continue");
getch();
closegraph();
return 0;
}
```

Note that the animation expects the list of images to be represented as an ordered collection. The element type of the ordered collection, in this case, **circl**, is also specified as a type parameter when the animation is created.

The operations for an animation include:
1. Create with specified images and delay time
2. Run
3. Add an image to the beginning or the end
4. Remove an image from the beginning or the end
5. Replace the entire list of images
6. Access the delay time
7. Modify the delay time

Declaring the Animation Class

The formal specifications of the operations for the animation class are left as exercises. The attributes of the animation class are
1. **myList** (the collection of images)

2. **myDelay** (the delay interval)
3. **imageType** (the type of image in the collection).

The class declaration module follows:

```
// Class declaration file: animate.h

#ifndef ANIMATE_H

#include "ordercol.cpp"

template <class imageType> class animation
{
    public:

    // Constructors

    animation();
    animation(const ordered_collection<imageType> &images,
            int time_delay);
    animation(const animation<imageType> &a);

    // Destructor

    ~animation();

    // Assignment

    const animation<imageType> & operator =
            (const animation<imageType> &rhs);

    // Accessor

    int delay_time() const;

    // Modifiers

    void set_list(const ordered_collection<imageType> &images);
    void add_first(const imageType &i);
    void add_last(const imageType &i);
    imageType remove_first();
    imageType remove_last();

    // Output

    void run();

    protected:

    // Data members
```

```
      ordered_collection<imageType> myList;
      int myDelay;
};

#define ANIMATE_H
#endif
```

We now explore some function implementations, leaving others as exercises.

Running an Animation

The function for running an animation draws and erases all of the images in its list. The function leaves the last image in the sequence, if there is one, visible on the screen.

```
template <class imageType>
void animation<imageType>::run()
{
      int len = myList.length();

      for (int i = 0; i < len; ++i)
      {
            myList[i].draw();
            delay(myDelay);
            myList[i].erase();
      }
      if (len != 0)
            myList[len - 1].draw();
}
```

Here once again, we see the power of overloading the functions **draw** and **erase**. Neither the list nor the animation knows anything about the particular kind of image being drawn and erased.

Modifying Images Within an Animation

The operations to add or remove an image from the beginning or the end of an animation resemble similar operations for ordered collections. Some examples follow:

```
template <class imageType>
imageType animation<imageType>::remove_first()
{
      return myList.remove_first();
}

template <class imageType>
void animation<imageType>::add_last(const imageType &i)
{
      myList.add_last(i);
}
```

■ Exercises 10.6

1. Using the animation class developed in this section, write code segments to create the following animation objects:
   a. Move a 10 × 10 rectangle 30 pixels horizontally to the right from the center of the screen.
   b. Move two circles of radius 10 in parallel. The first circle moves horizontally from the top left corner to the middle of the screen; the second circle moves vertically from the bottom middle to the top of the screen. The circles should appear to move in tandem.
2. Discuss the costs and benefits of using an animation object. Pay attention to the use of memory and the use of processing time.
3. An animation object can contain transformations of only one kind of object. Discuss the limitations of this constraint. Propose a way of animating several kinds of objects at once.

Focus on Program Design: Case Study

A Word Frequency Analyzer

As you saw in Chapter 7, much of word processing involves the use of strings to represent words or sentences. Many applications must maintain tables or dictionaries that are keyed by words that are associated with other information, like salaries or phone numbers. We now examine how to set up a table that allows an application to count the frequencies of all of the words in a file. The application will use the sorted collection class developed in Section 10.4.

The input to the program will be a text file. The output will be two columns of data. The first column will be an alphabetical listing of the words in the file. The second column will be integers representing the frequency of each word in the file.

To solve our problem, the program will need two classes of objects: one for representing a word and its frequency, and the other for representing a table of such objects. We can define a new class, called **entry**, to represent a word and its frequency. Because the words must appear in alphabetical order when displayed, the table of entries can be represented as a sorted collection.

An entry class will have two attributes: a string representing a word and an integer representing the word's frequency. The operation to create an entry will take a new word as a parameter, and set its frequency to 1. In addition, the entry class will support the following operations:

Operation	Action
word	Returns the word in the entry.
frequency	Returns the frequency in the entry.
increment	Increments the frequency by 1.
equality (==)	Compares two entries by word.
less than (<)	Compares two entries by word.
greater than (>)	Compares two entries by word.
assignment (=)	Copies one entry to another.

The completion of this class is left as an exercise. We now describe the design of the program. The general idea is to enter a loop that reads words from a file. As each word is input, the program searches the collection for an entry for that word. If no entry is found, the program creates one with the word and adds it to the collection. If an entry is found, the program indexes into the collection with the value returned by the search function, and sends the increment message to the entry for the word. When this process is completed, the program loops through the collection, displaying the word and frequency of each entry in an appropriate format. Therefore, we have two top-level program modules:

1. Enter the data from the file into the table
2. Display the data from the table to the screen

The main program block would be

```cpp
int main()
{
        sorted_collection<entry> table;

        read_table(table);
        print_table(table);
        return 0;
}
```

The **read_table** function prompts the user for a file name, opens it for input, runs the loop described earlier, and closes the file:

```cpp
void read_table(sorted_collection<entry> &table)
{
        ifstream in_file;
        apstring word, fname;
        int index;
        entry old_entry;

        cout << "Enter the file name: ";
        cin >> fname;
        in_file.open(fname.c_str());
        in_file >> word;
        while (! in_file.eof())
        {
                entry new_entry(word);
                index = table.index_of(new_entry);
                if (index == -1)
                {
                        table.add(new_entry);
                }
                else
                {
                        old_entry = table[index];
                        old_entry.increment();
                        table.remove(old_entry);
                        table.add(old_entry);
```

```
                        }
                    in_file >> word;
                }
            in_file.close();
        }
```

The **print_table** function displays a header and then loops through the table, displaying the word and the frequency of each entry on a line:

```
    void print_table(const sorted_collection<entry> &table)
    {
            entry next_entry;

            cout << setw(25) << "Word" << setw(5)
                << "Frequency" << endl;
            for (int i = 0; i < table.length(); ++i)
            {
                    next_entry = table[i];
                    cout << setw(25) << next_entry.word()
                        << setw(5) << next_entry.frequency()
                        << endl;
            }
    }
```

Running, Debugging, and Testing Hints

1. Make sure that all vector elements that are referenced for their values have been initialized. Avoid using loops with the capacity of the vector as an upper bound, unless you have initialized the entire vector. Use an integer variable to maintain the logical size of the vector. Better still, use an ordered collection to guarantee that references to uninitialized data in an array will be caught at run time.
2. The same precautions about references to uninitialized memory locations that are applied to vectors are applied to matrices also.
3. Use a sorted collection when you wish the data elements of an array to be maintained in sorted order. The use of this ADT is much more efficient than sorting an array of randomly entered data values.
4. Use an ordered collection when you wish to be able to add new data elements to the beginning or end of the collection (this cannot be done with sorted collections).

Summary

Key Terms

access adjustment	fill value	pointer variable
class template	logical size	sorted collection
contained class	matrix	substring
destructor	ordered collection	vector
dynamic memory	physical size	

Keywords

delete   **new**   **template**

Key Concepts

◆ A vector allows users to work with an array that supports run-time range checking.

◆ A class template allows users to specify the element types contained in objects of that class.

◆ A pointer variable can contain the address of a chunk of memory. This memory is known as dynamic memory, because it is allocated under program control. The form for declaring a pointer variable is

> <element type> *<pointer variable name>

◆ A destructor is a special member function that the computer runs automatically to return dynamic memory allocated for an object to the system.

◆ The operator **new** allocates storage for an object from dynamic memory. The form for its use with arrays is

> <pointer variable name> **=** **new** <element type> [<number of elements>]

◆ The operator **delete** is used to return dynamic memory from an object to the system. The form for its use with arrays is

> **delete [ ]** <pointer variable>

◆ The logical size of an array is the number of data elements currently stored in it; this size may differ from the array's physical size.

◆ An ordered collection enables users to work with just the logical size of an array of data elements.

◆ A sorted collection enables users to work with an array of data elements whose alphabetical ordering is maintained automatically.

◆ A matrix allows users to work with a two-dimensional array that supports run-time range checking on both dimensions.

Chapter Review Exercises

These exercises assume that you can make use of the classes developed in this chapter.

1. Declare variables with the following characteristics:
   a. a vector of 20 integers
   b. a vector of 10 characters, initialized to **'b'**
   c. a string, initialized to **"Hi there!"**
   d. an ordered collection of strings
   e. a sorted collection of integers
   f. a 20 × 20 matrix of integers
   g. a 10 × 10 matrix of integers, initialized to 10
   h. a 10 × 10 matrix of ordered collections of strings

2. Write formal specifications for the following operations:
   a. the concatenation (**+**) of two vectors
   b. the compound assignment (**+=**) of two ordered collections
   c. the operations **first** and **last**, which access the first and last elements in an ordered collection
   d. the operation **column**, which returns a vector containing the cells of a specified column in a matrix

3. Write code segments that do the following:
   a. Reverse the order of data stored in an ordered collection.
   b. Compute the sum of the values in a vector of integers.
   c. Compute the sum of the values in a matrix of integers.
   d. Copy data from a matrix into an ordered collection, moving row by row.
   e. Copy data from a matrix into an ordered collection, moving column by column.
   f. Return a vector containing the cells along the diagonal of a matrix (from position (0, 0) to position **(rows() - 1, cols() - 1)**

4. Define free functions, using the operator **<<**, that
   a. output the contents of a vector
   b. output the contents of an ordered collection
   c. output the contents of a matrix, row by row

5. Define the following type conversion functions, using the assignment operator (**=**):
   a. ordered collection to vector
   b. string to vector
   c. ordered collection to sorted collection
   d. string to sorted collection
   e. sorted collection to string

6. Discuss the security issues surrounding the use of classes developed in this chapter. Be sure to focus on run-time range checking, access to uninitialized memory cells, and encapsulation of private data.

Programming Problems and Activities

1. Vector arithmetic is commonly used in linear algebra applications as well as in many physics problems. Addition and subtraction are done component by component for vectors. For example, if the two vectors are $[x_1, y_1, z_1]$ and

$[x_2, y_2, z_2]$, then the difference of the two vectors would be the vector $[x_1 - x_2, y_1 - y_2, z_1 - z_2]$ and similarly for addition. Extend the vector class developed in this chapter by overloading addition (**+**) and subtraction (**−**) for vectors. The preconditions for the operations are that the two operand vectors contain numbers, have the same capacity, and have been filled with data values. Test your new functions with an appropriate driver module.

2. To streamline the testing of vector arithmetic operations, define two free functions, **>>** and **<<**, that expect a vector of doubles as a parameter. **<<** should output the vector in the form $[v1, v2, \ldots, vn]$. **>>** should accept input in the form $v1\ v2 \ldots vn$, filling all of the vector's cells with values. Incorporate these functions into the driver program from Problem 1.

3. There are two different types of vector multiplication. First, the dot product between two vectors is the sum of the products of the components of the two vectors. For example, the dot product of $v_1 = [x_1, y_1, z_1]$ and $v_2 = [x_2, y_2, z_2]$ is

$$v_1 \cdot v_2 = x_1 * x_2 + y_1 * y_2 + z_1 * z_2$$

which is a real number. Second, the scalar product of a vector and a real number is a vector containing the product of the real number with each of the components of the operand vector. That is, $f * [x, y, z] = [x, y, z] * f = [f*x, f*y, f*z]$. Note that the real number f can be either the first or the second operand. Thus, scalar multiplication requires two functions to be complete. Add these three functions to the vector class, and modify the driver program of Problem 1 so that it clearly demonstrates functions.

4. A stack is a collection of data allowing access to just one end, called the top. The **push** operation adds a data element to the top of the stack. The **pop** operation removes and returns the data element at the top of the stack. The **top** operation returns the data element at the top of the stack without removing it. The **empty** operation returns **TRUE** if there are no data elements in the stack, and **FALSE** otherwise. No other access or modifications to a stack are allowed. Any type of data may be stored in a stack, as long as all of the values are of the same type. Write formal specifications for a stack class, declare and implement these operations in a C++ library, and test the class with an appropriate driver program. (*Hint:* Use another class developed in this chapter to represent the data elements within a stack.)

5. A queue is a collection of data allowing access to one end, called the rear, for insertion, and to the other end, called the front, for removal. The **empty** operation returns **TRUE** if there are no data elements in the stack, and **FALSE** otherwise. No other access or modifications to a queue are allowed. Any type of data may be stored in a queue, as long as all of the values are of the same type. Write formal specifications for a queue class, declare and implement these operations in a C++ library, and test the class with an appropriate driver program. (*Hint:* Use another class developed in this chapter to represent the data elements within a queue.)

6. Using the sorted collection class developed in Section 10.4, write a program to read an unknown number of integer test scores from the keyboard (assume at most 150 scores). Print the original list of scores, the scores sorted from low to high, the scores sorted from high to low, the highest score, the lowest score, and the average score. (*Hint:* This is a rehash of Problem 1, Chapter 8.)

7. A one-key table is a collection of data in which each data value is accessed by specifying a unique key. A key can be an integer, a character, a string, or any other data type that supports comparisons. The set of keys in a given table must

be of the same type, and the set of values in a given table must be of the same type. An example of the operation to add a value to a table of integers keyed by strings would be **table.add("height", 60)**. An example of the operation to access a value at a given key in this table would be **table["height"]**. An example of the operation to remove a value at a given key in this table would be **value = table.remove("height")**. Other operations allow the user of a table to examine its length and test it for emptiness. No other modifications or access to a one-key table are allowed. Write formal specifications for a one-key table class, declare and implement these operations in a C++ library, and test the class with an appropriate driver program. (*Hint:* Use a sorted collection of structs to represent the data within a one-key table.)

8. A set is a collection of unique data values in no particular order. Operations on sets include:

Empty
Length
Add(an item)
Remove(an item)
Includes(an item)
Union (of two sets)
Intersection (of two sets)
Difference (of two sets)

No other modifications or access to sets are allowed. All of the data values in a set must be of the same type. The element type must support comparisons. The union of two sets is the set of elements in both sets combined. The intersection of two sets is the set of elements they have in common. The difference of two sets is the set of elements produced by combining the elements in the two sets and then removing the elements of the second set that are not contained in the first set. Write formal specifications for a set class, declare and implement these operations in a C++ library, and test the class with an appropriate driver program. Use the + operator for union, the * operator for intersection, and the - operator for difference. (*Hint:* Use another class developed in this chapter to represent the data within a set.)

9. The transpose of a matrix is a new matrix with the row and column positions reversed. That is, the transpose of matrix A, an $M \times N$ matrix, is an $N \times M$ matrix B, with each element $A[M][N]$ stored in $B[N][M]$. Write a function **transpose** that expects as a parameter an object of the matrix class developed in this chapter. The function should return a new matrix representing the transpose of the parameter. Test the new function with a driver program that allows you to input the values for two matrices of different dimensions, transpose them, and display the results.

10. A matrix is symmetric if it has the same number of rows and columns, and if each element $M[x][y]$ is equal to $M[y][x]$. Write a function **symmetric** that takes a matrix object as a parameter and returns **TRUE** or **FALSE** for this property. Test your function with an appropriate driver program.

11. Operations on matrices of numbers include addition, subtraction, and multiplication of two matrices, as well as scalar multiplication of a real number

with a matrix. The result of each of these operations is another matrix. For 3×3 matrices, these operations are defined as follows:

$$M + N = \begin{bmatrix} m_{11} & m_{12} & m_{13} \\ m_{21} & m_{22} & m_{23} \\ m_{31} & m_{32} & m_{33} \end{bmatrix} + \begin{bmatrix} n_{11} & n_{12} & n_{13} \\ n_{21} & n_{22} & n_{23} \\ n_{31} & n_{32} & n_{33} \end{bmatrix} = \begin{bmatrix} m_{11} + n_{11} & m_{12} + n_{12} & m_{13} + n_{13} \\ m_{21} + n_{21} & m_{22} + n_{22} & m_{23} + n_{23} \\ m_{31} + n_{31} & m_{32} + n_{32} & m_{33} + n_{33} \end{bmatrix}$$

$$M - N = \begin{bmatrix} m_{11} & m_{12} & m_{13} \\ m_{21} & m_{22} & m_{23} \\ m_{31} & m_{32} & m_{33} \end{bmatrix} - \begin{bmatrix} n_{11} & n_{12} & n_{13} \\ n_{21} & n_{22} & n_{23} \\ n_{31} & n_{32} & n_{33} \end{bmatrix} = \begin{bmatrix} m_{11} - n_{11} & m_{12} - n_{12} & m_{13} - n_{13} \\ m_{21} - n_{21} & m_{22} - n_{22} & m_{23} - n_{23} \\ m_{31} - n_{31} & m_{32} - n_{32} & m_{33} - n_{33} \end{bmatrix}$$

$$M * N = \begin{bmatrix} m_{11} & m_{12} & m_{13} \\ m_{21} & m_{22} & m_{23} \\ m_{31} & m_{32} & m_{33} \end{bmatrix} * \begin{bmatrix} n_{11} & n_{12} & n_{13} \\ n_{21} & n_{22} & n_{23} \\ n_{31} & n_{32} & n_{33} \end{bmatrix}$$

$$= \begin{bmatrix} m_{11} * n_{11} + m_{12} * n_{21} + m_{13} * n_{31} & m_{11} * n_{12} + m_{12} * n_{22} + m_{13} * n_{32} & m_{11} * n_{13} + m_{12} * n_{23} + m_{13} * n_{33} \\ m_{21} * n_{11} + m_{22} * n_{21} + m_{23} * n_{31} & m_{21} * n_{12} + m_{22} * n_{22} + m_{23} * n_{32} & m_{21} * n_{13} + m_{22} * n_{23} + m_{23} * n_{33} \\ m_{31} * n_{11} + m_{32} * n_{21} + m_{33} * n_{31} & m_{31} * n_{12} + m_{32} * n_{22} + m_{33} * n_{32} & m_{31} * n_{13} + m_{32} * n_{23} + m_{33} * n_{33} \end{bmatrix}$$

$$f * M = f * \begin{bmatrix} m_{11} & m_{12} & m_{13} \\ m_{21} & m_{22} & m_{23} \\ m_{31} & m_{32} & m_{33} \end{bmatrix} * \begin{bmatrix} f m_{11} & f\, m_{12} & f * m_{13} \\ f * m_{21} & f * m_{22} & f * m_{23} \\ f * m_{31} & f * m_{32} & f * m_{33} \end{bmatrix} = M * f$$

A precondition of the operations with two matrix operands is that the two matrices have the same number of rows and columns (for example, two 2×2 matrices or two 3×5 matrices). Add five functions to the matrix class developed in this chapter to support these operations. Test your functions with an appropriate driver program.

12. Another operation that can be defined on matrices is matrix-vector multiplication. The definition depends on which position the matrix takes in the operation, but in either case the result is a vector. In three-dimensional space, the two definitions are as follows:

$$M * v = \begin{bmatrix} m_{11} & m_{12} & m_{13} \\ m_{21} & m_{22} & m_{23} \\ m_{31} & m_{32} & m_{33} \end{bmatrix} * \begin{bmatrix} v_1 \\ v_2 \\ v_3 \end{bmatrix} = \begin{bmatrix} m_{11} * v_1 + m_{12} * v_2 + m_{13} * v_3 \\ m_{21} * v_1 + m_{22} * v_2 + m_{23} * v_3 \\ m_{31} * v_1 + m_{32} * v_2 + m_{33} * v_3 \end{bmatrix}$$

and

$$v * M = \begin{bmatrix} v_1 & v_2 & v_3 \end{bmatrix} * \begin{bmatrix} m_{11} & m_{12} & m_{13} \\ m_{21} & m_{22} & m_{23} \\ m_{31} & m_{32} & m_{33} \end{bmatrix} = \begin{bmatrix} v_1 * m_{11} + v_2 * m_{21} + v_3 * m_{31} \\ v_1 * m_{12} + v_2 * m_{22} + v_3 * m_{32} \\ v_1 * m_{13} + v_2 * m_{23} + v_3 * m_{33} \end{bmatrix}^T$$

A precondition of these operations is that the number of rows and columns in the matrix and the capacity of the vector must all be the same. Add two functions to the matrix class developed in this chapter to support these operations. Test your functions with an appropriate driver program.

13. A graph in the field of graph theory consists of a collection of vertices and edges. For example, the graph G

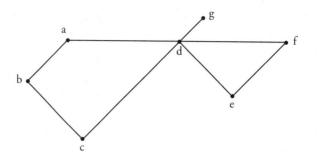

contains seven vertices and eight edges. Two vertices are adjacent if they are joined by an edge. In graph G, therefore, *a* is adjacent to *b* but *a* is not adjacent to *g*.

The adjacency matrix of a graph is a square matrix consisting of 1's and 0's. These values indicate whether or not two vertices are adjacent. If two vertices are adjacent, the corresponding entry is a 1; if they are not adjacent, the entry is a 0. For graph G, the adjacency matrix is as follows:

	a	*b*	*c*	*d*	*e*	*f*	*g*
a	0	1	0	1	0	0	0
b	1	0	1	0	0	0	0
c	0	1	0	1	0	0	0
d	1	0	1	0	1	1	1
e	0	0	0	1	0	1	0
f	0	0	0	1	1	0	0
g	0	0	0	1	0	0	0

Write a program that accepts as input the adjacency matrix of a graph G. Each input line represents one row of the matrix. Output should consist of the adjacency matrix with the vertices indicated for the rows and columns and a list of all the edges in the graph.

14. Using the animation class developed in Section 10.6, design and implement an application that simulates the launch of a spaceship. Inputs to the program should be the initial position, distance to travel, angle of launch, and speed. The program should construct the appropriate animation object from these data, and allow the user two launches per test.

Communication in Practice

1. Contact the mathematics teachers at your high school and discuss with them the use of vectors and matrices as data types. Ask what kinds of programming problems require their use, and what kind of abstract operations would be desirable. Give an oral report of your findings to the class.

2. Contact some programmers at a local business and discuss the use of data structures in the language that they use. Ask which ones are built-in, which ones must be programmer defined, and if any are represented as classes. Give an oral report of your findings to the class.

3. Select a programming problem from this chapter that you have not yet worked on. Construct a structure chart and write all documentary information necessary for the problem you have chosen. Do not write code. When you are finished, have a classmate read your documentation to see if precisely what is to be done is clear.

Linked Lists

Chapter Outline

Material in the previous four chapters has focused on using data structures such as files, arrays, structs, and classes to solve problems. You have learned how to choose an appropriate data structure, based primarily on the kind of information to be represented. For example, arrays are good for storing elements of the same type, whereas structs are good for storing elements of different types. The way in which these data structures are represented in the computer's memory has been a secondary concern. However, in Chapter 10, you saw how memory could be dynamically allocated to allow a C++ array to represent dynamic data structures such as vectors, matrices, and ordered collections. In the present chapter, we explore more sophisticated ways in which dynamic memory can be manipulated to build a more appropriate data structure, a **linked list,** to solve certain problems.

11.1 The Need for Linked Lists

Objectives

- to understand what kinds of problems require sophisticated methods of dynamic memory manipulation
- to understand the properties of a data structure that can solve these types of problems

To motivate our discussion of linked lists, let us consider two problems. The first problem is the file input problem. The second problem is the data movement problem. Both problems can be solved by using the kind of dynamic memory manipulations that we saw in Chapter 10. However, each problem reveals some shortcomings of those methods and points to the need for some new, more sophisticated techniques for dealing with dynamic memory.

The File Input Problem

The following sequence of operations is typical of many computer applications:
1. Input the data from a file.
2. Process the data.
3. Output the data back to the file.

625

linked list: *A list of data items in which each item is linked to the next one by means of a pointer.*

The data in the file can be of any type, such as integers, strings, or personnel records. The processing step transforms these data in some way. For example, at the end of the year, each employee's salary might be adjusted. Because the data are written back to the same file, they must be saved in temporary locations for processing before output. Several data structures can serve as candidates for this role:

1. A C++ array
2. A vector
3. An ordered collection

As we saw in Chapter 10, a C++ array is the worst choice of a temporary data structure for this problem. When the array variable is declared before the input step, the number of cells specified may be more than is needed to hold the data values from small files. This memory would be wasted. The number of cells may also be less than is needed to hold the data values from large files. This would cause a logic error, in that some data in the file would be missing from the list. Assuming an element type called **element** and an input file stream called **in_file**, the following code segment illustrates this point:

```
// Declare data for an array of 100 elements

const int MAX_LIST_SIZE = 100;
element list[MAX_LIST_SIZE];
int length = 0;
element data;

// Input no more than 100 elements from a file

in_file >> data;
while (! in_file.eof() && (length < MAX_LIST_SIZE))
{
        list[length] = data;
        ++length;
        in_file >> data;
}

// Display the consequences of the input operation

if (! eof() && (length == MAX_LIST_SIZE))
        cout << "Too bad, some data missing" << endl;
else if (length < MAX_LIST_SIZE)
        cout << "Too bad, some memory wasted" << endl;
else
        cout << "Lucky choice of size of array" << endl;
```

A vector is a better choice than an array for this problem, because a vector takes advantage of dynamic memory. When the vector variable is declared, no memory is allocated for any cells. As each data value comes in from the file, the vector is resized and the data value is assigned to the last cell in the enlarged vector. At the end of the input process, no memory will have gone to waste and no data will be missing. The following code segment solves the file input problem with a vector:

```
apvector<element> list;
element data;
in_file >> data;
while (! in_file.eof())
{
        list.resize(list.length() + 1);
        list[list.length() - 1] = data;
        in_file >> data;
}
```

An ordered collection is the best choice of the three. There is no change in the manipulation of dynamic memory, because an ordered collection uses a vector in its implementation. However, the details of this process are hidden in an abstract **add_last** operation, as shown in the following code segment:

```
ordered_collection<element> list;
element data;
in_file >> data;
while (! in_file.eof())
{
        list.add_last(data);
        in_file >> data;
}
```

Although the use of dynamic memory guarantees at least two solutions to the file input problem, each solution comes with a potentially heavy price. Recall that the data elements in a vector are stored in an array data member. The process of resizing a vector for each input value requires

1. The allocation of memory for a new array almost equal to the size of the old array
2. The copying of all of the data from one array to the other array.

For small files, these costs in memory and processing time are negligible. But for large files, the costs grow unreasonably. In cases where the individual data elements are also large, the costs may be prohibitive. In the worst case, the computer may run out of memory when a new array is created during the input of a single data value. Or a process may not be completed on time, because it took too long to copy a large number of data values from one array to the other during an input operation.

Here is a case where the overall solution of a problem is correct, but the means of getting there are too costly. When faced with such a problem, a computer scientist focuses on the cause—the way dynamic memory is manipulated—and proposes a solution: a new way of manipulating this memory. An ideal data structure for the file input problem would do these tasks:

1. Start in an empty condition.
2. Create just one cell of memory during the insertion of each input value.

3. Require the copying of just one data value—the input value—to the new memory cell.

4. Allow the processing of each data value in sequence, from the beginning to the end of the data structure.

We will soon examine a new ADT called a *linked list* that uses dynamic memory to meet these requirements.

The Data Movement Problem

Another common process in computer applications is the insertion or removal of a data value from a list. When a list is represented as an array (or vector or ordered collection), the insertion or removal of a data value can result in the movement of many other data values as well. An insertion requires all of the subsequent data values to be shifted to the right. A removal requires all of the subsequent data values to be shifted to the left. In the worst case, insertion or removal at the beginning of the list, the contents of the entire list must be moved. We have seen good examples of these cases with the operations **add_first** and **remove_first** of an ordered collection.

A special case of this problem is that of the insertion or removal of data from a file. We must first input all of the data from the file into a list (the file input problem). Then, we add or delete data from the list. Finally, we output the contents of the list back to the file. Clearly, an ordered collection would be a bad data structure for representing a list to solve this problem!

The ideal data structure for solving the data movement problem would allow insertions or removals without causing the physical movement of any other data values in the list. It turns out that the linked list ADT satisfies this requirement, as well as the others mentioned earlier. The use of dynamic memory allows a data value to be placed anywhere in a linked list with no physical movement of the other data in the list. We explore the concept of a linked list in the next section.

Exercises 11.1

1. Suppose we have *n* data values stored in a file, and a program reads these values into an ordered collection. Review the implementation of the **add_last** operation, and determine the total number of copy operations, in terms of *n*, that must be performed during the entire file input process for a file of *n* data values. (*Hint:* **add_last** is run for each input value in the process.)

2. Are there occasions for which we would still want to use an ordered collection to receive file input, despite the problems we have discussed in this section? If so, discuss the reasons why.

3. Describe the case that causes the least amount of work during a data movement process in an ordered collection. Does this occur during insertion or removal, and where?

11.2	The Concept of a Linked List

Objectives

- to understand the characteristics of a linked list that make it suitable for solving some kinds of problems but not others
- to be able to visualize the logical structure of a linked list
- to understand the operations on a linked list

logical structure: The organization of the components in a data structure, independent of their organization in computer memory.

node: A component of a linked list, consisting of a data item and a pointer to the next node.

null pointer (synonym: **empty link**): A special value that indicates that no node can be referenced.

external pointer: A special pointer that allows users to access the nodes in a linked list.

The Characteristics and Logical Structure of a Linked List

We have just seen two applications for which a linked list is ideally suited:
1. File input into a data structure in which the data can then be processed in sequence
2. Insertions or deletions of data from a data structure with minimal physical movement of data

A linked list works perfectly for these problems because it has the following characteristics:
1. It allows users to visit each data element in sequence from the first element to the last element.
2. It allows users to insert or remove a data element at a given position with no physical movement of the other data elements.
3. It uses only enough dynamic memory to store the data values inserted by the user.

To support these features, a linked list must have a special **logical structure.** Its logical structure describes the organization of data independently of how it is stored in the physical memory of a computer. The primary organizational element of this structure is called a **node.** In a linked list, a node contains two parts or *members*:
1. A data element
2. A *link* or *pointer* to the next node in the list.

The sequence of data elements in a linked list is thus linked by the sequence of nodes in which the elements are contained. Figure 11.1 shows a sequence of nodes in a linked list. Note that the data elements are labeled D1 through D4. Each link is an arrow coming out of the back of a node and pointing at the next node. Note also that the link component of the last node in the list is a little box with no arrow. This designates an *empty link*, or **null pointer,** indicating that there is no next node after this one in the list.

The logical structure of a linked list has four other components that support the implementation of operations on the list:
1. A *first* pointer to the first node in the list
2. A *current* pointer that can be moved to a desired node
3. A *previous* pointer that always points to the node before the current one
4. An *integer* representing the number of nodes in the list

The first three components are sometimes called **external pointers,** because they are not links that hold the sequence of nodes together. Their purpose is to give users access to different nodes in the list. Figure 11.2 shows the linked list from Figure 11.1 with these additional components, after the current pointer has been moved to the second node in the list. As we shall see shortly, this logical structure is just what we need to satisfy the requirements of a linked list mentioned earlier. Users can move through the list and visit each data element in sequence by moving the current pointer to the next node. Users can also insert or remove a data element from the list by redirecting some pointers at the appropriate nodes.

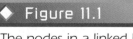

◆ Figure 11.1

The nodes in a linked list

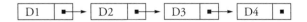

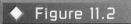

The external pointers of a linked list

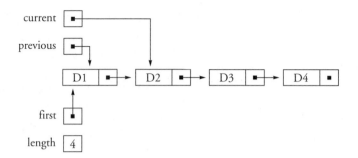

Linked List Operations

Let us now consider the abstract operations that the logical structure of a linked list makes possible. Each of these operations has a set of preconditions and postconditions. Most of these conditions concern the state of the external pointers in the linked list. In each of the following subsections, we provide an informal description of the operation, illustrate the operation with a figure, and state its preconditions and postconditions.

Creating a Linked List

When a linked list is created, it is empty and thus contains no nodes. However, the three external pointers and the length must all be initialized. Each of the pointers is set to null, as shown in Figure 11.3. The precondition of the **create** operation is that the linked list is in an unknown state. The postconditions are that each external pointer is null, and the length is zero.

◆ Figure 11.3

A newly created linked list

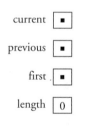

Detecting an Empty Linked List

An empty linked list looks just like the list shown in Figure 11.3. The precondition of the **empty** operation is that the list has been appropriately initialized. The postcondition is that the operation returns **TRUE** if there are no nodes in the list, and **FALSE** otherwise.

Moving to the Next Node

The **next** operation moves the current pointer to the next node after the current one. It also moves the previous pointer ahead one node. Figure 11.4 shows the states of a linked list before and after this operation, which moves the current pointer from the first node to the second node. Note that the previous pointer was null before the operation, and points to the first node afterwards.

◆ Figure 11.4

The effects of the **next** operation

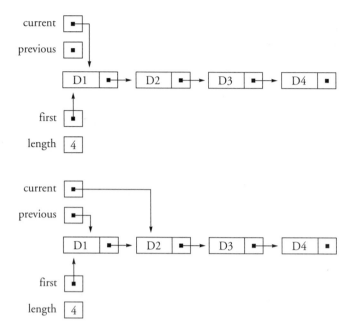

The **next** operation has one precondition. The current pointer must point to a node in the list. This will not be the case when the list is empty or after the **next** operation is run from the last node. The postconditions of the **next** operation are as follows:

1. The previous pointer is moved to the next node.
2. The current pointer is moved to the next node, unless this component is null. If that is the case, the current pointer becomes null.

Figure 11.5 shows the states of a linked list during a series of **next** operations to move the current pointer as far as it can go in the list.

Detecting the End of the List

To avoid running off the end of a linked list, users need a means of detecting when the current pointer can advance no further. For example, the **at_end** operation returns **TRUE** when a list is in the last state depicted in Figure 11.5. The operation also returns **TRUE** when the list is empty. When neither of these conditions is true, **at_end** returns **FALSE**.

Accessing and Modifying the Data in the Current Node

A typical application will move the current pointer to a desired node in a linked list, and then either access the data value in the node or modify it. These two operations, **access** and **modify**, assume that the current pointer is aimed at a node. In other words, **at_end** must return **FALSE**. **access** returns the data value in the current node. **modify** copies its parameter, a data value, into the data component of the current node. The result of an **access** operation to the contents of the last node is shown in Figure 11.6.

◆ Figure 11.5

Running the **next** operation to the end of a list

◆ Figure 11.6

The result of an access to the last node

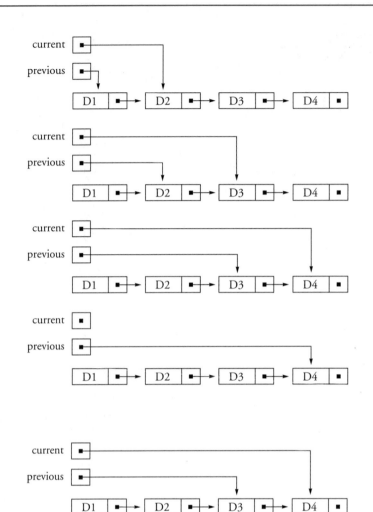

Moving to the First Node

Applications that process entire lists require an operation to move the current pointer to the first node in a list. The **first** operation assumes that the linked list has been appropriately initialized, but has no other preconditions. If the list is not empty, the operation aims the current pointer at the first node and sets the previous pointer to null. If the list is empty, **first** does nothing. Figure 11.7 shows the states of a linked list before and after the **first** operation.

Adding Data to the List

To add data to a linked list, a user moves the current pointer to the node before which the data should be inserted, and then invokes the **insert** operation. The only precondition of this operation is that the list has been appropriately initialized. The postcondition is that the node containing the new data element

Figure 11.7

The effects of the **first** operation

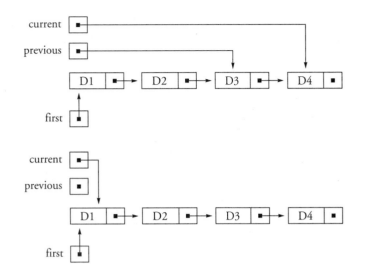

becomes the current node. The linked list handles an insertion of data in different ways, depending on the position of the current pointer.

Case 1: If the list is empty, the new data element is placed in the first node. This process is shown in Figure 11.8.

Case 2: If the current pointer points to the first node, the new data element is placed in a new node and inserted before the first node, as shown in Figure 11.9. The new node becomes both the current node and the first node.

Case 3: If the current pointer points to a node after the first node, then the new data element is placed in a new node that is linked into the list between the current node and the previous node, as shown in Figure 11.10. Once again, the current pointer is aimed at the node just inserted.

Case 4: If the current pointer has been moved past the last node in the list, the new data element is placed in a new node at the end of the list, as shown in Figure 11.11.

Note that in each case, the external pointers and the length are updated appropriately.

Figure 11.8

Inserting data into an empty list

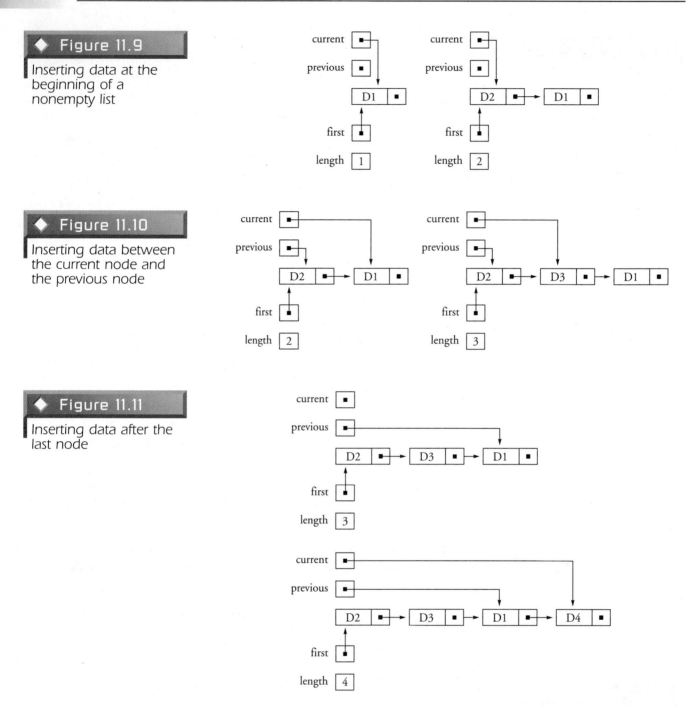

◆ **Figure 11.9**

Inserting data at the beginning of a nonempty list

◆ **Figure 11.10**

Inserting data between the current node and the previous node

◆ **Figure 11.11**

Inserting data after the last node

The following algorithm describes in detail the process of creating a new node and linking it into a linked list:

1. Create a new node
2. Set the data component of the new node to the new data element
3. Set the next pointer of the new node to null
4. If the list is empty or the current node is the first node

5.   Aim the first pointer at the new node

    Else

6.   Aim the next pointer of the previous node at the new node

7.   Set the next pointer of the new node to the current pointer

8.   Aim the current pointer at the new node

9.   Increment the length by one

The steps in this process for inserting a node into the middle of a linked list are depicted in Figure 11.12.

◆ Figure 11.12

The steps in the process of inserting a node into a linked list

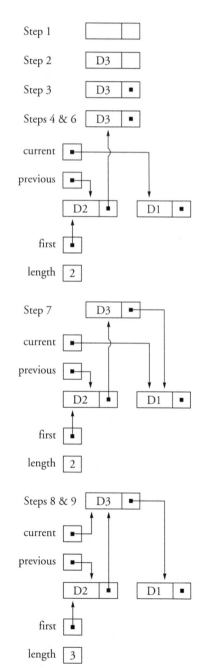

The order of steps 4 through 8 is critical. If this order is different, the new node will not be properly linked, and the logical structure of the linked list will be corrupted. Also note that these are the only steps performed during an insertion—regardless of where it occurs in the list. There is no loop to adjust the positions of other data elements, as with arrays. This is why a linked list solves the data movement problem.

Removing Data from the List

To remove data from a linked list, the user moves the current pointer to the desired node, and then invokes the **remove** operation. This operation assumes that the current pointer is pointing to a node (**at_end** returns **FALSE**). The operation unlinks the current node, returns its memory to the system, and returns the data element to the caller. At the end of the operation, the current pointer points to the node after the node just removed. The previous pointer remains unchanged. The first pointer may be updated as well.

The following algorithm describes in detail the process of unlinking a node to remove its data element from a linked list:

1. Save the data element in a temporary variable
2. Save a pointer to the current node
3. If the current node is the first node
4.   Set the first pointer to the next pointer of the current node
   Else
5.   Set the next pointer of the previous node to the next pointer of the current node
6. Set the current pointer to the next pointer of the current node
7. Use the saved pointer to return the old node to the system
8. Decrement the length by one
9. Return the data element to the caller

Once again, the order of the operations is important. The steps in this process for removing a node from the middle of a linked list are depicted in Figure 11.13. (See p. 638.)

The operations on a linked list are summarized in Table 11.1. (See p. 639.)

Using a Linked List to Solve Problems

Armed with a linked list abstract data type and knowing nothing about its implementation, we can now look at some examples of how it is used. We assume that the linked list ADT has been defined as a C++ class template. The type parameter for the linked list class is the type of the data stored in a list.

Example 11.1

The following program is a solution to an instance of the file input problem. The program reads integers from a file named **myfile** into a linked list. The program then increments each integer in the list. Finally, the program writes the contents of the list back to the file.

```cpp
// Program file: fileprob.cpp

#include <iostream.h>
#include <fstream.h>
#include "linklist.cpp"

int main()
{
      ifstream in_file;
      ofstream out_file;
      linked_list<int> list;
      int data;

      // Input phase - insert data at end of list

      in_file.open("myfile");
      in_file >> data;
      while (! in_file.eof())
      {
            list.insert(data);
            list.next();
            in_file >> data;
      }
      in_file.close();

      // Processing phase - increment all values
      //              in the list

      list.first();
      while (! list.at_end())
      {
            data = list.access();
            list.modify(data + 1);
            list.next();
      }

      // Output phase - write all values in the
      //          list back to the file

      out_file.open("myfile");
      list.first();
      while (! list.at_end())
      {
            out_file << list.access() << endl;
            list.next();
      }
      out_file.close();
      return 0;
}
```

◆ Figure 11.13

The steps in the process of removing a node from a linked list

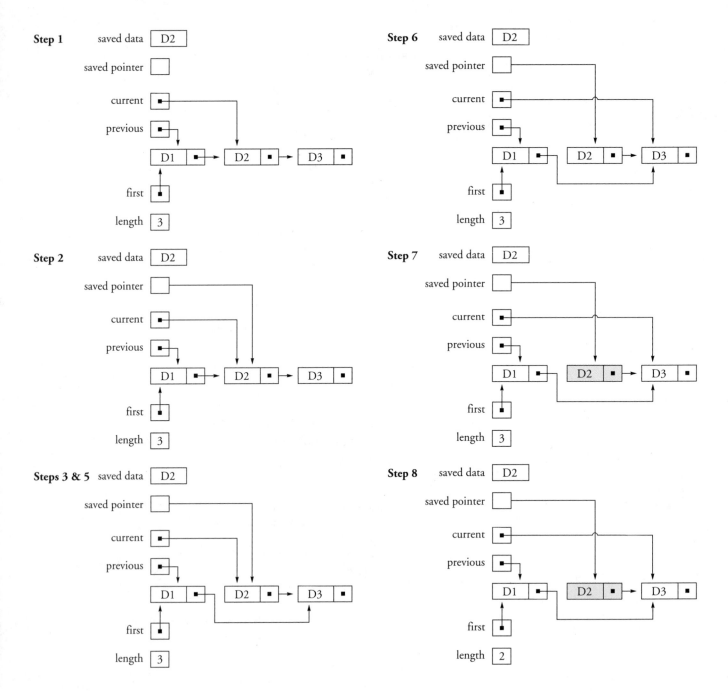

▼ **Table 11.1**

The operations on a
linked list abstract data
type

Operation	Preconditions	Postconditions
create	The list is in an unknown state.	The list is empty.
empty	The list is initialized.	Returns TRUE if empty, FALSE otherwise.
at_end	The list is initialized.	Returns TRUE if the current pointer has run off the end of the list, FALSE otherwise.
length	The list is initialized.	Returns the number of nodes in the list.
first	The list is initialized.	Moves the current pointer to the first node in the list.
next	The current pointer points to a node.	Advances the current and previous pointers ahead by one node.
access	The current pointer points to a node.	Returns the data element stored in the current node.
modify(new_data)	The current pointer points to a node.	Sets the data in the current node to the new data.
insert(new_data)	The list is initialized.	If **at_end** is true, then inserts the new data into a new node at the end of the list. Otherwise, inserts the new data into a new node before the current one. Makes the new node the current one
remove	The current pointer points to a node.	Removes the current node from the list, makes the node following this node the current one, and returns the removed data to the caller.

Let us examine the logic of each of the three main parts of the program of
Example 11.1.

Input phase: In this part of the program, the input file is opened, and we enter
a standard end-of-file **while** loop. The list is assumed to be empty at the
beginning of the loop. Thus, when the first data value is inserted, it goes at
the end of the list automatically. After the insertion, the **next** operation is
run. This has the effect of moving the current pointer beyond the last node in

the list. Thus, on the next pass through the loop, the new data will continue to be inserted at the end of the list. At the end of the input phase, the data in the list will be in the same order as they were in the file and be ready for sequential processing.

Processing phase: In this part of the program, the current pointer is moved to the first node to begin a **sequential traversal** of the list. This traversal consists of an end-of-list **while** loop. In the body of the loop, we access the data in the current node, process the data, and modify the node with the result. Then we move on to the next node, continuing the process until the end of the list is reached. Note that the control condition is tested at loop entry, to guard against the cases of the empty list and the end of the list.

sequential traversal:
The process of visiting each data item in a linked list, from beginning to end.

Output phase: This part of the program is similar to the processing phase. In this case, however, we traverse the list and simply access the data in each node for output to the file.

Example 11.2

Users would like to have a function named **reverse** that expects a linked list as a parameter and returns a new linked list with the contents of the parameter in reverse order. This is another instance of the data movement problem. The following C++ function solves this problem:

```
template <class itemType>
linked_list<itemType> reverse(linked_list<itemType> &list)
{
        linked_list<itemType> result;

        list.first();
        for (int i = 1; i <= list.length(); ++i)
        {
                result.insert(list.access());
                list.next();
        }
        return result;
}
```

The function in Example 11.2 illustrates two new ideas:

1. A count-controlled **for** loop can be used to traverse a linked list. The loop assumes that the current pointer is at the first node. The loop counts from 1 to the length of the list, and advances through the list by running the **next** operation.

2. The reversal of the data elements in the new list is automatically accomplished by inserting each value at the beginning of the list.

Note that the process of reversing the contents of a linked list is much more efficient than the process of reversing the contents of an ordered collection.

Communication and Style Tips

An entry-controlled loop that tests for the end of a linked list is an important idiom in programming. It resembles an end-of-file **while** loop and describes a similar process. In both cases, we are testing for the presence of a sentinel, using the functions **at_end** (lists) and **eof** (files). Also, in both cases, we advance to the next data value in a sequence by running the operations **next** (lists) and **>>** (files).

■ Exercises 11.2

1. Based on the operations for a linked list discussed in this section, describe how the linked list ADT differs from the ordered collection ADT.
2. Describe two applications for which a linked list is a suitable data structure.
3. Explain why so many linked list operations assume that the **at_end** operation returns **FALSE**.
4. Draw a picture of a linked list with three nodes. The current pointer should be aimed at the first node. Now draw pictures that show each step during the process of removing this node from the list.
5. Suppose that the length of a linked list is not maintained as a separate component of the data structure. How would this change affect the behavior of the **length** operation?
6. Describe the method used by a new linked list operation called **insert_last**. This operation expects a data element as a parameter and inserts it at the end of a linked list. The only precondition is that the list is initialized.
7. Describe how to overload the assignment operator for vectors so that one can assign a linked list to a vector. Why would this operation be useful?
8. Overload the **+** operator to define a C++ function that concatenates two linked lists and returns the result.

11.3 Defining the Linked List ADT as a C++ Class

Objectives

◆ to learn how to use pointers in C++ to manipulate dynamic data

◆ to learn how to create a dynamic data structure to represent a linked list

In the previous section, we examined the definition and use of a linked list as an abstract data type. We assumed the existence of a C++ class template that corresponds to that definition, and showed how that class can be used to solve some problems. Now it is time to develop the code for the C++ class template for a linked list.

The first step, declaring the operations and data members for the class, results in the following file:

```
// Class declaration file: linklist.h

#ifndef LINKLIST_H

#include "bool.h"

template <class itemType> class linked_list
```

```cpp
{
public:

    // constructors

    linked_list();
    linked_list(const linked_list<itemType> &list);

    // destructor

    ~linked_list();

    // assignment

    const linked_list<itemType>& operator =
            (const linked_list<itemType> &rhs);

    // accessors

    int  length() const;
    bool empty() const;
    bool at_end() const;
    itemType access() const;

    // modifiers

    void first();
    void next();
    void modify(const itemType &item);
    void insert(const itemType &item);
    itemType remove();

private:

    // Data members

    struct node;                // Definition of the node type
    typedef node *node_ptr;     // Definition of type pointer to node type
    struct node                 // Completion of the node type definition
    {
        itemType data;
        node_ptr next;
    };

    // External pointers to the list

    node_ptr myFirst, myCurrent, myPrevious;

    // The number of nodes in the list

    int mySize;
```

```
      // Member functions


      node_ptr get_node(const itemType &item);
};
```

```
#define LINKLIST_H
#endif
```

The declarations of the operations call for no comment. They have been translated directly from the abstract operations listed in Table 11.1.

The data members **myFirst**, **myCurrent**, **myPrevious**, and **mySize** represent the four external components, **first**, **current**, **previous**, and **length**, of the logical structure of a linked list discussed in Section 11.2. Each of the pointer data members is of type **node_ptr**. We now examine the definitions of this type and of the private member function **get_node**.

Defining a Pointer to a Node

As we saw in Section 11.2, each node in a linked list contains two parts: a data component and a pointer to the next node in the list. A struct is a logical choice for representing a node in C++. One component of the struct, the data element, is of type **itemType**. The other component of the struct, a pointer to a node, is of type **node_ptr**. Thus, the meaning of the definition of the **node** type

```
struct node                            // Completion of the node type definition
{
      itemType data;
      node_ptr next;
};
```

should be clear. However, the type name **node_ptr** must be defined before it can be used in the struct. As the name indicates, a **node_ptr** type should be defined as a pointer to a **node** type. As we saw in Chapter 10, C++ provides a special syntax for defining pointer types, as follows:

<type of object pointed to> * <pointer type name>

We apply this rule in the present situation to obtain the following definition of the **node_ptr** type:

```
typedef node *node_ptr;        // Definition of type pointer to node type
```

The asterisk ($*$) indicates that any object of type **node_ptr** will be a pointer to an object of type **node**.

Now we have a problem. No matter how we order the definitions of **node** and **node_ptr** in the class declaration file, one of these names will be undefined before it is used. To solve this problem, we introduce the name **node** as a struct before we define **node_ptr** and complete the definition of the struct. Thus, the complete set of type definitions looks like this:

```
private:

// Data members

struct node;                    // Definition of the node type
typedef node *node_ptr;         // Definition of type pointer to node type
struct node                     // Completion of the node type definition
{
      itemType data;
      node_ptr next;
};
```

Note that the type names **node** and **node_ptr** are declared as **private**. This means that they are of use in the implementation of the linked list class only. Users of the linked list class will have no awareness of them.

Declaring the get_node Function

Each time a data element is added to a linked list, three things must be done:
1. Allocate dynamic memory for a new node.
2. Set the data part of the node to the new data element.
3. Set the next pointer part of the node to null.

This task is complex enough to warrant the definition of a function to perform it. Because the function will be used only within the implementation of the linked list class, we declare it as **private**. The function expects a data element as a parameter. The function returns a pointer to a new node that contains the data element and a null pointer:

```
node_ptr get_node(const itemType &item);
```

Now that we have completed the declaration of the linked list class, we can turn to its implementation.

Creating a Linked List

Recall from Section 11.2 that a new linked list is empty. Thus, its external pointers **first**, **current**, and **previous**, should all be null, and its length should be zero. The default constructor does this:

```
template <class itemType>
linked_list<itemType>::linked_list()
: myFirst(0), myCurrent(0), myPrevious(0), mySize(0)
{
}
```

Note that the null pointer is represented in C++ as a zero. This value looks like a number, but it is used here as a pointer value. The null value indicates that the pointer variable does not currently point to a node.

The Copy Constructor for a Linked List

The copy constructor copies all of the data from the parameter list into the receiver list. The function makes use of the temporary pointer **probe** to traverse the nodes in the parameter list. It uses **insert** and **next** to place each data value at the end of the receiver list.

```
template <class itemType>
linked_list<itemType>::linked_list(const linked_list<itemType &list)
: first(0), current(0), previous(0), mySize(0)
{
        // Temporary pointer to first node in list
        node_ptr probe = list.myFirst;

        // Loop until end of list is reached

        while (probe != 0)
        {

                // Insert data from node in list

                insert(probe->data);

                // Advance to end of receiver

                next();

                // Move probe to next node in list

                probe = probe->next;
        }
}
```

This code is heavily commented to clarify each step. Note the following points:
1. The **probe** pointer starts at the first node of **list**.
2. The loop control condition (**probe != 0**) returns **FALSE** as long as **probe** points at a node in **list**, but returns **TRUE** when **probe** has reached the end of **list**.
3. The expression **probe->data** accesses the **data** component in the node pointed to by **probe**. This value is passed to **insert** to add it to the end of the receiver list.
4. The assignment statement **probe = probe->next;** sets **probe** to the value of the **next** component in the node pointed to by **probe**. This has the effect of advancing **probe** to the next node in **list**.

As you saw in Chapter 10, a pointer value can be compared to zero to determine whether or not it is null. The syntax for accessing a member of a node is new. Its form is

<pointer variable> -><node member name>

The *arrow operator* (->) directs the computer to follow the arrow from the pointer variable to the designated member in the node, as shown in our box and pointer diagrams. This process is accomplished in two steps:

1. A **dereference,** in which the node is located
2. A **selection,** in which the designated member is located in the node.

The same process could be accomplished by using the dereference operator (*) and the selector operator (.) introduced in Chapters 9 and 10. For example, the expressions

```
probe->next
```

and

```
*probe.next
```

have the same effect. Obviously, the use of the arrow notation simplifies the expression, so we prefer that.

dereference: The operation by which a program uses a pointer to access the contents of dynamic memory.

selection: The process by which a member of a struct or class is accessed.

Communication and Style Tips

The use of the arrow operator (->) with pointers is a bit like the use of the selector (.) with structs. However, you must exercise extreme caution when attempting to access the components of a node with the arrow operator. If the pointer variable is not initialized, or if the pointer variable is null, the use of the arrow operator could cause an error at run time. Remember that a pointer variable can point to a chunk of dynamic data (a node), but it need not. To protect your programs from bad pointer references, you should follow these guidelines:

1. Set all pointers to null when they are declared.
2. Test a pointer for the null condition before attempting to access the contents of a node with the arrow operator.

The Destructor for Linked Lists

The destructor makes use of the **first**, **empty**, and **remove** operations to return all of the nodes in the list to the system.

```
template <class itemType>
linked_list<itemType>::~linked_list()
{
      itemType item;

      first();
      while (! empty())
            item = remove();
}
```

The `first` and `next` Operations

After the **first** operation, the current pointer points to the first node and the previous pointer is null. The **first** operation thus modifies the current and previous pointers appropriately.

```
template <class itemType>
void linked_list<itemType>::first()
{
      if (myCurrent != myFirst)
      {
            myCurrent = myFirst;
            myPrevious = 0;
      }
}
```

The **next** operation moves the current and previous pointers ahead in the list by one node each. The precondition is that the current pointer must be pointing to a node.

```
template <class itemType>
void linked_list<itemType>::next()
{
      assert (myCurrent != 0);
      myPrevious = myCurrent;
      myCurrent = myCurrent->next;
}
```

Accessing and Modifying Data in a Node

Like the **next** operation, both the **access** and **modify** operations assume that the current pointer is pointing to a node.

```
template <class itemType>
itemType linked_list<itemType>::access() const
{
      assert(myCurrent != 0);
      return myCurrent->data;

}
```

```
template <class itemType>
void linked_list<itemType>::modify(const itemType &item)
{
        assert(myCurrent != 0);
        myCurrent->data = item;

}
```

As you can see from the last three function implementations, it is the responsibility of the user to test for the end of the list condition before running an operation that accesses the contents of a node. The **assert** function catches any failures to do so.

Testing for the End of the List

The **at_end** operation should return **TRUE** if the list is empty or if the current pointer has advanced to the end of the list. Otherwise, the operation returns **FALSE**.

```
template <class itemType>
bool linked_list<itemType>::at_end() const
{
        return empty() || myCurrent == 0;
}
```

Testing for an Empty List

The current pointer is null when the list is empty, but it is also null when it is at the end of a nonempty list. Thus, the empty operation compares the length of the list to zero.

```
template <class itemType>
bool linked_list<itemType>::empty() const
{
        return length == 0;
}
```

Inserting Data into a Linked List

The **insert** operation follows the algorithm presented in Section 11.2. The **get_node** function is used to create and initialize a new node with the new data element:

```
template <class itemType>
void linked_list<itemType>::insert(const itemType &item)
{
        node_ptr new_node = get_node(item);

        if (empty() || (myFirst == myCurrent))
            myFirst = new_node;
```

```
        else
                myPrevious->next = new_node;
        new_node->next = myCurrent;
        myCurrent = new_node;
        ++mySize;
}
```

Implementing get_node

Whenever a new node is needed for a linked list, the implementation invokes the function **get_node**. To allocate dynamic memory for the new node, **get_node** uses the **new** operator introduced in Chapter 10. In that chapter, a call to **new** took the form **new itemType [<number of items>]**. This expression allocates memory for an array of items and returns a pointer to the array. In the context of linked lists, we want **new** to return a pointer to a node. Thus, the form of the call to **new** should now be **new node**. The **get_node** function verifies that memory was allocated for the node by asserting that the new node pointer is not null. **get_node** then uses the pointer to initialize the contents of the new node with the new data element and the null pointer, and returns the pointer to the caller.

```
template <class itemType>
linked_list<itemType>::node_ptr linked_list<itemType>::get_node (const itemType &item)
{
        node_ptr new_node = new node;

        assert(new_node != 0);
        new_node->data = item;
        new_node->next = 0;
        return new_node;
}
```

Note a slight difference in the syntax of this function's heading from the headings of the other linked list functions. The scope specifier **linked_list <itemType>::** must also appear at the beginning of the heading. The reason for this is that the privately declared return type, **node_ptr**, would appear to be undefined if it were not preceded by the scope specifier of the class declaration module.

Removing Data from a Linked List

The **remove** operation follows the algorithm presented in Section 11.2:

```
        template <class itemType>
        itemType linked_list<itemType>::remove()
        {
                assert (myCurrent != 0);
                itemType data = myCurrent->data;
                node_ptr garbage = myCurrent;
```

```
        if (myFirst == myCurrent)
                myFirst = myCurrent->next;
        else
                myPrevious->next = myCurrent->next;
        myCurrent = myCurrent->next;
        delete garbage;
        --mySize;
        return data;
    }
```

Note that the function uses the operator **delete**, introduced in Chapter 10, to return the memory for the node to the system. In Chapter 10, the form for invoking this operator was **delete [ ] <pointer to array>**. In the present context, where we want to recycle just a node, we use the form **delete <pointer to a node>**.

■ Exercises 11.3

1. Implement the remaining linked list member functions.
2. State an algorithm for an **add_first** operation for linked lists, and write the corresponding C++ member function.
3. State an algorithm for an **add_last** operation for linked lists, and write the corresponding C++ member function.
4. Compare the processes described by **add_first** and **add_last**. Which one is more expensive to run and why?
5. State an algorithm and write a function for a subscript operation that allows access and modification of a data value at a given position in a linked list. Overload the operator **[ ]** for the function.
6. Describe the differences between the subscript operation defined in Exercise 5 for linked lists and the subscript operation for arrays.
7. Suppose that we drop the **mySize** data member from the definition of a linked list. Rewrite the function **length** so that it still returns the number of nodes in a list.

11.4 Pointers and the Management of Computer Memory

Objectives

- to understand the difference between the address of a memory location and the value stored in a memory location
- to understand how computer memory is organized to support different data types
- to understand how the logical structure of a linked list can be independent of its structure in memory
- to understand the costs and benefits of using linked lists

Thus far in this chapter, we have focused on the logical structure of a linked list and paid no attention to how the list is stored in computer memory. Even when we use the operators **new** and **delete** to manipulate dynamic memory, the operations are abstract, hiding any details of how the computer performs these tasks. In this section, we explore some of the concepts underlying memory management in C++ programs. In the process, you will gain a clear understanding of the costs and benefits of using linked lists.

Addresses and Values of Simple Variables

When we introduced the idea of a variable in Chapter 3, we illustrated the concept with little boxes and labels, as shown in Figure 11.14. As this picture shows, variables in C++ are named memory locations where values can be stored and accessed. However, the picture is abstract, in that it suppresses the details of

◆ **Figure 11.14**

Visualizing variables
and their values
abstractly

```
int x = 3, y = 4;
double d = 5.6;
```

x $\boxed{3}$

y $\boxed{4}$

d $\boxed{5.6}$

address: Often called
address of a memory
location, this is an
integer value that the
computer can use to
reference a location.

representing the memory cells and data at the machine level. When a program is loaded to run on a computer, each of the variable names is converted to a machine address, which is a binary number. The data stored in the memory cells are also represented as binary numbers. Thus, the variables shown in Figure 11.14 might be more accurately depicted as shown in Figure 11.15.

The binary numbers to the left of each memory cell in Figure 11.15 are called the **addresses** of the memory cells. The numbers inside of the boxes are the data or values stored there. Note that one cell is reserved for each integer value, but that two cells are needed for the real number. The whole part of the real number, 101 (5), is stored in cell 1101. The fractional part of the real number, 110 (6), is stored in the next cell. In general, the machine automatically computes the amount of memory needed for each type of data value and allocates that memory accordingly.

◆ **Figure 11.15**

Visualizing variables
and their values at the
machine level

1011 $\boxed{11}$

1100 $\boxed{100}$

1101 $\boxed{101}$

1110 $\boxed{110}$

Addresses and Values of Array Variables

The distinction between an address and a value stored at an address is one of the most important in computer science. This distinction also applies to array variables. In Chapter 8, we visualized an array variable as a block of adjacent memory cells, as shown in Figure 11.16. Note that in the abstract view of an array, the individual cells containing the data values are labeled with index values ranging from 0 to 4. The name **list** appears to label the entire block of cells.

At the machine level, the name **list** is translated to the binary address of the first cell in the array. The address of each subsequent cell in the array is one greater than the previous one, as shown in Figure 11.17. As you saw in a **Note of Interest** in Chapter 8, this arrangement allows the address of an array cell to be computed by adding its index value to the machine address of the first cell. (In cases where each data element requires several cells of memory, the index is first multiplied by this factor.) For example, if the machine address of **list** is 11100, the machine address of **list[2]** is 11100 + 10, or 11110 (using binary arithmetic). This method of computing the address of an array cell is the reason

◆ **Figure 11.16**

Visualizing an array
variable abstractly

```
int list[5];
for (int i = 0; i < 5; ++i)
    list[i] = i + 1;
```

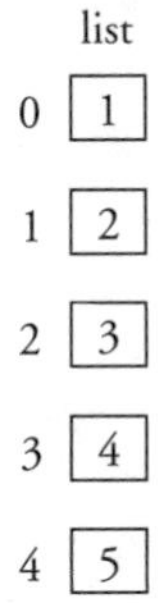

list

0 | 1 |

1 | 2 |

2 | 3 |

3 | 4 |

4 | 5 |

why array indexing is so fast, no matter where the cell is in the array. In fact, an array is called a *random access data structure,* because the time needed to access an array cell is independent of its position in the array. Put another way, it takes no more time to access the cell at **list[2]** than it does to access the cell at **list[0]**.

◆ **Figure 11.17**

Visualizing an array at
the machine level

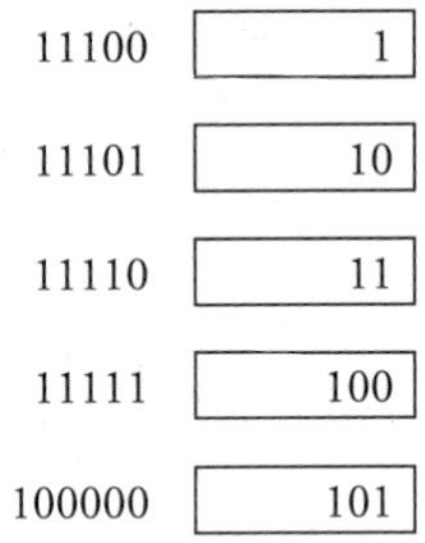

11100 | 1 |

11101 | 10 |

11110 | 11 |

11111 | 100 |

100000 | 101 |

Addresses and Values of Pointer Variables

The distinction between an address and a value is even more obvious when we deal with pointer variables. A pointer variable is a special kind of memory cell capable of storing the address of another memory cell. Thus far in this text, a pointer variable has contained either the null value (0) or a pointer to a chunk of dynamic memory (either an array or a node) returned by the **new** operator. However, we can use the **address-of operator** (**&**) to obtain the address of any C++ variable and store this value in a pointer variable. The restriction is that the variable whose address is assigned to the pointer must be of the same type as the base type of the pointer. For example, the following code segment accomplishes this for an integer variable:

address-of operator:
This operator, **&**, is used to access the address of a variable.

```
// Declare an integer variable and set it to 2

int x = 2;

// Declare a pointer to an integer variable
// and set it to the address of x

int *int_ptr = &x;
```

Figure 11.18 uses the abstract notation of boxes and arrows to distinguish the integer and pointer values stored in the variables **x** and **int_ptr**. Figure 11.19 shows what the contents of the memory cells might look like at the machine level. Study the binary numbers stored in the memory cells in Figure 11.19 carefully. They both appear to be integer values. However, the value stored in cell 1001 is the address of cell 1000, and thus is a pointer value.

◆ **Figure 11.18**

An integer variable and a pointer to this variable

x   2

int_ptr

The dereference operator (*****) is the inverse of the address-of operator. It expects a pointer value (an address) as an argument and returns the value stored at that address. Thus, the following code segment would display the machine address of **x** (in decimal) and then the value stored at that address:

```
// Declare an integer variable and set it to 2

int x = 2;

// Declare a pointer to an integer variable
// and set it to the address of x

int *int_ptr = &x;

// Display the address of x

cout << int_ptr << endl;

// Dereference int_ptr to display the value
// stored in x

cout << *int_ptr << endl;
```

Using the memory shown in Figure 11.19, when the computer evaluates the expression ***int_ptr**, it goes through these steps:
1. Looks up the value in memory cell 1001.
2. Uses the value from step 1, 1000, to look up the value in memory cell 1000.
3. Returns the value from step 2, 10.

◆ **Figure 11.19**

The variables of Figure 11.18 at the machine level

1000   10

1001   1000

Pointers and Dynamic Allocation of Memory

In all of the code examples shown thus far in this section, the computer allocates memory automatically for the variables. When this memory is no longer needed, the computer deallocates the memory by returning it to the system. Another example of this process is a function call. If the function has value parameters and locally declared variables, the computer allocates memory for these each time the function is invoked. When the function returns, the computer returns this memory to the system for other uses. Because the computer manages this memory automatically, the programmer can focus on the syntax of variable declarations and the scope rules for referencing the variables, without worrying about memory management.

As we have seen in the last two chapters, however, the programmer can become involved in memory management by using the **new** operator to allocate dynamic memory for data structures such as vectors and linked lists. When this memory is no longer needed, the programmer is responsible for invoking the **delete** operator to return the memory to the system.

To understand how **new** and **delete** work, we must take a more global view of the organization of memory in a computer. We can think of this memory as a giant block of cells, as shown in Figure 11.20. This block of cells appears to resemble a giant random access data structure. In fact, that is how it is treated when the computer is asked to look up or store a value at a given memory location. That is why this memory is called *RAM* (for random access memory).

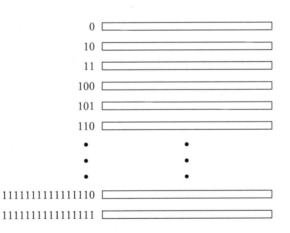

To simplify our discussion, we assume that the computer has a single user running a single C++ program. The memory of the computer at run time is divided into the following components:

1. An area of cells for the instructions and data of the computer's operating system
2. An area of cells for the instructions of the C++ program
3. An area of cells for the variables and data necessary for function calls, including the main program function; this area is called a **run-time stack,** and is discussed further in Chapter 12
4. An area of cells for representing dynamic data. This area is called a **heap** or *free store.*

run-time stack:
An area of computer memory reserved for local variables and parameters.

heap (synonym: **free store**): An area of computer memory where storage for dynamic data is available.

This organization of memory is depicted in Figure 11.21.

◆ Figure 11.21

The four parts of computer memory

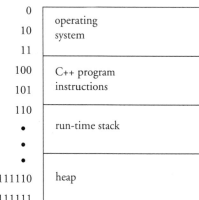

When a programmer runs the **new** operator to request a chunk of dynamic memory, the computer attempts to obtain the desired cells from the heap. If the heap cannot provide a block of these cells, the computer returns a null pointer to the caller of **new**. Otherwise, the computer returns a pointer to the first cell of the desired chunk of memory in the heap.

For example, consider the insertion of a new node into a linked list of integers. Each node requires a block of two cells, one for the integer and one for the pointer to the next node in the list. The **get_node** function asks for this memory and initializes it by running the statements

```
node_ptr new_node = new node;
assert(new_node != 0);
new_node->data = item;
new_node->next = 0;
```

Assuming that **item** has the value 3, an abstract view of the memory allocated for the new node is shown in Figure 11.22.

◆ Figure 11.22

An abstract view of a pointer to a node

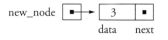

If the address of **new_node** is 1110 in the data area of computer memory and the address of the first available block of two cells in the heap is 1111111111111110, then the view of the node at the machine level is as shown in Figure 11.23.

Now suppose that the values 1 and 2 are inserted, in that order, at the beginning of an empty linked list at program start-up. After these operations, the chunks of memory for the two nodes in the heap will be adjacent to each other, as shown in Figure 11.24. Note that the positions of the two nodes in the heap are similar to the positions of two structs in an array. The positions are adjacent, and

◆ Figure 11.23

A pointer to a node at the machine level

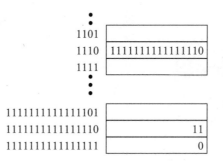

the physical order of the cells representing the nodes in memory is the same as the logical order of the nodes in the linked list. This situation might lead you to think that we could use indexing to access a data element at a given position in a linked list. However, this is true only in some cases.

Suppose that the same program removed the first data element (2) from the linked list, and reinserted it at the end of the list. The resulting situation is shown in Figure 11.25. The memory for the node containing the first data element is returned to the heap during the removal, and reused for a new node to contain the

◆ Figure 11.24

Memory allocated for two nodes in a linked list

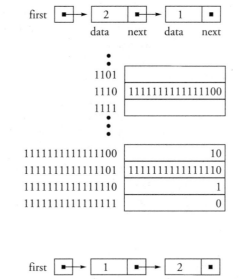

◆ Figure 11.25

Memory after removal of the first data element and reinsertion at the end of the list

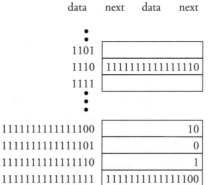

data element during the insertion. Even though the same cells of physical memory are used for the same numbers in both cases, the logical order of the data elements in the linked list has been reversed. This is indicated by the changes in the pointer values stored in the external pointer of the linked list and in the next pointers within the nodes. The number 2 comes after the number 1 in the linked list from the user's perspective, but in computer memory, the number 2 is stored before the number 1. Thus, we cannot count on the physical order of cells in the heap to reflect the logical order of nodes in a linked list. That is why we must treat the logical order of the nodes in a linked list as independent of their order in computer memory.

The Costs of Using Linked Lists

Now that you understand how linked lists are represented in computer memory, you are in a position to assess the costs of using them. The first cost concerns the access time for a given data element in the list. Because the logical structure of a linked list is independent of its physical structure in memory, we cannot generally use random access indexing with linked lists. This is why a linked list is called a **sequential access data structure.** To access a data element in this kind of data structure, we must start with a pointer to the first node and run a sequence of $n - 1$ **next** operations to reach the node at the nth position. The time of access to a given data element in a linked list depends on its position in the list. The value at the end of a linked list of 1000 elements will take about 1000 times as long to access as the value at the second position. By contrast, the access to a data element at the end of an array **a**, expressed as **a[length - 1]**, requires one or two machine instructions. The access to the last element in this array would be just as fast as the access to the second data element, expressed as **a[1]**.

The low cost of random access with arrays plays a role in highly efficient search strategies, such as the binary search to be discussed in Chapter 12. The high cost of sequential access makes the linked list a poor choice of an ADT for applications that must perform many searches for given data elements or must access data elements at specified positions. Also, some operations, such as insertion at the end of the list, require $n - 1$ **next** operations for a list of length n.

Another cost associated with linked lists is the use of memory. Each node in a linked list requires memory not only for a data element but also for a pointer to the next node. The memory needed to store one pointer value is not large (probably one cell). But a linked list of a million nodes would require a million such cells. By contrast, an array of the same logical size would require one million fewer memory cells.

One final cost of using linked lists has to do with the likelihood of program errors. The manipulation of pointers can be complicated and error prone, as compared with the range-checked indexing of arrays. Also, with dynamic data, the programmer has all of the burden of memory management. It is easy to ask for dynamic memory with the **new** operator, but also easy to forget to return it with **delete** when it is no longer needed. The failure to recycle this memory is called **memory leakage.** If it is severe enough, memory leakage can lead to a condition known as **heap underflow,** in which new dynamic memory can no longer be obtained from the heap.

sequential access data structure: *A data structure in which the time to access a data item depends on its position in the structure.*

memory leakage: *A condition in which dynamic memory is lost due to programmer error.*

heap underflow: *A condition in which memory leakage causes dynamic memory to become unavailable.*

Garbage Collection

Programs that make frequent use of dynamic memory can be error prone. One kind of error that can occur is the failure to return pieces of dynamic memory to the heap when they are no longer needed. If this failure occurs often enough, the program will run out of memory, perhaps at a critical point in its task.

To avoid the problem of memory leakage, some programming languages have been designed so that the programmer does not have to worry about returning unused memory to the heap at all. The run-time system for these languages has a special module called a **garbage collector** that automatically recovers unused dynamic memory when it is needed.

Two such languages, Smalltalk and LISP, rely on dynamic memory for all of their data structures, so an automatic garbage collector is an essential part of their design. In Smalltalk, a pure object-oriented language, dynamic memory is used to create new objects. In LISP, which supports a linked list as a standard data structure, dynamic memory is used to add data elements to a list. When an application in either of these languages asks for a new piece of dynamic memory, the computer checks the heap to see whether the request can be satisfied. If not, the garbage collector is invoked, and all of the unused memory locations are returned to the heap. Then the request is granted, if enough dynamic memory is available.

The garbage collection mechanism works roughly as follows: Every memory location is marked as either referenced by the application or not. A memory location is referenced if it is named by a variable or is part of a linked structure pointed to by such a variable. When memory is allocated for variables, it is marked as referenced. When memory becomes completely unlinked from any variable references in a program, it is marked as unreferenced. Thus, only unreferenced memory locations will be candidates for being returned to the heap.

Garbage collection in early versions of LISP and Smalltalk sometimes degraded the performance of a program. During a collection, an application would appear to pause for a moment while the mechanism did its work. This is one reason why Smalltalk and LISP applications have not received much play in industry, where efficiency in time-critical tasks is a priority. However, much research and development have produced very efficient garbage collection algorithms, so that LISP and Smalltalk programs now perform as well as programs written in languages without any garbage collector.

The Benefits of Using Linked Lists

As we saw in the first three sections of this chapter, the primary benefit of using linked lists is the low cost of inserting or removing a given data element. In each case, the process requires the rearrangement of at most three or four pointers. The number of these operations is close to the same, whether the data element is at the beginning of the list or at the end of the list. By contrast, a removal or insertion of a data element at position i in an array of n data elements requires that $n - i$ data elements be shifted (copied) by one position. When the data elements are large and the position is near the beginning of the array, insertions or removals can be very expensive.

Another benefit of using linked lists concerns the modeling of dynamic situations such as file input. In these situations, memory is allocated in a linked list for the incoming data incrementally, or node by node. By contrast, as we saw in Section 11.1, the use of vectors or ordered collections for these problems is expensive, in that n extra memory locations and n extra copy operations are necessary to accomplish each insertion into a list of length n.

To summarize, a linked list works very well for problems like the file input problem or the data movement problem. In this class of problems, random access is unnecessary, but we need a data structure that can grow or shrink incrementally with the size of the data. An array works much better when random access is needed, when we can predict how many data values will be input, and when the likelihood of movement of data within the array is small.

Exercises 11.4

1. Discuss the difference between an address and the value stored at that address.
2. Draw pictures of the computer's memory, with binary addresses and data values, that show the memory cells for the following statements:
   a. `int x = 2, y = 3, z = 4;`
   b. `double a = 4.8, b = 7.6;`
   c. `char ch = 'a';`
   d. `double list[5];`
   e. `double *real_ptr = 0;`
   f. ```
      struct
      {
          int first;
          double second;
      } a_struct;
      ```
3. Draw a picture of the array data member of a vector object with a size of 5 and a fill value of 3, after that object has been created. Your picture should show two views of the array: an abstract view that shows the integer indexes and values, and a machine-level view that shows binary addresses and values.
4. Write a program to test for how many nodes can be allocated for a linked list of integers until the heap has no more memory. You can accomplish this by writing a count-controlled loop whose upper bound is an input integer and which adds a new data element to the beginning of the list on each pass. Start with the input of a large integer, and if an error occurs, try another integer of half that size. If an error does not occur, repeat the input with an integer half again the size of the previous input. When your inputs can alternate between an integer that causes an error and an integer that is one less that does not cause an error, you will have determined how many nodes can be obtained for storing integers from the heap.
5. Simon Seeplus recommends that we use a linked list rather than a vector to implement the data member of the ordered collection class. He argues that the ordered collection class will then solve the data movement and file input problems very efficiently. Discuss his proposal. Does it violate any of the requirements of the ordered collection class?

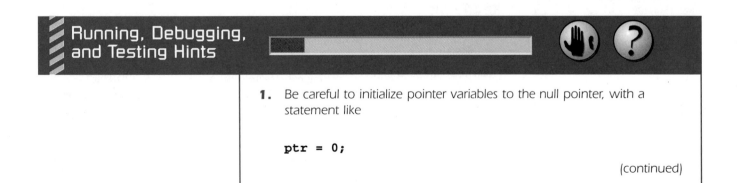

**Running, Debugging, and Testing Hints**

1. Be careful to initialize pointer variables to the null pointer, with a statement like

   `ptr = 0;`

   (continued)
      ```

---

2. Be careful not to dereference a pointer that is null. Thus, if the assignment

```
ptr = 0;
```

is made, a reference to ***ptr** or to **ptr->data** results in an error.

3. Always test a pointer to see whether or not it is null before attempting to dereference it. Use statements of the form

```
if (ptr != 0)
    process(ptr->data);
```

or

```
while (ptr != 0)
    ptr = ptr->next;
```

4. When a piece of dynamic memory is no longer needed in a program, use **delete** so that the memory can be reallocated.

5. After using **delete** with a pointer, its referenced memory is no longer available. If you use **delete ptr**, then ***ptr** and **ptr->data** are unpredictable.

6. When creating dynamic data structures, be careful to initialize properly by assigning the null pointer where appropriate and keep track of pointers as your structures grow and shrink.

7. Operations with pointers require that they be of the same type. Thus, exercise caution when comparing or assigning them.

8. Values may be lost when pointers are inadvertently or prematurely reassigned. To avoid this, use as many auxiliary pointers as you wish. This is better than trying to use one pointer for two purposes.

9. Be sure to declare and implement a destructor operation for a class that uses dynamic memory.

Summary

🔑 Key Terms

address (of a memory location)

address-of operator (**&**)

arrow operator (**->**)

dereference

external pointer

free store

heap

heap underflow

linked list

logical structure (of a linked list)

memory leakage

node

null pointer

random access data structure

run-time stack

selection (of a member)

sequential access data structure

sequential traversal

Key Concepts

- Values are stored in memory locations; each memory location has an address.
- A pointer variable is one that contains the address of a memory location; a pointer variable can be declared by

```
int *int_ptr;
```

where the asterisk (*) is used after the predefined data type.
- Dynamic memory is memory that is referenced through a pointer variable. Dynamic memory can be used in the same context as any variable of that type. In the declaration

```
int *int_ptr;
```

the dynamic memory is available after **int_ptr = new int;** is executed.
- Dynamic memory is created by

```
ptr = new base_type;
```

and destroyed (memory area made available for subsequent reuse) by

```
delete ptr;
```

- The success of dynamic memory allocation can be detected by examining the value returned by **new**. If it is **0**, then there is no more dynamic memory available.
- Assuming the definition

```
int *ptr;
```

the relationship between a pointer and its associated dynamic variable is illustrated by the code

```
ptr = new int;
*ptr = 21;
```

which can be envisioned as

    ptr   *ptr

- **0** (the null pointer) can be assigned to a pointer variable; this is used in a Boolean expression to detect the end of a list.
- Dynamic data structures differ from other data structures in that space for them is allocated under program control during the execution of the program.
- A linked list is a dynamic data structure formed by having each node contain a pointer that points to the next node.

◆ A node is a component of a linked list. Each node contains a member for storing a data element and a member for storing a pointer to the next node.

◆ References to the members of a node structure use the arrow operator **->**, as illustrated by

```
struct node
{
      int data;
      node *next;
};

node *ptr;

ptr = new node;
ptr->data = 45;
ptr->next = 0;
```

◆ When creating a linked list, the final component should have **0** assigned to its pointer member.

◆ Processing a linked list is accomplished by starting with the first node in the list and proceeding sequentially until the last node is reached.

◆ When a node is deleted from a linked list, it should be returned for subsequent use; this is done by using the standard operator **delete**.

Suggestions for Further Reading

Lambert, Kenneth A., and Naps, Thomas L., *Fundamentals of Program Design and Data Structures with C++*. Cincinnati, Ohio: South-Western Educational Publishing Company, 1998.

Chapter Review Exercises

Assume that the member names of a node are **data** and **next**, and that the external pointers **first**, **probe**, and **trailer** and the integer variable **number** have been declared and initialized as follows:

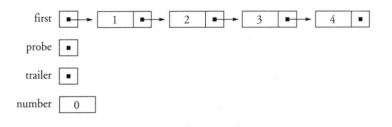

For Exercises 1–5, draw a picture of the state of these objects after the statements have been executed. Assume that the state of the objects carries over from one exercise to the next.

1. ```
probe = first;
trailer = first;
```

2. ```
while (probe->next != 0)
{
        trailer = probe;
        probe = probe->next;
}
```

3. ```
number = probe->data;
```

4. ```
delete probe;
```

5. ```
trailer->next = 0;
```

6. You could think of the statements of Exercises 1–5 as the steps of a single operation. What operation would you call this?

7. What are the preconditions and postconditions of the operation you named in Exercise 6?

8. Suppose that someone forgot to declare and implement a destructor for the linked list class. Describe a situation in which this omission is likely to cause problems.

9. Suppose that a bug has been introduced into the linked list implementation, so that linked lists of the following form are created:

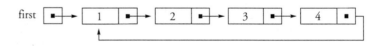

Describe the problems that this structure would cause for a sequential search for a given data element in the list.

## Programming Problems and Activities

1. An index for a textbook can be created by a C++ program that uses dynamic data structures and works with a text file. Assume that input for a program is a list of words to be included in an index. Write a program that scans the text and produces a list of page numbers indicating where each word is used in the text.

2. One of the problems faced by businesses is how best to manage their lines of customers. One method is to have a separate line for each cashier or station. Another is to have one feeder line where all customers wait and the customer at the front of the line goes to the first open station. Write a program to help a manager decide which method to use by simulating both options. Your program should allow for customers arriving at various intervals. The manager wants to know the average wait in each system, average line length in each system (because of its psychological effect on customers), and the longest wait required.

3. Write a program to keep track of computer transactions on a mainframe computer. The computer can process only one job at a time. Each line of input contains a user's identification number, a starting time, and a sequence of
```

integers representing the duration of each job. Assume all jobs are run on a first-come, first-served basis. Output should include a list of identification numbers, starting and finishing times for each job, and average waiting time for a transaction.

4. Several previous programming problems have involved keeping structures and computing grades for students in some class. If linked lists are used for the students' structures, such a program can be used for a class of 20 students or a class of 200 students. Write a record-keeping program that utilizes linked lists. Input is from an unsorted data file. Each student's information consists of the student's name, 10 quiz scores, six program scores, and three examination scores. Output should include the following:

   a. A list, alphabetized by student name, incorporating each student's quiz, program, and examination totals; total points; percentage grade; and letter grade

   b. Overall class average

   c. A histogram depicting class averages

5. Mailing lists are frequently kept in a data file sorted alphabetically by customer name. However, when they are used to generate mailing labels for a bulk mailing, they must be sorted by zip code. Write a program to input an alphabetically sorted file and produce a list of labels sorted by zip code. The data for each customer follow:

   a. Name

   b. Address, including street (plus number), city, two-letter abbreviation for the state, and zip code

   c. Expiration information, including the month and year.

   Use a linked list to sort by zip code. Your labels should include some special symbol for all expiring subscriptions.

6. As a struggling professional football team, the Bay Area Brawlers have a highly volatile player roster. Write a program that allows the team to maintain its roster as a linked list, ordered by player last name. Other data items stored for each player are

   Height
   Weight
   Age
   University affiliation

   As an added option, have your program access players in descending order of weight and age.

7. Write a program that allows the input of an arbitrary number of polynomials as coefficient and exponent pairs. Store each polynomial as a linked list of coefficient–exponent pairs arranged in descending order by exponent. These pairs do not need to be entered in descending order; it is the responsibility of your program to arrange them that way. Your program should then be able to evaluate each of the polynomials for an arbitrary number x and to display each of the polynomials in the appropriate descending exponent order. Make sure your program works for all "unusual" polynomials, such as the zero polynomial, polynomials of degree 1, and constant polynomials.

8. A linked list limits users to movement in one direction through the list. Occasionally, it would be useful to move backwards to the previous node, or start a process at the last node in the list. The operations **last** and **previous**,

the inverses of **first** and **next** could be used with a doubly linked list having the following structure:

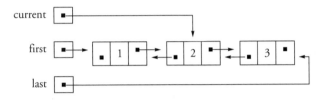

Note that a doubly linked list needs no external previous pointer. Write the specifications for the operations **last** and **previous**, and declare and implement a doubly linked list class in C++. The operations on singly linked lists should also work with doubly linked lists, but may be implemented differently. Test the new class with an appropriate driver program.

Communication in Practice

1. Select a programming problem from this chapter that you have not yet worked. Construct a structure chart and write all documentary information necessary for the problem you have chosen. Do not write code. When you are finished, have a classmate read your documentation to see if precisely what is to be done is clear.

2. Using a completed program from this chapter, remove all documentation pertaining to linked lists. Exchange this version with another student who has prepared a similar version. Write documentation for all linked lists in the other student's program. Compare your results with the program author's original version. Discuss the differences and similarities with your class.

3. Stacks and queues can be represented by using either arrays (with or without dynamic memory) or linked lists. Talk with a computer science teacher who prefers the linked list approach and with one who prefers the array approach. List the advantages and disadvantages of each method. Give an oral report to your class summarizing your conversations with the instructors. Create a chart to use as part of your presentation.

12

Advanced Topics: Recursion and Efficient Searching and Sorting

Chapter Outline

T he previous chapters presented techniques for developing programs to solve problems. Our choice of techniques has been guided by their usefulness in illustrating important introductory concepts in programming, such as the readability, maintainability, and correctness of programs. One other major criterion affecting the choice of problem-solving techniques in real-world programming is efficiency. Efficiency in computer science is a measure of the run-time and memory usage of computational processes. Frequently a solution that is clearest from a conceptual standpoint is not the most efficient one. Efficient solutions often require clever algorithmic design, and formal analysis is necessary to compare and predict how different solutions will behave with different data sets.

Although algorithm analysis is the subject of more advanced courses in computer science, we can give you a taste of the topic in this closing chapter. We first discuss how recursive algorithms are run on real computers and examine the resources—processing time and memory—used by recursive processes. We then introduce an improved algorithm for searching lists called *binary search,* and compare its efficiency to that of the sequential search algorithm introduced in Chapter 8. Next, we introduce an improved algorithm for sorting lists called *quick sort,* and compare its efficiency to that of the selection sort algorithm discussed in Chapter 8. Finally, we examine how linked lists lend themselves naturally to recursive processing.

In the chapter on repetition, you saw how to control iterative processes with **for**, **while**, and **do . . . while** statements in C++. Let's now examine how recursive processing works and how it differs from iterative processing.

12.1 Recursion

Objectives

- to understand how recursion can be used to solve a problem
- to be able to use recursion to solve a problem
- to understand what happens in memory when recursion is used
- to understand how algorithms can be analyzed for run-time and memory usage
- to be able to weight the costs and benefits of using recursion

Recursive Processes

recursion: The process of a subprogram calling itself. A clearly defined stopping state must exist. Any recursive subprogram can be rewritten using iteration.

Many problems can be solved by having a subtask call itself recursively as part of the solution. **Recursion** is frequently used in mathematics. Consider, for example, the definition of $n!$ (n factorial) for a nonnegative integer n. This is defined by

$$0! = 1$$
$$1! = 1$$

for $n > 1$, $n! = n * (n - 1)!$. Thus,

$$6! = 6 * 5! = 6 * 5 * 4! = 6 * 5 * 4 * 3! = 6 * 5 * 4 * 3 * 2! = 6 * 5 * 4 * 3 * 2 * 1$$

Another well-known mathematical example is the Fibonacci sequence. In this sequence, the first term is 1, the second term is 1, and each successive term is defined to be the sum of the previous two. More precisely, the Fibonacci sequence $a_1, a_2, a_3, \ldots, a_n$ is defined by

$$a_1 = 1$$
$$a_2 = 1$$
$$a_n = a_{n-1} + a_{n-2} \text{ for } n > 2$$

This generates the sequence

$$1, 1, 2, 3, 5, 8, 13, 21, \ldots$$

In both examples, note that the general term was defined by using the previous term or terms.

What applications does recursion have for computing? In many instances, a function can be written to accomplish a recursive task. If the language allows a subprogram to call itself (C++ does, early versions of FORTRAN do not), it is sometimes easier to solve a problem by this process.

| Example 12.1 |

As an example of a recursive function, consider the sigma function—denoted by $\sum\limits_{i=1}^{n}$ —which is used to indicate the sum of integers from 1 to n. A C++ function that performs this task is as follows:

```
int sigma (int n)
{
        if (n <= 1)
                return n;
        else
                return n + sigma(n - 1);
}
```

To illustrate how this recursive function works, suppose it is called from the main program by a statement such as

```
sum = sigma(5);
```

In the **else** portion of the function, we first have

```
return 5 + sigma(4);
```

At this stage, note that **sigma(4)** must be computed. This call produces

```
return 4 + sigma(3);
```

If we envision these recursive calls as occurring on levels, we have

```
1.   return 5 + sigma(4)
  2.   return 4 + sigma(3)
    3.   return 3 + sigma(2)
      4.   return 2 + sigma(1)
        5.   return 1
```

Now the end of the recursion has been reached and the steps are reversed for assigning values. Thus, we have

```
        5.   return 1
      4.   return (2 + 1)   (= 3)
    3.   return (3 + 3) (= 6)
  2.   return (4 + 6)   (= 10)
1.   return (5 + 10)   (= 15)
```

Thus, **sigma(5)** computes the value 15.

Before analyzing what happens in memory when recursive subprograms are used, some comments about recursion are in order:

stopping state: The well-defined termination of a recursive process.

1. The recursive process must have a well-defined termination. This termination is referred to as a **stopping state.** In Example 12.1, the stopping state was

```
if (n <= 1)
    return n;
```

recursive step: A step in a recursive process that solves a similar problem of smaller size and eventually leads to a termination of the process.

2. The recursive process must have well-defined steps that lead to the stopping state. These steps are usually called **recursive steps.** In Example 12.1, these steps were

```
return n + sigma(n - 1)
```

Note that, in the recursive call, the parameter is simplified toward the stopping state.

What Really Happens?

What really happens when a subprogram calls itself? First, we need to examine the idea of a **stack**. Imagine a stack as a pile of cafeteria trays: The last one put on the stack is the first one taken off the stack. This is what occurs in memory when a recursive subprogram is used. Each call to the subprogram can be thought of as adding a tray to a stack called the *run-time stack,* which we introduced in Chapter 11. In the previous function, the first call creates a level of recursion that contains the partially complete return statement

stack: A dynamic data structure where access can be made from only one end. Referred to as a LIFO (last-in, first-out) structure.

        return 5 + sigma(4)

This corresponds to the first tray in the stack. In reality, this is an area in memory waiting to receive a value for **5 + sigma(4)**. At this level, operation is temporarily suspended until a value is returned for **sigma(4)**. However, the call **sigma(4)** produces

        return 4 + sigma(3)

This corresponds to the second tray on the stack. As before, operation is temporarily suspended until **sigma(3)** is computed. This process is repeated until finally the last call, **sigma(1)**, returns a value.

At this stage, the stack may be envisioned as illustrated in Figure 12.1. Since different areas of memory are used for each successive call to **sigma**, each variable **sigma** represents a different memory location.

The levels of recursion that have been temporarily suspended can now be completed in reverse order. Thus, since the return

        return sigma(1) = 1

has been made, then

        return sigma(2) = 2 + sigma(1)

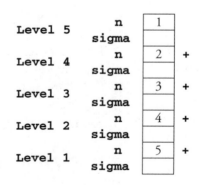

◆ Figure 12.1

Stack for the function **sigma**

becomes

```
return sigma(2) = 2 + 1
```

This then permits

```
return sigma(3) = 3 + sigma(2)
```

to become

```
return sigma(3) = 3 + 3
```

Continuing until the first level of recursion has been reached, we obtain

```
sigma = 5 + 10
```

This "unstacking" is illustrated in Figure 12.2.

◆ **Figure 12.2**

"Unstacking" function
sigma

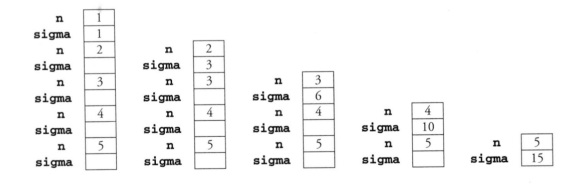

Example 12.2

Let's now consider a second example of recursion. In this example, a function is used recursively to print a line of text in reverse order. Assume the line of text has only one period (and this is at the end of the line); the stopping state is when the character read is a period. Using the data line

This is a short sentence.

a complete program is

```
// Program file: revprint.cpp

// This program uses a function recursively
// to print a line of text in reverse.

#include <iostream.h>
#include <fstream.h>

// Function: stack_it_up
// Prints a series of input characters in reverse
// order, up until a '.'
//
// Input: an opened input file stream
void stack_it_up(ifstream &in_file);

int main()
{
        ifstream in_file;

        in_file.open("sentence");
        stack_it_up(in_file);
        in_file.close();
        return 0;
}

void stack_it_up(ifstream &in_file)
{
        char one_char;

        in_file.get(one_char);
        if (one_char != '.')
                stack_it_up(in_file);
        cout.put(one_char);
}
```

Output from this program is

    .ecnetnes trohs a si sihT

In this program, as each character is read, it is placed on a stack until the period is encountered. At that time, the period is printed and then, as each level in the stack is passed through in reverse order, the character on that level is printed. The stack created while this program is running is illustrated in Figure 12.3.

◆ Figure 12.3

Stack created by
function **stack_it_up**

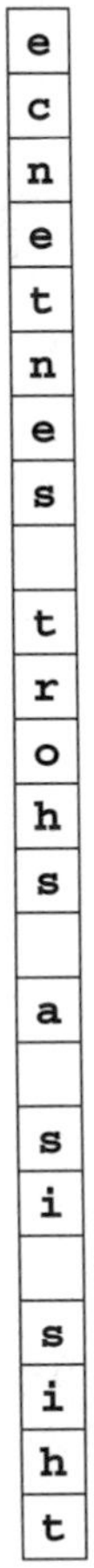

e
c
n
e
t
n
e
s
t
r
o
h
s
a
s
i
s
i
h
t

Example 12.3

Let's now consider another example of a recursive function. Recall that the factorial of a nonnegative integer, n, is defined to be

$$1 * 2 * 3 \cdots * (n - 1) * n$$

and is denoted by $n!$. Thus,

$$4! = 1 * 2 * 3 * 4$$

For the sake of completing this definition, $1! = 1$ and $0! = 1$. A recursive function to compute $n!$ is

```
int factorial(int n)
{
      if (n == 0)
            return 1;
      else
            return n * factorial(n - 1);
}
```

If this function is called from the main program by a statement such as

```
product = factorial(4);
```

we envision the levels of recursion as

```
1.   return 4 * factorial(3)
  2.   return 3 * factorial(2)
    3.   return 2 * factorial(1)
      4.   return 1 * factorial(0)
        5.   factorial(0) = 1
```

Successive values would then be assigned in reverse order to produce the following:

```
        5.   factorial(0) = 1
      4.   return (1 * 1) = 1
    3.   return (2 * 1) = 2
  2.   return (3 * 2) = 6
1.   return (4 * 6) = 24
```

Analyzing a Process for Running Time and Memory Usage

An efficient computational process solves a problem in a reasonable amount of time, using a reasonable amount of computer memory. An inefficient process solves a problem using an unreasonable amount of time and/or memory. What counts as reasonable or unreasonable may vary with user requirements and expectations. For example, a response time of one minute for searching a list of 10,000,000 names might be considered reasonable for some users but not others. Many times there is a trade-off between time and memory. Some users may be willing to pay more for extra memory if this allows data to be processed more quickly, while other users may have to settle for a slower processing time in order to economize on memory.

Computer scientists have discovered that some processes are inefficient regardless of who the user is. Some processes would take billions of years on the fastest processor to solve some problems (usually involving large data sets) or would use so much memory that a physical computer to run them would be too expensive to build.

One way to measure the efficiency of a process is to examine how long it actually takes on different data sets and to examine how many memory cells are actually used. A faster and much easier method is to examine the algorithm and data structures that describe the process. One can tell directly from the text of the code how many times a given instruction will be executed with a given data set, and compare potential runs of the algorithm on different data sets. From this pencil-and-paper analysis, a formal measure of the efficiency of any algorithm can be derived.

To perform such an analysis, we usually pick an instruction in the algorithm that will run more times or fewer times, depending on whether the data or problem size is larger or smaller. As the data size becomes very large, the work that this instruction does will dominate the work of the other instructions in the algorithm, so that the other instructions can be ignored. For example, a sorting algorithm might run a comparison on pairs of data elements in a list. The total number of comparisons performed for a complete run of the algorithm will vary with the size of the list and will dominate as the size of the list becomes very large. From this analysis, we can derive a general formula that can be used to predict the behavior of the algorithm on lists of any size. Analyzing memory costs works the same way: We pick an instruction that demands some unit of memory and analyze how that demand varies with the amount of data being processed.

Some standard relationships between processing time, memory use, and data or problem size have been discovered as a result of this kind of analysis. An algorithm has a **linear** behavior if the number of instructions executed or data units needed increases in direct proportion to the size of the problem. In other words, problems of size N require approximately N instructions to solve. An algorithm has **quadratic** behavior if the number of instructions executed or data units needed is proportional to the square of the size of the problem. In other words, problems of size N require approximately N^2 instructions to be executed. Other kinds of behavior that we will illustrate in our discussion in this chapter are called **logarithmic** ($\log_2 N$) and a combination of linear and logarithmic ($N \log_2 N$). As you can see from Table 12.1, logarithmic algorithms are the most efficient and quadratic algorithms are the least efficient of the algorithms we discuss. The numbers under the columns to the right of the data size column represent either the number of instructions that must be executed for a given data size or the number of memory units needed for a given data size. We will refer to this table as we analyze algorithms in the following sections.

linear: An increase of work or memory in direct proportion to the size of a problem.

quadratic: An increase of work or memory in proportion to the square of the size of the problem.

logarithmic: An increase of work in proportion to the number of times that the problem size can be divided by 2.

The Costs and Benefits of Recursion

You may have noticed that the previous recursive functions `sigma` and `factorial` could have been written using other iterative control structures. For example, we could rewrite the `sigma` function

```
int non_recursive_sigma(int n)
{
    int sum = 0;

    for (int j = 1; j < n; ++j)
        sum = sum + j;
    return sum;
}
```

▼ Table 12.1

Some standard efficiency relationships

| Data Size | Amount of Work Done | | | |
	Logarithmic	Linear	N log N	Quadratic
1	1	1	1	1
10	4	10	40	100
100	7	100	700	10,000
1000	10	1000	10,000	1,000,000
10,000	14	10,000	140,000	100,000,000

It is not coincidental that the recursive function **sigma** can be rewritten using the function **non_recursive_sigma**. In principle, any recursive subprogram can be rewritten in a nonrecursive manner. Let's compare the time and memory resources required by each kind of process.

In general, a recursive process that requires N recursive calls requires $N + 1$ units of stack memory and processor time to manage the process. For example, in the cases of the **sigma** function or a function for traversing a linked list, the size of the recursive process grows in direct proportion to the size of the argument number or length of the list (see Section 12.4). These processes therefore require a linear growth of memory. The memory needed by some recursive processes, such as the one generated by a recursive Fibonacci function, grows even faster than the size of their arguments.

An equivalent iterative process always requires one unit of stack memory and processor time to manage the function call, regardless of the size of the problem. Thus, recursion generally requires more memory and processor time than the equivalent nonrecursive iteration.

What are the benefits of recursion? There are several. First, a recursive thought process may be the best way to think about solving the problem. If so, it naturally leads to using recursion in a program. Recursive algorithms form a subclass of simple and elegant solutions known as **divide-and-conquer algorithms** that are used throughout computer science. A classical example is the Towers of Hanoi problem, which requires a sequence of moving disks on pegs. This problem is fully developed as our next example.

Second, some recursive algorithms can be very short compared to other iterative solutions. Some nonrecursive solutions may require an explicit stack (a programmer-defined data structure that is distinct from the system stack used to run a recursive process) and unusual coding. In some instances, use of a recursive algorithm can be very simple, and some programmers consider recursive solutions elegant because of this simplicity. The Towers of Hanoi problem in Example 12.4 provides an example of such elegance.

Third and finally, subsequent work in C++ can be aided by recursion. For example, one of the fastest sorting algorithms available, the quick sort, uses recursion (see Section 12.3). Also, recursion is a valuable tool when working with dynamic data structures (see Section 12.4).

Having now seen several reasons why recursion should be used, let's consider when recursion should not be used. If a solution to a problem is easier to obtain using nonrecursive methods, it is usually preferable to use them because a nonrecursive solution will usually require less execution time and use memory more efficiently. Using the previous examples, the recursive function factorial should probably be written using iteration, but reversing a line of text would typically be done using recursion because a nonrecursive solution is difficult to write.

divide-and-conquer algorithms: *A class of algorithms that solves problems by repeatedly dividing them into simpler problems.*

Example 12.4

A classic problem, called the Towers of Hanoi problem, involves three pegs and disks as depicted in Figure 12.4. The object is to move the disks from peg A to peg C. The rules are that only one disk may be moved at a time and a larger

◆ Figure 12.4

The Towers of Hanoi
problem

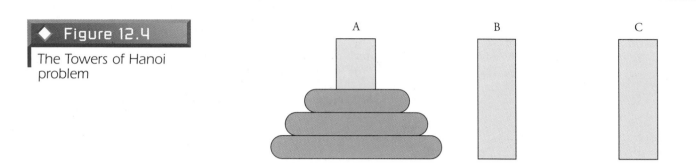

disk can never be placed on a smaller disk. (Legend has it that this problem—but
with 64 disks—was given to monks in an ancient monastery. The world was to
come to an end when all 64 disks were in order on peg C.)

To see how this problem can be solved, let's start with a one-disk problem. In
this case, merely move the disk from peg A to peg C. The two-disk problem is
almost as easy. Move disk 1 to peg B, disk 2 to peg C, and use the solution to the
one-disk problem to move disk 1 to peg C. (Note the reference to the previous
solution.)

Things get a little more interesting with a three-disk problem. First, use the
two-disk solution to get the top two disks in order on peg B. Then move disk 3
to peg C. Finally, use a two-disk solution to move the two disks from peg B to
peg C. Again, notice how a reference was made to the previous solution. By now
you should begin to see the pattern for solving the problem. However, before
generalizing, let's first look at the four-disk problem. As expected, the solution is
as follows:

1.   Use the three-disk solution to move three disks to peg B.
2.   Move disk 4 to peg C.
3.   Use the three-disk solution to move the three disks from peg B to peg C.

This process can be generalized as a solution to the problem for *n* disks.

1.   Use the $(n - 1)$-disk solution to move $(n - 1)$ disks to peg B.
2.   Move disk *n* to peg C.
3.   Use the $(n - 1)$-disk solution to move $(n - 1)$ disks from peg B to peg C.

This general solution is recursive in nature because each particular solution
depends on a solution for the previous number of disks. This process continues
until there is only one disk to move. This corresponds to the stopping state when
a recursive program is written to solve the problem. A complete interactive
program that prints out each step in the solution to this problem follows:

```
// Program file: hanoi.cpp

// This program uses recursion to solve the
// classic Towers of Hanoi problem.

#include <iostream.h>

// Function: list_the_moves
// Move num disks from start peg to last peg,
```

```
// using spare peg
//
// Inputs: The number of disks to move, the initial peg,
// the working peg, the destination peg

void list_the_moves(int num_disks, char start_peg,
        char last_peg, char spare_peg);

int main()
{
        int num_disks;

        cout << "How many disks in this game? ";
        cin >> num_disks;
        cout << endl;
        cout << "Start with " << num_disks
                << " disks on Peg A" << endl;
        cout << endl;
        cout << "Then proceed as follows:" << endl;
        cout << endl;
        list_the_moves (num_disks, 'A', 'C', 'B');
        return 0;
}

void list_the_moves(int num_disks, char start_peg,
        char last_peg, char spare_peg)
{
        if (num_disks == 1)
                cout << "Move a disk from "
                        << start_peg << " to " << last_peg << endl;
        else
        {
                list_the_moves (num_disks - 1, start_peg,
                        spare_peg, last_peg);
                cout << "Move a disk from " << start_peg
                        << " to " << last_peg << endl;
                list_the_moves (num_disks - 1, spare_peg,
                        last_peg, start_peg);
        }
}
```

Sample runs for three-disk and four-disk problems produce the following:

```
How many disks in this game?   3

Start with 3 disks on Peg A

Then proceed as follows:

Move a disk from A to C
Move a disk from A to B
```

```
Move a disk from C to B
Move a disk from A to C
Move a disk from B to A
Move a disk from B to C
Move a disk from A to C
```

```
How many disks in this game?   4
```

```
Start with 4 disks on Peg A
```

```
Then proceed as follows:
```

```
Move a disk from A to B
Move a disk from A to C
Move a disk from B to C
Move a disk from A to B
Move a disk from C to A
Move a disk from C to B
Move a disk from A to B
Move a disk from A to C
Move a disk from B to C
Move a disk from B to A
Move a disk from C to A
Move a disk from B to C
Move a disk from A to B
Move a disk from A to C
Move a disk from B to C
```

■ Exercises 12.1

1. Explain what is wrong with the following recursive function:

    ```
    double recur(double x)
    {
          return recur(x / 2)
    }
    ```

2. Write a recursive function that reverses the digits of a positive integer. For example, if the integer used as input is 1234, output should be 4321.

3. Consider the following recursive function:

    ```
    double a(double x, int n)
    {
          if (n == 0)
                return 1.0;
          else
                return x * a(x, n - 1);
    }
    ```

A Note of Interest

Recursion Need Not Be Expensive

We have seen that the use of recursion has two costs: Extra time and extra memory are required to manage recursive function calls. These costs have led some to argue that recursion should never be used in programs. However, as Guy Steele has shown (in "Debunking the 'expensive procedure call' myth," Proceedings of the National Conference of the ACM, 1977), some systems can run recursive algorithms as if they were iterative ones, with no additional overhead. The key condition is to write a special kind of recursive function called a **tail-recursive function.** A function is tail-recursive if no work is done in the function after a recursive call. For example, according to this criterion, the factorial function that we presented earlier is not tail-recursive, because a multiplication is performed after each recursive call. We can convert this version of the factorial function to a tail-recursive version by performing the multiplication before each recursive call. To do this, we will need an additional parameter that passes the accumulated value of the factorial down on each recursive call. In the last call of the function, this value is returned as the result:

```
int fact_iter(int n, int result)
{
        if (n == 1)
                return result;
        else
                return fact_iter
                        (n - 1,
                          n * result);
}
```

Note that the multiplication is performed before the recursive call of the function, when its parameters are evaluated. When the function is initially called, the value of **result** should be 1:

```
int factorial(int n)
{
        return fact_iter(n, 1);
}
```

Steele showed that a smart compiler can translate tail-recursive code in a high-level language to a loop in machine language. The machine code treats the function parameters as variables associated with a loop, and generates an iterative process rather than a recursive one. Thus, there is no linear growth of function calls and extra stack memory is not required to run tail-recursive functions on these systems.

The catch is that a programmer must be able to convert a recursive function to a tail-recursive function, and find a compiler that generates iterative machine code from tail-recursive functions. Unfortunately, some functions, like the one used to solve the Towers of Hanoi problem, are difficult or impossible to convert to tail-recursive versions, and the compiler optimizations are not part of the standard definitions of many languages, among them, C++. If you find that your C++ compiler supports this optimization, you should try converting some functions to tail-recursive versions and see if they run faster than the original versions.

---

    a. What would the value of **y** be for each of
       i. **y = a(3.0, 2);**
      ii. **y = a(2.0, 3);**
     iii. **y = a(4.0, 4);**
     iv. **y = a(1.0, 6);**
    b. Explain what standard computation is performed by function **a**.
    c. Rewrite function **a** using iteration rather than recursion.

4.   Recall the Fibonacci sequence 1, 1, 2, 3, 5, 8, 13, 21, . . . , where for $n > 2$ the nth term is the sum of the previous two. Write a recursive function to compute the nth term in the Fibonacci sequence.

5.   Write a function that uses iteration to compute $n!$.

12.2 Binary Search

Objectives

♦ to be able to use binary search to find a value in an array

♦ to be able to compare the costs and benefits of binary search and sequential search

binary search: The process of examining a middle value of a sorted array to see which half contains the value in question and halving until the value is located.

Searching relatively small lists sequentially does not require much computer time. However, when the lists get longer (for example, telephone directories and lists of credit card customers), sequential searches are inefficient. In a sense, they correspond to looking up a word in the dictionary by starting at the first word and proceeding word by word until the desired word is found. Because extra computer time means considerably extra expense for most companies where large amounts of data must be frequently searched, a more efficient way of searching is needed.

If the list to be searched has been sorted, a particular value can be searched for by a method referred to as a **binary search**. Essentially, a binary search consists of examining a middle value of a list to see which half contains the desired value. The middle value of the appropriate half is then examined to see which half of the half contains the value in question. This halving process is continued until the value is located or it is determined that the value is not in the list.

We must make two assumptions in order to use a binary search:

1. The list must be represented as an array. This will allow us to find the middle data element in the list in constant time, by dividing the sum of the first index position and the last index position by two and using the subscript operation. If the list were represented as a linked structure, finding the position of the middle element would require a linear search in linear time.

2. The list must be sorted. Maintaining a sorted list may incur some overhead, which must also be evaluated.

The basic idea of binary search can be expressed recursively. If there are elements in the list remaining to be examined, we compare the target value to the element at the middle position in the list. If the target value equals this element, we return the index position of the element. If the target value is greater than the element at the middle position, the target will be somewhere to the right of the middle position if it is in the list at all, so we recursively search the right half of the list. Otherwise, the target value will be to the left of the middle position if it is in the list at all, so we recursively search the left half of the list. If the target value is not in the list, we will run out of elements to consider at the end of some recursive process, so we return the value −1.

There are four input parameters to the problem: the target element, the list, the index value of the first position in the list, and the index value of the last position in the list. There is one value to be returned: −1, indicating that we have not found the target element in the list or an integer indicating its index position if we have found it. The initial value of the first position is zero. The initial value of the last index position is the number of data elements in the list minus one. A pseudocode algorithm for binary search is

If there are no more elements to consider then
      Return −1
  Else
      Set midpoint to (last + first) / 2
      If the element at index midpoint = the target element then
         Return midpoint

Else if the element at index midpoint > the target element then
  Return search the left half of the array
    (from indices first to midpoint − 1)
 Else
  Return search the right half of the array
    (from indices midpoint + 1 to last)

We assume that the program has defined a data type name, **list_type**, that specifies an array of elements that can be ordered. A C++ function representing the algorithm is thus

```cpp
int binsearch(element target, list_type list, int first, int last)
{
     if (first > last)
          return -1;
     else
     {
          int midpoint = (first + last) / 2;
          if (list[midpoint] == target)
               return midpoint;
          else if (list[midpoint] > target)
               return binsearch(target, list, first, midpoint - 1);
          else
               return binsearch(target, list, midpoint + 1, last);
     }
}
```

We might provide a simpler interface to the search function for users, who should not have to worry about providing the extra parameter for **first**:

```cpp
int search(element target, list_type list, int length)
{
     return binsearch(target, list, 0, length - 1);
}
```

| Example 12.5 | The following program is a test driver for the binary search function just developed. The program allows the user to input up to 100 integers in an array, and then allows the user an indefinite number of searches. |

```cpp
// Program file: binsearch.cpp

// A driver program for testing the binary search

#include <iostream.h>

const int MAX_LIST_SIZE = 100;

typedef int element;
```

```
typedef element list_type[MAX_LIST_SIZE];

int search(element target, list_type list, int length);

int binsearch(element target, list_type list,
     int first, int last);

int main()
{
     list_type list;
     element data;
     int length = 0;

     // Input up to 100 integers into the list

     cout << "Enter the next number or -999 to quit: ";
     cin >> data;
     while ((data != -999) && (length < MAX_LIST_SIZE))
     {
          list[length] = data;
          ++length;
          cout << "Enter the next number or -999 to quit: ";
          cin >> data;
     }

     // Allow an indefinite number of searches

     cout << "Enter the target or -999 to quit: ";
     cin >> data;
     while (data != -999)
     {
          int result = search(data, list, length);
          if (result == -1)
               cout << "Not found" << endl;
          else
               cout << "Position = " << result << endl;
          cout << "Enter the target or -999 to quit: ";
          cin >> data;
     }
     return 0;
}

int search(element target, list_type list, int length)
{
     return binsearch(target, list, 0, length - 1);
}

int binsearch(element target, list_type list,
     int first, int last)
{
```

```
        if (first > last)
            return -1;
    else
    {
            int midpoint = (first + last) / 2;
            if (list[midpoint] == target)
                return midpoint;
            else if (list[midpoint] > target)
                return binsearch(target, list,
                    first, midpoint - 1);
            else
                return binsearch(target, list,
                    midpoint + 1, last);
    }
}
```

Before continuing, let's walk through a binary search to better understand how it works. Assume **list** is the array

4	7	19	25	36	37	50	100	101	205	220	271	306	321

list[0]   list[13]

with values as indicated. Furthermore, assume **target** contains the value 205. Then initially, **first**, **last**, and **target** have the values

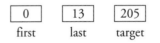

0	13	205
first	last	target

A listing of values by each call of **binsearch** produces

	first	**last**	**midpoint**	**list[midpoint]**
After initial call	0	13	6	50
After second call	7	13	10	220
After third call	7	9	8	101
After fourth call	9	9	9	205

Note that we need only four comparisons to find the target at the ninth position in the list. To illustrate what happens when the value being looked for is not in the array, suppose **target** contains 210. The listing of values then produces

Microprocessor Chips

Microprocessor speeds are changing rapidly. Processor speeds used to double about every 18 months. That was true in the early days when we were going from the 286 chip to the 386 and 486 chips. Now, doubling seems to occur in 9 to 12 months. In 1981, chips ran with a clock speed of 4.7 megahertz, about 1/40 of the current rate for off-the-shelf microprocessors.

Industry analysts predict that new technology will be required for processor speeds to continue to grow. Current developments include using gallium arsenide (potentially toxic) as a conductor, elaborate parallel designs, and searches for new ways to open and shut transistors within semiconductors.

Research is also being done to see if it is possible to use photons rather than electrons for tripping switches. Photons are both swifter and sleeker than electrons, but they are more difficult to control. Other schemes use beryllium atoms chilled to near absolute zero and photon streams colliding with streams of cesium atoms. Both of these efforts result in a switch that can be on and off at the same time, a result that makes it possible to do what is almost impossible! For example, with this technology, it is conjectured that a task that currently would require 1600 linked computers 800,000 years could be accomplished with one computer in 30 years.

	first	last	midpoint	list[midpoint]
After initial call	0	13	6	50
After second call	7	13	10	220
After third call	7	9	8	101
After fourth call	9	9	9	205
After fifth call	10	9	9	205

At this stage, **first > last** and the recursive process terminates.

Let's now examine briefly the efficiency of a binary search compared to a sequential search. There are two worst cases for sequential search: When the target is at the last position in the list and when the target is not in the list at all. In each case, sequential search requires N equality comparisons for a list of N data elements. Therefore, sequential search is linear in the worst cases.

Binary search has a single worst case: When the target is not in the list at all. How many comparisons will it take to discover this for a list of length N? On the first call of the binary search function, we make one equality comparison. On the second call of the function, we have essentially thrown away half of the original list and are performing a comparison in the remaining half. This process of throwing away half of the data elements occurs on each call of the function. Therefore, the number of comparisons in the worst case will be equal to the number of times we can divide the original length of the list by two, or $\log_2 N + 1$. Binary search describes a logarithmic process.

Binary search is definitely more efficient than sequential search, as Table 12.1 on page 675 illustrates. Binary search is also an excellent example of the benefits of using divide-and-conquer and recursive strategies in designing an algorithm. The only new cost of using this method is that we must assume that the array has been sorted. Maintaining a sorted array may take some extra time, so we must be careful to choose an efficient sorting algorithm. We will see another use of the divide-and-conquer strategy in designing an efficient sorting algorithm in the next section.

■ Exercises 12.2

1. Modify the binary search function by putting a global counter in the function to count how many calls are made when searching a sorted array for a value. Write and run a program that uses this version on lists of length 15, 30, 60, 120, and 240. In each case, search for a value as follows and plot your results on a graph.
   a. A value in the first half
   b. A value in the second half
   c. A value that is not there

2. Write an **index_of** function for sorted collections (see Section 10.4) that uses a binary search.

18	25	37	92	104

a[0]   a[4]

3. Suppose array **a** is
   Trace the values using a binary search to look for
   a. 18
   b. 92
   c. 76

4. Using a binary search on an array of length 35, what is the maximum number of passes through the loop that can be made when searching for a value?

5. Write a new version of the binary search function using a C++ loop rather than a recursive function. Compare the two versions for efficiency, examining their memory requirements as well as their processing times.

12.3 Quick Sort

Objectives

♦ to be able to use quick sort to sort the data elements in an array

♦ to be able to compare the costs and benefits of quick sort and selection sort

Several algorithms are available for sorting elements in lists. We worked with the selection sort in Chapter 8. This method works relatively well for sorting small lists of elements. However, when large databases need to be sorted, a direct application of an elementary sorting process usually requires a great deal of computer time. To demonstrate this point, let's do a brief analysis of the selection sort algorithm. Recall that the algorithm consists of a nested loop structure:

```
For each j from 0 to N – 2 do                    // Find the minimum N – 1 times
    Set index to j
    For each k from j + 1 to N – 1 do    // Find the index of the minimum
        If a[k] < a[index] then          // data value
            Set index to k
    If index does not equal j then       // Exchange values if necessary
        Swap(a[index], a[j])
```

The instruction that will do the most work and vary with the data size the most is the comparison **<** in the **if** statement in the inner loop. On the first pass through the outer loop, the comparison will be performed $N - 1$ times in the inner loop. On the second pass through the outer loop, the comparison will be performed $N - 2$ times. On the last pass through the outer loop, the comparison will be performed once in the inner loop. Thus, the total number of comparisons will be

$$(N - 1) + (N - 2) + \cdots + 1$$

or

$$\frac{N^2 - N}{2}$$

Because the quadratic term predominates in this formula, we can ignore the other terms and conclude that selection sort exhibits quadratic behavior. As you can see from Table 12.1, this kind of behavior is very unreasonable for large data sets.

One of the fastest sorting techniques available is the **quick sort**. Like binary search, this method uses a recursive, divide-and-conquer strategy. The basic idea is to separate a list of elements into two parts, surrounding a distinguished element called the **pivot**. At the end of the process, one part will contain elements smaller than the pivot and the other part will contain elements larger than the pivot. Thus, if an unsorted list (represented as array **a**) originally contains

quick sort *A relatively fast sorting technique that uses recursion.*

pivot *A data item around which an arrary is subdivided during the quick sort.*

14	3	2	11	5	8	0	2	9	4	20

a[0] a[1]   a[5]   a[10]

we might select the element in the middle position, **a[5]**, as the pivot, which is 8 in our illustration. Our process would then put all values less than 8 on the left side and all values greater than 8 on the right side. This first subdivision produces

pivot ⟶

4	3	2	2	5	0	8	11	9	14	20

a[0] a[1]   a[6]   a[10]

Now, each sublist is subdivided in exactly the same manner. This process continues until all sublists are in order. The list is then sorted. This is a recursive process.

Before writing a function for this sort, let's examine how it works. First, why do we choose the value in the middle position? Ideally, we would like to pivot on the median of the entire list. However, searching a list for the median element is at best a linear process, whose cost would more than offset the benefit of the divide-and-conquer process of quick sort. Therefore, we choose the value in the middle as a compromise. As in binary search, the index of this value is found by **(first + last) / 2**, where **first** and **last** are the indices of the initial and final elements in the array representing the list. We then identify a **left_arrow** and **right_arrow** on the far left and far right, respectively. This can be envisioned as

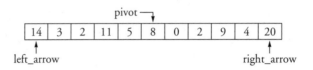

where **left_arrow** and **right_arrow** initially represent the lowest and highest indices of the array components. Starting on the right, the **right_arrow** is moved left until a value less than or equal to the pivot is encountered. This produces

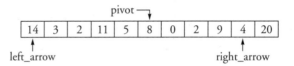

In a similar manner, **left_arrow** is moved right until a value greater than or equal to the pivot is encountered. This is the situation just encountered. Now the contents of the two array components are swapped to produce

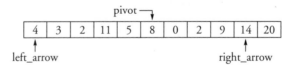

We continue by moving **right_arrow** left to produce

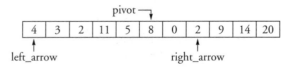

and moving **left_arrow** right yields

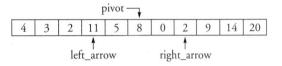

These values are exchanged to produce

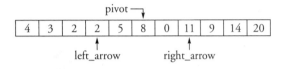

This process stops when **left_arrow > right_arrow** is **TRUE**. Since this is still **FALSE** at this point, the next **right_arrow** move produces

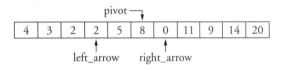

and the **left_arrow** move to the right yields

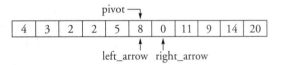

Because we are looking for a value greater than or equal to **pivot** when moving left, **left_arrow** stops moving and an exchange is made to produce

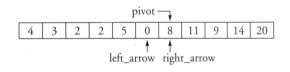

Notice that the pivot, 8, has been exchanged to occupy a new position. This is acceptable because **pivot** is the value of the component, not the index. As before, **right_arrow** is moved left and **left_arrow** is moved right to produce

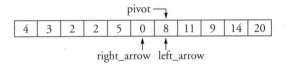

Since **right_arrow < left_arrow** is **TRUE**, the first subdivision is complete. At this stage, numbers smaller than **pivot** are on the left side and numbers larger than **pivot** are on the right side. This produces two sublists that can be envisioned as

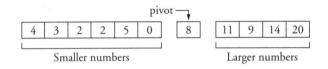

Each sublist can now be sorted by the same function. This would require a recursive call to the sorting function. In each case, the array is passed as a parameter together with the **right** and **left** indices for the appropriate sublist. We assume that the program has defined a data type name, **list_type**, that specifies an array of elements that can be ordered. A C++ function for this sort is

```cpp
void quick_sort(list_type list, int left, int right)
{
        int pivot, left_arrow, right_arrow;

        left_arrow = left;
        right_arrow = right;
        pivot = list[(left + right) / 2];
        do
        {
                while (list[right_arrow] > pivot)
                        --right_arrow;
                while (list[left_arrow] < pivot)
                        ++left_arrow;
                if (left_arrow <= right_arrow)
                {
                        swap(list[left_arrow], list[right_arrow]);
                        ++left_arrow;
                        --right_arrow;
                }
        } while (right_arrow >= left_arrow);
        if (left < right_arrow)
                quick_sort(list, left, right_arrow);
        if (left_arrow < right)
                quick_sort(list, left_arrow, right);
}
```

We might provide an interface function for users:

```
void sort(list_type list, int length)
{
        quick_sort(list, 0, length - 1);
}
```

Note that the two integer parameters specify the upper and lower bounds of the index values of elements actually in the array. Hence, the value 0 for the lower bound and **length - 1** for the upper bound are passed as actual parameters to **quick_sort**.

Now let's briefly analyze the quick sort algorithm for efficiency. We will assume the best case, in which the element at the middle of each sublist in the process happens to be the median of the sublist. This will cause the list to be split evenly around the pivot, so that each sublist will have close to $N/2$ elements. To carry out a partitioning of a list of N elements, each element other than the pivot must be compared with the pivot. Therefore, the first partitioning of an N-element list into two sublists that each have approximately $N/2$ elements requires approximately N comparisons. Each of these sublists will also be partitioned, together requiring another N comparisons. Therefore, each recursive level of the process requires N comparisons. How many levels will there be? Recall from our discussion of binary search that the number of times we can subdivide a list of length N evenly is $\log_2 N$. Thus, in quick sort, the N comparisons at each level are performed approximately $\log_2 N$ times, so quick sort exhibits $N \log_2 N$ behavior in the best case.

In cases where the middle element in a sublist is not also the median element, the sublists will not be evenly partitioned. The worst cases are where the middle element is also the largest or the smallest element. In these cases, one sublist will be almost the same size as the original list. This will cause more subdivisions to be made than in the ideal case. On the average, however, the middle element in a randomly ordered sublist should have a value that is somewhere within the range of values from the smallest to the median or from the median to the largest. On the average, then, the behavior of quick sort will be close to $N \log_2 N$. The analysis of the worst case behavior of quick sort is left as an exercise.

Exercises 12.3

1. Use selection sort and quick sort to examine their relative efficiency; that is, run them on arrays of varying lengths, count the number of comparisons, and plot the results on a graph. What are your conclusions?
2. Explain how an array of objects with a key field, **name**, can be sorted using a quick sort.
3. Modify function **quick_sort** to use the median of the first three elements in an array as the pivot rather than the middle element.
4. The worst case behavior of the quick sort algorithm depends on the configuration of elements in the original list. Describe what this configuration would be, why it would cause quick sort to behave that way, and derive a formula that expresses the behavior.

Gene Mapping: Computer Scientists Examine Problems of Genome Project

Deciphering the human genome is much like trying to read the instructions on a computer disk filled with programs written in the zeros and ones of electronic code—without knowing the programming language.

That was the message from molecular biologists to computer scientists at a meeting sponsored by the National Research Council. The biologists hope to involve the computer scientists in the U.S. Human Genome Project, a 15-year, three-billion-dollar effort to identify and locate the information contained in human chromosomes.

Computer scientists, with their experience in managing information and using arcane programming languages to store data and convey instructions, could be particularly valuable in helping to read and organize the three billion "letters" that make up the human genetic code, the biologists said.

"The entire program for making **me** is about 10 to the 10 bits," (about 10 trillion pieces of information),

said Gerald J. Sussman, a professor of electrical engineering and computer science at the Massachusetts Institute of Technology. "It is no bigger than the U.S. Tax Code, or the design documents for the U.S. space shuttle." Figuring out what that program is, he said, is a computer science problem.

Biologists said they needed computer scientists to accomplish the following:

◆ Design easy-to-use databases that can handle the millions of pieces of information that need to be correlated to fully understand genetics—and life.
◆ Design computer networks that will allow biologists to share information conveniently.
◆ Create functions that will allow biologists to analyze information pulled from laboratory experiments.
◆ Write programs that will let biologists simulate the formation and development of proteins.

12.4 Linked Lists and Recursion

Objectives

◆ to understand the natural fit of linked lists and recursive algorithms
◆ to understand the use of recursion to traverse a linked list in either direction
◆ to understand the use of recursion to accumulate a value while traversing a linked list

You may have noticed in Chapter 11 that a linked list is a **recursive data structure.** The structure of a linked list contains a component part that is either another list of the very same form or an empty list denoted by the null pointer. Recursive data structures lend themselves very naturally to processing by recursive functions. In this section, we examine some strategies and implementations of recursive list processing. For purposes of exposition, we define the following data structures for representing a linked list of numbers:

```
struct node;
typedef node *list_type;

struct node
{
      int data;
      list_type next;
};

list_type list;
```

Traversing a Linked List

Many operations on linked lists require us to visit each node sequentially. For example, we have seen that printing the contents of the nodes in a linked list

recursive data structure: A data structure that has either a simple form or a form that is composed of other instances of the same data structure.

involves this kind of process. We can describe a recursive algorithm for printing the contents of a linked list informally as

If the list is not empty then
      Print the contents of the current node
      Print the contents of the rest of the list

Note that the algorithm describes the two essential parts of a recursive process:
1. A termination of the process (when the list is empty)
2. A recursive step (where we run a process of the same form on a smaller data structure of the same form).

The termination condition in a recursive algorithm is usually handled by an **if** statement. The recursive step in the algorithm processes the data in the rest of the list. Therefore, it usually operates on the next pointer of the current node in the list.

Let us assume that the **list_type** is defined as above and that the function **empty_list** returns **TRUE** when the list is empty and **FALSE** otherwise. A recursive function for printing the numbers in a linked list with the logical structure defined in Section 11.2 is

```
void print_list(list_type list)
{
      if (! empty_list(list))
      {
            cout << list->data << endl;
            print_list(list->next);
      }
}
```

Searching for a target item in a linked list is a process that is similar to the process of printing all of the items, except that the search can stop when the target item is found. Moreover, this process should return a value to the caller, such as **TRUE** or **FALSE**. Assuming that the algorithm returns a Boolean value to the caller, a recursive search algorithm can be described informally as

If the list is empty then
    Return FALSE
Else if the item in the current node = the target item then
    Return TRUE
Else
    Return the result of searching the rest of the list

There are two possible termination conditions of the recursive process, each of which returns a simple Boolean value. If the process ever hits the end of the list, the list will be empty and the target item will not be found. If the process finds the item somewhere in the list, it can halt the search and return **TRUE**. The recursive step, which searches the rest of the list, also returns a Boolean value. A recursive search function is

```
bool search(int target, list_type list)
{
        if (empty_list(list))
                return FALSE;
        else if (list->data == target)
                return TRUE;
        else
                return search(target, list->next);
}
```

Accumulating a Value from a Linked List

Many problems call for processes that traverse a linked list to accumulate a value. Consider the problem of determining the length or number of nodes in a list. If we do not keep this value in a separate variable, we will need a process to count the number of nodes. A recursive algorithm for counting nodes would have two cases to consider:

1. The list is empty. In this case, the algorithm returns 0, the number of nodes in an empty list.
2. The list has at least one node. There may also be nodes in the rest of the linked list after this node. Therefore, in this case, the algorithm recursively counts the rest of the nodes in the list after this one, adds this count to 1, and returns the result.

The recursive algorithm can be described informally as

If the list is empty then
        Return 0
Else
        Return the length of the rest of the list + 1

Note that this recursive process both moves ahead through the list and accumulates a value whenever it returns from a recursive call. A recursive length function is

```
int list_length(list_type list)
{
        if (empty_list(list))
                return 0;
        else
                return list_length(list->next) + 1;
}
```

The problem of finding the sum of all of the integers in a linked list can be solved by a very similar recursive process. Briefly, if the list is empty, the process returns 0. Otherwise, it returns the sum of the integer in the current node and the sum of the integers in the rest of the list. Informally, the recursive algorithm is

If the list is empty then
        Return 0

Else

> Return the sum of the rest of the integers in the list
>> + the integer in the current node

The function is

```
int sum_list(list_type list)
{
        if (empty_list(list))
                return 0;
        else
                return sum_list(list->next) + list->data;
}
```

Moving Backwards Through a Linked List

Consider the problem of printing all of the items in a linked list in reverse order. We need a way of beginning at the last node in the list and working our way back to the first node. Unfortunately, the next pointers in each node point in the wrong direction for implementing this process in terms of a simple loop that would move through the list from the last node to the first. If we think in terms of a recursive process, however, we can find an easy and elegant solution to this problem.

Recall from our discussion of recursion in Section 12.1 that as each recursive call of a function is made, the system keeps track of the state of the caller on a structure called a stack. As the overall recursive process ends and starts to unwind, each call returns to the state of its caller on the stack. We can use this information to design a recursive algorithm for moving backwards through a linked list.

First, we move forward recursively through the list until we reach the end (where the list is empty). As we go, the system is saving pointers to previous nodes on its run-time stack. *After* each recursive call, we visit a node to do our processing of the data there. This means that the first data to be processed will be the data in the last node in the list. The next data will be the data in the node *before* the last one, and so on. In effect, we traverse the list in reverse as the recursive process unwinds. Informally, the algorithm is

If the list is not empty then

> Print the contents of the rest of the list in reverse
> Print the data in the current node

A function for solving this problem is

```
void reverse_print_list(list_type list)
{
        if (! empty_list(list))
        {
                reverse_print_list(list->next);
                cout << list->data << endl;
        }
}
```

■ Exercises 12.4

1. Write a recursive function to return the product of the integers in a linked list.
2. Write recursive functions to insert an item into a linked list and to delete an item from a linked list.
3. Write a recursive function that searches a linked list for a given item. The function returns a pointer to the item's node if it is found; otherwise, the null pointer is returned.

12.5 Graphics

Objectives

◆ to understand how recursive patterns can be represented graphically

◆ to be able to use a recursive function in a graphics program

Fractal Geometry

Fractal geometry as a serious mathematical endeavor began with the pioneering work of Benoit Mandelbrot, a fellow of the Thomas J. Watson Research Center, IBM Corporation. Fractal geometry is a theory of geometric forms so complex that they defy analysis and classification by traditional Euclidean means. Yet fractal shapes occur universally in the natural world. Mandelbrot has recognized them not only in coastlines, landscapes, lungs, and turbulent water flow but also in the chaotic fluctuation of prices on the Chicago commodity exchange.

The C-Curve

The **c-curve** that appears on the cover of this book is an instance of a fractal shape. It represents a series of recursive patterns of increasing levels of complexity. When the level is zero, the c-curve is a simple line segment, specified by the endpoints $(x1, y1)$ and $(x2, y2)$. A level-N c-curve is composed of two level $N - 1$ c-curves connected at right angles. Thus, a level-1 c-curve is composed of two perpendicular line segments, and a level-2 c-curve is three-quarters of a rectangle, which begins to resemble the letter c, as shown in Figure 12.5.

◆ Figure 12.5

C-curves of the first six levels

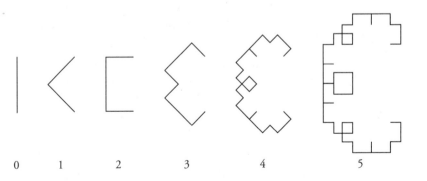

The level-12 c-curve on the cover of this book was generated on a graphics workstation by running the following recursive function written in C++:

fractal geometry:
A theory of shapes that is reflected in various phenomena, such as coastlines, water flow, and price fluctuations.

c-curve: A fractal shape that resembles the letter c.

```
void c_curve(int x1, int y1, int x2,
     int y2, int level)
{
     int xm, ym;

     if (level == 0)
          draw_line(x1, y1, x2, y2);
     else
     {
          xm = (x1 + x2 + y1 - y2) / 2;
          ym = (x2 + y1 + y2 - x1) / 2;
          c_curve(x1, y1, xm, ym,
               level - 1);
          c_curve(xm, ym, x2, y2,
               level - 1);
     }
}
```

Example 12.6

The following program allows the user to draw c-curves with the graphics system that we have used in this text. The program opens with prompts for the end points of the initial line segment. The program then enters a loop in which it prompts the user for the desired level of recursion. If the user enters a negative number for the level, the program quits. Otherwise, the program draws the c-curve with the specified parameters, and pauses to allow the user to view it.

```
// Program file: ccurve.cpp

// Displays a c-curve with an initial line
// segment and level specified by the user.
// Allows the user to test different levels.

#include <iostream.h>
#include <conio.h>
#include <graphics.h>

void c_curve(int x1, int y1, int x2,
     int y2, int level);

void draw_line(int x1, int y1, int x2, int y2);

int main()
{
     int start_x, start_y, end_x, end_y, level;

     // Obtain end point and initial level
     // from the user

     cout << "Enter the starting x coordinate: ";
     cin >> start_x;
```

```
        cout << "Enter the starting y coordinate: ";
        cin >> start_y;
        cout << "Enter the ending x coordinate: ";
        cin >> end_x;
        cout << "Enter the ending y coordinate: ";
        cin >> end_y;
        cout << "Enter the level of recursion, "
             << "or a negative number to quit: ";
        cin >> level;

        while (level >= 0)
        {
                // Set the graphics mode

                int graphdriver = DETECT, graphmode;
                initgraph(&graphdriver, &graphmode,
                        "c:..\\bgi");

                // Draw the c-curve

                c_curve(start_x, start_y, end_x, end_y,
                        level);

                // Pause for a key to be pressed

                moveto(0, 0);
                outtext("Strike any key to continue");
                getch();

                // Return to text mode for input

                closegraph();
                cout << "Enter the level of recursion, "
                     << "or a negative number to quit: ";
                cin >> level;
        }
        return 0;
}

void c_curve(int x1, int y1, int x2,
        int y2, int level)
{
        int xm, ym;

        if (level == 0)
                draw_line(x1, y1, x2, y2);
        else
        {
                xm = (x1 + x2 + y1 - y2)/2;
                ym = (x2 + y1 + y2 - x1)/2;
```

```
                c_curve(x1, y1, xm, ym,
                        level - 1);
                c_curve(xm, ym, x2, y2,
                        level - 1);
        }
}

void draw_line(int x1, int y1,
        int x2, int y2)
{
        moveto(x1, y1);
        lineto(x2, y2);
}
```

■ Exercises 12.5

1. Modify the program of Example 12.6 so that the user can enter the foreground and background colors as inputs.
2. Modify the program of Example 12.6 so that each lower level c-curve in a single run is drawn in a randomly chosen color. Be sure that this color is never the same as the background color.

Focus on Program Design: Case Study

Sorting a List with Quick Sort

A complete interactive program to illustrate the use of quick sort is given. The design for this program is
1. Fill the list
2. Sort the numbers
3. Print the list

The complete program follows:

```
// This program illustrates the quick sort as a sorting
// algorithm. The array elements
// are successively subdivided into "smaller" and
// "larger" elements in parts of the array. Recursive
// calls are made to the function quick_sort.

// Program file: qsort.cpp

#include <iostream.h>

const int MAX_LIST_SIZE = 30;

typedef int list_type[MAX_LIST_SIZE];

// Function: fill_list
// Reads numbers into list from keyboard
```

```
//
// Output: a list of numbers and its length

void fill_list(list_type list, int &length);

// Function: sort
// Sorts numbers in list into ascending order
//
// Inputs: a list of numbers in random order and
// its length
// Output: a sorted list

void sort(list_type, int length);

// Function: sort
// Sorts numbers in list into ascending order
//
// Inputs: a list of numbers in random order, 0,
// and list length - 1
// Output: a sorted list

void quick_sort(list_type list, int left, int right);

// Function: print_list
// Prints contents of list in a column on the screen
//
// Input: a list of numbers in random order and
// its length

void print_list(list_type list, int length);

// Function: swap
// Exchanges the values of two numbers
//
// Inputs: two integers
// Outputs: the two integers, exchanged in position

void swap(int &first, int &second);

int main()
{
    list_type list;
    int first, last, length;

    fill_list(list, length);
    cout << "The unsorted list is:" << endl;
    print_list(list, length);
    sort(list, length);
    cout << "The sorted list is:" << endl;
    print_list(list, length);
    return 0;
```

```cpp
}

void fill_list(list_type list, int &length)
{
      int data;

      length = 0;
      cout << "Enter an integer, -999 to quit. ";
      cin >> data;
      while ((data != -999) && (length < MAX_LIST_SIZE))
      {
            list[length] = data;
            ++length;
            cout << "Enter an integer, -999 to quit. ";
            cin >> data;
      }
}


void print_list(list_type list, int length)
{
      for (int index = 0; index < length; ++index)
          cout << list[index] << " ";
      cout << endl;
}

void sort(list_type list, int length)
{
      quick_sort(list, 0, length - 1);
}

void quick_sort (list_type list, int left, int right)
{
      int pivot, temp, left_arrow, right_arrow;

      left_arrow = left;
      right_arrow = right;
      pivot = list[(left + right) / 2];
      do
      {
            while (list[right_arrow] > pivot)
                  - -right_arrow;
            while (list[left_arrow] < pivot)
                  ++left_arrow;
            if (left_arrow <= right_arrow)
            {
                  swap(list[left_arrow], list[right_arrow]);
                  ++left_arrow;
                  --right_arrow;
            }
      } while (right_arrow >= left_arrow);
```

```
            if (left < right_arrow)
                  quick_sort(list, left, right_arrow);
            if (left_arrow < right)
                  quick_sort(list, left_arrow, right);
      }

      void swap(int &first, int &second)
      {
            int temp;

            temp = first;
            first = second;
            second = temp;
      }
```

A sample run of this program using the previous data produces

```
Enter an integer, -999 to quit. 14
Enter an integer, -999 to quit. 3
Enter an integer, -999 to quit. 2
Enter an integer, -999 to quit. 11
Enter an integer, -999 to quit. 5
Enter an integer, -999 to quit. 8
Enter an integer, -999 to quit. 0
Enter an integer, -999 to quit. 2
Enter an integer, -999 to quit. 9
Enter an integer, -999 to quit. 4
Enter an integer, -999 to quit. 20
Enter an integer, -999 to quit. -999
The unsorted list is:
14 3 2 11 5 8 0 2 9 4 20
The sorted list is:
0 2 2 3 4 5 8 9 11 14 20
```

Running, Debugging, and Testing Hints

1. When using recursion, make sure the recursive process will reach the stopping state.
2. When testing sorting algorithms, be sure to use data sets that reflect several different situations, such as the following:
   a. Data in random order, list of length 2
   b. Data in random order, list of length 3
   c. Data in random order, list of length 10
   d. Same three lists as a–c, but data in sorted order
   e. Same three lists as a–c, but data in inverse of sorted order

(continued)

3. When testing the binary search algorithm, be sure to use data sets that reflect the following situations (the data must always be in sorted order):

   a. A list of length 0

   b. A list of length 1, the target is in the list

   c. A list of length 1, the target is not in the list

   d. A list of an even-numbered length, data are consecutive (no gaps), target is in the list

   e. Same as d, but target is not in the list

   f. Same as d, but an odd-numbered length

   g. Same as e, but an odd-numbered length

   h. Repeat d–g, but allow gaps in the data, such as 3, 5, 7, 10.

Summary

🔑 Key Terms

binary search	logarithmic	recursive data structure
c-curve	pivot	recursive step
divide-and-conquer	quadratic	stack
algorithms	quick sort	stopping state
fractal geometry	recursion	tail-recursive function
linear		

🔑 Key Concepts

◆ Recursion is a process in which a subprogram calls itself.

◆ A recursive subprogram must have a well-defined stopping state.

◆ Recursive functions in most programming languages require the use of a run-time stack to maintain the input parameters and return values of each recursive call.

◆ Recursive solutions are usually elegant and short, but generally require more memory than iterative solutions.

◆ Binary search is one of the fastest searching techniques available. It can use recursion and is based on the idea of separating a list into two parts.

◆ A quick sort is one of the fastest sorting techniques available. It uses recursion and is based on the idea of separating a list into two parts.

◆ Linked lists are recursive data structures; they lend themselves quite naturally to recursive processing.

Suggestions for Further Reading

Recursion and sorting are subjects of numerous articles and books. This chapter provided some samples of each. For variations and improvements on what is included here as well as other techniques, the interested reader is referred to the following books, which many consider to be classics in the field.

Baase, Sara, "Sorting," Chapter 2 in *Computer Algorithms: Introduction to Design and Analysis*. Reading, MA: Addison-Wesley Publishing Company, 1978.

Gear, William, *Applications and Algorithms in Engineering and Science*. Chicago: Science Research Associates, 1978.

Horowitz, Ellis, and Sartaz, Sahni, "Divide and Conquer," Chapter 3 in *Fundamentals of Computer Algorithms*. Potomac, MD: Computer Science Press, 1978.

Knuth, Donald, *The Art of Computer Programming*. Vol. 3, *Sorting and Searching*. Reading, MA: Addison-Wesley Publishing Company, 1975.

Roberts, Eric, *Thinking Recursively*. New York: John Wiley & Sons, 1986.

Chapter Review Exercises

For Exercises 1–3, specify the number of comparison operations needed to find the target value of 11 in the list during a binary search.

1. 1 3 5 7 9 11
2. 1 3 11 12 24 56
3. 11 12 13 14 15 45

For Exercises 4–6, show where the midpoint will be at the end of a search for the target value of 11 with a binary search.

4. 1 3 5 7 9
5. 1 5 9 13 15
6. 10 12 13 12 15
7. What is wrong with the following recursive function?

```
// Returns the sum of the numbers between low
// and high

int sum(int low, int high)
{
        return low + sum(low + 1, high);
}
```

8. Write a correct version of the **sum** function in Exercise 7.
9. Explain how the divide-and-conquer strategy is used in the quick sort algorithm.

Programming Problems and Activities

1. Write a program to update a mailing list. Assume you have a sorted master file of records where each record contains a customer's name, address, and expiration code. Your program should input a file of new customers, sort the file, and merge the file with the master file to produce a new master.
2. The Bakerville Manufacturing Company has to lay off all employees who started working after a certain date. Write a program that does the following:

a. Inputs a termination date.

b. Searches an alphabetical file of employee records to determine who will get a layoff notice.

c. Creates a file of employee records for those who are being laid off.

d. Updates the master file to contain only records of current employees.

e. Produces two lists of those being laid off, one alphabetical and one by hiring date.

3. The Bakerville Manufacturing Company (Problem 2) has achieved new prosperity and can rehire 10 employees who were recently laid off. Write a program that does the following:

a. Searches the file of previously terminated employees to find the 10 with the most seniority.

b. Deletes those 10 records from the file of employees who were laid off.

c. Inserts the 10 records alphabetically into the file of current employees.

d. Prints four lists as follows:

    i. An alphabetical list of current employees

    ii. A seniority list of current employees

    iii. An alphabetical list of employees who were laid off

    iv. A seniority list of employees who were laid off

4. The Shepherd Lions Club sponsors an annual cross-country race for area schools. Write a program the does the following:

a. Creates an array of records for the runners. Each record should contain the runner's name, school, identification number, and time (in a seven-character string, such as 15:17:3).

b. Prints an alphabetical listing of all runners.

c. Prints a list of schools entered in the race.

d. Prints a list of runners in the race ordered by school name.

e. Prints the final finish order by sorting the records and printing a numbered list according to the order of finish.

5. The greatest common divisor of two positive integers a and b, GCD(a, b), is the largest positive integer that divides both a and b. Thus, GCD(102, 30) = 6. This can be found using the division algorithm as follows:

$$102 = 30 * 3 + 12$$
$$30 = 12 * 2 + 6$$
$$12 = 6 * 2 + 0$$

Note that

$$GCD(102, 30) = GCD(30, 12)$$
$$= GCD(12, 6)$$
$$= 6$$

In each case, the remainder is used for the next step. The process terminates when a remainder of zero is obtained. Write a recursive function that returns the GCD of two positive integers.

6. A palindrome is a number or word that is the same when read either forward or backward. For example, "12321" and "mom" are palindromes. Write a recursive function that can be used to determine whether or not an integer is a palindrome. Use this function in a complete program that reads a list of integers and then displays the list with an asterisk following each palindrome.

7. Recall the Fibonacci sequence discussed at the beginning of this chapter. Write a recursive function that returns the *n*th Fibonacci number. Input for a call to the function will be a positive integer.

8. Probability courses often contain problems that require students to compute the number of ways *r* items can be chosen from a set of *n* objects. It is shown that there are

$$C(n,r) = \frac{n!}{r!(n-r)!}$$

such choices. This is sometimes referred to as "*n* choose *r*." To illustrate, if you wish to select three items from a total of five possible objects, there are

$$C(5,3) = \frac{5!}{3!(5-3)!} = \frac{5*4*3*2*1}{(3*2*1)(2*1)} = 10$$

such possibilities. In mathematics, the number $C(n,r)$ is a binomial coefficient because, for appropriate values of *n* and *r*, it produces coefficients in the expansion of $(x + y)^n$. Thus,

$$(x + y)^4 = C(4,0)x^4 + C(4,1)x^3y + C(4,2)xy^2 + C(4,3)xy^3 + C(4,4)y^4$$

   a. Write a function that returns the value $C(n,r)$. Arguments for a function call will be integers *n* and *r* such that $n > r > 0$. (*Hint:* Simplify the expression $n!/[r!(n-r)!]$ before computing.)

   b. Write an interactive program that receives as input the power to which a binomial is to be raised. Output should be the expanded binomial.

 9. The twentieth century Dutch painter Piet Mondrian developed a style of abstract painting that exhibited simple recursive patterns. For example, an "idealized" pattern from one of his paintings might look like this:

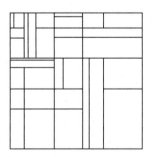

To generate such a pattern with a computer, an algorithm would begin by drawing a rectangle, and then repeatedly drawing two unequal subdivisions, as follows:

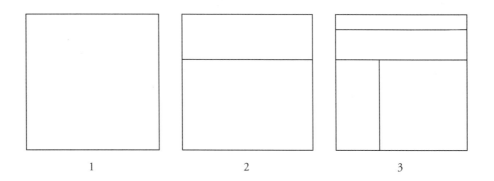

1   2   3

As you can see, the algorithm continues this process of subdivision for a number of levels, until an "aesthetically right moment" is reached. In this version, the algorithm appears to divide the current rectangle into portions representing $\frac{1}{3}$ and $\frac{2}{3}$ of its area and appears to randomly alternate the subdivisions along the horizontal and vertical axes. Design, implement, and test a program that uses a recursive function to draw such patterns. The user should be able to draw several pictures with different levels.

10. Modify the program in Problem 9 so that it fills the rectangular areas in the picture with randomly generated colors, as shown in shades of gray in the following examples:

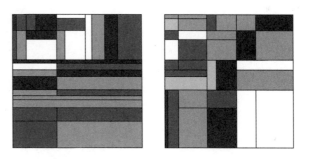

11. The programs in Problems 9 and 10 use constant factors of $\frac{1}{3}$ and $\frac{2}{3}$ to subdivide the rectangle on the recursive steps. Modify the program in Problem 10 so that the factors randomly alternate among $\frac{1}{5}$ and $\frac{4}{5}$; $\frac{1}{4}$ and $\frac{3}{4}$; and $\frac{1}{3}$ and $\frac{2}{3}$.

Communication in Practice

1. Select a programming problem from this chapter that you have not yet worked. Construct a structure chart and write all documentary information necessary for the problem you have chosen. Do not write code. When you are finished, have a classmate read your documentation to see if precisely what is to be done is clear.

2. Write a short paper that discusses the advantages and disadvantages of the selection sort and the quick sort.

3. Form a team of students (three or four) to identify some local business that has not yet computerized its customer records. The team should have a discussion with the owner or manager to determine how the customer records are used. After talking with the owner or manager, the team should design an information processing system for the business. The system should include complete specifications for the design. Particular attention should be paid to searching and sorting. The team should then give an oral presentation to the class and use appropriate charts and diagrams to illustrate its design.

4. Interview a teacher in the arts at your high school or local college. Ask the teacher about the use of computers to generate art works or to assist in their construction. Prepare a report on your findings to present to your class.

Glossary

absolute coordinates   The specification of a point in terms of x and y coordinates.

abstract   Simplified or partial, hiding detail.

abstract data type (ADT)   A form of abstraction that arises from the use of defined types. An ADT consists of a class of objects, a defined set of properties of those objects, and a set of operations for processing the objects.

access adjustment   A method of changing the access mode of an inherited member from within a derived class. For example, a derived class may inherit all members from a base class in protected mode, and then make some members public by means of access adjustments. *See also* **access specifier, base class, derived class,** and **inheritance.**

access specifier   A symbol (public, protected, or private) that specifies the kind of access that clients have to a server's data members and member functions. *See also* **private member, protected member,** and **public member.**

accessor   A member function used to examine an attribute of an object without changing it.

accumulator   A variable used for the purpose of summing successive values of some other variable.

actual parameter   A variable or expression contained in a function call and passed to that function. *See also* **formal parameter.**

address   Often called address of a memory location, this is an integer value that the computer can use to reference a location. *See also* **value.**

address-of operator   This operator, **&**, is used to access the address of a variable.

algorithm   A finite sequence of effective statements that, when applied to a problem, will solve it.

alias   A situation in which two or more identifiers in a program can refer to the same memory location. An alias can become the cause of subtle side effects.

application software   Programs designed for a specific use.

argument   A value or expression passed in a function call.

arithmetic/logic unit (ALU)   The part of the central processing unit (CPU) that performs arithmetic operations and evaluates expressions.

array   A data structure whose elements are accessed by means of index positions.

array index   The relative position of the components of an array.

ASCII collating sequence   The American Standard Code for Information Interchange ordering for a character set. The ASCII character set is listed in Appendix 4.

assembly language   A computer language that allows words and symbols to be used in an unsophisticated manner to accomplish simple tasks.

assertion   Special comments used with selection and repetition that state what you expect to happen and when certain conditions will hold.

assignment statement   A method of putting values into memory locations.

attribute   A property that a computational object models, such as the balance in a bank account.

base class   The class from which a derived class inherits attributes and behavior. *See also* **derived class** and **inheritance.**

behavior   The set of actions that a class of objects supports.

binary digit   A digit, either 0 or 1, in the binary number system. Program instructions are stored in memory using a sequence of binary digits. Binary digits are called *bits*.

binary search   The process of examining a middle value of a sorted array to see which half contains the value in question and halving until the value is located.

bitmap   A data structure used to represent the values and positions of points on a computer screen or image.

block   The area of program text within a compound statement that contains statements and optional data declarations.

Boolean expression   An expression whose value is either true or false. *See also* **compound Boolean expression** and **simple Boolean expression.**

bottom-up testing   Independent testing of modules.

buffer   A block of memory into which data are placed for transmission to a program.

buffered file input   The input of large blocks of data from a file.

bus   A group of wires imprinted on a circuit board to facilitate communication between components of a computer.

byte   A sequence of bits used to encode a character in memory. *See also* **word.**

call   Any reference to a subprogram by an executable statement. Also referred to as *invoke*.

cancellation error   A condition in which data are lost because of differences in the precision of the operands.

c-curve   A fractal shape that resembles the letter C.

central processing unit (CPU)   A major hardware component that consists of the arithmetic/logic unit (ALU) and the control unit.

character set   The list of characters available for data and program statements. *See also* **collating sequence.**

class   A description of the attributes and behavior of a set of computational objects.

class constructor   A member function used to create and initialize an instance of a class.

class declaration section   An area of a program used to declare the data members and member functions of a class.

class destructor   A function member defined by the programmer and automatically used by the computer to return dynamic memory used by an object to the heap when the program exits the scope of the object. *See also* **dynamic memory.**

class implementation section   An area of a program used to implement the member functions of a class.

class template   A kind of class that allows its component types to be specified as parameters.

client   A computational object that receives a service from another computational object.

client/server relationship   A means of describing the organization of computing resources in which one resource provides a service to another resource.

clipping rectangle   An area within which a graphical image is drawn.

code (writing)   The process of writing executable statements that are part of a program to solve a problem.

cohesive subprogram   A subprogram designed to accomplish a single task.

collating sequence   The particular order sequence for a character set used by a machine. *See also* **ASCII collating sequence.**

comment   A nonexecutable statement used to make a program more readable.

compatible type   Expressions that have the same base type. A parameter and its argument must be of compatible type, and the operands of an assignment statement must be of compatible type.

compilation error   An error detected when the program is being compiled. *See also* **design error, logic error, run-time error,** and **syntax error.**

compiler   A computer program that automatically converts instructions in a high-level language to machine language.

compound assignment   An assignment operation that performs a designated operation, such as addition, before storing the result in a variable.

compound Boolean expression   Refers to the complete expression when logical connectives and negation are used to generate Boolean values. *See also* **Boolean expression** and **simple Boolean expression.**

compound statement   Uses the symbols **{** and **}** to group several statements as a unit.

concatenation   An operation in which the contents of one data structure are placed after the contents of another data structure.

conditional statement   *See* **selection statement.**

conjunction   The connection of two Boolean expressions using the logical operator **&&** (AND), returning FALSE if at least one of the expressions is FALSE, or TRUE if they are both TRUE.

const function   A member function that does not allow changes to the attributes of an object.

constant   A symbol whose value cannot be changed in the body of the program.

constant definition section   The section where program constants are defined for subsequent use.

constant parameter   A method of declaring a formal array parameter so that the value of an actual array parameter will not change in a function.

constant reference   A method of declaring a formal parameter so that the actual parameter is passed by reference but will not change in a function.

constructor   A member function used to create and initialize an instance of a class.

contained class   A class that is used to define a data member of another class.

control structure   A structure that controls the flow of execution of program statements.

control unit   The part of the central processing unit that controls the operation of the rest of the computer.

coordinate system   A grid in which a point in space or a pixel on a computer screen can be located.

copy constructor   A member function defined by the programmer and automatically used by the computer to copy the values of objects when they are passed by value to functions.

counter   A variable used to count the number of times some process is completed.

data   The particular characters that are used to represent information in a form suitable for storage, processing, and communication.

data abstraction   The separation between the conceptual definition of a data structure and its eventual implementation.

data member   A data object declared within a class declaration module.

data type   A formal description of the set of values that a variable can have.

data validation   The process of examining data prior to its use in a program.

debugging   The process of eliminating errors or "bugs" from a program.

declaration section   The section used to declare (name) symbolic constants, data types, variables, and subprograms that are necessary to the program.

decrement   To decrease the value of a variable.

default constructor   A member function that creates and provides reasonable initial values for the data within an object.

dereference   The operation by which a program uses a pointer to access the contents of dynamic memory. *See also* **dynamic memory** and **pointer variable.**

derived class   A class that inherits attributes and behavior from other classes. *See also* **base class** and **inheritance.**

design error   An error such that a program runs, but unexpected results are produced. Also referred to as a *logic error. See also* **compilation error, run-time error,** and **syntax error.**

destructor   A member function that returns dynamic memory for an object to the system.

disjunction   The connection of two Boolean expressions using the logical operator || (OR), returning TRUE if at least one of the expressions is TRUE, or FALSE if they are both FALSE.

divide-and-conquer algorithms   A class of algorithms that solves problems by repeatedly dividing them into simpler problems. *See also* **recursion.**

do ... while loop   A post-test loop examining a Boolean expression after causing a statement to be executed. *See also* **for loop, loops,** and **while loop.**

dynamic memory   Memory allocated under program control from the heap and accessed by means of pointers. *See also* **heap** and **pointer variable.**

dynamic structure   A data structure that may expand or contract during execution of a program. *See also* **dynamic memory.**

echo checking   A debugging technique in which values of variables and input data are displayed during program execution.

empty link   *See* **null pointer.**

effective statement   A clear, unambiguous instruction that can be carried out.

empty statement   A semicolon used to indicate that no action is to be taken. Also referred to as a *null statement.*

encapsulation   The process of hiding and restricting access to the implementation details of a data structure.

end-of-file marker   A special marker inserted by the machine to indicate the end of the data file.

end-of-line character   A special character ('\n') used to indicate the end of a line of characters in a string or a file stream.

entrance-controlled loop   *See* **pretest loop.**

error   *See* **compilation error, design error, logic error, run-time error,** and **syntax error.**

executable section   Contains the statements that cause the computer to do something.

executable statement   The basic unit of grammar in C++ consisting of valid identifiers, library identifiers, reserved words, numbers, and/or characters, together with appropriate punctuation.

execute   To carry out the instructions of a program.

exit-controlled loop   *See* **post-test loop.**

explicit type conversion   The use of an operation by a programmer to convert the type of a data object.

exponential form   *See* **floating point.**

extended if statement   Nested selection where additional if . . . else statements are used in the else option. *See also* **nested if statement.**

external pointer   A special pointer that allows users to access the nodes in a linked list.

extractor   The standard input operator **>>**.

field width   The phrase used to describe the number of columns used for various output. *See also* **formatting.**

file   A data structure that resides on a secondary storage medium.

file stream   A data structure that consists of a sequence of components that are accessed by input or output operations.

fill value   A value that is used to initialize every component in a data structure.

fixed point   A method of writing decimal numbers in which the decimal is placed where it belongs in the number. *See also* **floating point.**

fixed-repetition loop   A loop used when it is known in advance the number of times a segment of code needs to be repeated.

floating point   A method for writing numbers in scientific notation to accommodate numbers that may have very large or very small values. *See also* **fixed point.**

for loop   A structured loop consisting of an initializer expression, a termination expression, an update expression, and a statement.

formal parameter   A name, declared and used in a function declaration, that is replaced by an actual parameter when the function is called.

formal specification   The set of preconditions and postconditions of a function.

format manipulator   A symbol that instructs the computer to display output in a specified format, such as right-justified.

formatting   Designating the desired field width when printing integers, reals, Boolean values, and character strings. *See also* **field width.**

fractal geometry   A theory about shapes that are reflected in various phenomena, such as coastlines, water flow, and price fluctuations.

free function   A function not declared within the scope of a class declaration module.

free store   *See* **heap.**

function   *See* **library function** and **user-defined function.**

function declaration   A form that contains a function's name, parameter declarations, and return type.

function heading   The portion of a function implementation containing the function's name, parameter declarations, and return type.

function implementation   A detailed, complete, and executable description of a function.

functional abstraction   The process of considering only what a function is to do rather than details of the function.

global identifier   A name that can be used by the main program and all subprograms in a program.

global variable   *See* **global identifier.**

hardware   The physical computing machine and its support devices.

header file   A C++ file that provides data and function declarations in a library to client modules.

heap   An area of computer memory where storage for dynamic data is available.

heap underflow   A condition in which memory leakage causes dynamic memory to become unavailable.

high-level language   Any programming language that uses words and symbols to make it relatively easy to read and write a program. *See also* **assembly language** and **machine language.**

identifiers   Words that must be created according to a well-defined set of rules but can have any meaning subject to these rules. *See also* **library identifiers.**

implementation file   A C++ file that provides the implementations of data and functions declared in a header file.

index   *See* **array index** or **loop index.**

infinite loop   A loop in which the controlling condition is not changed in such a manner as to allow the loop to terminate.

information hiding   A condition in which the user of a module does not know the details of how it is implemented, and the implementer of a module does not know the details of how it is used.

inheritance   The process by which a derived class can reuse attributes and behavior defined in a base class. *See also* **base class** and **derived class.**

input   Data obtained by a program during its execution.

input assertion   A precondition for a loop.

input device   A device that provides information to the computer. Typical devices are keyboards, disk drives, card readers, and tape drives. *See also* **I/O device** and **output device.**

input file stream   An input stream that is connected to a file.

input stream   A channel for receiving input data.

inserter   The standard output operator **<<**.

instance   A computational object bearing the attributes and behavior specified by a class.

integer arithmetic operations   Operations allowed on data of type **int.** This includes the operations of addition, subtraction, multiplication, division, and modulus to produce integer answers.

integer overflow   A condition in which an integer value is too large to be stored in the computer's memory.

interface   A formal statement of how communication occurs between the user of a subprogram and its implementer.

invariant expression   An assertion that is true before a loop and after each iteration of the loop.

invoke   *See* **call.**

I/O device   Any device that allows information to be transmitted to or from a computer. *See also* **input device** and **output device.**

iteration   *See* **loops.**

keyword   Either a reserved word or a library identifier.

l-value   A computational object capable of being the target of an assignment statement.

library constant   A constant with a standard meaning, such as **INT_MAX**, available in most versions of C++.

library function   A function available in most versions of C++. A list of useful C++ library functions is given in Appendix 2.

library header file   A file of source code, usually having a **.h** suffix, containing data and function declarations.

library identifiers   Words defined in standard C++ libraries. *See also* **identifiers.**

library implementation file   A file of source code, usually having a **.cpp** suffix, containing function implementations.

linear   An increase of work or memory in direct proportion to the size of a problem.

linear search   *See* **sequential search.**

linked list   A list of data items in which each item is linked to the next one by means of a pointer.

local identifier   A name that is restricted to use within a subblock of a program.

local variable   *See* **local identifier.**

locally declared data   Data declared within a block, usually the block of the main program or a function.

logarithmic   An increase of work in proportion to the number of times that the problem size can be divided by 2.

logic error   *See* **design error.**

logical operator   Either logical connective (**&&**, **||**) or negation (**!**).

logical size   The number of data items actually available in a data structure at a given time. *See also* **physical size.**

logical structure   The organization of the components in a data structure, independent of their organization in computer memory.

loop index   Variable used for control values in a loop.

loop invariant   An assertion that expresses a relationship between variables that remains constant throughout all iterations of a loop.

loop variant An assertion whose truth changes between the first and final execution of a loop.

loop verification The process of guaranteeing that a loop performs its intended task.

loops Program statements that cause a process to be repeated. *See also* **for loop, do . . . while loop,** and **while loop.**

low-level language *See* **assembly language.**

machine language The language used directly by the computer in all its calculations and processing.

main block The main part of a program.

main driver The main program when subprograms are used to accomplish specific tasks. *See also* **executable section.**

main (primary) memory Memory contained in the computer. *See also* **memory** and **secondary memory.**

main program heading A syntactic form that marks the beginning of the main part of a C++ program.

main unit A computer's main unit contains the central processing unit (CPU) and the main (primary) memory; it is hooked to an input device and an output device.

mainframe A large computer typically used by major companies and universities. *See also* **microcomputer** and **minicomputer.**

manifest interface The property of a function such that, when the function is called, the reader of the code can tell clearly what information is being transmitted to it and what information is being returned from it.

matrix A two-dimensional array that provides range checking and can be resized.

member A component of a struct or class.

member function An operation defined for a class of objects.

memory The ordered sequence of storage cells that can be accessed by address. Instructions and variables of an executing program are temporarily held here. *See also* **main memory** and **secondary memory.**

memory leakage A condition in which dynamic memory is lost due to programmer error.

memory location A storage cell that can be accessed by address. *See also* **memory.**

merge The process of combining lists. Typically refers to files or arrays.

microcomputer A computer capable of fitting on a laptop or desktop, generally used by one person at a time. *See also* **mainframe** and **minicomputer.**

minicomputer A small version of a mainframe computer. It is usually used by several people at once. *See also* **mainframe** and **microcomputer.**

mixed-mode Expressions containing data of different types; the values of these expressions will be of either type, depending on the rules for evaluating them.

modem A device that connects a computer to a telephone system to transmit data.

modifier A member function used to change the value of an attribute of an object.

modular development The process of developing an algorithm using modules. *See also* **module.**

modularity The organization of a program into independent units.

module An independent unit that is part of a larger development. Can be a function or a class (set of functions and related data). *See also* **modular development.**

module specifications In the case of a function, a description of data received, information returned, and task performed by a module. In the case of a class, a description of the attributes and behavior.

negation The use of the logical operator **!** (NOT) with a Boolean expression, returning TRUE if the expression is FALSE, and FALSE if the expression is TRUE.

nested if statement A selection statement used within another selection statement. *See also* **extended if statement.**

nested loop A loop as one of the statements in the body of another loop.

nested selection Any combination of selection statements within selection statements. *See also* **selection statement.**

network A group of computers that are linked to share resources.

node A component of a linked list, consisting of a data item and a pointer to the next node.

null character The special character (**'\0'**) used to mark the end of a string in C++.

null pointer A special value that indicates that no node can be referenced.

null statement *See* **empty statement.**

object A collection of data and operations, in which the data can be accessed and modified only by means of the operations.

object code *See* **object program.**

object-oriented programming The use of small, reusable components to construct large software systems.

object program The machine code version of the source program.

one-dimensional array An array in which each data item is accessed by specifying a single index.

opened for reading Positions an input stream pointer at the beginning of a file for the purpose of reading from the file.

opened for writing Positions an output stream pointer at the beginning of a file for the purpose of writing to the file.

opening a file Positions a pointer at the beginning of a file. *See also* **opened for reading** and **opened for writing.**

operating system A large program that allows the user to communicate with the hardware and performs various management tasks.

ordered collection A data structure that behaves like a vector, with the additional capability of adding data elements at the beginning and the end. The logical size of an ordered collection is always the same as its physical size.

ordinal data type A data type ordered in some association with the integers; each integer is the ordinal of a value of the type.

output Information that is produced by a program.

output assertion A postcondition for a loop.

output device A device that allows you to see the results of a program. Typically it is a monitor or printer. *See also* **input device** and **I/O device.**

output file stream An output stream that is connected to a file.

output stream A channel for sending output data.

overflow In arithmetic operations, a value may be too large for the computer's memory location. A meaningless value may be assigned or an error message may result. *See also* **underflow.**

overloading The process of using the same operator symbol or identifier to refer to many different functions. *See also* **polymorphism.**

parallel arrays Arrays of the same length.

parameter *See* **argument.**

parameter list A list of parameters. An actual parameter list is contained in the function call. A formal parameter list is contained in the function declaration and heading.

parameter mode The way in which a parameter is passed, such as by value or by reference.

passed by reference When the address of the actual parameter is passed to a subprogram.

passed by value When a copy of the value of the actual parameter is passed to a subprogram.

peripheral memory *See* **secondary memory** and **memory.**

physical size The number of memory units available for storing data items in a data structure. *See also* **logical size.**

pivot A data item around which an array is subdivided during the quick sort.

pixel A picture element or dot of color used to display images on a computer screen.

pointer variable A variable that contains the address of a memory location. *See also* **address** and **dynamic memory.**

polymorphism The property of one operator symbol or function identifier having many meanings. *See also* **overloading.**

portable Able to be transferred to different applications or computers without changes.

postcondition A statement of what is true after a certain action is taken.

post-test loop A loop where the control condition is tested after the loop is executed. A `do . . . while` loop is a post-test loop. Also referred to as an *exit-controlled loop.*

precondition A statement of what is true before a certain action is taken.

preprocessor directives Statements that tell the C++ preprocessor to perform such tasks as combining source program files prior to compilation.

pretest condition A condition that controls whether the body of the loop is executed before going through the loop.

pretest loop A loop where the control condition is tested before the loop is executed. A `while` loop is a pretest loop. Also referred to as an *entrance-controlled loop.*

primary memory *See* **main memory** and **memory.**

priming input statement An input statement that must be executed before a loop control condition is tested.

private member A data member or member function that is accessible only within the scope of a class declaration.

procedural programming A style of programming that decomposes a program into a set of functions or procedures.

program A set of instructions that tells the machine (the hardware) what to do.

program heading The heading of the main block of any C++ program; it must contain the identifier `main`.

program proof An analysis of a program that attempts to verify the correctness of program results.

program protection A method of using selection statements to guard against unexpected results.

program walk-through The process of carefully following, using pencil and paper, the steps the computer uses to solve the problem given in a program. Also referred to as a *trace.*

programmer-supplied identifiers Words defined by the programmer.

programming language Formal language that computer scientists use to give instructions to a computer.

prompt A message or marker on the terminal screen that requests input data.

protected member A data member or member function that is accessible only within the scope of a class declaration or within the class declaration of a derived class.

protection *See* **program protection.**

pseudocode A stylized half-English, half-code language written in English but suggesting C++ code.

public member A data member or member function that is accessible to any program component that uses the class.

quadratic An increase of work or memory in proportion to the square of the size of the problem.

quick sort A relatively fast sorting technique that uses recursion. *See also* **selection sort.**

r-value A computational object capable of being assigned to a variable.

random access data structure A data structure in which the time to access a data item does not depend on its position in the structure.

range bound error   The situation that occurs when an attempt is made to use an array index value that is less than 0 or greater than or equal to the size of the array.

reading from a file   Retrieving data from a file.

real arithmetic operations   Operations allowed on data of type float or double. These include addition, subtraction, multiplication, and division.

receiver object   A computational object to which a request is sent for a service.

recursion   The process of a subprogram calling itself. A clearly defined stopping state must exist. Any recursive subprogram can be rewritten using iteration.

recursive data structure   A data structure that has either a simple form or a form that is composed of other instances of the same data structure. *See* **linked list.**

recursive step   A step in the recursive process that solves a similar problem of smaller size and eventually leads to a termination of the process.

recursive subprogram   *See* **recursion.**

reference parameter   A formal parameter that requires the address of the actual parameter to be passed to a subprogram. The value of the actual parameter can be changed within the subprogram.

relational operator   An operator used for comparison of data items of the same type.

relative coordinates   The use of horizontal and vertical distances to specify a new point in relation to an existing point.

repetition   *See* **loops.**

representational error   A condition in which the precision of data is reduced because of the order in which operations are performed.

reserved words   Words that have predefined meanings that cannot be changed. A list of C++ reserved words is given in Appendix 1.

return type   The type of value returned by a function.

robust   The state in which a program is protected against most possible crashes from bad data and unexpected values.

round-off error   A condition in which a portion of a real number is lost because of the way it is stored in the computer's memory.

run-time error   Error detected when, after compilation is completed, an error message results instead of the correct output. *See also* **compilation error, design error, logic error,** and **syntax error.**

run-time stack   An area of computer memory reserved for local variables and parameters.

scaling   The modification of the size of an image by specified horizontal and vertical factors.

scattershot diagram   The plotting of points such that one coordinate represents a value and the other coordinate represents the index position of the value in a data structure.

scope of identifier   The largest block in which the identifier is available.

secondary memory   An auxiliary device for memory, usually a disk or magnetic tape. *See also* **main memory** and **memory.**

seed   An initial value used by a random number generator.

selection   The process by which a member of a struct or class is accessed.

selection sort   An algorithm that sorts the components of an array in either ascending or descending order. This process puts the smallest or largest element in the top position and repeats the process on the remaining array components. *See also* **quick sort.**

selection statement   A control statement that selects some particular logical path based on the value of an expression. Also referred to as a *conditional statement.*

selector   The operator (**.**) used to access a member of a struct or class.

self-documenting code   Code that is written using descriptive identifiers.

sender   A computational object that requests a service from another computational object.

sentinel value   A special value that indicates the end of a set of data or of a process.

sequential access data structure   A data structure in which the time to access a data item depends on its position in the structure.

sequential algorithm   *See* **straight-line algorithm.**

sequential search   The process of searching a list by examining the first component and then examining successive components in the order in which they occur. Also referred to as a *linear search.*

sequential traversal   The process of visiting each data item in an array or a linked list, from beginning to end.

server   A computational object that provides a service to another computational object.

short-circuit evaluation   The process whereby a compound Boolean expression halts evaluation and returns the value of the first subexpression that evaluates to TRUE, in the case of | |, or FALSE, in the case of **&&.**

side effect   A change in a variable that is the result of some action taken in a program, usually from within a function.

simple Boolean expression   An expression in which two numbers or variable values are compared using a single relational operator. *See also* **Boolean expression** and **compound Boolean expression.**

software   Programs that make the machine (the hardware) do something, such as word processing, database management, or games.

software engineering   The process of developing and maintaining large software systems.

software reuse   The process of building and maintaining software systems out of existing software components.

software system life cycle   The process of development, maintenance, and demise of a software system. Phases include analysis, design, coding, testing/verification, maintenance, and obsolescence.

sorted collection   A data structure that behaves like an ordered collection, but with the data items maintained in ascending order. *See also* **ordered collection.**

source program   A program written by a programmer.

stack   A dynamic data structure in which access can be made from only one end. Referred to as a LIFO (last-in, first-out) structure.

standard output stream   An object to which a program sends data for output to a device, normally the terminal screen.

standard simple types   Predefined data types such as `int`, `double`, and `char`.

statement block (synonym **compound statement**)   A form by which a sequence of statements can be treated as a unit.

statement section   An area of a C++ program where the executable statements are placed.

stepwise refinement   The process of repeatedly subdividing tasks into subtasks until each subtask is easily accomplished. *See also* **structured programming** and **top-down design.**

stopping state   The well-defined termination of a recursive process.

straight-line algorithm   Also called *sequential algorithm,* this algorithm consists of a sequence of simple tasks.

stream   A channel in which data are passed from sender to receiver.

string   A data type used to represent a word or a line of text.

string constant   A word or a line of text enclosed in double quotes.

string data type   A data type that permits a sequence of characters. In C++, this can be implemented using an array of characters.

string literal   One or more characters, enclosed in double quotes, used as a constant in a program.

struct   A data structure that can have components of different data types, accessible by name.

structure chart   A graphic method of indicating the relationship between modules when designing the solution to a problem.

structured design   A method of designing software by specifying modules and the flow of data among them.

structured programming   Programming that parallels a solution to a problem achieved by top-down design. *See also* **stepwise refinement** and **top-down design.**

stub programming   The process of using incomplete functions to test data transmission among them.

subblock   A block structure for a subprogram. *See also* **block.**

subprogram   A program within a program. Functions are subprograms.

subscript   *See* **array index** or **loop index.**

substring   A string that represents a segment of another string.

syntax   The formal rules governing construction of valid statements.

syntax diagramming   A method to formally describe the legal syntax of language structures. Syntax diagrams are set forth in Appendix 3.

syntax error   An error in spelling, punctuation, or placement of certain key symbols in a program. *See also* **compilation error, design error, logic error,** and **run-time error.**

system software   The programs that allow users to write and execute other programs, including operating systems such as DOS.

tail-recursive   The property that a recursive algorithm has of performing no work after each recursive step. *See also* **recursion.**

test program   A short program written to provide an answer to a specific question.

top-down design   A design methodology for solving a problem whereby you first state the problem and then proceed to subdivide the main task into major subtasks. Each subtask is then subdivided into smaller subtasks. This process is repeated until each remaining subtask is easily solved. *See also* **stepwise refinement** and **structured programming.**

trace   *See* **program walk-through.**

translation   The process of modifying the position of an image by a specified vertical and horizontal distance.

two-dimensional array   An array in which each data item is accessed by specifying a pair of indices.

type   *See* **data type.**

type cast   An operation that a programmer can invoke to convert the type of a data object.

type definition   The introduction of a synonym for an existing data type.

type promotion   The process of converting a less inclusive data type, such as integer, to a more inclusive data type, such as double.

underflow   If a value is too small to be represented by a computer, the value is automatically replaced by zero. *See also* **overflow.**

user-defined data type   A new data type introduced and defined by the programmer.

user-defined function   A new function introduced and defined by the programmer.

user-friendly   A phrase used to describe an interactive program with clear, easy-to-follow messages for the user.

value   Often called value of a memory location. Refers to the value of the contents of a memory location. *See also* **address.**

value parameter   A formal parameter that is local to a subprogram. Values of these parameters are not returned to the calling program.

variable   A memory location, referenced by an identifier, whose value can be changed during a program.

variable condition loop   A repetition statement in which a loop control condition changes within the body of the loop.

variable declaration section   The section of the declaration section where program variables are declared for subsequent use.

vector   A one-dimensional array that provides range checking and can be resized.

void function   A function that returns no value.

while loop   A pretest loop that examines a Boolean expression before causing a statement to be executed.

word   A unit of memory consisting of one or more bytes. Words can be addressed.

workstation   A powerful desktop computer that uses microprocessor technology.

writing to a file   The process of entering data to a file.

Appendixes

Reserved Words

The following words have predefined meanings in C++ and cannot be changed. The words in boldface are discussed in the text. The other words are discussed in Stanley B. Lippman, *C++ Primer,* 2nd edition, Reading, MA: Addison-Wesley Publishing Company, 1993.

asm	**double**	**new**	**switch**
auto	**else**	**operator**	**template**
break	enum	**private**	**this**
case	extern	**protected**	throw
catch	**float**	**public**	try
char	**for**	register	**typedef**
class	friend	**return**	union
const	goto	**short**	**unsigned**
continue	**if**	**signed**	virtual
default	inline	sizeof	**void**
delete	**int**	static	volatile
do	**long**	**struct**	**while**

APPENDIX 2   Some Useful Library Functions

Some of the most commonly used library functions in the first course in computer science come from the libraries **math** and **ctype.** Descriptions of the most important functions in each of these libraries are presented in the following tables.

math

Function Declaration	Purpose
`double acos(double x);`	Returns arc cosine for x in range -1 to $+1$
`double asin(double x);`	Returns arc sine for x in range -1 to $+1$
`double atan(double x);`	Returns arc tangent of x
`double atan2(double y, double x);`	Returns arc tangent of y/x
`double ceil(double x);`	Rounds x up to next highest integer
`double cos(double x);`	Returns cosine of x
`double cosh(double x);`	Returns hyberbolic cosine of x
`double exp(double x);`	Returns e to the xth power
`double abs(double x);`	Returns absolute value of x
`double floor(double x);`	Rounds x down to next lowest integer
`double fmod(double x, double y);`	Returns remainder of x/y
`double ldexp(double x, double exp);`	Returns x times 2 to the power of exp
`double log(double x);`	Returns natural logarithm of x
`double log10(double x);`	Returns base 10 logarithm of x
`double pow(double x, double y);`	Returns x raised to power of y
`double sin(double x);`	Returns sine of x
`double sinh(double x);`	Returns hyberbolic sine of x
`double sqrt(double x);`	Returns square root of x
`double tan(double x);`	Returns tangent of x, in radians
`double tanh(double x);`	Returns hyperbolic tangent of x

`ctype`

Function Declaration	Purpose
`int isalnum(int ch);`	**ch** is letter or digit
`int isalpha(int ch);`	**ch** is letter
`int iscntrl(int ch);`	**ch** is control character
`int isdigit(int ch);`	**ch** is digit (0–9)
`int isgraph(int ch);`	**ch** is printable but not ' '
`int islower(int ch);`	**ch** is lowercase letter
`int isprint(int ch);`	**ch** is printable
`int ispunct(int ch);`	**ch** is printable but not ' ' or alpha
`int isspace(int ch);`	**ch** is a whitespace character
`int isupper(int ch);`	**ch** is uppercase letter
`int isxdigit(int ch);`	**ch** is hexadecimal digit
`int tolower(int ch);`	Returns lowercase of **ch**
`int toupper(int ch);`	Returns uppercase of **ch**

APPENDIX 3   Syntax Diagrams

The following syntax diagrams correspond to the syntax forms used to describe the features of C++ discussed in the text. Two points of caution are in order. First, the diagrams in this appendix by no means represent an exhaustive description of C++. Second, many of the features discussed in this text have more than one syntactically correct construction (for example, **main** can be preceded by either **int** or **void**, but the C++ programming community prefers **int**). By confining your attention to preferred ways of using a small subset of features, we hope to place your focus on concepts rather than syntax. Students who want to learn more features of C++ or other ways of expressing them are referred to Stanley B. Lippman, *C++ Primer,* 2nd edition, Reading, MA: Addison-Wesley Publishing Company, 1993.

The terms enclosed in ovals in the diagrams refer to program components that appear in programs literally, such as operator symbols and reserved words. The terms enclosed in boxes refer to program components that require further definition, either by another diagram or by reference to the text. The syntax of terms for which there are no diagrams, such as **identifier**, **number**, **string**, and **character**, should be familiar to anyone who has read this text.

Main program module

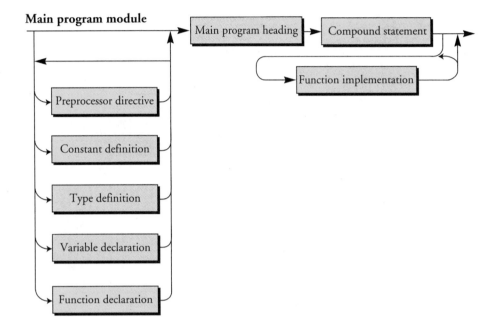

Preprocessor directive

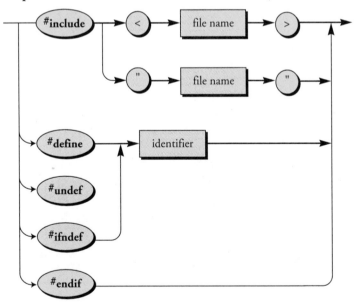

Constant definition

Type definition

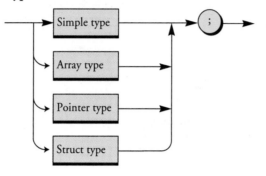

Simple type

Array type

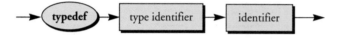

Pointer type

Struct type

List of members

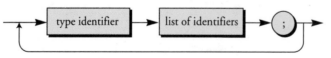

Variable declaration

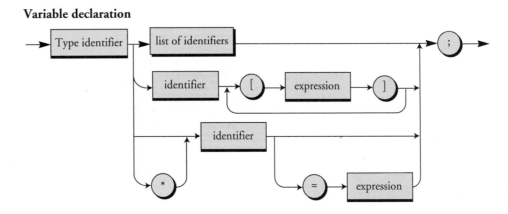

List of identifiers

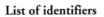

Function declaration

Main program heading

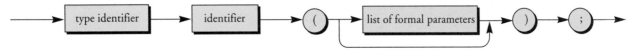

Compound statement

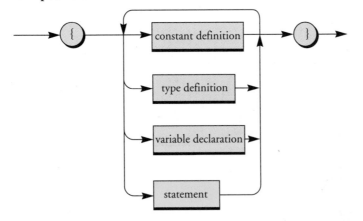

Statement

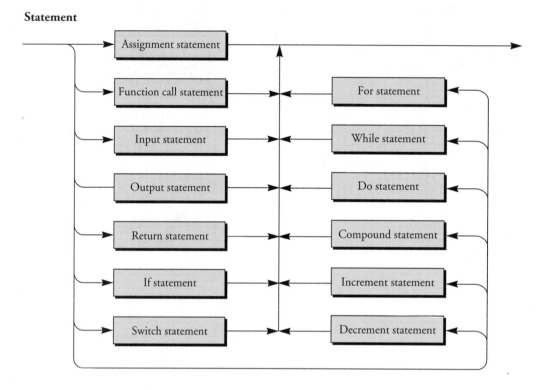

Assignment statement

Function call statement

Input statement

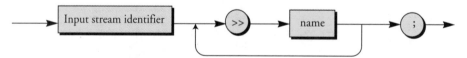

Output statement

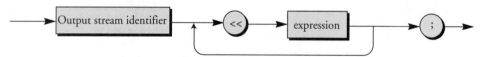

Return statement

If statement

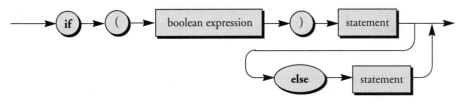

Switch statement

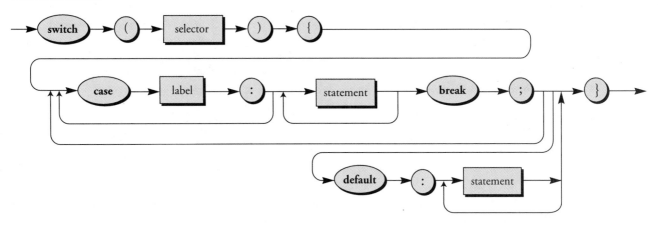

For statement

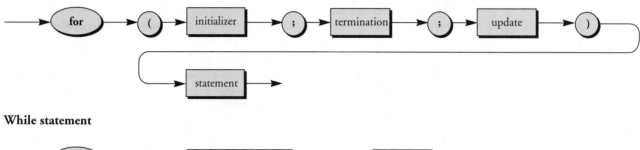

While statement

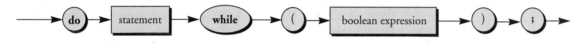

Do statement

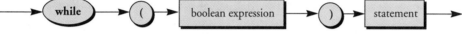

Increment statement

Decrement statement

Function implementation

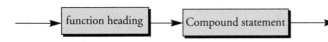

Function heading

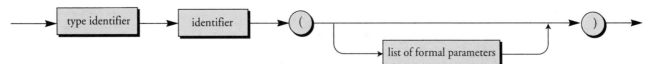

List of formal parameters

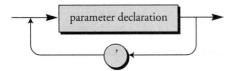

Parameter declaration

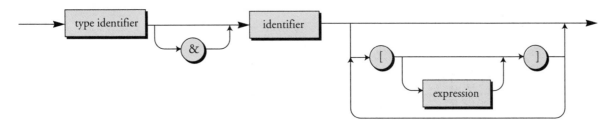

Expression

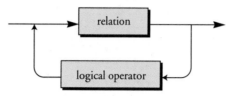

Relation

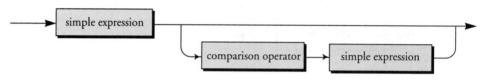

Simple expression

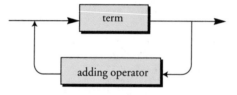

Term

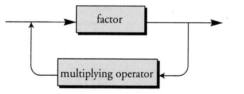

Factor

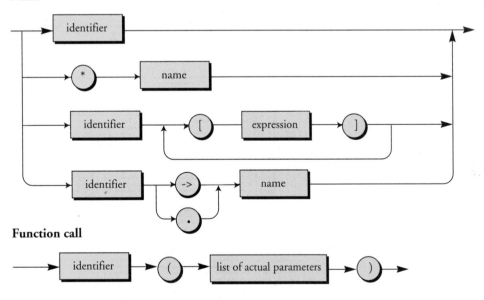

Primary

Name

Function call

List of actual parameters

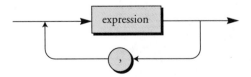

Logical operator

Adding operator

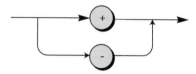

Comparison operator

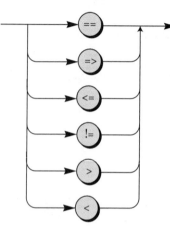

Multiplying operator

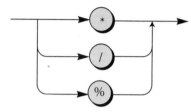

Class declaration module

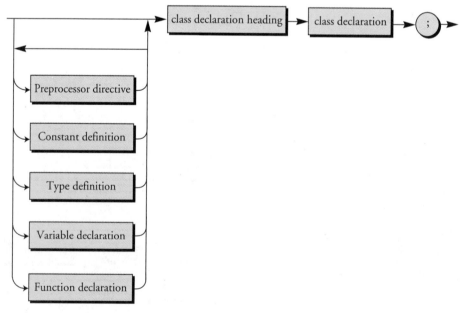

Class declaration heading

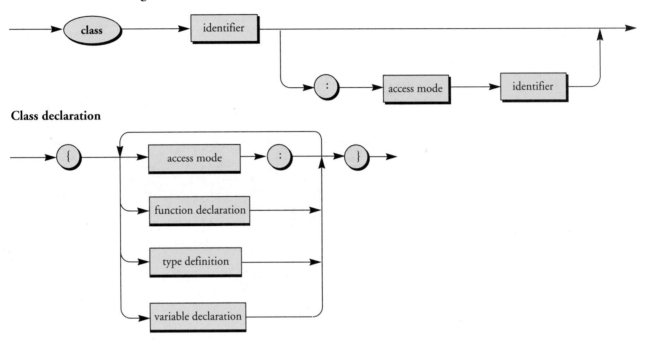

Class declaration

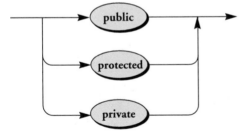

Access mode

APPENDIX 4

The ASCII Character Set

The table included here shows the ordering of the ASCII character set. The printable characters range from ASCII 33 to ASCII 126. The values from ASCII 0 to ASCII 32 and ASCII 127 are associated with whitespace characters, such as the horizontal tab (HT), or nonprinting control characters, such as the escape key (ESC).

The American Standard Code for Information Interchange (ASCII)

Left Digit(s)	Right Digit									
	0	1	2	3	4	5	6	7	8	9
0	NUL	SOH	STX	ETX	EOT	ENQ	ACK	BEL	BS	HT
1	LF	VT	FF	CR	SO	SI	DLE	DC1	DC2	DC3
2	DC4	NAK	SYN	ETB	CAN	EM	SUB	ESC	FS	GS
3	RS	US	SP	!	"	#	$	%	&	'
4	(	)	*	+	,	-	.	/	0	1
5	2	3	4	5	6	7	8	9	:	;
6	<	=	>	?	@	A	B	C	D	E
7	F	G	H	I	J	K	L	M	N	O
8	P	Q	R	S	T	U	V	W	X	Y
9	Z	[	\	]	^	—	`	a	b	c
10	d	e	f	g	h	i	j	k	l	m
11	n	o	p	q	r	s	t	u	v	w
12	x	y	z	{			}	~	DEL		

APPENDIX 5

Graphics Functions

Graphics Functions for PC/DOS Users

The graphics programs presented in this text were written for use with the BGI/DOS graphics system supported by Borland's Turbo C++. The programs in Chapters 2 through 9 and Chapter 12 can be run with Turbo C++ 3.0, which runs under DOS. The graphics programs in Chapter 10 require Turbo C++ 4.5, which requires Windows 3.1 or higher. Note that Borland's C++ compilers for Windows do not support BGI graphics. However, these compilers allow you to create a DOS overlay application, and this mode allows you to use BGI graphics.

Before compiling and running a BGI graphics program with Turbo C++, be sure that the compiler is configured to include the graphics library. In particular, you should perform the following steps:

1. Use the **Options/Directories** menu to place the path **TC:\\BGI** in the lists of **Include Directories** and **Library Directories.**
2. Use the **Linkers/Libraries** menu to check the **Graphics Library** box.
3. Place a copy of the file **EGAVGA.BGI** in the same directory as your source program files and project file.

A list of the commonly used BGI graphics functions is shown in the following table. You can find a complete list in your compiler's manual.

Function Declaration	Purpose
`void arc(int x, int y, int startangle, int endangle, int radius);`	Draws an arc with the specified attributes.
`void bar(int left, int top, int right, int bottom);`	Draws a bar with the specified attributes and fills it with the current fill pattern.
`void circle(int x, int y, int radius);`	Draws a circle with the specified attributes.
`void cleardevice();`	Clears the graphics screen.
`void ellipse(int x, int y, int startangle, int endangle, int xradius, int yradius);`	Draws an ellipse with the specified attributes.
`void fillellipse(int x, int y, int startangle, int endangle, int xradius, int yradius);`	Draws an arc with the specified attributes and fills it with the current fill pattern.
`void floodfill(int x, int y, int bordercolor);`	Using the current pen color, fills outward to the border color.
`int getbkcolor();`	Returns the current background color.
`int getcolor();`	Returns the current pen color.
`int getmaxx();`	Returns the width of the graphics screen.
`int getmaxy();`	Returns the height of the graphics screen.
`int getpixel(int x, int y);`	Returns the color of the pixel at $<x,y>$.
`int getx();`	Returns the x coordinate of the pen.
`int gety();`	Returns the y coordinate of the pen.
`void initgraph(int *graphdriver, int *graphmode);`	Sets up the graphics mode to allow drawing.
`void line(int x1, int y1, int x2, int y2);`	Draws a line with the specified attributes.

(continued)

Function Declaration	Purpose
`void linerel(int x, int y);`	Draws a line the given *x* and *y* distances from the current pen position.
`void lineto(int x, int y);`	Draws a line from the current pen position to <*x,y*>.
`void moverel(int x, int y);`	Moves the pen the given *x* and *y* distances from its current position.
`void moveto(int x, int y);`	Moves the pen from its current position to <*x,y*>.
`void outtext(const char *str);`	Draws the string at the current pen position.
`void outtextxy(const char *str, int x, int y);`	Moves the pen to <*x,y*> and draws the string.
`void pieslice(int x, int y, int startangle, int endangle, int radius);`	Draws a pie slice with the specified attributes.
`void putpixel(int x, int y, int color);`	Draws a pixel with the specified attributes.
`void rectangle(int left, int top, int right, int bottom);`	Draws a rectangle with the specified attributes.
`void sector(int x, int y, int startangle, int endangle, int xradius, int yradius);`	Draws a sector with the specified attributes.
`void setbkcolor(int color);`	Sets the background color to a color.
`void setcolor(int color);`	Sets the pen color to a color.
`void setfillstyle(int pattern, int color);`	Sets the fill style to a pattern and a color.
`setlinestyle(int style, int pattern, int thickness);`	Sets the line style to a style, a pattern, and a thickness.
`settextstyle(int font, int direction, int charsize);`	Sets the text style to a font style, a direction, and a font size.
`int textheight(const char *str);`	Returns the height in pixels of the string in the current text style.
`int textwidth(const char *str);`	Returns the width in pixels of the string in the current text style.

Graphics Functions for PC/Windows Users

The graphics functions for Windows applications are defined in the Windows API. Many of these functions have the same purpose and the same calling protocol as the BGI functions. For example, the Windows function **LineTo** corresponds to the BGI function **lineto**. Thus, Windows users should be able to run many of the graphics programs discussed in this text by defining a library of BGI functions that call the appropriate Windows functions. For further details, consult the documentation on the Windows API that comes with your compiler.

Graphics Functions for Macintosh Users

The graphics functions for Macintosh applications are defined in the Macintosh Toolbox. Many of these functions have the same purpose and the same calling protocol as the BGI functions. For example, the Toolbox function **LineTo** corresponds to the BGI function **lineto**. Thus, Macintosh users should be able to run many of the graphics programs discussed in this text by defining a library of BGI functions that call the appropriate Toolbox functions. A sample library and application for one compiler, Metroworks Code Warrior, is included in the disk that accompanies this text. For further details, consult the documentation that comes with your compiler and Apple Computer's *Inside Macintosh,* Volume I, Reading, MA: Addison-Wesley Publishing Company, 1985.

APPENDIX 6   The AP Classes

The AP classes for strings, vectors, and matrices have been developed by the Advanced Placement Computer Science Ad Hoc Committee on C++ to facilitate problem solving and programming with C++ classes. These classes are discussed in simplified form in Chapter 10. The following sections contain the complete listings of the class libraries for the AP classes. The AP classes are also available as source code files on the disk that accompanies the text. Documentation for the complete APCS C++ subset can be obtained on the World Wide Web at **http://www.cs.duke.edu/~ola/ap/prolog.html**.

The apstring Class

```
// File: apstring.h

#ifndef _APSTRING_H
#define _APSTRING_H

#include <iostream.h>
// uncomment line below if bool not built-in type
// #include "bool.h"
```

```
// ****************************************************************
// APCS string class
//
// string class consistent with a subset of the standard C++ string class
// as defined in the draft ANSI standard
// ****************************************************************

extern const int npos;   // used to indicate not a position in the string

class apstring
{
  public:

  // constructors/destructor

    apstring( );                       // construct empty string ""
    apstring( const char * s);         // construct from string literal
    apstring( const apstring & str );  // copy constructor
   ~apstring( );                       // destructor

  // assignment

    const apstring & operator = ( const apstring & str ); // assign str
    const apstring & operator = ( const char * s );       // assign s
    const apstring & operator = ( char ch );              // assign ch

  // accessors

    int     length( )                  const;   // number of chars
    int     find( const apstring & str ) const; // index of first occurrence of str
    int     find( char ch )            const;   // index of first occurrence of ch
    apstring substr( int pos, int len ) const;  // substring of len chars
                                                // starting at pos
    const char * c_str( )              const;   // explicit conversion to char *

  // indexing

    char   operator[ ] ( int k )       const;   // range-checked indexing
    char & operator[ ] ( int k );               // range-checked indexing

  // modifiers

    const apstring & operator += ( const apstring & str );// append str
    const apstring & operator += ( char ch );             // append char

  private:
    int myLength;                      // length of string (# of characters)
    int myCapacity;                    // capacity of string
    char * myCstring;                  // storage for characters
};
```

```
// The following free (non-member) functions operate on strings
//
// I/O functions

ostream & operator << ( ostream & os, const apstring & str );
istream & operator >> ( istream & is, apstring & str );
istream & getline( istream & is, apstring & str );

// comparison operators:

bool operator == ( const apstring & lhs, const apstring & rhs );
bool operator != ( const apstring & lhs, const apstring & rhs );
bool operator <  ( const apstring & lhs, const apstring & rhs );
bool operator <= ( const apstring & lhs, const apstring & rhs );
bool operator >  ( const apstring & lhs, const apstring & rhs );
bool operator >= ( const apstring & lhs, const apstring & rhs );

// concatenation operator +

apstring operator + ( const apstring & lhs, const apstring & rhs );
apstring operator + ( char ch, const apstring & str );
apstring operator + ( const apstring & str, char ch );

// ******************************************************************
// Specifications for string functions
//
// Any violation of a function's precondition will result in an error
// message followed by a call to abort.
//
// constructors / destructor
//
// string ( )
//    postcondition: string is empty
//
// string( const char * s )
//    description:   constructs a string object from a literal string
//                   such as "abcd"
//    precondition:  s is '\0'-terminated string as used in C
//    postcondition: copy of s has been constructed
//
// string( const string & str )
//    description:   copy constructor
//    postcondition: copy of str has been constructed
//
// ~string( );
//    description:   destructor
//    postcondition: string is destroyed
//
// assignment
//
```

```
// string & operator = ( const string & rhs )
//     postcondition: normal assignment via copying has been performed
//
// string & operator = ( const char * s )
//     description:   assignment from literal string such as "abcd"
//     precondition:  s is '\0'-terminated string as used in C
//     postcondition: assignment via copying of s has been performed
//
// string & operator = ( char ch )
//     description:   assignment from character as though single char string
//     postcondition: assignment of one-character string has been performed
//
// accessors
//
// int length( ) const;
//     postcondition: returns # of chars in string
//
// int find( const string & str)  const;
//     description:   find the first occurrence of the string str within this
//                    string and return the index of the first character.  If
//                    str does not occur in this string, then return npos.
//     precondition:  this string represents c0, c1, ..., c(n-1)
//                    str represents s0, s1, ..., s(m-1)
//     postcondition: if s0 == ck0, s1 == ck1, ..., s(m-1) == ck(m-1) and
//                    there is no j < k0 such that s0 = cj, ...., sm == c(j+m-1),
//                    then returns k0;
//                    otherwise returns npos
//
// int find( char ch ) const;
//     description:   finds the first occurrence of the character ch within this
//                    string and returns the index.  If ch does not occur in this
//                    string, then returns npos.
//     precondition:  this string represents c0, c1, ..., c(n-1)
//     postcondition: if ch == ck, and there is no j < k such that ch == cj,
//                    then returns k;
//                    otherwise returns npos
//
// string substr( int pos, int len ) const;
//     description:   extract and return the substring of length len starting
//                    at index pos
//     precondition:  this string represents c0, c1, ..., c(n-1)
//                        0 <= pos <= pos + len - 1 < n.
//     postcondition: returns the string that represents
//                    c(pos), c(pos+1), ..., c(pos+len-1)
//
// const char * c_str( ) const;
//     description:   convert string into a '\0'-terminated string as
//                    used in C for use with functions
//                    that have '\0'-terminated string parameters.
//     postcondition: returns the equivalent '\0'-terminated string
//
```

```
// indexing
//
// char operator [ ] ( int k ) const;
//    precondition:   0 <= k < length()
//    postcondition:  returns copy of the kth character
//
// char & operator [ ] ( int k )
//    precondition:  0 <= k < length()
//    postcondition: returns reference to the kth character
//
// modifiers
//
// const string & operator += ( const string & str )
//    postcondition: concatenates a copy of str onto this string
//
// const string & operator += ( char ch )
//    postcondition: concatenates a copy of ch onto this string
//
//
// nonmember functions
//
// ostream & operator << ( ostream & os, const string & str)
//    postcondition: str is written to output stream os
//
// istream & operator >> ( istream & is, string & str )
//    precondition:  input stream is open for reading
//    postcondition: the next string from input stream is has been read
//                   and stored in str
//
// istream & getline( istream & is, string & str )
//    description:   reads a line from input stream is into the string str
//    precondition:  input stream is open for reading
//    postcondition: chars from input stream is up to '\n' have been read
//                   and stored in str; the '\n' has been read but not stored
//
// string operator + ( const string & lhs, const string & rhs )
//    postcondition: returns concatenation of lhs with rhs
//
// string operator + ( char ch, const string & str )
//    postcondition: returns concatenation of ch with str
//
// string operator + ( const string & str, char ch )
//    postcondition: returns concatenation of str with ch
//
//*****************************************************************
#endif


// File: apstring.cpp


//  *****************************************************************
//  APCS string class   IMPLEMENTATION
```

```
//
//   see apstring.h for complete documentation of functions
//
//   string class consistent with a subset of the standard C++ string class
//   as defined in the draft ANSI standard
// ********************************************************************

#include <string.h>
#include <assert.h>
#include "apstring.h"

const int npos = -1;
const int MAX_LENGTH = 1024;          // largest size string for input

apstring::apstring()
// postcondition: string is empty
{
    myLength = 0;
    myCapacity = 1;
    myCstring = new char[myCapacity];
    myCstring[0] = '\0';               // make c-style string zero length
}

apstring::apstring(const char * s)
//description:    constructs a string object from a literal string
//                such as "abcd"
//precondition:   s is '\0'-terminated string as used in C
//postcondition:  copy of s has been constructed
{
    assert (s != 0);                  // C-string not NULL?

    myLength = strlen(s);
    myCapacity = myLength + 1;         // make room for '\0'
    myCstring = new char[myCapacity];
    strcpy(myCstring,s);
}

apstring::apstring(const apstring & str)
//description:    copy constructor
//postcondition:  copy of str has been constructed
{
    myLength = str.length();
    myCapacity = myLength + 1;
    myCstring = new char[myCapacity];
    strcpy(myCstring,str.myCstring);
}

apstring::~apstring()
//description:    destructor
//postcondition:  string is destroyed
{
```

```
        delete[] myCstring;                  // free memory
}

const apstring& apstring::operator =(const apstring & rhs)
//postcondition: normal assignment via copying has been performed
{
    if (this != &rhs)                        // check aliasing
    {
        if (myCapacity < rhs.length() + 1)   // more memory needed?
        {
            delete[] myCstring;              // delete old string
            myCapacity = rhs.length() + 1;   // add 1 for '\0'
            myCstring = new char[myCapacity];
        }
        myLength = rhs.length();
        strcpy(myCstring,rhs.myCstring);
    }
    return *this;
}

const apstring& apstring::operator = (const char * s)
//description:   assignment from literal string such as "abcd"
//precondition:  s is '\0'-terminated string as used in C
//postcondition: assignment via copying of s has been performed
{

    int len = 0;                      // length of newly constructed string
    assert (s != 0);                  // make sure s non-NULL
    len = strlen(s);                  // # of characters in string

    // free old string if necessary

    if (myCapacity < len + 1)
    {
      delete[] myCstring;     // delete old string
      myCapacity = len + 1;   // add 1 for '\0'
      myCstring = new char[myCapacity];
    }
    myLength = len;
    strcpy(myCstring,s);
    return *this;
}

const apstring& apstring::operator = (char ch)
//description:   assignment from character as though single char string
//postcondition: assignment of one-character string has been performed
{
    if (myCapacity < 2)
    {
        delete [] myCstring;
        myCapacity = 2;
```

```cpp
        myCstring = new char[myCapacity];
    }
    myLength = 1;
    myCstring[0] = ch;  // make string one character long
    myCstring[1] = '\0';
    return * this;
}


int apstring::length( ) const
//postcondition: returns # of chars in string
{
    return myLength;
}


const char * apstring::c_str() const
//description:   convert string into a '\0'-terminated string as
//               used in C for use with functions
//               that have '\0'-terminated string parameters.
//postcondition: returns the equivalent '\0'-terminated string
{
    return myCstring;
}


char& apstring::operator[](int k)
// precondition:  0 <= k < length()
// postcondition: returns copy of the kth character
{
    if (k < 0 || myLength <= k)
    {
        cerr << "index out of range: " << k << " string: " << myCstring
            << endl;
        assert(0 <= k && k < myLength);
    }
    return myCstring[k];
}


char apstring::operator[](int k) const
// precondition:  0 <= k < length()
// postcondition: returns copy of the kth character
{
    if (k < 0 || myLength <= k)
    {
        cerr << "index out of range: " << k << " string: " << myCstring
            <<endl;
        assert(0 <= k && k < myLength);
    }
    return myCstring[k];
}


ostream& operator <<(ostream & os, const apstring & str)
//postcondition: str is written to output stream os
```

```
{
    return os << str.c_str();
}

istream& operator >>(istream & is, apstring & str)
//precondition:  input stream is open for reading
//postcondition: the next string from input stream is has been read
//               and stored in str
{
    char buf[MAX_LENGTH];
    is >> buf;
    str = buf;
    return is;
}

istream & getline(istream & is, apstring & str)
//description:   reads a line from input stream is into the string str
//precondition:  input stream is open for reading
//postcondition: chars from input stream is up to '\n' have been read
{
    char buf[MAX_LENGTH];
    is.getline(buf,MAX_LENGTH);
    str = buf;
    return is;
}

const apstring& apstring::operator +=(const apstring & str)
//postcondition: concatenates a copy of str onto this string
{

    apstring copystring(str);          // copy to avoid aliasing problems

    int newLength = length() + str.length(); // self + added string
    int lastLocation = length();          // index of '\0'

    // check to see if local buffer not big enough
    if (newLength >= myCapacity)
    {
        myCapacity = newLength + 1;
        char * newBuffer = new char[myCapacity];
        strcpy(newBuffer,myCstring); // copy into new buffer
        delete [] myCstring;          // delete old string
        myCstring = newBuffer;
    }

    // now concatenate str (copystring) to end of myCstring
    strcpy(myCstring+lastLocation,copystring.c_str() );
    myLength = newLength;                 // update information

    return *this;
}
```

```
const apstring & apstring::operator += ( char ch )
// postcondition: concatenates a copy of ch onto this string
{
    apstring temp;          // make string equivalent of ch
    temp = ch;
    *this += temp;
    return *this;
}

apstring operator +(const apstring & lhs, const apstring & rhs)
// postcondition: returns concatenation of lhs with rhs
{
    apstring result(lhs);       // copies lhs to result
    result += rhs;       // concatenate rhs
    return result;       // returns a copy of result
}

apstring operator + ( char ch, const apstring & str )
// postcondition: returns concatenation of ch with str
{
    apstring result;     // make string equivalent of ch
    result = ch;
    result += str;
    return result;
}
apstring operator + ( const apstring & str, char ch )
// postcondition: returns concatenation of str with ch
{
    apstring result(str);
    result += ch;
    return result;
}

apstring apstring::substr(int pos, int len) const
//description:    extract and return the substring of length len starting
//                at index pos
//precondition:   this string represents c0, c1, ..., c(n-1)
//                0 <= pos <= pos + len - 1 < n.
//postcondition: returns the string that represents
//                c(pos), c(pos+1), ..., c(pos+len-1)
//
{
    if (pos <0)                             // start at front when pos < 0
    {
        pos = 0;
    }

    if (pos >= myLength) return "";      // empty string

    int lastIndex = pos + len - 1;       // last char's index (to copy)
    if (lastIndex >= myLength)           // off end of string?
```

```
    {
        lastIndex = myLength-1;
    }

    apstring result(*this);                 // make sure enough space allocated

    int j,k;
    for(j=0,k=pos; k <= lastIndex; j++,k++)
    {
        result.myCstring[j] = myCstring[k];
    }
    result.myCstring[j] = '\0';             // properly terminate C-string
    result.myLength = j;                    // record length properly
    return result;
}

int apstring::find(const apstring & str) const
//description:    find the first occurrence of the string str within this
//               string and return the index of the first character. If
//               str does not occur in this string, then return npos.
//precondition:  this string represents c0, c1, ..., c(n-1)
//               str represents s0, s1, ..., s(m-1)
//postcondition: if s0 == ck0, s1 == ck1, ..., s(m-1) == ck(m-1) and
//               there is no j < k0 such that s0 = cj, ...., sm == c(j+m-1),
//               then returns k0;
//               otherwise returns npos
{
    int len = str.length();
    int lastIndex = length() - len;
    int k;
    for(k=0; k <= lastIndex; k++)
    {
        if (strncmp(myCstring + k,str.c_str(),len) == 0) return k;
    }
    return npos;
}

int apstring::find( char ch ) const
// description:    finds the first occurrence of the character ch within this
//               string and returns the index. If ch does not occur in this
//               string, then returns npos.
// precondition:  this string represents c0, c1, ..., c(n-1)
// postcondition: if ch == ck, and there is no j < k such that ch == cj
//               then returns k;
//               otherwise returns npos
{
    int k;
    for(k=0; k < myLength; k++)
    {
        if (myCstring[k] == ch)
        {
```

```
            return k;
        }
    }
    return npos;
}

bool operator == ( const apstring & lhs, const apstring & rhs )
{
    return strcmp(lhs.c_str(), rhs.c_str()) == 0;
}

bool operator != ( const apstring & lhs, const apstring & rhs )
{
    return ! (lhs == rhs);
}

bool operator <  ( const apstring & lhs, const apstring & rhs )
{
    return strcmp(lhs.c_str(), rhs.c_str()) < 0;
}

bool operator <= ( const apstring & lhs, const apstring & rhs )
{
    return lhs < rhs || lhs == rhs;
}

bool operator >  ( const apstring & lhs, const apstring & rhs )
{
    return rhs < lhs;
}

bool operator >= ( const apstring & lhs, const apstring & rhs )
{
    return rhs <= lhs;
}
```

The apvector Class

```
// File: apvector.h

#ifndef _APVECTOR_H
#define _APVECTOR_H


// ******************************************************************
// APCS vector class template
//
// implements "safe" (range-checked) arrays
// examples are given at the end of this file
// ******************************************************************
```

```
template <class itemType>
class apvector
{
  public:

  // constructors/destructor
    apvector( );                           // default constructor (size==0)
    apvector( int size );                  // initial size of vector is size
    apvector( int size, const itemType & fillValue ); // all entries == fillValue
    apvector( const apvector & vec );      // copy constructor
    ~apvector( );                          // destructor

  // assignment
    const apvector & operator = ( const apvector & vec );

  // accessors
    int  length( ) const;                      // capacity of vector

  // indexing
    itemType &        operator [ ] ( int index );        // indexing with range
checking
    const itemType & operator [ ] ( int index ) const; // indexing with range
checking

  // modifiers
    void resize( int newSize );                // change size dynamically;
                                               // can result in losing values
  private:

    int  mySize;                           // # elements in array
    itemType * myList;                     // array used for storage
};

// ****************************************************************
//   Specifications for vector functions
//
//   The template parameter itemType must satisfy the following two conditions:
//     (1) itemType has a 0-argument constructor
//     (2) operator = is defined for itemType
//   Any violation of these conditions may result in compilation failure.
//
//   Any violation of a function's precondition will result in an error message
//   followed by a call to abort.
//
//   constructors/destructor
//
//     apvector( )
//       postcondition: vector has a capacity of 0 items, and therefore it will
//                      need to be resized
//
```

```
//   apvector( int size )
//      precondition: size >= 0
//      postcondition: vector has a capacity of size items
//
//   apvector( int size, const itemType & fillValue )
//      precondition: size >= 0
//      postcondition: vector has a capacity of size items, all of which are set
//                        by assignment to fillValue after default construction
//
//   apvector( const apvector & vec )
//      postcondition: vector is a copy of vec
//
//   ~apvector ( )
//      postcondition: vector is destroyed
//
/;  assignment
//
//   const apvector & operator = ( const apvector & rhs )
//      postcondition: normal assignment via copying has been performed;
//                        if vector and rhs were different sizes, vector
//                        has been resized to match the size of rhs
//
//   accessor
//
//   int  length( ) const
//      postcondition: returns vector's size (number of memory cells
//                        allocated for vector)
//
//   indexing
//
//   itemType &         operator [ ] ( int k)          -- index into nonconst vector
//   const itemType & operator [ ] ( int k ) const -- index into const vector
//      description: range-checked indexing, returning kth item
//      precondition: 0 <= k < length()
//      postcondition: returns the kth item
//
//   modifier
//
//   void resize( int newSize )
//      description:  resizes the vector to newSize elements
//      precondition: the current capacity of vector is length; newSize >= 0
//
//      postcondition: the current capacity of vector is newSize; for each k
//                        such that 0 <= k <= min(length, newSize), vector[k]
//                        is a copy of the original; other elements of vector are
//                        initialized using the 0-argument itemType constructor
//                        Note: if newSize < length, elements may be lost
//
//   examples of use
//       apvector<int> v1;           // 0-element vector
```

```
//       apvector<int> v2(4);      // 4-element vector
//       apvector<int> v3(4, 22);  // 4-element vector, all elements == 22.

#endif

//   File: apvector.cpp

// *****************************************************************
//   APCS vector class   IMPLEMENTATION
//
//   see vector.h for complete documentation of functions
//
//   vector class consistent with a subset of the standard C++ vector class
//   as defined in the draft ANSI standard (part of standard template library)
// *****************************************************************

#include <stdlib.h>
#include <assert.h>
#include <iostream.h>
#include "apvector.h"

template <class itemType>
apvector<itemType>::apvector()
// postcondition: vector has a capacity of 0 items, and therefore it will
//                need to be resized
    : mySize(0),
      myList(0)
{

}


template <class itemType>
apvector<itemType>::apvector(int size)
// precondition: size >= 0
// postcondition: vector has a capacity of size items
    : mySize(size),
      myList(new itemType[size])
{

}


template <class itemType>
apvector<itemType>::apvector(int size, const itemType & fillValue)
// precondition: size >= 0
// postcondition: vector has a capacity of size items, all of which are set
//                by assignment to fillValue after default construction
    : mySize(size),
      myList(new itemType[size])
{
    int k;
```

```
    for(k = 0; k < size; k++)
    {
        myList[k] = fillValue;
    }
}

template <class itemType>
apvector<itemType>::apvector(const apvector<itemType> & vec)
// postcondition: vector is a copy of vec
    : mySize(vec.length()),
      myList(new itemType[mySize])
{
    int k;
        // copy elements
    for(k = 0; k < mySize; k++)
    {
        myList[k] = vec.myList[k];
    }
}

template <class itemType>
apvector<itemType>::~apvector ()
// postcondition: vector is destroyed
{
    delete [] myList;
}

template <class itemType>
const apvector<itemType> &
apvector<itemType>::operator = (const apvector<itemType> & rhs)
// postcondition: normal assignment via copying has been performed;
//                if vector and rhs were different sizes, vector
//                has been resized to match the size of rhs
{
    if (this != &rhs)                              // don't assign to self!
    {
        delete [] myList;                          // get rid of old storage
        mySize = rhs.length();
        myList = new itemType [mySize];            // allocate new storage

            // copy rhs
        int k;
        for(k=0; k < mySize; k++)
        {
            myList[k] = rhs.myList[k];
        }
    }
    return *this;                                  // permit a = b = c = d
}

template <class itemType>
int apvector<itemType>::length() const
```

```
// postcondition: returns vector's size (number of memory cells
//                 allocated for vector)
{
    return mySize;
}


template <class itemType>
itemType & apvector<itemType>::operator [] (int k)
// description: range-checked indexing, returning kth item
// precondition: 0 <= k < length()
// postcondition: returns the kth item
{

    if (k < 0 || mySize <= k)
    {
        cerr << "Illegal vector index: " << k < < " max index = ";
        cerr << mySize-1 << endl;
        abort();
    }
    return myList[k];
}


template <class itemType>
const itemType & apvector<itemType>::operator [] (int k) const
// safe indexing, returning const reference to avoid modification
// precondition: 0 <= index < length
// postcondition: return index-th item
// exception: aborts if index is out of bounds
{
    if (k < 0 || mySize <= k)
    {
        cerr << "Illegal vector index: " << k << " max index = ";
        cerr << mySize-1 << endl;
        abort();
    }
    return myList[k];
}


template <class itemType>
void apvector<itemType>::resize(int newSize)
// description:  resizes the vector to newSize elements
// precondition:  the current capacity of vector is length(); newSize >= 0
// postcondition: the current capacity of vector is newSize; for each k
//                such that 0 <= k <= min(length, newSize), vector[k]
//                is a copy of the original; other elements of vector are
//                initialized using the 0-argument itemType constructor
//                Note: if newSize < length, elements may be lost
{
    int k;
    int numToCopy = newSize < mySize ? newSize : mySize;
```

```
                // allocate new storage and copy element into new storage

      itemType * newList = new itemType[newSize];
      for(k=0; k < numToCopy; k++)
      {
          newList[k] = myList[k];
      }
      delete [] myList;                        // deallocate old storage
      mySize = newSize;                        // assign new storage/size
      myList = newList;
}
```

The apmatrix Class

```
// File: apmatrix.h

#ifndef _APMATRIX_H
#define _APMATRIX_H
#include "apvector.h"

// ****************************************************************
// APCS matrix class
//
// extends apvector.h to two-dimensional "safe" (range-checked) matrices
// examples are given at the end of this file
// ****************************************************************

template <class itemType>
class apmatrix
{
  public:

  // constructors/destructor
    apmatrix( );                              // default size 0 x 0
    apmatrix( int rows, int cols );           // size rows x cols
    apmatrix( int rows, int cols,
            const itemType & fillValue );     // all entries == fillValue
    apmatrix( const apmatrix & mat );         // copy constructor
    ~apmatrix( );                             // destructor

  // assignment
    const apmatrix & operator = ( const apmatrix & rhs );

  // accessors
    int numrows( ) const;                     // number of rows
    int numcols( ) const;                     // number of columns

  // indexing
    const apvector<itemType> & operator [ ] ( int k ) const;  // range-checked
indexing
```

```
   apvector<itemType> & operator [ ] ( int k );              // range-checked
indexing

  // modifiers
    void resize( int newRows, int newCols );    // resizes matrix to newRows x
                                                // newCols
                                                // (can result in losing values)
  private:

    int myRows;                                 // # of rows (capacity)
    int myCols;                                 // # of cols (capacity)
    apvector<apvector<itemType> > myMatrix;     // the matrix of items
};

// ****************************************************************
// Specifications for matrix functions
//
// To use this class, itemType must satisfy the same constraints
// as for vector class.
//
// Any violation of a function's precondition will result in an error message
// followed by a call to abort.
//
// constructors/destructor
//
//   apmatrix( );
//      postcondition: matrix of size 0x0 is constructed, and therefore
//                      will need to be resized later
//
//   apmatrix( int rows, int cols );
//      precondition: 0 <= rows and 0 <= cols
//      postcondition: matrix of size rows x cols is constructed
//
//   apmatrix( int rows, int cols, const itemType & fillValue );
//      precondition: 0 <= rows and 0 <= cols
//      postcondition: matrix of size rows x cols is constructed
//                      all entries are set by assignment to fillValue after
//                      default construction
//
//   apmatrix( const apmatrix<itemType> & mat );
//      postcondition: matrix is a copy of mat
//
//   ~apmatrix( );
//      postcondition: matrix is destroyed
//
// assignment
//
//   const apmatrix & operator = ( const apmatrix & rhs );
//      postcondition: normal assignment via copying has been performed
//                      (if matrix and rhs were different sizes, matrix has
//                      been resized to match the size of rhs)
```

```
//
// accessors
//
//   int numrows( ) const;
//       postcondition: returns number of rows
//
//   int numcols( ) const;
//       postcondition: returns number of columns
//
// indexing
//
//   const apvector<itemType> & operator [ ] ( int k ) const;
//       precondition: 0 <= k < number of rows
//       postcondition: returns k-th row
//
//   apvector<itemType> & operator [ ] ( int k );
//       precondition: 0 <= k < number of rows
//       postcondition: returns k-th row
//
// modifiers
//
//   void resize( int newRows, int newCols );
//       precondition: matrix size is rows x cols,
//                     0 <= newRows and 0 <= newCols
//       postcondition: matrix size is newRows x newCols;
//                     for each 0 <= j <= min(rows,newRows) and
//                     for each 0 <= k <= min(cols,newCols), matrix[j][k] is
//                     a copy of the original; other elements of matrix are
//                     initialized using the default constructor for itemType
//                     Note: if newRows < rows or newCols < cols,
//                          elements may be lost
//
//   Examples of use:
//
//       apmatrix<double> dmat( 100, 80 );        // 100 x 80 matrix of doubles
//       apmatrix<double> dzmat( 100, 80, 0.0 );  // initialized to 0.0
//       apmatrix<apstring> smat( 300, 1 );       // 300 strings
//       apmatrix<int> imat;                      // has room for 0 ints


#endif


//File: apmatrix.cpp

// ******************************************************************
//  APCS matrix class   IMPLEMENTATION
//
//  see matrix.h for complete documentation of functions
//
//  extends vector class to two-dimensional matrices
//  ******************************************************************
```

```cpp
#include "apmatrix.h"
#include <stdlib.h>
#include <iostream.h>

template <class itemType>
apmatrix<itemType>::apmatrix()
        : myRows(0),
          myCols(0),
          myMatrix(0)

// postcondition: matrix of size 0x0 is constructed, and therefore
//                will need to be resized later
{

}
template <class itemType>
apmatrix<itemType>::apmatrix(int rows, int cols)
        : myRows(rows),
          myCols(cols),
          myMatrix(rows)

// precondition: 0 <= rows and 0 <= cols
// postcondition: matrix of size rows x cols is constructed
{
    int k;
    for(k=0; k < rows; k++)
    {
        myMatrix[k].resize(cols);
    }
}

template <class itemType>
apmatrix<itemType>::apmatrix(int rows, int cols, const itemType & fillValue)
        : myRows(rows),
          myCols(cols),
          myMatrix(rows)

// precondition: 0 <= rows and 0 <= cols
// postcondition: matrix of size rows x cols is constructed
//                all entries are set by assignment to fillValue after
//                default construction
//
{
    int j,k;
    for(j=0; j < rows; j++)
    {
        myMatrix[j].resize(cols);
        for(k=0; k < cols; k++)
        {
            myMatrix[j][k] = fillValue;
        }
```

```
    }
}

template <class itemType>
apmatrix<itemType>::apmatrix(const apmatrix<itemType> & mat)
    : myRows(mat.myRows),
      myCols(mat.myCols),
      myMatrix(mat.myRows)

// postcondition: matrix is a copy of mat
{
    int k;
    // copy elements
    for(k = 0; k < myRows; k++)
    {
        // cast to avoid const problems (const -> non-const)
        myMatrix[k] = (apvector<itemType> &) mat.myMatrix[k];
    }
}

template <class itemType>
apmatrix<itemType>::~apmatrix ()
// postcondition: matrix is destroyed
{
    // vector destructor frees everything
}

template <class itemType>
const apmatrix<itemType> &
apmatrix<itemType>::operator = (const apmatrix<itemType> & rhs)
// postcondition: normal assignment via copying has been performed
//                (if matrix and rhs were different sizes, matrix has
//                been resized to match the size of rhs)
{
    if (this != &rhs)                      // don't assign to self!
    {
        myMatrix.resize(rhs.myRows);       // resize to proper # of rows
        myRows = rhs.myRows;               // set dimensions
        myCols = rhs.myCols;

        // copy rhs
        int k;
        for(k=0; k < myRows; k++)
        {
          myMatrix[k] = rhs.myMatrix[k];
        }
    }
    return *this;
}

template <class itemType>
```

```
int apmatrix<itemType>::numrows() const
// postcondition: returns number of rows
{
    return myRows;
}

template <class itemType>
int apmatrix<itemType>::numcols() const
// postcondition: returns number of columns
{
    return myCols;
}

template <class itemType>
void apmatrix<itemType>::resize(int newRows, int newCols)
// precondtiion: matrix size is rows x cols,
//                 0 <= newRows and 0 <= newCols
// postcondition: matrix size is newRows x newCols;
//                 for each 0 <= j <= min(rows,newRows) and
//                 for each 0 <= k <= min(cols,newCols), matrix[j][k] is
//                 a copy of the original; other elements of matrix are
//                 initialized using the default constructor for itemType
//                 Note: if newRows < rows or newCols < cols,
//                     elements may be lost
//
{
    int k;
    myMatrix.resize(newRows);

    for(k=0; k < newRows; k++)
    {
        myMatrix[k].resize(newCols);
    }
    myRows = newRows;
    myCols = newCols;
}

template <class itemType>
const apvector<itemType> &
apmatrix<itemType>::operator [] (int k) const
// precondition: 0 <= k < number of rows
// postcondition: returns k-th row
{
    if (k < 0 || myRows <= k)
    {
        cerr << "Illegal matrix index: " << k << " max index = ";
        cerr << myRows-1 << endl;
        abort();
    }
    return myMatrix[k];
}
```

```
template <class itemType>
apvector<itemType> &
apmatrix<itemType>::operator [] (int k)
// precondition: 0 <= k < number of rows
// postcondition: returns k-th row
{
    if (k < 0 || myRows <= k)
    {
        cerr << "Illegal matrix index: " << k << " max index = ";
        cerr << myRows-1 << endl;
        abort();
    }
    return myMatrix[k];
}
```

Answers To Selected Exercises

This section contains answers to selected exercises from the exercise sets at the end of each section. In general, answers to odd-numbered problems are given.

CHAPTER 2

Section 2.1

1. a and c are effective statements.
   b is not effective because you cannot determine when to perform the action.
   d is not effective because there is no smallest positive fraction.
   e is not effective because you cannot determine in advance which stocks will increase in value.

3. a. 1. Select a topic
   2. Research the topic
   3. Outline the paper
   4. Refine the outline
   5. Write the rough draft
   6. Read and revise the rough draft
   7. Write the final paper

   c. 1. Get a list of colleges
   2. Examine criteria (programs, distance, money, and so on)
   3. Screen to a manageable number
   4. Obtain further information
   5. Make a decision

5. First-level development
   1. Get information for first employee
   2. Perform computations for first employee
   3. Print results for first employee
   4. ⎫
   5. ⎬ Repeat for second employee
   6. ⎭
   Second-level development
   1. Get information for first employee
       1.1 Get hourly wage
       1.2 Get number of hours worked
   2. Perform computations for first employee
       2.1 Compute gross pay
       2.2 Compute deductions
       2.3 Compute net pay
   3. Print results for first employee
       3.1 Print input data
       3.2 Print gross pay

   3.3 Print deductions
   3.4 Print net pay
   4. ⎫
   5. ⎬ Repeat for second employee
   6. ⎭
   Third-level development
   1. Get information for first employee
       1.1 Get hourly wage
       1.2 Get number of hours worked
   2. Perform computations for first employee
       2.1 Compute gross pay
       2.2 Compute deductions
           2.2.1 Federal withholding
           2.2.2 State withholding
           2.2.3 Social security
           2.2.4 Union dues
           2.2.5 Compute total deductions
               2.3 Compute net pay
                   2.3.1 Subtract total deductions from gross
   3. Print results for first employee
       3.1 Print input data
           3.1.1 Print hours worked
           3.1.2 Print hourly wage
       3.2 Print gross pay
       3.3 Print deductions
           3.3.1 Print federal withholding
           3.3.2 Print state withholding
           3.3.3 Print social security
           3.3.4 Print union dues
           3.3.5 Print total deductions
       3.4 Print net pay
   4. ⎫
   5. ⎬ Repeat for second employee
   6. ⎭

7. There are several ways to solve this problem, one of which follows:
   1. Get the numbers as input
   2. Put them in order: Small, Large
   3. Check for a divisor
       3.1 If small is a divisor of large
           3.1.1 gcd is small
           else
               3.1.2 Decrease small until a common divisor is found

4. Print the results

   3.1.2 can be further refined as

      3.1.2 Decrease small until a common divisor is found

         3.1.2.2 Do

               If **gcd_andidate** is a common divisor

                  gcd is **gcd_candidate**

               Else

                  Decrease **gcd_candidate** by 1

               While a common divisor is not found

Section 2.2

3. a is valid.

  b is a Pascal program heading.

  c is missing a return type and should omit parameters.

  d is missing a return type and should use lowercase letters.

5. a. **const char GENDER = 'F';**

  b. **const int AGE = 18;**

  c. **const double PI = 3.1416;**

Section 2.3

1. a, d, e, and g are valid.

  b has a decimal.

  c has a comma.

  f is probably larger than **INT_MAX**

3. a. 1.73E2

  b. 7.43927E11

  c. −2.3E-8

  d. 1.4768E1

  e. −5.2E0

5. a and d are integers.

  b, c, and g are reals.

  e and f are string literals.

7. a.
```
cout << setw(14) <<   "Score" << endl
     << endl;
cout << setw(13) << 86 << endl;
cout << setw(13) << 82 << endl;
cout << setw(13) << 79 << endl;
```
  b.
```
cout << setw(54) <<   "Price" << endl
     << endl;
cout << setw(54) << "$"   <<  setw(7)
     << 19.94 << endl;
cout << setw(53) << "$"   <<  setw(7)
     << 100.65 << endl;
cout << setw(54) << "$"   <<  setw(7)
     << 58.95 << endl;
```

CHAPTER 3

Section 3.1

1. a. 11   f. −64

  b. −49   g. 48

  c. 3   h. 108

  d. 24   i. −2

  e. 120   j. 7

3. a, b, c, f, g, and j are valid, type integer.

  e, h, and i are valid, type float.

  d is invalid.

5. Output will vary according to local implementation.

Section 3.2

1. a, b, c, e, f, and h are valid assignment statements.

  d is invalid. An operand cannot be on the left of an assignment statement.

  g is invalid. IQ/3 is a float.

3. a.

3	−5
A	B

  b.

26	31
A	B

  c.

−3	−5
A	B

  d.

9	9
A	B

5.
```
Gender       M
Age          23
Height       73 inches
Weight       186.5 lbs
```

7. column 11
```
*****************************
*                           *
*   Name      Age    Gender  *
*   ----      ---    ------   *
*   Jones     21       M     *
*                           *
*****************************
```

9.   column 10
```
           This reviews string formatting.
When a letterA is used,
           Oops! I forgot to format.
           When a letter A is used,
           it is a string of length one.
```

Section 3.3

1. **cin** is the name of the standard input stream. This stream is connected to the keyboard and allows data to be input from the user. **cout** is the name of the standard output stream. This stream is connected to the terminal screen, and allows data to be output to the user.

Section 3.4

1. a. ```cout << first;```
   b. ```third = first;```
   c. ```first = "";```
      ```second = "";```
      ```third = "";```
   d. ```cout << "Enter first string: ";```
      ```cin >> first;```
      ```cout << "Enter second string: ";```
      ```cin >> second;```
      ```cout << "Enter third string: ";```
      ```cin >> third;```

3. a. **word1** contains "567".
   b. **word1** contains " 567 is a small number".
   c. **number** contains 567.
   d. **number** contains 567 and **word1** contains "is".
   e. **number** contains 567 and **word1** contains " is a small number".
   f. **number** contains 567, **word1** contains " is a small number", and the computer waits for a second line of input.

5. a, b, and e are valid.
   c is invalid, because a string and a number do not concatenate.
   d is invalid, because at least one of the operands must be a string.

Section 3.5

3. a. ```const double PI = 3.1416;```
   b. ```const int CENT_TO_FAHR = 32;```
   c. ```const int RIGHT_ANGLE = 90;```
   d. ```const char LAST_LOWER_LETTER = 'z';```
      ```const char LAST_UPPER_LETTER = 'Z';```

Section 3.6

3. A programmer must know a function's name, the number, positions, and types of its formal parameters, and its return type in order to use it correctly.

Section 3.7

3. a. ```sqrt(a * a + b * b)```
   b. ```(- b + sqrt(b * b - 4 * a * c)) / (2 * a)```
      ```(- b - sqrt(b * b - 4 * a * c)) / (2 * a)```

7. ```
#include <iostream.h>

int main()
{
    for (int ascii_value = 'A'; ascii_value <= 'Z'; ++ascii_value)
        cout << char(ascii_value) << " " << ascii_value << endl;
    return 0;
}
```

Section 3.8

1. Relative coordinates specify the horizontal and vertical distances to move or draw from a given point. Absolute coordinates specify the coordinates of the destination point of a movement or drawing operation. **moveto(100, 100)** asks the pen to move to the point specified by the coordinates. **moverel(100, 100)** asks the pen to move the distances specified by the coordinates from the pen's current position.

3. a. ```moveto(150, 185);```
   b. ```lineto(110, 95);```
   c. ```moveto(20, 95);```
   d. ```lineto(95, 45);```

CHAPTER 4

Section 4.2

1. c and d are valid.
   a has no types for the parameters.
   b has no return type.
7. Parameters allow the user of a function to specify the data on which the function will operate.
9. General functions can be used in many different situations. Thus, a separate function does not have to be written for each new situation.

Section 4.3

1. a. Both parameters should be declared as reference parameters rather than value parameters.
   b. **width** should be declared as a value parameter rather than a reference parameter.
   c. **radius** should be declared as a value parameter rather than a reference parameter.
3. When a data object is passed as a value parameter to a function, a copy of the object is made and placed in a temporary storage location for the use of the function. Thus, changes to the parameter will not result in changes to the original data object. When a data object is passed as a reference parameter to a function, the name of the parameter and the name of the data object refer to the same storage location. Thus, changes to the parameter will result in changes to the original data object. When a data object is passed as a constant reference parameter to a function, the name of the parameter and the name of the data object refer to the same storage location. However, the compiler disallows assignments to the parameter inside the function, so no changes to the original object can occur.

Section 4.5

1. Global identifiers can be referenced from any point below their declaration in a program, unless they are redeclared as local identifiers. Local identifiers can be referenced from any point below their declaration in a program block (a region of text bounded by the symbols { and }), unless they are redeclared in a nested block.
3. Constants and functions are appropriate uses of global identifiers.
7. Identifiers for this program are represented schematically by the figure shown here.

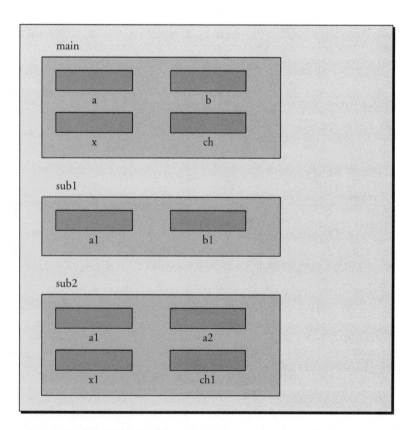

9. **10**
   20
   10

11. There are several syntax errors. **x1** is not visible in the main program block. **x** cannot be used as an actual parameter for function **sub1**, because **x** is a **double** and **sub1** expects an **int** as a parameter. **x** and **y** are not visible in the block of **sub1**.

Section 4.6

1. Users of these functions can access them simply by including the library in which they are defined, rather than copying the code from the functions into their own module. Also, when these functions are modified, users need only recompile their modules, rather than make the changes themselves.

3. **#include** instructs the preprocessor to include the source code from the argument file at the beginning of the current file. When the preprocessor encounters **#ifndef <symbol>** in an included file, it determines whether or not **<symbol>** has been defined. If so, the segment of the included file between **#ifndef** and **#endif** is skipped. If not, the segment is processed. During this processing, the preprocessor normally encounters **#define <symbol>**. Thus, if another module attempts to include the same file, the preprocessor will not process it again.

CHAPTER 5

Section 5.1

1. 1 1 0
   0

3. a and b are TRUE.
   c and d are FALSE.

Section 5.2

1. a. 10   5
   b. no output
   c. 5   Since **b** has no value, the result will vary.
   d. 10   5
   e. 15   4
      15   4
   f. 10   5

3. a. No error.
   b. **3 < x < 10** cannot be evaluated. This should be **(3 < x) && (x < 10)**.
   c. The two statements following the condition should be enclosed in braces:

```
if (a > 0)
{
     count = count + 1;
     sum = sum + a;
}
```

5. Yes.

9.
```
{
     cin >> num1 >> num2 >> num3;
     total = total + num1 + num2 + num3;
     cout << num1 << " " << num2 << " " << num3 << endl;
     cout << endl;
     cout << total << endl;
}
```

11.
```
cin >> ch1 >> ch2 >> ch3;
if (ch1 <= ch2) && (ch2 <= ch3)
     cout << ch1 << ch2 << ch3 << endl;
```

Section 5.3

1. a. **-14**
   b. **5025**
      175
   c. **105**
      50

Section 5.4

1. a. 38.15   763.0
   b. −21.0   21.0
   c. 600.0   1200.0
   d. 3000.0   9000.0
3. a.
```
if (ch == 'M')
    if (sum > 1000)
        x = x + 1;
    else
        x = x + 2;
else if (ch == 'F')
    if (sum > 1000)
        x = x + 3;
    else
        x = x + 5;
```
   b.
```
cin >> num;
if (num > 0)
    if (num <= 10000)
    {
        count = count + 1;
        sum = sum + num;
    }
    else
        cout << setw(27) << "Value out of range" << endl;
```
   c.
```
if (a > 0)
    if (b > 0)
        cout << setw(22) << "Both positive" << endl;
    else
        cout << setw(22) << "Some negative" << endl;
```
   d.
```
if (c < 0)
    if (a > 0)
        if (b > 0))
            cout << setw(19) << "Option one" << endl;
        else
            cout << setw(19) << "Option two" << endl;
    else
        cout << setw(19) << "Option two" << endl;
else
    cout << setw(19) << "Option one" << endl;
```
7. 8   13   104
     a   b   c

Section 5.5

3. a. Statement has semicolon rather than colon after third label and list of values as last label.
   b. Statement has no colon after first label, no semicolon after third label, and a list of values as last label.
   c. Statement has list of values as first label.
   d. Reserved word **case** is missing from all labels.
   e. Cases for 2 and 1 are missing statements.

CHAPTER 6

Section 6.2

1. a.
```
*
 *
  *
   *
    *
     *
```

b.

```
 1 :      9
 2 :      8
 3 :      7
 4 :      6
 5 :      5
 6 :      4
 7 :      3
 8 :      2
 9 :      1
10 :      0
```

c.

```
 2
 3
 4
 5
 6
 7
 8
 9
10
11
12
13
14
15
16
17
18
19
20
```

d.

```
 1
 2
 3
 4
 5
 6
 7
 8
 9
10
11
12
13
14
15
16
17
18
19
20
21
```

3. a.
```
for (int j = 1; j <= 4; ++j)
    cout << " *" << endl;
```
b.
```
for (int j = 1; j <= 4; ++j)
    cout << setw(j + 3) << "***" << endl;
```
c.
```
cout << setw(6) << "*" << endl;
for (int j = 1; j <= 3; ++j)
    cout << setw(6 - j) << "*" setw(2 * j) << "*" << endl;
cout << "**** ****" << endl;
for (int j = 1; j <= 2; ++j)
    cout << setw(7) << "* *" << endl;
cout << setw(7) << "***" << endl;
```
d. This is a "look ahead" problem that can be solved by a loop within a loop. This idea is developed in Section 5.6.

```
for (int j = 5; j >= 1; --j)
{
    cout << setw(6 - j)<< " ";            // Indent a line
    for (int k = 1; k <= 2 * j - 1; ++k)  // Print a line
        cout << "*";
    cout << endl;
}
```

5. a.
```
for (int j = 1; j <= 5; ++j)
    cout << setw(3) << j;
for (int j = 5; j >= 1; --j)
    cout << setw(3) << 6 - j;
```
b.
```
for (int j = 1; j <= 5; ++j)
    cout << setw(j) << '*' << endl
for (int j = 5; j >= 1; --j)
    cout << setw(6 - j) << '*' << endl;
```

7.
```
for (j = 2; j <= 10; ++j)
    cout << setw(j) << j << endl;
```

Section 6.3

3. a.
```
1
2
3
4
5
6
7
```

```
        8
        9
       10
  b. 1    0
     2    1
     3    2
     4    1
     5    2
  c. 54   50
```

```
  d. The partial sum is    1
     The partial sum is    3
     The partial sum is    6
     The partial sum is   10
     The partial sum is   15
     The count is 5
  e. 96.00    2.00
```

5. a.
```
while (num > 0)
{
    cout << setw(10) << num << endl;
    num = num - .5;
}
```

Section 6.4

1. A pretest loop tests the Boolean expression before executing the loop. A post-test loop tests the Boolean expression after the loop has been executed.
3. a. This loop is infinite, because the value of **j** is never changed within the loop.
   b. This loop terminates.
   c. This loop is infinite, because the value of **a** will always be a power of 2, and thus never equal 20.
   d. This loop terminates.

Section 6.6

1. a.
```
for (int k = 1; k <= 5; ++k)
{
  cout << setw(k) << ' ';
  for (int j = k; j <= 5; ++j)
        cout << '*';
  cout << endl
}
```
   c.
```
for (int k = 1; k <= 7; ++k)
    if (k < 5)
    {
        for (int j = 1; j <= 3; ++j)
            cout << '*';
        cout << endl;
    }
    else
    {
        for (int j = 1; j <= 5; ++j)
            cout << '*';
        cout << endl;

    }
```

3.
```
4   5   6   7
4   5   6   7
4   5   6   7
4   5   6   7
5   6   7
5   6   7
5   6   7

6   7
6   7
```

Section 6.7

1. a. This is an infinite loop.
   b. The loop control variable, **k**, is unassigned once the **for** loop is exited. Thus, the attempt to use **k** in the expression **k % 3 = 0** may result in an error.

CHAPTER 7

Section 7.1

1. a. The first two input statements read the two data values from the file, and they are displayed by the first two output statements. The third input statement also reads the second data value, because the end of file has been reached. Thus, the third output statement displays the second data value also.
   b. The first data value is read before the loop starts. It is output on the first pass through the loop, because the end-of-file condition is not yet true. Then the second data value is read at the bottom of the loop. The end-of-file condition is not yet true, so the loop is entered once more, where the second data value is output. At the bottom of the loop, the second data value is read once more, and the end-of-file condition becomes true, forcing an exit from the top of the loop.
   c. Because the **>>** operator must be run three times before the end-of-file condition becomes true, three outputs will occur. Thus, the second data value in the file is output twice to the screen.
3. We use the **apstring** library for strings. Note that all input can be received as strings.

```
// Program file: person.cpp

#include <iostream.h>
#include <fstream.h>
#include <assert.h>
#include "apstring.h"

int main()
{
        apstring string_var;
        ifstream in_file;

        in_file.open("myfile");
        assert(! in_file.fail());
        in_file >> string_var;
        cout << "Name: " << string_var << endl;
        in_file >> string_var;
        cout << "Address: " << string_var << endl;
        in_file >> string_var;
        cout << "Age: " << string_var <<endl;
        in_file.close();
        assert(! in_file.fail());
        return 0;
}
```

5. Note that the data for the person's name is received from a priming input, and also is received at the bottom of the loop.

```
// Program file: persons.cpp

#include <iostream.h>
#include <fstream.h>
#include <assert.h>
#include "apstring.h"

int main()
{
        apstring string_var;
        ifstream in_file;

        in_file.open("myfile");
        assert(! in_file.fail());
        in_file >> string_var;
        while (! in_file.eof())
        {
```

```
                cout << "Name: " << string_var << endl;
                in_file >> string_var;
                cout << "Address: " << string_var << endl;
                in_file >> string_var;
                cout << "Age: " << string_var << endl;
                in_file >> string_var;
            }
            in_file.close();
            assert(! in_file.fail());
            return 0;
        }
```

Section 7.2

```
1. void count_words(ifstream &in_file)
   {
       apstring word;
       int word_count = 0;
       in_file >> word;
       while (! in_file.eof())
       {
           ++word_count;
           cout << word << endl;
           in_file >> word;
       }
    cout << "Word count = " << word_count << endl;
    }
3. void count_words_and_average(ifstream &in_file)
   {
       apstring word;
       int word_count = 0, char_count = 0, average = 0;
       in_file >> word;
       while (! in_file.eof())
       {
           ++word_count;
           char_count = char_count + word.length();
           in_file >> word;
       }
       if (word_count > 0)
           average = char_count / word_count;
       cout << "Average length = " << average << endl;
   }
```

5. Defining functions for opening and closing files hides the details associated with these tasks, such as prompting the user for file names.

Section 7.3

1. a. Three characters are read from the file and displayed on the screen.
   b. All of the characters are read from the file and displayed on the screen.
   c. If the file is initially empty, the data read and processed will be undefined; if the file has at least one value in it, the last value read will be undefined.

CHAPTER 8

Section 8.1

```
1. a. const int MAX_SCORES = 35;
     typedef int score_list[MAX_SCORES];
     score_listscores;
   b. const int MAX_PRICES = 20;
     typedef double price_list[MAX_PRICES];
     price_list prices;
   c. const int MAX_ANSWERS = 50;
     typedef boolean answer_list[MAX_ANSWERS];
     answer_list answers;
```

d. `const int MAX_GRADES = 4;`
   `typedef char grade_list[MAX_GRADES];`
   `grade_list grades;`

3. a, b, d, e, f, h, and l are valid.
   c. Will run, but displays the address of the array.
   g. Uses three indexes, but the array expects one.
   i. Attempts to input a value into the address of the array.
   j. `list[100]` is a range error.
   k. Type names cannot be indexed.

5. waist_sizes

34	0
36	1
32	2
30	3
33	4

7. `for (int i = 0; i < 10; ++i)`
   `     list[i] = 0.0;`

Section 8.2

1. a.   list

0	0
0	1
0	2
1	3
1	4

b.   list   scores

4	0		1	0
5	1		1	1
6	2		2	2
7	3		2	3
8	4		2	4

c.   answers

TRUE	0
FALSE	1
TRUE	2
FALSE	3
TRUE	4
FALSE	5
TRUE	6
FALSE	7
TRUE	8
FALSE	9

d.   initials

A	0
B	1
C	2
D	3
E	4
⋮	
S	20
T	19

3. The code counts the number of scores that are greater than 90.

5.
```
const int MAX_CHARS = 20;
typedef char name_type[MAX_CHARS];
name_type name;
int length = 0;
char ch;

cin >> ch;
while (ch != '\0')
{
    name[length] = ch;
    ++length;
    cin >> ch;
}
```

7.
```
for (int i = 0; i < 100; ++i)
    a[i] = 0;
```

9.
```
cout << "Test scores" << endl;
cout << "-----------" << endl;
for (int i = 0; i < 50; ++i)
    cout << setw(2) << i << ". " << setw(3) << test_scores[i] << endl;
```

Section 8.3

1. a is valid.

  b is invalid, because arrays are declared as reference parameters.

  c is valid.

  d is invalid, because arrays are declared as reference parameters.

  e is invalid, because a type name is used to declare a parameter name.

  f is valid.

  g is invalid, because **name** has not been defined as a type.

  h is valid.

  i is invalid, because **name** has not been defined as a type.

  j is invalid, because arrays are declared as reference parameters.

3. a.
```
void input_scores(int scores[]);
input_scores(scores);
```
  b.
```
int char_count(char name[], char ch);
number = char_count(name, 'A');
```
  c.
```
void score_data(int scores[], int &length, int &count_90);
score_data(scores, length, count_90);
```

5.
```
void array_data(int data[], int &max, int &min, int &neg_values)
{
    max = INT_MIN;          // Initial maximum value.
    min = INT_MAX;          // Initial minimum value.
    neg_values = 0;         // Initial count negative values.
    for (int i = 0; i < MAX_ARRAY_SIZE; ++i)
            if (data[i] > max)
                    max = data[i];
            if (data[i] < min)
                    min = data[i];
            if (data[i] < 0)
                    ++neg_values;
}
```

Section 8.4

1. First pass Second pass

–20	0		–20	0
10	1		–2	1
0	2		0	2
10	3		10	3
8	4		8	4
30	5		30	5
–2	6		10	6

3. We use a new function, **find_maximum**, that locates the largest value in the unsorted portion of the array. On each pass, the largest remaining value will be placed at the end of the sorted portion of the array. Thus, at the end of the process, the array will be sorted from high to low.

```
void sort(int a[ ], int length)
{
        int min_index = 0;

        for (int j = 0; j < length - 1; ++j)
        {
                min_index = find_maximum(a, j, length);
                if (min_index != j)
                        swap(a[j], a[min_index]);
        }
}
```

5.
```
void sort(int a[ ], int length, int &count)
{
        int min_index = 0;
        count = 0;
        for (int j = 0; j < length - 1; ++j)
        {
                min_index = find_minimum(a, j, length);
                if (min_index != j)
                {
                        swap(a[j], a[min_index]);
                        ++count;
                }
        }
}
```

7. The sort of the test scores will have no effect on the order of the names. If the test scores are all the same, then there will be no change in the meaning of the table. Otherwise, the names will no longer always be correlated with their test scores.

Section 8.5

1. `double table[5] [4];`
3. `int table[30] [12];`

CHAPTER 9

Section 9.1

1. Arrays are data structures having elements that must be of the same type and are accessed by specifying a numeric position value, ranging from 0 to the size of the array minus one. Structs are data structures whose elements can be of different types and are accessed by specifying member names.

3.
```
struct book
{
        apstring author, title, date;
        double price;
};
```

11. Defining a set of functions for each new data structure helps to modularize a program. This in turn enhances readability, correctness, and maintenance.

Section 9.2

1. A class allows a programmer to associate functions with data in such a way that the data can be accessed only by means of invoking the functions. By contrast, a data structure allows direct access to its components.

3. A default constructor creates an instance of a class and runs any code implemented in the function to initialize its data to default values. A constructor with user-specified initial values allows the user to supply values to an instance's data when it is created. A copy constructor is invoked automatically when an object is passed as a value parameter or returned as the value of a function. This constructor runs the code defined in its body to copy data values to a new object.

5. We assume that private data members **name** and **password** have been added to the class declaration, and that appropriate modifications have been made to the declarations of member functions **deposit**, **withdraw**, and **get_balance**. The implementations are updated as follows:

```
double account::deposit(double amount, const apstring &your_name,
        const apstring &your_password)
{
        if ((your_name == name) && (your_password == password))
        {
                balance = balance + amount;
                return balance;
        }
        else
                return 0;
}


double account::withdraw(double amount, const apstring &your_name,
        const apstring &your_password)
{
        if ((your_name == name) && (your_password == password))
                if (amount > balance)
                        return -1;
                else
                {
                        balance = balance - amount;
                        return balance;
                }
        else
                return 0;
}

double account::get_balance(const apstring &your_name,
        const apstring &your_password)
{
        if ((your_name == name) && (your_password == password))
                return balance;
        else
                return 0;
}
```

Section 9.3

3. Total number of operations = M times N.

5. The following implementations cover all of the possibilities. If the rational number is already in lowest terms, then the implementations can be simplified and made more efficient.

```
bool rational::whole_number()
{
        return (denominator == 1) || (numerator % denominator == 0);
}

int rational::make_int()
{
        if (denominator == 1)
```

```
            return numerator;
      else
            return numerator / denominator;
}
```

CHAPTER 10

Section 10.1

1. a. `apvector<int> int_vector(20);`
   b. `apvector<char> char_vector(100, 'a');`
   c. `apvector<person> person_vector(50);`
   d. `apvector<apvector<int> > twenty_by_twenty(20);`

3. One indexing operation is a const member function that returns the value stored at the index position. The other indexing operation returns a constant reference to the value stored at the index position. Because the second operation returns a constant reference or the address of a cell in the vector, the caller can modify the contents of the cell. Thus, the second operation cannot be used in functions to which vectors are passed by value or constant reference. The first operation can be used in such functions, but for access only.

Section 10.2

3. A string object is an instance of a class, which means that users are restricted to the operations defined by the string class. A C-style string is an array of characters. In general, string objects are safer and more convenient to use than C-style strings.

5. The following function makes use of the **ctype** library function **toupper**:

```
apstring make_uppercase(const apstring &str)
{
      apstring result(str);
      int len = str.length();
      for (int i = 0; i < len; ++i)
            result[i] = toupper(result[i]);
      return result;
}
```

Section 10.3

1. The physical size of an array is the number of cells of memory allocated for storing data in it. The logical size of the array is the number of data values currently stored in it that have meaning for a program.

3. The addition of a Boolean flag to the removal operation places a slight burden on the implementer and makes the operation's interface more complex. However, removals will be more efficient, in that only one search will be necessary to determine that the target is in the collection and to remove it.

9. The following free function concatenates two ordered collections:

```
template <class itemType>
ordered_collection<itemType> operator +
      (const ordered_collection<itemType> &lhs,
      const ordered_collection<itemType> &rhs)
{
      ordered_collection<itemType> result(lhs);      // Copy lhs
      for (int i = 0; i < rhs.length(); ++i)         // Copy rhs
            result.add_last(rhs[i]);
      return result;
}
```

Section 10.4

3. The subscript operator for ordered collections allows references to elements as *l*-values or as *r*-values. A sorted collection object should not allow references to elements as *l*-values, because clients could then store elements that might violate the ordering of the elements in the collection.

5. The following function converts an ordered collection to a sorted collection:

```
template <class itemType>
sorted_collection<itemType>::sorted_collection(const ordered_collection<itemType>&oc)
      : ordered_collection<itemType>()
  {
      for (int i = 0; i < oc.length(); ++i)
            add(oc[i]);
}
```

Section 10.5

3. Both index values would be checked after the subscript operations for the underlying vectors are invoked.
5. The following function returns the sum of the numbers in a matrix:

```
double sum(const apmatrix<double> &m)
{
        double result = 0;
        for (int row = 0; row < m.numrows(); ++row)
                for (int col = 0; col < m.numcols(); ++col)
                        sum = sum + m[row] [col];
        return result;
}
```

CHAPTER 11

Section 11.1

1. The total number of copies required to insert n data values from a file into the end of an ordered collection is $1 + 2 + 3 + \cdots + n$, or $1/2n^2 + 1/2n$.
3. Removal of a given data value requires the most work, in that a linear search for the value must be performed. Otherwise, n copies must be performed for all insertions and removals.

Section 11.2

1. Ordered collections and linked lists both represent linear sequences of data values. Ordered collections allow access to data elements in constant time. Linked lists allow access to data elements in linear time. Ordered collections are resized in linear time. Linked lists are resized in constant time.
3. The **at_end** operation returns **FALSE** when the current pointer is referencing a node in the list. Only in this case is it safe to access, modify, remove, or move to the next node.
5. The length of the list would have to be computed by counting the number of nodes, thus resulting in a linear process each time the length is requested.
7. One could redefine the assignment operator for a vector so that a linked list is the parameter and the contents of the list are copied to the end of the vector. This operation would be useful to transfer data after input from a file to a structure more suitable for fast access times during processing.

Section 11.3

3. An algorithm for an operation to add a data value to the end of a linked list follows:

> While not at the end of the list
> > Move to the next node
> Run the insert operation

5. An algorithm for a subscript operation for a linked list follows:

> Assert that 0 <= index < length of list
> Move to the first node
> While index > 0
> > Move to next node
> > Decrement index by 1
> Return the data value in the current node

Note that the operation should return a constant reference to the data value, so that users can target the data cell for assignment.

Section 11.4

1. An address is the label of a cell in memory. The value stored at an address is contained in the cell labeled by the address.
3. If ordered collections were implemented as linked lists, they would solve the data movement problem. However, users would lose random access to data in the collections, making operations such as binary search ineffective.

CHAPTER 12

Section 12.1

1. There is no stopping state.
3. a.   i. $y = 9.0$
      ii. $y = 8.0$

iii. $y = 256.0$

iv. $y = 1.0$

5.
```
int iter_factorial(int n)
{
    int partial_product = 1;

    for (int next_factor = 2; next_factor <= n; ++next_factor)
        partial_product = partial_product * next_factor;
    return partial_product;
}
```

Section 12.2

3. a. **num = 18**

	first	last	mid	a[mid]	found
Before loop	0	4	Undefined	Undefined	FALSE
After 1st pass	0	1	2	37	FALSE
After 2nd pass	0	1	0	18	TRUE

c. **num = 76**

	first	last	mid	a[mid]	found
Before loop	0	4	Undefined	Undefined	FALSE
After 1st pass	3	4	2	37	FALSE
After 2nd pass	3	2	3	92	

5.
```
int binsearch(element target, list_type list, int last)
{
    int first = 0, midpoint = 0;

    while (first <= last)
    {
        midpoint = (first + last) / 2;
        if (target == list[midpoint])
            return midpoint;
        else if (target > list[midpoint])
            first =  midpoint + 1;
        else
            last = midpoint - 1;
    }
    return -1;
}
```

Section 12.4

1.
```
int product(list_type list)
{
    if (empty_list(list))
        return 1;
    else
        return list->data * product(list->next);
}
```
3.
```
list_type search(list_type list, element e)
{
    if (empty_list(list))
        return 0;
    else if (list->data == e)
        return list;
    else
        return search(list->next);
}
```

Index

Credits

PHOTOS

Page 11–13 Figures 1.4, 1.5a, 1.5b, 1.5c, and 1.6b: Courtesy of International Business Machines Corporation. Unauthorized use not permitted.

Page 12–13 Figures 1.5d and 1.6a: Courtesy of Apple Computer, Inc.

Page 14 Figure 1.8: Robert A. Barclay

NOTES OF INTEREST

Page 5: Ethics and Computer Science
From the *Minneapolis Star/Tribune,* October 14, 1990, *The Washington Post* reprinted with permission.

Page 16: Why Learn C++
Richard P. Gabriel ("The end of history and the last programming language," *Journal of Object-Oriented Programming,* July-August, 1993).

Page 27: Software Verification
From Ivars Peterson, "Finding Fault: The Formidable Task of Eradicating Software Bugs," *SCIENCE NEWS,* February 16, 1991, Vol. 139. Reprinted with permission from *SCIENCE NEWS,* the weekly magazine of science. Copyright 1991 by Science Services, Inc.

Page 69: Herman Hollerith
Reprinted by permission from *Introduction to Computers with BASIC,* pp. 27-28, by Fred G. Harold. Copyright 1984 by West Publishing Company. All rights reserved. Photos courtesy of IBM Corporation.

Page 86: Communication Skills Needed
From P. Jackowitz, R. Plishka, J. Sidbury, J. Hartman, and C. White, *ACM Press SIGCSE Bulletin* 22, No. 1, (February, 1990). Copyright 1991, Association for Computing Machinery, Inc. Reprinted by permission of Association for Computing Machinery, Inc.

Page 96: Defined Constants and Space Shuttle Computing
Communications of the ACM 27, No. 9 (September, 1984); 880. Copyright 1984, Association for Computing Machinery, Inc. Reprinted by permission of Association for Computing Machinery, Inc.

Page 106: Computer Ethics:
Copyright, Intellectual Property, and Digital Information. Adapted from *Communications of the ACM,* Vol. 39, Number 7, July 1996, pages 17-22.

Page 153: Computer Ethics: Hacking and Other Intrusions
Reprinted by permission from *Computers Under Attack: Intruders, Worms, and Viruses,* pp. 150-155, edited by Peter J. Denning, Article 7, "The West German Hacker Incident and Other Intrusions," by Mel Mandell. Copyright 1990, Association for Computing Machinery, Inc.

Page 215: George Boole
Adapted from William Dunham, *Journey Through Genius: The Great Theorems of Mathematics,* John Wiley & Sons, 1990. Photo: Courtesy of The Bettmann Archive.

Page 233: Artificial Intelligence
Reprinted by permission from *The Mind Tool,* Fifth ed., pp. 394-398, by Neill Graham. Copyright 1989 by West Publishing Company. All rights reserved.

Page 261: A Software Glitch
From Ivars Peterson, "Finding Fault: The Formidable Task of Eradicating Software Bugs," *SCIENCE NEWS,* February 16, 1991, Vol. 139. Reprinted with permission from *SCIENCE NEWS,* the weekly magazine of science. Copyright 1991 by Science Services, Inc.

Page 306: Charles Babbage
Reprinted by permission from *Introduction to Computers with BASIC,* pp. 24–26, by Fred G. Harold. Copyright 1984 by West Publishing Company. All rights reserved.

Page 313: Ada Augusta Byron
Reprinted by permission from *Introduction to Computers with BASIC,* pp. 26-27, by Fred G. Harold. Copyright 1984 by West Publishing Company. All rights reserved. Photo: Courtesy of The Bettmann Archive.

Page 335: A Digital Matter of Life and Death
From Ivars Peterson, "A Digital Matter of Life and Death," *SCIENCE NEWS,* March 12, 1988, Vol. 133. Reprinted with permission from *SCIENCE NEWS,* the weekly magazine of science. Copyright 1988 by Science Services, Inc. Photo courtesy of Ontario Hydro.